Crime and Punishment in Eighteenth-century England

UTSA DT LIBRARY RENEWALS 458-2440

DATE DUE

GAYLORD

D1021747

Crime and Punishment in Eighteenth-century England

Frank McLynn

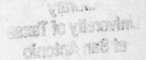
WITHDRAWN
UTSA LIBRARIES

Oxford   New York

OXFORD UNIVERSITY PRESS

1991

Oxford University Press, Walton Street, Oxford OX2 6DP
Oxford   New York   Toronto
Delhi   Bombay   Calcutta   Madras   Karachi
Petaling Jaya   Singapore   Hong Kong   Tokyo
Nairobi   Dar es Salaam   Cape Town
Melbourne   Auckland
and associated companies in
Berlin   Ibadan

Oxford is a trade mark of Oxford University Press

© Frank McLynn 1989

First published 1989 by Routledge
First issued as an Oxford University Press paperback 1991

All rights reserved. No part of this publication may be reproduced,
stored in a retrieval system, or transmitted, in any form or by any means,
electronic, mechanical, photocopying, recording, or otherwise, without
the prior permission of Oxford University Press

This book is sold subject to the condition that it shall not, by way
of trade or otherwise, be lent, re-sold, hired out or otherwise circulated
without the publisher's prior consent in any form of binding or cover
other than that in which it is published and without a similar condition
including this condition being imposed on the subsequent purchaser

British Library Cataloguing in Publication Data
McLynn, F. J. (Frank J.)
Crime and punishment in eighteenth-century England.
1. Crime and punishment England
I. Title
364.942

ISBN 0–19–285233–7

Library of Congress Cataloging in Publication Data
Data available

Printed in Great Britain by
The Guernsey Press Co. Ltd.
Guernsey, Channel Islands

Library
University of Texas
at San Antonio

To Pauline

Contents

Introduction

The Bloody Code is the name traditionally given to the English system of criminal law during the period 1688–1815. In these years a huge number of felonies punishable by death was added to the statute book. In 1688 no more than fifty offences carried the death penalty: the crimes so punishable were treason, murder, rape, and arson. By 1765 this figure had risen to about 160; an average of one new capital offence a year was added during the thirty-three-year reign of George II. A further sixty-five capital felonies added to the Code from 1765 to 1815 brought the number of crimes that bore the death penalty to about 225 by the end of the Napoleonic wars.[1] Even so, the number of capital offences was not co-extensive with the number of cases where the death penalty *could* be inflicted. On one calculation, the actual scope of the death penalty was about three or four times as wide as the capital provisions indicate.[2]

The other notably sanguinary feature (at least on paper) of the Bloody Code was that the new capital statutes deprived the felon of 'benefit of clergy'. Before 1706 it had been possible for members of the clergy and other literate persons to escape the death penalty in the case of lesser crimes by pleading an old form of ecclesiastical privilege; to obtain 'benefit of clergy' a person had to offer proof of literacy by reciting a passage of Scripture. An Act of 1706 abolished the literacy test.[3] Its abolition undoubtedly saved many illiterate men and women from the gallows since they were taken under the umbrella of equity. But what the state gave with one hand it took back with the other. As well as enlarging the scope of the death penalty, the authorities saw to it that the new capital offences were 'non-clergyable', that is, benefit of clergy could not be invoked.

The explosion of capital statutes marked a return to Tudor severity and was the product of a mentality that saw the gallows as the only deterrent to serious crimes. In functional terms the Bloody Code was the response of a society where capital enterprise was releasing new forms of wealth which could not be adequately protected without a regular police force. There is no need to posit a conspiracy to introduce draconian legislation *in general*. In terms of challenge and response, the Bloody Code was an organic process of adaptation by a society concerned to protect new forms

ix

of property and to restrict the benefits of a huge increase in wealth. The increase in commercial activity after the 'Glorious Revolution' of 1688 led to a plethora of laws on stolen property, receiving, embezzlement, fraud, and the obtaining of goods on false pretences. The modern law on theft may be said to date from this period.[4] The pattern was clear even in the reign of William and Mary. A law of 1691 made it a non-clergyable offence to take goods from a house while the owner was present and put in fear, and to break into houses, shops, and warehouses and then steal items to the value of five shillings.[5] Eight years later it was made a non-clergyable offence to shoplift any item worth more than five shillings or to steal articles of the same value from stables and warehouses.[6] In Queen Anne's reign it was additionally made non-clergyable to steal goods worth more than forty shillings from a house or outhouse, even if entry was secured without breaking and the owner was absent.[7]

It is a constant of human society that each age imagines itself more wicked than the preceding ones. Lord Chancellor Hardwicke remarked that the draconian provisions of the Bloody Code were made necessary by the egregious wickedness of the age.[8] And it is quite clear that, despite the hindsight assurances of later historians that the Hanoverians lived in a period of Augustan calm, the upper classes genuinely feared the mob, whether overtly criminal or not, and were quick to convert an increase in criminality into a threat to social order itself.[9] It was quite true that crimes against property *did* increase in the eighteenth century. Whether they increased at anything like the rate of trade or wealth, especially in real estate, is much more debatable. Those who argued for the singular wickedness of the age forgot the economic side of the social equation, just as they ignored urbanization, poor infrastructure, and (in the second half of the century), industrialization and population increase.

Yet while many members of the elite were prepared to countenance the Bloody Code as a necessary defence of social order against the evil anarchy of the mob, the violent, and the incorrigibly criminal, more thoughtful beneficiaries of the social system were disturbed by the Code's wild irrationality. In the first place, there was the element of 'overkill'. It was a capital crime to steal a horse (and after 1741 a sheep); to pickpocket more than a shilling; to steal more than forty shillings in a dwelling place or five shillings in a shop; to purloin linen from a bleaching ground or woollen cloth from a tenter ground; to cut down trees in a garden or orchard; to break the border of a fishpond so as to allow the fish to escape.

Second, there was the confusion arising from the fact that ancient statutes were not repealed, and that legislation long considered obsolete could suddenly be revived. The Bloody Code could become more severe in its effects simply through inflation. An Act that ordained the death penalty for stealing five shillings at the beginning of the eighteenth century could appear altogether harsher if revived unchanged at the end of it. As one historian has put it: 'While everything else had risen in its nominal value and become dearer, the life of a man had continually grown cheaper.'[10]

In addition, the same crime could be prosecuted under totally different statutes and penalties. Often a multiplicity of laws bore on the same crime. The theory and practice of the criminal law were light-years apart. Then there were the well-known anomalies in the Code. To commit a theft in a furnished house which was let as a whole was not an offence. Pickpocketing carried the death penalty but child-stealing, despite its high incidence, was not even an offence.[11] It was a capital felony to steal goods worth more than forty shillings from a ship on a navigable waterway, but not on a canal. To steal fruit already gathered was a felony; to steal it by gathering it was a mere trespass. To break a pane of glass at 5 p.m. on a winter's evening with intent to steal was a capital offence; to housebreak at 4 a.m. in the summer when it was light was only a misdemeanour. To steal goods from a shop and to be seen to do so merited transportation; to steal the same goods 'privately', that is, without being observed, was punishable by death.[12] In extreme cases parricide might receive the same punishment as the theft of five shillings.[13]

Some of the anomalies became notorious. A servant who had wounded his master fifteen times with an axe was executed, not for attempted murder, but for burglary, on the grounds that he had had to lift the latch of his employer's door to enter his chamber. In another case, an inveterate burglar was convicted and executed on the 'lesser' charge of cutting down trees.[14] The essence of the situation was that the Code worked by exemplary punishment, where the retribution did not fit the crime.

There are two obvious traps to fall into when discussing the Bloody Code. One is to underrate its ferocity; the other is to overrate it. On the one hand, for those unlucky enough to be caught up in the web of exemplary punishment the criminal Code was unjust, irrational, and exceptionally severe. There was some discrimination on grounds of age and sex, but not nearly enough. What there was attracted the censure of hardline defenders of the Code like Martin Madan, who deplored the fact that juries tended to be lenient towards young offenders.[15] The safeguards supposedly guaranteeing the liberties of Englishmen, like Habeas Corpus and the jury system, were inadequate to prevent miscarriages of justice. Judges often admitted that capital punishment did not fit a given crime or even that they had doubts about a particular person's guilt; nevertheless they continued to argue that the death penalty should stand even in such cases, since it served as an awful example and warning.[16]

Sir Erskine May famously described eighteenth-century justice thus: 'The lives of men were sacrificed with a reckless barbarity, worthier of an eastern despot or African chief, than of a Christian state.'[17] His words were an elegant gloss on the dithyrambic attack on the Code made in Parliament by Sir William Meredith in 1778. Meredith exposed the fallacies in the Code's premises in a *tour de force* of anti-deterrent rhetoric. Cruel laws encouraged crimes rather than preventing them. Since only half at most of all convicted felons were hanged, a thief might reckon the odds in his favour to be as much as twenty to one. And even if the odds were twenty to one on his being apprehended, criminal psychology was such that the felon could still argue that it was his fate to be the one in twenty. Moreover, the death penalty could be shown to be no deterrent even in the case of crimes that were never pardoned. Perpetrators of forgery and coining were virtually certain to be hanged under the Code, yet these were among the most common offences. Finally, Meredith pointed out, every new capital statute begat twenty more. If you hanged for sheep-stealing, logically you had also to hang the man who stole a cow or a goat. There would literally be no end to the crazy cycle of 'deterrence'.[18]

On the other hand, it would be a travesty of eighteenth-century history to suggest that the grisly ritual at Tyburn was inevitable and unending. One hundred executions a year in England was thought to be the limit the Code could order without bringing the entire notion of justice into disrepute. Judges and juries mitigated the law's sanguinary provisions by discretionary actions. Often juries would flagrantly flout the evidence placed before them in order to avoid sending a felon to the gallows. Indictments for grand larceny (carrying the death penalty on conviction) would be downgraded to petty larceny (where the maximum penalty was transportation) by valuing the stolen goods notionally, at less than one shilling. On one occasion it was clearly established that a large number of golden guineas had been stolen, yet the jury chose to reduce the charge from felony to misdemeanour by finding that less than forty shillings had been stolen![19]

Judges too played their part in the process of clemency by sometimes discharging the accused before their cases even came to trial. Such a discharge was quite distinct from acquittal by the jury *after* trial. Large numbers of petty criminals were pardoned without entering a court-room.[20] In the year 1791–5 it was estimated that 5,592 persons were discharged before trial, while 2,962 were acquitted after trial.[21]

The general rule of thumb discernible from an examination of the way the Code actually operated was that for the most part judges ordered capital punishment for the 'old' (pre-1688) offences, like murder and highway robbery, and handed down sentences of transportation for the 'new' capital offences added to the statute book after 1688. This tendency was particularly marked after 1750. By the 1790s, even when juries returned a guilty verdict for theft, they accompanied it with a plea for mercy, so that execution for stealing was uncommon. Where it took place, there were usually aggravating circumstances: armed robbery, demanding money with menaces, and so on.[22] Gang activities were particularly likely to elicit the full force of the Code.[23] But it must be emphasized that this was a relative pattern, not an absolute one. There was a proliferation of criminal statutes in the eighteenth century directed against forgery and counterfeiting. This was a response to the sustained lobbying of banks and other commercial interests, who were determined to secure protection for the new system of paper credit and exchange.[24] As a result, the crime of forgery was one great exception to the rule. Two-thirds of the century's convicted forgers were executed; except for murder, no crime was more relentlessly punished.

The central paradox of the Bloody Code was that a vast increase in capital statutes did not lead to higher levels of execution. This raises the question of what the ultimate intention of the framers of the Code actually was. The usual interpretation is that deep-seated resistance to a professional police force on the French model left the elite no choice but to use the deterrent horrors of Tyburn tree to protect its own property and privilege. The proliferation of capital statutes is then explicable in terms of lobbying by special interests to impose the death penalty for threats against their particular form of property. On this view, the fact that so many new offences were removed from benefit of clergy does not denote a ruling-class conspiracy or grand design by the Whig/Hanoverian ascendancy, but rather filling in the spaces of what has been described as a crude and rather mindless matrix. Blackstone adduced as the *locus classicus* of this process of piecemeal 'tacking' on to the Bloody Code by determined local pressure groups the 1741 Sheepstealing Act, the fruit of lobbying by a small group of farmers. Similar considerations apply to the passage of the 1731 and 1745 Acts against the theft of linen or cotton cloth, the 1742 Act against cattle theft, and the statutes of 1751 and 1765 directed against theft respectively from ships in a navigable river and from the mails.

It has not perhaps been sufficiently realized that the theory of the growth of the Code, as it were spontaneously and in a fit of absence of mind, as a functional response to the lack of a regular police force, does nothing to explain why the capital statutes were not more rigorously executed. Except for a few diehards like Madan, elite members of society themselves were fully aware that capital punishment could never fulfil the role of a police force. The theory that the Code was not inspired by a central intelligence but was an unconscious, quasi-organic adaptation to a new property-owning environment, also ignores the occasions when the elite did act in a concerted manner. The most famous such occasion was the 1722 Waltham Black Act, which in effect provided an overarching capital statute covering almost every conceivable criminal activity.

The truth is that, in explaining the explosion of capital statutes in the eighteenth century as a reaction to the absence of a police force, many historians have mistaken a symptom for a cause. The dislike of police was part of a cluster of attitudes, including hostility to a standing army, that stood at the heart of English political culture. This culture can be characterized as empirical rather than rational, relying on habit, custom, tradition, hunch, and intimation rather than reason. This tendency informs classical English political theory, providing a thread that runs from Hume and Burke in the eighteenth century to Oakeshott and J. L. Austin in the twentieth. A corollary of this empirical political culture is the aristocratic tradition and the cult of the amateur. Professionalism, being an aspect of rationalism, has always been suspect in England. 'Too clever by half' is a phrase that is inconceivable in French.

In terms of law enforcement, dislike of rationalism means a distaste for making the punishment fit the crime, in favour of general deterrence through exemplary punishment. A contemporary example may make the point clearer. The English law enforcement system favours the implementation of highway speeding regulations by means of the occasional ferocious example. There is no regular police patrol of the nation's motorways. In the USA, by contrast, a professional highway patrol rigorously enforces speed limits, so that speeding invites the certainty of detection. This reflects the differential experience of a society strongly influenced by Continental rationalism (the USA), with a written constitution and Bill of Rights, and a society accustomed to muddling through by 'intimations'. In a word, English law has always been concerned more with credibility and authority than punishment of each and every infraction.

That this political culture meshed beautifully with the requirements of the elite has been ably demonstrated by the most convincing explanation yet provided of the 'meaning' of the Bloody Code.[25] As Douglas Hay explains it, in eighteenth-century England the elite used a system of draconian punishments to allay its own anxieties over a number of issues: the real stability of their regime, the threat from Jacobites and later from Jacobins, the fear of the mob. The real motive was credibility. The sanguinary statutes were not meant to be implemented at all times and at all points. As Hay expresses it, they were more concerned with authority than property.[26] The principal aim was always to compel the deference of the lower orders. It was deference – an obvious aspect of the aristocratic tradition – that the authorities wanted, not one hundred per cent effectiveness in punishment or control of crime.

Yet there was a further subtlety to the elite use of the Code that made the superficially sanguinary criminal law system a masterpiece of social

control. The grip exercized by the eighteenth-century elite was precarious, reflecting the 'half-State' twilight characterized by parasitism when a
ruling class has not yet sunk its roots deeply enough. What was needed
was an ideology to provide social cement and legitimate the entire
system. With the decline in traditional beliefs, religion could no longer
play the required role. The great nineteenth-century ideology of market
liberalism was still in the future. To fill the ideological gap, the elite
invoked the law, insinuating the idea that every man was equal before the
law, that the law was dispassionate, impartial, and blind to social
stratification.[27] As Gramsci was later to explain it, social hegemony is
only truly attained when a ruling class can persuade those it rules that the
norms and sanctions of society, which in reality benefit only the privileged
few, are devised for the good of all.

The occasional exemplary ferocious punishment meted out under the
law would reinforce the majesty and authority of the allegedly trans-class
law courts. An insistence on meticulous punishment for each and every
transgression ran the obvious risk of giving the game away, of directing
attention to how the legal system actually operated. But it is important to
be clear that, in order to achieve this *pièce de résistance* of social control,
to promote the law as the central legitimizing ideology, the elite had to
accept very substantial limitations on its own freedom of operation. The
trick of conflating 'equality' with 'equality before the law' is a difficult one
to bring off.[28] It could be made convincing only if the authorities
themselves accepted the restrictions imposed on them by the 'rule of law'.
The ruling class had to be inhibited by its own laws from the use of
arbitrary imprisonment, torture, or the indiscriminate use of the military.
The occasional aristocratic victim like Lord Ferrers (see below p. 150)
had to be offered up. Sometimes, as in the Wilkes case, the government
retired from the courts defeated.

The social control achieved by the eighteenth-century elite was thus
always partial and relative. Quite apart from lacking the necessary
technology, the rulers of eighteenth-century England could not hope to
rival the power available to a modern totalitarian state. There is a very
great gap between ruling by a system of bad or imperfect laws, and even
bending or misusing those laws, as in a primitive authoritarian regime,
and simply inventing the law, as in modern totalitarianism. The English
elite possessed no 'death squads' or secret agents 'licensed to kill'. By and
large, the rule of law exhausted the range of its powers. This is a truth
obscured by a vulgar Marxism of base and superstructure, where law is
considered 'nothing but' the interest of the ruling class. The attitude of
Sir Robert Walpole and Lord Hardwicke to the rule of law may have
been the merest humbug; this does not mean to say that the concept of
the rule of law itself was. As E. P. Thompson has well remarked: 'We
may imagine how Walpole would have acted, against Jacobites or against

disturbers of Richmond Park, if he had been subject to no forms of law at all.'[29]

Some of the more puzzling features of the Code thus become clear. Its egregious absurdities are revealed as part of a general resistance to rationality by a political culture that was profoundly functional in its support of elite interests. Since these absurdities were widely known and widely debated, it might be asked why the Code was not tidied up. After all, the elite had its own overarching enabling legislation in the form of the Waltham Black Act. Why not lop away the surplus or obsolescent statutes? The answer is that their retention increased the obfuscatory effect of the Code and facilitated social camouflage, so that the special interest of the elite could masquerade as the General Good. The same 'mystifying' effect was achieved by the use of exemplary rather than certain punishments. There can be few more misleading assessments than this by Blackstone: 'It is moreover one of the glories of our English law that the species, though not always the quantity or degree of punishment is ascertained for every offence.'[30] Nothing could be further from the truth.

1

London

London joyned with Westminster, which are two great
cityes but now with buildings so joyned up it makes but one
vast building with all its suburbs.
                Celia Fiennes, *The Journeys of Celia Fiennes*

Dear, damn'd, distracting Town farewell!
Thy fools no more I'll tease
This year in Peace, ye Critics, dwell,
Ye Harlots, sleep at Ease!
  Alexander Pope, *A Farewell to London in the Year 1715*

That tiresome dull place! where all people under thirty find
so much amusement.
Thomas Gray, letter to Norton Nicholls, 19 November 1764

In eighteenth-century England crime was overwhelmingly a London
phenomenon. Outside the capital there was of course the natural quota of
murders and petty theft. But in the provinces what the London
authorities considered as crime was usually viewed very differently by the
local community, as in the case of coining, poaching, smuggling, or
wrecking. Here 'local mafias' conducted their illicit operations with the
implicit or explicit sanction of local folkways. Only in London was there a
distinct criminal subclass, sustaining itself by its own 'underworld' ethos,
at odds with the wider community in which it found itself.

London was different from the rest of the country both in degree and
kind. In 1700 England had a population of some five millions, two thirds
of whom were employed in one way or another in agriculture. During the
entire eighteenth century London contained at least one-tenth of the
population. Before the first official census in 1801 all estimates are
guesswork. But if we take the population of London in 1801 (900,000) as
the fixed point, the best conjecture produces a population steadily rising
from about 575,000 in 1700 to 675,000 in 1750, then accelerating more
rapidly thereafter.[1] Between 1720 and 1750 there were more deaths than

births in London, but after 1750 the death rate declined. In the first half of the century bad harvests followed by a rise in the price of bread combined with harsh winters to produce epidemics of disease that carried off large numbers, as in 1709-10, 1713-14, 1727-8 and 1740-1.[2] The fact that London's population rose during 1700-50 was attributable to the 'population implosion', the increasing flight from the countryside to the capital.

'The great wen' dominated England to an extent difficult to appreciate. In 1700 when London's population was already well over half a million, the second city in numbers, Norwich, contained no more than 20,000 souls, while Birmingham had no more than 10,000. Throughout the entire century London contained at least one-tenth of the nation's people. Paris provided at most one-fortieth of the population of France in the same period. By another index, London's domination was even more complete. It is estimated that by 1750 one sixth of the English population either was living in London or had lived there for significant portions of its lives.[3]

Early Hanoverian London (including the cities of London and Westminster) was a noisome farrago of cobbled, mud-covered streets. Overcrowded and pestilential, it sometimes resembled a gigantic market town, where animals wandered freely in the streets and their smells and noises were ubiquitous. It extended from modern Bond Street and St. James's Park on the west to Wapping in the east, and from Moorfields (Sadler's Wells) to St. George's Fields, Southwark in the south. Included in the population total of some 600,000 for the early period were the villages of Chelsea, Kensington, Hampstead, Islington, Bow, Stepney and Camberwell. Soho and Mayfair were largely pasture ground. But the sheer appetite for space of the 'monster city' was beginning to appal the most perceptive contemporaries. Daniel Defoe estimated that London would soon have a circumference of thirty-six miles and would include not only the cities of London and Westminster but Southwark, Deptford, Islington and Newington. Next, the moloch would consume Poplar, Greenwich and Blackwall in its maw; soon Chelsea, Knightsbridge and Marylebone would be devoured:

It is the disaster of London, as to the beauty of its figure, that it has thus stretched out in buildings, just at the pleasure of every builder, or undertaker of buildings, and as the convenience of the people directs, whether for trade or otherwise; and this has spread the face of it in a most straggling confus'd manner, out of all shape, incompact and unequal; neither long not broad, round or square, . . . one sees it in some places three miles broad, as from St. George's in Southwark to Shoreditch in Middlesex: or two miles, as from Petersburgh House to Montague House; and in some places not half a mile as in Wapping; and much less as in Redriff. . . . We see several villages, formerly

standing, as it were, in the country, and at a great distance, now joyn'd
to the streets by continual buildings, and more making haste to meet in
the like manner. . . . That Westminster is in a fair way to shake hands
with Chelsea, as St. Gyles is with Marybone; and Great Russell Street
by Montague House, with Tottenham-Court; all this is very evident,
and yet all these put together, are still to be called London: whither
will the monstrous city then extend? and where must a circumvallation
or communication line of it be placed?[4]

At the end of the century Horace Walpole confirmed Defoe's prognosis:

There will soon be one street from London to Brentford; ay, and from
London to every village ten miles around! Lord Camden has just let
houses at Kentish Town for building fourteen hundred houses – nor do
I wonder; London is, I am certain, much fuller than ever I saw it. I
have twice this spring been going to stop my coach in Piccadilly, to
inquire what was the matter, thinking there was a mob – not at all; it
was only passengers.[5]

The topography of London with its tangled lanes, hidden courts, dark
alleyways and sprawling suburbs provided an ideal nesting ground for
criminals of all kinds. As Henry Fielding remarked in a famous passage:

Whoever indeed considers the cities of London and Westminster with
the late vast addition of their suburbs, the great irregularity of their
buildings, the immense number of lanes, alleys, courts and bye-places;
must think that, had they been intended for the very purpose of
concealment, they could scarce have been better contrived. Upon such
a view, the whole appears as a vast wood or forest, in which a thief may
harbour with as great security, as wild beats do in the deserts of Africa
or Arabia.[6]

The situation was aggravated by the existence of criminal sanctuaries. It
had long been a practice for criminals to claim the right of sanctuary on
consecrated ground where the old dissolved monasteries had once stood.
By 1712 the authorities had effectively clamped down on this misuse of
ancient privileges. Only the Mint at Southwark, a refuge for debtors,
remained as the last of the 'bastard sanctuaries'. But the old sanctuary
areas continued to be popular criminal ghettoes. The most famous were
at Whitefriars and Alsatia (the area between Fleet Street and the river),
but there were many others: Whitechapel, Barbican, Smithfield,
Bankside, Covent Garden, Shoe and Fetter Lanes, parts of Holborn.
There were many notorious streets, feared and dreaded by the law-
abiding: Chick Lane, Thieving Lane (near Westminster Abbey), Petty
France, Orchard Street.[7] The riverside district from St. Katherine's to
Limehouse was widely considered a 'no go' area. Even the fields and

roads around London were unsafe except on Sundays, when crowds of people streamed out to the pleasure gardens and tea rooms.[8]

Into these ghettoes peace-officers ventured at their peril. Fielding recorded glumly 'it is a melancholy truth that, at this day, a rogue no sooner gives the alarm within certain purlieus, than twenty or thirty armed villains are found ready to come to his assistance.'[9]

Violence was endemic in London, especially in the first half of the eighteenth century. Cock-fighting, bear-baiting, goose-throwing, bare-knuckle fist-fighting were just some of the popular recreations. A culture of heavy drinking, bawdy houses, illiteracy and low life-expectancy bred an ephemeral, gambler's attitude to 'law and order'. This 'deviant' subculture even produced its own literature and had a strong influence on the productions of elite culture and literature.[10] The violence was compounded by the minions of the elite, notably by press gangs, whose strong-arm methods routinely provoked serious rioting.[11] The French traveller and mathematician La Condamine said that he had visited the most barbarous countries in the world (he instanced Russia, Turkey, Algiers, Tunis, Tripoli, Morocco and Egypt) and had never seen savages to equal Londoners. In his view, the inhabitants of the capital were more ferocious and fearsome than any other group of people from China to Peru.[12]

There can be no mistaking the general level of casual violence. On a single day in 1764 the following crimes were reported. A footpad was committed for stealing a hat and a wig; another for stealing a bundle of linen from a woman's head; a man was arrested who had stolen £500 worth of plate in Cavendish Square. A housebreaker wounded the occupant in a house in Gloucester Street and made off with £100. A man lost a watch and £12 to a robber between Kentish Town and St. Pancras. A woman was robbed when one member of a gang fell down in front of her; she tripped over him, and his accomplice made off with her bundle. Meanwhile a ship's master was brought from Bristol on a charge of murdering two blacks on the high seas.[13]

Six months later casual violence was just as evident. On a single day, in December 1764, the *London Chronicle* records the following. A sailor bumped into a porter in Threadneedle Street, begged his pardon but was struck. He struck back and killed the porter. Since he was not the aggressor, the crowd of onlookers let him escape. On the same day the woman servant of a tripe-man in Southwark cut her own throat. On the road from Guildhall to London a married couple got caught up in a furious row. The husband, a carpenter, in his fury threw himself into a pond and was drowned.[14]

It is tempting to conclude that everyday life was not far removed from Hobbes's state of nature – 'nasty, brutish and short' – and there is some truth in such a shorthand description. Yet observers detected a more nuanced attitude to other human beings, suggesting that human life was not held quite so cheaply as in the cliché picture of early Hanoverian London.[15] The traveller d'Archenholz noticed that London crowds were in general very considerate towards women and children.[16] It has to be remembered, too, that modern indices of stress factors predisposing people to aggression are cultural constructs. The same triggers would not necessarily have elicited the same responses in the eighteenth century. The inhabitants of London lived in overcrowded conditions, but so did the capital's upper classes. It is a mistake to read back modern notions of privacy into the eighteenth century.[17]

The species of London criminal feared most was the footpad, the armed robber operating on foot, usually in gangs. They infested London and the outskirts. The normal pattern of operation was to waylay people in one area and then to retreat to safety in the 'flash houses' (safe houses) of one of the notorious 'rookeries'. Favourite operating haunts of the footpads were around Knightsbridge and Tottenham Court Road, then surrounded by ditches and open fields.[18] After the robbery the favourite retreat would be one at Holborn, Gray's Inn Lane, St Giles, Great Queen Street, Long Acre, St Martin's Lane, Bedford Street and Charles Street. Such was the *modus operandi* of the notorious White Brothers (executed in 1758).[19]

Footpads would steal anything of value but different gangs had different specialities or 'lays'. Obadiah Lemon's gang, operating in the second decade of the century, specialized in stealing from coaches. At first they used fishing hooks and lines to whisk hats, whigs, and scarves out of coach windows. The coach owners retaliated by fitting their vehicles with perforated tin sashes, though one unwelcome consequence was that passengers then had to travel in darkness and stifling heat.[20]

The Lemon gang then developed a new expertise. They would jump on to the backs of coaches, cut through the roof and snatch hats, whigs and jewellery out through the hole. A much simpler ploy was simply to sever the leather straps supporting the coach. Then, when the coachdriver got down to see what was the matter, the footpads simply made off with the boxes under the driver's seat.[21]

Other footpad specialities were the waylaying of stage-coaches when they dropped speed. The difficulty of their robbing men on horseback was obvious, though many such attempts were made.[22] But when a coach slowed down to cross a bridge, an opportunity arose. In June 1792 Mr Fry of Wimpole Street and six young ladies in his company were held up at Richmond Bridge on their way home from Richmond theatre and robbed of four guineas and some silver. There were six footpads on the bridge, and they fired into the coach window to stop it. One of the shots grazed a lady's ear and carried off her earring.[23] The same gang had held up two post-chaises from Richmond three days previously in Kew Lane.[24]

Footpads were much more violent and far more dreaded than the better-known highwaymen. Their level of homicide during robberies was high, unlike that of the highwaymen, simply because the footpads were unable to leave the scene of the crime quickly and were thus tempted to decrease the odds against them by killing the witnesses to their robbery. This in turn led to severity on the part of the authorities.[25] A convicted footpad was unlikely to escape the gallows. Any form of demanding money with menaces of bodily harm was virtually certain to consign the offender to public hanging.[26]

Nor was there any residue of popular sympathy for the footpad, again unlike the highwayman. No footpad could hope to become a folk hero. Only the most extraordinary individual abilities would keep a street robber even fleetingly in the public mind. Such a one was 'Jumping Joe Lorrison' (executed 1792), so-called from his cat-like ability to leap into carts and wagons to rob them.[27] But in general the footpad was regarded with loathing and horror. A case in 1768 showed that public vindictiveness towards them could extend all the way to the gallows. A 19-year-old carpenter's servant was condemned to hang at Tyburn for footpad robbery. James Gibson, who was being executed at the same time for forgery, asked that Payne be allowed to accompany him in his mourning-coach, instead of being conveyed on a cart. This compassionate request was turned down contemptuously by the Sheriff.[28]

Three generalizations are possible on footpad robbery. One was that particular hatred was aroused if such a crime was committed by gypsies, whose very legal status was uncertain in eighteenth-century England.[29] Second, the level of footpad robbery rose in the demobilization of the immediate post-war periods. In 1784 a 'moral panic' in London, resultant on a number of murder and footpad cases, made people afraid to walk even the main streets of London after dark, to say nothing of the back alleys.[30] It was a matter of general rejoicing when a footpad was taken for exemplary punishment that year.

Third, the coming of turnpike roads made it easier for the footpad to range out of London to the lush villages in its environs, especially those lying on or near main traffic arteries. In 1778 Sir Richard Perrin was robbed at his own front door in Twickenham.[31] Sixteen years later, a gang of pedestrian footpads competed with the highwaymen by operating on Whitton Heath.[32]

The pickpocket was another London criminal type that excited the astonishment of contemporary observers. The poet William Shenstone ('nothing is certain in London but expense') related in 1743 that after 8 p.m. armed pickpockets in Fleet Street and the Strand routinely knocked down passers-by. In Covent Garden they came in large numbers, armed with knives, and waited for people to come out of the theatres.[33] London pickpockets were especially skilful. Frequenting race-meetings, theatres and (especially) public hangings, they snatched handkerchieves, snuffboxes, watches, pocket-books and bank notes.[34] Their favourite haunts within London were Drury Lane, Covent Garden and the Exchange.[35] On one occasion the Duke of Cumberland ('Butcher Cumberland') had his sword stolen as he entered a theatre. Elite groups of pickpockets, elegantly dressed for the occasion, specialized in winnowing the wealth of race-goers and visitors to county fairs.[36]

Some of the pickpockets were of rare ingenuity. Tom Gerrard (executed 1711) taught his dog to lift valuables from people's pockets.[37] Arthur Chambers's speciality was to do it while his victims' attention was elsewhere. His favourite trick was to enter a tavern and attract a crowd around him by speaking gibberish and pretending it was Greek. He always carried a Greek testament with him to 'prove' his claim. While the publican and his customers were trying to make sense of St. Paul in the original Greek, Chambers was able to pick their pockets with ease. He had many years of success before being caught and executed in 1706.[38]

Women featured prominently in this crime, largely as prostitutes picking the pockets of their comatose or slumbering clients. But in such cases pickpocketing was an adjunct to the main activity. Direct pickpocketing was largely a male preserve. It was traditionally the way for a young male to begin his criminal career; most of those apprehended were between 12 and 14 years old.[39] Usually these lads worked in gangs under the direction of an adult (much as Fagin's gang did in *Oliver Twist*).[40] A pickpocketing combination of sixteen very young boys was reported in 1764.[41]

But it was not just their youth that made it difficult to prosecute and convict pickpockets. In the first place it was difficult to detect them; in the second, even when a boy was caught in the act, he was most unlikely to incriminate his accomplices. Apart from the reluctance of individuals to press charges, especially in circumstances where they had recovered their property, the ferocious nature of the Bloody Code itself was a deterrent. In cases where a pickpocket was caught in the act, it was more usual to mete out punishment then and there. The most common treatment of young offenders was simply to beat them up.[42] When a pickpocket was discovered in the Strand in 1784, the crowd pursued him and recovered a snatched purse. After a severe beating, he was then released.[43] A refinement was for the crowd to hold such offenders under water until almost at the point of drowning before releasing them.[44] This vigilante law enforcement sometimes had tragic results. In 1784 a man was caught in a petty theft and taken by the crowd from pump to pump for a long succession of duckings. In the end the man's heart gave way and he dropped down dead in the road near Cheapside. There was general outrage, expressed by this newspaper correspondent:

It certainly is highly incumbent upon the magistracy to interfere, to prevent the administration of justice from being assumed by a lawless rabble; who are in general as unable to discriminate between the nature of the crimes as they are incompetent to the proportioning of punishment to the guilt of the criminal.[45]

But the farther the pickpocket progressed in his career and the more refined his skills became, the more difficult the task of the authorities became. The ability to pick pockets often extended to that of picking locks. In September 1764 a one-legged sailor and a notorious pickpocket broke out of Bridewell together. The pickpocket had been double-ironed with the fetters riveted. Three hours later he sent back the irons, saying he was much obliged to the keeper for their use but no longer needed them.[46] Only when Sir John Fielding began to organize his mounted patrols in the 1750s did the authorities start to gain some success in the war against pickpockets. His patrolmen caught nine of them in January 1764 as they waited for crowds to come out of the Covent Garden theatres. Another twelve were taken up in St James's Park at the end of that month in the same way.[47]

London criminals were nothing if not audacious. A favourite trick was to throw ash in the faces of the better-off, then to seize hats and wigs from the temporarily blinded victims. No one, whatever the status, was safe from criminal attention in London. George III himself was robbed of his watch money and shoe buckles one evening while walking in the gardens of Kensington Palace.[48] Some criminal behaviour verged on the compulsive or pathological. In September 1764, while two pickpockets were being examined before the Lord Mayor of London, one was found with his hand in the pocket of one of the witnesses![49]

But perhaps the greatest incitement to crime in London was the Thames itself. Theft and pilferage on the river continued at epidemic levels throughout the century. The wealth of the Port of London was a magnet to thieves, both casual and organized. The value of goods stolen in the port in 1749 and the first half of 1750 was estimated at £100,000.[50] The water-thieves or 'mudlarks' had accomplices among the sailors and lightermen working on ships at anchor in the Thames. They would tip goods overboard for the 'mudlarks' to retrieve at low tide. More audacious thieves would cut the hawsers of anchored barges at night, so that they floated on the tide to some remote spot where the goods could be unloaded with impunity.[51] The river thieves' favourite haunt was 'Alsatia', between Fleet Street and the river. Bursting with thieves, receivers, footpads, and prostitutes, Alsatia was immortalized by Hogarth in the 'Thieves' Kitchen'.[52]

The Customs and Excise and the West India Company tried vainly to staunch this outflow of goods by appointing special constables. But these men were themselves incompetent or corrupt and could easily be bribed to turn a blind eye to the most barefaced theft. Sugar was a particular target of the thieves. Near the end of the century the annual value of sugar lost through fraud on the river amounted to £70,000. All classes of men were involved in the fraud. While the ship waited for the necessary delivery papers, the crew would fill sacks and their trouser pockets with sugar and take some ashore three times a day when they went for their meal breaks. Coopers who came on board to repair broken casks would send out bags ostensibly to fetch the necessary nails; in reality the bags would be full of sugar. Much the same happened with other West India cargoes such as rum and indigo.[53]

After 1751 it was a capital crime to steal more than 40 shillings worth of goods from a ship on a navigable river or wharf. But since customs and other law enforcement officers were 'on the take', they rarely intervened. Only with the organization of an effective river police at the end of the century did the law claim its first victims. John Fisher, aged 23, convicted of stealing 800 lbs of sugar from the Dundee Wharf and executed in 1801, was the first case of a hanging for this crime recorded in the *Newgate Calendar*.[54]

It was estimated that nine-tenths of all crime in the Port of London was the work, not of professional criminals, but of people whose presence was authorized and bona fide: sailors, portworkers, watchmen, revenue officers.[55] But organized crime gradually increased its scope and significance as the century wore on. Foreign visitors had long noted that London was different from other European capitals in the number of criminal gangs it possessed, operating in footpad robbery, river theft, pickpocketing, receiving stolen property, and protection rackets.[56] And after the revelations of John Poulter in 1753, there was no longer any room for doubt. Poulter, a professional criminal facing the death sentence, produced a contemporary best-seller with his day-to-day record of criminal activities during 1749-53, which revealed the vast extent of organized crime.[57] How important a feature of eighteenth-century life, then, were the criminal gangs?

There undoubtedly was a hard core of professional criminals in London who lived off their 'earnings'. These men (and women) had their own private customs and lore, and even a private language, the 'canting' vocabulary of the underworld.[58] The professional criminal fraternity thus formed a subculture within a subculture of the more casual criminals. At the beginning of the century conditions were particularly propitious for them. There was a vast number of pawnbrokers, fences, and receivers on hand, who asked no questions about the ownership of goods. This made it easy to dispose of stolen loot.[59] In addition, the 'flash houses' in such notorious streets as Chick Lane, Cock Lane, and Black Boy Alley provided a safe refuge.[60] On the other hand, 'organized crime' conjures visions of twentieth-century criminal societies like the Mafia and to that extent introduces anachronistic perspectives.[61]

In the first place, the number of fully professional criminals was probably smaller than in the more perfervid estimates of Defoe and the Fieldings, who had obvious axes to grind. At the end of the century Colquhoun thought there were only about fifty or sixty large-scale receivers in London, plus several thousand small-time (and part-time) operators.[62] The underworld fluctuated as people drifted in and out of the gangs and of crime itself. There was nothing in eighteenth-century London corresponding to the military discipline and cell-like structure of the modern Mafia with its 'made men'. Oaths of allegiance and brotherhood were sometimes taken,[63] but these were largely ineffective and cannot be compared with the dreadful modern 'omertà' of the Mafia. Indeed the lack of a modern machinery of systematic terror and intimidation was the major weakness of the eighteenth-century gang. Criminal organizations had little defence against the temptations to betrayal provided by the huge rewards the authorities in this century offered for information.

Moreover, in modern terms the eighteenth-century gang was a very small-scale unit. The effective operating size of a gang was four or five members.[64] Larger organizations tended to be confederations. Occasionally gangs as large as fourteen were reported,[65] but even in these cases the organization tended to be of the self-help variety. In other words a gang of, say, fourteen footpads would work in twos for operating purposes and band together only for some degree of self-protection and rescue.[66] Even in this context, the bonds were very tenuous. If a gang was betrayed to the authorities, its members did not stick together to concoct a common story or alibi or to silence and intimidate witnesses. In such cases they tended to disintegrate very rapidly; it was every man for himself.

This looseness in organization extended to membership. People sometimes returned periodically or entirely to legitimate occupations. At one time the famous highwayman Ralph Wilson gave up his calling and returned to his mother's business, before being blackmailed to return to his old way of life.[67] Another man who committed more than one hundred robberies in London in 1740-1 had a spell off in the middle of his career, running a shoemaker's shop in Birmingham.[68]

There was also a gradation in the looseness of the gangs depending on the type of crime. Loosest of all were the combinations of footpads. The small bands of professional pickpockets and shoplifters tended to be more cohesive, partly because they were often units of an extended family, in which the criminal skills had been nurtured and handed down through the generations.

But the most persistent and tenacious type of organized criminal was the professional river thief, a class distinct from the sailors and lightermen and the more disreputable watermen who took to river piracy.[69] The gangs did not do anything very different from the casual or amateur pilferers; it was the scale and organization that marked them out. First of all, a network of skilled riverside receivers was organized. These receivers provided the 'licence to plunder' – the money paid to revenue officers to get them to turn a blind eye. These fees could be as high as twenty to thirty guineas a night. Then the river gangsters boarded the West India merchantmen after dark. They opened and resealed casks, having shovelled out quantities of sugar that were put in the 'black strip' – a bag large enough to contain one hundred pounds of sugar and dyed black so as to be invisible in the darkness.

Meanwhile the watermen in the organization would procure as many boats as necessary. Lumpers would unstow the casks, coopers take out the heads, all would then fill and remove the bags, taking not just sugar, but coffee, rum, ginger etc. 'Mudlarks' would prowl in the mud under the ship to receive from the lumpers and others miscellaneous articles. Everything would be taken immediately to the receivers so that a number of trips could be made in the course of a single tide.

Other useful members of these gangs were rat-catchers, since they were allowed on board ships at night to set traps. A particular ploy of the rat-catchers was to move a set of rats from one ship to another, thus getting paid for catching the same animals several times. All the while they would be carrying out reconnaissance missions for the gangs and sharing in the eventual plunder.[70]

London's criminal life was parasitic on the great and increasing wealth of the country. England's seaborne expansion and the rise of the joint-stock company were the main factors. Estimates of the wealth arriving in the mother country from foreign trading ventures tend to be impression-istic, but one study records that by the end of the seventeenth century a single trading company had extracted 100,000 slaves from Africa.[71]

The criminal scene in London did not remain monolithic and unvarying over the century. After about 1750 a gradual change can be discerned. As well as the major structural factors discussed below in chapter 16 and the wartime fluctuations dealt with in chapter 17, variables peculiar to London were involved. These were both negative and positive. On the negative side the most important was undoubtedly the grip exerted by the authorities on public drunkenness.

To ascribe significant social change to control of the nation's drinking habits seems like the argument of a temperancer but the respected social historian of London, Dorothy George, has this to say about the gradually improving quality of life in the capital after 1750: 'A pronounced setback, for instance, between 1720 and 1750 was almost certainly due to an enormous consumption of very cheap, fiery and adulterated spirits.'[72] Certainly the extent of alcoholic consumption in London up to the mid-century provides powerful circumstantial backing for this argument. Smollett's impression was that London 'teemed' with public houses.[73] More specific estimates endorse his judgement. In 1750 one in every fifteen houses in the City of London was a public house. In the City of Westminster the figure was one in eight, in Holborn one in five, while in St Giles every fourth house was a pub.[74] In the same year 50 per cent of the wheat sold weekly in the London markets was converted into alcohol.[75] The consumption of alcohol that year was estimated at 11,200,000 gallons.[76]

The spectacle of an impoverished population reeling intoxicated about the streets of London, then turning to petty crime to fuel its alcoholism had long worried the authorities.[77] In the mid-1730s the first attempts were made to grasp the nettle. The 1736 Gin Act required retailers selling less than two gallons of spirits at a time to obtain a £50 licence each year, with a further £1 payable on each gallon sold in lesser quantity. The penalty for retailing without a licence was to be £100. If implemented, this act would have been another 'noble experiment' – an eighteenth-century English version of Prohibition.[78] But, like Prohibition, the act proved to be a classic example of a law that could not be enforced, since it commanded no popular consensus. The situation was quite the reverse: there were very real fears of mass insurrection by the London mob.[79] And apart from the threat of riot, the Gin Act threatened to produce an army of informers, thus exciting the same sort of fears over the loss of traditional English liberties that had contrived to defeat Walpole's 1733 Excise Act.[80] More sagacious observers pointed out that the net effect of the Act would almost certainly be to raise the crime rate. Not only would a thriving bootlegging trade spring up, but the former publican class, unless it joined that illicit trade, would be reduced to penury, thus swelling the throngs of London's beggars.[81] It is no wonder that across the water the Jacobites looked forward with relish to the disastrous loss of popularity the Hanoverian regime would incur.[82] The Whigs themselves saw the point. After seven years of impotent attempts to enforce a licensing law that would really bite, they admitted defeat in 1743.

It is possible that the final defeat of the Jacobite threat in 1745-6 gave the regime a new confidence. Certainly by 1751 it felt strong enough to lock horns with the mob once more. The time was ripe. Choruses of lamentations about the ill-effects of spirituous liquors were again mounting.[83] This time the authorities pursued a triple-track strategy. Their first assaults were indirect. An Act of 1751 increased duties on drink.[84] Next year there was Parliamentary legislation aimed at brothels and disorderly houses.[85] Only in 1753 did the government show its hand openly by introducing another Act for licensing public houses.[86] This legislation was heavily influenced by the Fieldings' writings on crime. It succeeded where the 1736 Act had failed in tightening the screws on public inebriation. The power to withdraw licences was a sanction with real bite.[87]

By the mid-1750s the authorities had succeeded in turning the corner on public drunkenness. It would be a mistake to overdramatize their success, however. The endemic bribery and corruption of the eighteenth century soon lent a hand. By the 1770s venal magistrates were conniving at the free sale of drink. Throughout the second half of the century the battle to control public intoxication was more a see-saw affair than an outright victory for either side.[88] The really crucial turning point came in the 1790s when the pendulum swung back decisively in favour of the temperancers. The growth of Methodism and the influence of reforming societies (especially Wilberforce's) made decisive inroads on alehouses and gin palaces.[89] Clearly this was a battle that could never be totally won, but there seems no disputing the fact that this aspect of London life was different in kind in the two halves of the century.[90]

The positive elements in the improving picture of London crime over the century can be summed up as ameliorated technology, higher living standards, better policing and changing attitudes within society. Naturally, this progression was not direct; there were many zigzags caused by war and economic depression, as we shall see. The more old-fashioned ideas of ever onward and upward progress should be discarded.[91] But enough real change took place to warrant Dorothy George's remark that 'by the end of the century we are in a different world'.[92]

The most important aspect of improved technology in the capital was the revolution in street lighting. Between 1717 and 1750 London crime entered a dark period in more ways than one. The street lighting devised by Hemmings in 1680 (convex-glassed lanterns) had been subsidized by a tax. But after Hemmings lost his patent in 1717, the system fell into disuse. As a final absurdity, the lighting tax was increased even as the streets were in total darkness.[93] Henceforth bourgeois Londoners ventured out into the murk to dine or go to the theatre only if armed to the teeth. London householders felt unsafe unless their houses were fortified by palisades and redoubts and defended by an army of servants. Even if there had been an efficient police force in London before 1750, the murky, fuliginous light in the dim alleyways and noisome rookeries would still have made the job of catching criminals a chancy affair.[94] But from the mid-century, the streets began, by comparison, to be bathed in light. Fielding's comparison of the capital to the deserts of Arabia began to seem less telling.[95]

Improving technology fed into higher living standards. Better sanitation and drainage together with less drinking made Londoners healthier. The death-rate started to fall after 1750, then more rapidly still after 1780. In general there was more poor law relief, there were fewer cases of imprisonment for debt, less brutality, and fewer crimes of violence. At the end of the century London was still full of beggars and prostitutes. There was still much drunkenness and addiction to gaming and blood sports.[96] But impressionistic estimates suggest that the level of these peccadilloes had declined steeply since 1700. Crime tended to change its character. There was more burglary and less footpad robbery, doubtless in part reflecting the greater pickings possible from the planned robbery rather than from the mindless chance assault.

Most important of all, there had been a profound change in attitudes. We shall examine later the lessening commitment to violence in society as a whole over the century. At present it is enough to record the judgement that the simultaneous assault on violent attitudes by Methodism and Enlightenment thought, as it were in echelon, had a significant impact. This change in attitudes affected both rulers and ruled. Considerable scepticism was evinced by the end of the century about the efficacy of the Bloody Code. The draconian laws ordaining the death penalty for an immensely broad spectrum of offences had had no effect on violent crime, and even less deterrent power in the case of fraud, coining, counterfeiting, smuggling, and the receiving of stolen goods.[97]

Underlying the belief in the death penalty had always been a hard core of 'original sin' pessimism by the authorities. But under the impact of the Enlightenment, shrewder critics now began to point to obvious facts about society as the primary causes of crime. In the first place, it was much harder to sustain a rigid hierarchy of norms and values, especially that of deference, in London than in a village community. In the traditional community it was plausible to accept the myth of god-given social stations with every man in his proper place. A highly stratified system of inequality could be reinforced in a traditional, inelastic community. But not in London. There the working and serving classes confronted not just absolute but relative deprivation. They saw fortunes made by rogues who had not been born to wealth. And quite apart from the obvious temptations in the capital, the working and serving classes were prey to unemployment, underemployment, and disguised unemployment. It was clear that crime was more common in London than in the country simply because large numbers of people depended on casual and seasonal work. They were thus peculiarly vulnerable to economic fluctuations: to sudden contractions in the supply of jobs or to oversupply of labour.[98]

Most of all, the impact of Enlightenment thought was to alert increasing numbers of people to the fact that the sheer wealth of London was in itself a cause of crime. It was obvious that robberies were parasitic on wealth, highwaymen on the volume of prosperous traffic in and out of London and so on.[99] Similar considerations applied in the case of crime in the port of London. The immense wealth at anchor on the Thames, with no effective protection, was too great a temptation to crime. Thus the poet James Thomson described it:

> Then Commerce brought into the public Walk
> The busy Merchant; the big Warehouse built;
> Raised the strong Crane; choak'd up the loaded street
> With foreign Plenty; and thy Stream, O THAMES,
> Large, gentle, deep, majestic, King of Floods!
> Chose for his grand Resort. On either hand,
> Like a long wintry Forest, Groves of Masts
> Shot up their Spires; the bellying Sheet between
> Possess'd the breezy Void; the sooty Hulk
> Steer'd sluggish on; the splendid Barge along
> Row'd, regular, to Harmony; around,
> The Boat, light-skimming, stretch'd its oary Wings;
> While deep the various Voice of fervent Toil
> From Bank to Bank increased.[100]

The propensity to river crime was also aided by two features of general eighteenth-century English culture. One was that, irrationally, the pillage of commercial property afloat seemed to attract less opprobrium than other forms of theft. The other was that all crime by water tapped into the general resentment at excessively high duties that so favoured the smugglers.[101]

There is one final factor in London crime, clearly important, which however cannot be assessed with any exactitude: Durkheim's category of *anomie*. Living in the monster city seems to have induced feelings of fear and anxiety, a genuine feeling that social laws had gone into abeyance. Elite detestation of London is everywhere apparent in literature. 'This sinful Sea Cole Town', Lady Mary Wortley Montagu called it. 'May my enemies live here in summer!' Jonathan Swift recorded in his *Journal to Stella* (August 1711). Pope's verdict was equally savage:

> Yes; thank my stars! as early as I knew
> This town, I had the sense to hate it too.[102]

Even Samuel Johnson, famous for his remark that when a man was tired of London, he was tired of life, provided this description:

> Here malice, rapine, accident conspire,
> And now a rabble rages, now a fire;
> Their ambush here relentless ruffians lay,
> And here the fell attorney prowls for prey
> Here falling houses thunder on your head
> And here a female atheist talks you dead.[103]

Where elite anxiety and dread was so palpable, is it far-fetched to speculate that the 'lower orders' might also have perceived themselves to be in the chaos world and reacted accordingly? The Hobbesian jungle of *homo lupus homini* may well have possessed the same reality to those who lived in it as to those who merely observed it. Certainly, historians hitherto have underrated the psychic strain on mankind that results merely from living in a megalopolis.[104]

Increasing sophistication in attitudes and a lessening in the levels of violence were aspects of eighteenth-century society that altered only gradually, and in the short-term had little effect on the authorities' determination to continue to use the Bloody Code. What contemporaries noticed most after 1750 was the rise of policing bodies and a growing acceptance of the notion of police. It was in this area, rather than in their tirades against the taste for 'luxury' of the London poor, that the Fielding brothers were to make their most revolutionary contribution to London life.

2

Law Enforcement

Great crimes may raise a growing cause, but seldom retard
the fall of a sinking one.
    Horace Walpole to Sir Horace Mann, 22 October 1774

Who's to doom, when the judge himself is dragged to the
bar?

    Herman Melville, *Moby Dick*

No ceremony that to great ones 'longs
Not the king's crown, nor the deputed sword
The marshal's truncheon, nor the judge's robe,
Become them with one half so good a grace
As mercy does
    William Shakespeare, *Measure For Measure*, II.ii.59

At no stage in the eighteenth century did England possess a central police authority. The feeling that professional police on the French model would be the death of traditional English liberties was deeply rooted in the political culture.[1] The despotism of the Bourbon monarchs, sustained by an army of informers and secret policemen, was thought to be conclusive evidence on this point.[2] Consequently law enforcement was a patchwork process, carried on by a number of disparate bodies. Only at the very end of the century did the first glimmerings of a professional English police force appear.[3]

This resistance to policing amazed foreign observers. One of the first comparative social analysts, Le Blanc, when contrasting the English and French nations, recorded his opinion that the English would rather be robbed on the highways than in their houses, that is that they had a greater tolerance for footpads and highwaymen than for ministerial intrusions into their private lives.[4] But the morbid fear of organized bodies of government-funded officials struck a deep resonance in English political culture. It had implications beyond the issue of policing. The Hammonds went so far as to claim that as a consequence there was no effective central government control at all in the first decades of the eighteenth century.[5] What looks like an exaggerated claim comes to seem more soberly based when the administrative competence of central government is examined in times of crisis. The *locus classicus* is of course the Jacobite risings; here we find the nexus binding central and local government held together by the thinnest of gossamer threads.[6]

Such rudimentary law enforcement as did exist was carried out on an *ad hoc* basis by a number of bodies. Because fear and suspicion of the Army was one of the cluster of 'country' ideas involved in the resistance to policing itself, the authorities could use the military only in times of dire emergency: against organized gangs of well-armed criminals (especially those involved in smuggling and poaching) and in the cities against rioters.[7] Yet the military was a particularly blunt instrument: it was ill-equipped to respond quickly to anything save large-scale riots where magistrates gave army commanders discretionary powers. Even in the case of serious rioting, a time-lag of two to three days between the inception of the disturbances and the appearance of the military was not uncommon. In addition, military intervention in civil disturbances was unpopular at all levels. It increased the bitterness of the crowd and exacerbated social tensions; it was unpopular with the troops; it was regarded by army officers as a task beneath their dignity.[8] Besides, citizens hated having troops billeted on them. The very moment the disturbances were over they would petition for the army's withdrawal.

In theory, the militia could also be used as a peace-keeping body, but, certainly until the 1757 Militia Act, this was an ill-armed, amateur, purely nominal force with infrequent musters and uncertain legal status.[9] That left the official policing bodies. The King's Messengers were a purely political police force, answerable to the Privy Council. In the first half of the eighteenth century their role was restricted to surveillance of political subversives and penetration of the English Jacobite movement.[10] The Press Messengers similarly were entirely devoted to looking for publishers of seditious literature. The Court of Aldermen in the City of London possessed its own private police force – the City Marshals and their men.

The only general and permanent system of law enforcement in England at the beginning of the eighteenth century was provided at local level by the justices of the peace and their executive officers, the parish constables. JPs dealt with minor crime at quarter sessions and petty sessions. They were responsible for preserving public order, reading the Riot Act, calling in the military, issuing warrants, etc. The difference between an eighteenth-century magistrate and his modern counterpart lay in the power to issue warrants as part of *initiating* a prosecution. In this way the eighteenth-century JP was more like a US district attorney or a French *juge d'instruction*.[11]

Justices of the peace were pillars of the local community. But they were not evenly distributed nationwide, since men of sufficient wealth and status were not necessarily available in every locality. Also, not everyone with the right qualifications wanted to take the mandatory oaths of allegiance and supremacy.[12] Moreover, the burden of work increased alarmingly in the eighteenth century with the growth in the number of offences that magistrates could deal with summarily – a further disincentive to service.[13] This burden of work, even more pressing in London, led to the growth in the capital of the notorious 'trading justices' – magistrates who made a living by charging fees (especially bail fees) for their services. Nor was hard work the only deterrent to the would-be justice of the peace. The preservation of law and order could involve one in counter-litigation, especially in cases where magistrates called in the military as a panicky reaction to some little local difficulty, or ordered troops to open fire without good cause. Justices of the peace had to find the elusive optimum point: too much force, and they could be sued for damages; too little, and they would be accused of incompetence. There was an endemic danger of 'damned if you do, damned if you don't'.[14]

The parish constable was the magistrate's subordinate and executive officer. Constables could police 'night-walkers', gypsies, peddlars, fortune tellers, servants absent without leave, infractions of Sunday or gambling laws. They could punish mothers for bearing bastards, whip vagabonds, force the unwilling to work, uphold apprentice statutes, confine begging to those licensed to beg, restrain lunatics, and detain suspicious characters. They were also responsible for crime detection, raising the 'hue and cry', apprehending criminals and housing them once detained. Here too the burden of work was oppressive. Often those eligible for office paid to escape the chore or obtained a certificate of exemption. The most famous such exemption was the 'Tyburn ticket'. If someone brought to justice an offender likely to be sent to Tyburn (a burglar, horse-stealer, robber, etc.), he or she received a certificate giving exemption from compulsory service in the parish in which the offence had been committed.[15] Another way to evade service was to accept office and pay a deputy to do the job on one's behalf. Reluctance to serve as constable was compounded by the financial penalties ordained for wrongful arrest or escape from custody.

In London the system of the justice of the peace and constable received a few refinements. Chief of these were the institutions of Beadle and the Watch. The beadle (immortalized in Dickens's Mr Bumble) was a paid employee who took over the lesser duties of a constable. He implemented the Poor Laws, acted as town crier, kept order in church yards, and, most important, supervised the parish Watch.

The Watch was the egg from which the later police force hatched. The Watch House, supervised by the beadle, was an embryonic police station. Every evening the officers of the Watch reported to the Watch House, armed with lantern and cudgel. Each man was assigned a length of street and given a sentry box from which to oversee it. He was supposed to patrol the 'patch' every hour. The problem was that the officers of the Watch were just one precarious social notch above the criminals they were supposed to be deterring. They were paid very little, and therefore tended to be men who could get no other employment. Moreover, there was a glaring defect at the very heart of the system. There was usually an interval of some four to eight hours between the end of the night watch and the commencement of the day shift. The predictable consequence was that most crime was carried out during this time 'window'.[16]

It was the received opinion during the first half of the eighteenth century that the Watch was incompetent.[17] Both its personnel and administration were heavily criticized and there were calls for a drastic overhaul.[18] Only in 1735 was a small start made in this direction. The two parishes of St George's, Hanover Square and St James's, Piccadilly, in the City of Westminster (the location of many wealthy houses), were given permission by a local Act of Parliament to set a rate and use it to employ and pay more highly skilled watchmen.[19] A dramatic improvement in the service was at once noted. From then on watchmen left the snug apathy of their boxes to patrol their patch, checking that the doors on business premises were secure, much like the modern policeman.[20] The example caught on. The Watch steadily improved in efficiency in the second half of the century. Criminals, formerly openly contemptuous, came to regard it as a force to be reckoned with.[21]

Yet for most of the century it was not law-enforcement agencies that secured the arrest and conviction of criminals. The most obvious problem was that each peace-keeping body operated within severely restricted territorial limits. Eighteenth-century policing was vitiated on a small scale by the problems that beset the USA before the coming of the FBI and the creation of a class of federal offences. In other words, each officer could patrol his own parish but was not allowed to stray into his neighbour's 'beat', nor could he expect help from other forces.[22] There was rivalry and jealousy rather than co-operation and mutual help between the Watch, King's Messengers, Press Messengers, city marshals and sheriffs, and the other *ad hoc* bodies. This meant that the system of policing broke down when faced with organized crime or rioting. In the case of a serious robbery a sheriff or magistrate could proclaim a 'hue and cry' so that the *posse comitatus* could be formed.[23] But, quite apart from the rivalries and jealousies that had to be overcome before a credible fighting force could pursue armed robbers over great distances, there was an understandable reluctance by citizens to join in an unpaid adventure with the risks of armed conflict simply on the basis of the 'king's prerogative'.[24]

Some attempt was made by an Act in 1735 to strengthen the ancient principle of 'hue and cry'.[25] Two of the most notorious parts of the 'Code of Blood' – the 1715 Riot Act and the 1722 Waltham Black Act – tried to stiffen the notion of local collective responsibility by making the inhabitants of a 'hundred' liable to make good losses committed in that area.[26] The one thing central government would not do (*plus ça change*) was to provide the finance to make local initiatives truly effective. This ran counter to the whole tenor of eighteenth-century England and was the other main barrier to successful crime-fighting.

The endemic corruption of Hanoverian England meant that securing justice was always expensive. Since the Walpolian political system was based on sustained patronage and bribery, and all 'places' from the City Recorder to the merest turnkey in the Fleet prison had to be bought, citizens who petitioned for justice had themselves to line the pockets of those who had bought these 'places'. In addition, there was no system of public prosecution. A citizen was expected to do his own police work: obtain an arrest warrant from a magistrate, arouse the constable, and then, providing the manpower from among his own friends and acquaintances, find and arrest the criminal. Then he had to bear the costs of the prosecution. It is not surprising that many people simply found it too expensive to bring an offender to justice, especially when most crime involved offenders too poor for the prosecutor to recoup his costs from. And even though in fact most criminal gangs did not stay together long enough to intimidate witnesses or prosecutors, the fear that they might do so was another powerful disincentive in the minds of would-be prosecutors.[27] The fortunate ones were those who belonged to a prosecution association, which provided an early form of insurance.[28]

There were some who called for a system of public prosecution in London, where all charges were met by the authorities.[29] But these were largely voices crying in the wilderness. There was little conception of the public good or of civic duty in eighteenth-century England. The lack of any true civic *virtù* explains why fires were so dreaded. Fire-fighting above all depends on co-operative effort and a high degree of motivation. The lack of these in eighteenth-century England was often disastrous. A fire in Wapping in 1715 destroyed 150 houses and carried off fifty people. So far from tapping any residue of collective effort, such disasters merely provided even greater opportunities for the underworld to plunder with impunity amid the confusion. Hanoverian England was *par excellence* a society where you got only what you paid for. This is shown most clearly by an examination of the mechanism whereby most criminals were actually caught: the system of rewards.

Well into the nineteenth century the state relied largely on rewards as its main weapon against crime and public disorder. Walpole and his successors believed that every man had his price. It followed that cash benefits accruing to private individuals for the discovery and conviction of offenders was the most efficacious method of fighting crime. The financial rewards offered to informers were of a very high order by the standards of the day. The standard fee for information leading to the capture of a highwayman was £40.[30] In the case of damage to a turnpike, the reward for identifying the offender could go as high as £400.[31] When rioting broke out in 1795, the level of fear entertained by the elite about the revolutionary temper of the crowd was so great that £1,000 was offered for the 'discovery of any person endangering the safety of the Royal Person'.[32] However, in discussing rewards an awareness of chronology is all-important. After about 1750 the government cut back severely on the rewards it offered. This development was connected with the rise of new methods of policing, to be considered below. Thereafter the goverment offered rewards only for offences against its own property (for example, burglary on a government building).[33] But rewards continued to be offered by private individuals throughout the century.[34]

Along with rewards as an inducement to turn informer went a whole hierachy of pardons.[35] In this way the criminal fraternity could be turned against itself, shoplifters against burglars, thieves against receivers, footpads against highwaymen. The 'Tyburn ticket' was just the best known of these inducements.[36]

The high levels of crime, totally inadequate or non-existent policing, plus the lavish rewards offered for apprehension of criminals provided the ideal breeding-ground for that distinctive eighteenth-century phenom- enon, the thief-taker. The role of the thief-taker is best illustrated by an examination of the career of Jonathan Wild, who arguably had the greatest criminal mind of the century.[37] Born in Wolverhampton in 1683, Wild came to London first as a servant, then worked briefly as a 'setter' or 'bum bailiff' before being committed to prison for debt in 1710. As so often, prison turned a petty criminal into a hardened professional.[38]

Released in 1712 under the Act for the deliverance of debtors, he set up as a brothel-keeper with his common-law wife Mary Milliner (or Molyneux). His next step up the ladder was to serve as deputy to under- city marshal Hitchen. The two worked together up to a quarrel in 1717. During this period Wild discovered his talent as a receiver of stolen goods. His criminal career was a process of ever-increasing subtlety. At first he and Hitchen ran a crude protection racket, extorting money and valuables from guilty and innocent alike. Then Hitchen evolved a primitive receiving system. But he lacked the patience necessary for success in this *métier*. He would often sell stolen goods to other receivers or dispose of stolen banknotes at gaming houses, before the owner of the stolen property had been brought to the point of paying 'rewards' for its return. Also, Hitchen restricted himself to stuff that was easy to dispose of but hard to trace, like banknotes and watches, or that could be used for blackmail, like pocket-books and diaries. He had no outlet for jewellery, silver plate, fabrics, or furniture.[39]

This was where Wild's genius first manifested itself. His solution was to cut out the fences and pay a higher rate directly to the thieves. He covered his costs by charging the original owners a still higher fee. But his true subtlety lay in the way he avoided falling foul of the Receiving Acts. Hitchen had made the mistake of actually taking possession of the stolen goods in exchange for cash. Wild merely took the details of the loot from thieves. Then he would call at the owners' houses, saying he had heard that certain goods stolen from the house had surfaced, at a pawnbroker's, say. He would then offer to have the goods returned. If the proprietors turned him away, he would leave in a dignified huff, which usually had the effect of making the owner think again.[40]

Wild had other ways of making recalcitrant victims consent to use his services as middleman. He would place an advertisement in a daily newspaper. The following is a typical example:

> Lost, the 1st October, a black shagreen pocket-book edged with silver, with some notes of hand. The said book was lost in the Strand near the Fountain tavern, about seven or eight o'clock at night. If any person will bring the aforesaid book to Mr. Jonathan Wild in the Old Bailey, he shall have a guinea reward.

The subtext of this was clear to everyone who knew London; the phrase 'notes of hand' indicated that Wild knew who the owner was. The Fountain was a well-known brothel; therefore the owner would either have to retrieve his property or explain to his wife or mother what he was doing there.[41]

The final difficulty Wild had to surmount was how to return the property without compounding the felony. He did this by arranging direct meetings between thieves and owners at street corners, squares, or bridges. In the earlier part of his career Wild refused to accept a reward but took a share of the money paid to the thieves or pawnbroker.

More usually, however, the victim of theft or robbery was at once willing to co-operate with Wild. The victim would place an advertisement in the newspaper, naming Wild as his intermediary and specifying the reward. 'Going public' like this had a number of advantages for Wild. Placing the advertisement allayed any suspicions the owner, the public, or the authorities might have had that Wild might manipulate them: it proved that Wild did not possess the stolen goods himself; it informed the thieves that the owner was ready to come to terms; it made Wild's name familiar to the general public. In addition, in the rare cases where Wild genuinely did not know who had stolen the property in question, it brought new thieves into his circle.[42]

Pari passu with this ingenious system of receivership, Wild gradually brought the London underworld under his personal control, thus making himself in effect both chief of police and controller of organized crime.

His method was to suborn one member of a gang and bribe him to impeach two of his colleagues. Then he would suborn a fourth to lay charges against the first; in this way the whole gang collapsed like a house of cards. Thieves could not fathom that Wild had transferred the burden of risk to them. They were at risk while they had stolen goods in their possession; Wild, by contrast, was never in jeopardy. He could 'shop' them, but they were powerless against him. He lulled their suspicions by persuading them that they had nothing to fear from him, since he did not know their hideouts. But little by little he induced them to operate on regular 'beats' so that they could transfer goods to their owners more swiftly. In this way, and by bribing informers, he gradually got to know all their lairs.[43]

In 1716 Wild struck ruthlessly. With his private army of two executive assistants and a cohort of bodyguards, he broke up a number of gangs and captured a handful of wanted highwaymen, including the notorious James Goodman. Shortly after this, he arrested a gang of footpads who had been responsible for the murder of a Mrs Knapp. Since this crime was a contemporary *cause célèbre*, Wild's reputation as 'thieftaker-general' was now made.[44]

As time went on, Wild added further refinements to his system. With consummate impudence, he set up a 'lost property' office in the Old Bailey. This street, running north from Ludgate Hill, contained the famous open courthouse at which most of the sanguinary death sentences in London were pronounced. It also contained Newgate gaol. By this time Wild's fame had reached the point where he was able to give up calling at houses. He simply awaited the public in his office, charged them a search fee, and asked them to call again in a few days. At the second meeting he would say that he had discovered who the thieves were, but that they were threatening to sell to a pawnbroker unless they got a certain price. By this means he usually got his clients to raise the 'reward' to between two-thirds and three-quarters of the value of the goods. Once the reward was paid, Wild made arrangements for the property to be left at a particular place and time. He made sure that he never actually saw the loot himself.[45]

Wild's ingenuity did not go unperceived by the authorities. They knew in general terms how he operated, but could not prove anything. The best legal brains were cudgelled to find effective counter-measures. The result was the Receiving Act of 1717, which made it a felony for anyone to take a reward for returning stolen goods to their owner unless that person also arrested the thief and gave evidence against him.[46] The so-called 'Jonathan Wild Act' was at first thought to have decisively curtailed Wild's activities. But it did no such thing. Wild simply ceased to charge a fee for his services, but acted as go-between, informing the victims that if a certain sum of money was left at a particular place and time, the stolen goods would be restored. Since the sum to be left now had to include not just the thieves' share but Wild's own fee, it was crucial to him that those picking up the sum could not double-cross him. Wild solved this by employing as his agents in the field convicts who had returned from transportation. It was a bad blunder by the authorities to choose the same year for their Transportation Act and the 'Jonathan Wild Act'. Since the penalty for returning prematurely from transportation was death, Wild's agents could not testify against him without condemning themselves to death. So far from curbing Wild's activities, the 1717 Act simply made them even harder to bring to light.[47] In 1720 Wild impudently opened a second 'lost property' office in London.

Meanwhile he was consolidating his thief-taking empire. It was vital to suck all London criminals into the vortex of his circular system. The lost property offices depended on a continuing queue of clients, which in turn depended on a regular flow of thefts and robberies. The money made in 'rewards' financed the robbers in further robberies, thus keeping the cycle in being. But to prevent the London underworld from disposing of its booty through other outlets, all actual or potential threats to Wild's organization had to be smashed ruthlessly. With the help of his highly skilled assistants Abraham Mendez and Quilt Arnold, Wild engaged from 1720 to 1723 in a sustained bid to bring all London gangs under his control or destroy those that would not come to heel.[48]

Wild's success was phenomenal. In 1721 the notorious sept of London footpads, the Spiggott gang, was captured *en masse*. Spiggott himself at first refused to plead, but changed his mind after being pressed under an iron weight of 400 pounds. He and his accomplices were executed.[49] Then Wild turned his attention to his biggest challenge yet, the formidable Hawkins gang.

Although small (no more than six men), Hawkins's organization was the most feared of all. During the South Sea Bubble crisis of 1720 it had gone on the rampage. Sallying out to rob two or three nights a week that summer, Hawkins and his men made a special point of preying on the coaches and sedan-chairs of speculators leaving Exchange Alley. They were a particular challenge and affront to Wild, since they bypassed him and sold their booty in Holland.

The murder of a Dr Philip Potts in 1721 gave Wild his chance. He suborned a couple of Hawkins's men who had taken fright at the murder. Alarmed at his diminishing numbers, Hawkins meanwhile threw in his lot with Shaw's gang (thirteen strong). James Shaw was a much less subtle operator than Hawkins. He believed in murdering the people he robbed. Wild found it easy to make inroads into an organization whose members doubted their leader's judgement. By the end of 1721 bribery had done its work. Of the original gang only Shaw himself was left at liberty.[50]

Back-tracking out of the cul-de-sac into which he had placed himself,

Hawkins tried to revive his own gang. In 1722 a violent recrudescence of the Hawkins terror occurred, as his new band of cut-throats spread a reign of terror exceeding even that of summer 1720. Criss-crossing London, they committed over fifty highway robberies. On three successive nights they held up the Worcester, Bristol, Gloucester, Cirencester, Oxford, Ipswich, and Portsmouth stage-coaches.

But the net was closing on Hawkins. In 1722 Shaw was taken and executed. The only potential ally left for Hawkins now was Carrick's gang, thirty-two strong, a loose confederation mainly composed of Irish immigrants.[51] But before he could link with them, Hawkins's career ran into the ground. After robbing the Bristol mail, Hawkins and his men were pursued and run to earth in a London tavern. After a long trial, they were executed and hung in chains on Hounslow Heath, scene of the mail robbery.[52]

Now only the Carrick gang was left. On the face of it this was a formidable opponent even for Wild. Apart from its three outer layers, it possessed an inner nucleus of Irishmen, Carrick's praetorian guard. Yet Wild was propelled forward as much by the need to protect his own system as by motives of greed and empire building. Allies from an unexpected quarter came in 1722, the year of one of the great Jacobite conspiracies, the Layer/Atterbury plot.[53] As Irishmen, Carrick's gang were prime Jacobite suspects, and attracted the attention of the King's Messengers. Carrick was taken up on tenuous charges of Jacobitism, but in the paranoid atmosphere of 1722, it was easy to secure a conviction. Once Carrick himself was hanged, and after the fortuitous intervention of the secret police, Wild struck like a serpent at his followers. Between 23 July and 4 August 1722 he captured no less than twenty-two members of the once mighty Carrick gang, netting himself £900 in rewards into the bargain.[54]

Wild was now at the pinnacle of his success and was undisputed king of the London underworld. He had destroyed all his rivals. His thriving receiving business was intact. Yet even now ominous signs had appeared of the cracks in his organization that would eventually bring his downfall. Not even Wild could cover all his tracks and muzzle all the evidence against him. For the first time he was openly denounced in court by his victims and some of the men he had 'framed'.

It was while Wild was at his apogee and had not yet begun his downward descent that his name first became linked with Jack Sheppard. Sheppard was the perfect foil to Wild. In time he came to represent to the English public the forces of light ranged against Wild's prince of darkness.[55] Born in 1702, and just five feet four inches tall, Sheppard made an entry into a life of crime that was fortuitous. His mistress 'Edgeworth Bess' was arrested by a beadle. Sheppard took the law into his own hands, beat up the beadle and released her. He started robbing with the remains of Carrick's gang. His skills as carpenter and locksmith made him invaluable as a housebreaker.

A long run of luck in 1723-4 ended with Sheppard's arrest. He was imprisoned in St Giles's Roundhouse, but on his very first night of captivity burrowed out through the roof. Recaptured in May 1724, he was committed to the New Prison. Once again he broke out. This time his escape was the more spectacular as he had to take Edgeworth Bess with him (she had been gaoled with him). He lowered himself and his woman to the yard of the Clerkenwell Bridewell next door. Then he scaled a twenty-two-foot wall, hauled Bess after him, lowered her down on the other side, and then away.[56]

Wild now came into the picture. His fear was that Sheppard would emerge as the leader of a revived Carrick gang. Acting on the *cherchez la femme* principle, Wild tracked down Edgeworth Bess. In her cups she revealed Sheppard's whereabouts. The formidable Quilt Arnold armed himself to the teeth and burst in on Sheppard. Jack was taken to New Prison, then transferred to Newgate.

Sheppard was tried for three robberies, acquitted on two, and found guilty on the third on Wild's testimony. But on the very evening of the conviction Sheppard, assisted by Bess and another woman and his cell-mate cut away a bar in the door leading from the condemned-hold passage into the lodge. Then he squeezed through the gap, put on a long cloak, and sauntered out of the prison.[57]

He was free for just ten days before being recaptured by a posse on Finchley Common and brought back to Newgate. This time the keeper lodged him in the strongest room in the gaol and loaded him down with chains and fetters. Incredibly, Sheppard still managed to escape. To do so he had to break through six iron doors, all bolted and barred on the other side. He accomplished all this without tools or tinderbox in the pitch darkness and without alerting the guards. His only implements were the handcuffs and (later) an iron bar. Then he returned to his cell to knot together blankets so that he could shin down on to the roof of a neighbouring house.[58]

To escape under these circumstances seemed to defy physical laws. In an earlier era Sheppard might have incurred a charge of witchcraft. But his exploits created a sensation. Overnight he was the most famous man in England. Defoe related that most evenings you could not find a porter in London; they were all in the taverns toasting Jack. Sheppard himself listened amusedly in the alehouses as balladeers made up verses about his amazing deeds.

Such a famous and distinctive man could not remain at large for long unless he was a master of disguise or ingenuity. This was not Sheppard's forte. He was above all an escapologist of genius. Once again it took just ten days for Wild's men to track him down, dead drunk in a gin-shop in

Drury Lane. This time he was gaoled and weighted down with 300 pounds of iron. Not even Sheppard's great talents could save him this time. After being visited by thousands of sightseers, he was 'launched into eternity' on 16 November 1724. There were violent scenes at the foot of the gallows as two gangs of thugs fought over his body. When the rumour arose that his body was to be sold to the surgeons for dissection, an angry crowd formed and had to be dispersed by the foot guards with fixed bayonets.[59]

Although it was Wild's network of informers that had secured Sheppard on successive occasions, it was ironically Wild's very success that turned the public against him decisively. With his small stature and ready wit, Sheppard was the perfect 'Cockney sparrow'. It matters not that sober analysis shows him to have been a cold, unscrupulous ingrate. In the public perception he had been David to Wild's Goliath. This was the image created by that propagandist of genius, Defoe, and it was an image that stuck. In the nineteenth century Harrison Ainsworth put the crowning touch to Defoe's edifice. Ever afterwards Sheppard and Wild were locked together in a mythological embrace as symbols of good and evil.[60]

Perhaps the disillusionment of the London crowd would not have been so critical for Wild if he had not at the same time fallen foul of the authorities. Ever since Wild circumvented the 1717 Act, the elite had opted for making a virtue of necessity; after all, in his own way, Wild as thief-taker general performed a useful service. But this analysis began to be called into question when Wild failed an important test set by his political masters. One Roger Johnson was suspected of a major jewel robbery at Windsor Castle. The authorities looked to Wild to apprehend him and hand him over. But Wild, fearing the information Johnson could give about his own organization, hid him away in a safe house. This act of impertinence effectively sealed Wild's fate. By this time, too, he knew too much for comfort about the corrupt practices of the London magistracy. He seemed to be becoming too much like the sorcerer's apprentice. Word went out discreetly to the mandarins of the judiciary to find some way to bring Wild to book.[61]

The occasion was found in an apparently trivial charge, brought under an Act of 1706.[62] This stated that even if the original felon could not be taken, the receiver of any stolen goods could be tried for a misdemeanour and punished by a fine or corporal punishment. Wild was acquitted, as was expected, since in the case in question the principal felon had been arrested, convicted, and executed. But the charade bought time for the prosecution and prevented Wild from getting bail. Then the City Recorder presented to the court a 'Warrant of Detainer', which detailed a long list of Wild's crimes.[63] It was obvious that by showing his hand so openly, the Recorder was insinuating that at long last he had proof of the offences Wild was long known to have committed but which could never be pinned on him.

Sent back to Newgate to prepare his defence, Wild tried to read the prosecution's mind. The truth was that he was past his best mentally and allowed his enemies to bluff him. The old Jonathan Wild would never have allowed himself to be mesmerized in this way.[64] The first charge being brought against him was under the Shoplifting Act of 1699.[65] He was accused of stealing fifty yards of lace, value £40, from the shop of Catherine Statham. The defence pointed out that since Wild had never been in the shop, he could not be guilty of 'privately stealing'. At most he was an accessory, but this was a clergyable offence. Wild was acquitted.

But in securing the acquittal, he made a bad mistake and ran ahead to deal with matters in the Statham case, which he imagined was the prosecution's next ploy. He admitted accepting a reward of ten guineas from Mrs Statham for helping her to recover the stolen lace. Wild thought himself safe, since he had brought the culprit Henry Kelly to justice, so was not vulnerable under the 1717 Act. Since his own guilt or innocence was to be decided before Henry Kelly was tried, it seemed logical to assume that he could not be found guilty of receiving before the felony of theft itself was established.[66]

But the authorities were determined to hang him. Hurriedly they cobbled together a second charge, of receiving (under the 1717 'Jonathan Wild Act'). The judge dismissed as irrelevant the fact that Kelly had not yet been found guilty of theft. Whenever Wild tried to raise this obvious point, the judge silenced him. The fact was that neither Kelly nor the others involved in the crime could be found guilty first, simply because they had only agreed to give evidence in the first place in exchange for immunity. In any case, if found guilty, they could not (unless pardoned) legally give evidence against Wild. In strict justice the harshest penalty Wild could have expected was transportation.

Yet the elite were determined to have their pound of flesh. Wild was convicted of receiving before it was established that the primary felony had been committed. It was a classic case of the 'grin without the cat'. There was gross injustice in Wild's case, but it does not seem to have proceeded from a conspiracy, wherein the prosecution had the second charge ready if the first failed. What seems to have happened, rather, is that Wild was too clever by half. He brought nemesis on himself by pre-empting the charges he imagined were pending in the Statham case and thus alerting the prosecution to his Achilles' heel. The prosecution then prepared a second indictment at great speed to take account of his evidence. In effect Wild talked himself on to the gallows.[67]

Taken back to Newgate, Wild tried unsuccessfully to cheat the hangman by taking an overdose of laudanum.[68] On 25 May 1725 he was executed at Tyburn. So perished the greatest criminal entrepreneur of the century. Yet his achievements as thief-taker soon made themselves felt. After his death there was a dramatic fall in the rate of convictions and in the number of hangings.[69] Quite simply, a vacuum had been created. There was no one left to discover and denounce thieves. It was not long before the solid citizen started to have second thoughts and regret his passing. After his demise, there was no longer any easy way to recover stolen property. The government had got rid of a master criminal but in so doing appeared to have thrown out the baby with the bathwater.[70]

The fall of Jonathan Wild did not, however, mean the end of thief-taking. The criminality of the system had been exposed by the numerous 'Lives' of Wild that appeared in print after his execution but, failing, any proper system of police, the most effective method of control of crime had to be 'set a thief to catch a thief'. Until the 1750s thief-takers were part of the informal social system.[71] Still, there was uneasiness about a policy of official connivance that at once allowed confessed thieves to escape punishment and held out great rewards for the apprehension and conviction of criminals. Since the possibility for framing an innocent man so clearly existed, it became the custom for accused thieves to turn this on its head and claim in every case that they had been set up by thief-takers.[72]

The most commonly practised 'fit-up' of the innocent was the pseudo-robbery. A thief-taker would organize a gang, say four strong. His agent or 'decoy duck' would induce one of London's marginal drifters to commit a theft or robbery on another member of the gang. The offender would then be denounced and convicted and the reward paid over to the thief-taker. Sometimes the gang would double its gains by alleging that more than one person was involved in the crime. This left the door open to the subsequent framing of another innocent. Usually the victims were the very young or rank novices at crime. Their youth and rawness did not bother the thief-takers. They were quite prepared to swear away the life of some hapless, probably mentally subnormal, 'thief'.[73]

A refinement of the 'fit-up' involved the collusion of a corrupt constable. The ingenuity of this variant was that an independent victim would be involved, who had no connection with the thief-taking organization. A passer-by would see a person being robbed (in reality one of the gang) and run to his or her assistance. The parish constable would conveniently be at hand. Together the witness and the constable would chase and arrest the robber. They would all go together to the magistrate. There the constable would be joined by the other members of the conspiracy.[74] Together they would swear that it was the casual passer-by who had committed the robbery. Joshua Kidden, executed 1753, was one of the innocents framed in this way. The cruel nuance to this case was that it was a woman, Mary Jones, who told a heartrending tale of the brutal 'robbery'.[75]

The bubble of this especially nefarious form of 'thief-taking' was finally burst in 1756 by Joseph Cox, High Constable of the 'hundred' of Blackheath. The MacDaniel Gang were past masters at the 'thief-taking' of innocents. Their victims this time were Peter Kelly and John Ellis. Stephen MacDaniel, thief-taker extraordinary, arrested the two men for robbing a breeches-maker called James Salmon. Two witnesses, John Berry and James Egan, appeared and swore that Salmon had been robbed by Kelly and Ellis. But Constable Cox had information that the whole affair was a thief-taking 'scam', that Salmon himself was in on the conspiracy.[76] By diligent detective work, he tracked down a man called Blee, who did MacDaniel's fencing. In return for immunity for past criminal conspiracies, Cox persuaded Blee to turn king's evidence and reveal the entire workings of the MacDaniel 'thief-taking' operation. Cox then arrested the four principals in the conspiracy.[77]

Cox had hoped to get the men convicted on a capital felony, but the indictment failed because of legal technicalities over the concept of 'conspiracy'. Even when it was shown quite clearly that they had caused the death of innocent men, the judiciary preferred to turn a blind eye to their blatant perjury, lest a draconian stance against people who forswore themselves dried up the supply of willing informers in other cases.[78] Yet fate decreed that the men would suffer capital punishment by another route. The four were retried on a lesser charge of falsely obtaining rewards. Found guilty, they were sentenced to the pillory. Given the savage mood of the London crowd against these homicidal pseudo-thieftakers, this came close to being a death sentence in itself. MacDaniel and Berry were put in the pillory first and emerged at the end of an hour with severe injuries from the stone-throwing throng of spectators. Egan and Salmon fared even worse. They were pelted with stones, brickbats, potatoes, dead cats and dogs. Seeing the men in danger of their lives, the constables tried to intervene but were overpowered by the crowd. Both men's heads had swollen to an enormous size when they were finally extricated from the pillory. Egan was found to be dead. During the first half hour an enormous stone had crushed his skull. Salmon was not far from death himself. He and MacDaniel and Berry died soon afterwards in Newgate from lack of medical care following their ordeal in the stocks.[79]

The MacDaniel case destroyed whatever credibility had been left to thief-takers after Jonathan Wild. Inch by inch the English people were dragged unwillingly towards the concept of professional police, 'ancient liberties' notwithstanding. The ineffectiveness even of the improved Watch on one hand, and the impious corruption of thief-taking on the other, created a vacuum too great to be left unfilled. This was the gap the Fieldings tried to plug in the 1750s, when both brothers held the office of principal magistrate for Westminster.[80]

The crime wave following the end of the War of Austrian Succession convinced the novelist Henry Fielding and his blind half-brother John that the old bulwarks against violent crime were not enough. They painted an apocalyptical vision of the anarchy to come if the idea of police was not embraced.[81] The Fieldings saw that there was much to learn from the thief-taking experience, especially in the time of Wild. Wild had sent his lieutenants out of London, to Bristol and other cities, in pursuit of their quarry. This idea appealed to the Fieldings. The task was to dissociate the new kind of operative from the taint of association with the old thief-takers.

Henry Fielding began the crusade with his famous *An Inquiry into the causes of the late Increase in Robbers* (considered further in chapter 12) in 1751. Two years earlier he had set up the first of the 'Bow Street runners', operating from his magistrate's office at Bow Street.[82] He persuaded half a dozen former parish constables to put themselves under his command as a genuine thief-taker. At first they worked only for rewards, then they were paid a guinea a week plus rewards for every criminal successfully prosecuted. The first fruits of the new scheme came in 1753 when Henry Fielding broke up a notorious gang of homicidal robbers in London.[83]

There is no doubt that the Fielding magistracy, universally conceded to be the first totally uncorrupt one in London, marked a turning point in attitudes and approaches to crime. At first Henry Fielding's chief assistant was Saunders Welch.[84] Welch was High Constable of Holborn during Fielding's magistracy. Fielding thought him the finest collaborator imaginable, but for some obscure reason his enthusiasm was not shared by senior figures in the elite. Although Fielding recommended Welch as a JP in December 1753, he was not in fact appointed to the commission until April 1755, six months after Fielding's demise. After the novelist's sudden death in Lisbon in 1754 at the age of 47, it was his blind brother John (knighted 1761) who stepped into the breach. From 1754 and for the next half century (as principal magistrate for Westminster 1754-80) Fielding waged an implacable, at times fanatical, campaign.[85]

The 1750s saw a flood of publications issuing from John Fielding's pen. His abiding aim was a large-scale permanent force of 'runners'.[86] His early successes made good propaganda for the cause. 'Mr. Fielding's men' went as far afield as Bristol and Portsmouth in pursuit of villains. Fielding himself was a man of the J. Edgar Hoover stamp, as much in his zealotry as in his implacable hatred of crime and his contemptuous rejection of any 'liberal' justifications for criminal behaviour.[87] Another point of similarity was in the way he dragged the unwilling authorities in the direction of the creation of a national police force. Yet another was the way the successes of the operatives were 'talked up'. The truth was that the 'Bow Street runners' were no more than glorified bounty-hunters.

They were no better than the men they pursued and arrested, performed only when paid, and in general were 'self-seeking knaves'.[88] But, as with Hoover and the 'G-Men', John Fielding's relentless propaganda on the runners' behalf, portraying them as tireless paladins and crusaders for righteousness, paid a rich dividend. By the 1780s the Bow Street runners were already a national institution, even though in Fielding's time they did not wear the distinctive uniform that earned them the later sobriquet of 'Robin Redbreasts'.[89] The eighteenth century was rich in criminal legend. The Bow Street runners no more deserved their reputation than Dick Turpin or Jack Sheppard did.

By the end of the 1750s John Fielding could look back on some solid achievements. The law on receiving had been amended so as to disrupt the association of ideas between that offence and thief-taking.[90] Following suggestions from Fielding himself, pawnbrokers were compelled to keep detailed records of all goods brought to them for hock.[91] Later, in 1785, a further act required pawnbrokers to be licensed annually. Both these acts reinforced the principle first adumbrated in the 1717 'Jonathan Wild Act' – that receivers should be tried and punished irrespective of the fate of the principal felons.[92]

By this time Fielding had popularized the very word 'police'. In 1757 he floated the idea of having a regiment of light horse at the ready in London to pursue highwaymen.[93] This was clearly controversial, as it meant using the military for civilian police purposes; it also played into the hands of critics of both Fieldings who alleged that their ulterior aim was a French-style tyranny that would destroy traditional English liberties.[94] Besides, in wartime the crime rate was always low (see chapter 17). But when the Treaty of Paris in 1763 unleashed a horde of veterans on to the streets and lanes of England and the crime rate soared, the authorities looked more sympathetically on Fielding's proposal. He was given an experimental mounted patrol of eight men for six months.

The sequel should not surprise anyone familiar with central government niggardliness. When the post-war crime wave began to level off, the authorities began to carp about the costs. They suggested that the county should begin to assume the financial burden. When Fielding refused, they simply disbanded the horse patrol. But in the eighteen months of its existence, the patrol had proved itself. While not willing to bear the expenses of horses, Fielding financed a mobile foot patrol which could be sent out at a moment's notice to any location in London.[95]

This was not the end of Sir John Fielding's initiatives. In 1772 he produced a General Preventative Plan for an embryonic national police force. The plan envisaged a primitive 'National Reporting Centre'.[96] Such a national network was becoming increasingly feasible as the century's accelerating technology made its impact. The first signs of an inchoate consumer society were beginning to be seen with the coming of the necessary infrastructure: turnpike roads, postal services, improved communications.[97] Most of all there was the multiplication of printing presses and the proliferation of newspapers. This meant that it was easier to advertise for wanted criminals or stolen property.[98] The vast expansion of information and literature about crime and criminals represented a technological quantum jump over the old society of the 'hue and cry'. Fielding was determined to exploit these changes.

Fielding was particularly impressed by the way Samuel Lister, a justice of the peace in the West Riding of Yorkshire, had caught a well-known local forger (Edward Wilson) by widespread use of the new information technology.[99] The principal obstacle in the way of professional policing in England (again, a pre-echo of the early days of J. Edgar Hoover) was the ease with which an offender could escape justice by fleeing to a different part of the country. Not only did magistrates in the area where a crime had been committed have no powers outside that area; in most cases they did not even know the names and addresses of magistrates elsewhere to whom to apply, even if they knew where their criminal had gone. There was no means of passing on information about offenders between regions and counties; even if there had been, there was still the question of the expense of disseminating intelligence about wanted criminals. And nearly all newspapers of the period were geographically limited in their circulations.[100]

By making a strenuous effort to get round these obstacles, and committing time and money, Lister had run his man to earth. This gave Fielding the clue he needed. The first thing was to get all provincial magistrates to inform his office at Bow Street directly. Then it would be necessary to send all provincial newspapers, bearing the details of crimes and wanted criminals, to every single mayor and magistrate in the country. The next stage was to publish a national crime journal. Fielding's *Hue and Cry* was the first important fruit of his 1772 General Preventative Plan. *Hue and Cry* was posted in every market place of every corporation town from Cornwall to Edinburgh. In addition, Fielding circulated cumulative lists of all offenders still at large to every magistrate in the country. These lists appeared yearly or half-yearly.[101]

At first Fielding's innovations were acclaimed as an important breakthrough in the war against crime. But the enthusiasm soon died away when Fielding, heartened by the initial response, tried to go further, always seeking the Holy Grail of a national police force. His next proposal was that the office of High Constable should be turned into a *de facto* local chief of police. His idea was that for at least one hundred miles from London the High Constables in the hundreds through which the main roads ran should be resident on those roads and receive a salary and expenses, paid out of a tax on places of public entertainment.[102]

At this point the counties began to evince their distaste for Fielding's reforming zeal. From the task of collecting the county rate, the High Constables were being expected to switch to full-time criminal investigators. Not only did the new bearing proposed seem at odds with their original role; it also seemed to bring the dreaded spectre of professional police a step nearer. Moreover, it was precisely the kind of person in the counties, suffused with 'country' ideology that scouted executive intervention, that was being expected to play sleuth.

Unwittingly, Fielding had crossed the invisible dividing line between 'soundness' and fanaticism. The county authorities were very interested in anything that effectively prevented crime, but not if it meant reducing themselves to the undignified role of thief-taker, on behalf of a central government bent on destroying ancient liberties. In any case, Fielding misread the situation. Extrapolating from the London experience, he imagined that provincial authorities had the same crime rates and therefore the same obsession with crime. He was on the right lines, for as the century proceeded, the problems encountered in London tended to be reproduced elsewhere in England. But he was running ahead of himself. The time for the idea of a nationally-linked police force had not yet come. In any case, London, Middlesex, and Westminster possessed an institutional framework and a bureaucratic uniformity that did not exist elsewhere. Even at the level of administration, Fielding's proposed reform of the constables was probably impracticable because of the multipurpose nature of the local administrative apparatus of the time.[103]

Sir John Fielding died in 1780 with his dreams still unfulfilled. But the seeds he had sown bore fruit after his death. The Bow Street runners won the propaganda battle for hearts and minds. In 1792 seven more offices on the Bow Street model were established in London by Act of Parliament. Stipendiary magistrates were paid out of public funds; clients' fees thenceforth went into the public coffers, not the justices' pockets. By the end of the eighteenth century London possessed about fifty full-time detectives in eight or nine groups. The Bow Street office could be called in nationwide. It was the embryo of Scotland Yard.[104] In 1798 crime on the Thames resulted in the establishment of the River Police, following the proselytizing work by Patrick Colquhoun, who first revealed the staggering volume of riparian crime. Colquhoun publicly acknowledged his debt to the pioneering Fieldings.[105]

Amid the rapid change of the eighteenth century, a skein of continuity can be discerned. Colquhoun took over from the Fieldings the idea of a metropolitan police; the Fieldings took from Jonathan Wild the idea of a nationwide network. The great irony about the Napoleonic period from the policing point of view is that while England edged ever closer to the idea of a professional force of criminal investigators, France, by engaging the famous criminal Eugène Vidocq as *chef de sûreté* returned in effect to the system of Jonathan Wild.[106]

3

Homicide

What the dickens is the woman always a-whimpering about murder for? No gentleman is ever looked on the worse for killing a man in his own defence . . . murder is as fashionable a crime as a man may be guilty of.

John Gay, *The Beggar's Opera*

See how love and murder will out.

William Congreve, *The Double Dealer*

Her death was doubtful,
And but that great command o'ersways the order,
She should in ground unsanctified have lodg'd
Till the last trumpet

William Shakespeare, *Hamlet*, V.i.231

In all societies murder is the most sensational and gravely regarded crime and the one, above all others, considered by social conservatives to merit the death penalty. When contemplating the severe penalties prescribed for this offence against humanity as well as the law, the Englishman has traditionally consoled himself with the thought that, if accused of it, he is at least innocent until proved guilty. It comes as a shock, then, to realize that this was not the case in the eighteenth century. All cases of homicide were treated as murder. It was for the defendant to establish that the homicide was justifiable and hence not murder. There was no pre-trial winnowing of indictments by a police force so that a charge of either murder or manslaughter could be brought against a person accused of homicide. The onus of proof was on the defendant. In this sense he was guilty until proved innocent.[1]

Eighteenth-century murder trials crucially turned on 'malice aforethought'. This excluded as murder both manslaughter and justifiable homicide. Blackstone further subdivided justifiable homicide into the category proper and what he called 'excusable' homicide. The idea was that in justifiable homicide no blame whatever attached to the person

36

doing the killing. Examples included the shooting by peace officers of someone resisting arrest or trying to break out of gaol; also the killing by a woman of a man who was trying to rape her or the killing by a paterfamilias of anyone trying to rape his wife or daughters.[2] In the case of 'excusable' homicide some slight scintilla of blame did attach to the killer. Blackstone's excusable homicide is our 'killing by accident or misadventure'. Accidental killing was particularly likely to involve horses. (There were 8,000 private and public coaches in London in the middle of the eighteenth century, and many times more horses.)[3] The other form of 'excusable homicide' was self-defence.

Manslaughter was different again from both kinds of justifiable homicide. Blackstone distinguished them as follows: homicide by accident or misadventure involved unintentional killing while pursuing a lawful purpose (as when the head of an axe wielded by a woodchopper flies off and kills a bystander); manslaughter involves unintentional killing in the course of an 'idle, dangerous and unlawful sport', as, for example, during a boxing match, a duel, or a wrestling contest.[4] The eighteenth-century legal system interpreted this distinction very liberally. Beating servants or children was not regarded as dangerous or unlawful. If you killed a child or servant during a thrashing, you would not be found guilty of either murder or manslaughter unless you used an 'unusual implement', for example a club. Manslaughter meant that you had actually to be fighting at the time the mortal stroke was given.[5] The one exception was for a husband to find a man in bed with his wife. Although to catch adulterers *in flagrante* was not permitted as a pretext for justifiable homicide, the rule of thumb was that a slaying in such a case was manslaughter rather than murder, since adultery was regarded as the worst possible kind of provocation.[6]

To convert a murder charge into one of manslaughter was a consummation devoutly to be wished for any defendant in a homicide case. In contrast to hanging for murder, the law invariably prescribed burning in the hand for manslaughter in the first half of the century. Even transportation was considered too severe. After 1760 imprisonment became the normal manslaughter penalty, especially when burning in the hand was abolished in 1779. The reason for leniency was that manslaughter seemed a natural consequence of generally condoned social violence. Many such homicides occurred as the result of brutal bare-knuckle boxing matches. Tavern brawls and fatal quarrels in drink were also common.[7]

Yet verbal taunts alone did not constitute grounds for a manslaughter plea. Actual blows had to be struck and the retaliation had to be immediate, in hot blood, or the homicide was murder. A good example of the sort of situation that would have engendered manslaughter was seen at the Drury Lane theatre in the 1740s. Here the management hired professional boxers and prize-fighters to intimidate hostile audiences. When the curtain went up, the entire stage was often full of thugs armed with bludgeons and clubs, defying the audience to boo the production. On one occasion these desperadoes were introduced into the pit to knock down anyone who hissed. Since a professional fighter's hands are held to be a deadly weapon in law, there was an obvious risk of murder. But the crowd in the pit retaliated with blows and drove them out by sheer force of numbers.[8] Had anyone been killed in the mêlée, the jury's verdict would almost certainly have fastened on manslaughter.

The theatre was in fact often the occasion for homicide. James Quin was a celebrated tragic actor on the London stage. Another actor whom he had insulted waylaid him in Covent Garden piazza. In the ensuing struggle Quin ran his rival through with a sword and killed him. The popularity of Quin was undoubtedly a factor, along with the element of self-defence, in securing a manslaughter verdict.[9]

There was one main exception to the general rule governing manslaughter. The so-called 'Stabbing Act' of 1604 made it a capital non-clergyable offence to wound a person mortally with a knife, whatever the overall intent. In this way a species of manslaughter was declared to be murder.[10] To enter an affray with a knife carried the obvious risk that if you killed someone you could not plead manslaughter, whatever the provocation.[11] The obvious moral was never to carry a knife, but from the first to the last decades of the century men were hanged for stabbing in street fights.[12] By extension, the 'Coventry Act' governing mayhem removed benefit of clergy from anyone who maimed the person of another in the eye, ear, tongue, etc., even if death did not result.[13] There were several executions for mayhem during the century.[14] Hence was produced the curious result that to maim a servant was a capital offence but to beat him to death was not. Finally, not the least of the many absurdities of the notorious 'Waltham Black Act' was that it was a capital offence to fire a gun in a dwelling place, regardless of whether or not anyone was hurt.[15]

It will be clear that the 'end-product' of a dead body was far from being necessarily the most serious factor in the eighteenth-century approach to crime. And even where the law was crystal-clear, it was often disregarded by juries, who considered that their knowledge of local customs and insight into extenuating circumstances overrode the strict letter of the law. It was the jury that made the final decision on whether a homicide was justifiable, manslaughter, or murder.[16] A few case studies will illustrate this point.

In 1744 Lydia Adler was found guilty of manslaughter and burnt in the hand after killing her common-law husband by kicking and stamping him in the groin. The mitigating circumstances in this case were twofold. Her husband suffered from a rupture, and had he been in normal health, her kicks would not have caused his death. Second, Lydia was just one of four 'wives' Adler enjoyed, and it was a quarrel between Lydia and one of the others that led to the assault.[17]

On the other hand, it was murder when a Newcastle pawnbroker shot dead a keelman who was trying to scale the wall of his house. Not only was the intention of the intruder not clear, though felonious intent could be presumed; more important, the pawnbroker had had time to weigh his actions. He had called for his wife to bring him musket and powder and thus had had a 'cooling-off' period in which to contemplate his actions.[18]

Anti-Jewish prejudice clearly played a part in a manslaughter verdict in 1784. During the Jewish harvest festival in October some boys on their way home from the synagogue let off fireworks near the premises of Mr Porter Ridout, a coffee-house keeper in Duke's Place. Ridout called out to the boys to stop. When they persisted he went to an upstairs window and discharged a blunderbuss at them. Two boys fell dead on the spot and three more were seriously wounded; one was pronounced dead on arrival at hospital.[19]

Ridout's trial was presided over by Lord Loughborough. In his summing up, he provided some of the most interesting legal distinctions of the century between murder and manslaughter. According to Loughborough, you did not need to have selected a particular victim to be guilty of murder; shooting at a crowd with malice constituted murderous intent. Similarly, if you drew a bead on a particular individual in the crowd, but hit someone else instead, you were still guilty of murder, even though no intention was directed against that particular person. Nevertheless, his Lordship told the jury that if they concluded that the balance of Ridout's mind was disturbed when he shot at the boys, they should acquit him of murder. The jury took the hint and brought in a verdict of manslaughter without even retiring.[20]

The most famous case in the century involving a murder charge where the jury decided on manslaughter, was that of Giuseppe Baretti, Italian writer and critic, in 1769. As he walked through the streets of London, he was subjected to deliberate provocation by a young woman who kneed him in the genitals, hoping to cause a scene so that her male accomplice could 'intervene'. In the ensuing struggle, Baretti drew a knife and killed his assailant.[21] Baretti was in serious danger of seeing the murder charge against him sustained for two reasons. One was the natural xenophobia of the London juryman. The other was the fact that he had used a knife; the provisions of the 'Stabbing Act' seemed to allow no latitude to the jury, and Baretti's friend Samuel Johnson feared the likely outcome.

Yet the jury acquitted Baretti of murder. There were two main reasons for this. A host of eminent people came forward to attest to Baretti's character and accomplishments. These included, apart from Dr Johnson, Edmund Burke, David Garrick, Oliver Goldsmith, and Sir Joshua

Reynolds. Burke, Garrick and Reynolds stood bail for Baretti before the much-feared Lord Mansfield.[22] Second, the two factors initially predisposing a jury against Baretti cancelled themselves out. His defence established that it was universal continental practice to carry a knife, not for offensive purposes, but simply because it was the custom in the inns of Europe to provide only forks at mealtimes. The jury's acceptance of the lesser plea of manslaughter demonstrated both that jurymen were alive to the nuances of local folkways and regarded this as a key extenuating circumstance, and that they were impressed by a 'character' given by eminent and reputable witnesses.[23]

The common prejudice of juries against the military, however, made their verdicts in cases involving soldiers and peace officers unreliable and eccentric. Joseph Relph, one of the last men to be branded for manslaughter (in 1778), was lieutenant of a press-gang, and he killed a man after an affray when he lifted up a woman's skirt.[24] This was clearly a case of accidental death, and the jury returned the correct verdict. But there was no malice aforethought in another case where a jury brought in a murder verdict against a soldier. One day in 1723 William Hawkesworth was marching with a battalion of guards in St. James's Park. Hearing a woman call out an insult to his regiment, Hawkesworth left the ranks and hit the woman's male companion. The man fractured his skull and died. There was obviously no intent to murder but the jury found Hawkesworth guilty of murder and he was executed.[25] This was a blatant case of anti-military prejudice, but unlike other instances, the Army did not extend its protective mantle to the luckless soldier. Doubtless the authorities felt that after the jangling of civilian nerves in the crisis of 1722 (the time of the Layer/Atterbury plot), it was politic to throw an innocent to the wolves. In another case, in 1799, when a soldier murdered a comrade in an alehouse brawl, the verdict would almost certainly have been manslaughter if the combatants had been civilians. As it was, the jury found the soldier guilty of murder and he was executed.[26]

Another case evincing anti-military prejudice was that of William Riley. A soldier in the Foot Guards, he took part in the walking contests, hugely popular in the eighteenth century. Large sums were wagered on men being able to walk 300 miles in six days, and similar feats. On the last day of such a marathon walk in which he was trying for a record, Riley, anxious to succeed, lashed out at the crowd of spectators who were pressing around him and restricting his movements. One of them returned the blow. In exasperation Riley drew his sword and ran the man through. Again, although this was clearly manslaughter, the jury was determined to have its pound of military flesh. Riley was executed in 1750, aged 19.[27]

Apart from self-defence, justifiable and excusable homicide, and manslaughter, the only plea a defendant could bring to escape a murder charge was insanity. Yet the English legal system has always been suspicious of insanity pleas, if only because it means surrendering the supremacy of lawyers to another set of 'experts' (physicians, alienists, psychiatrists).[28] The eighteenth-century precedent in such cases was set by the judge in the 1724 Arnold case. Edward Arnold was being tried under the recently passed Waltham Black Act for shooting at Lord Onslow, and pleaded temporary insanity. But the judge restricted the area in which an insanity plea was operable. He distinguished between 'lunacy' – defined as a state of intermittent insanity – and 'idiocy' – a state of utter, incorrigible, unintelligent bestiality. Only 'idiocy' was to be allowed as a defence in murder cases. The Bloody Code had no use for 'dissociative reaction' or other versions of 'temporary insanity'. Arnold was found guilty, sentenced to death, but reprieved and gaoled for life.[29]

In the area of insanity pleas we may perhaps discern some influence of Enlightenment thought after 1760. It is estimated that such a plea was entered in about twelve cases a year in England and Wales in the 1750s and was successful in about a third of them. Thereafter both the frequency of the plea and its success rate increased.[30]

Yet in the majority of cases, manslaughter remained the most reliable defence to a murder charge.[31] This was because most murders took place in circumstances of hot blood, where intent was difficult to prove, and where it was absurd to imagine that the killer could have rationally contemplated the likely consequences of his act. In a word, as in all modern eras for which there is reliable evidence, in settled societies murder overwhelmingly takes place in a family context in its widest sense (including common-law partners, wives, and mistresses and taking in the 'extended' family).

A detailed study of murder in Surrey between 1678 and 1774 underscores this point strongly. Of all homicide indictments at the Surrey assizes in these years, roughly 13 per cent fell in the category of accidental death, 23 per cent were found to be manslaughter, 3 per cent justifiable homicide, some 13 per cent were murders committed during another crime, and 36 per cent were murders in the family. In other words, *two-thirds of the actual murders* involved people who had known each other intimately.[32] If we look at the numbers of people convicted in the same sample, we find that about half of those found guilty of murder knew the victim well. The gap between the percentage of *murderers* and the percentage of *murder cases* is explained by the fact that in the non-family murder cases usually more than one murderer was involved.[33]

The fact that, in the eighteenth century as in our own day, most murders took place in the family is one more reason why the sanguinary capital provisions of the Code stood no more chance (and probably a lot less) of deterring people from murder than from any other crime. Where capital punishment fails to deter in circumstances when the criminal *can* foresee the possible consequences of his crime, as with burglary, highway robbery, and so on, it is surely obvious that it will fail even more signally in those circumstances, such as with family murder, where he cannot. Moreover, as a phenomenon murder highlights a central paradox. In most cases, the supreme penalty cannot deter those with a motive to murder. Those whom it might deter, the cold-blooded, premeditating contract killers, are almost impossible to detect, precisely because they have no apparent motive. It is a commonplace of law enforcement that the contract killer or other motiveless murderer is virtually certain to escape scot-free, unless the police get the assistance of a well-placed informant. Once again we confront the fact that the only possible justification of capital punishment for murder must be the retributive one.

Murder was usually committed for a limited number of reasons and in a limited number of contexts. First, there were the murders within the extended family. Second, there were crimes of passion. Third, there was murder of masters by servants. Finally, there was murder in the course of another crime.

The sole surprising thing about murder committed during another crime was that there was not more of it. Since the Bloody Code prescribed the death penalty for trivial property offences *as well as* for murder, the logical expectation might be that burglars, footpads, and other criminals would always murder their victims. Montesquieu in his *L'Esprit des Lois* drew attention to this to demonstrate the absurdity of a uniformly harsh level of punishment in society.

> In China those who add robbery to murder are cut in pieces; but not so the others; to this difference it is owing, that though they rob in that country, they never murder. In Russia, where the punishment of robbery and murder is the same, they always murder. The dead, they say, tell no tales.[34]

Montesquieu then went on to confront the obvious objection to his theory. In England, the punishment for the two offences was substantially the same, yet the incidence of murder was very low. Montesquieu tried to solve this conundrum by saying that in England robbers had some hopes of transportation, while murderers had none. The psychology of this is most unconvincing. We are asked to believe that a robber, contemplating whether to murder his victim, was restrained by the thought that he *might* be transported instead. So he might. But he might equally be hanged. The very lack of certainty at the heart of the eighteenth-century theory of deterrence by capital punishment – which its critics so derided as it seemed to reduce the legal system to a lottery – cut the ground from under Montesquieu's explanation. *Some* robbers were hanged while *some* murderers were reprieved.

The flaw in Montesquieu's thinking is his overconfident assertion that in Russia robbers *always* murdered. This, too, is psychologically unconvincing. As countless psychologists and novelists have demonstrated, outside wartime and excepting psychopaths, the moral barrier to murder is deeply planted in the human mind. To override this profound inhibition is to gamble with one's own sanity. The motives that led men to highway and footpad robbery and to burglary were very different from those impelling to murder. The central fallacy in Montesquieu's system, and later in Bentham's, was to regard all crime as being homogeneous, differing in degree but not in kind. In Bentham's view a proper system of punishment would grade the degree of punishment according to the degree of the offence. It never seems to have occurred to him that some crimes are offences against nature as well as against the law and are therefore different *in kind*. The reason that there was relatively little murder in pursuit of another crime was that people who were driven by want, hunger, or greed to rob were not thereby disposed to murder, even when it might be expedient and prudent for them to do so. It was no thanks to the Bloody Code that murder rates were not higher. If human beings really were units in a felicific calculus, *à la* Bentham, the principle of 'dead men tell no tales' would have made a more potent impact.

As it was, those committing lesser crimes tended to murder when they panicked or when their victims resisted or fought back. A good example of panic was the Gardelle case of 1761. Theodore Gardelle, a German, killed his London landlady by accident after a quarrel. Having lost his head during the row, he then entered a mode of ice-coolness. Instead of decamping from the scene of the crime, he calmly cut up the body and started to burn it. The fire aroused the suspicions of neighbours. The constable was sent for, and the rest of the corpse discovered.[35]

Very severe sanctions were visited on those who committed murder in the pursuit of another crime and then acted with total lack of remorse. In 1723 Jacob Saunders was hung in chains after execution for the cold-blooded way he compounded his original crimes. First he ambushed a farmer and murdered him for £60 cash. Arrested on suspicion while calmly attending a church service near Reading, he framed two innocent small-time villains for the murder to save his own skin. All winter the two men languished in gaol until by pure chance firm evidence was found to convict Saunders.[36] Since the Code ordained capital punishment for robbery alone, the authorities were hard put to devise an extra penalty for robbery *with* murder. The usual solution was to execute the criminals and then, as with Saunders, to hang their bodies in chains.

The most open-and-shut murder cases were those where the accused had shot someone dead in the course of a robbery, usually of the footpad or housebreaking variety.[37] A Jewish gang led by Levi Weil had a successful record of housebreaking and robbery in London. But their run of luck came to an end during the pillaging of the Hutchins household in Chelsea (in 1771) when a servant was shot dead. Unfortunately for Weil he had enlisted some of his gang members over in Holland to do this particular job. When the usual rewards were posted, one of the Dutchmen decided to 'shop' his comrades. On his information six men were arrested. Two of the gang were acquitted, but Weil and three others went to the gallows.[38] The fact that Jews had been involved in a criminal organization led to virulent outbursts of anti-Semitism and to physical attacks on Jews in London.[39]

Many cases of murder in the course of another crime were on a more banal level. Usually they involved clients in brothels who were murdered when they awoke while the pimp or madam was going through their pockets. By extension, guests in inns were sometimes at risk from innkeepers, and tenants in boarding houses from their landlords. But a serious case in the first year of the eighteenth century provoked public anger not just because the offenders were foreigners but because of the degree of premeditation in the crime. The Van Berghen couple from Holland, who could barely speak English, robbed their tenant, then prevailed on their servant to murder him. Public anger was assuaged by executing all three responsible for the murder. The woman was burnt and the bodies of the two men hung in chains.[40]

That Montesquieu's analysis of the reasons for murder was wide of the mark can be seen from the very great public indignation at any murder that *had* been coldly premeditated. In 1735 a Bristol sailor poisoned himself to escape hanging after the murder of his wife (following a lengthily gestated plan). The enraged mob dug up his grave, poked out his eyes, then scattered his corpse over the highway.[41] Another case of cold callousness showed that the boot could sometimes be on the other foot in tenant/landlord relationships. In 1764 an American sailor, William Corbett, robbed his landlord, a Rotherhithe publican, of plate and money, then murdered him and his wife in their beds. First he strangled the man, then bludgeoned the wife. The cynical premeditation and the old age of the victims excited a frenzied public clamour. Corbett's execution on Kennington Common was attended by 20,000 people.[42]

A sub-species of murder in pursuit of another crime was to kill a law officer in the course of his duties. This could be a watchman, a constable, or, especially in the later period, a prison warder killed by convicts.[43] Lewis Avershaw (executed 1795) clearly stood no chance of clemency after shooting one police officer dead and seriously wounding another while resisting arrest.[44] In the first half of the century such an offence would have seen him hung in chains into the bargain. In 1713 William Lowther and Richard Keeler, who had been sentenced to two years' hard labour in the Clerkenwell Bridewell, refused to be chained while they worked. Their altercation with the gaolers led to a riot in which a number of prisoners escaped and a gaoler was shot dead. For being the 'authors' of this murder, Lowther and Keeler were executed and then hung in chains.[45]

The murder of law officers was long recognized as being in the same category as murder to promote another crime. As recently as 1957 in England the two offences were bracketed together as 'capital murder' for which the death penalty was thought justifiable. It might be thought that to kill a peace-keeping official was in itself a mandatory death sentence. But, as with everything else in the eighteenth century, this depended on other circumstances being equal. If you had powerful friends and backers, the majesty of the law went into abeyance. In 1770 two Irish brothers called Kennedy killed a watchman on Westminster Bridge after a drunken brawl. They were tried for murder and found guilty but then pardoned, through the influence of their *demi-mondaine* sister, Polly, whose lovers included powerful figures in the elite.[46] John Wilkes and his followers took up the case as a grotesque miscarriage of justice: 'The mercy of a chaste and pious prince extended cheerfully to a common murderer, because that murderer is the brother of a common prostitute.'[47] How, asked the Wilkites, could rioting weavers be executed for loom cutting, while the Kennedys, convicted murderers, walked free? Yet Wilkes and his movement ran into an aristocratic brick wall. Their best efforts were unable to contrive a legal appeal to reverse the pardon.[48]

Servants were another constant in eighteenth-century crime, but their contribution was not necessarily limited to petty domestic pilfering. A case in 1734 illustrates the point. Richard Cantillon, a wealthy London banker, was murdered at his house in Albemarle Street by his cook. The cook, who had been dismissed from Cantillon's service ten days previously, returned and climbed into the house by a ladder. After filling a portmanteau with valuables and stuffing his pockets with guineas, the cook murdered Cantillon, then burned the house to the ground to conceal his crime. He then rode to Harwich and took ship for the Hook of Holland. But once again the reward system proved its potency. A reward of £200 had been posted for the cook, once the details of the murder had been pieced together. The master of the fishing smack that bore the cook to Holland at the special price of eight guineas recognized him from the 'wanted' posters.[49] The murderer was arrested in Holland.

Since the slaying of a master by a servant was a species of 'petty treason', it was futile to expect mercy.[50] But any murder by a servant, even though not of the master, was unlikely to attract a reprieve. Daniel Blake (executed 1763) was an habitual frequenter of brothels; as a menial in a great household he was therefore living beyond his means, and over a period of time stole from the house to finance his activities. When the butler eventually confronted him with evidence of his defalcation, Blake killed him.[51] The fact that Blake used his embezzlement to pay for *filles de joie* was clearly not an extenuating circumstance any jury was prepared to entertain.

Yet sometimes murder charges were brought because the master killed the servant. The marquis of Paleotti was hanged in 1718 for running his valet through with a sword for impertinence. Paleotti went to the gallows still incredulous that he could actually be executed for such a 'peccadillo'.[52] In a sense he was right: had he beaten the man to death, the law would have found him within his prerogatives.

Another similar case the following year (1719) had a bizarre ending. Edward Bird stabbed to death a waiter called Loxton in an inn, because Loxton did not draw his bath the instant he demanded it. Bird was convicted of murder and reprieved; he was then made ready for transportation. The Loxton family protested at a miscarriage of justice. Bird's friends in turn rallied around him and discredited Loxton by proving that he had been a bigamist. But by this time the case had become a *cause célèbre*. The credibility of the law was thought to warrant a judicial review. As a result of the review the original sentence was ordered to stand and Bird was executed.[53]

A case in 1756 combined murder of a servant with anti-military prejudice, making the fate of the perpetrator certain. In this instance there was no injustice in the 'guilty' verdict. Lieutenant Lander murdered a post-boy on the run from Chatham to London simply because the boy was unable (naturally) to make his horses gallop up Shooters Hill in Woolwich.[54]

Overwhelmingly, though, murder took place within the family, between intimates or for reasons of sexual passion. We may distinguish four main types: murder of a relative for economic motives; murder of wife by husband (or more rarely vice versa) after a quarrel, when drunk, or in a mindless rage; murder of wife by husband as a result of sexual jealousy; and genuine *crime passionnel* by persons driven to homicide by infatuation or sexual distraction.

Moralists may care to speculate on the reasons why murder between intimates for financial reasons seemed to call forth a greater degree of violence than other homicides. Sometimes the economic motive for this sort of murder was trivial, as when Matthew Clarke (executed 1721) killed his girlfriend simply because she knew he intended to rob his employer.[55] But more normally large sums of money were involved, and the circumstances of the murder were more than usually violent. John Bond was hanged in 1798 at the age of 69 after a decade of systematic mental cruelty practised on his wife. She had inherited an estate but refused to liquidate it to provide her husband with cash for debauchery. As a result he beat her up constantly until, one day, going too far, he finally killed her. The chain of violent beatings cut the ground from under a manslaughter plea.[56]

Yet the Bond case seemed almost a bagatelle compared with other murders for money in the extended family. William Smith (executed at York in 1753) poisoned his stepfather and his two children with arsenic.[57]

A disputed estate in the Athoe family led in 1723 to a singularly disgraceful murder. Thomas Athoe and his son set on their two cousins, the beneficiaries of the disputed patrimony, castrated them and left them to bleed to death. One did, but the other was found by a passer-by and patched up by a surgeon. The Athoes father and son were tried and 'launched into eternity'.[58]

An even more dreadful case occurred in 1742. John Bodkin, an Irish ne'er-do-well, who failed to inherit what he thought was his due, engaged his father's cousin and his shepherd in a wicked scheme to destroy his parents-in-law. In a dire instance of mass murder, the trio of assassins wiped out all eleven people in the father-in-law's house by cutting their throats. Such was the insensate blood-lust aroused in the killers that they went quite berserk and killed all the cats and dogs in the house as well.[59] To the outraged public, this was another instance of 'hanging not punishment enough'.

Financial murders between intimates always seemed to have their singular aspect. Eugene Aram and Richard Houseman murdered their partner Daniel Clarke for money in February 1745 and buried his body in a cave. In 1758 someone dug up his bones by accident. Since Clarke had disappeared mysteriously thirteen years before and had last been seen alive in Houseman's company, a warrant was issued for the latter's arrest. Under questioning Houseman broke down and incriminated Aram as Clarke's murderer. Aram's defence was the obvious one that since the decomposed corpse could not be positively identified as Clarke's, there was no case to answer, since it had not been proved that a murder had even been committed. But the jury convicted Aram on circumstantial evidence alone. The night before his execution Aram tried to commit suicide by severing an artery, but botched the job. He was bandaged up and taken to the scaffold in a weakened state. After the execution he was hung in chains. He left a posthumous confession, admitting the murder.[60] Quite apart from its sensational nature, this case demonstrates clearly the sovereignty of jury decision-making. This was far from the only case where the jury was prepared to convict on the most tenuous, circumstantial evidence.[61]

The murder of wives by husbands was usually a result of intoxication and/or violent altercation. Nicol Brown (executed 1754) came home drunk, got into an argument with his wife, started a fire, then pushed his wife into it. She died of severe burns.[62] Another stabbed his wife to death in a public house.[63] James Massey (executed 1801) murdered his wife and then tried to throw their 10-year-old daughter into a mill-dam.[64] Unpremeditated murder of wives by husbands in a rage was a dreary staple of the 'ordinary' of Newgate's accounts and of the cases later printed in the *Newgate Calendar*.[65] Sometimes there was a slight twist to a family murder, as when Daniel Broom (executed 1801) killed his brother's wife with a hatchet.[66] The case of William Cannicott in 1756 is also interesting. Having left his first wife, he fell madly in love with another woman. To defeat her many suitors, he bigamously married her. When the first wife found out and tried to blackmail him, Cannicott murdered her.[67]

Otherwise the dreary catalogue of slayings of fathers by sons and of women by their lovers continued as the steady drip-drip background to the more trumpeted crimes of the century.[68] Occasionally a particularly noteworthy piece of butchery in the extended family would make the headlines. Anti-semitism was again fuelled by the 1793 case of Aaron Mendez, a rich merchant who was murdered (together with his housekeeper) by a gang of half a dozen cut-throats led by his own nephew. The nephew had provided himself with what he thought was a cast-iron alibi, but when unshakeable forensic evidence secured his conviction, he cheated the hangman by taking arsenic.[69]

There was often a sexual element underlying fatal quarrels in the family. In 1764 a shoemaker stabbed a rope maker to death in a tavern, ostensibly about who should buy the next round of drinks but really because of sexual jealousy.[70] A husband killed his wife because she found him in a brothel and rebuked him for his infidelity.[71] Thomas Wilford (executed 1752) married a prostitute but killed her when she did not mend her ways after marriage.[72] Robert Anderson (executed 1791) stabbed to death the woman he was living with when her husband, a sailor long thought dead, returned from the sea and she wanted to return to him.[73] There were also ramifications of sexual problems when the victim lay outside the family. John Bolton was a married man with six children. He seduced a young girl and got her with child. He then murdered her to prevent his wife's finding out about the girl's pregnancy but, finding himself in a trap of his own making, in 1775 committed suicide.[74]

The final main category of murder involves crimes of passion. John White (executed 1795) was besotted with a young schoolteacher Maria Bally. Miss Bally rejected his overtures. On the morning of 19 June 1795 the 19-year-old got up, loaded a brace of pistols and went to her schoolroom. In front of her charges he shot her dead.[75]

Sometimes the victim of frustrated love was the parent who had forbidden the daughter to marry. Thomas Oliver (executed 1795) shot dead a Staffordshire gentleman called Wood because Mr Wood opposed Oliver's suit for his daughter's hand.[76] An insanity plea was turned down at the trial, but this was a clear case of judicial bloody-mindedness. Oliver had shot down Wood in cold blood and he insisted to the moment of his death that he felt no remorse and could not understand what he was supposed to have done that was wrong. He was clearly a type of psychopath or 'moral imbecile'.

But the century's most spectacular *crime passionnel* was undoubtedly the slaying of Martha Ray in 1779. Ray, the daughter of a staymaker, had lived with the Earl of Sandwich for seventeen years and borne him nine children.[77] She was fervently admired by James Hackman, a 27-year-old clergyman and former army officer. In 1779 when she was 33, Ray foolishly hinted to Hackman that, since she could never hope to marry Lord Sandwich, she might consent to become a clergyman's wife. But, after a trip to Ireland she changed her mind.[78] This rejection unhinged Hackman. In the spring of 1779 he waited with a loaded pistol while Miss Ray emerged from Covent Garden Theatre after a performance of Isaac Bickenstaffe's *Love in a Village*. As she got into her coach, he shot her dead. Hackman was hanged at Tyburn in April 1779, the century's most potent witness to the madness wrought by unrequited love.[79]

The only other class of murders worth a cursory glance consists of the genuinely bizarre cases. In 1748 10-year-old William York murdered a 5-year-old girl in a workhouse in a most brutal and premeditated fashion, but because of his age he was reprieved from the death sentence and eventually pardoned.[80] William Jacques, a sailor who killed a fellow (Negro) mariner in a wood, was sincerely stupefied when he was arraigned for murder. He claimed that it had never entered his head that killing a black could be regarded as murder. But the Bloody Code was colour-blind; Jacques was hanged at Devizes in 1764 in front of 10,000 spectators.[81] And surely one of the most amazing murders ever was that by 23-year-old James Brodie in 1799. Though blind, Brodie murdered the poor lad who acted as his guide![82]

A large number of murders have been cited in order to illustrate the *variety* of eighteenth-century homicide. But it would be a mistake to infer that the general level of murder was high in England. Foreign observers were unanimous in the judgement that, as compared with continental Europe, the homicide rate was remarkably low.[83] This was so even in the early years of the century, when conditions in London, as we have seen, most clearly favoured a 'crime wave'.[84] The general consensus was that a very high level of crime against property coexisted with a very low level of murders and serious crimes against the person.[85] Once again it is abundantly clear that the death penalty, indiscriminately imposed for so many different crimes, had no deterrent effect at all, that the motives for crime were various, and completely independent of the punishments prescribed for them. Even the most purblind original sin theorist might have been given pause by this differential crime rate. If man were inherently and irredeemably sinful, he would presumably murder and rape more often, given that the death penalty had no effect on his behaviour. The inference is clear that the causation for *most* crime is the state of society – precisely the inference that members of the eighteenth-century elite did not want drawn.

The other question that arises about eighteenth-century homicide is whether the murder rate was declining and if so, why. This is peculiarly difficult to answer confidently, if only because of the impression of a *constantly* low rate given by foreign observers. On the one hand, technological progress and the spread of Enlightenment ideas certainly did seem to have made an impact on the general level of violence in England over the century. Some writers postulate important changes in the social psychology of the population from 1700 to 1800.[86] If murder can be correlated with *general* violence, then the inference must be that the murder rate dropped. And there is much evidence that points in this direction. It is also possible that the statistical evidence is muddied by social change. If the advent of a skeletal police force and better methods of detection led to a higher rate of crime reporting and higher 'clear-up' rates, then a statistically constant level of murder could mask a considerable actual decline. Certainly it seems that levels of acquittal on murder charges declined over the century, as behaviour that was previously tolerated came to be condemned.[87]

On the other hand, scepticism about a declining rate of murder can be reinforced from a number of directions. In the first place, the general level of violence existing at the end of the seventeenth century may have been exaggerated.[88] Second, there is some evidence that the rate of murder within the family – the 'heartland' for homicide – has remained a social constant in modern history.[89] Yet the best and most recent work on the subject seems to establish that the murder rate did decline as new attitudes towards violence made themselves felt.[90] This is a topic we shall explore further in chapter 16.

There was one species of homicide that did not fit into any of the foregoing categories and has to be assessed in its own terms: suicide. The degree of animus directed against self-slaughter in the eighteenth century is hard for a modern mind to grasp. Blackstone's contemptuous assessment was typical: 'Self-murder, the pretended heroism, but real cowardice, of the Stoic philosophers, who destroyed themselves to avoid those ills which they had not the fortitude to endure.'[91]

Before the eighteenth century religion overwhelmingly determined people's attitude to suicide. Self-killing was held to be an effect of diabolic possession, the result of intervention by Satan and his demons.[92] There were still traces of this attitude in the early eighteenth-century writings on the subject.[93] But the main focus of elite concerns lay elsewhere. To the eighteenth-century mind the suicide was a criminal on two counts. In the first place, he offended against the king, whose interests dictated the preservation of his own subjects. In the second, he blasphemed against the law of God, 'rushing into his immediate presence uncalled for', as Blackstone put it.[94] A very grave view was therefore taken of this felony (*felo de se*). Anyone assisting or acting as an accessory to a suicide was treated as a murderer. The judiciary would not accept mental illness as a mitigating factor; it was considered that the depressive or melancholic still retained the capacity to distinguish between right and wrong, so that his 'depression' had nothing to do with the matter.

The central problem in dealing with this 'crime' was obvious. As Blackstone put it: 'What punishment can human laws inflict on one who has withdrawn himself from their reach?'[95] The answer of course was, none. But society was determined that the suicide should not go unpunished. His reputation could be ruined and his memory desecrated. Hence arose the custom of burying suicides at crossroads with stakes driven through their bodies. This, and other peculiar folkways, was the elite's way of co-opting the common people into a detestation of suicide, even though its own motives were very different. Educated people by and large scoffed at such superstitions. But the ordinary people in the eighteenth century still feared Beelzebub and his demonic choirs.[96] As a recent student of the subject has remarked:

> The practice of burying suicides who were judged *non compos mentis* on the north side of churchyards, where excommunicants, unbaptized babes and executed criminals lay, seems in the eighteenth century to have satisfied a strong lingering antagonism to the legitimation of self-destruction.[97]

Yet it was not enough that the common man's life was not his own in the eighteenth century; even his death was, in a sense, the property of the elite. Even more vindictively, the Code prescribed forfeiture of the suicide's property to the king. It is often said that the worst aspect of suicide is its impact on survivors. In the eighteenth century this was true in material terms, literally with a vengeance.[98] No more striking a demonstration of the fanaticism with which the elite clung to the theory of deterrence can be seen than in this provision regarding the goods and chattels of suicides. It is difficult to know which attitude is the more barbarous: that a clinical depressive can be 'deterred' from the effects of his mental condition by dinning into him the consequences for his relicts; or that a judicial system that was prepared to execute for petty theft should pursue beyond the grave anyone who visited the supreme penalty on himself. Anyone who doubts that the Bloody Code was really about authority and credibility should ponder the elite's pathological behaviour in the area of suicide. It was not the fact of death that troubled them; what mattered was that *they* should decide who died. As a recent student of the subject has remarked with beautiful irony: 'The attitude of the English elite to suicide in the eighteenth century cannot accurately be described as humanitarian.'[99]

Visiting the sins of the fathers on their heirs in the form of confiscation seemed to many contemporaries even more outrageously unjustified than the attainder in the case of treason. [100] The more suicide cases there were, the more this principle came to be questioned. [101] More thoughtful social critics tried to steer between humanity and elite authority by suggesting a compromise. One suggestion was that the children of suicides should be allowed to keep their patrimony, but to show society's displeasure at their fathers' actions, the corpses should be anatomized. [102]

The absurdity of the authorities' attitude is enhanced when one considers that the 'rational' suicides, those who could in principle be deterred by the law's inhumanity towards their wives and children, overwhelmingly committed suicide because they were ruined financially; in such cases there was no property to be confiscated by the king anyway. Among these 'rational' suicides can be included the case of Henry Bromley, Lord Mountford, who shot himself in 1755 to escape a mountain of debt. [103] Similarly, Thomas Bradshaw, MP, shot himself in 1774 at the age of 42 when overwhelmed by debt, [104] as did the Hon. John Damer, eldest son of Lord Milton who blew his own brains out in a Covent Garden tavern, at the age of 32, when in hock to creditors for £60,000. [105] When a bank failed as a result of a speculative crash in 1772 and four leading bankers were ruined, two of them immediately took their own lives. [106]

Committing suicide to cheat the hangman when the death penalty was certain to be administered can also be construed as rational behaviour. Two cases from 1764 illustrate this. A soldier who had stabbed his mistress in Westminster then shot himself; a half-pay naval officer, discovered stealing from a family of friends, cut his throat. [107] A man of a higher social level threw himself out of a boat into the Thames in 1737 to avoid being convicted for forging a will. [108] Charles Price, swindler and banknote forger, went one better in 1786 when he committed suicide *before he could be prosecuted* by the Bank of England. [109]

But by far the most common cause of suicide was insanity or mental illness. Lord Fortescue had a long history of depression and made several suicide attempts between 1762 and 1765. [110] Lord Orford tried to commit suicide when suffering insanity in 1777. [111] John Powell, a noted account-ant in the Paymaster-General's office, took his own life in 1783 after a long period of depression. [112] An unusual suicide method used by Dr John Elliott in 1786 was death by hunger-strike. Elliott had been charged under the Black Act for discharging two pistols at Miss Mary Boydell, the object of his overweening passion. It was discovered at the trial that Elliott had a long history of psychosis. In a conflated pre-echo of E. E. Cummings and Flann O'Brien, he wrote a pamphlet dedicated to the proposition that the sun was a balloon, not a fiery orb at all, and that his own heat came from an 'ether' around his body. [113] It is indicative of the Hogarthian severity of eighteenth-century judges that such revelations affected their sentencing not at all.

Even more striking were the cases of temporary insanity, or suicide while the balance of the mind was disturbed. A Mr Skrine blew his brains out in a tavern in Newgate Street after losing heavily at cards at Brook's.[114] In 1780 Hans Stanley, diplomat and politician, cut his throat in Lord Spencer's park at Althorp. He was 58.[115] In 1778, 63-year-old Sir George Hay walked deliberately into the Thames at noon in full sight of fifty people and drowned himself.[116] Another man in this age group, William Fitzerherbert, 59, MP for Derby Borough, hanged himself immediately after witnessing the public prosecution of three forgers; he remarked to a companion that the trio seemed to feel little pain, then made his way to his stable and hanged himself with a bridle.[117]

The rash of suicides in England worried more thoughtful observers. Horace Walpole was convinced the French thought suicide a weekly event in England. He assuaged his own anxiety by levity, dubbing self-murder 'death à l'Anglaise'.[118] In this he was following up an idea first put forward half a century earlier by George Cheyne.[119] Walpole attempted to explain the frequency of suicide by the weather. He thought that the change in the pattern that he had observed in his lifetime, whereby the English summers had become hotter and more sultry, had something to do with the fact that July had replaced November as the favourite month for people to kill themselves.[120]

Explanations of social phenomena by means of the weather were popular after Montesquieu, but lack cogency for the modern sociologist. However, it is by no means self-evident that Walpole's ascription of a peculiarly high suicide rate for England was a myth.[121] The issue is immensely complicated by the difficulty in ascertaining true suicide rates. On the one hand, relatives of the deceased had a double motive for concealing suicide and passing it off as natural or accidental death: there was the social stigma and refusal of Christian burial; more pressingly, there was the forfeiture of goods. Suicides, therefore, tended to be concealed and underreported.[122] In the 1720s Isaac Watts conjectured that most people found drowned were in fact suicides.[123] To a large extent this was a class phenomenon, since the wealthy could more easily cover the tracks of a suicide; after all they could bring all kinds of social pressure to bear on coroners and in any case constituted a large proportion of coroners' juries. On the other, juries had motives of prudence for not passing suicide verdicts, since a pauperized family was a burden to the community.[124]

To what extent did attitudes to suicide change over the century? The first half of the century marks a turning point, away from the superstition and severity of the seventeenth century. From 1700 to about 1760 legal punctiliousness was tempered with mercy. In about half the cases an insanity verdict was recorded. Much depended on the attitudes of jury to the deceased, his family, and to suicide in general. But after about 1745, there was an increasing tendency for reliable barometers of the feelings of polite society, like the *Gentleman's Magazine* to counsel compassion towards suicides and their families. From 1760 onwards, *non compos mentis* was the usual jury verdict.[125] The reign of George III saw the decisive abandonment of the belief that suicide was diabolically inspired. Put simply, the eighteenth century saw the secularization of the crime of suicide.[126]

Since the eighteenth century lacks its Durkheim, any assessment of suicide must necessarily be highly impressionistic. One aspect of it that bears further examination is the failure of Enlightenment thought to make any great difference to the general consensus on this 'crime'. Juries were prepared to accept pleas of insanity. They emphatically drew the line at the suggestion that there could be a *rational justification* for suicide, even though voices were increasingly raised in England in that direction.[127]

All the major eighteenth-century social theorists took it for granted that suicide could not be justified, as it offended against the 'law of nature'. Indeed, many of the most notorious problems surrounding the 'social contract' arose from this very consideration. Since society consisted, according to the contract theorists, in surrendering to the civil power the rights one enjoyed in the 'state of nature', and society had no other rights than those made over by the individual, what could possibly justify the State's use of the death penalty? If the individual had no right to commit suicide in the state of nature, how could society have the right to mete out death to its members? Cesare Beccaria concluded that it did *not* possess that right. Rousseau, who retained the death penalty in *Du Contrat Social* argued that every man had the right to *gamble* with his own life.[128] It was not suicide when a man jumped out of an upper window to escape fire. The social contract with which an individual bound himself to society was like boarding a ship in the full knowledge of the risks of the sea. You know the ship *may* sink, but you do not board it in order to be lost at sea. Similarly, so as not to fall foul of murderers, we agree to die if we ourselves become murderers.

This was ingenious, and a good argument for social laws *in general*. The trouble was that, in terms of the passage from state of nature to civil society, it still failed to deal with the original objection, as the French theorist Brissot de Warville pointed out.[129] The fundamental problem was that, using the narrow premises of the social contract theory, any number of insoluble absurdities arose. As the Neapolitan theorist Filangieri demonstrated, if society possessed only those rights that an individual possessed in the state of nature, it was impossible to see how any form of punishment could be justified, unless the individual making the social contract was a self-conscious masochist and insisted on his 'right' to punishment being enforced by society.[130]

It has recently been suggested that the impact of the Enlightenment in France was such that the authorities there were reluctant to enforce the law against suicide.[131] Is there any sign of a corresponding Enlightenment impact in England? Any answer must be tentative. On the one hand, Enlightenment thought did contribute to the 'demystification' of suicide and led to an elite consensus that self-killing had to be regarded either as a function of mental illness or as an aspect of moral choice, rather than diabolic possession. On the other hand, there were aspects of continental Enlightment that clashed fiercely with the habit/experience nexus of English empiricist culture. And the contribution of the Enlightenment was not at its strongest in the realm of suicide, for the justifications advanced for self-slaughter tended to be rehashes of the well-known apologies in the classical authors. Certainly, with the few exceptions we have noted, English writing on the subject seemed to cleave to an older tradition of argumentation, alien to Enlightenment methodology.[132]

In the absence of any mainstream rationalist theory that would attempt to justify suicide, and the ringing denunciations of its sinfulness by the spokesmen of organized religion, it was left to the odd idiosyncratic figure to offer any comfort to the surviving relatives of the 'criminal'. Richard Baxter, a sixteenth-century Presbyterian divine, had preached that a suicide was not necessarily damned to Hell. If you lived a good life, you did not forfeit your chances of salvation by a spur-of-the moment suicide while the balance of your mind was disturbed.[133] But Baxter and his followers were voices crying in the wilderness. Much more typical of the eighteenth-century mentality was John Wesley who in 1784 wrote to Pitt to urge him to check the 'suicide wave' by hanging its practitioners in chains, in addition to the usual penalties.[134] One cannot but sympathize with the wag who wrote of this proposal six years later: 'The pious John Wesley has proposed a remedy for suicide, by gibbeting the unhappy victims of despondency. Would not a total extirpation of the gloomy and absurd tenets of Methodism be much more conducive to that purpose?'[135]

4

Highwaymen

'Wealth, howsoever got, in England makes
Lords of mechanics, gentlemen of rakes
Antiquity and birth are needless here
'Tis impudence and money makes a peer.'
Daniel Defoe, *The True-Born Englishman* 1701

Gamesters and highwaymen are generally very good to their
whores, but they're the very devil to their wives . . . a
highwayman's wife, like a soldier's, hath as little of his pay
as of his company.
John Gay, *The Beggar's Opera*

Be absolute for death: either death or life
Shall thereby be the sweeter. Reason thus with life:
If I do lose thee, I do lose a thing
That none but fools would keep: a breath thou art
William Shakespeare, *Measure For Measure*, III. i.5

The scene described by Horace Walpole was repeated on countless
occasions in England during the century. While he and Lady Browne
were driving in their coach in Twickenham in October 1781, the following
exchange took place.

HIGHWAYMAN: Stop! Your purses and your watches!
WALPOLE: I have no watch.
HIGHWAYMAN: Then your purse! (To Lady Browne) Don't be
frightened, I will not hurt you. No I give you my word I will do you no
hurt. (Collecting the purse, he tips his hat.) I'm much obliged to you, I
wish you good night.[1]

In popular imagination, the highwayman was the criminal scourge of
eighteenth-century society. This was a perception that gained wide
currency after John Gay's *The Beggar's Opera* (1728), whose hero was
the highwayman 'Captain' MacHeath, but it was moderated by the

countervailing image of the highwayman as gentleman that Gay advanced. The highwayman as chivalrous Robin Hood was finally entrenched as a collective image by the novelist Harrison Ainsworth in the nineteenth century. In *Rookwood* (1834) the gallant figure of Dick Turpin is as far removed from the historical personage as an advertising campaign for the tobacco industry is from the truth about lung cancer.

Since the highwayman was the leading protagonist of property crime, he attracted the same sort of ambivalence as the modern bank-robber. The violence of his methods was deplored, but he was considered the logical extension of a society that deified greed. The contrast between the fuss made over a highway robbery involving ten pounds and the insouciance with which society regarded the bribery and speculation of Sir Robert Walpole, involving hundreds of thousands of pounds, was a staple comment of the day, and appears explicitly in *The Beggar's Opera*. The Jacobites encouraged this line of reasoning. Since the post-1688 regime was illegitimate, it followed that in a sense all its property relations were bogus, and that the highwayman was merely claiming back what had been stolen. Anticipating Proudhon, the Jacobites insinuated the idea that all Hanoverian property was theft. The proposition that crime was a function of destitution, and destitution was itself a direct consequence of Whig economic policies, was a hardy annual in the reportage of the Jacobite journalist Nathaniel Mist.[2] A report to James Stuart the 'old Pretender' at the end of 1728 (the year Gay's opera appeared) made the point explicit:

> Highway robberies prevail in England more than in any other nation of Europe. Are not the persons who commit them frequently such as are unwilling to make their distress public, and, finding themselves sunk in spite of industry, grow desperate and run the risk of an ignominious death to satisfy these voracious harpies [the Whigs] that occasion all their misery.[3]

There was a Jacobite flavour to some of the early eighteenth-century highwaymen. Thomas Butler (executed 1720) fought for the Pretender and was employed as a spy in the 1715 rising by the Duke of Ormonde. When luxurious living exhausted his money on the Continent, Butler came to England and took up highway robbery. He and his trusted servant lived a double life for four years. They would alternate periods 'on the road' with residence in London, where they lived in some style and were received in polite society.[4] Thomas Neale, a highwayman who was hanged in 1749, invoked the Jacobite martyr Lord Balmerino, beheaded two years before, as a fellow-sufferer; both were victims of an illegitimate government.[5] This is an ingenious twist on the 'social crime' argument. According to this line of argument, the highwayman was a political criminal; as Chevalier Ramsay, the Jacobite ideologue had argued, if you deny the hereditary principle in kingship you cannot retain it in property. The highwayman, when taxed with his actions, can reply:

> Rich men have violated this contract; they have seized upon everything, nothing remains for me. I will enter upon my natural right. I will take it and seize upon that which naturally belongs to me. The hereditary right of lands is a mere chimera.[6]

Naturally, the custodians of the Bloody Code did not see it that way at all. The shrewdest way to combat Jacobite propaganda was not to add new laws against highwaymen to the statute book but to emphasize continuity by using the old ones. Highway robbery had been one of the earliest offences to be removed from benefit of clergy (in 1531). It remained as the offence most likely to attract the death penalty on conviction.[7] As Horace Walpole remarked: 'All the world agrees in the fitness of severity to highwaymen, for the sake of the innocent who suffer.'[8] New legislation against them largely consisted of tinkering with the technicalities of evidence. The so-called 'Highwayman Act' of 1693 permitted the evidence of accomplices in cases of highway robbery, with the proviso that the man who turned State's evidence could not claim his liberty unless at least two of his confederates were convicted. It also offered £40 to any member of the public who would take a highwayman and secure his conviction. Section 6 of the Act said that whoever took a highwayman could keep his horse, money, guns and other effects, provided these had not been stolen in the first place.[9]

Catch-all statutes like the Black Act provided a reserve power in case of need. Some felt that the need would indeed arise since technology favoured the highwayman. Flintlocks, introduced around 1635, had become widely used. This spread of hand-guns produced a 'democratization of violence'. The technological gap between determined criminals like smugglers, poachers and highwaymen and the law enforcers virtually disappeared.[10] And there was no question of stage-coaches being able to outrun their assailants. The atrocious eighteenth-century roads did not permit this. The highways were scarcely more reliable than in the Middle Ages. Quagmires of mud in winter, whorls of swirling dust in the summer, deeply rutted ridges full of water in the spring and autumn, the roads produced lamed horses, broken axles, overturned coaches, and lost luggage even when the stage-coaches were proceeding at a trot.[11] The perils of stage-coach travel are graphically illustrated by an episode in 1784 when the Hertford coach overturned. The accident was caused by the combined weight of *twenty-five* people riding on the outside.[12] The absence of a professional police force left the highwayman virtually a free hand to prey on these already stricken travellers. The situation was so widely accepted that in 1692 a highwayman named Whitney pushed it to its logical conclusion. In exchange for an annual fee and a free pardon, he offered to police a large mileage of road on the grounds that he controlled it already![13]

What was the social origin of the 'gentlemen of the road'? Almost without exception highwaymen were men who had fallen from a high social station through bankruptcy or gambling debts or were members of the aspiring artisan class, dissatisfied with the hard work and slender returns of the trade they had been apprenticed to. There is abundant evidence that highwaymen were of a higher social and educational level than other criminals.[14] Again and again the epithet 'of liberal education' occurs in the description of their trials. After all, relatively few people in the eighteenth century were literate. It was the fact that Dick Turpin could write that eventually ensnared him. All this was in contrast to Europe. The highwaymen of Italy, Spain, and Germany were largely army deserters, smugglers, men without a profession, and divers unsavoury and dissolute characters. Since the social origins of the English highwayman were much higher, the appropriate comparison is between English footpads and continental highwaymen.[15]

Parsons' sons featured largely in the lists of those executed for highway robbery. This is understandable. They were caught in the classical dilemma of having been brought up to certain expectations, having it dinned into them that they had to keep up genteel appearances, while not possessing the financial resouces to live in the style to which their upbringing had accustomed them. Such a one was Thomas Barkwirth. He had attained great proficiency in Greek, Latin, French, and Italian, and would happily have lived the life of a scholar if he had had a private income. Barkwirth was clearly a 'born loser'. Opting for life as a highwayman, he was taken just one hour after his first robbery on Hounslow Heath, in which he had uplifted just twenty shillings. Neither the trivial amount robbed, nor his educational attainments and the fact that it was his first offence availed him. He was hanged in December 1739.[16] Yet the very capriciousness and uncertainty in the way the law was administered makes all generalizations difficult. Another virtually identical case involved Nicholas Horner, a Devonshire minister's son, also captured on his very first highway robbery. Thanks to his father's influence, he received a seven years' transportation instead of the death sentence. Unfortunately the story does not end happily. Horner returned and resumed his calling. This time he was taken and hanged, in 1719.[17]

It was their superior social origins, plus their claim to be 'Robin Hoods' that secured the highwaymen's place in public affections. They were far less dreaded than urban footpads, since they rarely used violence. This was a case where circumstance and social status reinforced each other. Taking to the road was a calling a gentleman could turn to, since the virtues and accomplishments of the 'officer class': horsemanship, daring, skill with weapons, etc., could be brought into play. The horse was an important reason for the potency of the myth of the highwayman, just as it was for the American cowboy in the following century. Mounted, the highwayman felt no temptation to kill, maim or disable his victim. The footpad, by contrast, was unable to leave the scene of the crime quickly and was tempted to reduce the chances of being caught by killing all witnesses.[18] The objective circumstances of his superior social status (for horses were expensive) thus fed into the associated culture of that status. The highwayman could afford to be courteous and chivalrous. This courtesy cushioned the experience of the robbery for both robber and victim. The fact that honourable behaviour was possible encouraged other impoverished 'gentlemen' to go on the road. And in most cases a bitter struggle with the victims did not need to be anticipated, since the travellers who were robbed did not go in fear of their lives.[19]

The 'Robin Hood' aspect of highwaymen was clearly overdone. Some of them played up to their image; some of the repartee reported seems forced and overdone. But it was important to reinforce a favourable image in the public mind. For this reason the condemned highwayman James MacLaine, a clergyman's son (see below p. 64), while waiting for execution in Newgate composed a famous apologia, contrasting the 'good thief' (the highwayman) with the 'bad thief' (the footpad).[20] He evinced his own magnanimity and literacy, then spoke of the 'low behaviour' of his footpad cell-mate, one Ned Slinker, whom he claimed to have forced to pay back his ill-gotten gains. Slinker's particular crime, according to MacLaine, was to have robbed a poor labourer; this was something the high-minded highwayman would never do; he robbed only the rich. What MacLaine did not point out of course was that the footpad did not have the time or the opportunity to be discerning about his victims. There was also the fact that in many cases no hard and fast distinction could be drawn between the two kinds of robbers. Particularly in the first half of the century, criminal gangs would alternate the two activities, sometimes robbing on foot, sometimes on horseback, partly because of varied opportunities, partly to throw law officers off the scent. Moreover, a successful young footpad might at once buy a horse and graduate to highwayman, thus increasing his social status.[21]

Yet there clearly were 'Robin Hoods' among the highwaymen, as well as individuals of refined sensibility and exquisite courtesy. In the early 1720s Benjamin Child was one who conformed to the romantic stereotype. Child once made the chivalrous gesture of freeing all the debtors in Salisbury gaol by using the money he had uplifted to pay their debts. The more he emphasized the injustice of English society by his actions, the deeper became the malice of the English authorities towards him. They hired Jonathan Wild to apprehend him. Child was captured, executed and hung in chains on Hounslow Heath, even though his crimes did not warrant this aggravated punishment. Wild's role in compassing his downfall was one of the reasons for the plummeting of his popularity with the London crowd.[22]

Another instructive example is provided by 'Captain' Evan Evans. He began as a trainee attorney, then switched to highway robbery before going to Guernsey for a four-year 'cooling off' period as clerk to Sir Edmund Andrews, governor of the island. After that Evans returned to the road with his brother Will, specializing in robbery from Mile End and Bow to the Strand. On one occasion, in Surrey, on the Portsmouth Road, he came on a press-gang leading thirty wretched individuals all bound with rope to the garrison at Portsmouth. The gang of constables were to receive thirty shillings a head for their endeavours. Having ascertained the true situation, the Evans brothers rode off and ambushed the column farther along the road. They robbed the constables and left them tied up in a field and released all the prisoners. Captain Evans was executed in 1708, aged 29. His brother, who swung with him, was just 23.[23]

The courtesy of highwaymen was shown in various ways: politeness to women, avoidance of pointing guns directly at victims, lack of thorough searches of passengers, even the return of favourite items of sentimental value. One highwayman actually returned with his victim to his house so that he could buy back a stolen favourite watch for two guineas.[24] Another, mounted on a shabby grey mare, robbed a man near Oxford but gave him back a shilling so that he could pay the turnpike toll.[25] Another sensitive gentleman of the road constantly reappeared in the year 1764. On one occasion he held up a clergyman and his wife between Mottingham and Chislehurst. He robbed the parson but not his wife, saying he hoped he had not frightened her.[26] Thereafter the same mawkish masked man put in appearances on the road at regular intervals. Always he regretted the necessity of what he was doing and apologized to the ladies. When he held up a post-chaise near Epsom in August that year, he told the two ladies within that he hoped someone would soon put a bullet in his brain and put him out of his misery.[27]

Wit and repartee was also widely reported in these encounters. One highwayman told his victims he was heir to a great fortune and would repay the stolen money when he came into his own.[28] Another, in 1751, said he needed the money to go into mourning for Prince Frederick who had just died![29] Clergymen, in particular, seemed to bring out the wag in highwaymen. One parson was robbed of a large sum of money and his watch. The robber gave him back a guinea for his travelling expenses. Encouraged by this, the cleric asked if his watch could be returned. The highwayman refused, since 'he was at present without one himself, and as he often wanted to know how time passed away, he could not oblige him with it'.[30] Yet another parson was robbed at Colnbrook (between Windsor and London) of twenty-five shillings and a manuscript sermon.

When he asked to have the sermon returned, the highwayman replied that he was a bad fellow and meant to improve himself by reading the parson's doctrine.[31] Nor was the repartee all one way. One of Horace Walpole's friends joked with the highwayman as he was being robbed: 'You must have taken other pocket-books. Could you not let me have one instead of mine?'[32]

Courtesy towards women was another constant in the 'gentleman's code'. A good example of a 'knight of the road' in action can be seen in the career of Jack Ovet. A former shoemaker's apprentice, Ovet was both an expert swordsman and a model of chivalry. Once, when he was robbing a country squire, the man called him a coward for sheltering behind his guns. Ovet accepted the challenge, got down off his horse, and fought the squire with swords. The contest ended when Ovet ran his taunter through and killed him. Later, when he was robbing a stage, Ovet was smitten with *coup de foudre* for a beautiful young lady traveller. Audaciously, Ovet arranged a means of corresponding with her though a *poste restante*. In his letter to her he promised to reform if she would marry him. The young lady replied that she had no intention of being a 'hempen widow'. Downcast by this rejection, Ovet self-destructively allowed his guard to slip. Neglecting his usual precautions, he was soon afterwards (1708) taken and hanged, aged 32.[33]

Ovet corresponded to the chivalrous image. But not all men had his scruples. The tale of the brutal ex-Quaker Jacob Halsey is well known, but illustrates the other side of the coin. He compounded his robbery of a young woman with rape. According to the contemporary chronicler of highwaymen, Alexander Smith, Halsey first delivered the following speech: 'My pretty lamb, an insurrection of an unruly member obliges me to make use of you on an extraordinary occasion; therefore I must dismount thy alluring body, to the end I may come into thee.'[34]

Another reason for not over-romanticizing the highwayman is that the species was often not a pure form: criminals moved in and out of highway robbery and there was an interlock between this form of robbery and other types of crime. Two highwaymen taken near Bristol in 1764 gave an account of a career that made highway robbery seem merely the high point in a *cursus honorum* of crime. They began as footpads and robbed a young man on a road near London. With the proceeds they went to a London club, stayed until everyone else had left, then robbed £100 from the tellers' bureau. On being posted for this robbery, they took a coach to Birmingham, then swung south-west to Bristol. There they burgled a house before proceeding to a housebreaking in Bath. With the banknote they found in a pocket book in a desk drawer they were finally able to set themselves up as highwaymen.[35]

This movement in and out of highway robbery was common. John Bellingham (hanged 1699), a magistrate's son, switched from highway robbery to forgery.[36] Dick Bauf made his way up the greasy pole of crime from pickpocket and cat-burglar to highwayman before being caught and executed in 1702.[37] George Anderson first acquired his criminal record by gambling and perjury, for which he was pilloried. He graduated through pickpocketing to passing counterfeit. While in Newgate for a spell he systematically picked the other prisoners' pockets. Released on a technicality, he tried footpad robbery before achieving the status of 'gentleman of the road'. He was eventually executed in (1750) for a lesser crime: stealing ribbons in a London shop.[38] John Nelson, who was arrested in January 1764 after a long criminal career, led a gang that systematically mixed housebreaking with highway robbery.[39]

The highwayman can be brought into sharper focus by an examination of some of the most famous eighteenth-century members of the species. Perhaps the best-known highwayman of all time is Dick Turpin, immortalized (but also absurdly distorted) in *Rookwood*, by Harrison Ainsworth. Born in 1705 in Essex, the son of a farmer, Turpin was taught to read and write before being apprenticed to a butcher. He began his life in crime as a smuggler before joining the Gregory gang, which specialized in housebreaking with violence. After narrowly avoiding arrest when a large reward for the Gregory gang was posted, Turpin went solo for a time as a highway robber in Epping Forest.[40]

It was at this phase in his career that he had his famous meeting with another notorious highwayman, Tom King, who already knew him. On the Cambridge road Turpin solemnly told the man he had held up that he would receive instant destruction if he did not hand over his money. King burst out laughing. 'What, dog eat dog? Come, brother Turpin, if you don't know me, I know you, and shall be glad of your company.'[41] King and Turpin then joined forces and operated as a twosome in Epping Forest.

During this period in his life Turpin revealed himself to be a thoroughly unpleasant character, quite unlike the myth fostered by Ainsworth. It was King who was the more chivalrous of the two; while Turpin insisted on robbing women on their own, King was reluctant. But the success of the duo elicited the offering of a reward of £100 dead or alive. Turpin showed his ruthlessness when two bounty hunters tracked him down to the cave in Epping Forest that he and King shared; Turpin pretended to surrender, then seized his gun and shot one of them dead. The other decamped at high speed.[42]

In May 1737 Turpin shot King mortally during a scuffle with a constable. Since King was in imminent danger of being captured, there is a suspicion that this 'accident' might have been something more sinister: a way of making sure that King could not talk if taken into custody.[43] If so, it was a mistake, for King lingered on in agony for a week before dying. At all events, it was clear that the south of England was now too dangerous. Turpin went north until the heat of pursuit cooled. He made a living as a horse-dealer in Yorkshire and Lincolnshire.[44]

But now his own arrogance tripped him up. He shot a cockerel, got into an argument with its owner and was asked to give sureties for his good behaviour. It then came out that he had been living in the area for no more than a year and no one knew his past history. Alarmed that dangerous enquiries might be set on foot, Turpin wrote to his brother in Essex under the pseudonym John Palmer for help in finding the necessary character referees, but neglected to send sufficient postage. His brother, unwilling to pay the postage, rejected the letter. It was returned to the Essex postmaster's office where, by pure chance, the handwriting was recognized by the schoolmaster who had taught Turpin. He informed the magistrates that 'John Palmer' was in fact the notorious highwayman Dick Turpin.[45]

Turpin was taken up in York on the lesser (but still capital) charge of horse-stealing. As with Al Capone and the charge of income tax evasion, it was a technicality that destroyed him. The evidence against him for this offence was not strong and in normal circumstances he might have hoped that a jury would have found him not guilty or that if found guilty he would be pardoned. But there was no chance of this once the jury realized they were dealing with Dick Turpin himself. Turpin was sentenced to death and hanged at York in April 1739. The historical Turpin was a cold, ruthless figure. There was no overnight ride to York from London, no 'Black Bess', nothing in fact to commend him for the mythical pantheon. But, as in the similar case of Jack Sheppard, he found in Ainsworth a nineteenth-century champion to immortalize him.[46]

Another highwayman, equally famous in his own day but with no later propagandist to promote his claims, was James MacLaine. Born in 1724, MacLaine had the clergy as his lineage. His father was an Irish dean and his brother a Calvinist minister at the Hague.[47] He began as a grocer but his wife's death seems to have unhinged him. He sold up his business for £200 and when this was spent took to the road in company with William Plunkett, a journeyman apothecary. The two of them lived a double life. When not on the highway, they lived as London gentlemen. MacLaine had lodgings in St James's Street and another residence in Chelsea; Plunkett lived in Jermyn Street.[48]

Their tally of victims was impressive: Lord Eglinton, Sir Thomas Robinson, Mr Talbot.[49] In November 1749 they held up Horace Walpole in Hyde Park. MacLaine's pistol went off by accident. The bullet whistled past Walpole's head, grazing the skin of his cheekbone.[50] In June 1750 MacLaine challenged a half-pay officer to a duel at Putney. This worthy declined unless MacLaine could produce a certificate of his lineage![51] Eventually MacLaine was arrested when he tried to sell a laced waistcoat that he had stolen. Unfortunately for him he used a go-between, Loader by name, who took the article to the lace merchant from whom the original lace had been purchased. Loader was arrested and confessed all. MacLaine was tried at the Old Bailey in September 1750 and sentenced to hang.[52]

MacLaine's double life intrigued London high society. High-born ladies flocked to visit him in Newgate, including Lady Caroline Petersham and Miss Ashe and many members of the fashionable White's Club.[53] Walpole, who had recovered the watch MacLaine took from him and was touched by the apology he made for the accidental shooting, reported in amazement:

> The first Sunday after his condemnation, 3,000 people went to see him. He fainted away twice with the heat of his cell. You can't conceive the ridiculous rage there is of going to Newgate, and the prints that are published of the malefactors and the memoirs of their lives and deaths set forth with as much parade – as Marshal Turenne's – as we have no generals worth making a parallel![54]

When MacLaine was hanged on 3 October 1750, Walpole was genuinely regretful. He told Sir Horace Mann that he would like to have seen Maclaine saved but did not see how it was possible without setting a bad example.[55]

More typical than either MacLaine or Turpin, and for a short time much more successful, was William Page. One of the most ingenious of all highwaymen, Page made detailed maps of all roads, lanes, and tracks within a twenty-mile radius of London. When he had selected his location for robbery, he drove out of town in a phaeton and pair, dressed in lace shirts and an embroidered frock coat. Some way out of the capital he would park the phaeton in a wood and change into his 'work clothes'. When he had robbed a stagecoach or private carriage, he would return to his hiding place and change back into his gentleman's clothes. On many occasions he was stopped soon after the robbery when he was back in his finery and told to beware of a highwayman who was prowling in the area. As a variation, he would sometimes claim that the highwayman had already robbed *him*.[56]

In company with his friend Darwell, Page committed more than 300 robberies in the years 1755-8. In one six-month period he and Darwell notched up thirty 'hits'. Having once been outwitted by a female confidence trickster, he was particularly fond of robbing women. His most famous hold-up was that on Lord Ferrers, afterwards himself the subject of a *cause célèbre* (see p. 150) On being accosted Ferrers pulled out a pistol but he trembled so much that Page laughed and took the weapon from his shaking hand. Then he said quietly: 'My lord, I know you always carry more pistols about you. Give me the rest.'[57]

Page's luck nearly ran out on him once at Putney. After one daring robbery he was closely pursued by four armed men and had to cross the Thames to escape. Meanwhile some haymakers came on his coach containing his city clothes. When Page saw his property advertised, he wondered at first if this was a trap and the authorities had rumbled his scheme. The problem was that if no one came forward to claim such valuable effects, the authorities really would start to put two and two together. Page decided to take a chance. He presented himself as the owner of the property and pretended to have been robbed and stripped naked. He brought his tailor with him to give evidence about the suit of clothes. Suspecting nothing, the authorities returned his property. They then arrested the haymakers on suspicion of having been the original robbers. Page solved this problem by simply not appearing in court to give evidence against them.[58]

In 1758 Page's luck really did turn. He was arrested on suspicion at Hereford. Lord Ferrers appeared to testify against him. It seemed that the noose was already round Page's neck. But he had a brilliant card to play. Showing the instinct of a natural lawyer, Page did some research on Ferrers's past. Luckily for him Ferrers was already himself something of a questionable character. In 1757 Ferrers's wife had petitioned for divorce against him in the Bishop of London's consistory court on grounds of cruelty. The arrogant Ferrers was summoned to answer the charges but had haughtily refused to do so. He was then excommunicated for contempt of court. Page's defence was then simple: Ferrers could not give evidence against him as he had already been excommunicated for judicial malfeasance. The court had no choice but to accept Page's defence.[59]

But the elite never took kindly to the manipulation of the rule of law against itself, especially when it involved making public the disgraceful conduct of one of its own scions. Besides, this was Page's second acquittal; he had already survived an Old Bailey trial. From the day Page walked free at Hereford he was a marked man. The very next month the authorities secured evidence against him for a highway robbery at Blackheath. Page was tried, condemned and hanged at Maidstone in March 1758.[60]

Even more flamboyant in his dress than Page was John Rann, known as 'Sixteen-string Jack'. A former footman and coachman, the dapper, diminutive (five feet, five inches) Rann cultivated a foppish air. His nickname derived from the sixteen silk strings he tied to the knees of his breeches. In one version of the story this denoted the number of his mistresses; more plausibly, it was said to indicate his sixteen acquittals on charges of highway robbery.[61] Rann had a decided taste for the ladies. His principal mistress was Letitia Darby, a woman of extravagantly easy virtue, who later made a good marriage for herself (to Sir John Lade in 1777) and lived on until 1825.[62]

Rann's sumptuous clothing attracted widespread popular comment. His favourite outfit was a scarlet coat, tambour waistcoat, white silk stockings, and laced hat. His popularity derived from his self-conscious attempt to be a Robin Hood and rob only the rich. Even Samuel Johnson fell under his spell: he declared that 'Sixteen-string Jack' towered above the common mark of highwaymen.[63] Eventually Rann's run of acquittals came to an end. He was executed in 1774 for robbing Dr William Bell of his watch in Gunnersbury Lane.[65] Yet even at his death Rann played the fop. He was hanged in a new suit of pea-green clothes, his hat bound round with silver rings. He wore a ruffled shirt and had a huge nosegay in his buttonhole.[65] He showed the utmost unconcern for his coming end and was cheered to the echo by 'the whole vagabond population of London'.[66]

The century ended with a vintage example of the genus highwayman. Richard Ferguson, alias 'Galloping Dick' had been trained as a stable boy and had a wonderful way with horses. He was also a great favourite with the ladies. Hired as a postilion, he was dismissed after being found *in flagrante* with a maid servant.

Ferguson's father died and left him the far from princely sum of £57. For a while Ferguson lived as a gentleman gambler. He made the acquaintance of a high-class courtesan, Nancy, who also bestowed her favours on leading criminals, especially highwaymen, telling each of her lovers that he was the only one. Although Ferguson soon learned the truth, her skills in the boudoir were such that he was besotted with her. His money shortly afterwards running out, Ferguson was obliged to take a post as postilion, in which position he frequently saw on the road his rivals for the lady's favours.

His principal rival was one Abershaw. One day Ferguson's chaise was robbed by a party of highwaymen, among them Abershaw. By chance the wind blew the handkerchief from Abershaw's mouth. He and Ferguson gaped at one another in recognition before the approach of other travellers made Abershaw's party sheer off. But they were worried at having been recognized. Abershaw visited Ferguson and offered him a bribe to keep his mouth shut. The elated Ferguson accepted the cash, bought himself new clothes and betook himself to his Nancy. She was not expecting him, however, and Ferguson burst into her quarters to find her in the arms of another. In pique Ferguson threw in his lot with Abershaw's gang.

At first Abershaw used him as an informant. But when Ferguson had learned the tricks of the trade, he went on the road himself and soon achieved fame for his many daring escapades, all due to his skill in picking fast, sound horses. A great womanizer, Ferguson enjoyed many affairs with married women, specializing in publican's wives. One day he rode across Hounslow Heath and found Abershaw hanging in chains. Ferguson did not learn the lesson this gruesome spectacle was supposed to teach him and continued a successful career until he fell foul of the Bow Street runners in 1800.[67]

How widespread was highway robbery in the eighteenth century? Obviously it is extremely difficult to quantify the numbers of highwaymen involved. Generalizations based on the court records alone are difficult, since a man could be caught and hanged at his first venture onto the road. On the other hand, the Pages and their ilk might go for years before being caught, in which time they could have chalked up hundreds of robberies. But to judge impressionistically from newspaper reports of robberies committed, highway robbery was at epidemic level for much of the period.[68] This judgement receives the sanction of foreign observers of England. Samuel Johnson's friend Baretti (see p. 39), a great traveller, said he had had several experiences in England but had never met a highwayman in Europe.[69] The general consensus was that the forty-mile radius around London was 'infested' with them.[70] Some inference as to levels is possible from the number of times leading members of the elite encountered highwaymen. Horace Walpole was held up three times in a far from peripatetic career. Another interesting pointer is the fact that most middle- or upper-class criminals had earlier encounters with highwaymen as part of their history; Ferrers is one instance, Dr Dodd (see below p. 139) another. On the other hand John Wesley testified that he had travelled hundreds of thousands of miles all over England by day and by night for forty years and was never stopped by a highwayman.[71]

The great magnet for highwaymen was the system of trunk roads spreading out from London. The most important of these were the road to Bristol and the West, the road to Dover and the Continent, and the Great North Road. The favourite place to hold up traffic bound for Kent and the Continent was around Woolwich and Blackheath.[72] For northbound vehicles the preferred location for interception was Epping Forest or Finchley Common.[73] But the real Mecca for highwaymen was Hounslow Heath, a wild, bleak, windswept wilderness.[74] If a highwayman failed to make a hit there on inbound stage-coaches and carriages, he could double back to Turnham Green, also a heath in this era.[75]

The highwaymen chose their locations well. Shooters Hill at Woolwich was well known, even in the seventeenth century, as a particular haunt for such armed assailants. In her *Journeys* Celia Fiennes described it as 'esteemed as a noting robbing place'. Pepys recorded that it was customary to hang apprehended criminals there: '[we] rode under the man that hangs upon Shooters Hill; and a filthy sight it was to see how his flesh is shrunk to his bones.'[76] Defoe described Epping Forest as 'in winter scarce passable for horse or man'.[77]

By common consent highwaymen had a special feeling for the most desolate terrain. The favourite place to intercept traffic between London and the south-west was Bagshot Heath, described by Defoe as follows:

Those that despise Scotland, and the north part of England, for being full of vast and barren land, may take a view of this part of Surrey, and look upon it as a foil to the beauty of the rest of England . . . here is a vast tract of land, some of it within seventeen or eighteen miles of the capital city; which is not only poor, but even quite sterile, given up to barrenness, horrid and frightful to look on, not only good for little but good for nothing: much of it a sandy desert, and one may frequently be put in mind here of Arabia Deserta, where the winds raise the sands so as to overwhelm whole caravans of travellers, cattle and people together; for in passing this heath, in a windy day, I was so far in danger of smothering with the clouds of sand, which were raised by the storm, that I could neither keep it out of my mouth, nose or eyes; and when the wind was over, the sand appeared spread over the adjacent fields of the forest some miles distant, so that it ruins the very soil.[78]

Bagshot Heath was not the only 'Arabian' wilderness. In 1822 William Cobbett described Ashurt forest thus:

Verily the most villainously ugly spot I ever saw in England. This lasts you for five miles, getting, if possible, uglier and uglier all the way, till, at last, as if baren soil, nasty spewy gravel, heath, and even that stunted, were not enough, you see some rising spots, which instead of trees, present you with black, ragged, hideous rocks. There may be Englishmen who wish to see the coast of Nova Scotia. They need not go to sea; for it is here to the life.[79]

Well-mounted highwaymen, armed to the teeth with pistols, could prey on a variety of conveyances: the coaches of the rich, the curricles of farmers returning from market, above all stage-coaches and the mail service. As the turnpikes improved, so did their pickings. In the long term the turnpikes were to favour the forces of law and order, especially when mounted patrols operated in and around the capital. But for most of the century the improved road network, especially near London, simply played into the highwaymen's hands.[80] For by the end of the century the ameliorated communications meant that several stage-coaches a day left London for Manchester, Bristol, Edinburgh, and the other large cities.[81]

As well as providing targets, London also supplied a network of 'safe' public houses and inns, plus an ancillary back-up force of receivers, liverymen, and stablekeepers. The feebleness of the law governing places of public amusement that so enraged the Fieldings played into criminal hands. In some locales the 'safe house' was an open secret. Such was the case with the Blue Lion (or Blue Cat) in Gray's Inn Lane and the Bull and Pen in Spa Fields.[82] St George's Fields practically pullulated with highwaymen's dens. The Dog and Duck, the Shepherd and Shepherdess,

Apollo Gardens and Temple of Flora were the most notorious. People would wait to see famous highwaymen mount up and say goodbye to their women.[83]

The average highwayman set out on his endeavours with six or seven pistols. Usually he wore a black mask over his eyes and a silk handkerchief over his face to avoid recognition.[84] The Exeter stage was robbed in 1764 by 'a young man of middle stature, dressed in a blue surtout coat, brown cut wig, a black crepe mask over his face, mounted on a bright bay gelding'.[85] The solitary highwayman tended to concentrate on coaches, where he did not have to keep his eye on so many people at once. He would present a pistol in one hand and his hat in the other, asking for purses. The valuables would be put in the hat and the highwayman, if satisfied, would then ride off.[86] But there were distinct disadvantages to being a lone robber. Quite apart from the danger, it meant that in exercising normal caution he had to concentrate on coaches, which were not so good for money. The takings tended to be small purses, watches, silver buckles and other gewgaws. It was much better for him to have a comrade or two; he could then both attack bigger and richer targets and search the passengers thoroughly. For this reason, pedestrians or solitary travellers were not often stopped; this could explain John Wesley's experience.[87]

The most tempting target were the postboys who carried the mails. These were known to contain bank bills and negotiable paper. But this type of robbery was the most perilous of all. Not only was there the danger of being caught when passing the stolen notes; such crime also drew the attention of the King's Messengers and led to the posting of huge rewards by the Post Office. Ralph Wilson, chronicler of the Hawkins gang in the 1720s, testified that it was robbery of the mails that led to their downfall after a successful career as 'normal' highwaymen.[88] Hawkins and his men specialized in covering the maximum geographical space in the shortest possible time. They would make several attacks an evening two or three times a week for several months, then lie low for a long period. They had an agreement with a livery stable keeper who had horses ready for them at any hour of the day or night in return for a 'cut'. Yet Hawkins's very success led him to hubris. One morning he and his gang robbed the Cirencester, Worcester, Gloucester, Oxford, and Bristol stages in succession.[89] The problem here was the very scale of the success. The huge reward that the Post Office inevitably posted (this time, of £200) was bound to lead to treachery, since this was more than a gang member could make by non-stop robbery for a month. The sequel was predictable.

It was often said that highwaymen had favourite times of the year and of the day in which to operate. Autumn and 7 p.m. were mentioned respectively.[90] Yet it was quite clear that highway robbery could take place at any time when there were travellers on the road. Two JPs returning from sessions at Brentford were robbed in Twickenham at noon in October 1784 by a pair of foul-mouthed highwaymen who made off towards Isleworth.[91] There was another case of (literal) daylight robbery in Twickenham in 1791.[92] Lady Hertford was attacked on Hounslow Heath at 3 p.m. but her two mounted servants beat off the assailant.[93] A shoot-out occurred on the same heath at midnight in July 1764 after a chaise had been robbed. The Bristol one-day 'machine' with its passengers came on the scene minutes after the robbery. Forming themselves into an armed posse the passengers caught up with the two highwaymen. There was a furious exchange of fire before the highwaymen made good their escape in the darkness.[94]

Another canard was that the highwayman liked to rob on Sundays, both because the roads were quieter and he could escape more easily, and because the authorities were unlikely to exert themselves to catch him, since the Sunday Trading Act relieved them of any responsibility towards the victim. But to set against this there was the fact that commercial traffic was slender for precisely these reasons. Also, the roads were thronged with churchgoers and pleasure seekers of all ranks, which made the formation of a strong pursuing party easier.[95]

Although the methods and targets of the highwaymen were always much the same, a few enterprising individuals had slants of their own. Tom Rowland (executed 1699) always robbed while dressed as a woman.[96] Another went disguised as a bishop with four or five companions as his servants and chaplain. Others provided ingenious alibis for themselves. Isaac Darking was a sailor who took to the road on his periods of leave. He was caught near the scene of a robbery on one occasion and secured his release by pretending to be a foreigner: the knowledge of foreign parts he had acquired as a sailor made his story most convincing.[97] Another highwayman's alibi was breached only by passion. John Stretton (executed 1771) went to bed ostentatiously at night in his lodgings, then crept out, got on his horse, and robbed the northern mail-coach. He was seen to get up at breakfast-time, and thus had provided himself with a cast-iron alibi. Unfortunately the father of the girl Stretton wanted to marry opposed the match. To demonstrate his substance, and blinded by love, Stretton pulled out the drafts he had stolen. The suspicious father insisted on having the notes verified. In this way Stretton was apprehended.[98]

The one thing that would enrage a highwayman and lead him to reveal the violence beneath the usually polite surface was a pretence by his victims that they were not carrying any money or valuables. Such a claim would release a flood of vituperation; the eighteenth century had a richness to its foul-mouthed abuse that cannot be matched in our own day, and highwaymen were masters of the tongue.[99] In the 1720s the houses of the rich in London were actually leafletted with warnings not to leave home without at least £10 and a watch.[100] This led to the custom whereby the nobility always made sure they had enough money to pay the highwayman's levy when they set out on journeys.[101] Another response was to carry two purses, a small one for the highwayman and a large one containing the bulk of the money.[102] A riskier variant on the 'two purse' approach was to fill the highwayman's purse with counterfeit, though such trickery was very dangerous when dealing with a large gang who might take the trouble to inspect the contents of their haul.[103] Sir Horace Mann's sister-in-law fell foul of a 'gentleman of the road' in this way when robbed in New Park in 1782. She gave the highwayman a purse containing very little money and slipped her valuable watch into the coach's bag. Her robber was not satisfied with the contents of the purse and roared out that he would not be cheated. In high terror Mrs Mann's orphaned grand-daughter not only yielded up her own watch but extracted her grandmother's concealed one also and handed it over.[104]

Yet travellers were not always so willing to give up their money without a fight. It was then that the highwayman was forced to use the guns he carried normally for deterrent purposes. It has to be emphasized that this was a comparatively rare outcome.[105] The general lack of resistance to highwaymen was universally deplored. It was suggested that there was a link between this and the general loss of martial spirit among the gentry that prevented them, for example, from contesting the passage of the Jacobite army through England in 1745.[106] Dr Johnson in particular deprecated people's reluctance to shoot it out with highwaymen. He said it was better to kill a man in the very act of committing a crime than to swear his life away afterwards. Besides, he argued, you could be mistaken about the man you testified against at a trial; you could not be mistaken about the man who was actually robbing you. Boswell teased his mentor on this principle: 'So, sir, you would rather act from the motive of private passion than that of public advantage?' Johnson's reply was typical: 'Nay, sir, when I shoot the highwayman, I act from both.'[107]

But in his more reflective moments Johnson admitted that there was a problem about the guilt and remorse someone might feel if he actually shot a highwayman dead. This was not the only objection to the good doctor's prescription. In the first place, it *was* possible to be mistaken about the man to shoot. Two drunks called out to a stage-coach as it sped past them at Woodford in Essex in October 1764. One of the passengers, thinking the drunks were highwaymen, leaned out of the stage and shot one of them dead. To avoid the consequences of his precipitate action, he had to connive in the perversion of justice. At the inquest he solemnly swore that the dead man had no companion and had brandished a pistol first.[108] The other problem was that if the public carried firearms to defend themselves, they ran the risk of being taken up on circumstantial evidence of being highwaymen.[109] For all the risks and drawbacks, those who fought it out were usually applauded. An incident on Putney Heath in 1754, when a servant shot dead the highwayman who had just robbed his master, was described as having the deterrent value of a hundred hangings.[110]

Shoot-outs with highwaymen were by no means common, and often turned out to the highwayman's disadvantage. Tim Buckley was a former Lincolnshire shoemaker's apprentice, who specialized in holding up pawnbrokers and stockjobbers, thus reinforcing the 'Robin Hood' image. His career came to an abrupt end in 1701 when he was 29, following a ferocious gun-battle when he waylaid a stage outside Nottingham. First Buckley's horse was shot dead by a blunderbuss fired by one of the passengers. Buckley then returned fire furiously, using all eight of his horse-pistols. He dispatched a gentleman and a footman before being overpowered by weight of numbers and loss of blood.[111]

Similarly, Zachary Clare, who had already escaped the gallows by turning king's evidence to save his own skin and swearing away the life of his confederate Ned Bonnet, was caught as much through the ineptitude of his own companion as the resistance of Sir Humphrey Jennison. Jennison was carrying £1,000 with him in his carriage when he was ambushed. He ordered his footmen to fight to the death. Two of them were wounded, but then another shot Clare's horse from under him. At this Clare's accomplice panicked and fled, leaving Clare to be taken and executed.[112]

Ned Wicks (executed 1713) was luckier in his companion. In 1705 the occupants of the coach he and his comrade were robbing fought back. Wicks's friend was wounded by a blunderbuss but fought long enough for Wicks to make his escape. When overpowered, the desperate highwayman was found to have eight separate pieces of shot in him. In this maimed state he was tried and hanged.[113] The blunderbuss was often the rock on which highwaymen foundered. When two highwaymen held up the Nottingham stage at Highgate in 1764, one of them was shot from behind by a 'Brown Bess'. He made his escape and when passing through the next turnpike gate gave out that he had been wounded by a footpad. A week later he died of his wounds.[114] Sometimes the shoot-out produced unintended consequences. A highwayman who shot the guard of the Stourbridge machine through the head in 1764 was so dismayed by his own action that he rode on without stopping to rob the passengers.[115]

More usually the motive for resistance was that the intended victims were carrying large amounts of money. But the most spectacular cases involved hot-blooded scions of the aristocracy, determined that no highwayman would 'give them laws'. The Hon. Charles Fox, veteran of a duel with Adams (see below p. 142) was stopped by two men as he journeyed to London in 1781. The principal highwayman roughly demanded his money. Fox's footman opened fire. There was a rapid exchange of shots. The highwayman's second shot went through the footman's coat. There would surely have been severe bloodshed if the second highwayman had not decided to keep his distance. Emboldened by this, Fox then discharged a double-barrelled pistol at his principal tormentor. The wounded assailant rode off at full tilt towards Finchley Common.[116] Frederick Augustus, Lord Berkeley went one better when highwaymen called on his post-chaise to stop on Hounslow Heath in 1774. Berkeley and his servant opened up a brisk fire and shot the man dead.[117]

This sort of resistance led some highwaymen to shoot first and ask questions later. Isaac and Thomas Hallam believed in this course of action. Yet this strategy also had its perils, since it led to the 'shoot first' highwaymen becoming well known, with the consequent posting of large rewards for their capture – exactly what snared the Hallams in fact.[118] Dr Dodd, later a famous criminal himself (see p. 139), was held up in 1772 by a highwayman who fired at him first to show he meant business.[119] A more alarming experience was the lot of Dr (later Sir John) Elliott. A highwayman came up to his carriage near Gunnersbury Lane on the Brentford Road. Without speaking or giving any other warning he fired at the coachman once he was abreast of him. Elliott returned fire. The highwayman discharged his second shot, then seemed to falter. When his hat fell off and he rode away, Elliott realized he had winged him.[120]

The most distinguished recipient of the 'shoot first' policy was the Prime Minister Lord North in 1774. On the evening of Tuesday 4 October he was attacked at the end of Gunnersbury Lane by the same lone highwayman who had made the attempt on Elliott. The man shot his postilion first, then robbed North of his watch and money. In contrast to the usual *fainéant* attitude to highwaymen, this 'scandal' galvanized the elite into action. The offender was taken just two days later in Chandos Street after the intelligence services had been deployed to sniff out a possible concealed assassination bid.[121]

The risk of being shot in the very act of robbery was not the only peril that afflicted the highwayman. If the alarm was raised very quickly after a robbery, even an individual, if determined, could be dangerous. In 1764 in Somerset a highwayman successfully assaulted a squire's chaise but was caught soon afterwards by a neighbouring hunting squire who passed the scene of the crime minutes later.[122] The very same month a hop-merchant was on his way to London from Worcester when he was robbed by two travelling-companions who suddenly revealed their true natures. In pretended exasperation the merchant threw down some guineas on the ground, swearing he had no more. While the two were busy, he hurled a purse containing £50 into the wood. The highwaymen took his mare and departed. Thinking themselves safe, they turned her loose after a couple of miles. But the merchant had followed their tracks on foot. Regaining his mare, he mounted up and trailed his assailants to an inn in Beaconsfield, where he recognized their horses. Waiting until they were asleep, the merchant burst in on them with gun in hand and arrested them.[123]

A posse had a better chance than an individual of catching up with robbers, and the highwayman would normally be on his guard against groups of men, as he would not be towards an individual. The dangers from a group or a posse were more obvious. For this reason the ex-Tyneside clothier Tom Jones (executed 1702) always insisted that the servants of the man he had robbed ride out of sight in the opposite direction from the one he intended to ride in, so that the task of pursuit was made more difficult.[124]

A throng of people was fatally dangerous to a highwayman who robbed two ladies in a post-chaise while they were watching an execution, in Bath in May 1764. He was in plain sight of the gallows, then found his exit route blocked by the throng of spectators. The alarm was raised before he could fight his way through the mêlée, and he was caught.[125]

However pursuit could be a dangerous business. In Surrey in 1742 a man who had been molested but not robbed by two highwaymen ran ahead to the village of Ripley to give the alarm. An armed pursuit was begun and the two robbers were pursued to Ripley village green where a cricket match was in progress. The highwaymen soon found themselves in the middle of the pitch, surrounded by players. One of them made good his escape, but the other was knocked to the ground by a brickbat. As his pursuers closed in on him, the dismounted robber opened fire with his pistol. He shot one of the cricketers dead before being overpowered and taken into custody.[126]

Given that they considered highway robbery more serious than other crimes for which the penalty was death, the authorities faced the problem of how they could impart greater deterrent force to the death penalty. Hanging in chains was one solution, but this was usually reserved for those who had robbed mail-coaches.[127] Malefactors were supposed to hang in chains *after* execution, but sometimes a brutal community would mete out the dreadful penalty of hanging in chains while alive, leaving the condemned man to die of starvation. Such was the fate of the highwayman John Whitfield at Durham in 1777. He lingered for several days before a mailcoachman took pity on him and put him out of his misery with a single shot.[128]

In the light of such severity, it is surprising that highway robbery by no means always attracted the death penalty on conviction. The plea of a first offence was not the most potent one in such cases; usually the crucial factor was witnesses testifying to character and educational attainment. In

1740 the judge in the case of Gil Langley commuted the death sentence to transportation on account of his high educational achievements.[129] A clergyman's testimony that Francis Brightwell knew Latin and Greek was enough to save him from the gallows. Unfortunately the reprieve came too late: Brightwell died of gaol fever shortly after his trial.[130]

The snag about transportation as a punishment for highway robbery was that transportees so often returned before their time and took to the road again. William Field and his partner were both transported to America in the 1760s but returned and resumed their old ways. Field was caught and hanged in 1773, his companion the year after.[131] Martin Keys, ex-vintner's apprentice, who had fled from bankruptcy into highway robbery and was reprieved from death on condition of transportation, actually served with the English at Pondicherry after his term had expired, but was still tempted back to the highway when he returned to England.[132] Transportation often simply increased the volume of highway robbery. Henry Simms, who had been transported for petty robbery of a baker's shop, learned the arts of the road from his fellow transportees and returned to England for a long career ranging from Kingston to Epping Forest, before being caught and executed in 1746.[133] And stories of the rich pickings to be had on English roads encouraged the indigent of America who fell in with the transportees to try their luck in the Old World. One such, taken in 1764, had several musket balls lodged in his body like old harpoons in a sperm whale. Appropriately, the man was from New England.[134]

Until very late in the eighteenth century imprisonment was not a practicable long-term punishment. In any case, the authorities realized that many highwaymen were extremely resourceful and they wanted no repeat of the Jack Sheppard scandal. Their fears were justified. In July 1764 a highwayman escaped from Newgate by pulling bricks out of an upper wall until he had made a tiny hole, then squeezing through and lowering himself onto an adjoining roof by a pair of sheets knotted together.[135]

For all that, the London gaols were considered more secure than the provincial ones. Particularly notorious provincial highwaymen were often sent to custody in the capital. Samuel Gregory was brought from Winchester to Newgate with maximum precautions. He was handcuffed and chained under his horse's belly, and escorted by eight armed men.[136] One of the factors governing such expensive transfers was the ease with which an accomplished arsonist could burn down the crude provincial gaols. Tom Gray, a former tailor's apprentice, escaped by burning down Gloucester gaol. He was taken and executed only much later, after he had moved to London and made Highgate and Hampstead his 'beat'.[137] Gray's case is interesting in another way. When hanged in 1713 he was 50 years of age. Although highway robbery was largely a young man's occupation and most such villains apprehended were in their twenties, some of the 'old lags' actually were old.

In most cases, though, conviction for highway robbery meant death. There were very few loopholes other than compassionate transportation. Special pleading simply made a person a marked man in the authorities' eyes. Thomas Lympus, who specialized in robbing the Bristol and Bath mails, once twisted the tail of the elite in a singular (but ultimately unwise) fashion. Pursued to France by the King's Messengers, he escaped extradition by claiming to be a Catholic and claiming sanctuary from Holy Mother Church. Baulked of their prey this time, the authorities sanctioned an extra large reward to net Lympus if he should ever return to England. He duly returned into the trap and was taken and executed.[138]

The judiciary also took a dim view of those it had once pardoned on compassionate grounds who repaid mercy with recidivism. Jack Blewit secured a pardon from conviction as a highway robber by telling the court the story of his early life, which included being sold into slavery by pirates. The court's leniency seemed misplaced when Blewit was shortly afterwards found guilty of two murders in the course of highway robbery. This time there could be no extenuating circumstances. He was executed in 1713.[139]

One case where the judiciary itself offered a highwayman a deal illustrates the morbid fear of anatomization universally entertained. In 1763 a robber in his early twenties was offered his life after condemnation if he would consent to have his leg cut off, so that a new styptic could be tested. The highwayman refused the offer indignantly. 'What?' he said, 'and go limping to the devil at last? No, I'll be damned first!' He was duly hanged.[140]

Did highway robbery remain constant throughout the century? Was there any periodicity in its occurrence? Is an awareness of chronology important? Unlike most other crime, highway robbery seems to have remained inelastic to the pressures of economic boom and slump. To be a 'gentleman of the road' required considerable skills and a high initial outlay. It was not the sort of crime to which the man suddenly cast onto the labour scrapheap could easily turn. But highway robbery was very sensitive to change in two other variables: the impact of war and the level of policing. To illustrate this point, a brief survey of the century's peaks and troughs in this particular crime is useful.

The return of demobilized troops after the Treaty of Ryswick produced a crime wave just as the eighteenth century commenced. The campaigns in Flanders had been a useful training ground for future professional criminals. John Holliday learned his skills robbing churches in Brussels and Antwerp, then graduated to robbing King William himself of £1,000 while he was on campaign. Back in England he alternated highway robbery with housebreaking, and it was for the latter offence that he was condemned and hanged in 1700.[141] In the same year an anonymous social critic entered the following verdict: 'We shall shortly not dare to travel in England unless, as in the deserts of Arabia, it be in large companies and armed.'[142]

After the Treaty of Utrecht in 1713, and the release of a fresh horde of ex-soldiers, an even greater crime wave built up in London and the home counties, reaching a crest in the early 1720s. There were many strands in this new upsurge. The Jacobites were still a major threat, and there were continuing rumours of plots and invasions. There were riots by weavers and apprentices. There was an outbreak of farm-burning and cattle-stealing that would eventually culminated in the 1722 Waltham Black Act. There was the new fashion for 'Mohocking', a euphemism for upper-class hooliganism. It seemed to some observers that this was the underworld antiphony to the theme of 'white-collar crime', played so rousingly during the South Sea Bubble scandal. In this context of 'general crisis', highwaymen were said to be behaving with a boldness and ferocity not seen before.[143]

It was Jonathan Wild and his thief-taking activities that put an end to this brief highwayman's heyday. He made an impressive beginning by arresting two on the Oxford road in 1719.[144] Then he entered his 'golden age', culminating in the arrest of the Hawkins gang (see above p. 25). Because of the iron grip exerted by Wild and his thief-takers, highwaymen gave London a wide berth in 1723-5. There is not a single instance of a highwayman's being convicted or hanged at Tyburn in these years.[145]

With Wild's downfall in 1725, and the absence of war until 1740, highway robbery returned to 'normal' levels. The only factor of special significance before the 1740s was the flight of Irishmen from London to the roads. After the 1736 riots over the alleged preferential employment of 'low wage' Irish labourers over their English counterparts, employers were obliged to give the Irish a cold shoulder. Unable to find work, many of them turned to highway robbery.[146] Like ex-soldiers or troops who became exasperated by low pay in the army, the Irish had a martial tradition to draw on.

The next outburst of hyperactivity by highwaymen came at the end of the War of Austrian Succession in 1748. Ex-soldiers, their skills honed in eight years of international warfare, returned to plague the capital.[147] It was the boldness of the new breed of highwaymen that so astonished and frightened the wealthy burghers.[148] Highwaymen patrolled the whole stretch between Hounslow Heath and Piccadilly without let or hindrance. Knightsbridge joined Turnham Green as a favourite spot for a hold-up.[149] The boldest robbery of all was of a post-chaise in Clarge's Street, Piccadilly in September 1750.[150]

This spate of crime ground to a halt in the mid-1750s. First the 1754 elections led to tighter policing. Then the press-gangs played their part in keeping the highwaymen at bay.[151] It was universally recognized that war with France would be resumed; the Navy in particular wanted to be ready. When war came, in 1756, crime levels dropped as manpower was drained away to the armed services. But when war ended in 1763, the problem of highway robbery returned in an even more acute form. 'We swarm with highwaymen who have been heroes', Horace Walpole remarked ruefully.[152] On one single evening in June 1764 there were robberies at Gunnersbury, Syon Park, Turnham Green, Kew Bridge and Hammersmith.[153] The south-western environs of London, especially Twickenham, Hampton, and Teddington with their handy access to Hounslow Heath were fast becoming the favourite area for the men in masks.[154] Yet the audacious hold-ups on the very edge of built-up London continued. In November 1764 the Bath stage was intercepted between Knightsbridge and Hyde Park Corner.[155]

There were two main differences between the period following the Seven Years War and the earlier similar era after the Austrian Succession conflict. One was the activity of the highly effective but short-lived troop of light horse commanded by Sir John Fielding (see above p. 33). The spring of 1764 saw the roads out of London virtually cleared of highwaymen. But once the niggardly government abolished 'Mr Fielding's people', the robbers returned. Even after the disappearance of the Fielding horse patrol, the importance of such mounted bodies was vividly shown when two highwaymen, chased from Putney Heath by hue and cry, were overtaken and caught by a troop of light horsemen stationed at Kensington. One was pursued into Lord Holland's garden on the Hammersmith road where he was overpowered by the gardeners. The other was overtaken by the troop in Hyde Park.[156]

The other difference is that highway robbery did not sink back to the usual peacetime level after the immediate post-war boom. The reason is that the turbulence of the 1760s, when there were challenges to the government from weavers, coal-heavers, sailors, and the Wilkesites, provided cover for a sustained level of activity on the turnpikes. This was reflected in unprecedentedly high levels of convictions for this offence. In 1769 four men were hanged at Tyburn for highway robbery on the same execution day.[157] Needless to say, the invocation of the Bloody Code did nothing to stem the tide. Robberies became even more barefaced. In 1776 the Lord Mayor of London and retinue were held up at Turnham Green. And in 1773 highwaymen penetrated to the very heart of London to ambush Sir Francis Holbourne and his sisters in St. James's Square.[158]

Yet it was the war with the American colonists that produced arguably the century's greatest efflorescence of highway robbery. This conflict had more serious consequences for English society than the continental wars with France, as it choked off the destination point for both emigrants and transportees. The pent-up log-jam of antisocial elements was supplemented by the first of the disgruntled soldiers who began to arrive back after the surrender at Yorktown in 1781. Moreover, dozens of actual or potential highwyamen were released by the crowd during the Gordon riots when they burned down Newgate gaol and the Fleet, New and King's Bench prisons.[159] From 1781 to 1785 highwaymen enjoyed a halcyon period.

Horace Walpole's correspondence provides a good barometer of the 'moral panic' among the propertied classes in these years. In 1782 he recorded the following:

> I am sure, from the magnitude of this inconvenience, that I am not talking merely like an old man. I have lived here above thirty years and used to go everywhere round at all hours of the night without any precaution. I cannot now stir a mile from my own house after sunset without one or two servants with blunderbusses;

> the highwaymen have cut off all communication between the nearest villages: it is as dangerous to go to Petersham as into Gibraltar;

> who would have thought that the war with America would make it impossible to stir from one village to another.[160]

The actual signing of peace with the now independent American colonies increased the flow of highwaymen. A rash of fresh new robberies was reported.[161] People took to travelling to social engagements in large parties, with a heavy guard of servants armed with blunderbusses.[162] The following year a series of daylight robberies in and around Twickenham further shook the confidence of the owners of the villas of the southwest.[163] Walpole joined in the lamentations: 'When highway robberies are arrived at that pitch to be committed at noon-day, in a public road, in the sight of several passengers, who is safe from their depredations? Sunshine is now no security.'[164]

Walpole's prognostications about the likely consequences of the end of the war in America were not hyperbole. July 1785 produced a bumper crop: hold-ups at Cramford Bridge, Ealing Common, Islington, plus a whole clutch from the county of Middlesex.[165] It is no accident that this was the year of Madan's bloodthirsty *Thoughts on Executive Justice* (see below p. 25) The Code seemed to have no answer to this unprecedented crime wave. In the view of the hardliners, the only possible response was capital punishment for *every* felony, with no pardons or extenuating circumstances.

Curiously, in the last decade of the century, as the high tide of the mid-1780s slackened, the Code tended to be administered more leniently, not more savagely, towards highwaymen. It must be emphasized that this was only a very relative tendency. But Noah Pierce, who got a reprieve after robbing a coach in 1794, would certainly have been executed for the same offence a hundred years before.[166] An interesting nuance, too, was employed by the judiciary in the case of Robert Perry and his two sons. Perry himself was an old lag who had already worked off one sentence in the Woolwich hulks, so he was held for execution. But his two sons were reprieved on the ground that their father had led them astray.[167] Most of the capital cases encountered in the 1790s feature highway robbery with some aggravating circumstance, either wounding a coachman, robbing the mails, resisting arrest, or killing Bow Street runners in a shoot-out.[168] Shooting of Bow Street runners increasingly becomes an aspect of highway robbery cases as the century ends.[169] In response, the authorities tended to hang in chains those guilty of killing police officers.

The increasing presence of the Bow Street runners as principals in cases that came to court provides a clue to the more nuanced, less bloodthirsty attitude of judges at the century's end. It was not that Enlightenment thought had made an impact and influenced them to be merciful. It was rather that they felt greater confidence that the war against highwaymen was finally being won. The balance of power was subtly swinging against the knights of the road. Mounted police patrols and more professional constables were an important element in this transformation. An examination of a few end-of-century cases may help to make this clear.

The Bow Street runners were, by the 1790s, a force to be reckoned with. Thomas and Henry Williams, brothers who had been apprenticed as watchmakers, had a successful robbery career until they held up a coach on Maiden Lane, at the end of Gray's Inn Lane. Such audacity played into the hands of the runners. The two brothers got no farther than the fields around Kentish Town before they were hunted down.[170]

The runners were also tenacious. The famous highwayman Richard Ferguson (see above p. 67) was arrested by them several times and then released for lack of evidence. The Bow Street men kept plugging away at him until he made a mistake and robbed a coach in Aylesbury.[171] The runners also coaxed and cajoled the military into lending a hand in cases where they themselves did not have sufficient numbers to hand. A whole clutch of highwaymen, none of them older than 23, were 'launched into eternity' in 1801. This gang of four had just completed a most satisfactory robbery on Shooters Hill near Woolwich just after nine o'clock one morning. Two armed runners quickly got on their tail. They tracked them to a wood, then, having decided they were not strong enough to take them, raised the military at nearby Woolwich barracks. The troops surrounded the wood and began combing it. They flushed the four men out of cover before midday.[172]

The age of the highwayman was rapidly coming to an end and after the turn of the century, the 'gentlemen of the road' were in headlong decline. The last mounted highway robbery recorded took place in 1831.[173] Although the disappearance of the highwayman is sometimes linked to the coming of the railways, as cause and effect such a correlation is anachronistic. The highwayman was already played out as a social force long before the 'Rocket' made its historic run from Stockton to Darlington.

The ostler in George Borrow's *Romany Rye* made a famous threefold analysis of the reasons for the decline and fall of highway robbery. First, there was the authorities' refusal to license public houses that were known to shelter highwaymen; this spelt the demise of notorious 'safe houses' like the Dog and Duck. Second, there was the enclosure system that took many a wild heath out of the public domain. Third, there was the advent of the Bow Street runners and the permanent mounted patrol operating out of London.[174] To this list can be added other factors. Urbanization and industrialization meant both an extension of the built-up areas of cities, cutting down on the highwayman's famous lairs on the open ground, and an improvement in the turnpike system. Good riding surfaces made mounted pursuit easier. The highwayman, on the other hand, did not respond to this technological challenge with any significant innovations in his *modus operandi*.

Most of all, and appropriately for the regime introduced after 1688, there was the factor of money. There are two aspects to this. On the one hand, the authorities steadily increased the amounts of money offered as a reward for the apprehension of highwaymen. By 1755 offers of £240 plus a royal pardon were being made.[175] It was not just the total amount being offered that acted as a spur to informants, but the *scope* of the payments. At the Surrey Assizes in 1785 six claimants shared £85 reward for the conviction of two highwaymen. At the same sessions, £120 was shared out between eight people for the conviction of three more highway robbers. The victim/prosecutor got £60 and a Tyburn ticket, his wife got £20, three men who helped to arrest the robbers recived £20, £12, and £5, while three witnesses were paid £1 each for their evidence.[176] On the other hand, changes in banking legislation at the end of the eighteenth century made it unnecessary in the main for people to carry large sums of gold or notes with them on their travels.

It has sometimes been remarked that highwaymen faded away at the same time as the coming of milder punishments. This was simply the congruence of technology and more enlightened thought. There is no more suspicion of cause and effect in this relationship than there was any connection earlier in the eighteenth century between draconian punishments and levels of highway robbery. The fact is that crime and punishment operated almost entirely on different planes. If the age of the highwayman has any moral, it is merely to reinforce the lesson taught by the study of the century's crime in general: that to believe in the deterrent effect of capital punishment is to believe in a chimera.

5

Property Crime

England is a prison for men, a paradise for women, a
purgatory for servants, a hell for horses.
>   Thomas Fuller, *Holy State*, 1642

It is my belief, Watson, founded upon my experience, that
the lowest and vilest alleys of London do not present a
more dreadful record of sin than does the smiling and
beautiful countryside.
>   Sir Arthur Conan Doyle, 'The Copper Beeches',
>   *The Adventures of Sherlock Holmes*

The jury, passing on the prisoner's life,
May in the sworn twelve have a thief or two
Guiltier than him they try
>   William Shakespeare, *Measure For Measure*, II.i.19

The defence of property was a prime aim of eighteenth-century law. The
natural tendency is to see this defence as one conducted against the
spectacular criminals of the century: the highwaymen, smugglers,
poachers, and coiners. Yet the law operated largely at a less elevated
pitch. Most cases that came to trial and/or exercized the minds of
ordinary people were at the more mundane level of property crime. Yet it
is in the 'minute particulars' rather than the grand set-pieces of crime that
we see the most typical operations of the law. Some attention must
therefore be given to the less 'glamorous' manifestations of crime: arson,
burglary, theft.

Arson

The danger from fire in the eighteenth century was very great, since
besides the staircases, there was a lot of inflammable material in the
general structure of the houses.[1] Fire-fighting was primitive, and the fire
brigades private organizations run by the insurance companies, who
rarely acted with efficiency and dispatch.[2] A quick impressionistic picture

will help to convey the extent and variety of fires that derived from 'natural' causes or 'act of God', and the havoc they caused.

In 1745 the Duke of Kingston's seat at Thoresby was burned to the ground, complete with all his papers and documents.[3] In 1752 a fire in Lincoln's Inn New Square destroyed many legal premises and their contents.[4] Among these were the complete papers and library of Philip Yorke, Lord Chancellor Hardwicke's son.[5] In 1789 the Opera House or King's Theatre in the Haymarket was burned down,[6] as was the Pantheon Theatre three years later.[7] In 1789, too, the north wing of Houghton Hall, Norfolk, seat of Lord Orford, was gutted. The fire would have destroyed the whole building but for a stone arcade that divided the wing from the main building and the fact that the wind was not blowing north-south at the time. The Phoenix and Sun Fire insurance companies took a particular interest in this conflagration, as damage estimated at £50,000 was alleged to have been caused.[8]

It was not just theatres and great ancestral homes that were at risk. A raging inferno in HM Dockyards at Portsmouth in July 1760 was arrested only when a firebreak was made in the Ropehouse. Vast quantities of stores were consumed in the furnace, although (except for a shortage of sails and cables), enough remained to meet the Admiralty's wartime needs.[9] A similar kind of fire broke out in May 1785 in a turpentine warehouse in Southwark. The blaze consumed the original warehouse and four others, together with four private houses and a quantity of pitch and rosin. A feature of this fire was the ineptitude of the firemen, who took two hours to locate a source of water.[10]

Finally, fire was a recurring source of domestic tragedy. A stationer's wife said goodnight to her seven children in 1782 and left a candle by the curtain of one of the beds. The candle set light to the curtain and the entire house was consumed by fire, carrying off all seven children.[11]

Given the fearsome threat from fire, and the extent of the damage it could do, it is not surprising that eighteenth-century legislators punished the crime of arson with the utmost severity. All cases of starting fires deliberately that were treated by the law as arson were in the class of non-clergyable felonies.[12] The Waltham Black Act of 1723 included arson in its all-encompassing net, although in 1758 it was thought best to make the point explicit in a separate law.[13] A whole battery of statutes dealt with ancillary or dubious cases of arson. A 1737 act made firing pits or mines arson.[14] A 1772 act dealt with naval property, ships, and dockyards.[15] Arson was universally abhorred. Even the liberal reformer William Eden thought that very severe punishment was justified in this case; his complaint was that the existing statutes on arson were too blunt and inflexible.[16] So seriously was this offence taken that in 1738 a landlord whose barn had been burned offered a £20 reward for conviction of the arsonist. The authorities added a royal pardon for anyone who would give information leading to a successful prosecution.[17]

Overwhelmingly, cases of arson fell into three main categories: acts of revenge by servants against their masters; insurance frauds; and acts of political sabotage directed against major institutions. Arson by servants made up the majority of fire-raising cases recorded in the contemporary press and the *Newgate Calendar*.[18] In 1764 an apprentice was found to have set fire to his master's house by putting a red-hot poker in his bed; his three previous attempts at arson had failed.[19] In 1787 Elizabeth Sedgwick, a rare female incendiary, was executed for setting fire to two barns and a stable belonging to her master.[20] One of the best-known cases was that of James Sampson, convicted at the Old Bailey in 1768. He was himself a servant of the duke of Richmond but was married to a servant of Lady Aylesbury, in the household of General Conway. Sampson stole banknotes worth £925 from Conway, then set his house on fire to conceal the theft.[21] Incendiarism to conceal thefts by servants was a recurring feature of eighteenth-century arson cases.[22]

There must have been many 'natural disasters' that in fact were undetected arson by servants. The inference is strengthened by one of the most famous cases of the century. One Friday in early May 1763, between 4 and 5 a.m., the house of Lady Molesworth in Brook Street was burned to the ground in a conflagration as sudden and violent as it was inexplicable. Lady Molesworth, her two daughters, her brother and three servants all perished in the flames. The cause of the inferno remained a mystery.[23]

Eighteen years later, by a pure fluke, the truth came out. One of Lady Molesworth's servants had stolen a trunk full of plate and valuables, which he shipped to a friend in Ireland. Then he burned down the house to conceal his crime. Because of the terrible circumstances of the fire, the servant always feared to send for the trunk, lest he be discovered. But in 1781 the friend in Ireland died, the trunk was opened routinely, and the plate with the Molesworth arms on it discovered. The servant was taken up for questioning and admitted having started the fire in three places on that fateful May morning.[24]

The rise of the insurance company in the eighteenth century produced a symbiotic increase in cases of arson in order to collect on policies. Fifteen new insurance companies were formed between 1710 and 1800 in England alone.[25] Yet the law on arson contained a glaring loophole. Before 1803 it was not a capital offence to set fire to one's own house. It was made capital that year precisely to close the door on the most popular insurance fraud.[26] Burning one's own house was not even a misdemeanour unless it caused a nuisance to neighbouring property, and this even in cases where the criminal intent was palpable. In 1786 Thomas Hilliard set fire to his own house but was acquitted of criminality, even though his motive was obvious.[27] Only if neighbouring houses were actually burned, did 'self-arson' become a felony. This produced the absurd result that if a person gutted his house to get insurance money, he was punishable at most by fines and imprisonment, yet if he set fire to a stack of hay that belonged to another man, he was liable to the death penalty![28]

Among the fraudulent incendiarists were so-called custodians of law and order. In September 1764 a watchman refused to let firemen into the upper apartment where he lived, until the entire premises had caught fire. His fraudulent intent was obvious, but what secured his arrest was not the incendiarism to his own apartment, but the fact that he had stated that his personal effects were worth £200 and had insured them for that sum with the Sun Fire office; independent witnesses, however, testified that the said goods were not worth £5.[29]

The third, and least common, category of arson was political sabotage. Here the *cause célèbre* of the century was the case of John the Painter (real name James Aitken). A 24-year-old itinerant painter, Aitken was an enthusiastic supporter of the American Revolution. He hoped to win fame as one of America's heroes by a series of fires directed against English shipping.[30] On 7 December 1776 he set fire to the Ropehouse at Portsmouth naval dockyards.[31] On 16 January 1777 he burgled a house in Bristol and then started a blaze in a row of dockside warehouses. The fire began in the premises of Messrs Lewsley & Co in Bell Lane but ironically went on to destroy property belonging to American merchants.[32] At first the fires baffled the authorities. Sabotage by the Americans or their agents was suspected, but the colonists indignantly denied the charge and counter-accused that the arson was a 'set up' by Tory agent-provocateurs. When 'John the Painter' was apprehended shortly afterwards, the truth emerged. He was not in the pay of the Americans, simply a lone wolf who had taken it upon himself to promote their cause.[33] His execution in 1777 provoked cries for an even more draconian law against arson in naval dockyards. But the time was out of joint. By this time opinion was running strongly against any further increases in the capital crime schedule of the already swollen Bloody Code.[34]

A final category of arson, dealt with partly in other chapters, was fire-raising to conceal another crime. A case from Wells in Somerset in 1732 will illustrate this. Jonathan Hawkins borrowed money from his brother-in-law and gave him his bond as IOU for the money. When the time came to repay the money, Hawkins decided to evade his debts in spectacular manner. First he went to his brother-in-law's house at a time when he knew that only he and his daughter were there and cut their throats on the spot. Then he started a fire in several places and quickly left the scene, expecting the blaze to wipe out all traces of the murder. He proceeded to join a card game at a neighbour's house and was sitting there calmly when the general neighbourhood fire alarm was raised. The time-honoured hands around the parish pump contained the fire before it could burn the house down. The murdered bodies were discovered. A confession was quickly extracted from Hawkins and he went to the gallows for his sins.[35]

By contrast Edward Morgan (executed 1757) tried the same trick and got away with it. Having murdered an entire family and then successfully gutted the house to conceal the crime, Morgan was plagued by guilt and remorse and confessed all.[36]

Burglary and housebreaking

Breaking and entering private property with felonious intent was the most commonly encountered capital crime of the eighteenth century. Burglary, or housebreaking by night, in addition required that the property robbed was a 'mansion house'.[37] This crime was treated particularly harshly, as it violated privacy and exposed householders to assault. In addition to burglary proper, the Bloody Code also dealt severely with housebreaking by day. It was a non-clergyable offence to break and enter by day if anyone was put in fear by the act, or if goods worth more than five shillings were stolen, even if no one was present in the house.[38] The relationship of these offences to the Bloody Code is interesting. Burglary proper had been a capital offence before 1688.[39] Capital penalties for housebreaking by day (if the above criteria were met) were added by statutes in 1706 and 1713.[40] These provisions were extended to cover shops and warehouses in 1763.[41]

Burglary and its diurnal analogue, housebreaking, are the staple of property crime in more ways than one. Not only can the offences be committed by anyone from the rawest, youngest tiro to the most sophisticated, professional criminal organization; unlike, say, highway robbery, burglary is not historically determined. Highway robbery could be made obsolete by technological progress; burglary cannot be, at least within the foreseeable limits of human technology. Indeed, increasing prosperity coupled with the 'relative deprivation' of an inegalitarian society is likely to augment rather than diminish its occurrence. Far more insights into the nature of crime *sub specie aeternitatis* can be gained from a study of burglary than from that of coining, wrecking, or poaching. Yet it is, understandably, the 'glamorous' crimes, like highway robbery, which attract the greatest attention. But, as the annals of Newgate show, the humdrum, inert, unchanging rump of crime throughout the century was provided by housebreaking and its nocturnal twin, burglary.[42]

Some very young housebreakers, amateur and professional, suffered execution. Peter McCloud, a boy not yet 16, was executed for the offence in 1772.[43] Another youth of similar age, John Hall (executed in 1707), a chimney-sweep turned burglar, became a London folk-hero after his death.[44] Sixteen-year-old Roderick Audrey introduced a touch of ingenuity into his housebreaking. He had a trained sparrow that accompanied him on his forays. He would send it ahead of him to squeeze into half-opened windows. Once inside the house, Audrey claimed, plausibly enough, that he had merely entered the house to retrieve his sparrow. But neither the bird nor his extreme youth prevented him from suffering the hangman's noose in 1714.[45] Judges and juries were not always softened by the youth of the offender. What mattered was whether it was the accused's first offence and whether he could get reputable witnesses to speak for his character. Failure on these points condemned the Cook brothers, who, though still in their teens, were already 'old lags'.[46]

But the rich pickings to be obtained from carefully-planned burglaries attracted the big operators. In the 1720s Edward Burnworth burgled forty-one houses and shops before being caught, constantly changing his accomplices so that he could not be betrayed by informers.[47] Burglary was also a speciality of the Gregory gang, with which Dick Turpin was at one time associated.[48]

The attractions of burglary for the 'big' criminal were obvious. It was far more profitable than highway robbery, since there was necessarily a limit to the amount of 'loot' a highwayman could carry off. No such limit applied with a well-planned burglary. It was estimated that in Surrey in the years 1660-1800 fewer than a tenth of robberies by footpads or highwaymen brought in more than £10, whereas a quarter of the reported burglaries did so.[49] Burglars in London could hope for particularly rich returns. When the Archbishop of Canterbury's palace was burgled in 1788, no less than £1,200 worth of silver plate was uplifted.[50]

The easy pickings, plus the difficulty of prevention and detection, easily outweighed any deterrent value the sanguinary laws on burglary might have had. The level of burglary in eighteenth-century London was always high, and at times approached epidemic proportions. The period between the end of the Seven Years War and the outbreak of war with the American colonists (1763-75) was considered a time of 'burglary plague' by contemporaries, as housebreaking statistics steadily mounted.[51] Thirteen houses were broken into in London between Michaelmas 1766 and Lady Day 1767, and thirty-six between Lady Day and Michaelmas in 1767. The same periods in the following twelve months produced fifty-two and sixty-two break-ins respectively.[52] Between Michaelmas 1769 and Lady Day 1770, the figure went up to 104. The year 1770 seemed to contemporary observers to be the crest of this particular crime wave.[53] The proportions can perhaps be gauged from a comparison of the 1770 statistics for London and Middlesex with the twenty-year run from 1750 to 1769. Whereas from 1750 to 1769, 909 offenders were capitally convicted in London and Middlesex (with 551 executions), the same figures for 1770 were 91 (with 49 executions). Given that detection methods had not improved, this represents a doubling in the rate of burglary.[54]

The epidemic level of burglary and housebreaking in the early 1770s produced what social historians call a 'moral panic'. There was particular shock when the Earl of Ilchester's house in Old Burlington Street was broken into and stripped bare of plate and silver in January 1772.[55] Something of the flavour of elite panic can be perceived in Horace Walpole's letters. He mentions a daring attack by daytime housebreakers on Cassiobury Park in Watford in 1772 (narrowly beaten off by servants) and an associated assault on a lawyer's house.[56] From Twickenham in 1774 Walpole reported that dinner-table conversation turned on nothing else but the number of houses broken into and robbed.[57] Nor was there much that could be done about the 'crime wave'. Powerful watchdogs could deter rank amateurs, but old lags knew all about poisoning house-dogs.[58] Servants could be armed with blunderbusses, but in response new types of housebreaker arose, well armed and in large numbers. The most sophisticated breed of 'gentlemen housebreaker' went about in a coach and four, complete with 'servants'. In many cases he could be inside a property before the defending servants realized that anything was amiss.[59] The ultimate in housebreaking effrontery occurred when a man broke into Buckingham Palace, and was executed for it, in 1791.[60]

The curious thing about eighteenth-century burglary, given the penalties prescribed by the Bloody Code, was the relatively low level of associated violence and the absence of genuine class bitterness. Cases of violence during housebreaking were largely confined to those where the victim awoke unexpectedly. Where the victim was threatened deliberately, a large-scale gang was likely to be involved.[61] If a single individual threatened violence during housebreaking, he virtually signed his own death warrant.[62]

Naturally, there were exceptions to the norm of absence of violence. A gang of five broke into a wealthy farmer's house near Chester in 1752. They tied up the farmer and his elder daughter, but the younger one got away. She alerted her grown-up brother, who came back with a friend, well armed. They killed the guard posted outside and burst in on the gang to find them on the point of setting light to the farmer to force him to divulge the whereabouts of his money. After a furious shoot-out at close quarters, the four gang members escaped. Three of them were later apprehended and condemned to death. One made his escape in a gaol-break, but the ringleaders John McCanelly and Luke Morgan were hanged.[63]

Such a case was exceptional. The amateur burglars of the eighteenth-century largely stole out of need, out of absolute deprivation. There was none of the peculiar hatred associated with burglars of the 'relative deprivation' of the modern era (which, for example, leads them to defecate on the effects they are rifling). Horace Walpole was a famous beneficiary of this relative lack of asperity. In 1771 burglars broke into his Strawberry Hill 'castle'. Although there was £3,000 worth of goods inside, they took nothing. Walpole hailed the intruders as 'philosophers (for thieves that steal nothing deserve the title much more than Cincinnatus or I').[64] The burglars had spread out all his silverware for inspection but took nothing: 'you never saw such a scene of havoc as my first floor was, and yet £5 will repair all the damage . . . in short this is the first virtuoso that ever visited a collection by main force in the middle of the night.'[65]

Walpole's reflections on his experience also help to explain the psychological impetus behind the eighteenth-century's harsh attitude towards burglary. It was the invasion of privacy that then, as now, produced the greatest shock. Victims of burglary commonly describe the experience as being like a rape, both in the sense that their inner lives have been violated and that their private space has been penetrated. Walpole expressed it thus to the poet Gray:

> If you know any saint that dragged a beautiful young woman into a wood to ravish her, and after throwing her on her back and spreading open her legs, walked quietly away without touching her, to show his continence, you have a faint idea of my housebreakers.[66]

This observation prompts two reflections. One is that the assimilation of burglary to rape – an offence against property with an offence against the person – works purely on the principle of the association of ideas and thus overstates and understates the respective gravity of the offences. The other points to the deficiency of the Bloody Code and all other draconian systems, namely the assumption that it is the task of society and the judiciary to carry into law perfectly understandandable *individual* feelings of rage and desire for revenge. As Beccaria and others were to show, if the aim of law is the general good of society, there are few conceivable circumstances when *lex talionis* fits that requirement. Clearly the death penalty for burglary was one of the more egregious absurdities of eighteenth-century English law. Since the social factors underlying burglary and other property crimes are impervious to the *degree* of punishment, we should expect eighteenth-century experience to be exactly what it was: that crime in general was never seriously affected by the death penalty, but by wider social circumstances.

Theft

The dividing line between actual robbery and burglary was often a shadowy one. But there was a clear distinction between robbery, where violence was offered as the ultimate sanction to produce the intended effect, and simple theft, which depended on stealth, not force. The most common forms of theft were from dwelling houses, shoplifting, or the theft of animals.

Theft from dwelling houses was distinct from burglary and housebreaking, as it was usually done by servants, so that there was no breaking and entering. In general, the law laid down that the theft of goods valued at more than twelve pence was grand larceny, punishable by death but usually clergyable, in which case the punishment was imprisonment or burning in the hand. Theft of goods worth less than twelve pence was petty larceny, punishable by whipping, fines, imprisonment, or seven years' transportation.[67] But there were additional penalties in the case of theft by servants. An act of 1713 deprived servants of benefit of clergy if they stole goods worth more than forty shillings from their masters.[68]

A good example of the kind of theft that attracted the death penalty was the 1765 case of John Wesket. In 1762 Lord Harrington took Wesket on as a porter, unaware that he had a criminal past, particularly in association with his friends John Bradley and James Cooper. It did not take Wesket long in Lord Harrington's service to concoct what he hoped would be a foolproof crime, involving his old partners. In 1763 he let Bradley into his quarters while his patrons were out at the opera. When they had returned, and settled down for the night, he daubed a window-sill with his own dirty shoes, to make it look as though an intruder had entered the house.

Next Wesket and Bradley went to Harrington's study, where he kept his money. The two of them removed £3,000 in cash, banknotes, and valuables. Wesket then let Bradley out by the street door and left it ajar so that it would make no noise. Bradley reurned to Cooper's lodgings and together they hid the loot.

In the morning the theft was discovered. Wesket was immediately suspected of the theft, for he had made a stupid, elementary mistake. While daubing the window-sill on the inside, he had neglected to leave any shoe marks outside. Moreover, the yard outside the 'entry window' was surrounded by a five-foot wall which showed no signs of having been climbed. Yet nothing could be conclusively proved against Wesket. Lord Harrington contented himself with dismissing him.

The full story came out after Wesket jilted his girlfriend. Forced to turn to prostitution, she revealed Wesket's tale to a client. The client went with the information to Sir John Fielding's Bow Street office. Fielding took up Wesket and examined him, but again nothing could be proved.

The case was finally cracked after Bradley foolishly tried to pass a £30 banknote from the haul. Since Lord Harrington had already circulated its details, payment was stopped. The banknote was traced to one Walker, an alias of Bradley's. Patient sleuthing established that Walker and Bradley were one and the same. At this point Cooper was hauled into Bow Street. Under cross-examination he cracked and revealed all. A search in Wesket's cellar revealed some of the stolen items. Warrants were issued for the arrest of all three men. Bradley was caught, disguised as a sailor. When Cooper 'peached' against him, Bradley tried to incriminate Cooper in revenge. In this way the final details of the theft were revealed. Wesket and Bradley were hanged at Tyburn in January 1765.[69]

The Wesket case was an unusual one, because of the large amount of money stolen. Most aristocratic masters, when confronted by their servants' petty pilfering, did not bother to prosecute. They had other sanctions such as dismissal, the refusal to give a 'character', hence causing the disgrace of the servant in the local community. These seemed more appropriate penalties, especially when the possible end of the prosecution road was the death penalty. Most prosecutions for theft by servants were not by the rich but by middling farmers or traders, who wanted exemplary sentences to cow their employees, since they lacked the power or status to disgrace them informally.[70]

Most cases involving thefts by servants came to trial in the metropolis. This reflected a number of factors. There were more of the 'middling sort' in London, the servants were insulated from the informal sanctions of the agrarian community and, most important, the level of pilfering was higher simply because of the greater temptations of urban living, the greater need for spare cash, and the ease of disposing of stolen goods.[71] Yet even in London, there was a certain reluctance on the part both of would-be prosecutors and jurors to consign petty thieves to Tyburn. This tendency became particularly marked by the time of the Reforming era. By the 1790s juries were increasingly adding a recommendation to mercy to their guilty verdicts in such cases.[72] Overwhelmingly, for petty theft the capital provisions of the Code were ignored and transportation used instead.[73] A clear distinction emerged between robbery and its adjuncts, such as demanding money with menaces, and theft properly so-called. The leniency towards theft was balanced by mercilessness towards genuine robbers.[74] Yet even the leniency was exercised only if other things were equal. When George Griffiths, a legal clerk, stole a jewel from his master, that alone would not have consigned him to the gallows. What sealed his fate was the aggravated circumstance of having also seduced his master's daughter on a promise of marriage. He had projected himself to her as a man of property; in fact the only property he possessed was the stolen jewel![75]

Another very common petty property theft was shoplifting. A statute of 1699 made it a capital offence to steal goods valued at more than five shillings from a shop.[76] But this capital provision was seldom enforced and the crime itself was greatly 'underreported'. Few shoplifting cases reached the courts. The reasons for this were threefold. In the first place, shopkeepers did not want the expenses of prosecution; in most cases they had caught the offender red-handed and got their goods back. Second, it was bad business publicity if a prosecution ended with a hanging. Third, most offenders were women, and in general, indictments were pressed against the female sex only in serious cases.

The shoplifters who made the headlines tended to be the hardened recidivists. In January 1764 two Irishwomen, one aged about 50, the other 40, were caught after a six-month orgy of petty theft in stores in London and Southwark, in which they took jewels, rings, muslins, gauzes, and linens.[77] Two months later Sarah McCabe, an accomplished thief with a string of aliases, was run to earth after twenty years' sustained shoplifting. She had actually been transported for the offence in 1748 but had returned in 1752 and resumed her old ways.[78] An ingenious variant on shoplifting was provided in 1764 by an apprentice in a Cheapside store. Over a period of six years he stole £1,000 from the till and from overcharging customers. Following the contemporary exhortations to financial thrift and prudence, he invested his takings in the public funds![79]

Apart from women, shoplifting was the province of gangs of very young boys. It can thus be seen that there was a kinship between shoplifting and that other form of 'privately stealing', pickpocketing. Pickpocketing gangs sometimes rang the changes by bouts of shoplifting.[80] The age of the offenders helped to militate against prosecution. Although nominally a capital offence, the nature of the offenders meant that very few people were actually hanged for it.

There was no similar reluctance to prosecute in the case of stealing horses. Next to burglary, this was regarded as the most serious of the property offences. In a society where the only effective means of transport was by horse, it is not surprising that animals at once valuable and easy to steal had to be protected by very tough laws. Horse-stealing had been one of the first offences (in Elizabethan times) to be removed from clergy. It remained capital throughout the eighteenth century and was largely excluded from consideration by the liberal reformers who campaigned for a diminution of the death penalty. Executions for the offence remained at a fairly constant level.[81] But because of the harshness with which horse-stealing was treated, and the difficulty for an individual of making a successful, untraceable sale of the stolen animal, this crime was almost entirely the prerogative of organized gangs. Typically they would steal horses in the south of England and sell them in the north, or vice versa.[82] This was exactly the sort of crime Sir John Fielding's General Plan aimed to extirpate.

The stealing of sheep was not regarded as seriously as that of horses, largely because sheep were less valuable and more difficult to dispose of or to move around the countryside in large numbers. Sheep-stealing was the work of individuals, not gangs, and it could affect smallholders as well as big farmers.[83] But because it was relatively easy to detect and largely the result of individual need and desperation, it was not at first included among the capital statutes of the Bloody Code. Only in 1741, after an epidemic of such thefts following a period of acute economic depression, hardship, and want, did it become a non-clergyable offence.[84] Interestingly, though, the first victims of the statute were not starving cottagers who killed sheep to eat the meat. Patrick Bourke and George Ellis, hanged for the offence in 1744, used to extract fat from the carcasses which they then sold to a tallow-chandler.[85]

Miscellaneous property crimes

It will be convenient briefly to mention here other capital offences against property that do not fit easily into any other main category. Crimes committed while on the king's service particularly drew down the wrath of legislators. Robbery or theft while in the Army entailed a mandatory death sentence.[86] There was clearly an element of 'lèse-majesté' in the minds of the authorities here, as there was also in the peculiar offence of 'injuring the king's armour' which in 1749 ordained the death penalty for anyone serving in the Navy who unlawfully burned anything, even so little as a piece of tackle.[87] Impersonating servants of the Crown for gain was another serious offence. A man was hanged in 1764 for impersonating a sailor in order to draw his wages.[88] By implication, also, impersonating a police officer was thought to be an act of insolence towards the King's Peace and punished accordingly.[89] No mercy could be expected, either, for anyone tampering with His Majesty's mail. John Swinden, a post office sorter, was executed for secreting a letter in 1794.[90] A postman, John Williams, was sent to the gallows five years later for abstracting and opening a letter containing a £10 note.[91] Next year (1800) another postman, Thomas Chalfont, was executed for a near-identical offence.[92]

The century also had its quota of confidence tricksters. Although this was usually in this era a middle-class crime, exceptionally quick-witted individuals among the 'lower sort' could turn the elite notions of deference on their head. The career of Dick Adams is instructive. Adams started by getting a job as a duchess's servant in St. James's Palace. On several occasions he ordered silks and satins from a mercer on the Duchess's account, which were promptly paid for. Finally he ordered an extra large consignment of these fabrics. The mercer's men delivered them to the Palace. Adams, who had laid his plans carefully, asked them to wait outside, then decamped. After two hours' waiting, the mercer's men discovered the 'scam'.

About a month later the mercer lit by chance on an inebriated Adams and demanded instant restitution on pain of bringing felony charges. At that moment Adams saw the Bishop of London's coach passing in the street. With amazing mental agility Adams at once claimed to be the bishop's nephew and declared that his 'uncle' would make good the losses. Intrigued, the mercer allowed Adams to approach the bishop's coach alone. Doffing his hat, Adams addressed the bishop in awestruck reverential tones. His friend, he said (pointing out the mercer) was an amateur theologian who had become snarled up in his reading of the early Church fathers; would the bishop consent to grant him an interview to disentangle the finer points? Much flattered, the bishop agreed. Manipulated by Adams as to the form of words he should use, the bishop then called the mercer over and told him that he would resolve the matter that was troubling him if he called at his lodgings next day. Well satisfied, the mercer let Adams go. The next morning, as the bishop prepared a disquisition on the finer points of Clement and Origen, the mercer appeared with a bill for more than £200. The inevitable initial failure to communicate resolved itself when both men realized the extent to which Adams had bamboozled them. Unfortunately for Adams, his quick wits availed him little. Turning from urban theft to highway robbery, he was taken and executed in 1713.[93]

Throughout the century the most serious crimes against property remained highway and footpad robbery, burglary and housebreaking, and horse-stealing. There was as yet no sign of the modern crimes of bank, payroll, or bullion robbery. The primitive nature of the financial system did not provide the necessary preconditions. Yet a startling case at the very end of the century showed the shape of things to come. In the winter of 1798 James Turnbull attempted the most daring robbery yet. Turnbull was a private in the regiment of Guards that guarded the Mint. Part of his duties involved working the die for the coinage of guineas, so he knew in detail how the Mint system worked. One morning he pretended to go for breakfast but at once returned with an accomplice called Dalton. While Dalton watched the door, Turnbull clapped a pistol to the head of the apprentice left in charge of the coining room and demanded the keys of the chest where the finished guineas were kept. Turnbull and Dalton then made off with four bags containing 2,380 guineas and effected their escape before the alarm could be given.[94]

Such a crime was a direct affront to the authority and credibility of the entire social system. A massive dragnet was organized. On 5 January 1799 Turnbull was arrested at Dover as he tried to cross to France. He was immediately tried, found guilty and hanged. Yet his daring example sent a chill through the authorities. It was not just Irish rebellion, invasion threats, mutinies and Jacobin revolutionaries that seemed to portend a grave threat in this turbulent last decade of the eighteenth century.

6

Women (1)

The happiest women, like the happiest nations, have no history.

George Eliot, *The Mill on the Floss*

Women, indeed, are bitter bad judges in these cases, for they are so partial to the brave that they think every man handsome who is going to the camp or the gallows.

John Gay, *The Beggar's Opera*

Far be it, Sirs, from my more civil Muse,
Those Loving Ladies rudely to traduce,
Allyes and Lanes are Terms too vile and base,
And give Ideas of a narrow Pass;
But the well-worn Paths of the Nymphs of Drury
Are large and wide; Tydcomb and I assure ye.

Verses enclosed in Alexander Pope's letter to
Henry Cromwell, 25 April 1708

AS VICTIMS OF CRIME

In the eighteenth century there was a large twilight area between sin and crime, which affected both sexes, but particularly brought the spotlight to bear on women. It was a hardy perennial of conservative and reactionary social thought (and to a large extent still is) that the roots of crime were to be located in immorality, especially of the sexual kind.[1] The principal targets of such reformers were adultery and prostitution. For these critics, the Commonwealth, whatever its other faults, represented a golden age of austere morality. For ten years from 1650 adultery and brothel-keeping were capital crimes; even fornication, on a second offence, was a non-clergyable felony.[2] The Restoration had changed all that: one more reason, according to Henry Fielding, to hate the house of Stuart.

In his *Inquiry into the late Increase of Robbers* Henry Fielding advocated an all-out effort to destroy popular culture and the folkways of the 'lower orders'. In its place a new culture would arise: spartan, thrifty, dedicated to the reality principle, not the pleasure principle.[3] The theatre would be closely regulated. There would be censorship of 'subversive' works like John Gay's *The Beggar's Opera* – a particular target for the Fieldings (not surprisingly, as it brilliantly exposed the humbug of all they stood for). There would be a heavy clamp-down on the sale of alcohol, tight regulation of all public spectacles, strict licensing of gaming and brothels. Those, like Gay, who supported the detested popular culture, would have their works banned and be deprived of all hope of making a living from literature.[4]

Fielding considered that an essential first step towards the realization of his programme was to hit seducers hard and dampen down the fires of sexuality. In the *Covent Garden Journal*, which he founded in 1752 and which ran for eleven months, he advocated returning to the criminal code of the Commonwealth and making adultery a crime.[5] In making such a proposal Fielding tapped deep into a latent core of puritanism and hatred of sex. Even Blackstone felt that the law which made adultery a mere private injury was too lax.[6] Believing in the power of example, he accepted the argument that the sexual immorality of the toiling classes was attributable in part to the bad example set by their 'betters'. There was a wide consensus that adultery should be punished. Even if the bloody provisions of the Code were inappropriate, there should at least be fines and imprisonment.[7] Colquhoun was another who wanted adultery made a criminal offence and thought that the seducers of women should be liable both to corporal punishment and payment of damages.[8] Colquhoun underlined how the law so often worked to the disadvantage of women. He thought it very wrong that forcible abduction was a criminal offence only when made on women of estate and property.[9]

Fielding's advocacy triggered a strong movement in favour of the conflation of sin and crime. In 1771 a bill to prohibit adulterers from marrying within a specified period passed the Lords and was thrown out of the Commons only by a slender majority. The Adultery Bill, rejected in 1779, was another attempt to bring sexual morality within the compass of the criminal law.[10] The final attempt of the century, also a failure, was made in 1800.[11]

The theorists of moral outrage could muster an even bigger constituency for the campaign to do something about prostitution, which was a mere misdemeanour. The burgeoning Methodist societies for the improvement of manners and keeping the Sabbath holy particularly focused on prostitution and bawdy-houses after a speech by John Wesley on 30 January 1763.[12] The problem was *what* to do. Even the relatively unsophisticated social analysts of the eighteenth century were aware that prostitution played a vital role in siphoning off rampant sexuality. Because lower-class men married late for economic reasons, there had to be some outlet for libido.[13] If it was not in whorehouses, unmarried men might begin to prey on the wives and daughters of the respectable. This inference was strengthened by the known fact that those who committed sexual crimes, either on adults or children, were almost always the illiterate, the economically deprived and the unsocialized flotsam of the big cities who had grown up to regard sex as a merely animal activity.[14]

Yet the prejudice against prostitution ran deep. Even a normally commonsensical individual like Samuel Johnson began to splutter when Boswell used on him the argument that prostitutes kept down the level of rape against 'respectable' women.[15] Vehemently rejecting this line of reasoning, Johnson became almost Fielding-like in his belief that severely enforced laws against fornication would do the trick. He used the facile argument that theft is as much part of human nature as sexuality, yet we have laws against theft, so why not against fornication?[16] Apart from his confusion of the social with the biological, Johnson neglected to compare like with like. He failed to see that the laws against theft were a consequence of private property; of what general category, then, would the laws against fornication be a sub-class?

This was one area where Johnson departed signally from the thought of his mentor in social theory, Bernard Mandeville. Mandeville took the more modern view that prostitution was an inevitable concomitant of the human situation and that brothels should be licensed.[17] Johnson would have none of this, and singled out the licensed bordellos in Rome for especial excoriation. To the argument that severe laws against prostitution would not only harm the whores themselves but also 'respectable' women, since they would have to go everywhere chaperoned, Johnson claimed (without much evidence on his side) that taverns would always admit well-dressed women; it was the ladies of the night at which they drew the line.[18]

For all his blinkered attitude, Johnson's heart was in the right place. He was sorry for 'fallen' women and declared that illicit sex produced far more misery than happiness.[19] His attitude pre-echoes that of the great American lawyer Clarence Darrow: 'I may hate the sin, but never the sinner.' Fielding on the other hand hated the sinner more than the sin. When he had a chance to show the true value of his fulminations against 'disorderly houses' during the 1749 riots (see below p. 223), Fielding took the side of the brothel-keepers against the rioting sailors. In his Whig heart Henry Fielding knew that strong action against prostitutes ultimately meant tough measures against bawdy houses as *property*. As an outstanding student of those events has remarked: 'It appears that the magistrate's duty lay less in bringing down bawdy-houses than in keeping them standing. Indeed, where in July he (Fielding) quotes Coke against adultery and fornication, in November he quotes Hale to argue that the pulling down of bawdy-houses is high treason.'[20]

Midway between the Fielding and Mandeville positions stood Colquhoun. He baulked at going all the way with Mandeville and legalizing prostitution. But he was in favour of 'confining the evil', that is to say, keeping prostitutes strictly within a controlled and supervised 'red-light district'.[21] This idea foundered both on notions of untramelled individual freedom and more especially on the objections of the 'moral majority', who thought that such a step would be seen to condone prostitution. There is also a suspicion that male members of the elite were not happy with Colquhoun's even-handed approach. He did not want all the opprobrium for prostitution to fall on women. Instead, he proposed to make it a fineable offence for a man to make sexual overtures to a woman or to accept such overtures from her.[22]

How widespread was this problem that so exercised the best minds of eighteenth-century England? Clearly, little changed qualitatively in one hundred years. At the end of the 1690s John Dunton was publishing a monthly newsletter devoted to prostitution, in which he spoke of London as a second Sodom, where whoredom was an aspect of organized crime.[23] By the end of the 1790s much the same picture was being provided by pamphleteers: there was individual, free-lance prostitution and there were brothels run by gangs.[24] As for quantity, Colquhoun estimated that there were 100,000 prostitutes in England as a whole, of which 50,000 were based in the metropolis. On his own figures, this meant that 30 per cent of all criminals in the provinces, and 50 per cent in London were prostitutes.[25] It is hard to know what to make of these figures. Taken seriously, they meant that every third or fourth female was an acknowledged and professed whore. This seems implausible, to say the least. But Colquhoun was no hyperbolic Fielding: the fact that he set the figure so high means it probably was high, while not attaining the numerical proportions he imagined.

London was the Mecca of sexuality, offering every conceivable lubricious variety. On one occasion the constables cleared the streets around Covent Garden on a routine raid and trawled in twenty-two women plying their trade. When they were confined in the round house, two of them were found to be men dressed as women.[26] Dr John Arbuthnot, a noted physician and wit of the early eighteenth century, once poked fun at the wide range of carnal delights available by entering a high-class brothel and saying to the madam: 'a little of your plain fucking for me if you please!'[27] As the 1749 riots made only too clear, London was chock-full of bawdy-houses. Many of the favourite and most notorious ones were in Covent Garden.[28] There was a well-known red-light district off the Strand including 'Mother Wisebourne's house', where the girls were said to cost an incredible £250 a night (£2,000 in modern money).[29] Mrs Comyn's 'house' in St James's Street was another favourite haunt of young aristocratic bucks.[30]

Some social critics were content to follow Fielding and conflate sin and vice, arguing in effect that there should be laws against sin.[31] Fielding's friend and staunch lieutenant Saunders Welch added a new twist to the party line by arguing that it was the Irish who were chiefly responsible for the high levels of London prostitution; he too endorsed the Fielding plea for a systematic extirpation of popular culture.[32] Others emphasized the outrage to public decency by casual whores. Hyde Park was patrolled twice a night by the Watch, but the solid citizens with houses backing on to the Park complained that this was not enough. Common harlots, they alleged, knew the times of the patrol to a nicety and took their clients into the park. Lascivious writhings in the grass could be seen every night from their rear windows.[33]

More down-to-earth critics alleged that something had to be done about prostitution, not because it was immoral but because of the other crimes it invariably engendered. Encounters with women of the night either in brothels or in the open frequently led to serious disturbances of the peace. A man was thrown from an upstairs window in a Covent Garden brothel in 1764 after an argument with pimps, and died from his injuries.[34] In 1700 an argument over an 'orange woman' in Drury Lane ended in murder.[35] On one occasion thirty men set on a couple of constables in a brothel off Eagle Court, Strand, while they were executing a warrant, and gave them a severe beating.[36] Another crime associated with the 'houses' was waiting at the coaching stations and luring ingenuous young country girls, just arrived in London, into a life of 'pleasure'. There was a very disturbing case in May 1764 when it was discovered that Susannah Leach, just such an ingenue, had been lured to a brothel in Eagle Street, Strand, by a depraved couple. They kept her there on short commons, pandering to the lust of their clients, beating her betimes for not bringing in enough money.[37]

But far the most common crime associated with brothels was the robbery of clients, which frequently ended in murder if the victims awoke and saw what was going on. One such homicide came to light in a singular manner. An apprentice clog-maker who wanted to lead a virtuous life of industry confessed to his master the skeleton in his family's cupboard. As a boy he had lived with his elder sister in a bawdy-house off Chick Lane. One evening his sister brought home a client, went to bed with him, then began to rifle his pockets. The man awoke and caught her, then struck her hard across the face. She stabbed him through the heart with a knife, then, with the aid of the other whores, stripped him naked. Next they dug a hole with pick-axe and spade in a piece of waste ground behind the 'house'. There they buried him, and there the authorities found him when the shoemaker alerted them.[38]

Sometimes the overspill from London brothels seeped into high society itself. In 1778 there was an *opéra bouffe* row when the Spanish ambassador allegedly tried to avoid payment in a high-class 'bagnio'. When matters looked like turning ugly, the ambassador foolishly tried to disentangle himself by claiming that he was the *Venetian* ambassador, thus provoking a double scandal.[39]

Nor was the trouble confined to bawdy-houses. It was a favourite trick of the London petty criminal to get a female accomplice to lure victims into secluded alleyways where they could be robbed or pickpocketed. A favourite ploy involved the woman in locating a man's money and valuables while he groped her in some dark recess. The woman would then cough to tell her accomplice that she had found the 'goods'. A blow on the head from behind then knocked out the foolish client.[40] If there was more than one accomplice, the decoying and subsequent robbery could be done in an open field, such as the ones around Chelsea.[41]

What, then, was the solution to prostitution? Some attempt was made by an act of 1752 to regulate the worst excesses of bawdy-houses, though this legislation was widely considered ineffective.[42] Given that elite opinion would not tolerate the licensing of brothels, some form of deprivation of liberty seemed the only possibility. It had long been the custom to commit 'egregious' offenders to a house of correction, with or without hard labour. Sometimes this punishment would be meted out to female brothel-keepers as well, as when a madam of a brothel in Charterhouse Lane was committed to the Clerkenwell Bridewell. Her particular offence was the corruption of the young: her 'house' specialized in providing services for young apprentices, some of them not yet sixteen.[43] Saunders Welch suggested that any citizen should have the right to apprehend and deliver up to a constable any woman whom he found plying her trade on the streets or in public places. She should then be sent to a special reformatory or 'hospital'.[44] The problem was, as with all imprisonment, that such an experience converted an amateur sinner into a professional criminal. The passage from bawdy-house to work-house was, in terms of its effects, the transition from harlot to thief.[45]

Prostitution made a harsh impact on women in two main ways. In the eighteenth century it did not primarily represent a choice between a subsistence level of employment and something grander. It was sometimes the *only* way a woman could keep herself alive.[46] The story of Mary Adams, one of the century's first victims at Tyburn, shows how initial zero life-chances could lead one to the gallows almost without noticing it. Adams began in service in Reading, where she was seduced by the young master. After pregnancy and childbirth, she went to London and took another domestic post, where she was again seduced by the master and again became pregnant. The master promptly dismissed Mary so that his wife would not discover what was afoot. He maintained her in lodgings until the child was born, then told her he was no longer prepared to keep her. He suggested she go into service again. Twice bitten, she refused a third stint below stairs and instead threatened to expose her second lover to his wife. He bought her off with twenty guineas, with which she equipped herself with a 'lady's wardrobe'.

With the new clothes she bought, Mary was able to cut a figure and pass herself off as a woman of substance. On the strength of this imaginary substance and her good looks, she found herself a husband. When the newly-wed spouse learned the truth about her, he shipped out for foreign parts, leaving her to shift for herself. Gradually Mary drifted into prostitution, then started to steal from her clients as well. After she had stolen a banknote and the owner stopped payment at the bank, her fate was sealed. When she arrived at the bank to change the note, she was arrested, convicted, and executed (1702). None of her early experiences was held to extenuate the crime in any way.[47]

The other way women were victimized was in the assumption that the entire weight of social censure for 'illicit' sexuality should descend on them. Apart from a few lone voices crying in the wilderness (such as Colquhoun's), there was no suggestion that the male sex should have any share in culpability for prostitution. Like Adam, men always felt that the woman could be blamed for tempting them. It was supposed to be the responsibility of women to maintain a universe of sexual order and propriety. Whereas the law in general presumed a woman to act at the dictation of her husband, when it came to brothel-keeping this was not so. For this offence a wife could be set in the pillory alongside her husband. The reasons given by Blackstone for this exception to the general legal presumption is eloquent on eighteenth-century attitudes: 'for this is an offence touching the domestic economy or government of the house, in which the wife has a principal share; and it is also such an offence *as the law presumes to be generally conducted by the intrigues of the female sex.*' [italics are mine].[48]

As we shall see in the next chapter, it would be romantic and simple-minded to insinuate the idea of the essential 'niceness' of women, so that all female criminality was merely a reaction to being victimized. Yet it would also be foolish to deny that women genuinely were victims, of male brutality, harsh laws and patriarchal attitudes. The lines in Gay's *The Beggar's Opera* are instructive: 'All men are thieves in love and like a woman the better for being another's property.' And again:

> Virgins are like the fair flow'r in its lustre
> Which in the garden enamels the ground;
> Near it the bees in play flutter and cluster
> And gaudy butterflies frolick around.
> But when once pluck't, 'tis no longer alluring
> To Covent Garden 'tis sent (as yet sweet)
> There fades and shrinks and grows past all enduring.

Mistreatment of women by their husbands was commonplace. Severe beatings, often routinely administered on whim, were outside the pale of the law. Only when they ended in murder was the brutality deemed to be criminal. We have already seen some of these cases when considering homicide. Reginald Tucker, for example, murdered his wife in a fit of temper because he did not like the dinner she served up.[49] John Williamson (executed 1767) was a genuine sadist who tortured his wife and starved her to death; he was able to do this the more easily because she was a mental defective.[50]

Sexual jealousy and the 'double standard' were other factors that often led to the murder of women. John Stanley was a ladies' man whose perversity led him to the gallows in 1723. A war veteran and expert swordsman, Stanley specialized in introducing himself unbidden into company at taverns and then picking a fight so that he did not have to pay for what he had eaten and drunk. This hypertrophied egotism carried into his relations with women. His principal mistress was a Mrs Maycock whom he had seduced while she was still married. When her husband died, Stanley moved in with her and fathered three children on her. Habitually promiscuous himself, he insisted on her fidelity at all times. One evening he found her talking to another man in a tavern. On the way home a furious argument arose between them. Used to resolving disputes with the sword, Stanley ran her through with his rapier.[51]

Army officers, doubtless used to the stews and bordellos of barracks towns, seemed particularly 'undersocialized' when it came to pacific settlement of amorous disputes. George Cadell began his relationship with Elizabeth Price by seducing her, then leaving her to eke out a living by needlework when she was 'disgraced'. Later he came back to live with her. She became pregnant and, unwilling to face another dose of the community's contumely, urged him to marry her. Cadell had meanwhile found a truly desirable target for his affections in the form of a moneyed surgeon's daughter. Cadell told Price he was going to leave her to marry the surgeon's daughter. She threatened to reveal the truth about Cadell's liaison with her. Cadell solved the problem by cutting her throat.[52]

In the case of Elizabeth Mann, the mere fact of her becoming pregnant was enough to make her married lover murder her.[53] Yet it was not just sex that put women at risk. As is well known, certain forms of psychosis manifest themselves in the identification of women as evil incarnate. John Nichols, a 50-year-old hedge carpenter to the duke of Grafton, was the author of a singularly appalling crime. He encouraged his son Nathan to kill his 17-year-old sister (Nichols's daughter) and even provided him with the sharpened stake with which to do the deed. Nichols's dementia was clearly shown on the scaffold when he continued to claim that he had done nothing wrong.[54]

Women were also the victims of the law in more ways than one. The class and status of the assaulted woman often counted for more than the

actual offence against her. Rynwick 'Hunter' Williams was as clear a
candidate for execution under the 'Stabbing Act' as could be imagined
after he had shredded a girl's clothes with a knife and then cut her throat.
In the more enlightened climate of the 1790s it was cause for general
comment that the judge sentenced him to just two years' imprisonment.[55]
The hidden subtext was that his victim did not rate highly enough in the
social system. On the other hand, the most tenuous circumstantial
evidence would be accepted as good enough to hang a woman. There was
a notable miscarriage of justice in 1759 when Mary Edmondson was
hanged for murdering her aunt, when there was not a shred of real
evidence linking her with the crime.[56]

Another way in which the law penalized women was that it did not
protect them against their seducers (unless they were women of approved
social station) but reacted with ferocity if a woman tried to get revenge on
her own account. Elizabeth Jeffries was seduced by her uncle, but hit
back by acquiring a lover whom she persuaded to murder the uncle. For
this exploit the two of them were hanged, the lover in chains, in Epping
Forest.[57]

Execution of women for being accessories to murder was the Code's
way of serving a terrible warning on women who acted 'out of character'
for their sex. Any infringement of the unspoken set of rules by which
women were supposed to conduct themselves would incur the wrath of
judges. Deborah Churchill was hanged in 1708 for being an accessory to
murder. What had happened was that one Hunt, her lover, stabbed a
man to death one night and promptly escaped to Holland. Since Churchill
had been with Hunt on the night of the murder, she was 'deemed',
without further evidence, to have been his accomplice. The real reason
for the court's vindictiveness was an earlier episode in Churchill's life.
She persuaded a soldier to marry her, without revealing that she had
previously run up a mountain of debt. On the wedding night, she plied
her husband with drink and made her escape. With the certificate of
marriage, she could not be prosecuted for the money she owed, since a
husband is legally responsible for his wife's debts. It was this
contemptuous flouting of society's norms that drew down on her the full
weight of judicial revenge. Churchill commenced a desperate six-month
battle to save her life. She claimed that she was pregnant. In such cases a
panel of matrons would inspect the woman to verify the claim, since the
law did not permit the execution of pregnant women. Since the panel
could not decide, judgment was deferred for six months. When it was clear
that Churchill was not pregnant, the death penalty was implemented.[58]

The famous case of Mary Blandy showed how little the law was
disposed to give women the benefit of the doubt. Twenty-six-year-old
Blandy was infatuated with a Scottish army captain called Cranstoun.
Cranstoun was already married with children in Scotland but first

concealed the fact, then denied it to Blandy. Mary was convinced and prepared to marry Cranstoun, but there remained the obstacle of Blandy's father, who threatened to cut her off without a penny if she persisted. Cranstoun decided to remove the obstacle. Blandy's father was sick. Cranstoun sent her some powders, alleging that they were an efficacious Scottish folk-remedy. The artless girl mixed a potion for her father, unaware that the powder was poisonous. When her father expired in agony, Mary was arrested, tried, and convicted for murder. In vain did she protest that she had been an innocent dupe. The only one who could have saved her was Cranstoun, who decamped to France. Blandy was executed in 1752. The true villain, Cranstoun, died of fever in France later the same year.[59]

The law discriminated against women in other ways. There was a general feeling that the testimony of women in court was not as reliable as men's. A case in 1754 saw the collision of two sets of prejudices. Elisabeth Canning swore that she had been robbed by Mary Squires, a gypsy. But Squires's people proved conclusively that she had been elsewhere at the time. There was violent prejudice against gypsies at the time. A barrage of statutes sought (unsuccessfully) to banish them from the kingdom. It was a felony even to be in their company.[60] The conjuring trick the judiciary had to perform in this case was to reinforce the prejudice against female testimony without giving comfort to the Romanies. This it did by a 'solomonic' judgment stupefying in its illogicality. On the one hand, it accepted that Canning had indeed been robbed. Squires was convicted of robbery, then promptly pardoned. On the other, Canning was found guilty of perjury and transported![61]

Even more disgraceful was the viciousness of certain judges if women did not exhibit a proper 'womanly' deference in their presence. A 22-year-old girl was once on trial for having received a piece of checked cloth from an accomplice who had stolen it. Such crimes were hardly ever punished capitally. Yet the terrified girl drank liberally during the dinner break to fortify her spirits. Unfortunately she overdid the liquid courage and when giving evidence was 'impertinent'. Not receiving the proper deference, the judge retaliated by sentencing her to death. It was said that the prosecutor in the case died soon afterwards from a heart attack brought on by shock and remorse at this upshot.[62]

An important index to any society's attitude to women can be obtained from the level of rape and the way this dreadful crime is dealt with by the law. Certain generalizations about the eighteenth century seem in order here. First, it can be assumed that most rapes went unreported. Second, the century had a different cultural definition of rape from our own. Third, the level of rape by a stranger was relatively low.[63]

That most rape cases were not reported was partly a function of the general level of violence, which meant that violent crimes prosecutable in the twentieth century did not end up in court in the eighteenth.[64] More important, it resulted from the exhaustive (and expensive) legal processes involved. Since rape attracted the death penalty, and it was well known how easy it was to bring a false and malicious charge of rape, the courts were extraordinarily cautious.[65] A woman bringing a rape charge knew that every minute detail of the case would be held up to public scrutiny in court. A woman was deemed to have a very weak case if she did not report the rape within twenty-four hours, if she did not struggle or cry out, or if she was of 'bad character' or had had previous sexual experience. Robert Moody, a London waterman, was acquitted of rape in 1778 because his victim Sarah Bethell was considered a woman of easy virtue. Besides, Moody was able to find ladies of quality to vouch for his good behaviour.[66] Similarly, the year before Ralph Cutler was acquitted because his victim had often been seen drunk and was known to have a previous sexual history.[67]

Faced with these obstacles to a successful prosecution, few women (especially if they were without husband or father) brought their plight before a court. For this reason, newspaper reports are a more reliable guide to the phenomenon of eighteenth-century rape than court records. Even if a case came to court, a woman would often withdraw charges rather than relive the experience. A typical case of such withdrawal was that of a woman in Croydon in 1764 who had been raped by three men in a hayloft.[68] Cases that did surface tended to be ones where such serious injuries had been inflicted that forcible intercourse could not be doubted, or where the assault had been witnessed. In one instance in Surrey, a man was caught on Abinger Common, minutes after a rape on a 16-year-old girl, by a farmer and his son, who had been drawn to the scene by the girl's screams.[69]

Virginity was also a powerful circumstantial factor tipping the scales in favour of the accuser in rape cases. Colonel Francis Charteris was a notable ruffian and rake who turned his house into a brothel. Not content with housing established prostitutes, he tried to lure innocent young girls into his web. Anne Bond accepted a place as governess in Colonel Charteris's household. Charteris then revealed his hand and offered her money to sleep with him. When she turned him down, he raped her in the parlour, then had her thrown out of the house on a trumped-up charge of having stolen thirty guineas. Bond then took legal action for rape. Charteris's counsel tried to blacken her character but this tactic foundered on the well-attested fact that Bond had been a virgin when she went to work for Charteris. The ruffianly colonel was found guilty and condemned to death. At this point elite influence lent a hand. Charteris's son-in-law Lord Wemyss bribed Lord President Forbes of Culloden to secure him a royal pardon. This was achieved, on condition that Charteris settled a handsome annuity on Anne Bond.[70]

Apart from protestations of virginity, evidence of grievous bodily harm or witnesses to the event, women faced an uphill struggle to prove rape in a court.[71] The best way to obtain some satisfaction from her attacker, while protecting herself from the rigours of a blow-by-blow reliving of the case and relentless cross-examination, was for a woman to bring a charge of attempted rape. This had a number of advantages. It got round the problem of *proving* a rape; it was a misdemeanour and so did not attract the death penalty; and it was a less expensive form of litigation, since it could be heard at quarter sessions rather than the assizes.[72]

Cultural considerations are also of crucial importance in assessing eighteenth-century rape. The age of consent had been set at 10 in 1576. This meant that browbeating very young girls into intercourse would not necessarily be regarded as rape. 'Technical rape' – intercourse with a girl under 10 – was meant to be in clear contrast to 'forcible rape', but the very notion of such 'consent' in the case of 10- and 11-year-old girls was clearly specious. The testimony of such young females would in general be viewed with scepticism by judges and juries. 'Technical rape' itself was common enough – not surprisingly in a culture where nobody batted an eyelid at adults and children sharing beds.[73] The problem of accepting evidence from children under the age of reason made the law on this point seem theological and unreal. Usually 'technical rape' cases came to court only if the children involved contracted venereal diseases and further enquiries established a rape.

Apart from genuine incest cases, the young girls most at risk both from 'technical rape' and while in the twilight area between 10 and full nubility were publicans' daughters. Dennis Nugent was executed in 1798 for raping an innkeeper's 8-year-old daughter.[74] An 11-year-old, Anne Thacker, awoke one night to find Thomas Davenport in bed with her. He was a lodger who had bribed the female servant who normally slept in the child's room to leave. Next morning the girl was able to describe the rape to her publican father. Davenport was hanged in 1796, aged 26.[75] The year before Patrick Murphy had suffered the same fate for a similar rape on an 8-year-old.[76]

Another important cultural factor was that many cases involving intercourse without consent took place between masters and servants. The image of chambermaid as sexual fodder for the young master has become a cliché, but it was none the less true. The 'seduction' of parlourmaids by masters, or parish girl apprentices by their masters, clearly rape from the twentieth-century viewpoint, was regarded as a peccadillo. In its view of the correct relations between masters and servants, the eighteenth century was not light years away from *droit de seigneur*. In any case, even if a maid had the temerity to press on to a court hearing, it was extremely unlikely that jurymen would take her word against her master's. To do so would set at risk the entire fragile nexus of authority, obedience, and deference. Besides, such a plaintiff would never work again in that locality. The informal mafia of the 'unco guid' would see to that.

On the other hand, the cultural prejudices of the century could sometimes help victims of rape. Jane Bell, a 15-year-old milkmaid was raped one evening on Constitution Hill by John Briant. The case turned on the conflict of evidence between Briant's 'low-life' associates and Bell's master and mistress. The implications of social stratification made this no contest. The men who had given Briant an alibi were found guilty of perjury; Briant himself was found guilty and executed. Unfortunately, the rape had been so brutal that Jane Bell died a week later from its after-effects.[77] The jurymen's prejudice against the military, and the known licentiousness of soldiers, also meant that it was virtually impossible for troops to allege consent successfully. In any case, the brutalizing effects of war usually meant that raping soldiers left tell-tale injuries on their victims. Elizabeth Hagger, a 25-year-old maid and her sweetheart Peter Dodd were 'jumped' on a common in 1798 by two soldiers with 'naked' bayonets. Dodd was held at bayonet point and forced to watch as the soldiers took it in turns to rape his fiancée.[78] Even more brutally, a 57-year-old army veteran raped an 8-year-old in 1801.[79]

What seems incontestable is that the level of casual rape, where the parties were strangers to each other, was low in the eighteenth century. As we have seen, highwaymen rarely raped their female victims. The danger from casual rape was nothing like the risk run by contemporary hitchhikers from motorists. When this sort of assault did take place, it made news because of its extraordinary nature.[80] The inference is strengthened from a close reading of eighteenth-century literature. Heroines traversing country fields worry that their gowns will be dirtied, not that they will be raped. Even the crime-obsessed social critics like Defoe, Fielding, and Colquhoun, who fulminate against receivers, highwayrobbers, housebreakers, footpads, and river thieves, say nothing about rapists. This illustrates the fallacy of reading back the experience of North America in the 1970s and 1980s as a universal historical constant. It is a staple of modish feminism that rape is society's ultimate weapon for the control of women, that rapists are the shock-troops of the patriarchy. There is absolutely no evidence in the eighteenth century to support such a theory. The high levels of rape in the contemporary industrial world are better explained by the twentieth-century's reification of sexuality.[81]

Another pointer here is that the authorities were zealous avengers of the anonymous rape, where a counter-allegation of consent was implausible. In 1749 a young woman employed by a Southwark rug-maker was returning home from the annual employees' party when she was attacked in St George's Fields. In the pitch dark three men set on her and raped her brutally. The woman managed to crawl to St Thomas's hospital but died of her wounds a few weeks later. The horror aroused by the crime put pressure on the authorities to track down the guilty parties. There was a general feeling that such a homicidal rape could not be allowed to go unpunished. Casting around for an easy scapegoat, the authorities fastened on a man who had left the tavern with the dead woman but had a cast-iron alibi. The man was hauled into court. Despite the evidence, the jury took just two minutes to find him guilty. Two years after his execution, another man confessed to the rape. He and his accomplice were tried and hanged. The unfortunate original 'guilty' man was pronounced innocent.[82] If society really did connive at rapists as crack irregulars in the fight for the social control of women, it seems extraordinary that a jury should have rushed to judgment enough to hang an innocent man in a rape case.

Historically there had been some uncertainty in the English legal treatment of rape. For ten years in the reign of Edward I rape had been demoted from a felony to a mere trespass. The horrifying experience of that decade restored rape to the criminal statutes.[83] By the eighteenth century, if a rape could be proved, it was usually punished very severely. This was because the idea that rape was an offence against property was still prevalent. Aside from the offence against a woman, rape was a challenge to male ownership and authority.

The authorities took a particularly severe view of rape committed by officials or other persons in a position of trust, as this weakened the credibility of social hierarchy. John Lennard was executed in 1773 for ravishing Ann Boss, a woman who lived in the house where Lennard, a bailiff, had been sent to distrain on the owner's effects.[84] Even more serious as a breach of trust was Benjamin Russen's rape of a female pupil. Russen was a clergyman-schoolmaster, with a wife and six children.[85] This was especially grave, since eighteenth-century England held clergymen in peculiar esteem.[86] When someone as universally detested as a hangman fell into this trap, there was no hope of mercy. Jack Ketch, the public hangman, tried to rape a woman and when she resisted he beat her mercilessly and gouged out one of her eyes. She lingered in agony for four days before dying.[87]

However, there is some evidence that as the century drew to a close, more leniency was displayed towards rape. While for both rape and sodomy the conviction rate was low, the differential acquittal rate is significant. A survey of rape and sodomy in Surrey in the years 1660-1800 shows that a royal pardon was granted to 60 per cent of those found guilty of rape; in the same period all those found guilty of sodomy were hanged.[88] Partly this greater leniency may have been due to the population implosion towards the cities, leading to a feeling that the stricter standards of morality of the village community were no longer applicable; rape could therefore be considered a 'fact of life.' Partly it may have been due to a distorted Enlightenment perspective. There was a perception abroad at the end of the century that rape related to a barbaric age that it would wither away with increasing civilization, to be replaced by seduction. Certainly not even the Marquis de Sade was able to concoct the ghoulish twentieth-century fantasy that women *want* to be raped.[89] William Eden was one Enlightenment criminologist who thought that rape was the classical example of a crime where the royal prerogative of mercy could often be used, presumably because he thought it was about to die out anyway.[90]

Admittedly, the evidence on changing attitudes to rape is confusing. On the one hand, as women moved into the larger cities, they no longer brought rape charges to the same extent as in the villages of their birth. The organic solidarity of family and the knowable village community was very different from the anomie of the monster city, where such 'supports' did not exist. On the other hand, there seems to have been an increased willingness by women to prosecute, especially for attempted rape, as the century wore on.[91]

But the constant of women as property remained through the century. This can be seen clearly in the differential treatment of *rich* women. The abduction of heiresses carried a mandatory death sentence. This involved the kidnapping of an heiress who was then either married or raped. The law governing this was very severe, as befitted the defence of patrimony. Even if the woman later condoned her abductor's actions and stated that she had consented to intercourse or marriage, the abductor was still guilty of the offence. Numerous proposals to repeal this bloodthirsty law were all rejected. Edmund Burke argued that abduction was worse than murder, for a woman might have to live for ever with a man she detested if this law was tampered with.[92] Yet the most telling point about the abduction law was that it applied only to women with property. This was tantamount to an open declaration by the elite that property was far more important than chastity.

Money was also the key to another chapter of the Code where women were harshly treated: the laws on infanticide. This is not to suggest that the murder of infants can be justified. But what led women to commit this crime was their position in the class hierarchy. Eighteenth-century infanticide was partly a function of poverty and partly of the social opprobrium incurred by the unmarried mother. This opprobrium in turn derived from a consensus inculcated from 'above' on the social utility of marriage.[93]

For married women there was no distinct charge of infanticide. In the unlikely event of a respectable matron killing her child, she would be charged under the ordinary homicide laws. The particular offence the Code was concerned with was the killing of a child by an *unmarried* woman. Properly speaking, too, infanticide applied only to children a few weeks old.[94] The injustice of the law governing the offence was blatant. Under the relevant 1624 statute, if an unmarried woman gave birth to a child and concealed the fact, and the child was later found dead, she was presumed to have killed it. The penalty for such a crime was death.[95] The woman was in effect guilty until proved innocent. The prosecution did not have to prove murder, merely the fact of concealment. To defend herself effectively, the woman had to produce witnesses that the child had been born dead.[96]

A number of generalizations are possible about eighteenth-century infanticide. The babies were usually killed immediately after birth by their unmarried mothers. These unmarried mothers were overwhelmingly lower-class women, usually serving maids. The motive for the infanticide was avoidance of the social stigma of being considered 'of easy virtue' and of having produced a bastard. This motive was particularly important for female servants whose livelihood depended on getting a 'character' from their employers. Also, the sex of the infant was irrelevant. The oriental custom of exposing 'useless' girl babies did not enter into the matter.[97]

Why were servants so much associated with this crime? Partly it was because of the custom of late marriage in the eighteenth century, itself a function of financial pressure. Young women who hoped to be able to afford marriage and also make themselves a marriageable prospect needed perhaps a decade of domestic service to scrape together enough savings. This meant that about half of all unmarried women between the ages of 16 and 25 were employed as servants.[98] Yet at the same time women were, in John Paul Jones's words, going in harm's way. Nubile young women in service were regarded as fair game for seduction by their masters (and their sons). The danger was particularly acute if domestic service brought a woman into contact with numbers of young men. Elizabeth Butchill, executed at the age of 22 for infanticide in 1780, was a bedmaker at Trinity College, Cambridge.[99] It does not need the imagination of a novelist to reconstruct the events that led her to the gallows.

Women without a husband or financial means were in a dreadful dilemma when faced with an unwanted pregnancy. The primitive abortion techniques of the time meant that termination was much too dangerous. Adoption was excluded as a possibility by the official culture, which placed so much emphasis on blood lineage. The unmarried pregnant woman was thus caught in a social trap. If she brought forth a bastard child, society would castigate her for her brazen immorality, and she would be unemployable in 'polite society'. If, in order to avoid these disastrous consequences, she concealed the birth of an illegitimate child, she ran the risk of being executed for murder.[100] Even if the woman decided to brave the ridicule and contempt of society by openly admitting that she had given birth, social sanctions were still not exhausted. In theory both mother and father were responsible for the financial upkeep of the child. If they were in employment and the child was taken into care elsewhere, both were expected to contribute to its upkeep. In reality, because of the difficulty of proving paternity, only the woman paid. If she was not employed (as was most likely after the public admission of an illegitimate birth), and the bastard child was chargeable to the parish, the mother would be put in a house of correction.[101]

The only way to avoid the logical conclusion of infanticide with its terrible risks was to abandon the child at birth. Exposure on a church porch, in a basket at a marketplace or on the doorstep of a rich man's house ('dropping') was frequent in the eighteenth century. But infanticide was even more common and in the 1720s was at epidemic level according to Defoe.[102] The reason for this is that abandonment was not a viable option for servants. To jettison a child necessitated moving immediately from the place of abandonment, without having to worry about the baby's crying. This was not possible for servants, and accounts for the forced option of infanticide rather than the exposure of the child.[103]

Even when women were not immediately faced with the dreadful dilemma attendant on the birth of a bastard, so that the motive for infanticide at birth was absent, social pressures could still catch up with the mother. Elizabeth Chivers was a servant made pregnant by the master of the house. She was dismissed from her post, but the child was born because the master financially supported it and the mother and moved them both into private lodgings. But after three months the master's jealous wife found where Chivers was living and publicly exposed her to stigma and humiliation. Beside herself with shame, the woman threw her 3-year-old into a pond. The appropriate verdict would have been that the balance of Chivers's mind was disturbed. Society in 1712 knew no such niceties. She was found guilty and executed.[104]

A not wholly dissimilar case occurred in Molesworth, Hampshire, in 1764. A young girl, who had been seduced by her master and at first thought to be pregnant, was given the 'all clear' by a midwife she consulted. She then persuaded another man to marry her. The day after the wedding, she suddenly gave birth. On being reproached bitterly by her husband and his aunt, she ran out to a pond and drowned herself and the new-born child.[105]

Amazingly, as this would appear to be *par excellence* a woman's crime, not all infanticides were committed by women. A *cause célèbre* from 1754 shows the male taking a hand. William Horne, clearly a sufferer from satyriasis, capped a notorious career of seduction by having intercourse with his own sister. When the fruit of this incestuous union was born, in 1724, Horne and his brother exposed the child. Thirty years later the affair came to light. Horne was asked by his brother, who was desperate to emigrate, for just £5 passage money. Horne refused. The brother broke his long silence in revenge and the crime was revealed. On the evidence of his brother, Horne went to the gallows, aged 74.[106]

As with all eighteenth-century crime, an awareness of chronology is all-important when considering the murder of the new-born. In 1700 the Infanticide Act was seventy-five years old and at the height of its vigour. A 'proven' infanticide was almost always a hanging offence, and the standards of proof were derisory. A dead child could be found in a river, and it might then be recalled that a servant in the neighbourhood had cried out during an alleged illness. This flimsy causal line, not even strong enough to warrant the description 'circumstantial evidence', could be enough to hang her.[107]

But already by the 1720s courts were taking a more lenient line. There was growing disquiet about the 'guilty until proved innocent' provision of the 1624 Act and the risible level of proof required to secure a conviction. Besides, more acute social critics pointed out that the Act was fundamentally misconceived. Its framers had had immorality in their sights as much as infanticide, yet the Act signally failed to fulfill its founders' purpose. Since prostitutes had no good name or 'character' to lose, they did not kill illegitimate children. The full weight fell on servants: 70 per cent of the women charged with infanticide at the Old Bailey in a forty-year period were in service.[108]

The new judicial bearing first evident in the 1720s took the form of a partial step in the direction of 'innocent until proved guilty'. A favourite defence was to produce scraps of linen or other signs of the preparation of baby clothes as evidence that a woman had been looking forward to birth and had no intention of killing the child.[109] The obvious objection to this as a defence was that items of baby clothes could be got together after an infanticide or even prepared cold-bloodedly beforehand by a woman with full intention of killing her child. Hardliner as ever, Defoe mocked the credulity of anyone who would be taken in by such a transparent stratagem.[110]

Other forms of defence seemed more promising. Accidental death and still birth were the most common. There grew up the custom of testing for still-birth by the 'lung test'. This involved extracting the lungs from the dead child and putting them in a pail of water. If they sank, the child had been still born; if they floated, it was murder. This remained a popular defence until advances in medical science in the 1770s discredited the 'lung test'.[111]

The plea of accidental death was usually sustained by the evidence of midwives. They testified to the difficulty of survival in the case of an unaided birth and to instances of 'apparent death' which only a midwife or physician could spot.[112] Society's cant and humbug could be turned back on itself. Because of the disgrace attached to unmarried childbirth, it was merely common sense that servant girls, say, would attempt to deliver their illegitimate offspring themselves, with all the associated risks of accidental death through their inexperience in midwifery.

In the case of married women, even when the circumstantial evidence of premeditation was strong, a defence of 'temporary insanity' would usually be accepted, since it could be argued that there was no other presumptive motive.[113] A married woman in Norwich in 1724 who killed her child was adjudged 'temporarily insane' and imprisoned for a year. In 1751 when a married woman who had cut her child's throat was indicted on a common law murder charge, she claimed to have been deranged after the child's birth and to be unable to remember anything. The defence was accepted. In general, as long as the woman was respectably married she stood a far better chance than men did of having an insanity plea accepted.[114]

But in the eighteenth century even insanity had its class implications. Real insanity among the 'lower orders', which would not be accepted in a court of law – presumably on the grounds that mental illness is a luxury that only the prosperous classes can afford – manifested itself in more tragic ways, as in the case of the woman in Whitechapel in 1764 who hurled her new-born baby from an upper window.[115]

As the century wore on, juries were more and more disposed to accept all of these defences. By the 1760s most women were tried for infanticide under the normal laws of homicide rather than the 1624 Act. By Blackstone's time, presumptive evidence that the dead child had been born alive was required to sustain a charge under that Act.[116] The acquittal rate for infanticide rose. The presence of the 1624 law on the statute book was felt to be a blemish on a Code that promised due process to the truly innocent. In 1773 an attempt was made in Parliament to repeal the draconian Infanticide Act. As with most of the century's attempt to reform or amend the Code, this was a failure.[117]

Juries responded to this elite recalcitrance by extreme reluctance to convict. They wanted proof that a mother had murdered her baby, and therefore preferred that genuinely guilty infanticides should go free rather than the suffering by the innocent of the extreme penalty on mere suspicion. One result of this was that infanticide cases began to decline in frequency, especially in the more sophisticated cities, where the 1624 Act was almost universally considered a piece of anachronistic cruelty. Yet this tendency was a relative one. Although the level of indictments for the offence was very low when compared with the presumed actual rate of infanticide, probably not much more than one a year in each county, it would be a mistake to assume that Enlightenment thought swept all before it. Three executions of women for murdering their children were recorded in London: in 1794, 1795 and 1797.[118]

The long battle for the repeal of the Infanticide Act was finally won in 1803. As with so many other features of the Code, the repeal of draconian legislation did not affect the underlying phenomenon at all. Infanticide continued as the social problem it had always been, unrelated to the punishment prescribed for it.[119] Never was the unfairness to women of the eighteenth-century law more graphically demonstrated.

7

Women (2)

Most women have no characters at all.
> Alexander Pope, *An Essay on Man*

There is a mighty increase of dirty wenches in straw hats
since I knew London.
> Jonathan Swift, *Journal to Stella*, May 1711

Wedlock, indeed, haft oft compared been
To public feasts where meet a public rout
Where they that are without would fain go in.
And they that are within would fain go out.
> Sir John Davies, *Contention betwixt a Wife,*
> *a Widow and a Maid*

AS CRIMINALS

All facile notions that the lesser propensity to crime of women can be
attributed to their innate 'niceness' fail when we examine the record of
women as 'masters'. The story of 'parish children' taken into domestic
service does not redound to the credit of the female sex. It was the
custom to 'apprentice' orphan girls, previously in the care of the parish,
to propertied women as soon as the girls were of working age. This
meant, in reality, sentencing them to a nightmare of drudgery and
serfdom.

A case from 1796 is by no means untypical. Elizabeth Hall habitually
beat and assaulted her two 'apprentice' female children, aged 11 and 9.
She kept a rod soaking in brine with which she used to beat the children
every night when they undressed. The two girls had to start work at
4 a.m. and work until 11 p.m., undergoing constant beatings and often
being deprived of dinner and supper. On many occasions they worked for
nineteen hours on a diet of six unsalted potatoes. Eventually the children
could take no more and ran away. They were found roaming the streets
by the Watch at 10 p.m. When they told their story, the Parish took them

in and brought a prosecution against Hall. Found guilty, she was fined and ordered to spend a year in a house of correction. Those who attended the trial openly fumed at such lenient treatment. One man was heard to say that he wished Hall had killed one of the children so that they could hang her.[1]

There was an insane logic in the man's argument for, short of murder, it was very difficult to bring a successful prosecution against a woman employer who had been cruel to her 'apprentices'. And not even murder could be guaranteed to secure requitement. In 1748 one Elizabeth Dickens murdered her parish girl but was acquitted.[2] A much higher general level of brutality was accepted in the eighteenth century, and it took cruelty of a singular kind to consign its perpetrators to the gallows.

The two most notorious cases of cruelty to children, which did end in capital sentences, were those of Elizabeth Brownrigg and Sarah Metyard. Over a number of years Brownrigg routinely beat her apprentice girls to within an inch of their lives. Finally, in 1767, she went too far and killed one of them.[3] The horrific details that came out at her trial shocked a nation whose sensibilities were far from being refined.[4] Brownrigg's psychopathic brutality suggests that there is a certain kind of evil in human beings not reducible to social circumstances. In another age she would have fitted happily into a system of concentration camp guards and genocidal warders.

Another demon in female form was Sarah Metyard. She took in two sisters from the workhouse, and was then outraged to find that one of them was too ill to work. Metyard solved the problem of 'idle hands' by tying the girl up and starving her to death in an attic room. When her sister discovered what had happened, Metyard murdered her to prevent the truth from coming out. These atrocities only came to light four years later, in 1762, and then only because Metyard's daughter, who had colluded in her brutality and murder, broke rank. Shark-like, Metyard finally turned on her daughter and beat her up. The daughter revealed the full story of her mother's murderous rages to a male friend, not realizing that she herself was vulnerable as an accessory. At the trial the jury was treated to the unsavoury spectacle of the two Metyards rending each other with accusation and counter-accusation. The jurymen had no hesitation in finding them both guilty, and the two were sentenced to death. Finally realizing the trap into which she had cast herself, the younger Metyard 'pleaded her belly'. But on examination by the usual panel of matrons, she was found to be not pregnant. She joined her mother at Tyburn.[5]

It must be stressed, however, that most murders by women were not of the psychopathic type but arose within a family or intimate context. Women hardly ever featured in homicide cases outside this arena.[6] The slaying of husbands or lovers was the staple female murder. Some women, having taken one beating too many, took advantage of their husbands' drunken stupor to beat them to death; the poker was a favourite weapon. The motive here was all too obvious. In all ages a majority of women would certainly have left their husbands but for economic constraints, especially as until very recently most husbands thought mistreatment of their wives was a marital right.[7]

In the case of lovers, the usual motive for murder by a woman was that she had been seduced and abandoned. If the lover left her for another woman, the impetus of sexual jealousy might be uppermost. But in any case, there was a fundamental economic motive to female revenge for abandonment. Often the woman had not given herself to the man for love alone but with the prospect of marriage, or at any rate the betterment of her economic position by being set up as mistress in a comfortable house.[8]

When aroused, the homicidal instincts of women could be tigerish in their ferocity. In Surrey in 1774 a woman who had lived with a man for nineteen years and borne him eleven children, dashed his brains out with a poker after a quarrel. When reproached with her behaviour, she declared defiantly that she would do it over again.[9] But the law made an important distinction between killing one's husband, which was 'petty treason' and killing a lover. Petty treason as the name implies, was punished very severely. In the case of those who had lived in non-connubial bliss, the demeanour and history of the women was all-important in deciding how stiff was the sentence they received. Elizabeth Richardson killed her lover in a jealous rage in 1768 because she thought he was sleeping with other women.[10] The cardinal factor here was that Richardson was a former prostitute. It was this more than anything else that made the jury commend her to the gallows. In a similar case in 1723, Sarah Priddon stabbed her lover to death because she suspected that he was about to transfer his affections from her to her sister. As it turned out, the sympathy of the jury availed her nothing. She received a mild sentence of fines and imprisonment, but died after a month in Newgate.[11]

As we have seen above, as the century progressed, courts became more disposed to accept insanity pleas. Such a plea was accepted in the case of Anne Broadric in 1795; it was the only possible defence, as the premeditation was palpable. Broadric had been mistress to a Mr Errington. Errington fell in with a rich heiress and married her for her money. He made what he considered was a generous settlement on Broadric, but she was not appeased. She traced him to his country address and shot him down in cold blood with a horse-pistol.[12]

The law punished the murder of legal relatives more harshly than that of lovers since it reasoned that money was not a motive where there could be no legal claim. This was somewhat naïve since, as we have seen, the motive of revenge often has a concealed financial basis. But it did permit the Code to make some perfunctory informal gestures in the direction of *crime passionnel*. Where money was obviously a motive, the murder of relatives nearly always attracted the death penalty. This was the case for three women in 1794: Anne Scalberd was executed for the murder of her mother-in-law; Hannah Limbrick for killing her daughter-in-law; 15-year-old Elizabeth March for slaying her grandfather in his sleep.[13]

There was one type of murder by women that was regarded with peculiar horror, as a kind of violation of the fundamental laws of nature: poisoning. As in the case of witchcraft, the especial revulsion was connected with what was perceived as a distortion of a traditional female role: the preparation of food. A wife wishing to dispose of a husband yet in fear of the dreadful penalties for petty treason might well decide that her best course lay in slow poisons administered with meals. Poisoning was also detested because it tapped a profound male fear of female deviousness; it was the ultimate horror even to conceive of the possibility that the polite yet secretive female might harbour dark homicidal urges under the mask of gentility.[14]

Poisoning cases therefore carried a *de facto* mandatory death sentence on conviction, whether the simple punishment of hanging or the aggravated penalties prescribed for petty treason. In 1712 Elizabeth Mason, a servant, tried to dispose of her employers, two maiden ladies, with arsenic. She poisoned one and just failed with the other.[15] That was a hanging offence. But Anne Hale was tied to a stake, strangled, and burnt to ashes for the petty treason involved in poisoning her husband. A Mrs Whale had formed a lesbian attachment with Sarah Pledge, and together the 'sisters' did away with James Whale. Pledge was hanged.[16] Another case combining deviant sexuality and poisoning ended with the escape of the female principal. Patrick Ogilvie seduced his brother's wife, Catherine, then sent her poison with which to kill him. Found guilty, Ogilvie was executed in 1765 but the pregnant Catherine was given respite until childbirth. After the delivery, another order was issued for her execution but she broke gaol and fled to the Continent.[17]

The case of Mary Channel (executed 1703) was singular in that philosophically speaking her parents were the true authors of the crime she committed. Mary combined high intelligence, wit, and learning with a fundamental passivity, the result of having had her spirit broken in early childhood by domineering parents. Mary, who was 18 at the time of her death, had attracted many suitors. It was intense parental pressure that had led her to accept as husband a Dorchester grocer who revolted her. As soon as she had married him Mary regretted it. Finding him physically unendurable, she poisoned him with white mercury. At her trial she conducted a witty and ingenious defence that won the sympathy of the jurors. But this was a case of petty treason; the murder of a husband by a wife, whatever the circumstances, was held to strike at the very principles of natural order. There could be only one verdict.[18]

Sometimes in murder cases women were protagonists while not being the actual killers. The sensational Sayer case at the beginning of the century illustrates this sort of situation. In 1699 John Sayer, a member of the gentry, married Mary Nevil, a woman apparently of nymphomaniacal disposition. She soon pronounced her husband unsatisfactory as a lover and banished him from her bed. Sayer then took to consorting with prostitutes and contracted venereal disease. After a painful cure he was accepted back, but the next thing was that *both* of them had the disease. Sayer was adamant that his wife had been infected by one of her many lovers and had simply used him to mask her own promiscuity. In any case, she again threw him out.

Mary Nevil's mother was of a similar nature to her daughter. On her husband's death she married an army officer, Colonel Salisbury. When Salisbury made so bold as to tax his step-daughter with her infidelities, mother and daughter ganged up on him. In exasperation the colonel threw a dish of tea over Anne. The two women then tried to use this 'insult' to arouse Sayer against Colonel Salisbury. They hatched a plot (for once the cliché 'diabolical' is not out of place) to dispose of both men. First they induced Sayer to challenge the colonel to a duel. With one of the men dead, they hoped to produce their *pièce de résistance*: whichever of them was the widow would then give false evidence of homicide against the surviving male.

Salisbury was clearly made of sterner stuff than the pathetically uxorious Sayer. Sensing something of what was afoot, he persuaded Sayer to call off the challenge. Baulked of her prey, Mrs Sayer retreated to country life in Buckinghamshire where she quickly ran through a string of lovers. Her extravagance brought about a financial crisis, which Sayer brought in an attorney, Richard Noble, to solve. In a short time Noble and Mrs Sayer were lovers and the two of them were conspiring to defraud Sayer.

Noble began by pretending that the children he had fathered on Mrs Sayer were her husband's. Then he persuaded Sayer to sign a deed of separation with generous provisions for his wife. Under the pretence of getting Sayer to put his financial affairs in order, Noble inveigled him into spending a year in Holland while he lived with his wife and wasted his substance. When at the end of the year Sayer returned only to be told by his wife she wanted a complete divorce, he put a notice in the newspapers, repudiating his wife's debts.

Mrs Sayer's response was to assemble as large a pile of effects from the household as she could manage and to attempt to frame her husband into making over *all* his property. When this misfired, she, her mother, and Noble took refuge in the Mint, a sanctuary for debtors. By now Sayer's blood was up. He got round the sanctuary aspect of the Mint by having a warrant sworn out, ostensibly to allow him to search the Mint for a missing person, which he proceeded to do in the company of two constables. An altercation began between the hunters and the hunted; in the mêlée Noble drew his sword and stabbed Sayer to death.

Noble was taken up on a charge of murder; the two women were arraigned as his accomplices. The three of them further enraged public sensibilities by jury challenging. Every person indicted for a felony had the right to challenge twenty jurors (those indicted for petty treason could challenge thirty-five). Anne Sayer, charged with petty treason, got through thirty-five and the other two ran through twenty each in an obvious attempt to pervert the course of justice by exhausting the available supply of jurors. The tactic did not work, for a far-sighted sheriff had summoned more than a hundred. In an astonishing verdict, Noble was found guilty and hanged but the two women, the real authors of the crime, were both acquitted. The crowd was so enraged by the jury's decision that the women had to be escorted from the court by turnkeys for their protection.[19]

The murder of husband by wife, or master by servant (or ecclesiastical superior by inferior), was regarded as petty treason by eighteenth-century law. These crimes were thought to have a kinship with high treason because they violated the implicit contract between ruler and ruled.[20] Whereas the murder of wife by husband was simple murder, punishable by hanging, petty treason carried the penalty of hanging and burning. The most ferocious and bloodthirsty provisions of the Code were those that were designed to inculcate obedience, of discontented subjects towards the elite, servants towards tyrannical masters, wives towards oafish husbands. But once again the central fallacy of capital punishment as deterrent was demonstrated. When wives murdered their husbands, in most cases the slaying took place in hot blood, when there was no possibility of calculating the consequences. Even poisoning, a premeditated act, could be the result of desperation for which the law allowed no resolution, as the case of Mary Channel above shows.

For this reason there was no slackening in the rate of petty treason throughout the century.[21] In one of the cases, a kind of double petty treason was involved, for Anne Bedingfield (executed 1763) murdered her husband with the aid of a young male servant whom she had seduced.[22] Realizing the absurdity of the aggravated penalty for this crime, William Wilberforce brought a bill into the House of Commons in 1786 to abolish burning as a penalty for women found guilty of petty treason. As with all major attempts to reform the Code, this bill was thrown out.[23] Women continued to be burned for all varieties of treason. Whereas men were hanged drawn and quartered for high treason, women were committed to the flames after being hanged. Blackstone argued that the differential provision in treason cases derived from the greater consideration due to women:

> For as the decency due to the sex forbids the exposing and publicly mangling their bodies, their sentence (which is to the full as terrible to sensation as the other) is to be drawn to the gallows and there to be burned alive.[24]

In most cases women were not actually burned alive; the executioner made sure they were dead before consigning them to the flames.[25] But where the fury of the mob was aroused, the executioner's best intentions could be baulked. There were crimes involving particular outrage to public prejudices and sensibilities when the crowd insisted that the penalty be administered to the letter of the law.[26] In Scotland, the murder of master or mistress by servant excited peculiar indignation. In 1751 such a killer, Norman Ross, was sentenced to have his right hand chopped off, then be hanged, and afterwards have his body hung in chains. In addition, his right hand was to be affixed at the top of the gibbet together with the murder weapon (a knife).[27]

The most famous case of a crowd insisting that a woman be burned alive and not hanged first was that of Catherine Hayes in 1726. With the aid of two lovers Hayes played Clytemnestra to her husband's Agamemnon. After murdering him with an axe, she cut up his body and dropped the head into the Thames. Unfortunately for her, the head was recovered and put on public view in the churchyard at St Mary's, Westminster, in hopes that the murdered man could be identified. When the head was in danger of putrefaction after four days of exposure, a surgeon was ordered to preserve it in a glass of spirits to permit further examination. It was the length of time the head remained identifiable that doomed Catherine Hayes and her associates, for eventually someone did recognize the murdered man.

When Mrs Hayes was arrested, the singular depravity of the crime led George I in person to direct his own counsel to conduct the prosecution. Hayes was convicted and sentenced to be burnt for petty treason. On this occasion the crowd was so angry that it protested when the hangman tried the compassionate way. Whether in fear of the crowd, or for some other reason, the man bungled the job of strangling. Hayes was literally burnt alive.[28]

To sum up on women as murderers, certain conclusions are in order. In the case of indictments for wilful murder, the execution rate for men and women was much the same: about one-fifth of those tried. This reflected the constant of murders in the family or between intimates. But women featured far less in homicide cases *in general*, as might be expected. The reasons were obvious: men were much more likely to be in taverns, to drink too much, to feel their honour slighted, to feel compelled to give and accept challenges. They were also much more likely to be carrying a weapon. For this reason women were rarely found guilty of man-slaughter. An examination of a range of cases in Surrey in 1660-1800 produced a figure of only one in forty of manslaughter convictions involving women. Over the same period in the same area women formed just 9 per cent of principals and 11 per cent of accessories in murder indictments. They were in general much more likely than men to be discharged or acquitted of manslaughter.[29]

These of course are aggregate judgements and by no means imply the absence of real female aggression that could lead to murder. The female keeper of a lodging house was executed in 1796 for cutting the throat of her guest. What made this case a sensation was that the victim, Comte de Gripière, was an aristocratic French émigré, and the killer, Mary Knott, a 63-year-old woman.[30] Maria Phipoe had a long history of violence before the murder that led her to the gallows. In 1795 she managed to manacle John Courtois to the back of his office chair and then threatened to cut his throat if he did not sign over to her a promissory note for £200. When he signed it, she said she would kill him anyway, and gave him a choice of pistol, knife, or arsenic. Courtois managed to get free but cut his fingers on Phipoe's knife during the struggle. At the subsequent trial Phipoe was acquitted of the capital charge on a technicality, and received a mere twelve months imprisonment for common assault. Much heartened by the nugatory results of her brush with the law, Phipoe resumed her violent ways on release. She tried to sell some items of jewellery to Mary Benson. When Benson told her she was only prepared to buy part of the items, Phipoe lost her temper and stabbed her to death. Her previous record told heavily against Phipoe and she was executed in 1797.[31]

Women were also liable to be burned for offences other than murder. This was a result of the absurdity whereby offences against the coinage were considered on a par with Jacobite or Jacobin rebellion. A sensational case in 1777 brought this issue to a head. A 14-year-old girl who had abetted her master in coining by hiding whitewashed farthings in her stays, was found guilty of high treason and ordered to be burned alive. A reprieve was granted at the very last moment.[32] General outrage at the barbarity of the punishment prescribed in such cases was eloquently expressed by Sir William Meredith in the House of Commons: 'Good God, sir, we are taught to execrate the fires of Smithfield, and are we lighting them now to burn a poor harmless child for hiding a whitewashed farthing?'[33]

A spate of executions of women for the high treason of coining was the elite's answer to this impassioned advocacy: Isabella London in 1779, Phoebe Harris in 1786, and Christiane Murphy in 1789.[34] As we have seen, the Commons refused to follow Wilberforce when he advocated the repeal of the laws on burning women for treason. But attitudes did change over the century. Two cases make this plain. In 1721 Barbara Spencer was strangled and burnt at Tyburn for coining. While she tried to say her prayers at the gallows, the mob pelted her with dirt and stones.[35] Yet by the 1790s public opinion had forced a *de facto* abandonment of petty treason. When Anne Warner was executed in 1798 for colouring base shillings, she was hanged without accompanying 'refinements'.[36] That the revulsion was against burning rather than against the severity of the sentence for coining alone, was shown when Margaret Hughes was hanged the following year for poisoning her husband but not burnt; poisoning was the most feared and detested type of petty treason.[37]

Like most other felonies, female coining could sometimes be the 'lead-in' to other crimes. Jane Housden was in Newgate in 1712, awaiting trial on a coining offence that would almost certainly send her to the fire, because she had already been found guilty once of coining and been pardoned. On the day of her trial her lover William Johnson tried to visit her in Newgate. When the head turnkey refused him admittance, Johnson took out a pistol and shot him dead. In a curious way this secured Housden a lesser penalty. She was held as an accomplice in the murder by Johnson and on conviction was sentenced to hang rather than to the flames, as she would have been if found guilty on the coining indictment. Johnson was hung in chains after his execution.[38]

At a lower (but still capital) level of crime, offences by female servants against their employers was a constant characteristic of crime by women. These were both crimes of opportunity and of social revenge. Many a servant testified that it was his or her life of deprivation juxtaposed to the privilege of employers that provided the spur. Many women decided that they were just as deserving subjects of wealth and finery as their mistresses. Some took to prostitution to provide the funds for the tastes and aspirations aroused in them by domestic service. Others turned to theft within the household. There was an objective, as well as psychological basis to this. Boswell pointed out that female servants worked much harder than their male counterparts but were paid less, even though they were obliged to buy their own clothes while men were given free livery.[39]

But household theft was risky. Hannah Giffiths was executed for this in 1796.[40] Grace Tripp agreed to take part in her lover's robbery of her mistress's house, but the pair were interrupted in the middle of their pillaging by a housekeeper. In panic Tripp cut the housekeeper's throat, which guaranteed her passage to the gallows at the age of 19.[41] A less serious case in 1800 still placed the hangman's noose around the neck of Sarah Lloyd. She let in a friend in order to burgle the house, but the hotheaded young man set the house on fire as well. Lloyd was taken, tried, and condemned. For being an accessory to a crime in which no one was killed, the death sentence was considered unduly harsh. There was a considerable public outcry. Yet the Duke of Portland 'deemed' that the petitions in her favour had been signed by people actuated by ill-judged motives of humanity. He ordered the execution to stand. Despite an universal feeling that this was a miscarriage of justice, Sarah Lloyd was hanged.[42]

The death penalty was not the only supposed deterrent to theft by servants from employers. The ruin of one's reputation and the impossibility of getting a 'character' also weighed. This could lead to grim consequences. In 1764 Isabel Stephenson committed suicide in her cell simply because she had been taken up on suspicion of robbing her master.[43] Besides, even to be in the vicinity of an employer when his or her death occurred suspiciously was dangerous. When Jane Butterfield's mistress died suddenly in 1775, she had to endure the ordeal of a murder trial before it was established that the old woman had died of natural causes.[44]

Lesser crimes, where offender and victim did not know each other, fell into three main categories. There were women who stole out of real need; women who were accomplices of male criminals; and women who had evolved pickpocketing and shoplifting specialities of their own. The first category was the most common. The fate of such women when caught depended on the sympathies of the jury and the laws governing the offence. Because of the idiosyncracy of the Code, it was perfectly possible to be hanged for petty theft but to receive a lighter sentence (such as whipping) for a crime where the financial implications were far greater.[45] Even defenders of draconian deterrence were forced to admit the skew effects of the law. In his famous 1777 speech Sir William Meredith instanced the notorious case of Mary Jones, who was destitute and her children starving. She took a piece of raw linen off a shop counter but put it back when the shopkeeper saw her. For this alone she was hanged.[46]

But in general juries were sympathetic to the plight of women in genuine need. A case in Essex in 1740 involved a woman who stole five shillings. She told the court that she had done it only because her husband was a useless provider. The jury accepted the plea and reduced the value of the stolen money to ten pence, so that it was not a capital felony. The woman was then allowed to return for her family. This was not necessarily dispassionate altruism on the part of the jury. The jurymen knew very well that if the family disintegrated on the woman's execution, under the Poor Law system they would have to bear the cost of keeping the family on the parish.[47]

Women who were wives or mistresses of male criminals had sometimes been corrupted by their partner's example and had sometimes been attracted to them in the first place by a kind of underworld symbiosis. Anne Harris, executed in 1708 at the age of 20 for shoplifting, was already a 'hempen widow' twice over.[48] Mary Wild, Jonathan Wild's wife, had two husbands and a kinsman executed at Tyburn within ten years; in the same period her uncle, a Newgate turnkey, was murdered. After Wild's death she was said to have married his chief aide Quilt Arnold.[49] The principal thief-taker before Wild, Richard Yeomans, was married to a well-known female criminal called Moll Pines, who accompanied him to transportation in America.[50] Many women were accomplices to men in the 'buttock and thay' caper (see above p. 101)[51] Others accompanied their men on burglarious forays. In 1794 Mary Mallet escaped the noose while her male friend was hanged for burglary by pleading her belly. She was examined by a panel of matrons and found to be pregnant.[52] Finally, there was a category of women so browbeaten by their husbands that they went along meekly with their evil schemes; such was the wife of John Crouch, who helped him try to sell their 14-year-old niece on the London flesh market.[53]

But many women needed no male to perfect their criminal skills. They started young. Two 9-year-old girls began their burglary career in 1764 when they were let into a house by another 9-year-old female.[54] By the age of 17 or 18 such girls could be ace pickpockets or shoplifters.[55] Sarah McCabe had a shoplifting career of twenty years. She used four aliases and worked with two other women. Transported for seven years in 1748, she returned after four, was caught shoplifting again and brought to trial. But because she had changed her name, it was not noticed that she had returned from transportation. Her speciality was lace, silk, minionet, point, and mechlin.[56] Martha Tracey was dismissed from domestic serice for having 'ideas above her station'. She alternated prostitution with pickpocketing before being caught and executed in 1745.[57] The judiciary had no particular qualms about hanging female pickpockets. The only sure way to escape the hangman was to plead pregnancy successfully.[58]

Perhaps the most famous female exponent of the pickpocketing art was Mary Young, alias Jenny Diver. She was so adroit that she could remove a ring from a person's hand while shaking it. She once picked a man's pocket of £200 and received £130 from a fence the same day. Her most famous exploit was the 'pregnant pickpocket'. She had had a false pair of arms and hands made, and made herself look pregnant, concealing her real hands under her dress. Then she would seat herself at church between two elderly ladies, each of whom, say, had a gold watch. When the watches were later found to be missing, the ladies immediately dismissed the pregnant young woman from suspicion, since her hands had not left her lap all through the service.[59]

Sometimes Jenny varied her routine by employing male accomplices on more elaborate crimes. One of her favourite tricks was to dress up in the most sumptuous finery and knock at the door of a great house, accompanied by her lover, dressed as a footman. The footman would explain that his mistress was ill and crave the household's assistance. While the staff fussed around the 'poor lady', Jenny's lover would ransack the house for valuables. When his task was complete, Jenny would 'recover' and give the mistress of the house her card, with an invitation to dine.

Another favourite variant was to pretend to be a married woman forced by circumstance into part-time prostitution. She would bring back a man she had picked up in Covent Garden and the two of them would undress. Suddenly her maid would appear to say that the master of the house had returned unexpectedly. Jenny would then jump up and tell her victim to hide under the bed clothes so that if her husband entered the room, he would see nothing suspicious. Meanwhile she would take his clothes and hide them until the coast was clear. When her husband was settled, she assured her 'client', she would return them to him. Then Jenny and her accomplices decamped. Hours later, the bemused client would finally work out that he had been the victim of a confidence trick.

When Jenny was finally arrested and transported to Virginia, she returned immediately by getting an admirer to pay her passage back to England, then jumping ship at Gravesend. Unable to reassemble her gang of accomplices, Jenny went solo for a time but was caught again.[60] Again she was transported and again she returned. This time she was caught, sentenced to death, and executed in 1740.

Another similar female ace pickpocket, who sometimes claimed that it was she, not Jenny Diver, who had invented the false hands 'caper', was Moll King, the model for Defoe's Moll Flanders. Arrested in 1718 for pickpocketing and sentenced to death, she pleaded her belly. When the panel of matrons found her to be pregnant, she was transported for fourteen years. Returning from transportation, she was blackmailed by Jonathan Wild into working for him. Caught pickpocketing again, Moll was committed to Newgate and in obvious danger of hanging. Wild agreed to save her provided she acted as false witness against the members of a gang he was trying to crush. Wild's 'plea bargaining' was successful. After all the gang members had been convicted on Moll's evidence, she herself was brought into the dock. She was sentenced to death for returning from transportation but then immediately reprieved.[61]

The gamut run by Jenny Diver did not exhaust the female criminal imagination. Moll Hawkins was an expert practitioner of the 'question lay'. She made a habit of finding out which great ladies had placed an order for dressmaking. Dressing up as the apprentice of a milliner or seamstress, Moll would knock on the door of the lady's house and say that the materials for the dress were ready. While the servant went upstairs to consult his mistress, Moll would make a clean sweep of the valuables downstairs.[62] Another female swindler, Elizabeth Greeve, turned the pretensions of the gentry against them in a different way. An accomplished impersonator, Greeve would pose as Lady X and Lady Y in order to buy on credit. She was another who was transported twice and returned.[63]

How can we sum up on the criminality of women in eighteenth-century England? In the first place, they committed fewer and less serious crimes than men. They were also usually treated more leniently by juries and judges, who were more inclined to reprieve and pardon them when found guilty. On capital charges, they were more likely than men to be acquitted, more likely to be found guilty on a reduced charge, and if convicted more likely to be reprieved. Only 12 per cent of the accused in the home counties in 1782-7 were female. Yet female acquittal and partial verdict rates were nearly 40 per cent higher than average and their sentences relatively light, even when allowance is made for the fact that women tended to be accused of less violent crimes and less serious property offences.[64]

For the obvious reasons we have already noted, women charged with homicide were likely to be accused of murder. But apart from murder, women convicted of capital crimes had a better chance than men did of escaping the gallows. Out of 467 offenders executed in London and Middlesex in 1771-83, only seventeen were women.[65] In the years 1660-1800, 80 per cent of female offenders in property crimes in Surrey were reprieved.[66] Only two women were actually hanged in Surrey during 1749-76.[67]

This leniency extended to non-capital larcenies, where again women were more frequently acquitted and punished more lightly than men. If convicted, they were frequently found guilty of a lesser charge than the one on the indictment. Even in the area of secondary punishment, women *in general* received more favourable treatment. If they did not receive a clergyable discharge, they were more often whipped and imprisoned than sent for transportation.[68]

How can we explain this differential treatment of men and women? Part of the explanation is obvious. Women were generally perceived to be less dangerous to the community, less of a threat to authority and the social order. Some have attempted to explain jury partiality for women in terms of 'chivalry'.[69] Insofar as this played a part, it required the accused woman to behave with proper deference and submission. And it is doubtful if it extended to women of the 'lower orders'. A better explanation is in terms of deterrence. Because the perceived threat to the social order from women was less, even the purblind opinion leaders of the elite could see that the exemplary force of the death penalty was diminished. The hanging of a woman was more likely to excite pity for the victim than reinforce confidence in 'law and order'.[70]

Other factors played a part. The execution of pregnant women was suspended until they were delivered of the child. The respite usually induced feelings of mercy and compassion – after all, Fielding wanted execution to follow very closely on conviction precisely so that passions could not cool and the sentencers have time for dispassionate reflection. Moreover, in many cases women had committed offences in company with their husbands and were presumed to have acted at their behest.[71] Above all, women's crimes were usually the ones committed without violence and therefore the most difficult to detect. Even when they were detected, the injured parties were less likely to press charges against women than against men. In other words, large numbers of female offences were overlooked or condoned in the first place.[72] As for partial avoidance of transportation, women achieved this not only because their offences were in general less serious and less of a threat to life and property. There was also the hard financial fact that women transportees were worth less money than men as transportees.[73]

However, there was one circumstance that could overturn the normal pattern of leniency towards women in sentencing. This occurred when women broke the unspoken rules of gender and sex roles and acted 'mannishly', aggressively, or without due deference. There was little chivalry displayed towards women who came within the ken of the courts and had broken social taboos.

The kind of behaviour that was taboo was graphically illustrated in 1784, in an incident involving a dispute over seats at the Covent Garden Theatre. An angry altercation led to fisticuffs, in the course of which a well-dressed, elegant lady gave a constable a black eye, knocked out a watchman, and compelled a soldier with fixed bayonet to retreat. One eye-witness reported: 'The Amazon who fought so desperately in the green boxes at Covent Garden on Saturday evening, exceeds in her feats all the heroines that we ever saw within the pale of a theatre.'[74]

Women dressing as men excited particular horror. This was thought to be an offence against the Law of Nature and of God himself, following the proscription in Deuteronomy 22:5.[75] The woman who escaped from Shrewsbury gaol in August 1764 dressed as a man presumably had some excuse.[76] But there were no mitigating considerations in the punishment of the woman who was discovered later that year to have pursued a martial career for years. A 'sailor' wishing to transfer to the army went to a recruiting sergeant, took the bounty money and was attested before a magistrate. In a drinking session with the sergeant later, the 'sailor' revealed his female gender. She had served two years in the Navy and was discharged only after sustaining a gunshot wound. But she was adamant that she wanted to continue her career as a warrior, in whatever service.[77]

Other female activities that broke down gender stereotypes were severely frowned on. The Fieldings particularly detested female prize-fighters like 'Bruising Peg', who once fought another woman in a Westminster street for an hour just for a guinea.[78] This sort of 'masculine' behaviour was thought to encourage women to turn violent. Two women were brawling at noon in an Old Street Tavern in 1764 when one killed the other with a blow on the head from a quart pot.[79] In another incident, an oysterwoman returning from a ship at Deptford refused to pay a waterman threepence for bringing her ahore and stabbed him in the belly with her oyster knife.[80]

The initial reaction to violent crime by women was often stupefaction. When a man was held up by a female highway robber in Romford in 1735, it took him several minutes to work out what she wanted, so deeply ingrained were the conventional expectations about female behaviour.[81] But when this 'unnatural' behaviour manifested itself in purposeful rather than casual crime, society usually cracked down hard. There was no possibility of mercy for female footpad robber Mary Finlayson, executed in 1795.[82] When three women took part, alongside four men, in a brutal robbery in Southwark in 1785, they were ordered to be hung in chains in Kent Street, where the offence had taken place.[83]

Even more anger was excited by lesbianism and other deviant sexual behaviour. Dressed as a man, Mary Hamilton married fourteen women, then left them shortly after the wedding. Since she was in reality a woman, she could not be caught. It was only on the fourteenth 'marriage' that she was discovered. Her 'wife' confessed that she had no idea until recently that Hamilton was not a man. Hamilton had bamboozled her, like all the others, by using a dildo.[84]

Hamilton was whipped through town for her offence, but she was luckier than Anne Marrow, who committed a similar offence of 'marrying three times' while impersonating a man. Placed in the pillory at Charing Cross, Marrow was so savagely pelted by the crowd that she lost both her eyes.[85]

It was also a source of peculiar horror to the common eighteenth-century sensibility when women prisoners acted violently, in a way uncharacteristic of the 'gentle sex'. Hannah Dagoe, a Covent Garden basketwoman convicted of burglary in 1763, was a burly, masculine woman. On the way to Tyburn she managed to get her hands and arms untied and began to struggle with the executioner. Once arrived at Tyburn Tree she defied him to hang her and dealt him such a blow that she nearly knocked him out. While the hangman recovered his senses, Dagoe tore off all her clothes and threw them into the crowd, so that the executioner could not claim them. When the noose was finally looped over her, she threw herself out of the cart with such violence that she broke her neck and died instantly.[86]

An even more startling case at the end of the century showed that even evidence of insanity would not be readily accepted if a woman acted in such a way as to outrage popular conceptions on correct sexual behaviour. Jane Gibb had instituted a number of charges of theft against innocent passers-by on the patch where she worked as a prostitute before she murdered a client and the entire history of her previous violent behaviour came out.[87] As soon as she appeared in the dock at her trial it was obvious to all dispassionate observers that she was psychotic. Thus the *Newgate Calendar* described her behaviour:

> During the whole time of her giving evidence, she appeared to be in a violent passion: she frequently darted looks of fury and rage. . . . Her language was extremely low and vulgar; and the very tone of voice in which she delivered herself was disgusting. She seldom attended to the questions that were put to her, but poured forth a heap of words without much connection or meaning; and without any endeavour to guard herself against inconsistencies and contradictions . . . she pretended to be deaf, yet, in the course of her examination, she frequently heard what was said when not supposed to . . . at times trembling, fainting and pretending to be much affected at her situation, and then looking round the office with an expression of the greatest contempt and audacity towards the persons present.[88]

Gibb was taken to the Bridewell while the authorities considered her singular case. She had to be kept in a separate cell, as the other female prisoners threatened to beat her. During the next few weeks, as she was brought back and forth for further judicial hearings, the crowd attacked her on sight and tried to string her up,[89] and had to be held at bay by a much strengthened party of the watch. On one occasion in Bedford Square the mob came close to lynching her. They had torn all the clothes off her back before the constables rescued her.[90] Such was the horror and detestation caused by behaviour thought inappropriate to her sex. Gibb was eventually pronounced insane and put in Bedlam.

It was doubtless female behaviour of this 'unnatural' type that led hardliners to conclude that all female crime was in a sense unnatural. Such thinking lay behind the 1750 proposal that all women should be transported for a first offence, no matter how trivial.[91] But rigid sex roles cut both ways. When Catherine Jones was on a bigamy charge in 1719, she produced the ingenious defence that her second marriage was invalid, because the later husband was in fact a hermaphrodite. He was examined and found to be so. Jones was acquitted without more ado.[92]

Was there any impact on female criminality of social change over the century? Urbanization was one relevant factor. There was a higher level of indictments against women for property crimes in the large towns and cities. This reflected a number of things: the anomie of the urban environment, divorced from an organic knowable community; the greater wealth available in the cities; and the revolution of rising aspirations. Not only were opportunities and temptations for crime greater in the city; the magistrates there lacked the range of informal sanctions available in rural areas.[93]

The drift to the cities was connected with rural unemployment. Seasonal underemployment in agriculture particularly affected women, as it reduced family incomes and increased destitution.[94] This in turn explains female involvement in English food riots. Women had both a compelling motive for participation in these, and what seemed like an especial opportunity. The greater leniency of the Code towards women in normal circumstances led to a belief that they could not be arrested as easily as men. For this reason, some food rioters even dressed as women.[95] Also, in times of dearth more women resorted to petty theft. In response prosecutors became more punitive, more ready to indict women.[96]

The impact of war was mixed. On the one hand, female propensity to crime could be cut down, since they could get jobs from which they were normally excluded.[97] On the other, if war and dearth coincided, there were large numbers of abandoned wives and mothers left to fend for themselves and tempted to turn towards crime. As men returned from war, the crime rate in general soared while female criminality declined: one study shows the proportion of women indicted for capital crimes going down from 16 per cent to 10 per cent, and for clergyable felonies from 23 per cent to 12 per cent with the return of peacetime 'normalcy'.[98]

It is difficult to form a final judgement on the impact of the Bloody Code on women. The net advantage that females enjoyed over males in the area of formal indictments has to be balanced against the cultural toll imposed on women by patriarchal attitudes and rigid views on gender roles. Yet even patriarchy cuts both ways: it is seldom a one-way process; arguably the greater burden of instinctual renunciation demanded by civilization is borne by men. There were swings and roundabouts in eighteenth-century sexual relationships, as in all eras. Such an impressionistic answer will doubtless please neither the quantitatively minded historian nor the committed feminist. The solution, if any, will have to await greater historians.

8

Crimes of the Powerful

Behind every great fortune there lies a crime
> Honoré de Balzac, *The Thirteen*

I was told that the Privileged and the People formed Two
Nations.
> Benjamin Disraeli, *Sybil*

Yet, it was thought, the sword she bore
Check'd but the Desp'rate and the Poor;
That, urged by mere Necessity,
Were tied up to the wretched Tree
For Crimes, which not deserv'd that Fate
But to secure the Rich, and Great.
> Bernard Mandeville, *The Fable of the Bees*

In stratified societies the inevitably political nature of much crime produces a situation where the majority of criminals are young, poor males. Godwin once famously defined crime as 'those offences which the wealthier part of the community has no temptation to commit'.[1] Yet it would be a very lopsided review of eighteenth-century crime that failed to look at the crimes of the powerful. Power, 'the production of intended effects', as Bertrand Russell defines it, can range all the way from knowledge and education to vast wealth and direct political influence. To assess the crimes of the powerful we have to span the spectrum, beginning with *relative* power and ending with the near-absolute variety.

Since knowledge is power and since, further, most Englishmen in the eighteenth century were illiterate[2], the mere ability to read and write meant that a literate criminal could enter a higher domain from that occupied by the footpad and housebreaker. By definition, then, such offences as fraud and forgery were 'white-collar' crime. They were also peculiarly calculated to arouse the ire of the post-1688 elite. The development of banks, trading houses, and systems of credit in the eighteenth century made the entire financial system vulnerable to the arts of the forger. Since it was the preservation of this system that led to Jacobites being hanged, drawn, and quartered, and to the elevation of coinage offences to the status of high treason, it is not surprising that forgery evoked some of the most savage manifestations of the Bloody Code.

Forgery had not originally been a capital offence in English law. Traditionally it was punished by fines, the pillory, or, in extreme cases, by cutting off both the offender's ears and slitting his nose. Such a sentence was in fact passed on Japhet Cooke in 1731, in a rare exception to the otherwise hard and fast rule that conviction for forgery in the eighteenth century meant death.[3] Yet in the period between the later reign of Elizabeth and 1634 it became a hanging offence. By the middle of the eighteenth century there were over four hundred statutes directed at every conceivable kind of forgery; as soon as a loophole was discovered that might benefit a forger, it was closed.[4] The laws on forgery were consequently of hideous complexity. For this reason technical problems of evidence were acute and many times more people were indicted than were convicted.[5] On the other hand, those who were convicted were more likely to hang even than highway robbers. The dreary catalogue of executed forgers in the *Newgate Calendar* tells its own story.[6]

The sheer variety of forgery cases and the ingenuity they display is dazzling. The most basic forging technique was to buy a banknote and use a chemical preparation to change the denomination. Banknotes made out in the order of £11 were a great favourite. Forgers would leave the initial 'e' of 'eleven', erase the rest of the letters, then write in 'ighty' to make £80. It was then a question of changing the note into coin. Most such forgeries did not amount to more than £1,000.[7] One army veteran who was hanged for forgery, had merely counterfeited a £50 note to cover his gambling debts.[8]

More sophisticated forgers combined their counterfeiting with expertise learned elsewhere, in service or business. James Gibson, a 45-year-old attorney, forged receipts which enabled him to embezzle more than £900. He was hanged at Tyburn in 1768.[9] Henry Bogeard, a Frenchman, had been servant to Count Herman Wedel, son of the Danish ambassador. Having compiled a dossier on Wedel's financial affairs, he forged a bill in his name. When apprehended, he had a plausible story ready: he was a Frenchman and did not understand English, therefore could not possibly have compassed such a fraud. Unfortunately for Bogeard, this was the era of the Revolutionary wars of the 1790s. English xenophobia alone was dangerous enough. Even with a jury half composed of foreigners, the tide of prejudice swept away Bogeard's flimsy defences. He was found guilty and hanged.[10]

Often the motive for forgery was more than a generalized desire to rise in the world. Sexual passion brought Robert Franklin to the gallows in

1798. Thoroughly besotted with the beautiful but abandoned Mary Jones, and afraid of losing her to rival admirers, Franklin began to forge bank notes to cover the expenses of their luxurious life style together. Realizing that he was one step away from the scaffold, Franklin panicked and joined the navy, hoping to cover his tracks. Aboard HMS *Hydra* he seemed safe from the hangman.

But Mary Jones sent word that she was pining away for love of him. Franklin obtained leave and returned to her. When she pleaded poverty, he passed another forged note. On his way back to the *Hydra*, he stopped at an inn in Rochester, where he was robbed of £40 in forged banknotes. The men who uplifted them were caught as soon as they tried to pass the bills. Questioned at Bow Street, they revealed how they came by the money. The Bow Street runners then proceeded to trace Franklin from the Rochester inn to the *Hydra*. He was arrested, tried and convicted. But because of the complex rules of evidence in forgery cases, what hanged him was not the stolen money but the forged note he had given to Mary Jones.[11]

Forgery was often allied with general confidence trickery. A man who most spectacularly combined the two was Henry Griffin. Born in America, he held a commission in Washington's army during the colonists' war for independence. After the war he sold his commission and came to England to start a new life as an impersonator of nobility. He posed as a variety of aristocrats, most notably as Lord Massey and the Duke of Ormonde. For ten years he defrauded banks, nobility, and gentry of large sums of money. Finally he was caught after 'uttering' a bill of exchange for £1449 drawn on Coutts the bankers. This purported to be a payment from the Earl of Tankerville to 'Lord Massey'.[12]

The most seriously considered type of forgery was tampering with the stock of the great financial institutions: the Bank of England, the East India Company, or the South Sea Company. As early as 1721 legislation had been introduced to make frauds on public funds and the stocks of public companies a non-clergyable felony.[13] Three categories of offence were particularly underlined: forging letters of attorney or other authority to transfer stocks or receive dividends; forging the names of proprietors to such letters of attorney; and impersonating the proprietors of stock. The effect was that conviction of forgery offences against the 'big three' institutions virtually implied a mandatory death sentence.[14] The only consolation for forgers of bonds and securities was that there were many loopholes in the law, which the authorities continually tried to close with fresh legislation.[15]

Yet there were no loopholes big enough to save Henry Weston, the most spectacular swindler of the Bank of England. Weston was an inveterate gambler and the nephew of Sir Hugh Palisser. On one occasion he forged the name of General Tonyn to obtain £100,000 from the Bank of England, which he then lost in two nights' sustained gaming and gambling. Nothing daunted, Weston then got another tranche from the Bank by persuading his mistress to pose as General Tonyn's sister. Eventually the whirlpool of crime and indebtedness threatened to suck him down. He tried to escape to America and was actually on board ship at Liverpool waiting to sail when he was arrested. He was executed in 1796.[16]

The odds were in favour of the authorities rather than the major forger. Occasionally, to enhance the credibility of the Code by tempering justice with mercy, judges would decree a pardon, but this was always in minor forgery cases. One of the lucky ones was Captain Peter de la Fontane in 1752, whose death sentence was commuted to transportation.[17] By the 1790s it was not unknown for a forger to receive a free pardon.[18] But this was a prerogative exercised only for first-time offenders. Forgery following a long record of fraud still attracted the death penalty, unless some other circumstances came into play.[19] It was the extreme youth as well as the consummate cheek of Thomas Hawkins and Edward Underwood that got them a sentence of transportation instead of the gallows in 1800.[20] The fear of the hangman often led an individual to sink back in the criminal hierarchy. After a period as a forger, Will Chance decided he would run less risks as a footpad robber. Alas for him, his counterfeiting past was deemed to have compounded the gravity of his footpad robbery when he was caught in 1715. His attempt to play safe had merely secured him double jeopardy.[21]

Forgery cases became *causes célèbres* on four occasions in the eighteenth century. The case of John Ayliffe led to extensive bad publicity for the elite. Mrs Strangways Horner, previously Henry Fox's mistress, took up with a schoolmaster, John Ayliffe, and made him steward of some of her estates in Wiltshire and Dorset. But she soon became bored with him and in 1753 dismissed him. Meanwhile Ayliffe was living beyond his means on the strength of the legacy allegedly promised him by Mrs Horner. In 1758 she died, but left him precisely nothing. The estates were bequeathed to her former lover Henry Fox, later first Lord Holland.

The discontented Ayliffe tampered with some title deeds and mortgages and then forged a deed of gift of £3,000 to himself from Mrs Horner plus an annuity of £420. Shortly afterwards Ayliffe was arrested for debt and thrown into the Fleet prison. Lacking the time to paper over his forgeries, he was a sitting duck when indicted for the crime. He was executed in 1759. But a powerful rumour gained credence, to the effect that Fox had framed Ayliffe out of spite and sexual jealousy. The political opposition to Fox assiduously peddled the canard. The mud stuck; for the rest of his life Fox was never able to clear himself of suspicion.[22]

The John Rice case became subsumed in general Anglo-French

hostility during the Seven Years War. After forging £19,000 worth of South Sea stock, Rice fled to Cambrai. The French government refused to hand him back. Despite pressure from the great financial institutions, including the Bank of England, who feared what might happen if a precedent was set, the English government was less than keen to press for a formal extradition arrangement. They feared they would end up the losers in any reciprocal agreement.

So far Rice seemed to have pulled off the perfect crime. But it proved a mistake to go to Cambrai after all. When his wife tried (on his instructions) to bring over the bulk of the ill-gotten funds to Cambrai she was arrested by the English. And the French did not remain committed to the cause so advantageous to him. While hostilities lasted, he was a useful gadfly with which to sting London. But when peace came in 1763 the French saw him mainly as a very valuable bargaining counter. On the conclusion of the Treaty of Paris, perfidious Louis XV allowed Rice to be shipped back to certain conviction and execution.[23]

The two final forgery dramas of the century were even more sensational. The case of the Perreau brothers was especially 'good copy' since it turned on the evidence of a woman of doubtful reputation. Robert and Daniel Perreau were London wine merchants. Robert was a former apothecary of unblemished record, but Daniel had clearly been guilty of minor crimes in his career. In 1775 the two brothers were brought to trial on a charge of having forged a money bond for £7,500 in the name of William Adair.[24]

Behind this indictment lay a tangled web of human relationships. Daniel Perreau had a mistress called Margaret Caroline Rudd. Née Young in 1745, she had married Valentine Rudd in 1762, but left him soon afterwards to pursue the life of an adventuress. After liaisons with Wilkes and the Duke of Cumberland, in 1770 she became Daniel Perreau's mistress and bore him three children. But when Perreau was taken before Sir John Fielding for examination on a charge of forgery, Rudd gave evidence that she had forged a bond under duress because Daniel Perreau held a knife at her throat.[25]

Fielding quite improperly released her on bail, then admitted her as 'an evidence' against the Perreau brothers on a quite separate forgery charge. Fielding here demonstrated a shaky knowledge of the law he was so vehement to uphold. The whole point of being admitted as 'an evidence' was that one had to confess to being guilty of a crime before the charges were drawn up. Then, if the evidence convicted any accomplices at the trial, one was given a free pardon. Technically, then, Rudd was in no position to be 'an evidence'. She had pleaded guilty to one forgery under duress, but now the Perreaus were on trial for a *different* charge. Rudd had at no time confessed to being an accomplice in *the particular forgery* with which the Perreaus were charged. The prosecution saw the danger and did not call on Rudd to give evidence at the trial; nevertheless her widely-bruited accusations were well known to the jurymen. Her evidence in effect condemned both Perreaus to the gallows. The prosecuting counsel, Henry Howarth, pressed hard for a conviction and used all his wiles in a successful attempt to bamboozle the jury. The two brothers were sentenced to hang.[26]

It was quite clear that the brothers had been condemned on evidence improperly given, by a cold-blooded, treacherous *femme fatale*. Her former lover Wilkes thought it was monstrous that Rudd should go unpunished just because she had given evidence against the Perreaus. 'Devilling' by newspaper reporters threw up a story that she had been the clandestine mistress of the very William Adair who was the alleged victim of the Perreaus forgery.[27] It seemed likely to dispassionate observers that Rudd, tired of her relationship with Daniel, had framed the Perreau brothers. Robert was certainly innocent and Daniel, though no angel, was probably guilty of no more than peccadilloes. After the death sentence was handed down, seventy-eight bankers and merchants signed a petition for clemency to King George III.[28]

Yet the royal prerogative was not exercised. Despite great popular agitation, the death sentence was allowed to stand. In January 1776 the brothers, still loudly protesting their innocence, were taken to Tyburn for execution before a crowd of 30,000 people.[29] So unruly was the crowd and so hostile to the hangman that three hundred constables were needed to clear a space around the scaffold to allow him to perform his ghastly rites.[30]

Attention then switched to Mrs Rudd. Partly to appease public anger she was committed for trial on the forgery charge to which she had originally pleaded guilty. Lord Chief Justice Mansfield overruled Fielding's judgment, on the quite proper grounds outlined above. Since she was not an accomplice to the crime of which the Perreaus had been found guilty, she could stand trial on her own account. But now public opinion underwent one of its periodic, amazing, changes of mood. Rudd was a spell-binder, possessed of obvious sexual magnetism. At the trial she won over the public.[31] There was also behind-the-scenes elite manoeuvring on her behalf. Howarth, who again led the prosecution, was as weak and unconvincing in his arguments as he had been strong and cogent when hounding the Perreaus. To cheers from the public gallery, Rudd was found not guilty.[32]

After the trial Rudd showed her true colours. Once free she scorned her many supporters and disappeared from London with her new lover Lord Lytton, who had been exercising discreet and hidden influence at the trial. More than ever now people began to conclude that Robert Perreau, at least, had certainly been innocent. But such was the allure and notoriety of Mrs Rudd that the public could not stop reading about her. Her memoirs, published in 1777, became a best-seller.[33] She continued her lubricious career until 1797, at one time adding James Boswell to her long list of lovers.[34]

The year 1777 produced an even more famous forgery trial that still attracts detailed treatment from writers today: the case of Dr William Dodd.[35] Dodd was a clergyman, and had also been tutor to the young Lord Chesterfield. His first brush with fame followed a highway robbery in Tottenham Court Road in 1773. Dodd was a principal witness at the trial of William Griffiths, who was hanged for this and other robberies.[36] By 1776, Dodd was in debt, with no prospect of the ecclesiastical preferment he yearned for. When his creditors pressed for payment, Dodd forged the signature of his former charge, Lord Chesterfield, on a bond for £4,300.[37]

Very soon after the bond was cashed, an investigator who worked for the company that accepted the bond noticed an irregularity in the signature. The bond was shown to Lord Chesterfield, who disowned it. Dodd was questioned and then sent for trial. There was general distaste at the thought of a well-known clergyman being sent to Tyburn. Dodd's influential friends, including Samuel Johnson, rallied round him.[38] But despite their lobbying and a huge groundswell of popular support, the jury at Dodd's trial took just ten minutes to find him guilty.[39]

Efforts were now concentrated on securing a pardon for Dodd and 100,000 signatures in favour of exercising the royal prerogative of mercy were collected. But there were two things that barred Dodd's path to the king's favour. One was the implacable hostility of Lord Chief Justice Mansfield, who was determined that Dodd should hang.[40] The other was the unfortunate precedent of the Perreaus. George III had let the death sentence stand then; how could he commute Dodd's sentence now? As the monarch remarked in bewilderment: 'If I pardon Dodd, I shall have murdered the Perreaus.'[41]

It soon became clear that Dodd was doomed. Samuel Johnson visited the cleric in Newgate to prepare him for the worst. Wesley too visited him and attempted commiseration with a fellow preacher.[42] When all avenues of supplication and appeal were exhausted, Dodd was executed. The crowd at Tyburn surpassed anything seen before: an estimated 100,000 saw the luckless clergyman go to his doom.[43]

The aftermath of the Dodd case was a mixed picture. On the one hand, the king was soon after obliged to let a royal favourite hang for forgery, in order to sustain the precedent set by Dodd and the Perreaus. William Ryland became a man of considerable fortune after his appointment as the royal engraver. Tempted into forgery none the less, he would in normal circumstances have entertained high hopes of a royal pardon from his patron. But George III's hands were effectively tied by the two great forgery trials of the mid-1770s. Ryland too met his end at Tyburn.[44]

On the other hand, elite dismissal of the public's wishes in the Dodd case led to a significant backlash against the death penalty. One of the beneficiaries of this shift in opinion was a minor forger, John Harrison; he received a pardon for an offence that, before the shift in opinion, would certainly have consigned him to the gallows.[45] In general, the Dodd case was harmful to the elite. Not only did the majesty of the law seem a hollow sham when public opinion was so signally flouted, but it was felt that Mansfield's personal animus had been elevated to the status of Law. Moreover, Lord Chesterfield's conduct disgusted most observers. Although Dodd had shown particular interest in him as a charge, Chesterfield did not lift a finger on his old tutor's behalf. The harsh, uncaring face of the elite, demonstrated by the behaviour of Mansfield and Chesterfield, seemed counterparted in a mindless use of the death penalty which seriously affected its credibility and that of its exponents.[46]

Forgery was the most important 'white-collar crime', but there were many others of significance. The rise of the limited company in the eighteenth century made it necessary for laws to be framed that prevented fraudulent insolvency. An Act of 1732 made it a non-clergyable felony for bankrupts to fail to present themselves to the proper authorities within forty-two days of being given notice to do so.[47] It was also a hanging offence to refuse to submit to examination by a commission of bankruptcy or to hide one's effects. A creditor could require a debtor to produce a true schedule of his effects, under pain of death for refusal or falsification. New laws were passed during the century to tighten up on the many loopholes relating to insolvency, since certain rogues turned the law into a laughing stock.[48] They preferred to go to prison for debt and live in the Fleet or Marshalsea like kings rather than pay their debts.

Curiously, most of the victims claimed by the gallows for infraction of the bankruptcy laws were taken in the first half of the century. The usual conviction was defrauding creditors under a commission of bankruptcy or concealing assets.[49] The plethora of bankruptcy cases during the century more usually led to suicide. Executions for fraudulent insolvency after the middle of the century tended to involve a complicating factor, as when Thomas Sherwood in 1778 compounded forgery with absconding when a commission of bankruptcy was issued against him.[50] The diminishing execution rate belied the trend of the times, for in the years 1740-77 there was a veritable explosion of failed companies and bankrupted individuals.[51]

Insurance frauds were another staple 'middle-class' crime. The favourite felony was the destruction of ships by their masters to collect on insurance money.[52] This crime was specifically removed from benefit of clergy by two Acts of 1717 and 1724.[53] But it was still a thriving industry at the end of the century, as the case of Captain William Codlin in 1802 demonstrated. Codlin, master of the brig *Adventure* was executed for attempting to defraud the insurance underwriters by boring holes in his ship so as to sink her.[54]

Blackmail by letter, again an offence for which literacy was a prerequisite and previously a misdemeanour, was made non-clergyable by the Waltham Black Act. One of the first to be hanged under the relevant clauses of this Act was Jepthah Big in 1729.[55] His crime was to demand money with menaces. Since these provisions of the Black Act were widely taken to refer to *extortion* by letter alone, a further Act of 1754 made it explicit that to send *any* threatening letter, not just about money, was a capital offence.[56] The main purpose for the passage of the second statute was to deal adequately with those who sent threatening letters as a primitive form of social protest. As E. P. Thompson has said in his study of this phenomenon:

> The anonymous threatening letter is a characteristic form of social protest in any society which has crossed a certain threshold of literacy, in which forms of collective organised defence are weak, and in which individuals who can be identified as the organisers of protest are liable to immediate victimisation.[57]

As soon as we ascend the social scale above the middle sectors, the very concept of crime becomes problematical. As one critic has written: 'Crime in the eighteenth century was after all an act of the streets rather than the suites. Generally speaking, men like the Duke of Newcastle or Sir Robert Walpole succeeded in abstaining from street robbery or the theft of wood, and they thus escape our attention in the court records.'[58] But there was one elite activity that was, at least formally, recognized as a crime by the Code: the practice of duelling.

Duelling as a custom first took a hold in England in the late Elizabethan era. It was particularly popular during the Restoration. Leaders of society like George Villiers, second Duke of Buckingham, set a fashion for solving disputes by the pistol and rapier. The duel became a recognized part of the aristocrat's 'code of honour'.[59]

In theory the law recognized no distinction between killing a man in a duel and premeditated murder. Even if a man ran through an opponent who was pressing him too closely, he could not evade the *general* premeditation involved in agreeing to meet for a duel in the first place.[60] The fulminations of Blackstone set out the official stance of the law on duelling as murder with malice aforethought:

> Where both parties meet avowedly with an intent to murder: thinking it their duty, as gentlemen, and claiming it as their right, to wanton with their own lives and those of their fellow creatures; without any warrant or authority from any power either divine or human, but in direct

contradiction to the laws both of God and man; and therefore the law has justly fixed the crime and punishment of murder on them, and on their seconds also.[61]

That was the theory. The reality was rather different. Jurymen overwhelmingly accepted the plea that duelling was a proper way for 'gentlemen' to resolve their disputes. As long as the 'rules of honour' had been obeyed, they would not find a murder charge proven. The maximum sustainable charge was manslaughter.[62] In six cases in a ninety-five-year study of eighteenth-century Surrey where one gentleman had killed another in a duel, there were five acquittals and one conviction for manslaughter.[63] Even in the rare cases where the letter of the law was upheld, the 'code of honour' intervened. It was common practice for a combatant in a duel who had received a mortal blow publicly to forgive his opponent. An interesting case from the middle of the century showed this clearly. Captain Clarke RN killed a brother officer, Captain Innis, in a duel after a violent disagreement over evidence given to a court martial. In the duel Clarke had used screw-barrelled pistols, seven inches long, as against Innis's common pocket pistols, half that length. This was considered perfectly permissible by the 'code of honour', but the prosecution convinced the jury that it demonstrated an excessive determination on Clarke's part to kill his opponent. Clarke was found guilty of wilful murder and condemned to die. Then his friends petitioned the monarch, pointing out that Innis had forgiven Clarke before expiring. The king immediately granted Clarke a free pardon.[64]

It is hard to escape the conclusion that eighteenth-century England suffered from duelling mania. In February and March 1764 there were four major duels. In February a surgeon was shot dead in Hyde Park by an officer of marines.[65] Three days later an army captain and the chaplain of Bland's dragoons duelled in Epping Forest; the chaplain later died of his wounds.[66] Two weeks later a duel came to an abrupt end when an exploding pistol shattered the hand of one of the combatants.[67] At the beginning of March a duel at Stroud Green, Newbury, was stopped by the magistrates after the first of the customary two shots had been exchanged.[68]

Duelling was an instance where the elite clearly committed acts declared criminal by their own Code. Three eighteenth-century prime ministers fought duels: Fox with Adam, Shelburne with Fullerton, Pitt with Tierney. In 1779 Fox, in a vehement attack on Lord North's American policy, tore to pieces a speech by William Adam.[69] Adam then challenged him to a duel. Fox was willing to give all reasonable satisfaction, but Adam was spoiling for a fight. After the first exchange of shots, Fox asked Adam if he was satisfied. The hotheaded Adam rejected the olive branch and fired again, slightly wounding Fox in the groin. To show his contempt for such behaviour, Fox wasted his last shot by discharging his pistol in the air.[70]

Three months later Lord Shelburne and Mr William Fullerton duelled in Hyde Park. Like Fox, Shelburne was wounded in the groin. Coincidentally, the same pistol produced both wounds, since Adam had borrowed Fullerton's weapon for his earlier joust with Fox.[71] Fullerton's second shot passed through Shelburne's waistcoat pocket. As the pocket was full of papers, the bullet was deflected and lodged farther down his body. Shelburne laughed off his wound, saying: 'Why, I don't think Lady Shelburne will be the worse for it.'[72]

Most duel-prone of all elite figures, not surprisingly perhaps, was John Wilkes. In October 1762 he fought a duel with Lord Talbot on Bagshot Heath. Neither man was hit.[73] The following year he fought in Hyde Park against Samuel Martin over Martin's use of the phrase 'cowardly scoundrel'. Martin was said to have put in six months of target-practice before meeting Wilkes on the field of combat.[74] Martin's preparations paid off, up to a point, for on the second exchange of shots Wilkes was wounded under the navel.[75] Earlier the same year (1763), Wilkes had been challenged to yet another duel by a Scotsman John Forbes, arising from Wilkes's well-known hatred of Scots. Since the venue for the duel was in Paris, this time Wilkes declined, on the grounds that the French rules made duelling too dangerous to enter into on such a trivial pretext.[76]

All these incidents caused serious concern to more thoughtful members of the elite. Sir James Lowther pointed out in the House of Commons in 1780 that if Parliamentary proceedings were made the occasion for duels, all claims to freedom of debate and expression would have to be abandoned.[77] If a member could call out another member for a critical speech, the hallowed sovereignty of Parliament, for which a civil war had been fought, would be reduced to the rule of the bully-boy. Oratory would give place to swordsmanship, logic to the long-barrelled pistol. For some writers, duelling was a more sophisticated form of attempted suicide and thus contrary to reason.[78] It is interesting, incidentally, to observe the impact of the Enlightenment on this debate. In the 1770s it was conducted on the basis that duelling was an affront to Reason. Fifty years earlier, the argument had been that duelling, like suicide, was an offence against God and thus an implied form of atheism.[79]

It was in the 1770s that battle was joined in earnest between supporters and opponents of duelling. Horace Walpole wrote of that era: 'The rage of duelling had of late much revived, especially in Ireland, and many attempts were made in print and on the stage to curb so horrid and absurd a practice.'[80] Yet the thinking classes were not at one on the issue. Many aristocratic apologists argued that the outcome of duels depended on God's providence and that duelling was thus like the medieval trial by combat. God, it was alleged, gave the victory to the just, not the most skilful. Accidents occurred to upset the calculations of the most expert swordsmen and crack shots: a stumble, a change in the direction of the wind, even the respective presence of mind of the combatants.

Support for duelling was an issue that united the Tory Samuel Johnson and the Whig Henry Fielding. Fielding famously defended the practice in *Tom Jones*.[81] Johnson found duels permissible on two grounds. In the first place, every individual had the right to self-defence and to avoid the stigma of cowardice that would drive him out of polite society.[82] Second, if it was allowed that the 'just war' existed and that public warfare was therefore legitimate, in order to be consistent with morality private warfare must also be allowed.[83] Johnson's argument, curiously, had a distinct Humean flavour (normally Johnson did not care for Hume's social philosophy). He thought there could be no rational justification of the practice, but that custom and habit, plus the excuse of self-defence, made it an acceptable social convention.[84] Boswell supported his mentor to the hilt on this issue. His eldest son was killed in a duel, and he himself was prepared to fight one in 1785.[85]

Where no powerful intellectual consensus had formed on the issue, the elite felt itself under no pressure to reform its ways. Duelling mania continued. Two impressions of eighteenth-century combat are striking: the poor level of marksmanship and the triviality of the issues on which most duels were fought.

In December 1770 Lord George Germaine and Governor Johnstone emerged without a scratch after both men had fired twice and missed.[86] Lord Bellamont received no more than a graze from his duel with Lord Townshend in 1773.[87] It was the same story with the Duke of York and Colonel Lennox. Sometimes the incompetence of the elite manifested itself in indiscretion that prevented the duel from even taking place. After George Townshend had challenged Lord Albemarle to a duel in 1760 (over allegations concerning his conduct the year before at Quebec), he asked Lord Buckingham to be his second. Buckingham's garrulous behaviour alerted the authorities. On the day appointed for the duel, the Captain of the Guard arrived on the scene. After apologizing to the duellists as his superior officers, he placed them both under arrest.[88]

Serious injuries were usually sustained in duels only when both sides agreed to continue with swords after the two shots apiece had been discharged. In December 1773 the banker William Whateley fought a duel in Hyde park with John Temple, surveyor-general of customs. Whateley had accused Temple of removing some documents while searching his brother's papers. After all four shots had been fired without effect, the two men set to with swords. Temple emerged with superficial wounds, but Whateley was badly cut up and had to be hospitalized.[89]

The most common pretexts for duels were disputes over women or slights to one's 'honour'. Augustus Townshend fought a duel in 1741 because his opponent merely mentioned a lady's name.[90] In 1778 a quarrel over a woman led two old friends into tragedy. Over their cups in a Bath tavern the 29-year-old Vicomte du Barry clashed bitterly with his friend James Rice over a fair unknown. After making arrangements for the satisfaction of their honour, they sat in a coach until daybreak, then went with their seconds to the appointed ground. In the combat Rice was seriously wounded but du Barry was killed outright. The matter became something of a *cause célèbre*, since du Barry was nephew of the famous Madame du Barry, Louis XVI's mistress.[91]

Since army officers were the most weapon-happy and pugnacious, it is not surprising to find that their duels over women were sometimes expressly designed as fights to the finish. During the American war two army captains fought to the death because one of them whistled the tune to a ditty derogatory to the other officer's wife. Captain Tollemache, on whose wife the aspersions had been cast, challenged the other captain, Pennington to mortal combat with pistols and swords. When (inevitably) the two sets of pistols had been fired with no effect, the two men slashed at each other with swords. Pennington was wounded seven times but he eventually dispatched Tollemache with a thrust through the heart.[92]

To fight over a woman was at least consistent with a debased notion of chivalry. Yet many (if not most) duels were fought over issues of extreme triviality. In 1743 Horace Walpole's uncle wounded William Chetwynd in an 'affair of honour' that turned on a picayune political dispute.[93] William, fifth Lord Byron, killed William Chaworth in an improvised duel in the back room of a Pall Mall tavern in January 1765. The occasion for the combat was a dispute about which of them had more game on his manor! Byron was convicted of manslaughter by the Lords but saved from punishment by the privileges of his rank.[94] Small wonder that particular enthusiasm for duelling was evinced by the certifiably insane, like Lord Pomfret.[95] And a case in 1742 seemed to vindicate those like Ayscough and Watts who argued for a link between suicide and duelling. When Lord Windsor refused Charles Nourse's challenge to a duel on the grounds that Nourse was too old, Nourse responded by going home and cutting his own throat.[96]

The fact that the elite gave its informal sanction to a practice explicitly condemned by the Code allowed unscrupulous, belligerent adventurers to turn the 'rules of honour' to their own advantage. The most famous exponent of 'coat-trailing' was George Robert Fitzgerald, grandson of Lord Hervey.[97] In 1775 Fitzgerald trumped up a charge that a Mr Thomas Walker owed him money. Knowing Fitzgerald's fearsome reputation as a duellist, Walker tried to avoid him. But Fitzgerald tracked Walker down at the Ascot race-meeting and gave him a public thrashing with a cane. To save face, Walker then had no choice but to issue a challenge. He survived the duel with the Irishman with no more than a superficial wound.[98] But Fitzgerald's usual habit was to kill those who stood in his way, by challenging them to single combat. He was a crack shot and expert swordsman, and the code of honour in effect granted him licence to kill. In 1786, while he was lying in Castlebar gaol in Ireland awaiting trial on one of many duelling charges, the relatives of the man he murdered broke into the gaol, determined to apply lynch law. They left Fitzgerald for dead, but he survived. This did him little good, for this time he was found guilty of murder and executed.[99]

The mania for duelling infected polite society. Many women pressed to be taken to observe the dawn ritual, as if it were part of the social round.[100] Even religious leaders were not immune to the lure of showing themselves to be men of honour, despite the obvious biblical prohibitions.[101] In Ireland a Mr Taafe changed his religion so as to be able to fight a duel; under the Penal Laws it was an offence for a Catholic to wear a sword.[102] When he was conducting his anti-slavery campaign William Wilberforce was challenged to a duel by a West India sea captain.[103] Eventually it became the custom for tradesmen whose bills were not paid to insult the scions of the upper crust. The hope was that the aristocrats would at least give them satisfaction with pistol or cutlass. Usually the elite response to this ploy was to reply disdainfully that it was beneath their dignity to soil their hands with mere 'mechanics'. Yet sometimes the provocation worked. In 1784 there were both fatal and near-fatal duels fought over bills from a haberdasher, a shoemaker and a milkman.[104]

Yet far the greatest volume of duelling was done by army officers, for whom the use of weapons was an everyday affair. In 1778 an army colonel was killed by a brother officer in a duel in Devonshire.[105] In September 1783 Colonel Thomas of the Guards was killed while fighting according to the code of honour. The case attracted attention, since Thomas left a testament in which he declared that duelling was morally wrong, but that the insane 'rules of honour' left him no choice but to fight if he wished to escape the taint of cowardice.[106] Earlier in 1783 two army officers shot each other dead in a duel. Mr Riddell of the Horse Grenadiers mortally wounded Mr Cunningham of the Scots Greys by shooting him through the breast on his first volley. After a two-minute pause Cunningham returned the fire and wounded Riddell so seriously that he died the next day.[107]

Because of this endemic duelling in the Army, as well as generalized anti-military sentiment, juries tended to be harsher on the officer class and less disposed to acquit them. In 1752 there was a duel between two Guards officers over accusations of cheating at gaming. Lord Lempster killed his accuser Captain Gray on the spot. The coroner's inquest brought in a verdict of manslaughter. Lempster was then tried for this crime at the Old Bailey, found guilty, and burnt on the hand.[108] Horace St Paul killed William Dalton, a law student at the Inner Temple, in a duel fought over a triviality. The dispute turned on a snuffbox belonging to Dalton's fiancée, Miss Green, which she playfully gave to St Paul. After a coroner's verdict of wilful murder, St Paul fled to Paris and was outlawed. In 1756 he entered Austrian service and was created a colonel and an Imperial Count. Pardoned in 1765, he became an English diplomat.[109] Miss Green meanwhile died of grief and shame after she had been accused in the newspapers of being the cause of Dalton's death.[110]

The generalized brutality and lack of subtlety in the life of many eighteenth-century officers led them to embrace the code of honour as a cloak to legitimate their rough-hewn behaviour. Chafing at the restrictions to which the military were subject in England, a commander of Hessians billeted in Hampshire once challenged a local magistrate to a duel for committing one of his troops for disorderly behaviour.[111] Another cross-grained character, General Braddock, a favourite of 'Butcher Cumberland' was the veteran of several duels. In one of them he put out the eye of the Jacobite Lord Clancarty. In another he was disarmed by Colonel Samuel Gumley but refused to plead for his life.[112]

Often quick-tempered army officers could not be bothered to wait for a properly constituted duel before settling their differences. In 1782 two of them got into an argument over a game of 'even and odd', then fought in Pall Mall with drawn swords. Other officers joined in the fracas; when the crowd tried to separate the milling combatants, a general affray developed. All the windows in the houses adjacent to the gaming house were smashed, and one of the guards called out to quash the riot was killed.[113]

It was doubtless memories of this incident that influenced the judge in another duelling case later that year. The Reverend Bennett Allen was convicted of killing a man in a duel in Hyde Park and sentenced to six months in Newgate. The jury tried to have him excused on the grounds that this was not a fitting penalty for a 'gentleman', but the judge insisted. The grudge was an ancient one, he declared, and the two duellists had gone looking for trouble.[114] By the end of the century, with a growing distaste for blatant violence in society at large, it was becoming more difficult to get away with the elite crime of duelling.

When members of the elite were indicted for crimes widely recognized as such, like rape, robbery, or theft, they were usually acquitted. Political influence, family patronage, jury deference, the skill of expensive counsel, all played their part. Behaviour that would not have been tolerated in the 'lower orders' was deemed to be merely 'letting off steam' on the part of gentlemen. Brutal assaults, sometimes including rape, by gangs of idle youths from upper-class families were commonplace in the streets of eighteenth-century London. These so-called 'Mohawks' drew on a long tradition of aristocratic misbehaviour and gratuitous violence.[115] The Mohawks uniquely combined mindless hooliganism with staggering spending power. Sixteen of them once held a dinner in Covent Garden with their girlfriends. The bill for the riotous affair came to £117.9.6 (some £3,000 in present-day money, for one meal).[116]

Since it has sometimes been suggested that the Code treated the wealthy more harshly, because they could not plead poverty as a mitigating factor,[117] it is necessary to give some examples of the way in which the law was warped for the benefit of the rich and powerful. In 1747 a coroner's court brought in the verdict that a servant found in an Oxford college with his skull fractured had been murdered 'by persons unknown'. In fact it was known that when last seen the murdered servant had been made drunk and was being used as a plaything by a quartet of young 'bloods'. These were Lord Abergavenny, Lord Charles Scott, Sir Francis Blake Delaval, and the Reverend Sackville Spencer. The murdered servant was found in the morning at the foot of Lord Abergavenny's staircase.[118] All the circumstantial evidence pointed in the same direction. But clearly indictments against such a powerful quartet were out of the question.

Well-born people guilty of shoplifting and pickpocketing, crimes that could consign the poverty-stricken to the gallows, were invariably bailed or acquitted.[119] The trial of Viscount Dungarvan for pickpocketing in 1791 is instructive. It was abundantly clear from the circumstantial evidence that Dungarvan had committed the crime. But his defence discredited the plaintiff, Elizabeth Weldon, by digging up her past. In addition, he packed the court with character witnesses in Dungarvan's favour, including the Dukes of Portland and Devonshire. Sufficiently browbeaten by this display of the elite out in force, the jury brought in a verdict of 'Not Guilty'. The judge capped the farcical proceedings by delivering a eulogy on Dungarvan's character![120]

Similar elite influence saved Sir Simon Clarke in 1731. He and Lt. Robert Arnott were caught red-handed after a highway robbery near Winchester. Clarke pleaded economic necessity and won the sympathy of the local gentry. The High Sheriff and Grand Jury took into account the worth and dignity of Sir Simon's ancestors. They petitioned the king to reprieve the two men. A reprieve *sine die* (tantamount to a pardon) was granted. So great was the influence of Clarke's connections that they almost succeeded in suppressing all reporting of the case.[121]

Even more despicable behaviour would be condoned by the elite if one of its own sons was at risk, as a case heard at Kingston, Surrey, in 1764 shows. Frederick, Lord Baltimore, was determined to gratify his lusts on Sarah Woodcock, a milliner of a strict Dissenter sect. He enlisted the services of a singular trio of debauchees: a corrupt German physician, his wife, and a prostitute/procuress. They lured Sarah from her shop on the pretext of a bogus order for millinery, then kept her captive at Baltimore's seat. For three days the four villains tried to break her will. Fearing that she would be raped if she dozed off, Sarah did not sleep for three nights, nor did she eat the food offered her, in case it was drugged. On the fourth night she was too weak for further resistance. The two depraved women undressed her and bore her away to a bedroom where Lord Baltimore was waiting. He then raped her twice.

Following the rape, the quartet continued their task of psychological demoralization, to the point where Woodcock was willing to sign a letter saying she had been at Baltimore's house of her own free will. She later testified that she would have signed anything just to get out of his clutches. This letter, written under duress, formed the basis of Baltimore's defence when Sarah told her story and a charge of rape was brought. The jury seemed unconvinced at the trial, so the judge intervened. He directed the jury that they could not find Lord Baltimore guilty when it was simply Sarah Woodcock's word against that of an aristocrat and three other people. The jury duly returned a verdict of 'not guilty'.[122]

The arrogant attitude to the law taken by the sons and daughters of the elite demonstrated that they were in no doubt that they were above it, and that their being brought to trial at all was the gravest impertinence. In 1776 Elizabeth, Duchess Dowager of Kingston, was tried in the Great Hall of Westminster before her peers on a charge of bigamy. It was quite obvious that she had been bigamously married, but instead of expressing regret or showing contrition, or even producing witnesses, the duchess simply ranted and raved at the court for its insolence.[123] Incensed by her behaviour, the Attorney-General pressed to have her burnt on the hand when she was found guilty. Once again, behind-the-scenes pressure was exerted on the judges. The penalty was waived. The duchess remained impudent and unrepentant. When, to uphold the credibility of the law in the face of such blatant special pleading, the judges issued a writ of *ne exeat regno* to prevent her leaving the kingdom, the duchess pointedly ignored it and travelled to France. Even Horace Walpole, no radical, was led to comment: 'So all this complication of knavery receives no punishment but the loss of the duchy.'[124]

There was clearly a danger that the blatant favouritism exhibited towards the aristocracy by the courts could lead to debasing of the coinage. It would no longer be possible to use the Law as the central ideological myth in the social system, if it was obvious to everyone that there was one law for the rich and one for the poor. This placed the elite in a dilemma. One way out was to visit the full wrath of the Code on the 'middling sort', hoping that the poor would make no distinction between them and the aristocracy. This was undoubtedly one of the factors underlying the execution of Dodd and the Perreaus. Another victim of this sort of skewed thinking was Thomas Carr, executed with his common-law wife in 1738 for stealing ninety-three guineas. When pronouncing the death sentence, the judge said it was merited because Carr was a lawyer and had abused his trust.[125] This was convenient camouflage. The unspoken basis of the judge's remarks was that members of the 'middling sort' had occasionally to be sacrificed in order to protect the greater villains in the aristocracy.

Yet there were very rare occasions when a member of the elite committed crimes that were so dreadful that the full weight of the Code had to be used against him, in order to maintain the overall credibility of the Law. Such a case was that of Earl Ferrers, often mistakenly cited to prove that the Code was impartial, that there really was genuine equality before the law. Ferrers has already crossed our path (see above p. 65). He had a long record of violence. It was his habitual beating of his wife that enabled her to obtain a legal separation through Act of Parliament. On another occasion he set about a groom with a horsewhip because the man did not have his horse immediately available.[126]

It was the separation from his wife that precipitated Ferrers into one of the crimes of the century. One of his stewards, Johnson by name, sent Ferrers's wife £50 to tide her over until the receivers could secure her a proper allowance from the Ferrers estate. When he heard this, Ferrers summoned Johnson and made him kneel on the ground in front of him. He then shot the steward through the head. It was 3 p.m. Ferrers compounded his villainy by taunting the mortally wounded man until he finally expired at 1 a.m. the next morning.[127]

When Ferrers was arrested, he shocked the authorities by declaring that he was glad he had shot Johnson and would do the same thing again. This made a very bad impression on his fellow peers before whom he was tried. They were also concerned to impress foreign observers, whose interest in the case was intense, with the grandeur and impartiality of the English legal system.[128] They were therefore in no mood to accept the plea of insanity advanced by Ferrers's defence. Skilful cross-questioning from Lord Hewley demolished this defence and lost Ferrers any lingering sympathy the Lords might have had for him. He was found guilty and condemned to death.[129]

Normally, high expectations could have been entertained for a royal pardon. But when Ferrers's mother and family presented two petitions, the king replied that since the House of Lords had found Ferrers guilty, the monarch could not intervene. It was very soon clear that the elite intended to make an example of Ferrers. His petition to be beheaded, according to the traditional privileges of his rank, was turned down. When he asked to have his mistress with him in gaol, this too was denied.[130]

Of Ferrers it can indeed be said that nothing in his life became him like the leaving of it. The day before his execution he took leave of his four daughters with great dignity. Next morning he put on his wedding clothes and proceeded to Tyburn in a landau and six.[131] The crowd was surprisingly friendly. By this time they had largely forgotten the enormity of his crime, and in their awe at seeing a peer of the realm sent to the gallows, their mass emotion was nearer pity than anger. Again, despite expectations, Ferrers died bravely.[132] But the elite intended his death to be exemplary, and they had the last word. Ferrers's dead body was taken back to the surgeon's hall to be dissected.[133]

The only way elite crime could be dealt with, other than unsatisfactorily through the courts, was by impeachment before Parliament. Usually this procedure was employed in purely political trials, like that of Sacheverell or the defeated Jacobites after the risings of 1715 and 1745. On very rare occasions impeachments were brought for what were, at any rate on the surface, legal offences. Obviously this could happen only when the elite was itself divided. The 1725 trial of the Lord Chancellor was the most famous instance. Thomas, Earl of Macclesfield, was impeached in Westminster Hall for having taken bribes and embezzling public money to the value of £100,000 (about £3,000,000 in contemporary terms). His particular crime was to put Masterships in Chancery up for sale. Macclesfield was found guilty and fined £30,000. Most of this was paid on his behalf by George I; the rest he had no difficulty finding from his ill-gotten gains.[134]

Macclesfield's trial prompts comparison with the near-impeachment of President Nixon in 1974. In both cases what was at issue was not corruption *per se* but corruption in the wrong area. The adjudication of property rights in the Court of Chancery, like the burglary of the Watergate building, went beyond the pale of acceptable sharp practice. More significantly, perhaps, Macclesfield was attached to the wrong political faction and was hated by Walpole.[135] Yet the Macclesfield case brought to a head widespread resentment at the differential treatment of elite crime.

There were two main strands in the journalistic critique of the Macclesfield affair. One centered on the political nature of his impeachment; the other drew attention to the differential treatment meted out to 'high' and 'low' criminals. The Jacobite Duke of Wharton pointed out that if Macclesfield was arraigned for £100,000, how much more urgent was it that Sir Robert Walpole himself should be in the dock? There was a deficit in the Exchequer of £8 millions that had never been accounted for.[136] Other critics pointed out that 1725 had seen two major criminal trials, one of Jonathan Wild, the other of Lord Macclesfield. Wild had been hanged for making an estimated net £25,000 out of an entire criminal career; Macclesfield had merely had fingers wagged at him for making four times as much.[137] This unsavoury comparison underlay much of the subversive humour in Gay's *Beggar's Opera*:

> Since the laws were made for every degree
> To curb vice in others as well as me,
> I wonder we hadn't better company on Tyburn tree!
> And as the law works speedily
> For malefactors worse than me
> 'Tis strange there's not better company
> On Tyburn, on Tyburn tree!
> But gold from law can take the sting,
> And if rich men like us should swing
> 'Twould thin the land such numbers to string
> On Tyburn tree!

Gay's satire was justified: morally speaking there was nothing to choose between the two types of crime. As E. P. Thompson has remarked: 'The 'subculture' of the Hanoverian Whigs and the 'subculture' of Jonathan Wild were mirror images of each other.'[138] The Duke of Wharton returned to the issue of his *bête noire* Walpole and suggested that instead of hanging Wild, the elite should have set him on the trail of the missing eight millions.

In 1725 popular animus against Walpole was still very vehement because of his presumed association with the South Sea Bubble fiasco five years earlier. The South Sea directors had been allowed to get away with bare-faced fraud, and the public knew it. Passions ran very high on this issue. Robert, Viscount Molesworth, thought that the South Sea directors should be declared guilty of parricide by parliamentary fiat. They should then be subjected to the ancient Roman punishment for that crime: to be sewn up in a sack with a monkey and a snake and then drowned.[139]

Even worse was the fact that when the public complained about being defrauded, they were threatened with the Riot Act. As one member of the crowd exclaimed in July 1721: 'You first pick our pockets, then send us to jail for complaining.'[140] A particular target for resentment was Walpole. He was widely suspected of having been bribed in the South Sea scandal, but the bribe did not come to light. His significance was that he was the only senior Whig politician who could not be *proved* to have been bribed. Again, a comparison with the Watergate events throws up interesting parallels. The 'internal coup' whereby Ford replaced Nixon is not unlike the process whereby Walpole came to power. It was necessary for the blame to be put on individuals, not the system. For one thing, the royal mistresses were among those bribed. Walpole's accession to power provided a means of papering over the cracks left by the South Sea fiasco without discrediting the regime itself. A genuine reformer coming to power would turn over too many stones. Walpole's appointment led the Duke of Wharton to enquire why a highwayman should be hanged while the likes of Walpole were applauded for their clandestine depredations.[141]

The South Sea scandal entrenched the popular idea that the only difference between ordinary criminals and elite politicians was the class position they occupied. Gay notably highlighted the situation: 'I cannot but wonder that the talents requisite for a great statesman are so scarce in the world, since so many of those who possess them are every month cut off in the prime of their age at the Old Bailey.'[142] Bernard Mandeville went farther, stating that elite criminals were even more reprehensible, since there were no extenuating circumstances attendant on their crimes. 1720, he wrote, was a year 'prolific in deep villainy and remarkable for selfish crimes and premeditated mischief'. These crimes, he added, were committed not by 'poor ignorant rogues that could neither read nor write' but by 'the better sort of people as to wealth and education . . . great masters in arithmetic, and [who] lived in reputation and splendour'.[143]

Smuggling was a particular target for law enforcement by the elite, yet the aristocracy itself was among the worst offenders against excise laws. The Venetian and French ambassadors were frequent culprits. In 1780 Count Haslang, the Bavarian Minister in London, who had carried on a large-scale tea and coffee smuggling business for forty years, refused permission to the Excise to search his premises. Yet the truth came out shortly afterwards when the Gordon Rioters looted his house.[144] But this sort of thing was not confined to foreign diplomats. Walpole himself used an Admiralty barge to run smuggled wine up the Thames.[145]

The result of this sort of elite corruption was the deepest cynicism among the thinking and talking classes. A spoof advertisement in the 1769 *Middlesex Journal* made the point very well.

Whereas a gang of notorious robbers have for some years past infested the neighbourhood of St James and the Treasury, and have in a daring manner, and in open defiance of the laws of the land, plundered the public of several millions sterling, to the great loss of his majesty's liege subjects; and have lately absconded loaded with their plunder. These are therefore to require all good and well disposed people . . . to apprehend such traitors and robbers and bring them to justice.[146]

It was a short step from such cynicism about the rulers of eighteenth-century England to the proposition that all rulers in all eras were simply legalized criminals. *The Craftsman* in 1732 made the point trenchantly: 'Alexander, Caesar, and most of the great conquerors of old, were not better than Imperial cut-throats or Banditti; who robbed and murdered in gangs, too strong to be opposed, and escaped the gallows, which they deserved, by being above the law.'[147]

It is significant that elite crime was also associated with another great institution of the Glorious Revolution: the East India Company. The so-called 'nabobs' were those who enriched themselves while in the Company's service in India. The other great impeachment of the century was that of Warren Hastings in 1787. His trial at the bar of the House of the Lords began in February 1788 and ended in April 1795 with his acquittal on all charges of high crimes and misdemeanours while in India. He was, however, financially ruined, since the £80,000 of spoils he had brought back from India were entirely consumed in legal expenses. The East India Company partially compensated him with a generous pension.[148]

Hastings was only the most famous of the 'nabobs'. Even more spectacular in his pillaging was Sir Thomas Rumbold, who brought home from India fifteen lakhs of pagodas: each lakh contained 100,000 pagodas and each pagoda was worth eight shillings. Rumbold's total haul amounted to a staggering £600,0000 (roughly £20 million in today's money). In April 1782 Henry Dundas, Lord Advocate of Scotland, introduced two bills into the House of Commons. One sought to prevent Rumbold from leaving the kingdom for a year, pending investigations for extortion; it also ordered an investigation of his estate and instituted measures to stop him transporting or alienating any of his effects. The other was an accusation of high crimes and misdemeanours while Rumbold was governor of Fort St George in India.[149]

Dundas made little headway with either bill. The bill of pains and penalties against Rumbold was held up at every stage on its passage through the Commons. A year later the affair was still hanging fire. In May 1783 Dundas complained of the thin attendance in the chamber whenever the subject of the Rumbold bill was raised.[150] After twelve more Parliamentary sittings in May and June, the bill was again deferred for three months in July 1783.[151] Horace Walpole had scant sympathy for Dundas. His attempt to impeach Rumbold, he thought, was merely the pot calling the kettle black: 'The Lord Advocate of Scotland, who has sold himself over and over, is prosecuting Sir Thomas Rumbold for corruption at Madras!'[152] Walpole had a keen sense of the absurdity of the affair and his animadversions on Dundas's venality were soon proved correct. The Lord Advocate was bribed to be lenient, and his bill was eventually dropped.[153]

There was very high tolerance for 'nabobery' in the eighteenth-century English elite, even though the 'middling sort' detested them as upstarts.[154] Samuel Johnson, however, was prepared to defend them, on two very different grounds. The first, cynical, ground was that the nabob was simply the *reductio ad absurdum* of the regime of money introduced after 1688: 'Why, sir, the nabob will carry it by means of his wealth, in a country where money is highly valued, as it must be where nothing can be had without money.'[155] The other 'refutation' of the nabob as criminal was a primitive version of 'the white man's burden'; one could not apply English standards in India: 'Where bad actions are committed at so great a distance, a delinquent can obscure the evidence till the scent grows cold . . . I am clear that the best plan for the government of India is a despotick governor; for if he be a good man, it is evidently the best government; and supposing him to be a bad man, it is better to have one plunderer than many. A governor whose power is checked lets others plunder that he himself may be allowed to plunder.'[156]

A very different attitude was taken by Johnson's enemy Horace Walpole. In 1785 he contrasted the draconian treatment meted out in France to the Rohan-Guéméné family, following the famous 'Queen's necklace' affair with the leniency habitually extended to the nabobs in England.[157] The sage of Strawberry Hill was beginning to conclude that elite ideology was cant and humbug: 'We talk and write of liberty and plunder the property of the Indies', he wrote to Sir Horace Mann in April 1783 at the height of the Rumbold scandal.[158] There is a delicious irony in the fact that the son of the avatar of corruption, Sir Robert Walpole, was so incensed by the crimes of the powerful, but there is no doubting his indignation. Ten years before, when speaking of a rash of highwaymen in England, he remarked caustically: 'In short all the freebooters that are not in India have taken to the highway.'[159] Such testimony from a crusty 'law and order' oligarch is worth a dozen theses from modern deviance sociologists.

9

High Treason

Treason doth never prosper: what's the reason?
For if it prosper, none dare call it treason.
                              Sir John Harrington, *Epigrams*

Ye towers of Julius, London's lasting shame
With many a foul and midnight murther fed
                              Thomas Gray, *The Bard*

God bless the King, I mean the Faith's Defender,
God bless – no harm in blessing – the Pretender;
But who Pretender is or who is King,
God bless us all – that's quite another thing.
                              John Byrom, *To an Officer in the Army*

The English law relating to high treason was a heterogeneous collection of ancient statutes, dating from the very early days of English monarchy, and specifically post-Revolution (1688) Acts designed to safeguard the Protestant succession. The ancient statutes prescribed a traitor's death for anyone who compassed the death of the king (or his queen and eldest son) or raped his female relatives; for anyone who levied civil war against the king or supported the king's enemies; for anyone who counterfeited the king's great seal or his coinage or who killed his magistrates. To this had been added a series of treasonable offences directed against Catholics after the Reformation.[1]

Yet overwhelmingly in the eighteenth century high treason meant one of two things: coinage offences or crimes against the Protestant succession. In other words, treason was politically directed against the Jacobites. Only in the final decade of the century, when Jacobinism replaced Jacobitism as the mortal threat to the regime, was the political content of high treason significantly redefined.

That the exiled House of Stuart was *the* target for eighteenth-century treason law emerges clearly from the number of statutes enacted after 1688, specifically aimed at the Pretender and his adherents. In 1701, after

156

Louis XIV recognized James II's 13-year-old son James Francis as 'James III' it was declared high treason to correspond or liaise in any way with the Pretender or his agents or to recruit money for his cause. The Pretender himself was declared guilty of treason from the mere fact of his claim to the English throne.[2] The Act of Settlement in the same year ordained that any one opposing the Protestant succession was guilty of high treason.[3] On the outbreak of the War of Spanish Succession another Act laid down that any officer serving outside England by land or sea who corresponded with 'any rebel or enemy' would be guilty of high treason.[4] In 1707 there was a further addition to the list of treasonable offences: the declaration in any form that anyone other than those denoted in the Act of Settlement had a right to the throne, and the denial of the political legitimacy of the King-in-Parliament.[5] This was a double-barrelled broadside at Jacobitism, both because James the Old Pretender was a Catholic and hence debarred by the Act of Settlement, and because the doctrine of the sovereignty of Parliament, making kingship a form of trust, was aimed at the heart of the Jacobite tenet of indefeasible right.

When the Jacobite threat intensified with the coming of age of the 'Young Pretender' (Charles Edward Stuart), the law on treason was tightened to avoid any possible ambiguity. After the French invasion scare of 1744, a new statute was passed which stated that if the sons of the Pretender landed or attempted to land in Great Britain or Ireland or were found anywhere therein, they would be attainted for high treason and suffer the prescribed penalties.[6] Similarly, anyone holding a commission in a rebel army raised by the Pretender would be adjudged traitor.

Since the penalty for high treason was the dreadful one of being hanged, drawn and quartered, these Acts had a particular significance. But the treason laws were merely, as it were, the law's shock troops in the fight against Jacobitism. Below the level of high treason there was another echelon of capital offences directed against the adherents of the House of Stuart. In 1736 it was made a non-clergyable felony to recruit for the French service or to serve in the French army as a soldier.[7] This was directed principally at the crack Irish Brigade – half a dozen regiments formed from Irish Jacobite exiles, the legendary 'Wild Geese'. At the beginning of the Seven Years War, a further act extended the same penalty to *officers* of the said regiments.[8]

The failure of the 1745 Jacobite rising not only brought the century's most spectacular treason trials, but added to the aggregate of capital offences for Jacobitism. In 1747 an attempt was made to close the obvious loophole whereby Jacobite rankers sentenced to transportation simply evaded the punishment by returning from the New World to France or Spain. Henceforth this would carry a mandatory death sentence, which would also be visited on all who helped or corresponded with the returnees.[9]

This battery of anti-Jacobite laws claimed its fair quota of victims. William Gregg was executed for high treason following the abortive attempt at a Jacobite rising in 1708.[10] During the Sacheverell riots Daniel Damaree and George Purchase were promised a traitor's death for heading a pro-Sacheverell mob only to be reprieved at the last minute by the Harley ministry.[11] The failure of the rising of 1715 netted a further crop of 'treasonous' Jacobites.[12] The two star victims were the Earls of Derwentwater and Kenmuir; a third, Lord Nithsdale, was scheduled for execution but made good his escape. The privileges of rank did at least secure for the condemned Jacobite lords the executioner's block rather than Tyburn tree.[13]

The pressure continued after the '15 until the failure of the Layer/Atterbury plot in 1722 convinced the authorities that they had been granted a breathing-space from Jacobite plots. In 1718 James Sheppard was executed on a charge of having tried to kill George I.[14] In 1719 came a treason trial that produced almost universal sympathy for the victim. John Matthews was found guilty of high treason simply for printing a Jacobite pamphlet. Particular indignation was aroused in the general public from the fact that the authorities had used a general warrant to search his premises.[15]

The execution of Christopher Layer in 1723 after the plot sometimes named for him[16] saw the end of political treason trials for a quarter of a century. In 1746-7, after the failure of the most dangerous of all the Jacobite risings, the law of treason seemed in danger of running amok. Under an Act of Attainder in June 1746, the rights of trial were dispensed with. Forty-one named individuals were declared guilty of high treason, their titles were annulled and their properties confiscated. This meant that they could be executed summarily if apprehended.[17] Normally attainder came into being *after* sentence of death for treason had been pronounced following trial. This was made clear by Blackstone:

> When sentence of death, the most terrible and highest judgment in the laws of England, is pronounced, the immediate inseparable consequence by the common law is attainder. For when it is now clear beyond all dispute, that the criminal is no longer fit to live upon the earth, but is to be exterminated as a monster and a bane to human society, the law sets a note of infamy upon him, puts him out of its protection, and takes no further care of him than barely to see him executed. He is then called attaint, *attinctus*, stained or blackened.'[18]

For those who had served in the Jacobite Manchester regiment, it was thought best to conduct a show trial that would terrify all potential rebels by its awesome example. The Englishmen who had volunteered for Charles Edward Stuart's service at Manchester were solemnly paraded through Southwark Courthouse and found guilty on the evidence of a contemporary 'super-grass' Samuel Maddock – a member of the

Manchester regiment who had turned king's evidence to save his own skin. Then the dread sentence of death by hanging, drawing and quartering was pronounced.[19] 1746 saw the 'Bloody Code' at its apotheosis. It also exposed its fundamental absurdity. There could be debate about the efficacy of the Code as a deterrent to general crime (although in fact, as we shall see, the draconian laws on non-clergyable felonies had no deterrent effect whatever). There could be none in the context of treason, the most clearly political of all aspects of the criminal code. By definition, 'political crime' cannot be deterred by the death penalty.[20] As Sir William Meredith pointed out in 1777: 'You might as well bring in a bill to prevent the appearance or regulate the motions of a comet.'[21]

There were also four rebel peers to be tried, and their trial provided the legal spectacle of the century. Lords Balmerino, Cromartie, and Kilmarnock, all Jacobites captured at the time of Culloden, were tried in the House of Lords in July 1746.[22] Lord Lovat, who was taken only later, after a period of hiding in the Highlands, was impeached in the House of Commons in March 1747.[23] All four were found guilty, Lovat on the testimony of Murray of Broughton, the 'Young Pretender's secretary, who also turned king's evidence to save his own life.[24] The 80-year-old Lovat and 58-year-old Balmerino, who claimed the peer's privilege of decapitation rather than hanging, went bravely to their end on the block. Kilmarnock recanted in hopes of a reprieve, but he too was beheaded. Only Cromartie escaped execution, after his wife swooned theatrically at George II's feet.[25]

This was not quite the end of Jacobite immolations, either for treason or the 'lesser' capital offences. Paul Tierney was executed in 1751 for persuading one John May to join the French army. Although the judge had doubts about his guilt, his crime was thought to be of 'national concern'.[26] And in 1753 Dr Archibald Cameron, apprehended in the Highlands when trying to organize the ill-fated and absurd Jacobite 'Elibank Plot', was executed on the original 1747 Act of Attainder.[27] This action, seven years after the Jacobite rising had been decisively crushed, was widely regarded as an act of judicial murder, a characteristic piece of Hanoverian vindictiveness.[28]

Why, it may be asked, did the Whig elite cling so tenaciously to the notion of treason (already somewhat anachronistic)?[29] Why was there such a mortal fear of Jacobitism, if it was true that Jacobitism, far from being a serious threat to the Hanoverian regime, was after 1722 an obsolete, discredited ideology? The answer is, first, that on the contrary, the Jacobite challenge *was* a formidable one right up to the failure of the 1745 rising, and that its enemies were uncomfortably aware of this. Second, it was the only political or social movement that posed a *total* threat to the post-1688 social system.

It was the reality of the fearsome danger to the regime from Jacobitism that arrested all movements towards the abolition of forfeiture as a penalty for treason. The eighteenth-century elite had to put up with a law that showed its own political values to be humbug because of 'the king over the water.' Forfeiture of lands and chattels punished the heirs and descendants of a traitor; but visiting the sins of the father on the sons was widely considered unjust.[30] In 1709 Parliament came close to abolishing the practice. An impassioned speech by Bishop Burnet in the House of Lords made a deep impression when he argued that forfeiture had never been a mark of a free government: 'it was neither just not reasonable to set children to begging for their father's faults."[31] Parliament was within an ace of heeding his advice when the spectre of the exiled Stuarts was pressed into service by exponents of harsh treason laws.

The significance of the Jacobite threat was not only that it challenged a notion of legitimacy that seemed to have a very adventitious, *ad hoc* air about it – the king was whoever Parliament decided was its trustee. Beyond that, it confronted the new order over the entire spectrum of activities newly designated as 'crime' by the Bloody Code. The poacher threatened absolute rights of property, the smuggler threatened commerce, the forger and coiner threatened the new financial regime. Only Jacobitism formed an over-arching system that called in question the legitimacy of the entire capitalist triumph, in all its manifestations, agrarian, commercial and financial. It issued the challenge, moreover, in the name of the still cogent doctrine of divine, indefeasible right – cogent because the new regime could score no convincing ideological victory over it, but instead relied on the smear tactics of black propaganda.[32]

The question of land titles was one of the hidden but profound issues in the opposition to Jacobitism in England.[33] Many of the eighteenth-century Whig families, the Hollises, Pelhams, Russells, (and dozens of other aristocratic families) enjoyed property which had once belonged to the Catholic Church at the time of the Reformation – the so-called 'Abbey lands'. Naturally they were fearful about what might happen to these lands if the Stuarts were restored. There even existed a special law, *praemunire*, second only to high treason itself in gravity, aimed at the Pope and all his works. One of the factors constituting a *praemunire* was 'to molest the possessors of Abbey Lands.'[34]

These fears were largely chimerical. It was already two hundred years since the dissolution of the monasteries, and the 'Abbey lands' had been sold and resold, divided and subdivided many times since. Even if the Jacobites had wanted to restore them, the task would have been impossible. What mattered was not that such fears were irrational but that they existed and could be exploited to make political capital.

Nobody was unaware of the immense significance of the land issue to the outcome of the dynastic struggle between Stuart and Hanoverian. It was said that some Jacobite magnates drew back from outright rebellion in 1715 because of worries on this score.[35] Louis XV's agent James Butler pointed out in 1743 in a report to the French court that Cumberland was a county totally committed to the Hanoverians because former Crown lands had been alienated to the local aristocracy.[36] Great play was made of the issue of 'Abbey lands' during the 1745 rising. That masterly propagandist Henry Fielding devoted a good deal of attention to it in his *Serious Address*.[37] Horace Walpole remarked to Sir Horace Mann in September 1745 that, with the Young Pretender already in Scotland, priests would already have set out from Rome in expectation of repossessing the 'Abbey lands'.[38] Such was the emphasis placed on this issue that Charles Edward Stuart himself wrote from Perth in September 1745 expressing great indignation that the Whigs should have attempted to smear him by imputing to him the purpose of restoration of Church lands.[39]

The Jacobites themselves were well aware of their vulnerability to hostile propaganda on this issue. They realized that even if they could overcome the Byzantine complexities involved in restoration, they would simply cause hardship and suffering to hundreds of powerful families and thus drive them into eventual revolt. Yet the fear that these fertile lands, about one-third of all the real estate in England, might one day be restored, had always been the economic base on which the ideological superstructure of 'antipopery' had been built. To get round this, James's advisers put it to him in 1724 that he should obtain a decree from the Pope, in which the Catholic Church renounced all claim to these lands.[40] The advice was never acted on, for a number of reasons. James felt that such a disclaimer would harden rather than weaken the opposition to Jacobitism in England, as it would be construed as a preemptive bid to win hearts and minds, prior to a Jacobite invasion. Others raised the possibility of later popes annulling such a decree. William Shippen the English Jacobite objected that if James obtained such a decree, he would make himself seem more, not less, of a Papal poodle; he would appear to be a man who did no more and no less than what the Pope ordered him to do. The issue was left in limbo, to provide wonderful propaganda for the Whigs.

The Jacobites were even more vulnerable on the score of the national debt. It was an abiding canard in anti-Jacobite propaganda that if restored, the Stuarts would attempt to dismantle the post-1688 economic system. The enemies of the House of Stuart had ingeniously linked the fortunes of the Protestant succession with the national debt. They argued that to oust the Hanoverian dynasty was not just a matter of revoking the Act of Settlement (which could in principle be done by Parliament); it was to bring ruin on thousands, since the national debt stood or fell with with the Protestant succession. Quite apart from the problems this would cause with traditional allies like the Dutch (who were major debt bondholders), cancellation of the national debt would mean destroying wealth; the author of the 1745 *Calm Address* argued that the Debt was an interest-bearing form of wealth which the public owned.[41]

In a proclamation dated 10 October 1745, uttered in Edinburgh, Charles Edward Stuart gave the most explicit Stuart statement on the national debt:

> That it has been contracted under an unlawful government, nobody can disown, no more than that it is now a most heavy load upon the Nation; yet in regard that it is for the greatest part due to those very subjects whom he promises to protect, cherish and defend, he is resolved to take the advice of his Parliament concerning it.[42]

That was the nub of the matter. By increasing the number of bondholders battening off the national debt, the post-1688 elite had co-opted them into the new political and dynastic system. The countervailing lever the Jacobites had to play on was the interest of the gentry, who had to pay the land-tax to service the debt. Jacobite propaganda concentrated on the increasing load of tax that had to be paid for this purpose. The crushing burden of taxation adversely affected agricultural production, made English trade goods dearer and thus enabled England's rivals to undercut her in world markets. For this reason many of James's advisers counselled him to repudiate the debt altogether. Mere cancellation with compensation to debt-holders was too onerous.[43]

It was estimated in the early 1730s that if James Stuart was restored and wished to liquidate the national debt, he would have to raise £3,000,000 a year in compensation. At the same time he would have to raise £1,500,000 yearly to pay for the army and foreign mercenaries and another £500,000 for the civil list and to maintain foreign diplomatic representation. A Stuart monarch would then be faced with the option of cutting down the latter expenses and thus losing popularity fast or repudiating the debt. The hardliners among James's counsellors advised him that squeamishness over repudiation would cost him dear. The bondholders he repaid would merely use the money to conspire against him. Besides, Jacobites had been deprived of the fruits of their estates since 1688; it was time for the Whigs to suffer for their beliefs.[44]

Meanwhile, a very shrewd move would be to win over the landed classes to the Stuarts by making an outright gift of those entailed estates that came into the hands of certain great families in the reigns of Edward VI and Elizabeth I. Many noble families without a male heir lost estates worth £20,000 a year when the entailed estates reverted to the Crown. Such a gesture would turn the tables on the propagandists of 'Abbey lands' and conciliate sectors of the aristocracy.[45] With an alliance of non-bondholding gentry and aristocracy the way would be clear for repudiation of the national debt. It can be seen, then, that on this issue there was some foundation to Whig economic fears.

The final economic fear entertained about the Jacobites was that in return for having their king restored, they would make unacceptable trade concessions to France and thus hand victory in the global struggle for commercial hegemony to the French. France had its eyes particularly on the *asiento* concession to trade in Spanish America granted by England to Spain in the 1713 Treaty of Utrecht. In return for helping the Stuarts back on to the throne of England, France would first of all demand the renegotiation of this treaty. Then she would demand the repeal of the import duties on French wines and other goods and the recognition of her paramountcy in Canada. Spain meanwhile would wrest from the Stuarts as a *quid pro quo* for its diplomatic and financial support the fortresses of Gibraltar and Port Mahon in Minorca. This allegation that the Stuarts were bound to France by ties of gratitude that overrode the English national interest caused particular bitterness during the 1746 treason trials.[46] But, as the French themselves saw, the idea of such concessions being made to them by the restored Stuarts was a mere pipe-dream.[47]

Only in the context of the national debt, then, did English fears (and thus Whig propaganda) about the Jacobites have any solid foundation. What mattered was not that the Jacobites actually intended to restore Church lands or hand over global commercial supremacy to France, but that they were widely *perceived* to have such intentions. There was undoubtedly widespread fear that in the event of the return of the Stuarts to the English throne, many (possibly even a majority) of the great post-1688 fortunes would be annihilated. This accounts for the peculiar animosity towards the Jacobites at the 1746 treason trials. The savagery of the punishment meted out shows the fear the elite had lived with during the rising. It also demonstrates why the law on treason was a living force in the first half of the eighteenth century. The object of eighteenth-century punishment was always at bottom the safeguarding of property. Highwaymen and smugglers were parasitic on the system and could be held in check by the occasional outburst of ferocity. But an ideology that seemed to threaten the very notion of private property itself required the implementation of the ultimate resources of the Bloody Code.

It is a world away from the arena of high politics to the other context in which the eighteenth-century law of high treason was exercised. Even to contemporaries it seemed palpably absurd that the same awful majesty of the law and the same bloodcurdling punishments should be invoked for political crimes like Jacobitism, which really did pose a threat to the security of the regime, *and* for the comparatively trivial offence of tampering with coinage. Yet to coin or clip the current English gold and silver coin or to possess tools for that purpose were high treason, just as much as rising in rebellion for the Pretender.[48] The absurdity was heightened at the margin. A rebel lord like Cromartie could win a reprieve and escape the axe, while a poor serving maid who coloured a farthing to make it look like sixpence or a shilling would go to a traitor's death.[49]

Absurd or not, the law that regarded coining as treason was taken very seriously indeed in the eighteenth century. So far from amending the ancient statutes that made these offences treasonable, the proponents on the Bloody Code added to them. An Act of 1697, made permanent in 1708, declared it to be high treason to counterfeit the coin of the kingdom with similar letters, marks or figures to those used by the Mint.[50] Another Act in 1742 made it treasonable to make shillings and sixpences resemble guineas or half-guineas, or to make half-pennies or farthings resemble shillings or sixpences.[51] Conviction on a coinage offence (counterfeiting gold and silver coins, diminishing them or possessing appropriate coining tools) was virtually a sentence of death. For this reason there was a distinct reluctance by jurors to convict on coining offences unless overwhelming evidence was presented.

Counterfeiters abounded in London, but there were some very successful coiners operating in the provinces also; a number of illegal mints were reported in Birmingham in 1744. Naturally the coiners' activities focused on the more valuable coins. Forgers of illegal gold coins were the most harshly treated. There was no public tolerance at all for them (hardly surprising considering the loss to be taken). In 1733, when the old worn 'broad pieces' were being bought up for recoinage, it was made high treason to manufacture copies of them.[52]

Until 1771 counterfeiting of coinage meant abuse of gold and silver coins. Penalties for striking coins of lesser value were correspondingly less severe. This was just as well, for it was comparatively easy for coiners to counterfeit shapeless, worn or defaced silver coins. Before 1771, when the offence was raised to felony status, counterfeiting of copper was a misdemeamour only, carrying a penalty of two years imprisonment.[53] One consequence was that in the 1750s half the copper in circulation in England was said to be of false coin.[54] The forgery of copper was seasonal and largely suspended during harvests or hop-picking. It was also an activity commonly associated with the Irish. When figures for prosecutions became available after 1786 it was found that counterfeiting increased in times of depression and decreased during a boom.[55]

To produce bogus gold and silver coins required the considerable skill of mixing base metals to make an intrinsically worthless imitation, and the necessary equipment, especially melting pots and crucibles.[56] Another technique was to plate low denomination coin with a chemical wash.[57] In addition, the successful counterfeiter needed specialized, heavily capitalized premises at which to carry on the trade. The risks of detection and prosecution were considerable.

Actually to clip a coin, however, involved no more than cutting a thin sliver of gold from the edge of a guinea, restoring the milling with a file, then returning the diminished coin into circulation. The rule of thumb was to remove about two shillings' worth of gold from the guinea. Anyone possessing a special pair of scissors could clip; the important thing was to find an entrepreneur who would buy the clippings for reabsorption into a counterfeited coin.[58]

It was the coiner who provided the specialized service. Coining usually involved one of three processes: the production of fake gold and silver coins from base metals; the production of a new diminished guinea from gold clippings; or the overstamping of coins.[59] The most popular such process was to heat up guineas, half and quarter guineas, and overstamp them with the die of a *moidore* (or half or quarter *moidore* respectively), thus increasing their face value by 30 per cent. Overstamping guineas could, in principle, be carried out in any house with a fire. The most damning evidence against counterfeiters was to show that they had dies, anvils, or hammers in their possession for this purpose.[60]

The most famous individual eighteenth-century counterfeiter – as distinguished in his field as Jonathan Wild had been in receiving and thieftaking – was Thomas Lightowller. Lightowller is a fascinating example of the kind of highly talented individual a rigidly stratified society, based on corruption and patronage and dedicated to the hereditary rather than the meritocratic principle, will marginalize and force into crime. An undoubted mechanical genius – and later recognized as such by Maria Theresa of Austria – Lightowller used his outstanding skills as metalworker to establish a chain of coining workshops in Britain during the middle decades of the eighteenth century. He produced counterfeits of gold and silver coins from mixed or base metals in shops in South Wales, the West Midlands, Lancashire, Yorkshire, and the Isle of Wight. His operations came to an end in 1756 when he was tried on two counts of high treason. At Lancaster the jury pronounced him not guilty despite the most damning evidence; at Coventry he was discharged without prosecution.[61]

Apart from actual counterfeiting of coinage, the other main offence was 'clipping', cutting, or filing of a small quantity of gold from the edge of a guinea. The accumulated filings could then be melted down and reconstituted. There was much greater public tolerance for coin clipping than outright counterfeiting, since inept government financial policy meant that most gold coins were already seriously under their official weight simply after the wear and tear of being in circulation for a century.[62]

It was a supreme irony that the regime of money ushered in after 1688 employed a coinage that was defective both in quality and availability.

The lack of an international monetary system meant that silver was overvalued in England relative to its continental neighbours. Where it might take fifteen units of silver to redeem one unit of gold in England, the same gold could be purchased for fourteen units or less in Europe. Not surprisingly, the great financial institutions tended to export their silver bullion. What remained in circulation in England was an old, worn and underweight silver coinage. There was also an acute shortage of gold coin, only partially mitigated by the influx of *moidores*, tiny Portugese gold coins, which were imported to England in 1700-60 in settlement of England's massive trade surplus with Portugal. The reasons for this currency crisis were various: hidebound, dogmatic monetary and fiscal policies; a morbid fear of inflation; and the greed and incompetence of those who held sinecures at the Mint, which was the sole institution capable of providing a sound gold and silver coinage.[63]

The incompetence of the financial authorities provided counterfeiters and clippers with an arsenal of plausible excuses and justifications for their activities. They claimed that far from being 'traitorous', they did no harm and, arguably, a lot of good to society, since in increasing their own income, they created further employment and income in turn. Moreover, they claimed only to have come into existence in the first place as a result of the shortage of coin, which was the fault of the authorities. In any case, they argued, past governments had themselves practised deliberate debasement of the coinage to increase the income of the sovereign. So far from producing inflation, such tinkering with the coinage had merely a deflationary effect: there was augmented unemployment but no increase in prices. Above all, the mere fact that governments were prepared to tackle the problem piecemeal in this way meant that they were being pharisaical for punishing individuals who did so.

These arguments had a powerful effect on juries, who showed themselves markedly sympathetic to those accused of coinage offences. Since juries were composed of freeholders, farmers, tradesmen and manufacturers who knew all about the inconveniences of an inadequate legitimate coinage, they were likely to find much merit in the argument that it was the incompetence of the sinecurists of the Mint monopoly that had caused the root problem in the first place. This inference is strengthened when one considers that the law officers of the Crown allowed coining prosecutions to proceed only when they were thought certain to succeed. Yet for all that, the top rate of convictions in such cases was only some 60 per cent.[64] Quite apart from a natural reluctance to convict in cases of high treason, where the prescribed penalties were so awesome, capital coinage cases tapped into a deep reservoir of resentment among jurors over the general management of the currency. There were several instances of juries finding those accused of coining not guilty against the evidence, and of judges losing their temper with jurors.

In one 1746 trial of a serving maid at the Old Bailey, the judge antagonised the jury by losing his temper with the maid's mistress and saying he wished he could hang her. The jury responded to this outburst of petulance by immediately bringing in a 'not guilty' verdict.[65]

The underswell of general antagonism to the authorities in coinage cases was added to when local folkways and mores sanctioned coining as part of a legitimate local culture. This was notoriously the case with the Yorkshire coiners of the 1760s and early 1770s, where a local mafia defied the forces of law and order in the name of cultural autonomy.[66] This case bears close examination, not least because it is often cited as a prime example of 'social crime'.[67]

The precondition for the explosion of counterfeiting in the West Riding of Yorkshire and the nearby areas of Lancashire in the 1760s was the acute cash shortage in the country in general, as gold bullion prices continued to keep well ahead of the Mint's price for gold. The particular precipitant in the West Riding was the steep decline of the woollen industry, centred on Halifax but extending from Rochdale east to Leeds and Wakefield, and from Huddersfield north to Skipton. After a boom during the Seven Years War, post-war recession, especially in the crucial North American market, bit deep. Whitehall's efforts to force the American colonists back into the mercantilist fold merely exacerbated the misery of the West Riding.[68]

In these circumstances arose the 'yellow trade' – a combination of clipping and coining. The rise of this counterfeiting epidemic was as sudden as the slump that engendered it. Gold clippings were remanufactured into counterfeit *moidores* and other gold coins. Guineas were recirculated that were 25 per cent deficient. This illegal trade and its products were widely and openly supported in the 'coining heartland' (between Halifax and Rochdale). People were prepared to accept greatly diminished and counterfeit coin as the sole means to conduct business in face of the dire local shortage of specie. The coining itself was regarded locally as being every bit as legitimate as the stricken textile trade.[69]

The activities of the Yorkshire coiners differed from that of great individual showmen like Lightowller both in degree and kind. Lightowller was out to line his own pocket and used base metals to counterfeit silver and gold coins. His artefacts were accepted unknowingly by a general public. The Yorkshire coiners manufactured their counterfeits, not from base metals but from gold itself. They drew a clear distinction between their own activities and those of the base- or mixed-metal counterfeiters. There was no question of deception. The local population accepted and circulated the counterfeits since the acute shortage of legal currency left them no realistic alternative. They also made extra money by selling clippings directly to the 'yellow piecemakers'. Since they were paid in clipped or counterfeit coin, the circulation and acceptability of the 'queer' was thereby enhanced. Like smuggling, from which it differed by being more localized and shorter-lived, the Yorkshire coining was a kind of *reductio ad absurdum* of official government financial policy, which because of its absurdity and widely perceived injustice simply produced a backlash in the form of 'social crime'.

Yet the conceptual limitations of regarding the Yorkshire coiners as 'primitive rebels' *philosophically* speaking (as opposed to sociologically) comes through clearly when we realize that this activity too produced its 'great men'. Paradoxically, the heroes of Yorkshire coining, the allegedly 'social criminals', were more clearly mere entrepreneurs than was Lightowller, who self-confessedly worked for his own profit. David Hartley, alias 'King David', the most famous of the Yorkshire coiners, was a businessman pure and simple; he had none of Lightowller's technical genius. Hartley stood at the apex of a pyramid of coining establishments in the West Riding. In his organization, the mark of one's status and position in the hierarchy depended on how many coining shops, and how many facilities in each, one was empowered to use according to the rules of the association.[70]

For a long time, massive public support in the West Riding meant that the coiners pursued their activities with impunity. No law can ever be enforced effectively or for long if it does not enjoy the consent of the governed. The people of the West Riding perceived their livelihoods to be bound up with the yellow trade and resisted all attempts by the authorities to curtail it. Magistrates and constables were marginalized and, where necessary, intimidated if they tried to intervene. Yet in 1769 the backlash came, largely under the impetus of those large-scale worsted manufacturers who had to sustain lines of credit outside the West Riding. The attempts, from 1769 to 1773, to curb the yellow trade led to some of the most serious confrontations of the century between the central government and local Mafias.[71]

It was the energy of William Deighton, supervisor of the Halifax excise district from 1759 to 1769, that brought matters to a head. He hired informers to infiltrate the yellow trade. Their intelligence, plus that obtained by the private police employed in Bradford (outside the 'coining heartland') by the worsted manufacturers netted four suspects, committed to York castle in autumn 1769 to face trial. Having inserted this entering wedge, Deighton tried to prise open the coining organization by offering large-scale rewards and pardons to break down the customary wall of silence in the West Riding. In October 1769 Deighton secured his greatest coup. One of his long-time informers finally summoned up the courage, after a *douceur* of £100 from Deighton, to inform against 'King David' himself. Hartley was arrested and taken to York Castle, charged with clipping.[72]

It was now that the Yorkshire coiners revealed that they were quite unlike the London footpad gangs and nearer in nature to the modern Mafia. Instead of wilting under Deighton's inroads, they girded themselves for counterattack. After their browbeating of Deighton's witness to change his evidence had failed to get the York magistrates to release 'King David', they decided on a grimmer solution. A contract of £100 was put out for Deighton's assassination. Two weavers, Matthew Normanton and Robert Thomas, accepted the commission . They waylaid Deighton at 1 a.m. on the morning of 10 November 1769 and shot him dead.[73]

'King David's' men had hoped to cow the opposition with this bloody demonstration of their local power. But they succeeded only in waking the sleeping tiger. The elite in London was prepared to turn a blind eye to local malpractices and to terrify by the occasional sanguinary example. What they would never tolerate was a direct threat to their credibility. The entire ideological superstructure of deference, status, power, and authority that provided the social cement in eighteenth-century England was challenged if organized criminals could be seen to murder an exciseman and get away with it.[74] Indeed the murder of Deighton was the most self-destructive act the Yorkshire coiners could have committed.

In London the Secretary of State authorized a royal proclamation of a pardon and £100 reward to anyone who would discover the murderers. Deighton's original informer, James Broadbent, who knew all the secrets of the yellow trade, incriminated the two murderers and another man who was innocent. The three, plus Broadbent, were whisked away to the safety of York Castle. Meanwhile Whitehall gave the Marquis of Rockingham, lord lieutenant and *custos rotulorum* of the West Riding, discretionary powers, including the right to summon troops in order to deal with any public manifestation in support of the arrested men. Rockingham rightly declined the offer of troops, convinced that the credibility of the civil authorities was in jeopardy if they could not deal with this case without the aid of the military. But he and the magistrates in the West Riding combined to put on a theatrical show of strength and pomp in Halifax just before the coining trials, to convince the population that he and London meant business.[75]

At the 1770 Yorkshire Lent Assizes 'King David' and two other luminaries of Yorkshire coining were convicted, then executed near York in April. The three men charged with Deighton's murder were indicted in August and acquitted. Local solidarity manifested itself in another conspiracy of silence. Although the authorities knew well enough that two of the men were the actual murderers, they could not obtain unimpeachable proof.[76]

This failure led to a change of tack by the campaigners against the yellow trade. The fact that 'King David's' execution had not broken the back of the trade, but seemed rather to have stiffened local resistance, led the authorities to lose confidence in their ability to crush coining activities by a calculated show of terror and the draconian implementation of the ferocious coining laws. They were forced into the one measure they had always shrunk from: reform of the coinage.[77] In 1773 a statute was enacted 'for the better preventing of the counterfeiting, clipping and other diminishing of the gold coin in the kingdom'.[78]

The 1773 Act, followed by two others in 1774 and 1776, brought the standard of gold in coins in circulation into line with weights and values established at the Mint.[79] All coins deficient in value by more than 2d were withdrawn from circulation and recoined. Over four years gold coin valued at over £16.5 millions suffered this fate. It now became the universal practice to weigh all gold coins before accepting them. Since few coins in Yorkshire came up to the new mark, and thus would be rejected in trading and dealing, the effect of this reform of the coinage was to kill off the yellow trade at a stroke.

The death of the Yorkshire coining trade returned the West Riding to its former condition of economic depression. The local rate of burglaries, thefts, and robberies soared. With local resistance destroyed, the authorities were able to return to the festering sore of the two murderers of Deighton who had escaped justice. In 1774 Normanton and Thomas were convicted on the lesser charge of having robbed Deighton's body after the murder. They were executed publicly at Tyburn near York. To give expression to the frustration in having failed to convict them in 1770 and to serve as an awful warning, the judge ordered the two men's bodies to be hung in chains.[80]

The 1773 recoinage did not, of course, end all coining, either in the West Riding or elsewhere. Many of the yellow traders simply switched from making coins from clippings to the older style of counterfeiting from mixed and base metals. Moreover, the incidence of capital coining offences had been artificially increased even as the 1773 Act destroyed the yellow trade in Yorkshire. An Act of 1771 made counterfeiting copper a felony. Capital punishment had never deterred the coiners of gold, yet the moment recoinage cut the ground from under them, it reintroduced a new source of fodder for Tyburn by making counterfeiting of copper a non-clergyable felony.[81]

Coining offences brought together a heterogeneous collection of people, 'traitorous money makers', people just as guilty of high treason as Jacobites in the official view on one hand, potential 'social criminals' in the view of some twentieth-century historians on the other. Both perceptions are distorted. Quite apart from the magnates like 'King David', the Yorkshire coiners involved in the yellow trade in the 1760s and early 1770s were very different from the poachers and smugglers to whom they have sometimes been compared. The yellow trade lasted no more than fifteen years; it was a localized short-term response to a peculiar set of non-recurrent circumstances. The people of the West Riding did not attempt to legitimate their activities by appealing to ancient custom or prescriptive rights. They had no particular hostility to coinage laws as such but only to the financial position in which the West Riding found itself at the beginning of the 1760s. Nor did the yellow trade co-opt all classes as, for example, smuggling did. The working man, at the bottom of the social pile, and the big manufacturer at the top, were largely exempted from its benefits. Yorkshire coining as an organized illegal activity was overwhelmingly the province of the small local capitalist, the 'middling sort'.[82] The Yorkshire coiners were the unique product of a particular historical conjuncture; it is stretching the evidence to read any ulterior significance into them.

Ironically enough, the conjunction of 'high treason' and genuine 'social crime' did sometimes occur, as when bills of high treason were found against two Gloucestershire colliers for riot in 1753.[83] This was one of the few occasions before the 1790s when the treason laws were used for purposes other than combatting Jacobites or coiners. After 1790, of course, with the rise of the Jacobins and the threat from Revolutionary France, high treason made a roaring comeback (see chapter 17).

By the 1770s, as Enlightenment ideas began to make increasing inroads on English consciousness, the exaggerated character of the laws against treason and the ferocious penalties ordained led many to clamour for substantial reforms. Blackstone pointed out that the very wide spectrum of offences to which treason applied simply increased the element of judicial discretion and to that extent weakened the law by making it appear uncertain.[84] William Eden advocated making the law of treason more rational by using it as an ultimate deterrent for high political crimes and excluding from it the lesser matters that were out of place under such a rubric: the killing of magistrates, offences against religion, and coinage offences.[85] Montesquieu argued that to include coinage offences in the same category as political offences was itself to 'debase the coinage', as such a conflation removed the flavour of particular horror that should be associated with the idea of high treason.[86] Yet here, as elsewhere, the champions of the Bloody Code held firm against reform. The treason laws were used in a particularly savage way against three Derbyshire peasants as late as 1817.[87] And to this very day the law of treason remains on the English statute book.

10

Smuggling

England, where men and the sea interpenetrate, so to speak
– the sea entering into the life of most men, and the men
knowing something or everything about the sea.

Joseph Conrad, *Youth*

The slavery of the tea and coffee and other slop-kettle
William Cobbett, *Advice to Young Men*

But the ae best dance e'er cam to our lan,
Was- the De'il's awa wi' the Exciseman.
Robert Burns, *The De'il's awa wi' the Exciseman*

The years from 1713 to 1775 were the classic era of the smuggler in
English history. Out of a population of eight millions, some 20,000 people
were said to be engaged full-time in smuggling.[1] The contraband trade
never dies, if only, as one student of crime has remarked, because where
the danger of being found out is not great, the number of transgressions is
bound to be large.[2] But there were particular reasons why the 'industry'
was so thriving in the eighteenth century. High rates of duty on imports
and exports plus a host of bureaucratic controls produced a smuggling
epidemic.

Eighteenth-century fiscal policy was largely self-defeating. As Adam
Smith observed, because of contraband, high levels of taxation invariably
generated less revenue for the government than moderate ones.[3] Staunch
pillars of the squirearchy like Horace Walpole constantly lamented that
the smuggler was above the law.[4] But Adam Smith thought that this kind
of hand-wringing was humbug. For him, a smuggler was

a person who, though no doubt highly blameable for violating the laws
of his country, is frequently incapable of violating those of natural
justice, and would have been, in every respect, an excellent citizen had
not the laws of his country made that a crime which nature never meant
to be so.

172

Smith was scornful of those who took a high moral tone on contraband:

> To pretend to have any scruple about buying smuggled goods would in most countries be regarded as one of those pedantic pieces of hypocrisy which, instead of gaining credit with anybody, serve only to expose the person who affects to practice them to being a greater knave than most of his neighbours.[5]

In eighteenth-century England a distinction was usually drawn between smuggling proper, the *import* of goods while evading the duty payable, and 'owling' or the export of items (principally wool) without payment of duties. Following modern usage, however, we shall use the term 'smuggling' to apply to both activities. But it is true that smuggling in the old sense was far the most important aspect of contraband criminality. It is also true, as might be expected, that this smuggling overwhelmingly centred on London. Well over half the brandy, gin, tobacco, tea, coffee, silks, and linens imported illegally went to the capital. Tea landed in Yorkshire, spirits brought ashore in Cornwall, tobacco and silks unloaded at Bristol and Liverpool, all made their way to the monster city. The roads to London were spangled with dumps of smuggled goods. The smugglers used pits, haystacks, barns, and (especially) woods. Most notorious of all 'dumps' was the Fleet prison, since this was where convicted smugglers were mainly lodged. Once it was suspected that contraband was being concealed in the Fleet, excisemen accompanied by troops made several visits there. All the forays were fruitless: either the inmates beat off the intruders with stones and missiles, or the warden and turnkeys colluded in the concealment of the merchandise in return for a 'whack'.[6]

If London was the smuggler's Mecca, the domain of his operations took in the entire sea-coast of Great Britain. The sheer amount of coastline, with its jagged inlets, winding creeks, sheltered coves, and hidden caves, made effective control of smuggling impossible. Government policy concentrated on seizures and deterrent punishments rather than interception. The exemplary punishment of the Code, elsewhere embraced by the elite by choice, was here accepted as a necessity. Only those regions close to London or to regular Royal Navy patrols went in any fear of the authorities. Seizures were unheard of in Cornwall and Devon. As the century progressed, the West Country became more and more out of control. It was said that if all the goods smuggled at Falmouth in a single year had paid their dues, the Crown would have collected more than twice the annual land-tax for the entire kingdom.[7]

The struggle between smugglers and authorities can thus be presented in shorthand form as an ever widening net being thrown out from London to ensnare the initiators of contraband. The conflict with the Sussex smugglers reached its height in the late 1740s (see below p. 186) In the

1730s smugglers had virtually complete control of the East Anglian coast. Yet by 1749-50 government pressure had led the Suffolk smuggling gangs to diversify into armed robbery to sustain themselves.[8] As a consequence, the contraband boom shifted farther north. Hull, Bridlington, and Cleveland became new centres.

By 1775 cutters in the customs service made severe inroads into the smuggling nests between Falmouth and Plymouth. The large-scale smugglers moved farther west, to Mount's Bay. But on the north Cornwall coast, especially around Newquay, it was still open season for contraband. The smugglers' organization was much tighter in the far west. Whereas in Kent and Sussex, the actual smuggling operation was one thing and the distribution of smuggled goods (carried out by middlemen) another, in Cornwall there was complete 'integration' in the process: the smugglers owned the boats, brought in the cargoes, and then distributed them.[9] This made it harder for the authorities to crack the illicit activity by exploiting divisions among the various criminal groups. Arguably, it was Methodism that did most to break up the Cornish contraband gangs. After 1750 Wesley's preaching began to make a distinct impact on Cornwall, even though his moral prescriptions struck at the roots of the local economy by outlawing both smuggling and wrecking. Although smugglers began by stoning his meetings, they soon had to acknowledge that the mass conversions to Methodism made their position precarious.[10]

Because of the peculiarity of their relationship to the United Kingdom, the Isle of Man and the Channel Islands posed particular problems for customs and excise officers. The fiscal rights of the Isle of Man were held by the Duke of Atholl until 1765, when the English government purchased them. But until 1765 the Manx island, with its sheltering inlets, was a paradise for smugglers. There wsas a thriving re-export trade in tobacco from Liverpool, Whitehaven, and Glasgow, ostensibly bound for the Continent.[11] Another ploy was to get the plantation shipments for Bristol, Liverpool, Lancaster, and Whitehaven to call at Man first, where cargoes for shipment to Europe would be clandestinely unloaded. Brandy, tea, and silk were imported in foreign ships from France, Holland, and Scandinavia. Rum was brought in directly from the Americas, and sugar and spices from India. It was estimated that a single smuggling vessel from the Isle of Man would carry 12,000 gallons of brandy.[12]

Manxmen were well aware that their prosperity came from contraband and fiercely resisted any attempt to impede the trade. An incident in 1750 is instructive. Captain George Dow, commanding the revenue cruiser *Sincerity* found himself opposed by the entire island, including the governor, when he tried to seize a Dutch ship carrying contraband. Dow overhauled the Dutchman off the island only to find himself staring into the muskets of 150 Manxmen when he opened the hatches to reveal the contraband. Gow and his men were taken to the island as prisoners and released only when he made full restitution of all seized goods. To add salt to the wound of their contempt, Manxmen were fond of drinking the health of the Pretender even as Jacobitism was declared extinct in Britain.[13]

For many years the English government tried to staunch the fiscal haemorrhage through the Isle of Man. They made their first attempt to purchase the fiscal rights in the island from the Earl of Derby in 1725. Niggardliness proved the government's undoing, and in 1736 the rights passed to the Duke of Atholl through his wife, a Stanley. After Gow and other captains had reported the real dangers to any revenue cutter visiting Manx waters, the English authorities started to make more determined efforts at purchase. The negotiations dragged on. In desperation some proposed that the example of Wesley in Cornwall be followed. The Companies of Drapers and Clothworkers proposed a grant for translating the Bible into Manx.[14] But before this project could come to fruition, the government had finally bitten the bullet and purchased the rights to the Isle of Man for £70,000. That was the end of an era. Smuggling on Man came to a halt as if by magic. But there was a price to pay. Not until the present century did the island recover from the economic depression caused by the passing of smuggling.

Another great contraband centre, which could not be choked off by a payment of £70,000, was the Channel Islands, especially Guernsey. While the Kent and Sussex coasts were convenient for cross-channel dashes to French and Flemish ports (especially Dunkirk and Ostend), Jersey and Guernsey provided safer sanctuaries for the loading of wines and brandy, the repacking of tobacco, or the preparation of Continental goods for landing.[15] Everyone who lived on Guernsey in the eighteenth century was in some way connected with smuggling. In 1798 contraband goods emanating from the Channel Islands that were seized in provincial English harbours amounted to £124,351 in value. Since an estimated nine out of ten cargoes escaped seizure, it is clear that the 'traders' of Guernsey and the other islands were depriving the Crown of well over £1 million in revenue each year.[16]

Although Guernsey was the pack leader, the other islands were not wanting in commitment to illicit trading. All 250 families in Alderney manufactured kegs for spirits. The governor actually demanded compensation from the London government for the cost of eliminating smuggling. When the Lord of Sark was asked his terms for co-operation with the English authorities, he cited the costly precedent of the Duke of Atholl and the Isle of Man. No further feelers were put out to him. Smuggling reached new heights during the Revolutionary and Napoleonic wars. It was ended after 1815 only when a draconian tightening-up by London led to mass emigration. But, unlike on Man, the problem on the Channel Islands was never completely eliminated, even in the nineteenth century.

An incident in 1764 provides some of the flavour of Channel Islands smuggling. A revenue cutter, the *Laurel*, caught a smuggling lugger as it came out of Guernsey harbour. Excisemen boarded the cutter but were fiercely repelled and thrown overboard. After great difficulties these struggling men were rescued by a boat lowered from another revenue cutter. Both ships then crowded on sail and pursued the smugglers. This time the two crews managed to overhaul and overpower the smugglers. Alas for their efforts, when the *Laurel* docked at Weymouth in bad weather, every single one of her captives escaped.[17]

It was only in the 'tight little, right little island' that the authorities had any hope of keeping smuggling within some limits. Smuggling was abetted by local elites and mafias throughout Wales, especially in Aberystwyth, Milford Haven, and Swansea. Ireland was a virtual free-trade zone. The slender customs resources here produced a situation of utter farce, where heavily outnumbered revenue cutters went through the motions of deterring the export of contraband wool in activities more redolent of Ealing comedy than serious policing. In return for its huge illicit wool trade with France. Ireland received from the French brandy, wine, tea, and silks.

In Scotland smuggling was a more serious affair. The proximity of the Isle of Man and the Jacobite sentiment of many of its people provided both motive and opportunity to tweak the noses of the hated English. North of the border English customs law was especially detested. The defiance of the authorities by smugglers was regarded as heroic and became conflated with Jacobitism and Scottish nationalism. But what was comedy in Ireland was altogether more sombre in Scotland. It was the arrest of a smuggler that led to the long bloody sequence of the Porteous riots in 1736.[18]

This brings us to one of the most interesting questions about smugglers in the first half of the eighteenth century. How far were they motivated by Jacobite sentiment, and how far was Jacobitism merely a cloak to legitimate activities that would probably have been declared illegal whatever the regime? The main thrust of the Jacobite case, as we have already seen, is that taxes were high because of the burden of the national debt. It was possible to argue, then, that with no debt-holders to service, there would be moderate taxation and hence, as Adam Smith postulated, little smuggling.

There were good objective grounds, then, for the loyalty to the exiled Stuarts that many smugglers professed. Historians have generally been very quick to assert that manifestations of popular Jacobitism by the criminal classes must always have been spurious, but there is much evidence that the relationship was more 'organic' than has usually been supposed. For example, it has been demonstrated that some of the Waltham Blacks had strong Jacobite connections. So did some of the 'owlers'. In at least some cases, 'Blacks', 'owlers', and Jacobites were one and the same.[19] It is also possible that the Irish Jacobite Comte de Lally was the mastermind behind the famous raid on Poole custom-house (see below (p. 187).

Furthermore, the exiled Jacobites retained regular contacts with smugglers.[20] Since many of the exiles specialized in privateering this is not altogether surprising. Smugglers were instrumental in the many Jacobite schemes (and some actual enterprises) for landing arms in the Highlands. In 1727 the Jacobite David O'Brien wrote James the Old Pretender a long memoir, explaining how arms bought in Holland could be taken to the Western Isles with the help of their smuggler friends. The memoir reveals a deep knowledge of the entire contraband trade from Barbados to Hamburg.[21]

A closer look at the different types of smuggling will throw into relief the myriad problems the authorities faced in the impossible, sisyphean task of halting the flow of contraband. First, the 'owling' of wool. The eighteenth century opened with England still reeling from recent revelations about the extent of illegal exports of wool to France. In 1697 eight 'owlers' were earmarked for solemn impeachment. They escaped by making a full confession and paying a total of £20,000 in fines.[22] Parliament then rushed through an act forbidding anyone who lived within a fifteen-mile distance from the sea from buying wool unless he could produce documentary evidence that he intended to sell it inland from the 'exclusion zone'. To enforce the legislation, the government appointed a number of 'riding officers'. The first surveyor-general of riding officers, Captain Henry Baker, wanted to mount a vigorous campaign against the owlers. Among his plans was the hiring of spies and double agents in Calais and Dieppe. During his incumbency wool smuggling in Sussex and Kent was drastically reduced. But his successor lacked his crusading zeal. In any case, after the 1707 Act of Union anti-smuggling resources were switched away from England to Scotland.[23]

The scope of the task faced by Baker and his ilk can soon be appreciated. It was estimated that 150,000 packs of wool were illegally shipped from Britain each year.[24] The normal 'owling' method was to send combed wools as well as shearings by road to 'co-workers' who owned houses or cellars on the south coast of England. The merchandise was then loaded on to specially constructed craft and taken to ships lying offshore. Another method was to use barges on the large rivers, load them with contraband, then float the barges down the estuaries to a pick-up point, where sea-going ships that had already cleared customs would be waiting for them. Some wool and yarn was also pressed into bales and passed through customs as drapery. Other woollen items were taken out by passengers bound for the continent; the wool was tightly packed in their baggage, sometimes in false bottoms.[25] Favourite export points for wool were Kent, Sussex, and Hampshire, but some bales were sent to Scotland for shipment to France and Holland; this was particularly the case with Irish wool.

By the 1740s owlers were exporting more than £1 million in contraband wool. But such was the demand for the products of the Continent (which English smugglers were importing) that this impressive-looking sum (just less than the total annual proceeds of the customs and excise) could not purchase even one-half of the tea, brandy, and tobacco for which there was such an urgent desire in England. [26] The importance of the Isle of Man before 1765 can be gauged from the fact that in the winter of 1763 5,000 packs of wool were sent to the Manxmen from north-western ports to be located on to French and Dutch ships. A rueful observer recorded that a Viking raid on the Isle of Man conducted by revenue officers would uplift more than £100,000 in seizures.[27]

In the case of smuggling proper (the *import* of prohibited items), the most important contraband merchandise was tea. Legal imports of tea were controlled by the East India Company, which enjoyed a monopoly, limited sales, and set prices far above those obtaining in Hamburg or Amsterdam. Consequently an illegal trade in tea grew up that rivalled the sale of alcohol under Prohibition in the way it commanded universal acceptance.[28] The poet Gray referred in passing to 'run tea' as if it were the most commonplace aspect of eighteenth-century society.[29]

A few eloquent statistics attest to the folly of the East India monopoly and the company policy of keeping supplies low and prices high. In 1733 the average price of tea was five shillings a pound, of which four shillings and nine pence was duty. That this was prohibitively expensive can be seen from a comparison with Holland, where tea cost an average of six pence a pound.[30] Clearly there were vast profits to be made from contraband. The Dutch could sell tea to smugglers for two shillings a pound; the smugglers could then resell it in England for between four shillings and six pence and eight shillings, depending on quality. Every year at least three million pounds were run ashore, of which only about 0.3 per cent was seized.[31]

The vast extent of tea smuggling was obvious to anyone capable of simple arithmetic. The Dutch and other European nations brought back 15,500,000 pounds of tea each year, but consumed only a third of it themselves. Across the Channel was a nation, 90 per cent of whose people drank tea twice a day. The combination of high duties and demand of this level, plus the bribes paid to complaisant East India captains, made it apparent that almost all the tea consumed in England was illegally imported.[32] In desperation, the East India company sometimes tried to outpoint the smugglers by paying 'spot prices' for the entire European tea surplus at Ostend.[33] On one occasion this tactic spectacularly backfired. In 1785 an enormous fire at Southwark destroyed acres of buildings and some ships. Among the magazines of turpentine, pitch, tar, and hemp that contributed to the inferno were 15,000 huge chests of tea, valued at £150,000, which the East India Company had purchased at Ostend to anticipate the smugglers.[34] The particular irony was that Pitt's legislation, just passed in 1785, made such a pre-emptive move unnecessary.

In 1745 Henry Pelham grasped the nettle and cut excise duty on tea to a shilling a pound. The bottom threatened to fall out of the smugglers' market.[35] Pelham's action was one of the triggers for the violent behaviour of the Hawkhurst gang, and particularly the attack on the Poole customs house in 1747 (see below p. 187). But war, the mother of increased taxes, undid Pelham's work. After 1759 in particular the rate of duty began to escalate. By 1783 there was a tax of 119 per cent on tea.

The year 1783 was a key one in the history of tea smuggling. On taking office in the Fox-North coalition, Edmund Burke called for a report on contraband from the Board of Customs. The Board reported an extraordinary threefold increase in the practice since 1780, and estimated the annual volume of illicitly imported tea at 21,132,000 pounds.[36] Inland detection methods were severely criticized and several blatant frauds exposed. Before 1760 tea smuggling had mainly been the province of small-scale importers with little capital or credit.[37] But as prices rocketed after the Seven Years War, large-scale affluent entrepreneurs moved in. In the most obvious type of fraud London dealers simply took out an excise permit for sending some of their tea and brandy to a coastal warehouse. Then they would allege 'convenience of trade' as a pretext for bringing back 'the same' goods. In one week alone the Board discovered that 21,242 pounds of tea and 76,420 gallons of spirits had been sent by permit from London to Deal to mask fraudulent imports.[38] These findings were endorsed by the accountant of the East India Company. In 1784 he estimated that only one-third of the tea consumed in Britain had been legally imported.[39]

The reforms that Burke had set in hand were continued under the next government, headed by Pitt. Pitt realized that the contraband trade in tea was even more of a menace to the economy than the official reports were suggesting, since tea's illicit import was used by professional smugglers as cover for bringing in other items that would not have been worth smuggling on their own.[40] Pitt decided to eliminate the problem at a stroke. He reduced the 119 per cent tax to 12 per cent. The results were immediate. Whereas in 1784 only 4,962,000 pounds were entered in the customs for home consumption, in 1785 (the first year of reduced duties), the volume rose to 16,307,000 pounds.[41] This was a stunning demonstration of the accuracy of the statistics worked out by the East India Company accountant.

The smuggling of brandy and wine was first cousin to tea smuggling, since it was also usually run ashore on coasts – in contrast to the illicit trade in tobacco and silks, which was mainly carried out in the ports. The wars of William and Mary revived liquor smuggling, and thereafter it throve until the 1780s. High taxation and high demand made this a gilt-edged business. In 1735 French wines, rum, and brandy were supposed to pay the amazingly high duty of £1 a gallon.[42] At the same time the greater part of the alcoholic produce of Holland went to England illegally. Two-thirds of the 3,867,500 gallons of spirits distilled annually at Schiedam found its way across the Channel.[43] Calais-based Frenchmen were the principals in brandy smuggling. Guernsey led the field as a centre for contraband in fine French wines.[44]

The French were equipped to pursue this trade. Their sixty-ton ships could each carry 400 casks of brandy. The violence with which these sloops would defend their interests was well-known.[45] They openly assisted English smugglers in their battles with revenue cutters. Armed Frenchmen sailed right up the Tyne in 1729 to reinforce their self-appointed exclusive right to contraband trade with the Newcastle colliers. They were also active in the harbours of Essex and Suffolk.[46]

The impudence of the French led to many grave passages of arms with English law-enforcement. In 1721 brandy smugglers from Calais captured a customs officer and forced him to drink a huge quantity of brandy. When he was semi-conscious, the smugglers took a funnel and poured another five pints of brandy into him before tying him on a horse and whipping it away.[47] In another incident in Sizewell Bay, a customs smack saw three French ships riding at anchor, obviously preparing to land brandy. An ingenious officer pretended to trade for the brandy and outbid the smugglers. Once he had secured possession of the brandy, he informed the Frenchmen that he was confiscating it as seizure. The French responded by training their big guns on the smack and threatening to blow her out of the water. The customs officer returned the brandy.[48]

Each type of smuggler had his own peculiar tricks of the trade. The brandy smuggler was no exception. To evade the revenue patrols, they liked to carry clearing certificates made out from Calais or Amsterdam for Bergen. Then, if apprehended in the Channel, the smugglers could justify their presence there. Another tactic was to entice customs men with a small cargo. While the officers were occupied with that, the smugglers would bring in a really large consignment.[49] The importance of Guernsey for wine smugglers was that it enabled smugglers to mix French wines with port brought from Lisbon. Then the entire consignment could be passed through customs on payment of the lower duty levied on port.

In the 1720s the leading wine smugglers operated under the cover of legitimate business. Port was sold at two shillings and six pence a gallon at a time when no legitimate merchant could import it at less than four shillings. The corresponding figures for rum were five shillings and eight shillings and six pence. Messrs Boyes and Hatch kept a stable of about twenty tame witnesses, ready to swear that any wines seized by the authorities had been purchased in fair sale at the customs house or elsewhere. Boyes and Hatch bribed court officials to discover the Crown's evidence, then used their own 'witnesses' to discredit it. Usually the Crown would have no more than two witnesses. It was relatively easy to blacken their characters, otherwise discredit them, or at the very least induce doubt in the minds of jurymen.[50]

The smuggling of brandy and wine was to some extent symbiotic with the trade in contraband tea. When Pitt decided in 1784 to act decisively against the tea smugglers, he also struck at the thriving illicit trade in French wines.[51] First he cut the duty on all French wines from £90.3.10 a tun to £43.1.0. A Bonded Excise scheme – a modified form of Walpole's ill-fated 1733 Excise Bill – simplified accounting procedures and abolished differential tariffs for the same goods. Having cut the ground from under the smugglers at the demand end, Pitt then moved to restrict the supply. The key was his 'Hovering Act' of 1784.[52] This allowed the confiscation of all ships under sixty tons carrying wine, tea, or coffee found within three miles of the English coast. The same penalty was ordained for ships of any size that carried spirits in casks of less than sixty gallons capacity. All small cutters and luggers that operated without a licence were to be forfeit to the Crown. To obtain the said licence an operator had to give full security against the use of his vessel for contraband. Henceforth, too, shooting at naval officers or revenue patrols was punishable by death.[53]

Tobacco smuggling was another permanent headache for the authorities. About seven and a half million tons were smuggled into Britain annually, mainly from Ostend and Guernsey. The smugglers bought tobacco on the Continent for three pence a pound. After adding a further five and a half pence a pound for overheads and expenses, they were still able to make a handsome profit by selling it in England for one shilling and seven pence a pound.[54] The annual loss to the crown was estimated at £3 million.

A good deal of contraband tobacco was brought into England by seamen who secreted small bundles about their person. The authorities tried to prevent this by decreeing that no tobacco could be imported from the plantations nor loaded on ships there except in casks or chests of at least two hundredweight capacity.[55] But a more subtle method of smuggling was to persuade the 'land waiters' or officials who oversaw the landing of cargo to desert their posts or connive at illicit unloading. 'Socking' tobacco, that is, stealing it from ships at anchor before it was unloaded, was common, as were other frauds committed while the ship was in port.[56] For this reason it is as difficult to distinguish smuggling from port and river pilferage as it is to differentiate privateering from piracy.

Frauds were particularly rampant in tobacco re-export. Since tobacco was one of the items that was allowed a discount of customs duty on condition of immediate re-exportation, the criminal methods practised were almost predictable. After the debentures for export had been obtained, the tobacco was unloaded and sold for home consumption at the market price. After clearing port, venal captains would either transfer the tobacco to smuggling sloops or take it themselves to some deserted part of the coast. The tobacco would then be sold in the capital's coffee houses, and by hawkers and peddlars in the countryside. In London the bogus 're-export' trade was particularly blatant. Merchandise loaded in the port of London for, say, Rotterdam would be transferred to smaller boats a mile beyond Gravesend.[57]

By 1750 the tobacco trade had all but broken down under the impact of contraband. The Tobacco Bill of 1751 represented an unsatisfactory attempt to break the grip of the smugglers. This Act set up a Department of Register-General of Tobaccos to keep a strict accounting of all tobacco imports.[58] But in the 1770s the customs commissioners estimated that they still lost £200,000 a year on fraudulent 'drawback'. It was clear that as long as the drawback system on tobacco re-exports was permitted, abuses would continue.

As with the other types of smuggling, contraband in tobacco was a subject of long thought and deep concern to William Pitt in the early 1780s.[59] He was repeatedly urged to deal with the problem by cutting duties, as he had done in the case of tea and wines. Instead, he brought in a Tobacco Act (1789) which introduced a comprehensive warehousing scheme for the commodity. Henceforth London, Bristol, Liverpool, Glasgow, and seven other named ports were the only centres where legal import of tobacco could take place. The Act also regulated the tonnage of ships allowed to ply the trade and the minimum size of consignments (120 tons and 450 pounds respectively). The Tobacco Act did not eliminate smuggling, but it did make it more difficult. Unfortunately for Pitt, the upper hand he had gained in the war against the smugglers in the 1780s was lost in the war against France in the 1790s. Duties had to rise again to pay for the war. With a 96 per cent tax on tea by 1806, and a duty of three shillings and two pence a pound on tobacco by 1815, smuggling naturally revived.[60]

The smuggling of lace did not become a matter for concern to the authorities until after 1750. Until then the smuggling of fabrics had largely been concerned with calicoes.[61] Three separate factors then led to an intense battle between authorities and smugglers throughout the 1760s. With the expansion of the Post Office, diamonds and threadbare lace were increasingly smuggled into the country in postal packets.[62] Cambrics, Lyons silk, and Valenciennes lace joined the ever-lengthening list of contraband items in demand in England.[63] Second, an expansion in East Indies trade after the Seven Years War led to a great surge in the smuggling of silk and lace. This was an area particularly associated with foreign ambassadors claiming diplomatic immunity.[64] During Grenville's premiership (1763-5) a fresh batch of investigators was added to the strength of the customs department. In one incident an agent tracked a suspect all the way from Wapping to the Haymarket before making an arrest. A quantity of French and Brussels lace was found hidden inside a hollow loaf of bread.[65] In another case, customs officers followed a man who came ashore at the port of London and appeared to be a Turk. When they stopped him on suspicion they found that he was an Englishman who had blacked up and then wound a roll of French lace into his turban, sash, and gown.[66]

But what most encouraged the authorities to stiffen the laws against contraband lace was a *cause célèbre* when Lady Holdernesse was caught in possession of 114 Parisian silk gowns.[67] Shortly afterwards Lord Holdernesse became governor of the cinque ports. His wife proceeded to carry out a private smuggling enterprise based at Walmer castle on the Kent coast. Here, in open defiance of the law, she imported French gowns and furniture, ostensibly for her own use.[68] The backlash from this was felt mainly by travellers going on the grand tour. Walpole's friend Cole complained to him: 'At Dover they are strict at the custom-house in searching for laced clothes, and rummage the boxes quite to the bottom.'[69] This meticulous supervision by the revenue eventually paid off. In 1773 riding officers and troops made the most valuable seizure of the century near Hythe in Kent when they found French silks and lace worth £15,000.[70]

Given the deep inroads into government revenue made by smuggling of all kinds, it is surprising to find that, with a single major exception, until Pitt brought in his stern measures in the 1780s, the elite did not use the full weight of the Bloody Code in an attempt to crush the smugglers. In the early years of the eighteenth century there was a distinct tendency to regard the offence as a peccadillo. The usual penalty was fines, amounting to several times the worth of the smuggled goods, plus the confiscation of all boat, horses, and equipment used in the enterprise. The 1718 Act laid down that any ship under fifty tons that was laden with tea, French silks, pepper, or brandy, and that was found hovering near the English coast, was *liable* to seizure. But there was no mention of individual penalties.[71]

Three years later the law was stiffened. The minimum size of all vessels engaged in overseas trade was raised from fifteen to forty tons. Any ship not meeting this requirement could be burned. The 1721 Act also declared that any boat of more than four oars found on the coasts or below London Bridge was to be forfeit. For the first time transportation was prescribed: seven years would be the normal penalty for anyone resisting revenue officers or for any person who went armed or masked when passing forfeited goods.[72]

After the stick came the carrot. The 1736 Act of Indemnity for Smugglers allowed smugglers to obtain a free pardon for past offences, provided they fully disclosed them and gave the names of their fellow-conspirators. The snag was that the Act did not provide an amnesty for armed riding. Whatever else a smuggler confessed to, he could still be hanged under the Waltham Black Act if it was proved that he had gone armed. Also, in section 7 of the Act came the first mention of the death penalty specifically for contraband offences. Smuggling was declared a non-clergyable felony for anyone who had previously claimed benefit of clergy on conviction for the crime.[73] The death penalty was also stipulated for the wounding of customs officers. In 1739 a further Act prescribed capital punishment for the specific crime of resisting customs officers during the seizure of smuggled wool.[74]

Yet it was not until 1746 that the Code was used for the first full-blooded assault on smugglers. Henceforth death rather than transportation was to be the usual punishment for smuggling. It was a capital offence for three or more persons to assemble for the purposes of smuggling, to land or carry away uncustomed goods or to rescue such goods after seizure; to prevent the capture of smugglers or to rescue them, or to maim, wound, or shoot at customs officers. There was also to be collective punishment on the community if offenders were not convicted within six months. If any impounded goods were rescued, the county was liable to a fine of £200. A wounded revenue officer would cost the county £40 and a dead one £100.[75] The preamble to the Act threw a clear light on the smuggling epidemic that gripped England in the mid-1740s.

Each piece of legislation enacted halted the spate of smuggling temporarily. But once the novelty of changed law had worn off, the smugglers resumed their old ways. The main effect of the 1746 Act was to ensure that bloody clashes were more likely, since smugglers now went armed. There were in addition other reasons why the flow of legislation had little impact before the 1780s. The 1746 Act was widely criticized for its imprecision and sloppy drafting. Initially enacted for seven years, it very soon became a dead letter. An able lawyer could exploit its imprecisions to get his client acquitted. Sir William Eden thought that the 1746 Smuggling Act conflicted with traditional liberties since it punished with death accessories to an action that was previously clergyable for the perpetrator himself.[76]

In addition, draconian laws against smuggling collided with the general political culture that held illicit trading to be a peccadillo caused solely by inept government fiscal policies. The London crowd was always on the side of smugglers and regularly intervened to prevent seizures. In July 1768 tea weighing 500 pounds was seized at night in a field at Stockwell. In a trice more than sixty men armed with staves and brickbats appeared as if from nowhere and drove off the excisemen.[77] A single riding officer was rash enough to intervene at Hurst Beach near Southampton when fourteen armed smugglers were running a cargo. He suffered concussion of the skull and weeks in hospital from the thrashing he took.[78] After a number of bad beatings, revenue officers eventually did not dare to venture out after dark unless they had more than half a dozen well armed men. Another deterrent to law enforcement was that revenue men who killed smugglers could expect no mercy from local juries. When Pitt's 1784 Act made it a capital offence not to surrender to revenue officers when called upon to do so, it was found necessary to amend the law so that the officers could not be tried before a jury for the killing of smugglers who resisted arrest.[79]

The genesis of the 1746 Act, marking a distinct hardening in official attitudes towards smuggling gangs, can be sought in the unprecedented wave of violence that swept over Sussex in the 1740s as a new type of plebeian smuggler came to the fore. The turbulence of 1740s Sussex was a compound of wartime opportunity, the Jacobite threat, and the gradual replacement of property-owning 'owlers' by a new organization of tea smugglers drawn from the 'lower orders'.[80] The core of the new smuggling network was the Hawkhurst gang, based on the town of Hawkhurst, ten miles north of Hastings. These were men who were not prepared to bow the head to the elite and they were a force to be reckoned with. It was reliably reported that 500 well-armed men could be assembled at Hawkhurst within half an hour.[81]

Though close to London as the crow flies, Sussex in the 1740s presented the same 'Arabian' aspect that Defoe noted on Bagshot Heath. In 1749 Horace Walpole recorded his impressions:

If you love good roads, conveniences, good inns, plenty of postilions and horses, be so kind as never to go in Sussex. We thought ourselves in the northest part of England; the whole country has a Saxon air, and the inhabitants are savage, as if king George the second was the first monarch of the East Angles. Coaches grow there no more than balm and spices; we were forced to drop our postchaise, that resembled nothing so much as a harlequin's clash, which was occasionally a chaise or a baker's cart. We journeyed over Alpine mountains, drenched in clouds, and thought of harlequin again, when he was driving the chariot of the sun through the morning clouds, and so was glad to hear the *aqua vitae* man crying a dram.[82]

It is not, I hope, to fall victim to the 'pathetic fallacy' to point out the relationship between man and landscape and to correlate the wildness of Sussex and Bagshot with the violence of those who operated in that sort of terrain.

Pelham's reforms were a direct threat to the livelihood of these men of wild Sussex. In 1747, the *annus mirabilis* of the Hawkhurst gang, Sussex was convulsed with large-scale violence. The escalation had something to do with a change of leadership of the gang. Arthur Gray was replaced by William Kingsmill after Gray was arrested for highway robbery; the authorities, however, could not pin enough on him to hang him.[83] Kingsmill was a more energetic leader with a taste for quick, violent solutions, but his escalation of the struggle simply accelerated a clash that was inevitable anyway.

Adam Smith had this to say of contraband: 'The most hazardous of all trades, that of the smuggler, though when the adventure succeeds, it is likewise the most profitable.'[84] For most of the century smuggling revealed only the profitable side. 1747 saw the danger at its highest. The year began with a pitched battle at Goudhurst between the Hawkhurst gang and a rival sept that had doublecrossed them over some contraband tea. Shortly after this, Kingsmill led ninety-two men and a pack of vicious dogs to victory in a pitched battle with the burghers of Folkestone.[85] Flushed with this triumph, Kingsmill let the citizens of Goudhurst know that in future he expected no further trouble from them and, if necessary, would burn down the town to compel their obedience. But instead of buckling under this threat, the men of Goudhurst organized themselves into a militia under 'Captain' Sturt. The stage was set for a bloody clash.

It came on 20 April 1747. When Kingsmill and his men arrived at the outskirts of Goudhurst, they were greeted with 'popping shots' from Sturt's men, concealed behind doorways and in the church tower.[86] A ferocious shoot-out ensued. After brisk firing, the smugglers retired, leaving behind them two dead, including George Kingsmill, William's brother.[87] This reverse hardened the attitude of the Hawkhurst men. In August that year, as they passed through Rye, they carried off one young man who showed too great curiosity in their activities, and threatened the local printers with death if they continued to print 'wanted' notices for the gang.[88]

But the Hawkhurst men's greatest exploit was still to come. The gang's chief agent in France was Richard Perrin. He was bringing over a cargo of tea and spirits from Guernsey when his craft *The Three Brothers* was intercepted by a revenue cutter. Perrin made his escape, but the ship with its cargo was taken to Poole. Since the haul was thirty hundredweight of tea, valued at upwards of £500, the impoverished Hawkhurst men could not shrug off its loss. At Perrin's urging, Kingsmill decided to break into the customs house at Poole and regain the loot.[89]

The raid was planned in concert with the West Sussex gang, also potential beneficiaries from the *Three Brothers* cargo. On the night of 6 October 1747 the two groups met on the edge of Charlton forest for the last leg of the journey to Poole. At full strength the joint party would have consisted of about sixty men. But once at Poole the West Sussex men lost their nerve and tried to back out. The dogged Hawkhurst men held them to it, however. The raid was set for the night of 7 October. As it transpired, they broke open the customs house with remarkable ease and recovered their tea. They then proceeded in triumph through Hampshire to their base in Sussex. A division of the spoils provided twenty-seven pounds of tea for each man who had taken part in the enterprise.[90]

This was a bare-faced attack on the credibility of the government. By a twist of fate the authorities were soon able to take a terrible revenge. During their triumphant procession back to Sussex, the Hawkhurst gang had stopped for breakfast in the village of Fordingbridge in Hampshire. One of the smugglers happened to throw a bag of tea in the direction of a local shoemaker Daniel Chater. This made Chater valuable to the authorities, as he was one of the few who could clearly identify gang members. He was immediately recruited for the customs service.[91]

On 14 February 1748 Chater set out with William Galley, a riding officer in the excise service, for Chichester, where he was to make a deposition before magistrates and customs officials. At midday they stopped for refreshment at the White Hart at Rowland's Castle. The landlady, who was in league with the smugglers, became suspicious of the travellers and alerted the local chapter of the Hawkhurst gang. The leaders of this were Ben Tapner and John Cobby. These two immediately assembled their men and went straight to the White Hart.[92]

Tapner's men pretended to fall into conversation with Chater and Galley. Drinks were ordered, then further rounds called for. When Chater and Galley were thoroughly drunk, the Hawkhurst men revealed their hand and took them prisoner. After some division of opinion as to what to do with the captives, it was decided to kill them. After beating the two men, the gang tied them to horses and led them out into the countryside. They whipped horses and victims all the way from Rowlands castle to Lady Holt Park. Galley was described as riding 'with his head under the belly of the horse . . . wounded, bruised and hurt'. One of the gang members got his sport by periodically squeezing Galley's genitals. By 2 a.m. he was near death. They stopped in a remote spot and cut off Galley's nose and testicles. When the wretched man seemed to have expired from the experience, they dug a hole in a fox earth and buried him, possibly still alive. Chater lingered on for another three days, chained up in a lonely shed. Then he was taken to Lady Holt Park and strangled with a rope. He was then thrown down a well near Harting in

Sussex. To try to ensure that the dead man would tell no tales, the gang threw boulders and two large gate posts down the well.[93]

When the bodies of the two murdered men were found, the authorities moved heaven and earth to find the culprits. The case was grist to the mill for those like the Fieldings, who argued that smuggling was not just a venial sin; its logical ending place was murder. The Duke of Richmond decided to stake his reputation on bringing the murderers to justice. He also intended to hang those responsible for the Poole customs house break-in, the origin of the evil.[94] He began by obtaining authorization for a special commission so that judges could be brought down from London to try the murderers of Galley and Chater. The justices of West Sussex could not be trusted to convict smugglers. The large rewards Richmond dangled before the public produced the desired results. All the men involved in the bloody affair at the White Hart were apprehended. After a three-day trial before the special commission, the jury found five men (Tapner, Cobby, Carter, Jackson, and Hammond) guilty of murder as principals and two other men guilty as accessories. They were condemned to the aggravated penalty of being hanged in chains after their execution.[95]

Meanwhile Richmond's largesse had netted the three ringleaders in the 1747 'rescue' of tea from the Poole customs house. At the Old Bailey in april 1749 Kingsmill, Perrin, and William Fairall were convicted and later hanged at Tyburn.[96] Other Hawkhurst men were rounded up later in the year following information laid by ex-smugglers seeking a free pardon.[97] By the time of his death in 1750, Richmond's two-year campaign had secured thirty-five executions; another ten died in gaol while waiting to be hanged.[98] After his death the winnowing continued. In 1751 a pitched battle between dragoons and the remnants of the gang ended with the execution of the gang's last leader.[99]

Richmond's pogrom against the Hawkhurst gang has puzzled many historians who can see no clear motive for the money and energy he was prepared to expend on his campaign except an (unexplained) hatred of smugglers. Yet the explanation was almost certainly his fanatical anti-Jacobitism. Richmond was a staunch defender and friend of the Pelhams.[100] It is perhaps not fanciful to correlate Pelham's anti-smuggling measures of 1745 with the Jacobites; after all, this was the year when the threat from the Stuarts was at its greatest. Smuggling went hand in hand with Jacobitism not just in Scotland but in the Channel. The smugglers were a vital source of intelligence for French military planners in the two invasion attempts of 1743-4 and 1745-6.[101] Pelham's papers occasionally reveal that fear of the Jacobites was one of the motives in the crusade against the smugglers.[102] And Horace Walpole thought that the ending of the purge against the battered Sussex men by the Duke of Newcastle came about because Newcastle had 'turned' the smugglers in his war against the exiled Stuarts.[103] This inference would be greatly strengthened if it could be proved that the Jacobite Comte de Lally really was, as he boasted, the brains behind Perrin's proposal to break into the Poole customs house.

The one thing Richmond's crusade did not do was to break Sussex smuggling forever, although it is true that the destruction of the Hawkhurst gang led to a noticeable decline in smuggling on the south coast.[104] Even so, Horace Walpole in 1752 found Sussex still stiff with smugglers and complained that the inns were thronged either with customs men or dealers in contraband.[105]

But the Richmond crusade against the smugglers, and its resulting death toll, were atypical. For much of the century the smuggler had the upper hand in the struggle with the authorities. The government had three lines of defence against him, but all were vitiated by corruption, inadequate funding, and inter-departmental or service rivalry. The three tiers were the customs officer at port, the revenue cruisers at sea or in the Thames estuary, and the land guard. The riding officers of the land guard had powers very like those of a modern VAT inspector: they could make unannounced visits to inns and warehouses and inspect on demand for uncustomed or uncertified goods.[106]

Corruption was a perennial problem in the fight against the smugglers. As early as 1698, when 300 new officers were appointed, principally to check the illegal export of wool, this was apparent. Nearly all of them were later found to be corrupt: they connived at illicit trade and shared the high rewards offered for seizures with the smugglers themselves.[107] This was partly a consequence of the low salaries paid to customs officers, but was also due to defects inherent in the system of seizures and rewards. Demoralization among customs men was always likely to lead to their collusion with the smugglers, and this demoralization was enhanced by the knowledge that it was the sea-borne cruisers that were likely to scoop the pool. Seizures by law-enforcement officers rose from £40,000 in 1762 to £80,000 in 1782. Of the latter figure, £50,000 was accounted for by the cruisers, which were acknowledged to be the only effective peacetime deterrent.[108]

But the greater capability of the revenue cruisers was not the only reason for demoralization by customs officers at the ports. They lacked the credibility of thief-takers or the glamour of the Bow Street runners. Everyone knew that their seizures were a mere flea-bite. On paper the statistics looked impressive. From 1713-23, 192,515 gallons of brandy were seized, together with 1,061,268 pounds of tobacco and 102,041 pounds of tea. Yet this was estimated to be less than one-tenth of the smuggler's total haul of brandy, and far less in the case of tea. For every ounce of tobacco impounded by the revenue, at least a pound got through; for every pound of tea taken, more than three hundredweight went scot-free.[109] Moreover, the sales of seized goods often generated little revenue, so that the very system was called into question.

A further question-mark against the cost-effectiveness of the seizure system was provided by the cost of paying rewards. The going rate for informing on simple smuggling activities was anything from £20 to £50. Upwards of £50 was awarded for apprehending smugglers who had resisted arrest by revenue officers. Yet even these rewards were not large enough when violent gangs like the Hawkhurst men were on the rampage. The Duke of Richmond secured his great 'triumphs' by offering rewards up to £500. In addition, money had to be provided to compensate members of the public who sustained physical injury during the arrest of smugglers.[110] Moreover, rewards for seizures, in order to be effective, often had to be larger than the value of the shipment seized. The situation was tailor-made for collusion between customs officers and smugglers.

Because of the known ineffectiveness of the customs officials at the ports, much was expected of the riding officers of the land guard. Mounted patrols were particularly important in the fight against smugglers in wartime when the navy had other duties. Riding officers in the north of England were particularly involved in guarding the passes from Scotland into England.[111] In peacetime the riding officers were supposed to co-ordinate closely with the cruisers at sea. But the land guard never made a serious dent in contraband activity. The central government did not provide enough money to employ a full-time force of professionals. As a result, the posts of riding officers were filled by apothecaries, brewers, and other tradesmen, who carried out their duties in their spare time in a manner totally convenient to themselves, falsifying records if necessary.[112] Some were in league with the smugglers they were supposed to be tracking down. But not even the honest ones were brave or numerous enough to deal with armed smuggling gangs. As a contemporary remarked: 'Nor could they be increased to render effectual service unless one half of the inhabitants could be hired to watch the other.'[113]

The third line of defence for the authorities was the flotilla of revenue cruisers. By 1763 there were twenty-two of these in service. Here the system was twofold. Either the Crown provided a free vessel to a contractor, who then paid for all crew and upkeep costs out of the seizures. Or the contractor himself provided the ship in return for a monthly allowance and agreed to pay the costs out of seizures.[114] The snag was that often the contractors *were* the customs officials: in other words they were controlling and reporting on themselves. Moreover, there was widespread collusion with the smugglers. The very most the majority of contractors were prepared to do was to seize goods, while allowing the smugglers to escape in their boats.[115]

In fact it is arguable that the commanders of revenue cruisers spent more time trying to evade the meticulous instructions laid on them by the customs collectors at the ports than in trying to hunt down smugglers. In theory the captain of a revenue cruiser was answerable to the collectors. The captain had to keep a daily journal, maintain his crew on full alert at all times and ensure that his ship was in constant motion. He was never to go into port, except to make the briefest possible call for provisions. There was to be a system of signals by day and fires by night to warn of contraband activity. The captains had powers to seize any boat at anchor or 'hovering' within two leagues of the coast. Whenever their cruisers entered a bay, the commanders were to lower a boat and send a party of armed men ashore in search of any smugglers who might be lying low in the creeks or inlets, waiting for an opportunity to slip out to sea.[116]

Such was the pious theory. In practice the cruiser commanders, rugged individualists all, deeply resented the fact that a customs 'landlubber' could give them orders. Invariably relations between the two sets of 'law-enforcement officers' were tense. The captains also hated being permanently at sea and found myriad excuses (the need for provisions, repairs, or medical attention) to run into shore. The customs service hit back by making it illegal for a captain to land without reporting in or to go to sea without taking a month's provisions with him. Naturally, in retaliation for the closing of these loopholes, the cruiser commanders often took their revenge by making sure the actual smugglers escaped whenever they made a seizure.[117]

Another barrier to effective control of smuggling was jealousy and rivalry between the various government departments involved. The Secretary of War and the Secretary to the Treasury had at times to work closely with the Customs and Excise, as did the Admiralty, which lent its warships to the task of surveillance in return for help from the customs Department in pressing seamen.[118] The customs were particularly involved in decision-making when judges passed on requests for pardon for condemned smugglers for their consideration. Naturally, the different government departments had different aims and hence different perspectives. To make matters worse, the institutions most closely involved in the fight against smugglers were themselves divided. There was a Customs Board and a quite distinct Excise Board; Adam Smith felt that it was the excise laws, rather than those of the customs, that posed the real threat to contraband.[119]

In addition to the divided administrative command that faced them, the smugglers were also able to maintain a technological edge over the authorities throughout the century. When bigger and better cutters, cruisers, and six-oared boats were added to the customs fleet, the smugglers hit back by using light, open craft that could enter shallow waters unnavigable by the revenue boats. At one time the contraband runners used a lug-sail vessel that allowed them to land their goods and sail out to sea immediately, while the customs vessel with its ordinary sail lay to, becalmed and impotent.[120] Other smuggling gangs used great armed cruisers of 100 or 200 tons, with carriage guns and scores of men in their crews. Only Admiralty ships of the line could make any headway against these leviathans.[121] In 1783 it was estimated that 120 large armed vessels and 200 smaller ones were employed on a regular smuggling business. Smuggling gangs hundreds strong were so confident that on parts of the coasts they had erected batteries to provide covering fire for their vessels.[122]

Whenever the customs closed the technological gap in ships, the smugglers switched tactics. They possessed amazing ingenuity; sometimes their methods changed almost daily. A favourite ploy was to equip a vessel with false bulkheads, containing brandy, rum, or tea, that could escape detection in a search of the ship. The code of the sea and worldwide shipping practice also favoured the smugglers. Even if found in suspicious circumstances, they could wriggle off the hook if they possessed the correct paperwork. Manifests ostensibly for landing goods in Europe and America could mask an intended landing on the English coast.[123]

So far did the smugglers outstrip the authorities in technical innovation that when the first crossing of the Channel by balloon was made in 1785, Horace Walpole in all seriousness thought that the exploit would herald a new era of contraband, with the illicit traders once again vaulting over the law enforcers and opening up a further technological gap.[124] One of the few members of the elite with any real ideas for combatting smugglers proposed a primitive version of Martello towers, to be erected at strategic points on the coasts of Kent, Sussex, Suffolk, and Norfolk.[125]

The generally received opinion in the eighteenth century was that the struggle between smugglers and the authorities was an uneven one which the forces of law and order could never win. A number of considerations prompted this conclusion. The costs of guarding against contraband were very heavy. At the same time the sale of seizures brought in little revenue and badly dented the credibility of the system.[126] And, quite apart from the intimidating power and organization of the smuggling gangs and the corruption of officialdom, the rule of law itself posed formidable problems for the elite. The law was slow and costly; biased justices and juries often failed to convict on the most straightforward evidence. Even apart from juries that were genuinely sympathetic to smugglers, there were others that could be suborned or terrorized. Bribery produced a host of false alibis, witnesses who 'disappeared', had convenient lapses of memory, or changed their stories in the witness box. There was also the danger of counter-suits by the runners for wrongful arrest; the commanders of revenue cruisers had strict orders not to stop vessels except on the strongest presumptive evidence.[127]

Lavish rewards to informers might have seemed the obvious answer. There are good grounds for thinking that paid informers always posed more of a threat to smugglers even than the Army and Navy.[128] Some observers even felt that the lavish rewards offered for giving evidence of contraband would lead to perjury on a massive scale.[129] This was to overstate the case. Even with well paid informers there were difficulties. Aside from the cost of the rewards, counter-bribes or intimidation could get informers to change their story. In Yarmouth in the years 1742-4 there was a running battle between smugglers and authorities over one particularly important informer. After he had laid his first tranche of evidence, the smugglers set him up so that he was impressed on a man-of-war. When he was released through the intervention of the Customs Board, the smugglers struck back by resurrecting an ancient felony of which the informer had been guilty. When the witness was found guilty on this charge and imprisoned, the Customs again used its influence to get a free pardon. Exasperated, the smugglers finally solved the problem by giving the man a savage beating and leaving him half dead as a warning to others.[130]

Against determined, violent smugglers in large numbers only the Army could make any impression. Yet the Customs department was always reluctant to call in the military. Quite apart from widespread fear and loathing of soldiers by civilians whom the revenue men could not afford to alienate, the Customs oficials stood to take a financial loss if the military were involved.[131] Troops who took part in seizures were paid between one-sixth and a half of the Crown's share, plus two-thirds of the Customs officers' share, depending on how many infantrymen or dragoons were used. The financial implications of seizure were very important and added to the unimpressive general performance of Customs officers. Two-thirds was the customary share of all seizures paid to the military (including captains of Royal Navy ships) in any joint operaton in which they took part. Since informers had to be paid out of the remaining one-third left to the Customs officers, the combined use of informers and the military could leave the revenue men literally with nothing at the end of the seizure.[132]

Yet there were times when the customs department had no choice but to call on the secretary of War or the Admiralty for troops and ships with which to combat the more formidable smuggling gangs.[133] But not even the intervention of the military could curb the spirit of the larger gangs. An attempt by Sussex smugglers in 1740 to rescue a cargo of seized tea led to a sustained shoot-out, in which the Customs officer who had ordered the dragoons to open fire was killed by a smuggler's bullet.[134] After the Seven Years War the military were more often in evidence in the battle with the smugglers. Regular detachments were at last stationed along the coast. But they were too few in number to cut down the inflows. From the Wash to Land's End in 1772 just 552 cavalrymen and 104 foot soldiers were on anti-smuggling duty.[135] These duties were singularly unpopular with rankers, who took bribes or 'worked to rule'. Nor did the distribution of prize monies in proportion to rank do much to whet the bounty-hunting appetites of privates.

The other drawback about the use of the military was that they liked to smuggle themselves and resented taking orders from civilians. Sometimes there were disputes and even fights between Royal Navy vessels and revenue cruisers, both trying to seize the same cargo.[136] Royal Navy captains often smuggled in their own right and behaved with overweening arrogance towards Customs officials who wanted to search their ships.[137] The revenue commanders learned to accept the amused contempt in which naval officers held them, for 'going it alone' could be dangerous. The danger did not come just from armed smugglers. In September 1764 an excise cutter chased a lug-sail smuggling boat carrying tea, tobacco, and brandy into Lundy Bay. In the high easterly surf both craft were soon pounded to pieces.[138]

As the screws tightened on the smugglers, roughly from the beginning of the American War of Independence in 1775, clashes with the military became bloodier and more frequent. In July 1778 a pitched battle was fought beween Orford's militia and an armed gang who landed under the cover of a fusillade from a twelve-gun smuggling cutter. On this occasion regular army reinforcements won the day for the militiamen.[139] When the war ended and Pitt launched his campaign to abolish contraband, the very worst encounters took place. In 1783 there was a bloody battle on Southwold beach in Suffolk between Customs men and dragoons on one side and over seventy 'blacked' smugglers on the other; amazingly only one smuggler was killed after a grim shoot-out. It was this incident that made General Conway suggest his pilot scheme for Martello towers.[140]

In 1784 the customs department again had to call for troops to deal with the smugglers of Deal. This was a town that long possessed an unsavoury reputation. 'What a very pitiful town Deal is!' was Pepys' judgement in 1660. One and a half centuries later Cobbett endorsed this opinion: 'Deal is a most villainous place. It is full of filthy-looking people. Great desolation of abomination has been going on here.'[141] Since the mayor and citizens of Deal openly took the side of the smugglers against the authorities, the incident had some of the flavour of a genuine rebellion.[142] Pitt reacted with a taste of the controlled terror he was to unleash more fully in the 1790s. Like other subtle exponents of social control through repression (Heydrich in Czechoslovakia in 1941-2 comes to mind), Pitt alternated the carrot with the stick. After reducing taxes to cut the ground from under 'rational' smuggling, he was prepared to deal very harshly with those who still opposed his will. In January 1785 he learned that heavy gales in the Channel had forced the local smugglers to lay up their boats. At once he marched a regiment of foot to Deal; the Army was sent in regimental strength deliberately to intimidate the people there. The hostile inhabitants took down all signs indicating inns and taverns and pretended that there was no accommodation in the town. The commanding officer promptly rented a barn on a two-year lease. The next morning he took his men down to the beach and burned every boat in sight.[143]

The Pitt reforms closed the classic era of eighteenth-century smuggling. As the attitude of the elite to other crimes tended to become more relaxed (until the French wars of the 1790s put the clock back), its posture towards smuggling became much tougher. Three cases can be taken as illustrative of the new mood. In 1784 John Shelley was executed for carrying away 350 pounds of tea that had been seized by an excise officer.[144] In 1798 two Customs officers, William Hewlings and Josiah Oliver, were hanged for stealing 400 pounds of raw coffee from *The Three Sisters* as she lay at anchor in the Thames.[145] And in 1800 Thomas Potter was 'launched into eternity' at Execution Dock for killing a Customs officer in a shoot-out two years earlier. In 1798 a revenue cutter had intercepted Potter's contraband gang off Pen Point and called on them to surrender. Potter had been the prime mover in the gang's resistance to arrest.[146] These tough measures were counterpointed with the appointment of Customs collectors of a much higher intellectual and moral calibre. One of the first of these was William Arnold, father of the famous Rugby headmaster. Arnold effectively ended contraband on the Isle of Wight. As Collector there from 1777 to 1801 he waged a vigorous campaign against the smugglers; he even commissioned an extra revenue cutter out of his own pocket. By the end of the century the smugglers had moved on elsewhere.[147]

It is a moot point whether smuggling should be regarded primarily as an economic or a social phenomenon. Economically there can be no doubting the role played by smuggling in eighteenth-century England. A shorthand encapsulation of its vast extent can be obtained from one single statistic. In the years 1760-85 the average annual *net* receipts from seizures (after reward monies and the costs of prosecution had been deducted) amounted to 5 per cent of the yearly total paid into the Exchequer by the Receiver-General.[148] This suggests the existence of a parallel economy with a vengeance, given the estimated proportion of seizures to actual contraband!

Sophisticated econometric studies of major shifts in demand shows the economy clearly in thrall to the illicit trade, with demand oscillating according to the fluctuations in the level of smuggling.[149] This could scarcely be otherwise, when smugglers accounted for one third of the share of English commerce with France and Holland.[150] It is no exaggeration, therefore, to see contraband as a hidden factor greatly contributing to the growth of commercial capitalism.[151] The effect on local economies was particularly severe. In the littoral counties the rates paid by smugglers to casual labourers to convey their goods inland – said to be at least half a guinea for the simplest journey – led to serious labour shortages on coastal farms.[152]

The social importance of smuggling largely hinges on whether the activities of the smugglers can be construed as 'social crime' – a struggle against the encroachments of capitalism by 'primitive rebels' determined to assert local autonomy against central government, and to uphold the prescriptive rights hallowed by custom and tradition against the might of the market. It is quite true that smuggling was not regarded as a crime by most people in the great smuggling regions: Kent, Sussex, Dorset, Cornwall, the Isle of Man. And the plebeian social origins of the Sussex smugglers of the 1740s have been definitively established.[153] But unless we allow sociological relativism to have the last word, it must be recognized that there are distinct problems in recognizing smuggling as 'social crime'.

On one hand, as we have seen, contraband had an ambivalent relationship to capitalism. It both helped and hindered its development. On the other hand, at a more profound level smuggling must be seen as parasitic on the official economic system, if only because the aim of its practitioners was to make profits, not to transform society. Moreover, even at the level of local folkways, it is difficult to see the smugglers as disinterested defenders of a local way of life. The battle of Goudhurst shows that the inhabitants of Kent and Sussex were divided among themselves; it was not a simple matter of local customs against the new modalities of the central government. Much of the exaggeration of the social role of smuggling comes from extrapolating from the special case of the Sussex smugglers. In their purposive violence, social composition, and their rhetoric the Sussex smugglers were as atypical of eighteenth-century smuggling as a whole as the Duke of Richmond's sanguinary crusade against them was atypical of elite response.

One of the obvious problems in regarding smuggling as a form of primitive rebellion is that it was so widely practised by members of the elite themselves. This was not just a question of support by members of local elites, like the mayor of Romney or the magistrates in Wigtown in 1708. Scions of the upper class were often smugglers in their own right. There are many well-known instances. During the Gordon Riots, hoards of smuggled goods were uncovered when the crowd sacked the Bavarian ambassador's 'chapel'.[154] Virtually every upper-class traveller to France casually smuggled back quantities of burgundy.[155] Even the King's Messengers smuggled German millinery as they travelled backwards and forwards between London and Hanover. Lady Holdernesse's illicit trade in silks has already been mentioned. An even more notorious upper-class smuggler was Sir Matthew Blakiston. He had been caught red-handed in Sir Robert Walpole's time and given a free pardon. Returning to his old ways he was caught again and fined £5,000.[156] We need not labour the obvious contrast between his fate and that of the Sussex smugglers. But his experience does cast immediate doubt on any typology that would make smuggling *in itself* an act of social rebellion.

In addition there is evidence that smugglers were able to diversify quite easily into other forms of crime. There was significant movement in and out of contraband trading. We have noted the movement between highway robbery and smuggling in the case of Dick Turpin, and also the lesser known one of John Poulter.[157] Another very interesting case is that of Bli Gonzalez, alias 'Spanish Jack'. After serving in the Navy in the War of Austrian Succession, he put his specialized knowledge to good use as a member of smuggling gangs in Sussex and Kent. When these were temporarily dispersed by Richmond's pogrom, Gonzalez lowered his sights and took to 'privately stealing'. He was eventually caught and executed in 1756 for stealing a silver tankard.[158]

The movement into other forms of crime was particularly significant after concerted efforts by central government, either fiscal or military, to win the struggle with the smugglers. The 1719 Smuggling Act forced Jacobite owlers (who brought back wine, tea, and brandy from France with the proceeds of the 'run' wool) into poaching. In this way it can be demonstrated that some of the Waltham Blacks had both a Jacobite and smuggling background.[159] Those forced out of the contraband business by Pelham's 1745 reforms were responsible for a number of footpad robberies in the environs of London in 1746-7.[160] The military crackdown in 1749-50 led to a series of armed robberies by ex-smugglers in Suffolk.[161] Suffolk was again a depressed area after Pitt's reforms of 1783-4. The military was despatched to the county to contain the depredations of desperate former smugglers, who had been forced into housebreaking when Pitt's fiscal reforms cut the ground from under them.[162]

The ease with which smugglers were able to diversify into other felonies argues against their status as primitive rebels and makes them appear more as professional criminals. Much better candidates as social criminals were the wreckers and coiners whose activities were firmly embedded in local folkways rather than in universal activities (like smuggling) and who therefore could not shift readily into fresh areas of criminality.

There is, however, one area where a partial rehabilitation of the socio-political importance of smugglers is feasible. The coincidence of serious hunger riots in 1757 with a recrudescence of smuggling on the outbreak of the Seven Years War suggests a common basis in social protest.[163] The tradition of violence in smuggling provided a context for the food rioters' vehement defiance of the authorities. This tendency was reinforced during the hunger riots of the late 1760s. Rioting took place in areas where smuggling was also rife: in Canterbury, Exeter, Kings Lynn, Norwich, Suffolk, Dorset, Tiverton, and the coast of Cornwall. Some of the bloodiest encounters between troops and rioters took place in Devizes in 1766 – a notorious smuggling area.[164] Both phenomena had a common origin in wartime consequences. The economic depression produced the hunger riots; the discharge of skilled seamen into unemployment virtually guaranteed that some of them would turn to contraband. The rise in smuggling meant that the government had particular difficulty in enforcing its embargo on the export of grain (introduced in September 1766).[165]

Yet in general eighteenth-century smuggling was too heterogeneous an activity to be pinned down in any one category. The Janus-face of contraband is everywhere apparent. If the defiance of the Hawkhurst gang and their plebeian origins suggests 'class struggle without class', the alien cynic can reply that their organization, division of labour, intelligence system, and distribution network makes them the prototype of the organized crime of a later era. It is not for nothing that we have chosen to speak of 'local mafias'. All in all, it is safe to conclude that there are better candidates for the title of social criminal than the 'gentlemen' of the English coast.

One of the most notorious eighteenth-century crimes that received the sanction of the entire local community was wrecking: either pillaging the contents of ships wrecked through natural disaster of 'act of God' or the deliberate luring of ships on to the rocks so that they could be destroyed and then despoiled.[166] This was a felony particularly associated with Cornwall, as in Ethel Smyth's opera The Wreckers, and it is true that only in Cornwall did the practice receive the endorsement of virtually tne entire community. But wrecking by no means took place only in Cornwall. It was also, along with smuggling, a feature of Sussex life.[167] In 1765 one of Horace Walpole's friends described the practice as being endemic in Sussex, though this can be taken lightly, as a typical example of the kind of hyperbole that was batted to and fro in correspondence with the lord of Strawberry Hill.[168]

Wrecking was also particularly associated with North Wales and the Wirral peninsula (especially Hoylake).[169] The whole of the North Wales coast was reported roaring drunk in 1758 after a vessel with a huge cargo of wines and spirits ran aground on the Welsh approaches to Liverpool.[170] More usually, though, wrecking on the Wirral peninsula was a hard-headed business venture. The men of Hoylake sold their ill-gotten goods to dealers in Liverpool. It was said that wrecking was a full-time occupation for the inhabitants of the stretch of coast from West Kirby to what is now New Brighton. The villagers of Hoylake practised a rigid endogamy in order to keep the business 'in the family.'[171]

Wrecking involved a clear-cut defiance of the law in the name of the sovereignty of local folkways. The law differentiating private property from the public domain of shipwreck proper dated back to Henry II. Crucial to the distinction was the survival of passengers or crew from the ship.[172] It followed, therefore, that one way to establish a 'wreck' was for the wreckers to make sure that no one escaped from the ship alive. In this way a law designed to protect private property effectively imperilled survivors from shipwreck. What the sea had not destroyed, the hand of the wrecker would.

Naturally, we owe the few extant stories of the brutality of the wreckers to the handful who were pillaged but not murdered. One such case followed the destruction of the *Charming Jenny* on the coast of Anglesey in 1774, when the wreckers put out false lights to lure the ship on to the rocks.[173] The sole survivors were the captain and his wife, who carried 170 guineas on to the shore with her. The captain takes up the story:

> Nearly exhausted they lay for some time, till the savages of the adjacent places rushed down upon the devoted victims. The lady was just able to lift a handkerchief up to her head, when her husband was torn from her side. They cut his buckles from his shoes, and deprived him of every covering. Happy to escape with his life, he hastened to the beach in search of his wife, when horrible to tell! her half-naked and plundered corpse presented itself to his view.[174]

That sort of experience was common in encounters with the wreckers, even though the Act of 1753 made it a non-clergyable felony to kill or impede anyone from trying to escape a wreck. It was also a capital offence to put out false lights to draw a ship on to the rocks or into any other danger.[175] Yet the wreckers persisted in their belief that it was the law, not their activities that was wrong. In some ways wrecking was the century's most dramatic assertion of the supremacy of customary rights to statute law.[176]

Although wrecking was not a purely Cornish activity, its practice elsewhere paled into insignificance alongside the example of Cornwall and the Scilly Islands. Defoe, in a dithyrambic attack on the islanders, said that anyone wrecked on the extreme south-westerly coast of England would soon discover 'the rocks themselves not more merciless than the people who range about them for their prey'.[177] Not even John Wesley, for all his fulminations, was able to make significant inroads into something so deeply embedded in the local culture.[178]

It is no exaggeration to say that the entire economy of Cornwall was fuelled by wrecking.[179] Cornish tin miners used the proceeds from despoiling wrecked ships and their half-dead survivors to supplement their basic income. The term 'wreck' was interpreted liberally. Any vessel temporarily stranded but refloatable on the next tide was regarded as fair game by the Cornishmen. When ships ran aground in Cornwall, the problem for their captains was not to refloat them but to do it quickly, before the inevitable crowd of vultures, armed with clubs and poleaxes, arrived to claim their 'rights'.[180]

The depredations of the wreckers were a clear threat to the shipowning community, the insurance companies, and the merchant class in general. From the mid-1730s their representations to the government became more vociferous and insistent.[181] It was their combined pressure that led to the 1753 Act.[182] This Act tightened the existing legislation by dealing with 'indirect' wrecking, such as putting out false lights. It also made it a non-clergyable offence to loot wreckage, even if no one had survived a shipwreck.

The 1753 Act was the most obvious dead letter in the history of eighteenth-century legislation. Consequently, the authorities sometimes called out the military to deal with particularly serious challenges to its authority. Detachments of troops sometimes stood guard over stranded ships bearing particularly precious cargoes; this was often the case with East Indiamen that ran aground. If the wreckers persisted in their attempts to exercise their 'rights', the troops had orders to open fire. There were several such confrontations during the century. In one shoot-out between soldiers and wreckers near Bridgend in 1782, the casualties amounted to a dozen, with three killed.[183]

Occasionally, too, the elite, who normally turned a blind eye to an activity so firmly embedded in local communities, decided that an exemplary death sentence was necessary.[184] But nothing more clearly underlines the general attitude towards crime and punishment than the fate of Burke's 1776 attempt to put the law of wrecking on a rationalistic footing. His idea was to compel the community (technically the 'hundred') to compensate all injured parties for all losses taken as a result of wrecking.[185] The bill was defeated by a small majority on the ground that collective responsibility did not provide a suitable remedy for the offence, and that the innocent would be punished together with the guilty. Significantly, in rejecting Burke's bill, the House did not so much as suggest ways in which the existing law could be properly enforced.[186] The elite attitude to wrecking revealed English empiricism, 'hunch theory', 'muddling through', 'the pursuit of intimations' at its apogee. There is a considerable irony in the perishing of Burke by his own sword, for it was he more than anyone who habitually championed the idea that custom and tradition were always superior to reason.

The fate of Burke's wrecking bill also demonstrates that elite credibility was a key factor in the decision to enforce the criminal law. Those who explain eighteenth-century fondness for the exemplary sentence in terms of the absence of a professional police force need to explain why there was not a single mention of the difficulties of enforcement in the 1776 debate. The discussion turned entirely on matters of principle. The reason for elite complaisance is clear. Serious affrays (that is, threats to the authority of the central government) were rare. Wrecking was, outside the mercantile community proper, generally considered a bagatelle. The reformer Sir William Eden even wanted the repeal of the 1753 Act, since he considered capital punishment inappropriate for the offence.[187] As a recent student has put it:

> Wrecking attracted less persistent attention from the authorities than poaching or smuggling. It was an offence against property, but not, like poaching, a violation of the sacred property of the landed magistracy. Nor, like smuggling, did it offer the insult of an offence against the royal revenues.[188]

Wrecking takes us straight to the heart of the whole 'social crime' issue. It is difficult to assign the activity to the class of 'primitive rebellion' for two reasons. First, although wrecking was mainly a rural plebeian activity, in the communities where it was entrenched it was engaged in by all classes.[189] The local magistrates connived at the practice; in Cornwall even the clergy joined in.[190] The defence of local folkways against the legislation of a distant central government is a very different matter from inchoate class warfare. Second, unless we accept a red-blooded version of cultural and ethical relativism, there are no moral grounds on which the vicious and inhumane behaviour involved in wrecking could be justified or condoned. That the custom was far removed from the domain of morality can be seen from the telling anecdote involving a Cornishman whose wife informed him that Wesley had condemned wrecking. His reply: 'Wesley? What do 'ee knaw 'bout wrecking?'[191]

11

Poaching

Thy Forests, Windsor! and they green Retreats,
At once the Monarch's and the Muse's Seats
                    Alexander Pope, *Windsor Forest*

Windsor Forest . . . as bleak, as barren, and as villainous a
heath as ever man set eyes on.
                    William Cobbett, *Rural Rides*

He did not know that a keeper is only a poacher turned
outside in, and a poacher a keeper turned inside out.
                    Charles Kingsley, *The Water Babies*

In Nottinghamshire there is a very heptarchy of little
kingdoms elbowing one another, and the barons of them
want nothing but small armies to make inroads into one
another's parks, murder deer and massacre park-keepers.
                    Horace Walpole to Richard Bentley, August 1756

In all eras poaching is one of the most powerful collective images evoked
by the entire structure and ideology of property relations.[1] Taking their
cue from Genesis, where it is stated that animals were created by God for
the use of *all* men, opponents of aristocratic privilege in game have
always stressed that restrictions on the common appropriation of animals
for food offend against the law of God and nature. Against this, absolute
monarchy entrenched the idea that hunting rights were peculiarly vested
in the king himself. Blackstone instanced this as the classic triumph of
Norman feudal law over the ancient Saxon system.[2] For hundreds of
years, then, there was a latent submerged conflict between feudal
privileges and the 'race-memory' of ancient rights and customs. In the
eighteenth century a new variable was added: the rights of property,
triumphant in the Glorious Revolution. This three-way process was one
of the reasons for the awesome complexity of the game laws, famously
commented on by Blackstone.[3] In the eighteenth century the laws on

poaching were Janus-faced. On the one hand, the feudal residue of the king's sole right to hunt game impacted with the absolute right of private property; on the other, strict legal title to land conflicted with customary rights of commoners and cottagers. If the 1671 Game Act was the genesis of the first conflict, the notorious Waltham Black Act of 1722 provided the cockpit for the second.

In a sense, then, there were two separate conflicts involving poaching in the eighteenth century. There was genuine class conflict between the landed classes and their tenants who attempted to supplement their livelihood by taking animals illegally. And there was a 'contradiction' between men of wealth who did not possess the necessary property qualification to hunt game and those who did. The antagonism caused by this anomaly led to a certain fluidity in class relations and to *ad hoc* trans-class coalitions. The obfuscation caused by these cross-cutting rhythms of conflict was heightened by the definition of 'game' laid down in the 1671 Act. Strictly speaking in terms of that Act, 'game' meant hares, partridges, pheasants, and moor fowl. Deer, rabbits, wild ducks, badgers, otters, foxes, etc. were not regarded as game, but fell in the normal ambit of private property. No special property qualification was needed to hunt them.[4]

A closer look at the 1671 Act will help to clarify matters. This statute forbade anyone to hunt game who did not possess a freehold worth £100 a year or a leasehold worth £150 a year, was not the son and heir of an esquire or the owner of parks, warrens, chases or free fisheries.[5] Such provisos represented considerable privilege. The sum of £100 in the eighteenth century was roughly ten years' income for a labourer. This meant that without such a property qualification a man could not kill game, even on his own land. On the other hand, hunters with the qualification could follow game on to another's land or even invade it for the purpose of hunting. The only sanction possessed by the owner of the land was an action for trespass. In this way, the rights of hunting overrode those of private property, and this remained the case in law until an Act of 1831.[6]

This feudal residue was one of the few (outside Scotland) to hold up the triumph of the moneyed interest after 1688. The passage of the Game Act in the reign of Charles II is itself significant, as it represented the last fling of the old guard. One of its chief purposes was to reassert the cultural and economic supremacy of the country landed interests against the city merchants and financiers.[7] But, as Blackstone pointed out, whereas the old Norman forest laws 'established only one mighty hunter throughout the land, the game laws have raised a little Nimrod in every manor'.[8]

The property qualifications of the 1671 Act provoked particular bitterness. On the one hand, there was the absurdity that a man who did not possess the property qualification but who had invested, say, £10,000 in the public funds, could not hunt game. This absurdity approached a limit in one case of a former poacher who went one better than 'poacher turned gamekeeper' by inheriting property and thus qualifying for game huntsman status; he made the most of his sudden social ascent by taunting the gamekeepers who had previously tracked him on his illegal forays.[9]

The other main irritant to farmers whose crops were trampled by the gentry in pursuit of hares was that 'game' could not be bought. This was a case of the 'unspeakable in pursuit of the unsellable', for *noblesse oblige* dictated that it was beneath the dignity of a true gentleman to hunt game for commercial profit.[10] Such 'banausic' attitudes were for farmers or others of the 'middling sort'. A 'sportsman' did not sell his 'bag', however big. One of the most prized privileges of the gentry was enjoying a monopoly on game and sending the catch to their friends as a gift. The same consideration applied to venison, even though it was not strictly 'game'.[11]

Yet although yeomen suffered irritation and humiliation as a result of the game laws, they were not the main targets of the 1671 Act. The principal objective was the 'idleness' of the poor. The aim of the game laws was to prevent the poor from subsisting without working and to prevent the emergence of a 'black economy' based on game. As the eighteenth century progressed, it also became increasingly important to inculcate work discipline into the toiling classes.[12] The sacrifices that farmers had to make in ceding their absolute right of property to 'sportsmen' could thus be presented as a trade-off to keep the lower orders in their place and increase social stability. The problem, from the point of view of the yeomanry, was that the landed gentry were achieving this desirable end while making no sacrifices themselves.

The desire to choke off traditional 'perks' and thus subject the labour force to a rigidly controlled wage economy underlay the progressive tightening of laws relating to the hunting of wild animals not properly regarded as game. An Act of 1692 forbade anyone to take deer or rabbits without the permission of the relevant landowner. At first the punishment for killing deer was £30 or a year's imprisonment, but after 1717 the usual eighteenth-century penalty for killing a deer without permission was seven years' transportation.[13] For killing rabbits in warrens or for keeping dogs or snares, the punishment was £5 or three months in gaol.

While the taking of deer was originally considered a peccadillo, a spate of such poaching in the royal forests in the early eighteenth century led to a dramatic stiffening in the authorities' attitude. The royal parks and forests had always stood outside the general system of property and law.[14] Poaching in the king's domains smacked of *lèse-majesté*. These royal parks were regarded as hallowed ground in more ways than one.

Some of the medieval rights of sanctuary still attached to them. An ingenious aristocrat who enjoyed the royal favour could use these ancient rights to evade the law. The example of George Fermor, second Earl of Lempster, is instructive here. In 1752 he was convicted of manslaughter after killing a man in a duel. Rather than take the consequences, he took refuge in the royal parks, knowing that his father was not long for this world. There he skulked until 1753 when his father died. On succeeding to the peerage, Lempster's immunity was complete.[15]

Another reason for the hardening of elite attitudes was that the posts of Hereditary Forester and Ranger in many of the great forests were increasingly sought after for the prestige they conferred. It became a status symbol to dine off umble pie – made from the umbles or entrails of deer – the traditional perquisite of the huntsman. Horace Walpole's friend George Montagu managed to secure this position in the forest of Rockingham in Northamptonshire, though not entitled to it by the strict principles of descent (it was supposed to devolve on other members of the Duke of Montagu's family).[16] Naturally, when great effort went into securing the right to special status symbols, their recipients did not take kindly to the enjoyment of those privileges by mere poachers.

Consequently, the last years of the eighteenth century's second decade saw a tightening of the noose around poachers in the great English forests. Rewards were offered for the apprehension of poachers in Sherwood, Macclesfield, Windsor, and New Forest.[17] The sum of £100 was offered for the capture of deer-killers in Windsor Forest in 1719 and 1722.[18] But what finally showed that the authorities meant business was the 1722 Waltham Black Act.

Nothing more clearly demonstrates the centrality of poaching as a collective image in the nexus of property relations than the fact that an Act ostensibly passed to deal with poachers, should, together with the Riot Act, have become the central point of the Bloody Code. As we have seen, the Black Act had a much wider sweep than a statute intended merely to protect the royal forests. It was not a response simply to deer-slaying. Depredations in Windsor Forest provided the occasion for draconian legislation; they were not its cause. Nevertheless, on the face of it the main group of capital offences included in the Act had to do with poaching. It was now a felony to hunt, wound or steal red or fallow deer, to poach hares and conies or to break the heads of fishponds; if these offences were committed in the royal forests, the felony was non-clergyable. If poachers went armed, disguised, or with their faces blacked, even if the poaching was not conducted in the royal forests, they were also committing a capital crime. This part of the Act struck at the long tradition of blacking up when poaching.[19]

The first group to fall foul of the Waltham Black Act were the so-called Waltham Blacks themselves (named after their practice of blackening their faces). The principal of deterrence once again proved a flop. The Act did not end poaching and affrays in the forests. What it did was to bring social tensions to a peak and to make the struggle between poachers and gentry much more bitter. Initially, Walpole solved the problem by branding the gangs of poachers operating in Windsor and other forests Jacobites. This was Walpole's invariable way with opponents. The Layer/Atterbury plot of 1722 enabled him to round up poachers in Windsor, using general warrants. The actual connection of poaching gangs with Jacobitism was slight. What they sometimes did was to use the 'king over the water' as a legitimating slogan for their illicit activities. But some 'Blacks' bitterly objected to being called Jacobite.[20]

In the struggle between Blacks and gamekeepers in Windsor Forest from 1720-3, the Blacks had the upper hand. The passage of the 1722 Act turned the tide, especially when the poachers made themselves especially vulnerable by shooting dead a gamekeeper's son in Windsor Forest.[21] A new pattern of escalating violence was evident. After a shoot-out between Blacks and keepers in September 1723, four poachers were taken prisoner. There was a similar affray at roughly the same time in the Forest of Bere. By the end of September the authorities had seven Blacks on their hands from the two incidents. They decided to make a terrible example. The prisoners were tried away from their locality, in a strange county, by juries who knew nothing of their local folkways. All seven were found guilty and executed.[22]

The utter inability even of sanguinary legislation like the Black Act to deter was shown by the spate of violence that broke out in the wake of these executions. It was not just the Windsor Blacks who were involved. There were also the Farnham Blacks, more formidable and with a natural leader, 'King John'.[23] More seriously, there was an overspill from London crime. The London poachers were active in Richmond Park and on Enfield Chase. They tended to hunt without horses and with crossbows, armed to the teeth and with packs of dogs. Immediately after the 'exemplary' sentence of the seven Blacks, in 1724-5, there occurred the worst outbreaks of violence yet. In April 1724 there was a shoot-out between rangers and poachers in Richmond Park which left one man dead.[24] Shortly afterwards, one of the leading London poachers, John Guy, was taken in ambush and executed under the Black Act, in April 1725. Three months later there was another major armed clash between poachers and keepers on Enfield Chase. An Edmonton blacksmith, Vulcan Gates, was hanged for his part in this.[25] Another victim was Aaron Maddocks, one-time associate of Jonathan Wild. Caught poaching on Enfield Chase, he was arrested and died in captivity in Newgate.[26]

What the Waltham Black Act undoubtedly did was to bring hatred and resentment of gamekeepers to the boil. Defoe, usually a staunch defender of the Whigs and all their works, considered that keepers and rangers were worse offenders against game conservation than the poachers themselves.[27] But it was not just the humbug of gamekeepers that made them feared and detested. Under the law their licence to kill extended to more than just game. To kill a poacher who 'resisted arrest' was justifiable homicide under the rubric of the 'advancement of public justice'.[28] A particularly grisly case in Cheddar in 1764 showed what resisting arrest could sometimes mean. The keeper of a rabbit warren and his three assistants opened fire on two men on suspicion of their being poachers. One was shot dead instantly. The other, who was wounded, threw down his gun and surrendered, but the keepers peppered his body with guns loaded with square pieces of lead 'which tore his body in a shocking manner'.[29] With such trigger-happy keepers to deal with, it is hardly surprising that poachers went armed and fought it out with keepers if intercepted. The ten years after the passage of the Black Act saw ferocious encounters between them, in Windsor Forest, in Sussex, Kent and Essex, in Oxfordshire and Northamptonshire.[30]

The keepers' greatest weapon, however, was not their firepower but their right to search for the illegal 'engines of destruction': guns, dogs, nets, and snares. None of these items could be possessed legally except by landlords and keepers. Carrying search warrants, gamekeepers could swoop on the cottage of a suspected poacher and destroy all staff nets, wire snares, greyhounds and lurchers they found there.[31] Needless to say, this increased the level of violence between keepers and poachers. The destruction of dogs was a particularly embittering experience. These were valuable animals, carefully bred and trained. Keepers, who were subject to routine threats and actual thrashings from the poachers, took a particular delight in despatching them. In one unsavoury scene in a Staffordshire ale house, a keeper who was struggling to wrest a dog from eight women, cut its throat before they could rescue it. Usually keepers shot the hounds on the spot, but when the local JP thought that the community poachers needed to be taught a hard lesson, he would arrange for lurchers to be ritually hanged in mimicry of Tyburn.[32]

It was clear from all this that one way to deal with poachers was to tax dogs at source by forcing breeders to be licensed. After all, for what purpose did poor cottagers incur the extra expense of keeping and feeding a dog if not for poaching?[33] In 1784 a tax of £1 for each greyhound or lurcher was proposed.[34] Such a tax was often suggested but, curiously, never implemented. A dog-tax was introduced only in 1796.[35] It seems that there is another instance of the eighteenth-century resistance to any tax that would increase the number of officials and bureaucrats empowered to interfere with 'ancient liberties'.

Tension between gamekeepers and the rest of the community did not end with the poor labourers who poached to supplement their meagre incomes. Many of the most committed opponents of the game laws were 'middling' men, who had wealth and property yet were 'unqualified' because they lacked the £100 per annum from freehold. And even where men were qualified, a local grandee who claimed privileges of free chase and free warren would use his keepers to keep them off his land. Rich farmers thus debarred would retaliate by killing all deer and hares that came onto their land, whatever the strict letter of the law.[36]

Conflict between these men of middle rank and gamekeepers was particularly serious, since these wealthy 'poachers' could afford to mount a legal defence. One farmer who snatched back the hare a gamekeeper took from him, counted it money well spent when he paid a £5 penalty and five guineas damages for the privilege of horsewhipping the keeper.[37] It was a common complaint of these men of middle status that the keepers behaved 'impertinently' to them. But they had one easy means of revenge. The jurors at quarter sessions and assizes were overwhelmingly made up of farmers and tradesmen. When a case involving the game laws was tried before them, they nearly always refused to convict, since they regarded these laws as an infringement of their own property rights.[38] Moreover, even if the farmers had been willing to convict poaching labourers to keep the lower orders in their place, their own infringements of the game laws made them vulnerable to having information laid against them by the labouring poor.[39]

The game laws thus provided one of the most glaring 'contradictions' in eighteenth-century society. They alienated a whole group of men who in other circumstances were ardent champions of the rights of property and the punishment of thieves. The game laws also superficially weakened the social cement binding masters and men by putting a powerful weapon in the hands of the servants and labourers of those farmers (an overwhelming majority) who flouted those laws.[40]

Beyond the game laws themselves there was the antagonism caused by those territorial magnates who held rights of free chase and free warren, giving them the sole privilege to hunt game over huge tracts of land. Some of these magnates gave their keepers discretionary powers to enforce their rights even against members of the gentry who did possess the landed qualification demanded by the game laws. Not surprisingly, the keepers availed themselves of this unique opportunity to tweak the noses of their social 'superiors'. Querulousness from the middle farmers about the 'impertinence' of game keepers seemed mild alongside the deluge of similar complaints that poured in from aggrieved gentlemen who sometimes saw their own hounds shot on their own land by keepers trespassing after wandering deer from a neighbouring estate. The Earl of Uxbridge, who jealously guarded his manorial rights on Cannock Chase, and encouraged his keepers in a hard-nosed attitude to neighbouring gentry, was a notorious target for legal actions brought by affronted 'gentlemen'.[41]

By the mid-century the game laws and their associated ideas had produced a situation of rare confusion. Except in circumstances where the central government exerted itself to manipulate the legal system and pervert the normal course of justice, as with Walpole and the Blacks in 1725, the Waltham Black Act remained largely a dead letter as a deterrent to poaching. It was far too blunt a weapon. Juries would convict under it in capital cases only when the national interest was brought into the picture, as when Walpole muddied the waters by dubbing the Blacks Jacobites, and even then he had to remove the accused from their localities to get the required verdict. The reason was simply that the men who largely composed the juries hated the game laws. By the 1730s the problem of poaching in royal forests, which the Black Act was supposed to end once and for all, was as acute as ever.[42] Rewards for the apprehension of poachers in royal forests once again started to appear.[43]

Failure to secure convictions by jury trials meant that the game laws either had to be abandoned or some other means of punishing poachers had to be found. The solution hit on was to transfer jurisdiction over most game cases from quarter sessions to two justices of the peace sitting in summary sessions.[44] But the trade-off for evading the prejudices of a jury in this way was that the JPs could not pass capital sentences; they were restricted to awarding fines or detention in houses of correction.[45]

The central absurdity of the game laws continued to be that they were a relic of Norman feudalism, incompatible with an era of absolute property rights. If all poachers had been labourers and servants, the middling sort would have made common cause against them with the aristocracy and gentry. This possibility was ruled out by the property qualification for 'sportsmen'. And if the laws governing hunting and shooting had been restricted to the laws concerning 'game' properly so-called, the gentry and aristocracy could have closed ranks against all classes below them. What prevented *this* in turn was another class of feudal residues: baronial rights and royal franchises awarded centuries earlier to great territorial magnates. Ordinarily those with the property qualification were free to shoot or course game anywhere, even on another's land; the only possible sanction they faced was an action for trespass. In this sense game belonged to the propertied, though no one owned it. But game within chases or warrens or parks or free fisheries belonged to the owner alone.[46] Moreover the game in such preserves continued to belong to the owner even if it strayed outside his property limits. This was the excuse, or justification, for sending gamekeepers after it into other gentlemen's parks. The ultimate insult added to this injury occurred when a royal franchise explicitly gave the title-holder exclusive game rights over hundreds of acres of *the property of other qualified men.*[47]

It is the extreme complexity of the many laws and customs surrounding game in the eighteenth century that makes it difficult to generalize at all about poaching. The social composition of the poacher was as various as the laws that converted him into a poacher. A man taking game illegally could be a member of an organization of Blacks making forays into the royal forests.[48] He could be a starving cottager setting a snare, as in the stereotypical image.[49] He could be an 'unqualified' farmer killing game on his property. Or he could be a 'qualified' sportsman straying onto the individual preserve of an aristocrat holding a royal franchise.

For this reason there was no overall consensus on the criminality of poaching. It was *sui generis* in more ways than one. For a start, there was very little interlock between poaching and other forms of crime, even among the 'common poacher'. One of the executed Blacks in 1725 was a former highway robber. And one of Jonathan Wild's ex-thieftakers, Aaron Maddocks, turned to poaching.[50] Otherwise the poacher was largely a member of a traditional community exercising a customary right in defiance of the formal legal code. Among the labouring classes there was a universal belief that poaching was not theft, that the animals of the earth were a form of common wealth that had been illegitimately appropriated by powerful interests. All sectors in society suffered from theft, but only those who defied God's law suffered from poaching.

The only people likely to accept the justice of the laws on poaching in their entirety were the great aristocrats and their hangers-on. Horace Walpole, one such, typically defended the game laws and the ancient prerogatives as an integral part of the British Constitution.[51] Walpole was a great one for annexing anything that redounded to his advantage, like a supply of venison from his aristocratic friends, as part of 'English liberty'. His testimony can be largely disregarded. The impoverished rural labourer had a much keener sense of the genuine content of these ancient liberties than the lord of Strawberry Hill.

Higher up the social scale from the cottager, the attitude of the middle farmer was that poaching of one's animals by the lower orders was theft but that one's own taking of the game 'belonging' to a qualified gentleman, when it was on one's own property, was not. Finally, among the qualified sportsmen, the attitude to the aristocrats who claimed ancient prerogatives was that they were breaking the informal gentleman's code. To enjoy coursing and shooting mutual indulgence was necessary; freedom to pursue hares and pheasants onto another's land implied the corresponding freedom on your neighbour's part. Men like the Pagets and Uxbridges on Cannock Chase, on this view, wanted rights but refused to acknowledge duties. To the gentry the great aristocrats were therefore social cheats. The aristocratic rejoinder to this was succinctly expressed by a pamphleteer in 1772, the flavour of whose remarks accurately pins down the cynicism of the great magnates: 'What man of sense or sensibility would form a contract of copartnery in the article of wives, or to allow every one of his neighbours all rights and privileges with his spouse, because he had the same with theirs?'[52]

To this already complex web of social relations fresh skeins were added by the pace of economic and social change after 1750. The middle sectors of society, especially in London, were becoming increasingly 'gentrified'. Part of this process involved a taste for the culinary delights of the gentry, especially hare and venison. There was a demand for exactly the products explicitly barred to the unqualified by the Act of 1707.[53] This had added to the 1671 'qualifications' by imposing a ban on the *sale* of game. At the same time, as firearms increasingly replaced hawks and nets in the countryside, it became easier to kill animals and their numbers diminished. There was thus a clear conflict between technology and culture. Firepower was reducing the supply of animals even as the demand for game and venison augmented. To prevent the diminishing of the game stock by the widespread use of guns, Parliament enacted new legislation, tightening up on the loopholes affecting the sale of game. In an attempt to enforce this, the gentry formed themselves into 'game associations'.[54]

The effect of an absolute prohibition on the sale of game at the precise moment that the demand for it was intensifying was predictable. As with Prohibition in the USA in the 1920s, organized gangs arose to satisfy the demand. From 1755 onwards, the poaching gang increasingly displaced the lone poacher. The gentry's Gaming Association fought a losing battle with these gangs. This was not surprising. Outside their own ranks, the gentry could command no support for a monopoly that seemed merely a glaring instance of selfish privilege. By the late 1760s the Association virtually conceded defeat in the struggle to shut down the black market.[55]

The general resentment of the gentry's game privileges meant that it was comparatively easy for the gangs to organize their illicit trade. The natural link between the poachers and their urban customers was the 'higgler' or itinerant poultry dealer. Poorly paid stage-coach drivers were also more than willing to act as middlemen and carry contraband cargoes to the metropolis. The illicit trade in game burgeoned. In the 1780s no less than 500 heads of household in the county of Norfolk were said to be principally involved in organized poaching.[56]

Another aspect of social change favouring the growth of poaching gangs was enclosure. As the century wore on and game became more precious, landowners began to fence in and enclose their stocks. This was also an aspect of the conflict between property rights and hunting privileges. The effect of fencing was to restrict the theoretically unimpeded right of the sportsman to follow game on to private land. The development of what were in fact game reserves played into the hands of the organized poacher. It was easier to catch the animals since they were not running free; more important, the pickings in one enclosed area were rich enough to support a large gang.[57]

The increasing value placed on hares, partridges and wild fowl extended to other animals not strictly 'game'. The 1750s saw much harsher treatment of illegal rabbiting – catching rabbits without the landowner's permission (since the game qualification was not required). This was because the great territorial magnates were finding investment in rabbits increasingly profitable. The Earl of Uxbridge began to turn Cannock Chase into a huge rabbit warren and to forbid cottagers to graze their sheep and cattle on his lands, despite their centuries-old customary right. This was because sheep were in direct competition with rabbits and hares; all three were close croppers of the grass.[58]

The result of all this was exacerbated social tensions in the countryside. Great landowners turned commercial entrepreneur denied the poor farmers and labourers their traditional grazing rights. Meanwhile a vicious and bloody conflict was waged between the authorities and the poaching gangs. Attitudes hardened on all sides. The capital provisions of the Waltham Black Act could be exercised only through juries who were reluctant to convict on offences relating to game or deer. All that was left for the magistrates sitting in summary session was to order the harshest possible secondary punishments. Instead of fines and imprisonment, JPs now often ordered whippings. For stealing a hare, one young man in Reading in 1773 received the most severe whipping the locality had witnessed for generations.[59]

The conflict over customary rights was relatively short-lived. At first the labourers and yeomen scored some striking victories over the great territorial barons. A sensational instance was on Cannock Chase. On 28 December 1753 some 200 to 300 men commenced a two-week campaign to destroy the Earl of Uxbridge's 'illegal' rabbit warrens. Using clubs and ferrets to kill the rabbits and spades to fill in the burrows, by mid-January 1754 they had destroyed five of the six warrens on the chase plus between 10,000 and 15,000 rabbits. The total damage was assessed at more than £3,000.[60] The local magistrates were unwilling to do anything about the slaughter, both because they feared a blood-bath on the chase if they ordered in the military and because of political enmity towards Uxbridge; in addition, Uxbridge had banned one of them from hunting on the chase! Yet this was only a respite for the commoners. The sheer political influence of Uxbridge and the immense costs of litigation (which he could afford but the small farmers could not) led to his complete victory. In 1756 Chief Justice Lord Mansfield handed down his decision in the Court of King's Bench. The judgement was that a landlord had an absolute right to put conies on his own land; the commoner could not destroy a lord's estate just to preserve his own right of common.[61] This precedent spelt death to customary rights all over England. While sheep were displacing clansmen in the Highlands of Scotland, in England rabbits were displacing sheep.

Yet the struggle over common rights came nowhere near the ferocity of the battle between poaching gangs and the authorities. Significantly the greatest loss of life came, not in the class struggle over open access to grazing lands, but in the war over privilege between selfish gentry and profiteering gangs. The old-style poacher had used his skills at netting and snaring (usually taught him by his father) to get the better of gamekeepers in a battle of wits. The new organized poacher largely relied on the main force of guns and numbers. Violence bred violence. The keepers had instructions to shoot to kill. The poachers retaliated in kind. There were many shoot-outs between the two sides. In 1781 there was a pitched battle between poachers and gamekeepers on the Duke of Buckingham's estates in Norfolk; one keeper was killed.[62]

The hard-liners wanted to extend the Bloody Code to deal with this challenge to their authority from the poaching gangs. New laws were directed against night poaching, prescribing two-year terms of imprisonment for members of gangs. Some elite members wanted to go further and amend the Waltham Black Act so as to make night poaching a capital offence, on the ground that poaching at night was tantamount to going 'blacked' or in disguise.[63] But by the time the threat from the poaching gangs was felt acutely, opinion was already running strongly against the Black Act. A statute of 1776 modified the capital provisions regarding deer: instead of death, the penalty for killing or carrying away a deer was to be a fine for the first offence and seven years transportation for the second.[64] It was thought better in general to keep the Black Act out of the picture and attempt to deal with the problem by new, specific laws, such as the 1786 tax on hunting, which required the purchase of a hunting licence.[65]

At the same time the insolence of the poaching gangs could not be seen to go totally unpunished. The authorities looked round for a bloody example that would serve as an awful warning. The chance came in 1779 after a shoot-out between poachers and gamekeepers in Norfolk. Although no one was actually killed in the affray, so that the charge could not even be manslaughter, let alone murder, all the reserve powers of the Code were brought into play to make an example of one of the poachers. Shoemaker Thomas Bell was the unlucky one chosen to make the ritual procession to the gallows.[66]

But for the most part owners of game ignored the law and turned to weapons of destruction to deter the poachers. The principal deterrents were man traps and spring guns. Man traps had iron jaws with sharp teeth which, when sprung, caught and held the leg of the victim. They could weigh as much as eighty-eight pounds and have teeth one and a half inches in length. Spring guns were first introduced in the late 1770s. They were mounted on pivots and controlled by wires that extended out into the ground round about. When one of these wires was pulled, the gun would swing round in the direction of the disturbance and fire its charge. Four poachers were killed by a combination of these traps in a single night in Suffolk in 1785.[67]

The use of such fearsome devices argues for increasing desperation by the gentry. When charged with a cynical disregard for human life, they replied that they prevented an even greater loss of life in shoot-outs between poachers and gamekeepers, although the relative figures on fatalities provide no substance for this argument. What the spring gun and the man trap really represented was the gentry's contempt for urban culture – both the rising aspirations for new meats that led to the illicit trade in the first place, and the hamfistedness of the urban practitioners of the new poaching. There had been a mutual grudging respect between the old-style poacher and the country squire. The indigenous villager had enough skill to circumvent crude killing machines like the man trap and the spring gun. But the 'townie' with his reliance on guns and manpower lacked the woodcraft to deal with them. In that case, thought the squirearchy, the alien interlopers deserved their fate. In the late eighteenth century the gentry had the edge in this technological battle. It took until early in the nineteenth century for the 'new' poacher to master the crude man-killing devices.[68]

The game laws were in some ways a classical example of eighteenth-century law. In others they were an anachronism. Their most anachronistic feature was that they denied the absolute rights of private property; this anomaly was rectified only in 1831. Their organic relationship with other eighteenth-century law was shown by the huge discretionary element allowed to magistrates in their implementation and by their blatant class nature.

The standard accusation against the game laws is that they were singularly harsh.[69] One disgruntled critic wrote:

> There is not a worse-constituted tribunal on the face of the earth, not even that of the Turkish Cadi [sic], than that at which summary convictions on the Game Laws constantly take place; I mean a bench or a brace of sporting justices.[70]

In the sense of being unjust, the charge can be sustained. But they were neither especially severe by the standards of the Bloody Code, nor were they rigorously enforced. The harshest aspects of the law were the capital penalties relating to stealing deer after dark, but these were rarely invoked. Otherwise the laws against poultry stealing were in general harsher.[71] Nor is there much evidence that magistrates bent the law in favour of those qualified to hunt game. In fact, as E. P. Thompson has famously pointed out, with the 'rule of law' the eighteenth-century elite made a rod that often beat their own backs.[72] In contrast, the ordinary poacher had available to him a well-known legal loophole called the 'friendly denunciation'. If a man's friend laid an accusation of poaching before the magistrates, he could forestall a similar pending prosecution by the keepers. When about to be prosecuted, a man could arrange for his friend to denounce him. The JP would fine the poacher and then pay the fine to the informant as a reward. The informant (that is, the friend) would then return the 'fine' to the poacher. In this way a poacher could circumvent the law by means of a quiet chat over a pint in an alehouse.[73]

The accusation that the game laws were class legislation, on the other hand, cannot be rebutted. Most eighteenth-century law defended property, that is to say, it united the elite and middle sectors against the propertyless. What infuriated those who did not benefit from the game laws and the other laws governing manorial rights was that these were in no sense primarily a defence of *property* but of feudal rights. In that sense, the game laws were out of true with the rest of the Bloody Code. The most recent student of the subject has ingeniously defended them on just those grounds.[74] In the first place, there had to be *some* legislation to protect wildlife. With an expanding population, a total absence of laws on game would have led to its being wiped out in a single generation. Given then that there had to be laws on the subject, better by far that they should have been the anomalous ones of 1671 and other pre-1688 statutes than the sanguinary laws against property as such that were the scandal of eighteenth-century England. If the undergrowth of law on game had been cleared up, as Blackstone proposed, punishment could only have been harsher.

Yet it would be a mistake to infer from this that the game laws did not serve the interests of the elite. Simply *because* they did not protect property *tout court*, they served the other, arguably more important, function of the Code, reinforcing authority and deference. One of the reasons why night poaching was not dealt with more severely was that it did not involve overt defiance to society's norms. Theft at night was compatible with deference in the daytime; night poaching therefore did not seem to merit the toughest penalties.[75]

Moreover, precisely because the game laws were so widely unpopular in so many strata, they were the perfect means of promoting the ideology of 'equality before the law'. Gentlemen as well as commoners received summonses for poaching offences; there seemed no class favouritism there. The alliance between landowning farmers who did not possess the hunting qualification and the common labourer, both in poaching itself and in providing alibis for each other, created an artificial trans-class coalition that 'mystified' and obfuscated the true, partial, unequal nature of the law. By smoothing relations between labourers and farmers in this way and uniting them in opposition to the gentry, the game laws may well have increased stability and reduced tensions in rural society. The over-arching class nature of the Code in general could be obscured.[76]

Even the legal loopholes could be turned to advantage by sophisticated elite leaders. The very impotence that even great lords had to suffer on occasions by working through the rule of law could be masked by appearances of clemency. Territorial magnates could appear to act wisely and compassionately, when in fact their 'mercy' was simply the fact that they lacked enough evidence to secure a conviction.[77]

Similar nuances have to be considered when we weigh up whether poaching can be admitted into the canon of 'social crime'. In one sense this is an open-and-shut issue, since by definition the 1671 Game Act laid down that certain actions were not crimes in themselves but only became so because of the social class of the offender. *With* the property qualification, you could shoot hares with impunity even if you threw the carcasses away to rot; *without* it, you were deemed to be a criminal if you took one hare when your family was starving. It is tempting to leave the matter there. When a law is generally held in contempt and only half-heartedly enforced, one is drawn to conclude that it is scarcely a true law at all; therefore its transgressors can hardly be criminals, whether 'social' or of any other stripe, except through the pettifoggery of 'the law is the law is the law'.

Yet the issue bears further investigation, if only because the game laws were so widely regarded as unjust. Where so many people in so many different strata broke the law, it follows that if we wish to pursue the 'social criminal' tack, some distinctions will have to be made if the concept is to retain any meaning. The meaning usually assigned has to do with the distinction between legitimacy and legality. Thus, according to the law of the land it was illegal to coin, to smuggle, to wreck. Yet according to the local customs and folkways of, respectively, Yorkshire, Sussex, and Cornwall it was not. There was thus a geographical and cultural homgeneity about the 'criminals'. Such a distinction does not work with poaching. Poaching went on from Cumberland to Kent and from Land's End to Tyneside, by middle and labouring classes alike.

To refine the notion of social crime, we have to establish further subdivisions. To return to our original *philosophical/moral* definition, as opposed to a sociological categorization, it is clear that those who were concerned to defend customary rights against the Code simply to sustain a traditional way of life must be viewed in a different light from those who poached simply to make a profit. The Waltham Blacks and the cottagers of Cannock Chase would thus appear in one category; the large-scale post-1750 poaching gangs would appear in another.

Sceptics have from the earliest times asserted that poachers did not differ in any significant respect from other criminals. On this view, a man who poached would be just as likely to housebreak or commit highway robbery. In the 1780s the pampleteer Zouch classified poachers as the lowest form of life, alongside prostitutes and pawnbrokers.[78] A similar attitude seems to underlie the attitude of some modern scholars towards the Waltham Blacks.[79] Yet the case for 'King John' and the others has been convincingly been made out by E. P. Thompson.[80]

It is otherwise when we turn to the large poaching gangs of the second half of the century. This is not a sociological issue, for the social composition of the poaching gangs was remarkably close to that of the Blacks. By no means all were rural labourers 'on the make'. Weavers, miners, and other 'mechanics' went into the countryside to kill for the market. A wide variety of industrial workers can be found among known poachers: watch-makers, ribbon weavers, stocking-makers.[81] The important thing about the gangs was that they hunted not in support of a traditional way of life or out of simple need but to supply the tables of the new bourgeoisie in the cities. The 'pursuit of profit by other means' is very far from being the same thing as primitive rebellion. It was not their *group* activity but their commercial intentions that debars the poaching gangs from the status of 'social criminal'.[82]

The most striking thing about the laws on poaching is their relationship to general social factors. The way capitalism burst the fetters of traditional society can be seen in the increasing role of the market. On Cannock Chase the Earl of Uxbridge began to turn himself into a commercial entrepreneur to supply the demand for new types of meat. In the countryside poaching gangs arose to satisfy the tastes of the new urban bourgeoisie. These were tendencies that bypassed the game laws. Yet even these anomalous and widely unpopular laws had their role to play in the formation of a new society based on wages and prices. Laws against poaching were necessary not just to restrict the supply of desirable goods to the privileged, but to keep the poor in their proper appointed station. Wage discipline could be inculcated only if all means of supplementing the income of the poor were sealed off. The most obvious source of such a 'black economy' was poaching. Ironically, in this process of subjecting the working population to the impersonal dictates of the market, the authorities' most potent ally was the poaching gang itself. The gangs and the traditional impoverished lone poacher were in competition for the same animals, the one to make a profit, the other to supplement a subsistence diet. There was no question about who would have the upper hand in such a struggle. Once again, the inadmissibility of the gangs into the ranks of 'social criminal' is clear.

12

Rioting

The greatest inconveniences of Bristol are, its situation, and the tenacious folly of its inhabitants.

Daniel Defoe, *A Tour through the Whole Island of Great Britain*

I would there were no age between ten and three and twenty, or that youth would sleep out the rest; for there is nothing in the between but getting wenches with child, wronging the ancientry, stealing, fighting.

William Shakespeare, *The Winter's Tale*, III.iii.58

Nor should we listen to those who say, 'The voice of the people is the voice of God', for the turbulence of the mob is always close to insanity.

Alcuin (735-804), *Epistolae*

And yet no Nation produces so many drunken Quarrels, especially among the lower People, than in England (for, indeed, with them, to drink and to fight are almost synonymous terms). I would not methinks have it thence concluded that the English are the worst-natured People alive. Perhaps the Love of Glory only is at the bottom of this; so that the fair Conclusion seems to be, that our Countrymen have more of that Love and more of Bravery, than any other Plebeians.

Henry Fielding, *Tom Jones*

In many ways rioting is the core issue of 'social crime'. The attitudes it engendered also take us to the heart of the Bloody Code in more ways than one. For the 1715 Riot Act was, with the Waltham Black Act, one of the two main pillars of the Code. Any discussion of 'class warfare without class' must focus on the laws governing rioting. The enormously important role of Jacobitism in English life of the first half of the century also becomes clearer.

The irony of the Riot Act was that it was mainly *used* to deal with challenges to the regime from the masses (whether we designate them 'the crowd', as sympathetic witnesses do, or, in the old-style, 'the mob') but was *devised* to deal with a purely *political* challenge from the Jacobites. The first half of the century, when Jacobitism was a dangerous living force, saw few threats to the regime from 'below'. The century's early riots (up to about 1720) were mainly about the exiled Stuarts. Crowds demonstrated violently on their behalf, drank the health of the Pretender, tore down Dissenter meeting houses. In response anti-Stuart mobs burned the Pretender in effigy, beat up Scots and Irishmen, destroyed the homes of Catholics.[1]

The dynastic struggle reached crisis in 1714-15, the years of the Hanoverian succession and the great Jacobite rising of the '15. It was this, rather than any general perceived threat from 'the mob' that led to the passage of the Riot Act.[2] Henceforth it was a non-clergyable felony for more than twelve people to assemble and not to disperse within an hour after a magistrate had read out the said Riot Act. The Act also made it a capital offence for the twelve or more people to try to prevent the proclamation by the magistrate or to do any damage to property before it was actually read.

There were many absurdities attached to the Riot Act. The twelve people or more could demonstrate their contempt for the Act by dispersing at the fifty-ninth minute. Eleven people were outside its ambit altogether. Nevertheless, to political reactionaries like Henry Fielding, the Riot Act combined the virtues of Solon and Solomon. It was necessary, Fielding thought, because urban existence had broken down the organic solidarities of the old rural communities, where social control was exercised through the parishes and the hundreds.[3] The Riot Act alone, according to Fielding, stood between social order and anarchy. Especially welcome was the power given to magistrates to call in the military if a crowd refused to disperse.[4] The use of the military in a domestic context, or anything redolent of a professional police, so abhorrent to most eighteenth-century Englishmen, was always embraced with avidity by Fielding. In every age there is a type of mind that sees the most effective solution to social problems in 'the man on horseback'. Fielding was the most representative eighteenth-century type of this species.[5]

The first half of the century, and especially from 1715 to 1749, was relatively riot-free.[6] There were three main reasons for this. From 1722 to 1745 Jacobitism in England was moribund. From 1713 to 1749 England did not have to face the dislocating transition from wartime to peacetime. And before 1750 the rate of change in society in general was slight; this was the classic period of the 'Augustan calm'. Yet it must be stressed that the freedom from riots was relative only. Hunger riots took place in the

provinces in 1709, 1727-8, and 1740.[7] There *were* many serious disturbances, but they did not rival in frequency and intensity those of the
second half of the century.

A sign of things ahead came in 1719 with the calico riots in Spitalfields.
The fashion for wearing printed calicoes had been brought from Holland
with William and Mary in 1688. Calicoes were a cool and colourful
substitute for woollens and cost just one-eighth of the price. The threat to
the woollen trade was clear. An Act of 1700 banned the import of printed
calicoes. The loophole was that the import of plain calicoes was left
untouched. The fashion for wearing these grew in popularity. In 1719
there was a head-on collision between fashion and the interests of the
weaving trade. Riots by silk-weavers in Spitalfields had to be dispersed by
the Guards.[8]

The entire textile industry was affected by trade fluctuations, but silk-
weaving was more vulnerable than any other branch. Its raw materials
came from abroad and the supply was often interrupted. The trade,
though heavily protected, went in constant fear of French competition.
Smuggling was another peril. The silk-weaving industry was subject to
periods of over-expansion and sudden contraction as it tried to deal with
violent seasonal and fashion fluctuations. It was much more sensitive to
oscillations in demand than the highly capitalized clothing trade, where
'vertical integration' was the norm; the clothier undertook all the
processes of manufacture, from the buying of raw wool to the selling of
cloth. Silk-weaving entrepreneurs would regularly dispense with fifty to a
hundred workers at once; the trade was chronically overstocked with
workers.[9]

Not surprisingly, the severe depression of 1717-19 led to violent
reactions. The first wave of rioting in Spitalfields in June 1719 was
followed by a second in July. Women wearing the new calico fashions
were attacked in the streets. This outburst of violence was ended only
when autumn made it too cold for the wearing of calicoes and people
turned back to woollens. The authorities, fearing a fresh outbreak in the
summer of 1720, decided to enact a statute imposing a total ban on the
wearing of calicoes. Unfortunately, this bill was held up in the Lords in
February 1720, so that summer came and there was still no legislation to
protect the weavers. In May the predicted recrudescence of rioting began.
Once again women wearing calicoes had the garments torn off their
backs. The legislaton was rushed through. The total ban on *all* calicoes
retrieved the situation.[10]

Yet it was characteristic of eighteenth-century England that the
authorities should have been irritated at the lack of deference exhibited
by the weavers during this dispute. Plans were laid to make it harder for
them to be 'insolent' again. To disguise this offensive, a precedent was set
in laws directed at another urban group: the tailors. An Act of 1720 made

labour combinations illegal and prescribed two months' imprisonment for anyone in such a union.[11] Then in 1725 an Act was passed specifically aimed at the weavers. This was a much tougher piece of legislation. Henceforth any weaver or woolcomber guilty of 'bodily hurt' against his master or of sending him threatening letters would receive seven years' transportation. But the penalty for entering premises with intent to cut looms or other tools used in the woollen trade was death.

The next conflict between weavers and authorities arose over the Irish. It was a persistent canard throughout the century that the Irish were prepared to sell their labour cheaply so as to enable employers to undercut the domestic labour force. In 1736 at Spitalfields the rumour gained credit that Irish weavers and building labourers were prepared to work at half the normal wage rates. The native labour force rioted; Irishmen were assaulted. The magistrates read the Riot Act, but the crowd refused to disperse. It took several companies of guards dispatched from the Tower to contain the situation.[12]

The 1736 Spitalfields riot was just one of many popular disturbances directed against the Irish during the century. In 1740 it was the turn of London butchers to indulge in fisticuffs with them. In 1763 there was an affray between a large party of sailors and a group of Irish chairmen in Covent Garden. In 1774 English haymakers fought pitched battles with Irish harvest workers at Kingsbury, Edgware, and Hendon.[13] Apart from popular prejudice against the Irish for being 'dirty and verminous' – the standard accusation against those at the bottom of the social heap – the Irish were detested because they supported (or were thought to support) the exiled Stuarts; it was a staple of London alehouse gossip that the Irishmen in London were not bona fide work-seekers but merely cowardly deserters from the Irish Brigade in France. Besides, the Irish were Catholics: they gave their primary allegiance to a 'foreign prince' – the Pope. Thus, in the popular view, the Irish were treacherous in all three spheres: economic, political, and religious.[14]

The other main source of popular disturbances in the first half of the century was the new turnpike roads. It is significant that the one real outward sign of social change in the 'Augustan' period should have been the trigger for riots. The essence of the widespread resentment against turnpike roads was that carriers had to pay tolls to do what they had previously done free. But the authorities took a very serious view of the destruction of turnpike gates and toll-houses. An Act of 1735 made it a capital offence to destroy turnpikes, floodgates or river banks.[15] To show that it meant business, the government posted rewards for the apprehension of turnpike rioters.[16] Thereafter a veritable barrage of acts was directed against the destruction of turnpikes.[17]

It was not long before the Code claimed its first victims. In 1736 two colliers, James Baylis and Thomas Reynolds, were condemned to death for cutting turnpikes in Herefordshire. It would have been difficult to secure a conviction under the recently passed Turnpike Act, so the prisoners were tried under the catch-all provisions of the Black Act. Both men were found guilty and condemned to death. Baylis, who truckled and showed the right signs of deference and 'repentance' was reprieved, but Reynolds, who remained defiant, was executed.[18]

This case was interesting on two counts. It demonstrated intimately that the Code worked on the basis of 'awful examples' and that one way to blunt its sanguinary force was to make obeisance to its authority. It also showed that the Black Act was a weapon the elite could use to bring in capital sentences virtually at will. The alleged intention of the Act was to make 'blacking' an offence when a poacher went armed. But, by successive judicial decisions, 'blacking' was gradually detached from 'going armed' to form an offence in itself. The next stage was to empty the notions of 'in disguise' and 'blacked up' of all significant content, so that the phrases could mean almost anything. In time 'disguised' was construed to mean going about without a wig and with unpowdered hair. In the case of Reynolds and Baylis, the crucial piece of damning evidence was that they had gone about their work of turnpike cutting while 'blacked'. This was 'proved' by their having coal-dust on their faces (hardly surprisingly as they were colliers!). By the same dreadful logic, if their faces had been cleanly washed, it would have been open to Lord Chancellor Hardwicke, who accepted the prosecution's 'reasoning', to have declared that this constituted 'disguise', since the norm for colliers was blackened faces![19]

Colliers were particularly associated with the long resistance to turnpikes. A twenty-year struggle between the Kingswood colliers and the authorities reached its apogee with riots in Somerset in 1749. Troops were called in to suppress the disturbances. Eighteen men were tried by jury at Taunton in 1750 but all were found not guilty. The authorities took the point. An example *in terrorem* had to be made. The very next turnpike rioters would be tried away from their locality, as the Waltham Blacks had been.

The inevitable upshot came in 1753. Two of the Kingswood colliers were caught and executed for destruction of turnpikes.[20] This underlined yet another elite device. There was always the danger that the authorities would upgrade rioting to high treason – in the sense of levying war against the king – as had happened in the case of the London apprentices' riots in 1601. In 1753 this is precisely what happened. The colliers were indicted not under the Riot Act, but under the laws of treason. This was another clear perversion of justice. Yet the 'men of God', as ever in the eighteenth century, looked the other way. All the egregious John Wesley could find to say when he visited the condemned men in Newgate was

'They would not hear the gospel while they were at liberty. God grant they may profit by it now!'[21]

The government now possessed an arsenal of weapons to use against rioters. The most draconian parts of the Bloody Code were in the front line in the battle: the Riot Act, the Black Act, the laws against high treason. It is not altogether unexpected, then, that the most grotesque miscarriages of justice should have occurred in the context of rioting. The 1749 Strand riots produced one of the century's darkest *causes célèbres*.

The root cause of the Strand riots was the collision of demobilized seamen returning from service in the War of Austrian Succession, with the parasites hoping to batten on them: publicans, brothel-keepers, sneak-thieves, and confidence tricksters. The trigger was the theft from some sailors of their end-of-service gratuity by the keeper of a bawdy-house in the Strand. Failing to receive satisfaction from the bawd, the sailors returned with reinforcements and ransacked the 'house'. Elated with their depredations, the sailors declared that their aim was now the destruction of all brothels. Their numbers swelled to 400.[22]

Slow and ineffective action against the rioters at the beginning led to overreaction when the disturbances gathered momentum. When the sailors dealt sharply with the few constables who tried to intervene, Henry Fielding panicked and sent for the military, alleging the threat of general insurrection in the city. Yet it was increasingly clear that the sailors had no ulterior motives. Their target was the bawdy-houses and other property of known parasites. Fielding found himself out on a limb. When the dust settled, his judgment, on which he so prided himself, was likely to be subjected to close and critical scrutiny. To protect himself, Fielding began to collect circumstantial evidence that would buttress his bogus case that the Strand Riots were part of a general popular uprising.[23] This was particularly urgent, since the sailors dispersed once the military appeared in force, showing that their grievances had a limited scope.

It was at this juncture that a servant, Bosavern Penlez, was found lying dead drunk in an alleyway in possession of a number of items of lacewear, caps, handkerchiefs, aprons, ruffles. He could remember nothing of how the items came to be in his possession. No evidence could be produced that Penlez had been a rioter or in the company of the sailors. The clear inference was that one of the actual rioters had planted the stuff on a drunken Penlez to avoid being found in possession himself.[24] Yet Penlez was manna to Fielding. If it could be proved that he had participated in the riot with the sailors, this would be *prima facie* evidence that the population at large had taken part in the rioting and that his (Fielding's) decision to call in the military had been correct.[25] Penlez was tried on trumped-up charges of premeditated looting. The vengeful brothel-keeper whose theft from the sailors had sparked off the rioting in the first place, testified falsely with his wife that the items had been stolen from him during the demolition of his house and that he remembered Penlez being in the thick of the rioters. The best comment on Fielding's 'proof' was provided by a witness deeply versed in local folkways who said of the brothel-keeper and his wife: 'For my own part I would not hang a cat or a dog upon their evidence.'[26]

By pressing hard for the conviction of Penlez, and blowing up the riot out of recognizable proportions in his memoir on the affair, Fielding managed to save face. Only the most sagacious observers saw that his *A True State of the Case of Bosavern Penlez* was a farrago of self-justifying falsehood and special pleading. Their insights did not save Penlez. He was found guilty of aggravated rioting and sentenced to death. Despite hundreds of petitioners who pleaded with the king to overturn such a gross miscarriage of justice, George II allowed 'the law to take its course'. The real reason for the elite's backing of Fielding in this disgraceful way was their abiding fear of the London mob. When Charles Edward Stuart and his army stood at Derby in December 1745, the Whig rulers knew in their hearts that if it came to a battle for London, the 'lower sort' would not support them. Coming so soon after that time the Strand riots tapped into the deep trauma caused to the Whig elite by the '45 and its associated ideas. This was the hidden subtext to their blatant condoning of injustice in this case.

The 1749 Strand riots marked a turning point in the history of popular disturbance in the eighteenth century. The combination of social stop-go between warfare and painful peacetime readjustment plus the quickening pace of social change meant that rioting now became more frequent, more enduring in its peaks and more violent.

In the provinces the agitation over food prices became especially acute as this double impact fuelled the wildness of market fluctuations. And the Seven Years War, which produced the 1757 Militia Act, precipitated a number of serious disturbances concerning militia service.

There was a long history of food riots to stop the sale above regulation prices of corn and other staples. A favourite device of 'entrepreneurs' was to hoard grain and then force prices up in time of dearth. Often the violent opposition to this sort of profiteering was led by women, who were in the front line in the struggle to put food into mouths. There were provincial disturbances of this kind in 1727. And in 1740 Norwich was convulsed for five days during a riot over the price of mackerel.[27] In the 1750s these outbreaks became increasingly bitter and violent. There were widespread serious protests against hoarders and black-marketeers in the provinces in 1756-7.[28] In 1766-7 food riots in Somerset and Wiltshire led to the despatch there of 3,000 troops.[29]

A substantial number of these outbursts took place at ports, market towns, or trans-shipment points. The key factor in the disturbances was the transport network and the relationship of local markets to those of London and the growing manufacturing towns. Another important element in the riots was the presence of a large non-agricultural population dependent on the local market for supply and hence peculiarly vulnerable to rapid price fluctuations.[30] The Kingswood colliers perceived a causal link between the turnpike system and wild oscillations in basic food prices. But they were not the only provincial group to be so affected and to show their teeth. Similar considerations applied to the keelmen and pitmen of Tyneside, the tin-miners of Cornwall, the cloth workers of Yorkshire, the miners of Somerset, and the weavers of East Anglia and the West Country.[31]

The one notable absentee from food rioting was London. There were three main reasons for this. In the first place, London was in a nodal position in the national food trade and had a well-developed supply system. Second, the abiding fear of the London mob that we have already noted made the magistrates particularly vigilant over bread prices, and prepared to clamp down on hoarders. Third, there was the influence of geography. Paris was ringed by peasant communities, so that any uprising in the environs was likely to spread very quickly into the capital. London was protected from the 'contagion' of provincial food rioting by a *cordon sanitaire*, the protective shield of the semi-urban county of Middlesex. In this way the provincial riots were less of a threat than they might otherwise have been, since it was difficult to fan the flames of revolt and carry them to the metropolis.[32]

The other serious provincial revolts in the 1750s and 1760s were centred on the militia issue. People liable to service in the militia often feared that they would have to serve outside their own localities and communities. Since service was determined by draft ballots, there was the additional suspicion of corruption in the choice among those eligible. Newcastle colliers were in the van of the militia riots at Hexham in March 1761. In a particularly ugly confrontation between the crowd and militiamen, an officer and three militiamen and twenty-one demonstrators were killed.[33]

So far London seemed to have weathered the storm of popular disturbance remarkably well. True, there had been the 'half-price' or Fitzpatrick riots at the beginning of 1763, when considerable damage was done to London's theatres.[34] But these riots had a very specific provenance: the theatre managements in Drury Lane and Covent Garden ended a long-established practice and refused to allow half-price admittance after the second act. There was no recurring 'structural element' here. Against all the odds and paradoxically, London appeared to be breasting the flood of economic and social change better than the provinces.

This appearance proved to be merely the marble sea before the typhoon. Agitation by weavers fearful of foreign competition coalesced with provincial food riots. Soon coalheavers, sailors, and others were locked in conflict with their employers. By the end of the decade English society was in turmoil.

The snowball began to roll in 1765. Once again London's weavers provided the initial push. Silk-weaving had enjoyed great prosperity during the Seven Years War because of new market opportunities and the reduction of foreign competition. When peace came in 1763 these favourable circumstances were thrown into reverse, and a protective tariff was not erected in compensation. The silk-weavers were at the mercy of market forces in a depression – their ultimate nightmare. In a slump the acute vulnerability of the silk-weavers was dramtically underscored. Not only did the volatility of overseas markets leave the industry with a vast surplus of labour; in times of depression the first thing people stopped buying was luxury goods.[35] And the labour surplus was swollen by recent recruits to the trade, especially the hated Irish. Silk-weaving required relatively little skill, so during the Seven Years War many new hands had been taken on.

High unemployment among silk weavers in 1763-5 came at the very time the returning troops were raising the aspirations of the labouring classes. High food prices exacerbated the problem. The post-war economic depression in the mid-1760s led to a clamour for protectionism. A bill to prohibit the import of all foreign silks was introduced in the House but defeated in the Lords after intervention from the Duke of Bedford.[36] As soon as this news was learned, the weavers organized a formidable campaign. On the very day (13 May 1765) of the defeat of the Bill, they marched on Parliament to present a petition to the king.[37] When this produced no result, the weavers determined on sterner measures. Provincial weavers were invited to the capital to take part in demonstrations. It was made clear that the pressure would not end until there was a guarantee that no more silk would be imported from France.[38]

The sheriff of London began to spread alarmist rumours: the weavers were combining with the tailors and dyers, cutlasses were being issued, they intended to plunder all the mercers' shops in the capital, etc.[39] These dire forecasts seemed borne out when the weavers mobbed peers leaving the House of Lords in their carriages on 15 May.[40] Two days later rioting proper commenced. Only the intervention of the Guards saved the Duke of Bedford's house from destruction. The authorities used the military to restore order. Troops were brought in from provincial barracks and held in readiness.[41] But normality returned only after a pledge to rush another Bill through Parliament to prohibit all foreign silks. In addition, as a *douceur*, the price of bread was lowered and a promise extracted from silk-merchants to cancel orders already sent to France.[42] The weavers' discontent was temporarily stifled. The interesting thing was that the authorities had to supplement military measures with economic conciliation.

But the conflict, like the 1719-20 calico affair, seemed to point to a different lesson to the weavers. This was that violence alone wrested significant concessions from employers and their political guardians. There are many circumstantial pointers to growing bitterness in London labour in the 1760s and to an increasing readiness to solve disputes by force. First there was an unprecedented level of tension between the Irish and other labouring groups. An incident in September 1764 demonstrates the powder-keg nature of London proletarian society. An Irish journeyman was taken up by a peace officer for an assault on a weaver at a tavern in Spitalfields. The alarm was given in a tavern frequented by Irish bakers. They at once rushed out and attacked everyone they met on the street who could conceivably be identified as weavers. One weaver was killed and several others wounded before order was restored.[43]

In addition, the weavers themselves were learning greater sophistication. The bitter battles during the century had bred militancy in the bones of the weavers of Spitalfields, Stepney, and Bethnal Green. They had learned to discriminate in their choice of targets. In October 1763 during a wage dispute some weavers disguised as sailors broke into the homes of journeymen who had refused to join them in their strike, and smashed their looms. Industrial sabotage frightened the authorities in a way that mere rioting did not, as it struck at the heart of capital. In 1764 'cutting' or the smashing of looms was made a capital offence.[44]

Meanwhile agrarian hunger riots in the market towns and rural parishes of southern England had led to the disaffection of the industrious poor of most of southern England and the Midlands by the autumn of 1766. At the same time Wilkes and his radical supporters were locked in combat with the elite. As the price of wheat rose nationwide, the stage was set for the great 'general crisis' of 1768-9.

The year 1768 saw a disastrous breakdown in the much-vaunted Hanoverian stability. There were a number of heterogeneous elements in this. There were the Wilkite riots, though these were really the pursuit of mainstream politics by other means. The street protests on behalf of 'Wilkes and Liberty' were an unusual excrescence of City radicalism, choked off from its proper Parliamntary focus by the unusual circumstances surrounding John Wilkes and the Middlesex elections.[45] There was the lapping at the gates of London of the ripples caused by the distant agrarian riots. Most of all there was industrial unrest in London on a scale never seen before. The complexity of the political scene was enhanced by the way the Wilkite riots and the industrial troubles fed into one another. As the most distinguished student of the 1768 'general crisis' has remarked: 'There is no strict division, no wall of Babylon, separating the one from the other.'[46]

The other thing to note about the events of 1768-9 was the span of activities embraced by the rioters and their multitudinous occupational provenance. Demonstrations, marches, armed conflict with the military, strikes and assaults on machinery were all in evidence; their perpetrators were sailors, watermen, coopers, hatters, glass-grinders, sawyers, tailors, coal-heavers, and silk-weavers. Such a motley and broad-based selection of the 'lower sort' conjured visions of a general social crisis. Even the whores in London brothels rioted over the exorbitant 'cuts' demanded by bawds, pimps, panders, tavern-keepers, and waiters.[47]

In some ways the coal-heavers' dispute was the most serious of all, as it conflated the issue of the Irish with the struggle of labour. The unloading of coal from Thames lighters was mainly done by Irish Catholics, some of them with organizational experience with the Whiteboys in Ireland. Their employers tried to cut costs by farming out the registration of labour to agents or 'undertakers'. The net result of this labour scheme would be a cut in rates at the very time the coal-heavers needed a wage increase to compensate for the rise in the price of bread. The coal-heavers struck.[48]

One of the agents, William Russell, was a notable hard-liner who wanted to crush the strike by invoking the full vigour of the law against the coal-heavers. His orders to this effect to his deputy John Green, master of the Roundhouse Tavern, led to angry confrontations with the strikers. Green's life was threatened if he would not desist.[49] When Green persisted, a crowd of coal-heavers besieged him in the Roundhouse tavern in Gravel Lane, Shadwell. From 8 p.m. to 5 a.m. on the night of 20-1 April 1768, Green and two sailors held his assailants, said to number two dozen, at bay in a sustained shoot-out.[50]

It was the acute criticism directed at the authorities for not having intervened rather than the fact of a gun battle on London streets that led the elite to make an example of the coal-heavers.[51] Seven of the party who had assaulted Green's tavern were found guilty of affray and sentenced to death at the Old Bailey. They were hanged before a crowd of 50,000 in Stepney; the pattern of executing wrongdoers at or near the scene of their crimes was reinforced.[52]

This particularly bloody chapter in the Bloody Code did nothing to discourage the coal-heavers. In June a regiment of Guards had to be sent for after the Irishmen rampaged through Wapping.[53] Some other solution had to be devised. The authorities returned to the oldest trick in the book of social control: divide and rule.

Early 1768 had also seen serious trouble with merchant seamen who struck for increased wages to match the sudden price rises. By early May 1768 all ships in the Thames were strikebound.[54] Yet the sailors did not turn to riot and plunder. Calmly they set about petitioning Parliament.[55]

This pacific approach worried the authorities more than an efflorescence of violence would have done. The discipline and organization of the seamen seemed to bespeak a new and frightening level of political consciousness. Temporary concessions were made.[56] Then the happy idea was hit on to turn the sailors against the coal-heavers. This was particularly ingenious, since at the beginning of the coal-heavers' strike both sailors and sawyers had shown signs of joining them in sympathy.[57]

New improved wage rates were offered to the seamen on condition that they would agree to unload the coal-lighters. Once the sailors agreed to strike-break, they were on a collision course with the coal-heavers.[58] Armed conflict between the two groups became commonplace. Exchange of gunfire between ships and shore became a continuous feature of London life. The level of violence and bitterness was particularly intense because of the sailors' strike-breaking. This has always been the cardinal sin in the code of the labouring classes. For weeks Wapping was virtually a 'no-go' area. Anarchy was prevented only by the intervention of the Guards in battalion strength.[59]

The tension had now been screwed up to breaking point by the authorities' playing off one group against another. Desperation led to escalating violence. Armed parties of Irishmen boarded the lighters to beat up the strike-breaking sailors, and in one of these affrays a young sailor, John Beatty, was killed. Then the 'majesty of the law' was invoked. The army conducted a massive dragnet through the coal-heavers' ghettoes, and the culprits were brought to trial, sentenced, and hanged at Tyburn.[60]

Meanwhile there was equally serious trouble with the silk-weavers. The origin of the third, and final, great eighteenth-century disturbance in this industry was a dispute between single-hand weavers and those operating the engine loom which had been introduced from Holland. By being able to do six times the work of the old-style weavers, the engine-loom men threatened their livelihood. In retaliation armed gangs entered the premises of journeyman weavers in Spitalfields and destroyed looms and silk-works.[61] In August 1768 the swathe of destruction by the weavers entered a new phase when a 17-year-old lad was shot dead during a loom-cutting raid. The military were called in. Pitched battles took place in which the weavers attacked soldiers with old cutlasses and bludgeons. After one affray forty weavers were arrested.[62]

As the violent coal-heaving dispute petered out, the struggle between weavers and authorities moved up a notch in bitterness to occupy the centre stage just vacated by the Irishmen. From the beginning of 1769 a strike fund was set up by the weavers, to which employers had to contribute or see their looms cut. From March to September there was a spate of loom-cutting incidents.[63] When troops were sent in to contain the situation, the weavers showed no signs of backing off. On 30 September

1769 a gunfight at the Dolphin alehouse in Spitalfields left one trooper killed, two weavers dead and several wounded. One of the weavers' leaders Daniel Murphy was arrested and sentenced to death.[64]

In October there were further armed clashes between weavers and soldiers. This time there were five killed and dozens wounded.[65] The authorities decided on further bloody examples. On 6 December two more weavers' leaders (Valline and Doyle) were hanged on Bethnal Green. An attempt by the weavers to recue their comrades was nipped in the bud by the London sheriffs. Hearing that there was to be a general meeting after which the weavers would march on Newgate to break out their leaders, the sheriffs had the Riot Act read. Valline and Doyle were then taken from Newgate to the place of execution at Bethnal Green in a deliberate show of authority.[66]

By this time the Wilkesite agitation was subsiding and the elite were able to turn all their big guns on the weavers. Finally cowed, they subsided and, politically speaking, went underground for the rest of the century. As a Parthian shot, the weavers cut and destroyed a few more looms. Yet they were not to be allowed even this face-saving show of defiance. Three of the cutters were tracked down and sentenced to death.[67] To reinforce the point, when the informer who had 'peached' on the silk-weavers' combination or protection-racket in 1769 was murdered, the authorities left no stone unturned until they had tracked down the two killers and hanged them too.[68]

What general conclusions can we come to about the popular disturbances of the 1760s? The principal difference from the riots of an earlier epoch lay in the tighter organization and more sophisticated direction of the sailors, coal-heavers, and silk-weavers. There was as yet no class consciousness and awareness of the mutuality of interest between the protesting groups; loyalty was to the band of workers in a given trade not to the urban worker considered as an entity. But there was at least 'trade union consciousness' – the realization that the only way to combat the elite's control of armed force, wealth, the law, and information was in organized numbers. The fact that men like the Irish ex-Whiteboys knew enough to time their industrial action so as to coincide with the Wilkesite disturbances, and were tightly disciplined, was in itself a worrying development in the eyes of the authorities.[69]

Elite response was itself surprisingly nuanced, given the overall crudities of the Bloody Code. A clear distinction was made between demands *within* the system, such as higher wages and adherence to traditional working practices, and attacks on the system, like the frame-cutting campaign. From the point of view of the government, the silk-weavers were far the most dangerous opponents, as their industrial sabotage seemed to challenge the social system itself. Whereas the coal-heavers' and sailors' agitation represented conflict *within* the regime, the silk-weavers seemed to be engaged in conflict about the regime.[70]

There was thus a graduated response to the three types of London riots. The weavers' actions were considered the most serious, and were therefore dealt with most harshly, by execution and transportation. Slightly less severity was admissible in the case of the coal-heavers' functional demands, so that imprisonment was the norm. Finally, with the Wilkes riots, the authorities virtually conceded that these represented structural dysfunction. The system had failed to filter demands that could normally have been accommodated through the Parliamentary process. Wilkes's supporters were driven on to the streets by a freak maladaptation. How far Wilkes and his radicals were from any revolutionary threat to the regime was seen ten years later in the Gordon riots, when arguably the most reactionary anti-rioter figure in London was Wilkes himself.[71]

The relative indulgence shown to the Wilkes riots can be discerned in the role of the military. Firing on rioting mobs was always a tricky business in the eighteenth century. Both the soldiers and the magistrates who ordered them to open fire could be brought to court on capital charges if it was considered that they had overreacted. The famous constitutional lawyer Dicey, best known for the doctrine of the 'rule of law', summed up the military dilemma as follows:

> The position of a soldier may be, both in theory and practice, a difficult one. He may, as it has been well said, be liable to be shot by a Court-Martial if he disobeys an order, and to be hanged by a judge and jury if he obeys it.[72]

This dilemma became a matter of acute controversy during the Wilkesite disturbances of 1768. When a crowd gathered in St George's Fields and refused to disperse, the Surrey magistrate Samuel Gillam ordered the soldiers to open fire on them. Six people were killed and fifteen wounded.[73] By common consent Gillam had been in error and had acted in panic. The coroner's inquest on the dead brought in a verdict of wilful murder. If the case had gone to a jury, both Gillam and the soldiers would undoubtedly have been found guilty of murder. To get round this, the judge at Gillam's trial immediately acquitted him, so as to baulk the jury of their prey. Since the *primum mobile* had been cleared of all charges, it followed that the troops themselves could not be tried. From the point of view of the ignorant army rankers, this decision arguably contained some raw justice. The troops were so jumpy and trigger-happy by 1769 that when seven or eight hundred merchants went in procession to present a loyal address to George III, *condemning* the Wilkesites, they were mistakenly set on by several regiments of foot who pelted them with mud![74]

The important aspect of the Gillam case was not so much the legal sleight of hand whereby the judiciary made a mockery of the jury system; it was rather the fact that the case had come to court at all. Nobody thought of arraigning the military for murder when they gunned down coal-heavers and weavers. The reason was obvious. Striking workers and loom-cutters were beyond the pale of sympathy of the middling men who sat on juries. Wilkes's radicals were not, they were often indeed men from the very same social stratum as the juryman. No clearer demonstration can be given of the way in which contemporaries very closely discriminated between the different types of rioters in the hurly-burly that the later historian sees as 'general crisis'. To the jurymen the coal-heavers and weavers were criminals; the Wilkesite radicals were not.[75]

Formidable as were the disturbances of the 1760s, from the vantage point of the Gordon riots they seemed the merest bagatelle. The years 1779-81 were ones of profound stress for the Hanoverian ascendancy. The war in America was a haemorrhage that could not be staunched; it became increasingly obvious that the colonists could not be beaten. And in 1779 unprecedented naval weakness in the Channel enabled a Franco-Spanish invasion fleet to come close to capturing Portsmouth; it was their own ineptitude rather than the skills of the Royal Navy that prevented this. The elite in English society seemed to be losing its grip, perhaps suffering from a loss of nerve. This was the context in which the submerged frustrations of a hundred abortive labour disputes and popular disturbances came gushing out like larva.

The beginnings of the traumatic events of 1780 were modest enough. The repeal in 1778 of certain disabilities affecting Roman Catholics led to the formation of a Protestant Association, of which Lord George Gordon was elected president. Late in May 1780 a petition for the cancellation of the Toleration Act of 1778 was drawn up by the Association.[76] Gordon, then 29 years old, gave notice of his intention to lead a protest march to Parliament, both by personal statements in the House and by inserting advertisements in the newspapers. Then, on the morning of 2 June 1780, Lord George led a multitude of 'middling sort' Protestants in a four-column march of protest to Parliament. While Gordon went inside to present his petition bulging with signatures, the crowd of demonstrators remained in Parliament Square.[77]

Inside the chamber Gordon had a frosty reception. The tenor of the House of Commons was hostile. Edmund Burke was in the van of those who rejected the petition with contempt. Several times during the day Gordon came to the top of the gallery stairs and harangued his supporters, telling them of the lack of success their petition was enjoying and singling out Burke by name.[78] The atmosphere in Parliament Square became increasingly tense. Violence was in the air. It was almost as though by their threshing about in the House, Burke and his followers attracted the attention of the sharks. Scenting trouble, and seething with past humiliations, weavers and other members of the 'lower sort' joined the waiting crowd. Its mood grew ugly as the day wore on and still the tales of parliamentary obstruction filtered out from the House.[79]

Meanwhile it had dawned on those who rejected Gordon's petition that the price they had to pay for their support of the Catholic Relief Act was to run the gauntlet of the angry crowd outside. The Commons and Lords became aware of being besieged. It was rumoured that they would not be allowed to leave until they had accepted the petition. The first to test the temper of the crowd confirmed all the worst suspicions. Although it was the Commons and not the Lords that had rejected the petition, the crowd made no distinction of rank. Lord Willoughby was jostled and pummelled.[80] Lord Boston was dragged out of his coach and in danger of being torn limb from limb.[81]

Seeing that matters were now running dangerously out of control, Lord George Gordon addressed his followers in an emollient tone. He realized by now that unless he pacified them, there could be a massacre.[82] But the time was gone for soft words, and anyway the crowd was already swollen by men who owed no allegiance to Gordon. Defeated, Gordon retreated inside to find scenes of panic among the members. In their fear they turned on him. Colonel Murray, uncle of the Duke of Atholl drew his sword, held it at Gordon's body and said 'I see many lives will be lost, but, by God, yours shall be one of them!'[83]

The last straw for the restless crowd came when a battalion of Guards cleared a passage for the besieged parliamentarians. This was too much. Not only had the authorities treated their petition with contempt. They had also, as so often, answered reasoned argument with the use of force. The floodgates of violence were opened. The crowd went on the rampage.

The first objective was the Roman Catholic chapels. The chapels of foreign legations were not subject to the English penal laws against 'papist' places of worship; consequently they were habitually thronged with London's Catholics. The Sardinian church of SS Anselm and Cecilia in Duke Street, Lincoln's Inn Fields (now Sardinia Street) made a tempting target. At 10 p.m. an irate mob broke all the windows of this chapel, then set fire to it. When the fire-engines belonging to the insurance companies arrived at the scene, the crowd would not allow them to play their water on the chapel; they did, however, permit the extinction of the flames that licked over onto neighbouring buildings.[84]

The weekend that followed saw an orgy of looting of Catholic mass-houses and residential property. The Bavarian chapel in Warwick Street, Golden Square, was attacked and stripped of its adornments. The civil disturbance was clearly gathering dangerous momentum, but still the authorities did nothing. On the principle of not getting between a dog and its bone, they allowed the mob to ransack and loot, hoping that it would spend its wrath against a target (the Catholics) for whom the elite had no great liking. Only the most dire crises can force the British parliamentarian to forego his long weekend. At this stage the Gordon riots were not perceived in such a grave light. Even though they had been besieged in the House on Friday night, MPs still cavalierly held to their original plans not to reassemble before Tuesday 6 June.[85]

Over the weekend of 3-4 June, the Gordon riots subtly changed their character. It was almost as though the process through which revolutions normally pass had been telescoped within a few days. The change in consciousness that took three years in France after 1789 took no more than three days in England in 1780. What began as a large-scale manifestation of traditional anti-Catholicism became by Tuesday 6 June a broad river of social protest into which the small previously dammed-up streams of strikes, riots and industrial sabotage flowed. The size of the crowds on the streets of London on the morning of Tuesday the 6th showed the reassembled Parliament that they had dangerously underestimated the threat to social order. Quickly adjourning in panic, MPs looked to the dreaded Riot Act to quell the dangerous flood.[86]

At 5 p.m. on 6 June Justice Hyde solemnly read the Riot Act and ordered the Horse Guards to disperse the crowd, opening fire if necessary. This simply infuriated the crowd and worked them up to a new pitch of frenzy. A new purposiveness appeared in their actions. Elite figures were now singled out as targets. Justice Hyde's house in St Martin's Lane was at once pulled down in retaliation. His other house in Islington was destroyed the following night. Sir John Fielding's much-hated magistrate's house in Bow Street was another victim of mass fury.[87] Lord Sandwich's coach was stopped and he was within an ace of being lynched when he leapt out into the protection of a party of guards.[88]

With a collective political will born of osmosis, the crowd next surged through Long Acre and Holborn to Newgate gaol. All 300 prisoners were released, including four footpads under sentence of death who were due to be executed next day. All the prison buildings were then ransacked and gutted.[89] But the climax of Wednesday night's depredations was the attack on Lord Mansfield's house in Bloomsbury Square. The crowd set fire to the house, having first pulled all the furniture and effects into the streets. It was while they were busy ripping up the prized possessions of the detested Chief Justice that first blood was drawn. A detachment of horse and foot soldiers disturbed the looters in their work. Mindful of the St George's Fields affair, they first sent for a magistrate who gave them the proper authorization to open fire. Their volleys killed four men and a woman and seriously wounded many others.[90]

Yet this military intervention brought problems of its own. When the fire engines arrived to try to salvage something of the blazing inferno that was now Mansfield's house, the firemen at once realized that they would be sandwiched between a maddened crowd and trigger-happy troopers with a licence to kill. They refused to fire-fight until the soldiers were withdrawn. The officer called off his men, and the firemen prepared to play their hoses on the flames. Once again the crowd refused: the firemen were quite welcome to save Mr Hotham's house next door, already menaced by flames from the Mansfield fire, but the Lord Chancellor's house had to be burned to the ground as an example.[91]

The Gordon riots reached their zenith on Wednesday 7 June. Having demolished Newgate, the crowd turned its attention to London's other gaols. The King's Bench prison, together with three adjoining houses, the tavern behind them and the New Bridewell were put to the torch and totally destroyed.[92] Next it was the turn of the Fleet Prison. The crowd delayed just long enough to allow the prisoners to remove their effects.[93] As the flames licked around it, a fire engine from the Royal Exchange Insurance Company was dispatched to the Fleet to quench the fire. The crowd immediately consigned the engine itself to the inferno.[94]

Flames were carried on pitch-tipped flambeaux from the Fleet to Blackfriars Bridge. The halfpenny toll to cross this bridge had long been a festering grievance with London's poor. The torches carried from the Fleet were set to the toll-gate and the toll-gatherers' houses. All was soon reduced to ashes. A great mound of halpennies was found in the smouldering ruins and confiscated by the crowd.[95]

The fiery apogee of 'Black Wednesday' was the arrival of the crowd at the premises of Thomas Langdale (a Catholic distiller) between Holborn and Field Lane. Stored there were 120,000 gallons of gin in two distilleries. The more mindless elements at once began to gorge themselves on the alcohol. Some died here not from military firepower but from drinking non-rectified spirits.[96] But the more thoughtful members of the crowd simply put the entire distillery to the torch. The vats ignited and a general inferno of blazing alcohol engulfed nearby buildings.[97]

Yet casualties were beginning to mount as the authorities' resistance stiffened. At the Mansion House and Royal Exchange there was heavy loss of life as the soldiers poured volley after volley into the crowd.[98] There was similar carnage, though of shorter duration, at the Bank of England, where troops beat off two attacks from the rioters, one just before midnight on Wednesday night, the other during the early hours of Thursday morning.[99]

But to the casual onlooker the crowd seemed to have London firmly in its grip. On Wednesday night there were fourteen fires raging in the city at the same time. As the orange hue lit up the darkening summer sky, Horace Walpole recorded a sombre verdict: 'I remember the Excise and Gin Act, and the rebels at Derby, and Wilkes's interlude and the French at Plymouth – or I should have a very bad memory – but I never till last night saw London and Southwark in flames!'[100]

Thursday 8 June was the turning point. Although the riots continued, focusing particularly on the property of rich Catholics in Southwark and Bermondsey, the government now had 10,000 troops in the capital and was determined to crack down hard. There was further bloodshed when a detachment of horse and foot took fifteen rioters prisoner in the ruins of the Fleet prison.[101] While casualties mounted on the streets, the elite had spent 'Black Wednesday' working out the appropriate response to the crisis. Some members of the government wanted an immediate declaration of martial law. Others warned that this would set them down in history as tyrants, and that their credibility would ever afterwards be damaged. While the cabinet dithered, the Attorney-General gave his opinion that riotous assembly could be dispersed by military force without the reading of the Riot Act.[102] It was therefore decided to grant discretionary powers to the military. A proclamation to this effect was issued on 9 June.[103] A furiously protesting Lord George Gordon was arrested and lodged in the Tower.[104] The Army, freed from the usual shackles of civilian control and authorized to shoot to kill, quickly brought the situation under control, though with further loss of life. By Friday 9 June there were 11,443 regular troops in the capital and another 6,000 armed men from voluntary defence associations.[105]

The Gordon riots were the greatest civil disorders in England (as opposed to Scotland) since the 1685 Monmouth rebellion. No domestic commotion since has led to greater bloodshed or destruction of property. More than three hundred rioters were killed in the disturbances, mostly from gunshot wounds, but also from excessive drinking of neat alcohol or when houses collapsed around them.[106] Seventy-five people died later, from wounds, and 210 bodies were found; others were estimated to have been burnt in the ruins. In addition, there were 173 wounded. There was *not a single casualty* among soldiers or property victims of the riots. Seventy-two houses and four gaols were destroyed or seriously damaged; £100,000 was paid out in compensation by the insurance companies.[107]

Prisoners taken by the military numbered 450. Of these 160 were brought to trial, fifty-nine capitally convicted, twenty-five hanged and twelve gaoled.[108] The rest were pardoned.[108] Gallows were set up all over London so that the condemned could be hanged near the scene of their crimes. The gibbet adorned sites at Tower Hill, Bishopsgate, Bow Street, Holborn Hill, Bethnal Green, Whitechapel, Moorfields, Old Street, St George's Fields, Bloomsbury Square, and the Old Bailey.[109]

What astonished everyone was the extreme youth of those brought to trial and the number of women among them. Charlotte Gardiner was one of those hanged, guilty of having been the ringleader in pulling down a house.[110] Of the twenty-five executed, most of them apprentices, seventeen were under eighteen and three not yet fifteen.[111] As Horace Walpole remarked sardonically, 'The bulk of the criminals are so young that half a dozen schoolmasters might have quashed the insurrection.'[112] All in all, it was the convicts released from Newgate who came off best. Only one was returned for execution, one respited, and the other pardoned.[113]

Intense interest focused on the eventual fate of the prime mover himself, the enigmatic Lord George Gordon. The elite decided that only a treason trial matched the gravity of his offences. A grand jury found a true bill of high treason against him and he was arraigned on that charge. But in February 1781, after being out for no more than half an hour, the jury found Gordon not guilty.[114]

The authorities had been shaken to the roots by the Gordon riots. At one time, as reports of riots in Bath and Bristol came in, the entire country seemed on the brink of insurrection.[115] The spectacle of the mob plundering the capital for days without let or hindrance left an indelible impression. The immediate reaction was to cast about for scapegoats. The magistrates were severely censured: it was their reluctance to sign their names to authorizations to troops to open fire that had enabled the riots to catch fire.[116] Lord Mayor Kennett was forced from office. His particular offence was that he had not allowed the military to fire on the crowd while it was gutting Newgate.[117] These criticisms were unfair, even in strictly legal terms. It was widely believed by justices of the peace that troops could not be used before the Riot Act was read; soldiers themselves, fearful of possible jury trials later, endorsed this interpretation. Moreover, some magistrates thought that the law required an hour to elapse after the reading of the Riot Act before action could be taken.[118]

Elite trepidation meant that the Gordon riots were a turning point in a more profound sense. The old inhibitions about a professional police force were to a large extent broken down. The causal line connecting the Gordon riots to the 1785 London and Westminster Police Bill is very strong.[119] Indeed, the readiness to grant the military discretionary powers, and the fact that the soldiers did not leave their camps in St James's Park and Hyde Park until mid-August deeply worried the typical eighteenth-century squire, concerned about traditional liberties.[120] But for most propertied men fear overrode scruples. The Gordon riots alerted those previously sympathetic to radicalism of the potential horrors of 'the mob'. Like the 1871 Paris Commune, the events of June 1780 concentrated the minds of intellectual radicals on the likely consequences of 'power to the people'. Confronted with the reality, the radical wing of the elite closed rank with the reactionary sector; most of the links between city radicalism and the London crowd were severed forthwith. The proposed reforms of the great radical the Duke of Richmond (annual parliaments and universal suffrage to all over eighteen) were killed stone dead.[121]

How should we assess the Gordon riots? The old view was to see them as no more than violent anti-Catholicism and mindless ochlocracy: 'Those demonstrations of stupid and destructive violence that, for decades, militated so much against all notions of entrusting the populace [sic] with universal suffrage';[122] 'the reasons for riot were of little concern to the mob, which joined in for the fun or the looting, the chances of free drink or free women, or perhaps free food for starving families':[123] such assessments are typical of the traditional, 'old-guard' view.

A more sophisticated view is to see the riots as aimed ultimately at compelling the elite to end the war in America.[124] The rumour was current from the very beginning of the disturbances that the French or the Americans had fomented the riots. It was even said that the French would take advantage of them to relaunch the invasion that had failed the year before.[125] Interestingly, Horace Walpole, usually an avid defender of the status quo, scouted both these notions. He did not believe in the canard of French and American plotting and thought that anti-Catholicism had played a very small part. What had happened, in his view, was that the government had used the pretext of the riots to insinuate a general social conspiracy and have virtual martial law declared, with the object of crushing all political opposition, especially to the American war.[126]

The more persuasive revisionist view is to see the riots as revolution *manquée* – the nearest thing to the French Revolution in English history.[127] At first sight far-fetched, this interpretation becomes more convincing the closer one analyses the disturbances and their social content. The principal target of attack in the early days of the riots was the property of *wealthy* Catholics. Catholic labourers and craftsmen, of the same social stratum as the rioters, were left alone.[128] The riots were never a pogrom, even in the first few days, but they quickly developed into an assault on symbols of elite authority: prisons, banks, toll-gates, the houses of judges. The rioters deliberately ignored the opportunities for looting in the great mansions in the parts of London under their control to go out to Kenwood to attack Lord Mansfield's country residence. Similarly they sought out Justice Hyde's second house in Islington. The one thing the crowd was manifestly *not* concerned with was indiscriminate plunder.[129] Even Walpole, aghast at the spectacle of London in flames, paid tribute to the selectiveness of the crowd. He described their actions as a 'mixture of rage and consideration in the mob . . . much appears to have been sudden fury, and in many places the act of a few. In other lights it looks like deep premeditation – whether it will ever be unravelled I know not; or whether, like the history of darker ages, falsehood will become history.'[130] In view of the readiness of most later historians to swallow the 'official' version of the Gordon riots whole, we must account Walpole a true prophet.

The venom aroused by 1780, and the fact that the elite had shown itself quite willing to implement the Code to hang very young boys, exhausted, almost, the century's potential for popular disturbances. The decade of the 1790s ideally needs to be considered apart, as the impact of revolutionary ideas from France muddied the waters. The Priestley riots at Birmingham in 1791, ostensibly religious in origin, and suppressed by the military, were alleged by the authorities to have a Jacobin flavour.[131] Jacobinism in the final decade of the century came to be what Jacobitism had been in its first half: a handy excuse that allowed the authorities to take short cuts in the implementation of the law and to bend the rules under the guise of 'national emergency'. But it was the economic depression introduced by the war with revolutionary France, not Jacobin ideals, that caused most of the rioting in the 1790s. The 1795 food riots fell into this category; so too did the 1793 Bristol Bridge riots. Here, as so often with eighteenth-century disturbances, the issue was a demand for restoration of ancient rights, not a demand for revolutionary new ones. The unexpected renewal of a toll that was supposed to lapse in the month of September 1793 caused a crowd to assemble at the bridge and threaten the toll-takers. The magistrates were called and ordered the militia to open fire. Eleven people were shot dead and forty-five wounded.[132]

There was one significant development at the end of the century that was a harbinger of unfortunate things to come. In December 1798 upwards of thirty Irishmen and women were holding a *ceilidhe* in the King's Arms public house in London. Suddenly, a detachment of Bow Street runners commanded by 'Captain' Duncan Grant burst in on them with drawn cutlasses. It was a clear case of overzealousness by the police. In the ensuing mêlée Grant was killed. In terms of the notion of premeditation, it was inconceivable that the charge could be other than manslaughter. Yet already the precedent was becoming established that the death of a police officer was always to be considered as murder, rather than manslaughter. In this case anti-Irish prejudice made the outcome certain. An example was made of three of the Irishmen. Timothy Brian, Patrick Holland, and John Sullivan were found guilty of murder and executed.[133] This was the first clear example in English history of something that has since become entrenched in the fabric of society and disfigured English justice: the desire of the authorities to back the police right or wrong, especially where minorities are involved.

Those guilty of popular disturbances in the eighteenth century have had a bad press from most historians, yet arguably they present the most clear-cut example of 'social crime'. Revisionist historians have suggested that the terms in which these outbursts have been traditionally considered are loaded. Rudé argues that 'mob' is a term from above and prefers to use the neutral 'crowd'.[134] Similarly, E. P. Thompson suggests that 'popular disturbance' is a value-free concept where 'riot' is pejorative.[135] We began our examination by considering 'rioting' in terms of the legal code (that is, from 'above'). It remains now to consider 'popular disturbances' from 'below'.

'Rioting' properly considered has the strongest claim of all eighteenth-century felonies to be considered 'social crime'. There are two reasons for this, one sociological, the other philosophical. In the first place the rioter was the only one of the alleged 'social criminals' to utilize a primitive political consciousness. Poaching, coining, wrecking, smuggling were all trans-class phenomena, in which the 'middling sort' participated. But there were no middle-class rioters. This is because in an inarticulate, inchoate way the rioters were voicing demands that when forced through the prism of later class-consciousness would be seen to be class demands.[136] It is not a cogent objection to point out that the rioters generally fought with trade and union solidarity, rather than as a class. True self-conscious class conflict did not appear in history until the French Revolution. It would be anachronistic to expect to find it ready-formed in the England of the 1760s or 1780. For this reason, too, the rioters tended to look to the past for their inspiration: to customary law, Olde England, the Anglo-Saxon constitution. Their aims tended to be concrete, defensive and limited to the restoration of past rights.[137] Thus the grain rioters did not want the abolition of private property or workers' ownership of the grain market; how could they? – the dawn of these ideas had not yet risen. But they did want justice. There was a notion of a 'just price' and what E. P. Thompson has called a 'moral economy'.[138] Only when the triumph of the profit motive and the market displaced the medieval notion of 'value' was this 'moral economy' abandoned. But by then the battle lines were drawn and class conflict was self-conscious and overt.[139]

Yet the fact that the rioter was a forerunner of the later class warrior, a proletarian *avant la lettre* is not the only reason for regarding him as the sole unsullied candidate for the palm as 'social criminal'. Only the rioter's actions were 'other directed' rather than 'inner directed', or, to use John Stuart Mill's terminology, 'other regarding' rather than 'self regarding'. We have seen how the Gordon rioters chose to assault the symbols of authority rather than feather their own nests in an orgy of plunder. The rioter alone cannot be suspected of doing what he did for his own *immediate and exclusive* benefit. And what he did was done against the privileged, unless the privileged managed to obfuscate the issue and set proletarian against proletarian, as with the sailors and the coal-heavers in the 1760s.

A comparison with the other 'social criminals' may make this clearer. Poaching as we have seen, was a trans-class phenomenon, and utilized by many as a source of personal profit. So was coining. Smuggling was universal and explicitly financial in its aims. Wrecking scarcely qualifies for inclusion at all, except on the basis of sociological relativism; what the wreckers did was beyond the moral pale by any standards. The one activity that satisfies the moral criterion of altruistic social resistance was 'rioting' – representing a kind of *cri de coeur* by the dispossessed who had no means of processing their demands through the closed political system. This is in no way to romanticize those who took to the streets in protest against the Hanoverian supremacy. They simply exercised the only option open to them. In another age the same kinds of people and the same kinds of demand could have been filtered through unionism or a socialist party.

13

Theories on Crime and Punishment

Of all nations in the world the English are perhaps the least a nation of pure philosophers.

Walter Bagehot, *The English Constitution*

The whore and gambler, by the state
Licensed, build that nation's fate
The harlot's cry, from street to street,
Shall weave old England's winding sheet.

William Blake, *Auguries of Innocence*

And love th'offender, yet detest the offence

Alexander Pope, *Eloisa to Abelard*

There are no people so obviously made as the English. The French, the Italians, have great follies, great faults; but then they are so national, that they cease to be striking. In England tempers vary so excessively, that almost everyone's faults are peculiar to himself. I take this diversity to proceed partly from our climate, partly from our government: the first is changeable, and makes us queer; the latter permits our queernesses to operate as they please.

Horace Walpole to Richard West, 24 January 1740

The spectrum of views on the causes of crime has always ranged from those who believe that crime is a constant in human society as a result of man's original sin, and those who see it as entirely socio-economic in causation.[1] The latter view in turn bifurcates into those who believe that crime is a reality that can be accounted for in economic terms and those who hold that 'crime' has no meaning as a distinct type of human activity; it follows, then, that a search for the 'causes of crime' has no meaning.

The 'progressive' interpretation is a modern phenomenon. Crime as the consequence of class struggle and social stratification was a notion unknown in the eighteenth century. Only at the very end of the century were there the first glimmerings of a modern approach to the causes of criminality, when William Godwin pointed to the institution of private property as *the* first cause of crime.[2]

In the second half of the century, as Enlightenment ideas began to make an impact in England, penal theorists increasingly concentrated on the environment as the key to crime and punishment. Man on this view was not inherently sinful; he was a mere *tabula rasa* on which very different imprints could be made depending on society's influence. This was a theory of social optimism, starkly contrasting with the intrinsic pessimism of 'original sin'. Yet it would be simple-minded to view the century in terms of a neat division between original sin theorists (first half) and Enlightenment thinkers (second half). The entire subject of the impact of Enlightenment thought on English penal theory in the eighteenth century is problematical.[3] And no one view ever held predominance at any one time. Some of the century's reformers believed in original sin. As Michael Ignatieff has remarked about two of the leading lights on prison reform, 'Howard and Bentham both denied criminal incorrigibility, but from diametrically opposed positions – one accepting the idea of original sin, the other denying it. One insisted on the universality of guilt, the other on the universality of reason.'[4]

It might be thought that in the first half of the century, before the first wave of the Enlightenment rolled onto these shores, there would have been uniformity on the causes of crime. But in this era an ideological battle was fought between those who thought that the innate evil of man was enhanced by the opportunities opened up by 'luxury' and those who denied that the said 'luxury' had anything to do with the matter. This was part of the 'court' versus 'country' debate, but with significant transmogrifications.[5] In discussions of crime, the philosophical content of 'country' ideology was detached from its political base. 'Country' was supposed to be the foundation from which the Whig supremacy was assaulted, and the denunciation of 'luxury' a cornerstone of 'country' thought, yet Fielding, a notable propagandist for the Whig supremacy, embraced the idea that luxury was harmful, while Samuel Johnson, who detested the Whigs, scouted the idea that luxury had anything to do with crime.

Even the most casual observer could not fail to notice how the commercial and financial revolution of 1688 had increased wealth and prosperity in England. This increase in wealth was thought to contribute to crime in various ways. It increased the amount of money and 'portable property' in circulation; it gave rise to new forms of entertainment on which the new wealth could be spent; it encouraged idleness and inefficiency; worst of all, it introduced a 'revolution of aspirations'. As Pope expressed it:

Time was, a sober Englishman wou'd knock
His servants up, and rise by five a clock,
Instruct his Family in ev'ry rule,
And send his Wife to Church, his Son to school.
To worship like his Fathers was his care;
To teach their frugal Virtues to his Heir;
To prove that Luxury could never hold;
And place, on good Security, his Gold.
Now Times are chang'd, and one Poetick Itch
Has seiz'd the Court and City, Poor and Rich:
Sons, Sires and Grandsires, all will wear the Bays,
Our wives read Milton, and our Daughters Plays,
To Theatres, and to Rehearsals throng,
And all our Grace at Table is a Song.[6]

In a word, the rise of an inchoate consumer society placed new temptations in the way of the poor and dispossessed. They were less and less content to accept living on a pittance in the midst of so many good things (especially in the cities) that could be obtained only with money. Therefore they turned to crime. In this way the rage for 'luxury' fed into man's inherently depraved nature and increased the crime rate.[7]

Such was the analysis provided by the most able apologist for the Whig/Hanoverian regime, Henry Fielding in his *An Inquiry into the causes of the late increase in Robbers*.[8] But Fielding was astute enough to see that a general 'country' denunciation of luxury might seem to impugn his own political masters. He therefore produced that hardy perennial of elite thinking: certain things are desirable in themselves *but should not be permitted to the lower orders*. Whereas a lord or squire might use wealth to construct a house or park that would be an adornment to the age, the riff-raff would merely spend any extra money they received on amusements, gaming, and drunkenness. Therefore 'luxury', though harmless in the upper classes, was a kind of social larva if allowed to the mob; the torrent would sweep away property itself if left unchecked.[9]

Behind the kind of thinking laid out clearly in 1751 by Fielding was a plethora of unspoken assumptions that had informed the policy of the authorities since the beginning of the century. The most astonishing aspect of the Fielding line, to a modern mind, is its total confusion of symptoms and causes. This had underlain the great movement to get places of public entertainment licensed by the Lord Chamberlain in the 1730s.[10] The thinking was that it was taverns, theatres, amusement parks *in themselves* that increased crime, by enhancing and eliciting man's inherent sinfulness. Naturally, in some unexplained way, this endemic evil was deemed to have bypassed the upper classes, who were therefore immune to any deleterious consequences from theatres and public spectacles. Even Defoe, usually at one with Fielding on social matters, lampooned this attitude as humbug. Why was it, he asked, that the Reforming societies were so concerned with the immoral actions of the poor, yet turned a blind eye to the debauchery of the rich?[11]

It is worth noting that there was an overwhelming consensus in eighteenth-century England that for the 'lower sort' to view 'dubious' material in a theatre was to expose themselves to the risks of crime. Throughout history there have been two main paradigms on the effects of an audience's viewing violent or pornographic material, the Platonist and the Aristotelian. Naturally, in their pristine form these paradigms were extreme. Plato thought that to see a murder on stage was unacceptable, for it conjured thoughts of murder in the minds of the audience. This Platonist view was taken over by the early church fathers, especially Tertullian. Aristotle, on the other hand, considered that the vicarious experience of such things as murder and revenge in a tragedy was cathartic: the violent emotions were purged by pity and terror. To a large extent, these two paradigms, in attenuated form, are still with us in the continuing debate about the social effects of sex and violence on television.

Without any question, the eighteenth century was Platonist by temperament. The *locus classicus* for this argument was the debate over John Gay's *The Beggar's Opera* (which continued throughout the century from its first appearance in 1728). The work was generally considered to have a depraving effect in two ways: the highwayman MacHeath is reprieved and therefore the ill-doer is not punished; and MacHeath is presented as a gentleman and hence as a good role model for young men potentially drawn to a life of crime.[12] Astute criminals, under accusation of highway robbery, would sometimes plead in extenuation that they had been seduced from the paths of righteousness after seeing *The Beggar's Opera*.[13]

Not surprisingly, the Fieldings were among the foremost in maintaining that Gay's masterpiece depraved and corrupted the lower orders. In the 1770s Sir John Fielding fought a running battle to have *The Beggar's Opera* suppressed whenever theatre managements wanted to put it on.[14] The allegedly mimetic effects of the work split intellectual London.[15] Boswell thought the example of MacHeath was indeed pernicious, but so admired the brilliance and wit of the opera that he confessed he would hate to see it suppressed. Samuel Johnson himself hedged. While he did not think anyone was ever made a rogue by being present at its performance, he thought it might make the character of a highwayman more familiar and more pleasing to the public.[16]

The libertarians argued that *The Beggar's Opera* could actually have a beneficial effect, by refining the ferocity of highwaymen and making them polite and gentlemanly. One of Boswell's acquaintances went so far as the call Gay the 'Orpheus of highwaymen'.[17] Others more sagaciously pointed out that highwaymen and housebreakers seldom frequented the theatre anyway. Even if they did, it was inconceivable that any sane person could imagine he would be able to rob with impunity just because he saw MacHeath reprieved on the stage. Naturally, the Fieldings and their ilk pounced on any exceptions to this rule and pronounced that they were the rule. Much play was made out of the fact that the condemned highwayman Isaac Darking confessed that Gay's work was his favourite reading.[18]

Yet the critique of the Fieldings and their allies on the harmful effects of 'luxury' were by no means confined to the theatre and places of public entertainment. Behind their fulminations lay the 'country' thesis that luxury softened and weakened a nation. Gibbon's *Decline and Fall* was the apogee of this thesis. The model for such theorists was Sparta, where asceticism and civic *virtù* were at their height. Yet, quite apart from the inconvenient historical fact that Sparta was a glorified army barracks, while 'country' ideology condemned a standing army as the greatest conceivable threat to liberty, there was another, more serious, problem. It was simple nonsense to exhort people to return to austere modes of living in a society devoted to getting rich quickly. Sparta had been able to eschew luxury precisely because property was held in common and there were no glaring inequalities between rich and poor in the citizen body (the helots were another matter). As Dr Johnson pointed out more than once, theft was not considered illegal in Sparta.[19] There could not be Spartan asceticism *and* the worship of money within a single society. Yet this was the kind of nonsense the Fieldings committed themselves to in their exclamations against luxury *in the lower classes alone*.

In any case, critics of the Fieldings and those who thought like them maintained that the so-called 'luxury' was beneficial to society rather than the reverse. Bernard Mandeville, who shared Henry Fielding's obsessive fascination with crime, popularized the notion of 'private vice, public benefit' – a kind of pre-Keynesian idea that the higher the level of expenditure on sumptuous buildings and 'follies', the more the employment and the greater the income.[20] Like Keynes, Mandeville excoriated the situation of 'private affluence, public squalor' he found all around him. For him, the social hero was the prodigal son who inherited the careful savings of his father and squandered them in a gigantic spending spree.[21] The real social villain was the miser. Mandeville held that if a miser worth £100,000, and who normally spent just £50 a year, was robbed of £1,000, this money when disbursed would create a multiplier effect in employment and prosperity. The theft actually redounded to the public good, but society's rules required that the men who uplifted the money from the miser should be hanged.[22]

The Shavian flavour of this argumentation was too strong even for Dr

Johnson, but he agreed with Mandeville both that the English had not degenerated and that even if they had, luxury had nothing to do with it. He strongly dissociated himself from the Fieldings: in his view public entertainments distracted people from crime rather than encouraging them to it.[23] Johnson thought that Mandeville was not careful enough in his formulation, that he had allowed the doctrine of 'private vice, public benefit' to run away with him and allowed it to apply to *all* vice, not just luxury. He criticized Mandeville for being too facile in his assumption that *all* vice had a beneficial spin-off and suggested that he had not worked out the utilitarian consequences carefully enough.[24] Nevertheless, he was at one with him in dismissing the idea that luxury in any way impaired a nation, whether in its physical well-being or its mores. He suggested that the whole debate was somewhat unreal, as, *pace* the Fieldings, luxury was beyond the reach of most Britons. Even if it was within their grasp, it would help, not mar them. As a good 'country' thinker Johnson was more concerned about the effects of luxury on the martial spirit. He felt that commerce and manufacture introduced a division of labour such that lopsided (sometimes even physically so) individuals were produced, to the detriment of the 'whole man'.[25]

Yet Mandeville's merit was that he was one of the few eighteenth-century writers with a serious reputation who suggested that there might be some connection between the (perceived) high crime levels of eighteenth-century England and the general high levels of elite corruption under the Walpolian system.[26] The elite should have been more sympathetic to this argument, since *noblesse oblige* involves ruling by example. As it was, too often attention was drawn away from corruption to the peculiar *form* in which it manifested itself in England. American theorists speculated that a republican form of government might be more crime-free than a monarchical regime. The evidence for this seemed to be the lesser incidence of hanging in North America![27]

One man who emphatically rejected Mandeville's thesis that luxury warded off rather than encouraged crime was John Wesley.[28] Interestingly, it was one of Wesley's followers, Patrick Colquhoun, who pushed the eightenth-century debate on the causes of crime forward a few notches by relating it to poverty. It was still a long time before anyone would talk of alienation, class conflict, or social anomie as the causes of crime, but to deal with material circumstances rather than attitude and temptations in itself represented an advance in criminological thought.

Colquhoun wrote at the very end of the century, when Enlightenment thought had increasingly popularized the idea that crime and social rowdiness in general were connected with population increase, urbanization, increase in wealth and general lack of education. Clearly, Colquhoun thought, there had to be some connection between crime and poverty. But for him, the key concept was not poverty itself but *indigence*. If poverty was accepted as the root of crime, it followed that crime was ineradicable. Colquhoun worked within a conceptual framework that considered poverty inevitable ('the poor you have always with you'). But it did not follow from this, in his view, that *crime* was inevitable. The solution lay in distinguishing between poverty and indigence. It was *indigence* that caused crime. Indigence was to be distinguished from poverty, since poverty meant the adequate ability to produce a subsistence but no more. Indigence, on the other hand, was the utter or inadequate ability to produce such a subsistence.[29]

Out of an estimated population of ten and a half millions, Colquhoun reckoned that the indigent and criminal classes comprised 1,300,000 souls. This meant that one-eighth of the population were actual or potential criminals. In London the corresponding figures were one million and 115,000.[30] Crime was a crucial subject, not just because some £2 millions a year were lost through its direct agency, but because it contributed to the spread of lawlessness and social chaos encouraged by the French Revolution.[31] The events of 1789 onwards had opened up the floodgates to a tide of debauchery that threatened the very foundations of religion and morality. Remove indigence by better Poor Law relief, thought Colquhoun, and you got to the roots of crime at a stroke; you thereby also preserved civilization itself, threatened as it was by the chaos principle.

Colquhoun's example is an interesting one. So often in the pre-socialist era liberal reformers traced social ills back to their source only to discover that their eradication ultimately implied the dismantling of the structure of class and privilege of which they were themselves beneficiaries. At this point, either consciously or unconsciously, they would change tack and concentrate on symptoms rather than causes. Colquhoun was on the right track in beginning his investigation with poverty. But he soon found himself in a dilemma. Either he could admit that poverty was eternal and ineradicable, and with it its twin, crime. Or he could accept that to eliminate crime, you must eliminate poverty. But the very existence of a highly stratified society, with a tiny elite of great wealth at the top, necessarily involves either absolute or relative poverty, so that the circle of rising aspirations and crime cannot be broken. The concept of 'indigence' looks like an escape-route through the back door of original sin. Examined more closely, 'indigence' comes to seem a conflated species of all Wesley's old enemies: drink, gaming, amusements, public follies.[32] Having started from promising socio-economic premises, Colquhoun ducks the conclusions and takes refuge in conventional Methodist bromides. After hovering around a seminal idea, that of poverty, Colquhoun reverted in effect to the strictures of the Fieldings.[33]

The division between those who analysed the roots of crime superficially and those who took a more thoughtful, balanced view carried over into penal theory proper.[34] There are three main perspectives on the theory of punishment. There are those who hold that the end of punishment is to deter prospective offenders by exemplary sentences; there are those who feel that the aim of punishment should be retributive, 'to make the punishment fit the crime'; and those who hold that the only rational purpose must be that of rehabilitating the criminal. Clearly, in discussions of justification of the death penalty, by definition rehabilitation is excluded. And since nearly all felonies under the Bloody Code were non-clergyable, it followed that the theoretical debate tended to focus on retribution versus deterrence.

Social pessimists who believed in original sin and the consequent corruption of the 'lower orders' by luxury were fervent exponents of the deterrent theory. Undisturbed by the sanguinary provisions of eighteenth-century English law, they argued that the large number of non-clergyable offences was necessary to keep the monstrous *canaille* in check. Henry Fielding's arguments are typical. He believed that the way to deal with crime was to tighten both general social control and the criminal law in general. Social control was best achieved by reforming the hitherto ineffective poor laws and clamping down hard on the idle, the vagabond, the mendicant, and the workshy.[35] As for the criminal law, it was full of loopholes that favoured the 'dangerous classes': there was the impunity enjoyed by receivers; the connivance at the practice of advertising for the return of stolen goods; the unjustified use of frequent pardons.[36] Fielding popularized the notion that has become a staple of conservative critics of the law: that it is weighted in favour of the guilty, that far more attention is paid to the rights of criminals than to the plight of their victims.[37]

Fielding's views had many avid supporters. One of them, Thomas Alcock in his 1754 pamphlet *Observations on the Defects of the Poor Law* had this to say: 'Most pickpockets, housebreakers, street robbers and footpads have once been idle vagrants . . . You may hang or transport or cut off a number of felons at this sitting, but like Hydra's heads, there will be more spring up by the next, and ever will do so, as long as idle vagrants, who continually furnish a fresh supply, are suffered to go as they do, unmolested.'[38]

In essence Fielding and his followers eagerly embraced the Bloody Code and argued that it should be made more difficult to avoid its sanctions. He wanted strict enforcement of all capital statutes and more rigorous use of capital punishment. The only reform Fielding was prepared to countenance was the abolition of public executions. The carnival-like atmosphere of the procession to Tyburn, he felt, was prejudicial to the dignity of justice, and militated against the deterrent function of punishment. Quick, private executions would strengthen the idea of deterrence.[39]

Once punishment was made more certain and terrible, the use of the royal prerogative of mercy was cut down drastically, and the rights of the accused were generally curtailed, then, Fielding felt, a workable deterrent code would certainly be implemented. He was a zealot where deterrence was concerned. He quoted approvingly the words of a judge who replied to a man who protested against the injustice of being condemnned to death merely for stealing a horse: 'You are not to be hanged, sir, for stealing a horse, but you are to be hanged that horses may not be stolen.'[40]

The blinkered nature of Fielding's approach to crime is clear. So obsessed was he by the efficacy of capital punishment that he said nothing whatever about secondary punishments; it is only at this level that the concept of rehabilitation can even arise, but the very notion is absurd to Fielding, as to all original sin theorists. Similarly, Fielding thought that the attempt to make the punishment fit the crime was a palpable nonsense. For this reason he simply could not understand why jurors were reluctant to convict in many capital cases.

Wholesale reliance on capital punishment as deterrence was open to a whole barrage of counter-arguments, which Fielding's critics were not slow to deploy. In the first place, they said, he failed to understand that principles of intimidation and prevention are often, if not always, in conflict. He was blind to the negative, counterproductive aspects of draconian legislation. As Beccaria later pointed out, severity is self-defeating. If the penalty for a crime is increased from imprisonment to being broken on the wheel, after a hundred years people are only as much afraid of the wheel as they were a century before by imprison-ment.[41] Moreover, if the *sole* purpose of punishment is to deter, and it is absurd to try to make the punishment fit the crime, does this not, at the margin, dispense with the distinction between guilt and innocence? Hanging an innocent man has as much *deterrent* effect as hanging a guilty one as long as people *think* him guilty. Actual guilt, then, becomes an 'optional extra'.

Fielding is a very good example of the way in which a defective theory of the aetiology of crime will entail a defective theory of punishment. Those who followed in the Fielding tradition largely repeated his mistakes without adding anything significant to his hard-line severity. William Paley in his *Principles of Moral and Political Philosophy* (1785) merely expressed the Fielding thesis in a more systematic form.[42] He shared with other conservative anti-reform theorists the conviction that the sole purpose of punishment was to deter and its sole criterion its efficacy in deterrence. To his credit, Paley was prepared to follow where the absurd premises of his argument led him. He supported the death penalty in the controversial areas of horse-stealing and sheep-stealing, simply because the property was more exposed and easier to steal; it therefore needed the deterrent terror of capital punishment to protect it.[43] By the same logic, the difficulty of detecting writers of anonymous letters in itself provides the rationale for their severe punishment. Interestingly, unlike Fielding, Paley explicitly rejects the concept of rehabilitation. No non-capital punishment ever devised, he says, left the malefactor better than before. Prison, for example, simply transforms an amateur criminal into a professional hardened one.[44] The essence of Paley's approach is to justify the Bloody Code on the ground that it swept into its net every crime which under any conceivable circumstances could deserve death. It was then left for the executive to exercise its discretion on the actual choice of punishment in individual cases.

The *reductio ad absurdum* of the Fielding doctrine was reached however, in a work that appeared in the same year as Paley's, Martin Madan's *Thoughts on Executive Justice* (1785). Madan argued that capital punishment could deter only if it was enforced without exception in all non-clergyable felonies. The English system worked on the basis of making an occasional terrible example; the statutes of the Bloody Code were largely reserve powers, the 'ultimate deterrent' to crime. But precisely for this reason, thought Madan, they failed to deter. A criminal, even if apprehended, could reckon that there was a sporting chance he would be found not guilty, or, if sentenced to hang, that he would be pardoned or reprieved. The only way to cut through this, Madan suggested, was to make the death penalty mandatory for all non-clergyable felonies. It was the *certainty* of death alone that deterred. Madan, in short, argued for the full implementation of the provisions of the Bloody Code. At present it was forty to one against a man convicted of sheep-stealing or horse-stealing actually being hanged. Madan wanted it to be certain that he would hang in future.[45]

Madan's ideas represented an advance even on the draconian provisions of Paley. Paley believed that capital punishment, even if sparingly used, always acted as a deterrent. He wanted to amend the Bloody Code to take out the death penalty for pickpocketing. And he accepted the need for frequent reprieves through the royal prerogative to correct cases where there had been a miscarriage of justice.[46] Madan, on the other hand, thought that the death penalty only worked if there were *never* any exceptions to its being carried out for transgression of a capital statute. Blackstone famously ridiculed this posture:

> It is a kind of quackery in government and argues a want of solid skill, to apply the same universal remedy, the *ultimum supplicium* to every case of difficulty. It is, it must be owned, much *easier* to extirpate than to amend mankind: yet that magistrate must be esteemed both a weak and a cruel surgeon, who cuts off every limb, which through ignorance or indolence he will not attempt to cure.[47]

The eighteenth-century reformers, on the other hand, were largely social optimists who believed in the corrigibility if not the perfectibility of man and the sovereignty of Reason. By and large English legal reformers tried to graft elements of European Enlightenment thought onto the English empiricist tradition. In penology the two most important continental influences were Cesare Beccaria and the Baron de Montesquieu.[48]

In his masterpiece *L'Esprit des Lois* Montesquieu introduced two ideas that are now commonplaces but in the 1740s were major strokes of originality. In the first place, he insisted that harsh punishments such as those in the Bloody Code were always self-defeating, because criminals simply adjusted their consciousness to encompass the draconian penalties. This was a similar notion to Hume's celebrated 'association of ideas'. In other words, Montesquieu argued that the amount of fear inspired by a particular punishment derived from a *comparison* between it and other familiar punishments. It followed that if the general level of punishment could be reduced to mildness, no punishment need be very severe.[49]

Second, he insisted that deterrence was an idea that applied, if and when it did apply, to punishment in general. It gave no rational information on how a *particular* punishment should be applied. In a sense, then, Madan and the hardliners were right, given certain premises. The only way in which the *general* theory of deterrence could be made useful as a guide to particular crimes was by dispensing with all notion of the individual circumstances surrounding a given crime. By their insistence on royal pardons and judicial discretion where there were extenuating circumstances, Paley and the less rigid deterrence theorists were in effect admitting that deterrence was a clumsy bludgeon where in most cases what was needed was a subtle rapier. In other words, Montesquieu argued, unless you were prepared to follow the *reductio ad absurdum* road that Madan later took, you had to admit that the real purpose of punishment was to make it commensurate with the crime. It was absurd to prescribe the same penalty for murderers and highwaymen, and even more so if the offence was the theft of a sheep.[50]

It followed from this that two aspects of the Bloody Code were firmly fixed in Montesquieu's sights as grotesquely inappropriate. The first was the death penalty as a punishment for such a wide variety of offences. In his view, only murder and other serious violent crimes against the person should be punishable by death.[51] Crimes against property should merely attract imprisonment, exile, or fines. Second, the sins of the father should not be visited on the sons, as they were under the English law of treason when the estates of rebels were confiscated and not restored to the rebels' sons.[52]

Beccaria, in his classic *Crimes and Punishments* (1764), took over Montesquieu's main ideas and developed them. It was obvious, he thought, that severity was self-defeating. The bloodiest crimes and the most severe punishments were usually concomitant, showing that draconian penalties had no effect whatever and had to be construed purely as acts of social revenge.[53] He agreed with those who stressed that punishment must be certain but, unlike Madan, saw that the logic of this led towards moderation. The key weakness of excessive penalties was their very uncertainty. Punishment should always be moderate and should be administered as soon as possible after the crime, to take advantage of the 'association of ideas'.[54]

Like Montesquieu, Beccaria emphasized that punishment could never be a panacea for crime. This was the central fallacy of Fielding's position. The Enlightenment thinkers saw that crime was a general social problem, not an alternating point in some yin and yang of crime and punishment. Like Montesquieu, too, Beccaria agreed that punishment should fit the crime. So, for example, a theft without violence should be punished by a fine, theft *with* violence by a fine plus corporal punishment and a period of forced labour.[55] But he went far beyond Montesquieu in advocating the abolition of the death penalty. Montesquieu would have retained it for murder, but Beccaria argued that it was doubly inappropriate: both because it was ineffective, and because the state had no right to impose it.[56] The abolition of the supreme penalty even in cases of murder was Beccaria's most radical prescription. Not even Rousseau, the most original thinker of the century, was prepared to go that far.[57]

The works of the English legal reformers, from 1770 on, show clearly the influence of Beccaria and Montesquieu, but demonstrate also the limited extent to which Enlightenment rationalism could ever dent the English empiricist tradition. William Eden's *Principles of Penal Law* accepted the Paley/Madan thesis that the principal object of punishment was to deter, while at the same time trying to incorporate the Montesquieu/Beccaria axiom that the punishment must suit the crime.[58] In the main Eden came down on the side of Beccaria and Montesquieu. He rejected Blackstone's (and Paley's) argument that the severity of punishment should be increased to match the ease of the offence (as in sheepstealing), calling this a 'perversion of distributive justice'.[59] Eden also took to heart Montesquieu's strictures on the treason laws and advocated changes to prevent the crimes of the father ruining the patrimony of the sons.[60]

Blackstone, too, presents a mixed picture. He was deeply influenced by Beccaria's arguments on capital punishment, conceded the absurdity of the vast numbers of capital statutes in the Bloody Code, but drew back from following Beccaria in arguing for the abolition of the supreme punishment.[61] He scouted retributivism and believed wholeheartedly that the purpose of punishment was deterrence. That much allied him firmly to the English empirical tradition. But, unusually for the time, he was interested in exploring the possibilities of criminal rehabilitation, and argued for prison reform as the principal means of achieving this.[62] And he anticipated Eden in arguing that the treason laws be reformed so that sons were not penalized for the sins of their fathers.[63]

Other English legal theorists of the late eighteenth century exhibit the same ambivalent or half-digested attitude to Enlightenment ideas. Sir Samuel Romilly wrote his 1786 *Observations on the late publication entitled Thoughts on Executive Justice* explicitly as a counterblast to Madan. He argued that Madan's sanguinary ideas were already having a malevolent influence on English justice. In 1783 there had been fifty-one executions in London. After the publication of Madan's tract, this number shot up to ninety-seven.[64] There are reasons for thinking that other factors were at play (see below pp. 329–33), that Romilly's argument were a variant of *post hoc* reasoning. But whatever the truth, the stimulus of Madan prompted Romilly to one of the most searing attacks yet on the Bloody Code. Romilly revived Eden's argument that the death penalty was inappropriate for property offences; in particular Romilly wanted repeal of the notorious Waltham Black Act.

Romilly took over Enlightenment thinking in his conviction that the excessive severity of penalties was itself one of the *causes* of crime rather than any kind of deterrent to it.[65] But his analysis was one-dimensional. He did not follow Montesquieu and Beccaria in identifying criminality as a general social product. He was concerned merely to refute Madan on his own deterrent ground by showing that excessive punishments caused rather than cured crime.

In a similar way the great prison reformer John Howard reached much the same conclusions as Romilly while starting from very traditional premises. Howard was concerned with the analogues or extensions of original sin: shame and guilt. The idea was that punishment should tap the residue of guilt that existed in both criminal and public. Punishment should not be so severe that it alienated the offender or the overseeing public, or the legitimacy of punishment would be lost – precisely the error committed by hotheads like Madan. Excessive punishment merely excited the compassion of the public for the criminal; the indignation naturally due towards the original offence was diluted or dissolved.[66]

It is clear, then, that the growing tendency to query both the justice and the efficacy of the Bloody Code in the late eighteenth century can be ascribed only partially to the ideas of the Enlightenment. Cartesian rationalism of the Montesquieu/Beccaria variety could make only limited headway in the alien English political culture. English reformers took an eclectic approach to the Enlightenment. They tried to fuse its more progressive ideas with the staples of English empiricism. This process of fusion reaches its apotheosis with Jeremy Bentham.

In one sense, utilitarianism, 'the greatest good of the greatst number', with its emphasis on consequences, is the most extreme form of empiricism. One might have expected Bentham, with his fanatical zeal about making the punishment fit the crime, to have followed the path of Continental rationalism. Penalties truly commensurate with crimes would have to take into account extenuating circumstances. To establish these we should need to examine *motive*, as Kant did, not consequences. Yet Bentham thought the punishment could be made to fit the crime by a utilitarian calculation of consequences. He genuinely thought a utilitarian balance could be struck between the evil of a crime and the pain of punishment.[67]

Such zealotry led Bentham to espouse some very odd doctrines. A transmogrified Cartesianism undoubtedly underlies his famous 'felicific calculus'. The core idea here was that pleasure and pain could be *measured*. This meant that, in principle, the harm caused by a crime could be balanced by a corresponding amount of pain meted out as punishment. Bentham's uncompromising stance on this principle meant that he was prepared to countenance mutilation and castration for certain crimes. On the other hand, he was opposed to capital punishment except in murders where there were no conceivable extenuating circumstances or in cases of mass murder. And his willingness to follow where his eccentric premises led him meant that he had no compunction about espousing the idea of a professional police force. Once again we can discern the influence of Continental rationalism in Bentham's unconcern about 'traditional English liberties'. Even reformers like Romilly drew back when the idea of professional police was raised.[68]

Enlightenment rationality, too, rather than sturdy English 'common-sense' empiricism underlay Bentham's notion that humanity in punishment could be achieved only with impersonality. Bentham genuinely believed that punishment could become a science, every bit as impersonal as physics. Punishment would then match crimes as exactly as prices matched commodities. Given that Bentham accepted the measurability of pain, it followed that it was not beyond the task of science to devise machines that could inflict the exact measure of pain. He was interested in the possibility of developing a whipping machine. It seemed to Bentham that whipping was unjust in practice, but not in principle, because its severity depended on the physical strength of the person who inflicted it, as well as on the degree of indignation that the offender aroused in the crowd of onlookers. This meant that the punishment depended, not on the gravity of the offence, but on the emotions of flagellator and onlookers. What ought to happen, according to Bentham, was that the exact number of strokes should be determined by the felicific calculus, having regard to the amount of pain caused by the original crime. A machine turning a rotary flail (made of canes and whalebone) should then lash the backs of offenders with the same unvarying force.[69]

Bentham's attempt to make punishment into a science received its most outlandish expression in the sketch of a penitentiary he outlined in

Panopticon (1791). In this blueprint for the ideal prison, he placed both prisoner (in solitary confinement) and guard under the constant surveillance of an inspector patrolling a central inspection tower. From this vantage point the inspector could clearly see the prisoners in their cells and the guards on their rounds. In this way the inspector solved the conundrum of 'who guards the guards?' Members of the public, in turn, would be given open access to the tower to inspect the inspectors.[70]

Eighteenth-century penology offers an interesting perspective on the debate over capital punishment that was to continue for nearly two centuries after the century's close. Those who argued that the purpose of punishment was deterrence were overwhelmingly the conservatives and reactionaries. Those who wanted to make the punishment fit the crime were the progressives. Although the evidence was overwhelming, as Beccaria and his successors pointed out, that the death penalty did not deter, the conservatives clung tenaciously to the myth that the supreme penalty *did* deter and was the only barrier between civilization and order and the barbarism of the masses. The pressure for law reform in the late eighteenth century was successfully resisted by the champions of the Bloody Code, not because they necessarily sincerely believed in the actual deterrent power of the death penalty (though obviously some did) but because their own credibility was bound up in it.[71] The complex network of hierarchy, authority, and deference could be held in being only if the elite reserved the ultimate weapon as an awful example. In other words, the penal policy of the elite was primarily *ideological*, not instrumental.[72] Nowhere is the gulf between intuitive empiricism and continental rationalism more clearly seen.

This explains the paradox that in the twentieth century the emphasis on deterrence has largely been the prerogative of progressives, while the retributive stance has been espoused by political conservatives. Except in the case of a handful of diehards, the pretence that capital punishment actually deters has been abandoned. Instead the grounds for the retention of the death penalty have been shifted to retributivism: that a death requires a death in return, that society cannot allow a murderer to go unpunished (the assumption is that imprisonment is not 'real' punishment). Only with a far less sophisticated population can the political camouflage involved in 'ideological deterrence' of the eighteenth-century type be sustained.

The other point is, of course, that the eighteenth-century state lacked the technology for complete legitimation through co-optation (as in Gramsci's 'hegemony'). The open bribery and corruption of eighteenth-century England classically denotes a society at the half-way point between social control by violence and by 'hegemony'.[73] As we shall see later, no satisfactory account of crime in eighteenth-century England can be given that neglects the dimension of social structure.

14

Execution

> The only possible form of justice, of the administration of justice, could be, and will be, the form that in a military war is called decimation. One man answers for humanity. And humanity answers for the one man.
>
> Leonardo Sciascia, *Il Contesto*

> Those good old customs of the good old times which made England, even so recently as the reign of the Third King George, in respect of her criminal code and her prison regulations, one of the most bloody-minded and barbarous countries of the earth.
>
> Charles Dickens, *American Notes*

> One to destroy, is murder by the Law;
> And gibbets keep the lifted hand in awe;
> To murder thousands, takes a specious name,
> War's glorious art, and gives immortal fame.
>
> Edward Young, *Love of Fame*

The heart of the Bloody Code was its extensive provision for capital punishment. The years after 1688 saw a return to the Tudor policy of enlarging the scope of the death penalty. Large numbers of offences were removed from benefit of clergy; new crimes bearing the death penalty were added to the statute book. In 1688 the death penalty was ordained for about fifty distinct crimes. By 1765 this number had risen to at least 165 and to about 225 by the end of the Napoleonic wars.[1] This increase represented a determined defence of property by men who thought that hanging was the only real deterrent to crime.

The logical expectation, then, would have been a dramatic increase in the rate of public executions. But the level of hangings remained low. There were four times as many executions in the early seventeenth century as in 1750.[2] Only 10 per cent of those indicted in London in the years 1700-50 ended up on the gallows.[3] The general level of execution decreased further in the late eighteenth century. About twenty people a year were hanged in London and Middlesex at the end of the century, as compared with 140 a year two hundred years earlier. By 1800 only about a third of those condemned to death in London were executed. The number of capital statutes (more than 200) began to overtake the number of people (about 200) hanged every year in England and Wales.[4]

How can this apparent contradiction be explained? It is true that the severity of the Code was not matched by the efficiency of law-enforcement. There was no professional police force, indictments depended on private prosecutions by the victims, and the rules of evidence and code of criminal procedure led to many acquittals on technicalities. But none of this would explain the comparatively low rate of *executions carried out* compared with death sentences pronounced. The functional answer is that the rate of reprieve and pardon was high. As one student of the subject has summed it up: 'Many offenders went uncaught: if caught, unprosecuted, if prosecuted, unconvicted; and if convicted, unhanged because of the granting of a pardon.'[5]

The deeper answer is that the death penalty was not regarded by the elite as *primarily* a deterrent to crime. The deterrent effect of laws against crime rests on the *certainty* of prosecution. This was the point that so exercised and irritated Madan, who repeatedly called for a system of capital punishment based on certainty. He failed to understand that deterrence was not the primary purpose of the elite. What they aimed for, above all, was an ordered hierarchy of authority, deference, and obedience. The rulers of eighteenth-century England valued the discretion and uncertainty inherent in the Bloody Code. They did not want every single offence visited with a *certain* punishment. Their principal aim was social control. Pardons played an important role in this, for 'acts of mercy helped create the mental structure of paternalism . . . mercy was part of the currency of patronage'.[6] In other words the elite was well aware that 'overkill' was counterproductive. The full force of the Code should be kept in reserve as the ultimate deterrent; meanwhile, mercy and the granting of pardons should be used theatrically to show the 'justice' of the system.

Naturally, the rate of executions fluctuated with the actual or perceived level of crime. The panic over the crime wave in the early 1720s led to a higher than normal application of the supreme penalty. For instance, in Surrey in 1722-4 fifty-two persons were sentenced to death and forty-one executed (78.9 per cent) as compared with twenty-one and eight respectively (38.1 per cent) in 1732-4.[7] A 'normal' peace-time rate of death *sentences* in London would be something like the seventy recorded at the Old Bailey in 1732.[8]

The rate of execution to capital sentence tended to be higher in London, doubtless because the exemplary effect of a Tyburn hanging was thought to be greater than a similar ritual in the provinces. Of 527 people sentenced to death in London and Middlesex between 1749 and 1758, some two-thirds were executed.[9] On the other hand, in the Norfolk and West Midlands circuits in 1750-72, under a quarter went to the gallows (233 out of 952).[10] The average figure (for the mid-century years) of some 50 per cent actual executions out of death sentences passed, that is, a roughly 50 per cent pardon rate, masks differential levels in London and the provinces.

After 1750 growing doubts about the efficacy of capital punishment tended to reduce the level of executions. The influence of the Enlightenment was important here, especially that of Beccaria. Blackstone accepted his argument that the indiscriminate use of the death penalty for such a wide range of crimes was self-defeating.[11] Doubts about the supreme punishment were not limited to theorists of jurisprudence. The growing trend among judges to find an alternative punishment in the case of minor offences (but which were non-clergyable) showed that some of them too were sceptical. Juries also evinced dissatisfaction with the Bloody Code. They frequently convicted those accused of grand larceny (a capital offence) of petty larceny instead. This they did by undervaluing the stolen goods.[12] This in turn weakened the deterrent effect of the Code. Small shopkeepers and merchants were already reluctant to bring charges on minor offences when the penalty might be death. The effective commutation of the sentence by juries further discouraged would-be plaintiffs.

The general tendency in the second half of the eighteenth century was for juries to show a greater reluctance to convict even as the Code itself became more draconian on paper. The ratio of executions to capital convictions fell. Between 1790 and 1799 only a third of 745 capital convictions were carried out. In general, the *proportion* hanged decreased as the century wore on, but the *numbers* did not, since the rate of detection, prosecution, and conviction were all rising at the same time. A general consensus formed that as an exemplary punishment hanging simply did not work. When Lord Gordon was found not guilty of high treason after the 1780 riots, Horace Walpole wrote to one of his confidantes: 'I am better pleased that Lord George Gordon escaped the punishment he deserved. Matters of religion should be suppressed with the least *éclat* possible. Had he been executed, the Scotch would have made a martyr of him, and sanctified his memory for having set London on fire in defence of Protestantism, and the Pope would still send him to the devil for prosecuting his Catholics.'[13]

One event only arrested the drift towards decreasing use of the supreme penalty. The hanging rate suddenly shot up in the years 1783-6, the years when the last real attempt to impose law and order through terror was made. The outbreak of 'moral panic', was consequent on the end of the American war. This disgorged a flood of discontented veterans into England. The crime rate soared. With the ending of transportation to America, the gaols were full.[14] The authorities struck back with the most sustained use of hanging since the 1720s. Between 1771 and 1783 there had been 467 executions in London and Middlesex. Between 1783 and 1787 the rate of executions was 82 per cent higher than in the previous five years. In those years 348 people died on the gallows; in 1785 there were ninety-seven hangings from the Old Bailey sessions alone.[15] The percentage of those found guilty and sentenced to death at the Old Bailey jumped from 17 per cent in 1770-4 to 26 per cent in 1780-4.[16]

The publication of Madan's *Thoughts on Executive Justice*, came in 1785, advocating still stiffer punishments. Yet the elite saw that it had reached the limit of acceptable terror. More than a hundred executions in London alone would destroy the credibility of the Code. So many prisoners were awaiting execution that if they were all dispatched it was said that England would receive worldwide notoriety as 'the Bloody Country'.[17] It has to be remembered that in Amsterdam, with a population of 250,000 (nearly a third that of London) John Howard found that there had been just five executions in an eight-year period.[18] With the bursting of the crime bubble in 1786 the trend away from capital punishment continued.

The overall trend towards fewer hangings was always only a relative one. Although by the end of the century enlightened critics already thought of hanging as 'cruel and unusual punishment' and its deterrent value was widely discredited, the authorities clung to its retention tenaciously. In their minds the belief persisted that the Law had to have terrifying weapons as the ultimate deterrent. A balance had always to be struck between too much leniency, which would encourage crime, and too many hangings, which would discredit the Code, to say nothing of hardening the hearts of those who were supposed to be influenced by exemplary punishments. But as a symbol of authority the death penalty had to stay. This is why a sustained reform movement beat in vain against the adamantine rock of elite opinion.[19] The informal compromise usually adopted by the authorities was to hang people found guilty of the old pre-1688 capital crimes. In Surrey in 1660-1800 two-thirds of the men hanged had been convicted of either robbery or burglary.[20] But any attempt actually to repeal the capital provisions on individual statutes was stubbornly resisted. In 1770 Parliament rejected the abolition of the death penalty for gypsies and army deserters as a proposal at once immoral and subversive.[21]

It has been necessary to enter a number of qualifications and caveats when discussing the Bloody Code so as not to seem to veer too close to sensationalism in highlighting the instances where the supreme penalty was inflicted. Whatever the relative tendencies in the eighteenth century, there is no denying the fact that thousands of men and women went to a cruel and inhumane death, at Tyburn, Kennington Common, Execution Dock (East Wapping), Smithfield and dozens other locations in London and the provinces.[22] Although, as we have seen above, there was some rationality in the relationship between capital sentences and actual executions, often condemned criminals were the victims of luck, jury fallibility or a judge's caprices. No one entering the Old Bailey on a non-clergyable felony charge could be certain that the end of the road would not be Tyburn tree.

A vast gulf, in administrative practice if not time, separated the criminal act from its eventual punishment. For our purposes we must vault over the middle terrain: patterns of prosecution, trial procedure, and the court-room battle – to arrive at the point where the criminal is about to be sentenced to punishment.[23] A key element in determining whether that punishment was to be capital was the jury.

Juries were largely composed of 'middling' men and shared the prejudices of that social sector. As instruments of justice, jurymen were potentially deficient in a number of ways: they might lack the intellectual ability to follow a recondite legal argument; they might exercise their discretionary powers in an arbitrary way; or they might simply be inattentive to the proceedings. The conviction and execution of the innocent was not uncommon.[24] Juries were also particularly susceptible to circumstantial evidence, even when the judge instructed them to disregard it. A classic case was that of Jonathan Bradford, an Oxford innkeeper executed in 1743 because one of his guests was found murdered in his bed. The jury convicted Bradford because he was found in the dead man's room with a knife. What actually happened was that Bradford entered the room with intention to murder the guest for his money, only to find that someone else had already had the same idea and had beaten him to it. The real murderer, the dead man's servant, later made a death-bed confession.[25]

Another well-known problem about trials on capital charges was that they usually took place in the afternoon, after the jurymen had dined and drunk liberally. Many fell asleep during the proceedings and were prodded awake merely to give a verdict on evidence they had not heard ('and wretches must hang, that jurymen may dine', as Pope (*The Rape of the Lock*), put it, continuing the vicious circle).[26] But jury whims undoubtedly had their beneficial side. When the facts of a case could not be denied, and a guilty verdict was necessary on a point of law, the jury sometimes signified their disquiet with the law by uttering the verdict *sotto voce* or in a faltering accent. When Ann Flynn stole a shoulder of mutton from a Whitechapel butcher, and the butcher prosecuted, Flynn told the court that her husband was ill and her children starving when she committed the theft. When this was corroborated, the jurors pronounced the 'guilty' verdict in a mumbling tone. The judge replied: 'Gentlemen, I understand you.' Ann Flynn was then discharged with a one shilling fine which the jury paid.[27]

But few juries had any patience with old lags or with serious property crime like highway robbery, burglary, or forgery. This was when the road to Tyburn truly began for the condemned criminal. The judge pronounced the dreaded death sentence: 'The law is, that thou shalt return from hence, to the place whence thou camest, and from thence to the place of execution, where thou shalt hang by the neck till the body be dead! dead! dead! and the Lord have mercy upon thy soul.'[28]

The response by the prisoner to these terrifying words ran the entire gamut from oath-filled defiance to catatonic submission, often caused by an advanced case of gaol fever or exanthematic typhus. In Maidstone in 1784 a man who had just had sentence of death passed on him gave three loud cheers. In retaliation the judge ordered him to be chained to the floor of the dungeon until his execution.[29] There was something essentially nauseating about the way eighteenth-century judges lectured their victims on duty and justice and delivered devotional homilies to the audience before pronouncing a death sentence.[30] Martin Madan, the hardest of hardliners, described the scene, surely with unconscious irony:

> Methinks I see him (namely, the judge) with a countenance of solemn sorrow, adjusting the cap of judgement on his head . . . . His Lordship then, deeply affected by the melancholy part of his office, which he is now about to fulfill, embraces this golden opportunity to do most exemplary good. He addresses, in the most pathetic terms, the consciences of the trembling criminals . . . shows them how just and necessary it is, that there should be laws to remove out of society those, who instead of contributing their honest industry to the public good and welfare, have exerted every art, that the blackest villainy can suggest, to destroy both . . . . He then vindicates the *mercy*, as well as the *severity* of the law, in making such examples, as shall not only protect the innocent from outrage and violence, but also deter others from bringing themselves to the same fatal and ignominious end . . . . He acquaints them with the certainty of speedy death, and consequently with the necessity of speedy repentance – and on this theme he may so deliver himself, as not only to melt the wretches at the bar into contrition, but the whole auditory into the deepest concern. Tears express their feelings – and many of the most thoughtless among them may, for the rest of their lives, be preserved from thinking lightly of the first steps to vice, which they now see will lead them to destruction. The dreadful sentence is now pronounced – every heart shakes with terror – the almost fainting criminals are taken from the bar – the crowd retires – each to his several home, and carries the mournful story

to his friends and neighbours; the day of the execution arrives; the wretches are led forth to suffer and exhibit a spectacle to the beholders, too aweful and solemn for description.[31]

A devotee of refined cruelty of this kind was Judge Page who once dismissed a horsethief's plea that he had 'found' the horse he was accused of stealing with these words: 'Thou art a lucky fellow. I have travelled the circuit these forty years and never found a horse in my life; but I'll tell thee what, friend, thou was more lucky than thou didst know of; for thou didst not only find a horse but a halter too, I promise thee.'[32]

Once back in Newgate, or some other gaol, the condemned person was left to contemplate his fate. If the bid for a reprieve or pardon failed, the only way out was to cheat the hangman by suicide. This was not as common as might be supposed, given that self-murder was supposed to be the 'English disease'. More cases are recorded towards the end of the century, possibly because the diminishing level of execution itself bred a peculiar despair in the victim at having been 'uniquely' singled out. In 1777 Joseph Armstrong, a Newgate prisoner took this way out.[33] In 1784 two men condemned for robbery at Ashbourne hanged themselves in Derby gaol.[34] In such cases the usual hysteria directed towards suicides was heightened at the thought of the 'double damnation'. A stake would be driven through the heart of the suicide to prevent the ghost of the dead criminal from returning to earth.[35] Then the corpse would be buried at night in a deep pit at the crossroads or at a place of public execution. Sometimes people who were dying slowly from attempted suicide were still taken out and hanged.[36]

Female prisoners had a better chance of receiving a last-minute pardon. While awaiting execution the women were herded together in a huge cavernous ward on the top floor of Newgate.[37] From here the object was to find men who would impregnate them so that they could plead their belly. Since this was literally a matter of life and death, the level of soliciting and its overt manner was one of the things that habitually shocked the 'unco guid' visitors to Newgate.[38]

Yet in the eighteenth century condemned men and women were considered entitled to more than the final hearty breakfast. The authorities at Newgate and other gaols connived at all forms of dissipation and debauchery when a criminal lay under sentence of death.[39] Orgies and vast carousing sessions were common. The greatest restriction on condemned men was being in effect exhibited during the day to gaping spectators. The turnkeys at Newgate made a small fortune out of charging polite society sums of money to view celebrated criminals like Jonathan Wild, Jack Sheppard, or Maclaine the highwayman.

The other ordeal for most condemned men was having to put up with the ministrations of the 'ordinary' or prison chaplain. Most such men were humbugs or reprobates and utterly failed to make any impression on their spiritual 'charges'.[40] They added to their unpopularity by selling 'inside stories' of famous criminals in tracts sold on the day of the execution. Paul Lewis, a highwayman hanged at Tyburn in 1763, was so infuriated by the prating cant of the ordinary of Newgate that he tried to kill him.[41] Samuel Johnson testified that in general only Catholic priests or Methodist preachers could get close to their condemned co-religionists or bring them any comfort.[42] Yet Johnson joined Wesley in singling out the best known ordinary of Newgate, Reverend Mr Villette, for praise.[43] Few others of their contemporaries concurred in this judgement.

Yet the dreadful day soon came. Most Newgate prisoners would catch their last glimpses of the world during the traditional procession to Tyburn. The day appointed for the execution was known popularly as the 'hanging match'. It is significant of the central place occupied in popular culture by public executions that there were more than a hundred cant names for the gallows. Only the names for money were more numerous, symbolizing the gradual triumph of the capitalist ethos in the eighteenth century. Until the 1780s we are still in a world where the fact of death could be faced head-on. The total triumph of capitalism by the nineteenth century led to the obfuscation of death. Since death was the one aspect of humanity that could not be turned into a commodity by the remorseless pressure of exchange-value, it had to become instead the 'nasty little secret' of the modern era.

The centrality of death by hanging as a collective image in popular culture can be seen by the richness of vocabulary used to describe it. The 'hanging match' was also a 'hanging fair', 'Paddington Fair', a 'collar day', the 'Sheriff's Ball'. To hang was 'to swing', 'to dance the Paddington frisk', 'to morris', 'to go west', 'to ride up Holborn hill', 'to dangle in the Sheriff's picture frame', 'to dry cockles', 'to ride a horse foaled by an acorn'. It was also to be jammed, frummagemmed, collared, noozed, scragged, twisted, nubbed, backed, stretched, trined, cheated, crapped, tucked up, or turned off.[44]

The plethora of euphemisms and descriptive phrases alerts us to the importance of public hangings. On average one could be expected every six weeks.[45] On a hanging day factories and workshops would be deserted. The working city would be like a ghost town. In London crowds would line the route from Newgate to Tyburn. The prisoners would dress either in their best clothes or in shrouds, according to temperament. It was common for the condemned to be hanged in frock coats or wedding suits.[46] Thus Swift describes his condemned villain Tom Clinch:

> His Waistcoat and Stockings and Breeches were white
> His cap had a new Cherry Ribbon to ty't.[47]

At the prison gate at Newgate the prisoner's chains were struck off and they were ready for the *via dolorosa* to Tyburn.

Before the cavalcade left for Tyburn's fatal tree, the bell-man would pronounce an exhortation from the wall of a churchyard (St Sepulchre's in the case of Newgate). Those who were able to hear his words over the hubbub and din of the crowd could perceive the following formula:

> All good people pray heartily to God for these poor sinners, who are now going to their deaths; for whom this great bell doth toll. You that are condemned to die, repent with lamentable tears. Ask mercy of the Lord for the salvation of your own souls, through the merits, death and passion, of Jesus Christ, who now sits at the right-hand of God, to make intercession for as many of you as penitently return unto him.

The bellman then repeated three times 'Lord have mercy upon you! Christ have mercy upon you!'[48]

The procession to Tyburn or the other places of execution was either by public cart or private carriage. Lord Ferrers drove to his death in a landau and six. The famous female criminal Mary Young drove to Tyburn in a private coach.[49] But usually the condemned would be conveyed in carts, seated on their own coffins and accompanied by the ordinary. In a theatrical gesture calculated to impress onlookers with the majesty of the law, the authorities provided a solemn escort. First would come the City Marshal on horseback, followed by the Under-Sheriff with a posse of mounted peace-officers. Next marched a body of constables armed with staves. Then came the carts, with more constables on foot at either side. A company of javelin men brought up the rear. In the rare cases when the authorities feared public intervention, as with Dr Dodd and the Perreaus, a body of troops was held in readiness.[50] Sometimes the more fire-eating representatives of authority would rub salt in the wounds of the condemned. In 1739 when two men were executed at Kennington common for highway robbery, the prosecutor rode at the tail of the cart, jeering and insulting the victims all the way to the place of execution.[51]

The reactions of the condemned men at this stage were immenseley varied. When Samuel Richardson mounted a horse to follow the cavalcade to Tyburn, he afterwards recorded the following impressions:

> The criminals were five in number. I was much disappointed at the unconcern and carelessness that appeared in the faces of three of the unhappy wretches. The countenances of the other two were spread with that horror and despair which is not to be wonder'd at in men whose period of life is so near, with the terrible aggravation of its being hastened by their own voluntary indiscretion and misdeeds.[52]

The route to Tyburn tree ran through Smithfield, into the heart of the densely populated St Giles, thence through St Andrew's Holborn and onto Tyburn road to the gallows. The carts carrying the condemned would make a leisurely two-hour procession to Tyburn. On the way they would make frequent halts for ale and spirits at public houses or to allow the prisoners to converse with friends and relatives in the crowd. Unless the condemned were unpopular, the crowd would shower the cart with fruit and flowers to show their sympathy with the prisoners.[53] The frequent stops for liquid refreshment, especially at traditional taverns like The Bowl in St Giles, meant that prisoners usually arrived at Tyburn intoxicated.[54] As Swift recorded of Tom Clinch:

> As clever Tom Clinch, while the Rabble was bawling,
> Rode stately through Holbourn to die in his Calling;
> He stopt at the George for a Bottle of Sack,
> And promis'd to pay for it when he'd come back.[55]

It was deemed essential to the exemplary nature of capital punishment in the first-three quarters of the eighteenth century that hangings should be public. Tyburn tree, near present-day Marble Arch, was well-chosen to make a sombre impression, situated as it was on the edge of Hyde Park, then a byword for dusty desolation.[56] At the beginning of the eighteenth century Thomas Brown described the area thus: 'Here people coach it to take the air, amidst a cloud of dust able to choke a foot-soldier, and hinder'd as from seeing those that come thither on purpose to show themselves.'[57] But on an execution day dust was no deterrent to the excited crowd. At Tyburn thousands of people, and often tens of thousands, would crowd around the execution ground to witness the spectacle. There were 30,000 at the execution of the Perreaus, though the record is said to have been held by a hanging at Moorfields in 1767 when 80,000 spectators were present.[58] Parties would arrive on horseback and in coaches. Men and women would throng the adjoining streets. Others climbed ladders, sat on the wall enclosing Hyde Park or crowded into the cow pastures around Tyburn to try to get a glimpse of the proceedings.[59] Choice vantage points were much sought after. An enterprising cowkeeper's widow called Mrs Proctor erected a number of boxes on her own land around the gallows for the more affluent spectator.'Mother Proctor's Pews' were a lucrative investment: they were said to have brought her more than £500 on the day of Lord Ferrers's execution alone.[60] In general, you had to pay to get a position near the hanging. If a reprieve was granted on execution day, you lost your money. This sometimes resulted in serious rioting.[61]

Public executions were one of the rare occasions when the classes mingled. The upper strata vied for a good view with the underworld and the wretched and dispossessed.[62] This 'equality' was of course part of the artifice of public hangings, suggesting that all men were alike in the dispassionate gaze of the majestic law. But the usual scenes of crowd violence were more in the spirit of the people below than the people above. Nietzsche once remarked that mankind was only truly itself at bullfights and executions. He would have found support from eighteenth-century Tyburn. The brazen theatricality of public hangings seemed to excite popular blood lust. Here if anywhere, the 'crowd' became the 'mob'. Pugnacious, aggressive, combative, and abusive, the onlookers struggled and jostled for pride of place by the gallows.[63] If barriers were erected, they were soon swept away by the press of the crowd. Spectators often suffered broken limbs and had their teeth knocked out. Some were crushed to death.[64] This risk was especially acute for women and children. (It was thought particularly instructive for young children to witness hangings. Often they were taken home and beaten afterwards lest they forget the awful example.[65])

Public executions were occasions both for further violence and for further crime. A case from 1764 makes the point. Seven men were hanged at Tyburn. First pickpockets systematically worked through the crowd who stood in Newgate Street to watch the cart go by. Meanwhile one of the seven condemned, who had been sentenced to death for returning from transportation, harangued the crowd about the butcher who had been the chief witness against him. The incensed mob tried to pull down the butcher's house and had to be dispersed by troops. By the time the cart arrived at Tyburn, the same gang of pickpockets had worked through the spectators around the gallows.[66] These were not the only sorts of peril attending executions. During the beheading of Lord Lovat in 1747 a number of people climbed a scaffold at the bottom of Tower Hill for a better view. The scaffold collapsed, seven people were killed and many more severely injured.[67]

Samuel Richardson described the turmoil around Tyburn Tree:

At the place of execution, the scene grew still more shocking; and the clergyman who attended was more the subject of ridicule, than of their serious attention. The psalm was sung amidst the curses and quarrelling of hundreds of the most abandon'd and profligate of mankind: upon whom (so stupid are they to any sense of decency) all the preparation of the unhappy wretches seems to serve only for the subject of a barbarous kind of mirth, altogether inconsistent with humanity.[68]

The taste for public hangings was singular, as it did not seem to square with other aspects of English culture. As a distinguished student of the eighteenth century once remarked:

It is a curious illustration of the caprice of national sentiment, that English opinion in the eighteenth century allowed the execution of criminals to be treated as a popular amusement, but at the same time revolted against the continental custom of compelling chained prisoners to work in public, as utterly inconsistent with English liberty.[69]

Even more bizarre was the fondness for attending public executions evinced by the upper classes. Since their lives were not 'nasty, brutish, and short' like those of the mob, the phenomenon seems to suggest a form of morbid curiosity. But there is no doubting its existence. Lady Townshend was said to have taken a villa at Paddington expressly to be near at hand for the Tyburn executions.[70] George Selwyn, one of Horace Walpole's friends, had a particular fondness for attending executions. He was also a devotee of abnormal psychopathology and seems to have come close to necrophilia in his passion for examining disfigured corpses.[71] He is said to have made a special journey to Paris to see Damiens broken on the wheel for (allegedly) trying to assassinate Louis XV.[72]

The most famous of all such execution-watchers was James Boswell, who described his ghoulish hobby as follows:

> I must confess that I myself am never absent from a public execution. . . . When I first attended them, I was shocked to the greatest degree. I was in a manner convulsed with pity and terror, and for several days, but especially the night after, I was in a very dismal situation. Still, however, I persisted in attending them, and by degrees my sensibility abated; so that I can now see one with great composure. . . . I can account for this curiosity in a philosophical manner, when I consider that death is the most aweful object before every man, whoever directs his thoughts seriously towards futurity. . . . Therefore it is that I feel an irresistible impulse to be present at every execution, as I there behold the various effects of the near approach of death . . . the curiosity which impels people to be present at such affecting scenes is certainly a proof of sensibility, not callousness. For it is observed, that the greatest proportion of spectators is composed of women.[73]

On arrival at the gallows, the condemned man would ascend the scaffold, accompanied by the ordinary. This was the time for the 'dying speeches', often disseminated later in pamphlet form to the great financial advantage of the chaplain. The person about to hang could state whatever he liked. He could damn the government and the regime to the devil, or confess his sins and hope that those watching would benefit from his example. He could make a speech himself or hand a prepared text to the ordinary to read. In the case of famous criminals, the 'dying speech' could become a best-seller. The proceeds would go to the ordinary, who was deemed the legatee of the deceased in this respect, in return for the 'spiritual comfort' he had given the condemned.[74]

Then it was time for the hangman to do his gruesome work. Hangmen were by common consent the lowest of the low. In London a chief executioner and his assistant were retained at a salary of £50 a year plus a guinea for each execution carried out. At their best they were efficient butchers, showmen, and ham actors; at their worst, drunken, brutal incompetents. In 1738 an inebriated hangman tried to put the noose around the ordinary's neck and was persuaded to desist only with difficulty.[75] Many had criminal records and ended on the gallows themselves. The most famous such character was John Price, alias Jack Ketch. He began as a pickpocket with a gang of gypsies and was whipped for that offence. He joined the merchant navy and continued his pickpocketing activities at the expense of fellow seamen. This time he was whipped at a gun, pickled in brine, and keel-hauled. On discharge he was again convicted of petty larceny and whipped at the cart's tail. Finally, he achieved 'respectability' by becoming hangman for the county of Middlesex. One night, in a drunken stupor, he beat up a watchman's wife who was selling pies. She later died of her wounds and Ketch was executed for murder in 1718.[76]

The hangman's job was not just brutalizing, it was often dangerous. Condemned persons, like Hannah Dagoe (see p. 130 above) could get free of their ropes and attack the executioner. The crowd could turn nasty and vent its anger on the hangman; in 1768 a stone-throwing mob seriously injured the master of the Tyburn ceremonies.[77] Again, in 1769, after the execution of the weavers Doyle and Valline, the hangman came close to being lynched. Very occasionally, no one could be found to turn off the prisoners who were taken to public execution. In 1721 two prisoners shivered in the cold for two hours under the gallows until the Sheriff gave up and took them back to Newgate. Their old quarters had already been reallocated. More out of administrative convenience than mercy, their sentence was changed to transportation.[78]

In theory the executioner's task in the case of a simple hanging was straightforward. The scaffold consisted of three posts, ten or twelve feet high, held apart by three connecting cross-beams at the top. Twenty-four could be hanged at the same time. The prisoner was made to mount on a very wide cart, the cord was tied around his neck, and the end of the rope was fastened to the gibbet.[79] The chaplain and the man's relatives mounted the cart and stayed about fifteen minutes, whispering words of encouragement or mouthing homilies. Then all save the prisoner got off the cart. The executioner covered the eyes and face of the prisoner, and a handkerchief was dropped as the signal for the hanging to commence. The hangman got down and lashed the horses. The cart shot forward, the victim was left dangling. Death came slowly by asphyxiation. The friends of the executed man often laid hold of his legs while he was writhing and twisting at the rope's end and pulled at them to speed up the lingering death.[80]

So it transpired if all went according to plan. A sober hangman executed a sober victim without fear or favour and the victim died. But there were many departures from the putative norm at every stage of the proceedings. Many prisoners died bravely, fully conscious to the end. But many were too drunk to know what was happening. Some were in a state of religious ecstasy.[81] Elizabeth Jeffries fainted before the rope was tied, and so was hanged unconscious.[82] Sometimes the rope broke and the victim had to be strung up again. On many such occasions the crowd prevented the prisoner from being rehanged. In 1736 a man was saved in this way, but he died shortly afterwards of heart failure from the shock of anticipated death.[83] In 1763, on Kennington Common, a rare attempt was made by the crowd to rescue the condemned man. The military was sent for, and there was furious hand to hand-fighting between soldiers and spectators before the execution was finally carried out at eight o'clock in the evening.[84]

Since death from hanging was by asphyxiation, there was little possibility of survival unless the hangman had been bribed. But there were several instances of 'spontaneous' survival.[85] Margaret Dickson, hanged for infanticide at Musselburgh near Edinburgh in 1728, sat up in her coffin on the way to the burial ground. Since she could not be tried twice for the same offence, she was deemed to be a beneficiary of divine providence. She was still alive twenty-five years later.[86] William Duell was hanged for murder, cut down, and then taken for anatomization to Surgeon's Hall. Observing some signs of life in him, the surgeons revived him. He recovered and was given a sentence of transportation instead.[87] Most fortunate of all who escaped death by the rope was 'half hanged Smith', a felon hanged in 1705. He was taken down after fifteen minutes, dangling, and recovered rapidly. Smith went on to face two further capital charges and in both cases he proved singularly lucky. In the first of them he was acquitted after a 'special verdict' by a hung jury. In the other, the prosecutor died before the case came to court.[88]

The most common reason for survival of a hanging was that friends or relatives of the condemned had bribed the hangman to tie the knot in a certain way or to cut the hanged man down sooner than usual; it was at the discretion of the hangman to decide when someone was 'dead'. Asphyxia could result in temporary unconsciousness rather than death if the knot was tied at the front or the back of the neck rather than at the side. The hangman in the Dodd case was bribed to adjust the noose to give the victim a better chance of survival.[89] If a man hanged in this way could be cut down quickly, put in a warm bed and bled, and possibly given a pint of porter or other alcoholic liquid, it was thought he had a good chance of survival. There were enough cases of survival in the early eighteenth century to warrant such a belief.[90] But some of the 'survival techniques' were for the credulous only. In the early 1730s a surgeon, after doing experiments with dogs, evolved a theory that if an incision was made in his windpipe, a hanged man could recover if taken down quickly from the scaffold. The first 'beneficiary' of this theory underwent the necessary surgery and was taken down three-quarters of an hour after being turned off. Alas for him and the theory, he was already dead.[91]

The legends attaching to those who had been thus miraculously 'resurrected' fed into and reinforced the other superstitions about hangings and hanged men. It has been convincingly demonstrated that high mortality rates in the eighteenth century did *not* mean that the 'lower orders' were indifferent to death.[92] What it did mean was that the fact of death could not be obfuscated or fudged as in the modern world. Forced to confront death as a daily imminent possibility, the average uneducated eighteenth-century Englishman embraced superstition as a means of allaying fears and enhancing hopes. To touch the body of a hanged man was considered efficacious.[93] The clothes of the dead man and the rope itself were also thought to have magical properties. The fact that these items were regarded in law as the property of the hangman accounts for the many violent struggles at the foot of the scaffold between executioner and relatives of the hanged person.[94] In 1797 there was a murderous fracas over the body of the rapist John Briant between two factions, both led by women. Unfortunately, the imagined therapeutic effects of the corpse could never be verified, since the legs, arms, and head were all pulled off in the mêlée.[95]

Yet the greatest single cause of physical conflict in the immediate aftermath of a hanging was conflict with surgeons' messengers. This involved a head-on clash between science and popular culture. The advance in medical science involved the dissection of corpses. Yet the anatomization of one's body was popularly regarded as a worse fate than hanging.[96] The consequence was that corpses for surgical investigation became as rare as gold-dust. Body-snatchers arose to fulfil the demand. Yet the surgeons could never achieve a cheap and regular supply of bodies. Their best hope lay with purchasing the bodies of executed criminals from the hangman.[97] This was easily enough done in the case of notorious criminals detested by the crowd, like Jonathan Wild.[98] But in most cases it was easy enough for the family of the hanged man to whip up the crowd into a swell of indignation against the surgeons. The result was violence and pitched battles between the crowd and the representatives of 'law and order'.

One such fracas was described by Samuel Richardson:

As soon as the poor creatures were half-dead, I was much surprised, before such a number of peace-officers, to see the populace fall to haling and pulling the carcasses with so much earnestness, as to occasion several warm rencounters, and broken heads. These, I was told, were the friends of the person executed, or such as, for the sake of tumult, chose to appear so, and some persons sent by private surgeons to obtain bodies for dissection. The contests between these were fierce and bloody, and frightful to look at.[99]

It is difficult to overrate the fear and loathing occasioned by the thought of surgical dissection in the eighteenth century. Apart from the obvious fact that it was impossible to revive a corpse that had been anatomized, a deeper superstititious undertow was at work. To be cut up was worse than execution itself, since hanging did not of itself preclude the hope of eternal life, as the ordinary never ceased to point out on the procession to Tyburn.[100] But in what sense could there be resurrection of the body, as promised by the Christian ritual, if the parts of the corpse were dissected and scattered to the winds? This was why hardened criminals, who did not fear Tyburn, quailed at the thought of going under the surgeon's knife afterwards.[101]

This superstitious dread of anatomization also explained the authorities' use of the penalty to 'top up' the death sentence. Since the penalty for so many trivial offences was the same as for murder under the Code, hardline apologists for the Code constantly sought to entrench in law aggravated forms of the death penalty. Among such people there was an undercurrent of fury that the death penalty had not had the desired deterrent effect. Not only did many of the condemned go defiantly to their deaths; more seriously, all exemplary impact was lost in the carnival-like atmosphere of public hangings. Aggravated penalties, it was thought, would restore the terror of the supreme penalty.

The century was not one year old before this notion was canvassed. The anonymous author of Hanging Not Punishment Enough made a number of hardline proposals. Trials should take place immediately after arrest; those found guilty should be kept in solitary confinement on bread and water; hanging should follow as soon as possible after the trial; the condemned should be hanged in prison uniform. If all this did not sufficiently cow the criminal classes, they should be hanged in chains or starved to death.[102] These bloodthirsty proposals were supplemented by advocacy of the French punishment of being broken on the wheel.[103] Whipping criminals to death, hanging them in chains, and starving them to death continued to be popularly peddled options in the first half of the century.[104] Knowing the popular horror of surgical dissection, some strongly pushed this as the most efficacious form of aggravated death penalty.[105] Others advocated castration as a penalty for non-capital crimes and death by rabies for capital ones. The idea was that the condemned man would be deliberately subjected to the bite of a mad dog, so as to induce the most painful death. Medical science would also benefit from the inspection of cadavers dispatched in this way.[106]

Sometimes the authorities chose to put the bodies of executed people on public exhibition as a warning in terrorem. The corpse of Mrs Phipoe, a murderesss executed in 1797 in front of Newgate was publicly displayed on a structure erected in the Old Bailey.[107] On another occasion the bodies of two murderers were exposed in a stable in Little Bridge Street. The most widespread form of aggravated penalty was to hang in chains the bodies of executed offenders. Although in the past offenders had sometimes been hanged in chains alive, so that they died of starvation, in the eighteenth century hanging in chains was a penalty for a person already dead.[108] This was a fate second only to surgical dissection in the fear it created, although Blackstone produced the bizarre argument in its favour that 'it is a comfortable sight to the relations and friends of the deceased.'(!)[109]

Before 1752 hanging in chains was a means whereby the state could express its particular detestation of a given criminal; it had no place in law. But the Murder Act of 1752, an attempt to increase the deterrent effect of capital punishment, ordained that the judge could order dissection by surgeons or hanging in chains as additional punishments for those condemned to death for heinous murders.[110] The Act was not aimed at murders committed in hot blood within the family but at homicides of the cold-blooded kind.[111] A couple of examples will perhaps make the point clear. In 1792 John Day was hanged in chains after execution for cutting both his parents' throats and then murdering a maidservant who witnessed the act.[112] And a case from the 1750s underlines the cold-bloodedness aspect. A Hertfordshire farmer claimed to have been bewitched by a woman who threatened that the Pretender would 'have' him and his hogs. The woman was accused of witchcraft by her local community. In fear of the consequences she took sanctuary in the church. A lynch mob dragged her out and killed her by ducking. The ringleader of the mob was convicted, escorted back to the scene of the crime by nearly 200 soldiers, executed, and then hanged in chains.[113]

Hanging in chains excited loathing and curiosity in equal measure. Such was the detestation of the punishment by families of criminals, *pace* Blackstone, that it was found necessary to prevent the removal of the body hanged in chains by studding the post of the gibbet with thousands of nails.[114] Yet the morbid fascination of the public for the practice was so great that in 1795 London was said to be like a deserted city when hundreds of thousands trooped out to Wimbledon Common to see a body hanging in chains.[115]

Even so, the ultimate horror for the man going to the scaffold was that his body would be dissected by surgeons. It is significant that there is no record of riots at places of public execution over the bodies of those condemned to hang in chains. The reason is that hanging in chains was reserved for crimes that excited a peculiar popular horror, while anatomization was a routine function of the market economy. There seemed little point in judges expressly ordering that the body of an executed criminal be given over to the surgeons, when that was likely to happen anyway. Nevertheless, many judges did make that specific recommendation after 1752, in an attempt to stiffen the deterrent effect of capital punishment. In 1786 William Wilberforce tried to extend the penalty beyond murder so as to make it apply in cases of rape, arson, burglary, and robbery.[116]

The other notorious form of aggravated death penalty in the eighteenth century was that prescribed for treason. The sentence pronounced on the prisoners of the '45 says it all:

> Let the several prisoners return to the gaol from whence they came; and from thence they must be drawn to the place of execution; and when they come there they must be severally hanged by the neck, but not till they be dead, for they must be cut down alive; then their bowels must be taken out and burned before their faces; then their heads must be severed from their bodies, and their bodies severally divided into four quarters; and these must be at the king's disposal.[117]

By the eighteenth century the crueller parts of this sentence had gone into abeyance. A sledge or hurdle was allowed, to preserve the traitor from the torment of being dragged along the ground. The practice of bribery of the executioner made sure that the condemned man was dead before being disembowelled.[118] And, whereas the heads of the '45 rebels were displayed on gateways as a warning to the disaffected, by the end of the century this practice too was considered barbarous. The executioner would still cut off the head and display it aloft, saying 'This is the head of a traitor.' But thereafter it was customary for both head and body of the person executed for high treason to be put straight into the coffin.[119]

There were two very important changes in the mechanics and administration of capital punishment during the century. The first was the advent of the 'drop', replacing the old system of 'launching into eternity' from the cart. As we have seen, the traditional method involved death by asphyxiation when the cart on which the prisoner was standing was drawn away. In 1759 a new system was introduced at Tyburn, whereby the person being hanged was actually killed by falling through a trapdoor in a platform. The fall broke his neck, making death instantaneous. The technical change was that the old triangular gallows was replaced by a moveable one, erected on the day of execution and taken down afterwards.[120] It was said that Earl Ferrers was the first to be executed by the 'drop' method. However, the drop system did not become universal until 1783, when the other great innovation was introduced.

From very early times doubts had been expressed about the desirability of public executions. The theory was that the crowd of onlookers would be so deeply impressed by the awesome spectacle of the law taking away the lives of malefactors that they would 'go and sin no more'. In fact, as we have seen, public executions became simply an excuse for a public holiday and a pretext for behaviour that would not normally have been tolerated. It was felt that public hangings increased, not decreased, the crowd's inherent wickedness. Bernard Mandeville believed that the ribald and riotous lawlessness at Tyburn gallows led instead to the sullying of the law's majesty. It also increased the inefficacy of hanging as a deterrent.[121] The traditional procession to Tyburn was a particular target of the sceptics. Fielding was convinced that the carnival atmosphere, the condemned's gaudy clothing, the general carousing and drinking, all contributed to break down the central deterrent notion of a link between death and shame. Most criminals on the procession to Tyburn were regarded by the crowd as heroes not villains. This utterly defeated the purpose of the ritual.[122] Here are Samuel Richardson's comments:

> The face of everyone spoke a kind of mirth, as if the spectacle they had beheld had afforded pleasure instead of pain, which I am wholly unable to account for. In other nations, common criminal executions are said to be little attended by any beside the necessary officers, and the mournful friends, but here, all was hurry and confusion, racket and noise, praying and oaths, swearing and singing psalms. I am unwilling to impute this difference in our own from the practice of other nations, to the cruelty of our natures; to which foreigners, however, to our dishonour, ascribe it. In most instances, let them say what they will, we are humane beyond what other nations can boast; but in this, the behaviour of my countrymen is past my accounting for; every street and lane I passed through, bearing rather the face of a holiday, than of that sorrow which I expected to see, for the untimely deaths of five members of the community.[123]

Yet public executions had powerful intellectual allies. Samuel Johnson thought that an execution that could not be witnessed by the people at large could by definition have no deterrent effect. It was necessary actually to see a twisting, gasping, convulsed figure on the gibbet: the mere idea of hanging had no imaginative power.[124] Paley added the ingenious argument that unless society had a highly ceremonial demonstration of a sovereign's wrath to deter potential offenders, there would be no option but recourse to that ultimate horror, a professional police force.[125] Moreover, it was argued, in a private execution – which to most people would mean a mere association of ideas – deterrence could be achieved just as well by execution of the innocent as the guilty; it seemed to remove the link between the crime and the punishment. In addition, it opened the way for rich malefactors to bribe the hangman not to execute them, or at least to execute someone else in their place. For these reasons, the Fieldings' advocacy of a totally private execution within the prison gates received little initial support.[126]

Nevertheless, the main thrust of the argument of Mandeville and

Fielding gradually made an impact. There could be little question but that the Tyburn hangings had become, not an awestruck acceptance of the remorseless majesty of the Law, but a ritual of defiance of that very Law. The authority and credibility of the elite was seen to be ultimately at stake. But it took the crime wave of 1782-3 to jolt the authorities into action. The boisterous crowd disturbances at the increasingly frequent executions conjured unpleasant memories of the recent Gordon riots. It was time for decisive action. The last hanging at Tyburn took place on 7 November 1783.[127] Executions thenceforth were switched to the yard in front of Newgate. At a stroke the carnival of the Tyburn procession was ended. The use of the drop became universal. On 9 December the first Newgate executions were carried out: ten men were hanged in the yard.[128] Alas for the authorities, the crowd simply switched its attention to Newgate. True, it was deprived of the Tyburn procession, but its behaviour outside Newgate continued as unruly as ever.[129]

15

Secondary Punishment

You know the custom, sir. Garnish, captain, garnish!
John Gay, *The Beggar's Opera*

On the whole our intercourse with America has been little
else than interchange of vices and diseases.
Thomas Love Peacock, *Gryll Grange*

Australian history is almost always picturesque . . . it does
not read like history, but like the most beautiful lies . . . it
is full of surprises and adventures, and incongruities and
incredibilities, but they are all true, they all happened.
Mark Twain, *More Tramps Abroad*

To be found guilty of a non-clergyable felony did not necessarily mean
the procession to the gallows. Courts made wide use of reprieves and
pardons to palliate the excesses of the Bloody Code. Reprieval was the
temporary suspension of sentence. Judges used their powers of reprieve
to overturn jury decisions in cases where they considered the jury had
convicted wrongfully, where the defendant had become insane between
the crime and the conviction, and, in the case of female defendants,
where the condemned person was pregnant.[1] Reprieves often led to
pardons; this was almost invariably the case when women 'pleaded the
belly'.[2]

Roughly half of all people condemned to hang in the eighteenth
century were pardoned and given some form of secondary punishment.
Pardons were of three kinds: those granted by judges after a jury verdict;
those formally granted under the royal prerogative of mercy to overturn a
judicial sentence; and *de facto* pardons when courts or plaintiffs
downgraded the category of offence. Pardoning was always controversial.
We have seen how Madan argued that the royal prerogative should never
be exercised, as it usurped the certainty of punishment and thus
destroyed the credibility of the supreme penalty as deterrent. For Madan,
the frequency of pardons made the deterrent value of the death sentence

no more than that of 'a scarecrow set in a field to frighten the birds from the corn.'[3]

Both Fielding and Colquhoun argued strongly that pardons should be used very sparingly.[4] There was particular concern over pardons emanating from the monarch under the royal prerogative of mercy, not just on the grounds that society might appear 'soft on criminals', but through fear that the prerogative could be used to win popularity or undue parliamentary influence for the king.[5] The motives of a compassionate monarch were regarded with deep suspicion. George II was said to have had a generally merciful attitude, provided the crime was not murder.[6] Yet Samuel Johnson regarded him as cruel, barbarous, and unrelenting; his so-called humanity Johnson took to be mere self-serving camouflage.[7]

Opposition to the royal prerogative did not come from hardliners alone. Beccaria, who was opposed to the death penalty in any form, argued that in a proper system of crime and punishment, the infallibility of punishment should be the key notion. It followed that the uncertainty introduced by a royal pardon could not be entertained.[8] But Beccaria advocated the abolition of the royal prerogative *pari passu* with the abolition of the death penalty. Madan, and to a lesser extent Fielding, wanted its abolition while the draconian aspects of the Bloody Code were retained.

Sometimes more subtle arguments were advanced for the retention of royal pardons. Blackstone thought that they provided a further mystical link in the nexus binding monarch and subjects.[9] This pre-echoed Bagehot in insisting that the power of kingship lay primarily in its symbolic and emotional appeal. George III was particularly impressed by this argument and paid scrupulous attention to the cases brought before him.[10] The other subtle elite consideration was that pardons reinforced the ideology of mercy, itself a pillar of the multifaceted majesty of the Law, designed to mystify and obfuscate.[11] Very nice judgements were called for as to how many pardons could be granted and in what context, without affecting the credibility of the whole system. On one occasion, the equlibrium point between necessary punishment and the appearance of humanity was especially finely gauged. George III, in commuting the death sentence on a highwayman to transportation, ordered that the pardon be announced to the prisoner on the brink of execution, *à la* Dostoevsky.[12] This, incidentally, highlights the important role of transportation. Pardons were more frequent and more palatable to the elite when a tough secondary punishment like transportation could be used to blunt charges of 'softness'.

Pardons were freely given. Colquhoun calculated that four-fifths of the hundred persons gazetted for execution in 1785 had been pardoned, either on condition of being transported, or of joining His Majesty's forces, or absolutely unconditionally. From August 1792 to June 1794 he estimated that 1,002 pardons, absolute or conditional, had been granted.[13]

De facto pardons, on the other hand, arose because courts and litigants reshaped the Code in the direction of mercy. This could either take place by the court's use of precedents or through the discretionary actions of the plaintiff. Successive legal decisions had given the nod to those who wished to temper justice with compassion in minor offences. Non-clergyable felonies were reduced to clergyable ones: for example, it was established that you could not pickpocket someone who was drunk, or be guilty of burglary if you broke into a house at night before the owners or tenants had moved in.[14] Also, the attitude of the plaintiff was crucial. In 1788 one of the Duke of Devonshire's servants was accused of a multiple felony for which he would normally have been capitally indicted. The Duke saved his life in effect by reducing the charge to a single felony, of which the servant was found guilty and sentenced to seven years' transportation.[15]

What determined whether a pardon was granted? There were two supremely important factors. One was the degree of violence used during the perpetration of the crime. The other was the reputation or 'character' of the prisoner. In Surrey during 1660-1800 about three-quarters of those convicted of murder were hanged, but only about 38 per cent of those found guilty of property offences.[16] The theory behind this was that the occasional dreadful example would serve as a deterrent against minor thieves and pilferers, but sterner measures were called for against serious offenders. In property offences, in turn, more severity was visited on the criminals who terrorized their victims. In Essex during 1748-1800 capitally convicted burglars and highway robbers were about twice as likely to be hanged as horse thieves.[17] Of course local cultures played a part here. In some localities, horse-stealing would actually be considered a worse crime than highway robbery.

Yet the most important factor of all in securing a pardon was the 'character' of the prisoner. A pardon was fairly likely if an offender's respectable neighbours spoke up for him; it was *probable* if a member of the nobility or gentry intervened on his behalf. The opinion of pillars of the local community was crucial in securing pardons. It followed that those most at risk from hanging were old lags or those who could find no one to speak for them. The same considerations applied to the obtaining of a softer sentence. Testimony to one's good character was of overwhelming importance to one's chances of survival, especially since insanity was rarely accepted as a plea.[18]

There was one other consideration that could lead to a pardon or a lesser sentence in the case of a non-clergyable offence. Since the remaining family of an executed man, had to be supported by the parish, and since, further, males married relatively late in the eighteenth century, men aged between 30 and 40 had a better chance of evading the hangmen than really young men. In addition, the plea of being driven unwillingly to crime by poverty was more plausible from a married man with family responsibilities than a young single man.[19]

Conviction on one of the major felony charges tended to lead either to the gallows or to a pardon. What were the punishments available to the judiciary for lesser or mitigated offences? At the beginning of the century these were limited to fines or corporal punishments. Torture was unknown in England. In this respect the exponents of 'English liberty' had a sound case, since torture was widespread on the Continent and was not abolished in France until the Revolution. It was accounted a great breakthrough for civilization when Frederick the Great forbade it in Prussia in 1742.[20]

Yet England retained a form of torture in cases where the accused refused to plead. There was no right to remain silent in eighteenth-century England. To stand mute in a case of high treason incurred an automatic 'guilty' verdict. In other cases, the accused was subjected to *peine forte et dure*.[21] He was taken to a dungeon, chained spreadeagled to the floor, then loaded with a gradually increasing weight until he died or agreed to plead. The punishment was still being applied in 1770.[22] To the immense satisfaction of Blackstone, the procedure was abolished two years later.[23]

Yet the absence of torture in all other cases did not please the bloodthirsty champions of the Code. The author of *Hanging not Punishment Enough* (1700) wanted all non-capital punishment to consist of torture and branding followed by lifetime servitude in the colonies.[24] Thirty years later, a like-minded Draco wanted to introduce the French custom of breaking criminals at the wheel. He proposed to solve the problem of vagrancy by rounding up all able-bodied vagrants and exporting them as slaves, either to the American plantations or to the Mediterranean galleys.[25]

The eighteenth-century judiciary chose a Solonic rather than draconian path. By the late 1770s judges had very wide discretionary powers in non-capital cases. They could choose to award whippings, fines, detentions in a house of correction for between six months and four years. They could order direct prison sentences of up to five years or transportation for fourteen years. How did this wide spectrum of punishment become available? Let us examine the types of secondary punishment available, in ascending order of importance.

Corporal punishment was the point at which the eighteenth century most clearly linked with the past. Clergyable felons were traditionally branded on the thumb so that they could not plead clergy again. The penalty was not meant to disgrace the offender: the brand could be seen only by close inspection; its sole purpose was for the benefit of the authorities. But during the 'moral panic' at the end of the seventeenth century, an attempt was made to upgrade the penalty. By the 1699 Shoplifting Act it was ordained that branding would henceforth be on the left cheek near the nose.[26] But after seven years it reverted to the thumb because it was found that facial branding merely produced hardened criminals. Since no one would employ a person with the marks of criminality so clearly on his face, the first offender was forced into a life of crime. Facial branding was held as a reserve power for criminals who 'only just' escaped the gallows. Such a one was Joseph Crook, convicted in 1731 of the forgery of certain conveyancing documents. The public hangman cut both his ears, sliced his nostril and branded him on the nose.[27]

Whipping represented the next punishment in the ascending hierarchy of corporal punishments. Fines were often used in minor assault cases. But there was a proviso attached, that the fine should not be larger than a man could pay without endangering his livelihood.[28] When, therefore, a fine was not levyable or a heavier punishment was called for, as with vagrancy, a prisoner would be whipped, either by a gaoler within the confines of a prison, or in public by a hangman or constable. The sort of offences that elicited whipping as a punishment can be briefly illustrated. In 1790 Samuel Hinchcliffe pretended to be a porter in an inn to get tips from customers for imagined future services.[29] John Holmes and Peter Williams stole corpses which they then sold to the surgeons.[30]

The most common form of public flagellation was 'at the cat's tail': the prisoner would be tied to the back of a cart, stripped to the waist and whipped until the blood showed on his back. This was a mobile punishment. The man would be whipped over a certain route at a time of day best calculated to pull in the biggest crowds. The theory of the peculiarly exemplary quality of public floggings was taken over from the military.[31] But there was one important difference. In civilian floggings, unlike military ones, the number of strokes was not specified. It was this arbitrary quality that made Bentham so dislike the practice, but not the principle, of whipping. The constable could lay on the strokes softly or strongly, the cart could proceed slowly or very fast, the itinerary could be very short or unduly protracted. Besides, the punishment was meted out for wildly dissimilar offences. In 1772 two men were whipped around Covent Garden. One had seduced his own niece, while the other had merely stolen a bunch of radishes![32]

But Bentham, with his concentration on pleasure and pain, slightly missed the point about public floggings. Their principal aim was the inculcation of shame: shame especially at being publicly humiliated in front of people who knew you; this of course removed much of the force of the penalty in an urban context. For this reason, too, 'gentlemen' were never whipped for their misdemeanours; it was felt that the loss of honour sustained would be too great. From the elite point of view, whipping constituted a happy compromise between excessive leniency and the overreaction of the death penalty. An analysis of this punishment shows it increasing in the 1760s and 1770s for the punishment of grand larceny as doubts about capital punishment and the future of transportation grew, even though there was never any suggestion that whipping could actually *replace* transportation for more serious offences.[33]

Potentially the most serious form of corporal punishment was the pillory. This was used for offences that aroused a high degree of public indignation: hoarding, speculation, dishonest shopkeeping, cheating at cards, pretended fortune telling, and all minor forms of confidence trickery. Women were sometimes pilloried for brothel-keeping.[34] The object was both to chastise the offender and to warn the public of his identity. The prisoner was exhibited, usually for an hour, on a platform in the market-place, with his hands and head fixed in a wooden structure (the 'stocks').

The actual level of punishment depended on the disposition of the crowd. When the offence was one which the crowd did not consider criminal, the prisoner did not suffer at all. The 'punishment' could backfire on the authorities if they misjudged the popular mood. In 1703 Defoe was pelted with flowers when in the stocks for writing a satire on the Church. The same 'fate' was meted out to Jacobite rebels in Catholic Lancashire. In Cheapside in 1738 the crowd cheered a man set in the pillory for refusing to pay the duty on soap.[35] In extreme cases the crowd would release the prisoner from the stocks, as happened to many of the 1790s radicals and to those guilty of political offences such as speaking seditious words against the Hanoverian succession.

A very good example of the sort of person with whom the crowd sympathized was one Parsons, inventor of the 'Cock Lane Ghost'. In order to settle scores with a man who had sued him for debt, Parsons got his daughter to fake a phantasmal apparition. The 'ghost' accused Parsons's enemy of having poisoned his sister-in-law and vowed it would end its spectral wanderings only when the man was hanged. When the imposture was revealed and Parsons placed in the stocks, so far from pelting him, the crowd gave him money to pay his debts.[36]

However, some social analysts felt that, however kindly one was treated in the pillory, the stigma attached to the punishment made it impossible for a person thereafter to move in polite society. When Boswell mentioned a man who had been well treated in the stocks and alleged that he had not been dishonoured, Samuel Johnson riposted at once 'Ay, but he was, sir. He could not mouth and strut as he used to, after having been there. People are not very willing to ask a man to their tables who has stood in the pillory.'[37]

When the crowd was indignant at the person(s) pilloried, the prisoners were in grave danger of their lives. Thomas Lyell and Lawrence Sydney were pelted with sticks and stones until bloody in 1742. Their crime was to have made £4,000 by playing with loaded dice.[38] In 1732 John Waller was killed in the pillory after giving false information to get a reward. The angry crowd pulled the pillory down, stamped on Waller, broke all his ribs and fractured his skull.[39] We have already noted (see chapter 2) the fate of the four bogus 'thief-takers' who were placed in the pillory in Smithfield in 1756. On 5 March McDaniel and Berry were pelted with oyster-shells and saved from death only by determined efforts by the Keeper of Newgate and a sheriff. Three days later, when Eagan and Salmon stood in the pillory, the crowd stoned Eagan to death and mortally wounded Salmon.[40]

Informal judicial murder by means of the pillory did not fade. In 1771 the crowd stoned to death a man thought to be an informer.[41] In 1780 another pillory death led Edmund Burke to question the entire practice. His speech in the House of Commons was followed by an impassioned letter to the Attorney-General.[42] Yet the authorities continued to believe that pillorying was an ingenious means of co-opting the public into reinforcement of the Code. Law as overarching ideology was strengthened by this semblance of participation. Place suggested a compromise between maintaining due process and indulging public outrage. The sheriff and his men should form a protective circle around the pillory. Women only would then be allowed into the circle as licensed tormentors of those in the stocks.[43]

Some of the offences for which people were pilloried evoked mere indifference in the crowd; here very clearly we can discern the difference between the popular and elite perceptions of what constituted crime. In such cases the authorities used the pillory merely as a 'first base' punishment, and added more severe ones later. Moses Moravia and John Manoury, who sank a ship to defraud the insurers, were pilloried prior to being fined and imprisoned in 1752.[44] For 'blasphemy', that is, denying the literal truth of the Bible, Peter Arnet was pilloried and fined before being sentenced to a year's hard labour in the Bridewell.[45] For perjury William Chandler was placed in the stocks as a prelude to seven years' transportation.[46]

The pillory was particularly associated with two categories of crime most calculated to arouse the anger of the crowd: blackmail and sexual deviancy. The two crimes tended to feed into each other, since most blackmail took the form of extorting money under threat of laying a charge of paternity or of sodomy.[47]

A reading of eighteenth-century newspapers gives the impression that there were more cases of homosexuality, including rape, than of crime of a heterosexual nature.[48] In one year there were two cases of homosexual rape and a plethora of commitments for homosexual activity.[49] Buggery was regarded with peculiar horror as an offence against the very laws of nature. Blackstone's attitude is instructive. He cannot bring himself to name the crime in English and offers a Latin substitute that is itself evasive:

> I will not act so disagreeable a part, to my readers as well as myself, as to dwell any longer upon a subject, the very mention of which is a disgrace to human nature. It will be more eligible to imitate in this respect the delicacy of our English law, which treats it, in its very indictments, as a crime not fit to be named; *'peccatum illud horribile, inter christianos non nominandum'*.[50]

Homosexuality was a familiar part of the London scene.[51] The capital had its own 'gay' clubs.[52] Sixteen soldiers were charged in 1764 when such a club among the footguards was uncovered.[53] Buggery in the armed forces was a continuing problem throughout the century, and offenders were severely punished, often by death.[54] Sodomy, that is, actual anal intercourse, was a non-clergyable felony. Indictments were rarely brought because of the difficulty of proof, but anyone convicted of the crime stood no chance at all of escaping the gallows, as statistics from Surrey make clear.[55] The case of Robert Jones, sentenced to death for sodomy in 1772, but pardoned on condition of lifetime exile from England, seems to have been the exception that proved the rule.[56]

In the case of suspected, attempted, or known homosexual activity for which there was no clinching proof sufficient for a capital indictment, offenders were placed in the pillory. The same held good for those guilty of bestialism or other sexual crimes.[57] A good example of other sexual crimes can be supplied from Malmesbury, where a farmer maimed and castrated two of his apprentice boys, aged 8 and 16. One night when they went to bed, he proceeded 'to wicker them, after the manner in which poor rams are treated.' At his trial it emerged that he had made a practice of buying up bastard children from the workhouse, then gelding them for use in the opera.[58]

To be pilloried for homosexual offences could be virtually a death sentence in itself. A sodomite was always a favourite target for the London mob. Charles Hitchen, the marshal for whom Jonathan Wild had been deputy in his early years and who later quarrelled with him, was seized *in flagrante delicto* in a Charing Cross tavern and taken to Newgate. Because actual penetration had to be proved to secure a capital sentence, Hitchen was found guilty instead of attempted sodomy, and sentenced to a fine of £20, six months' imprisonment, and an hour in the pillory. Knowing the likely response of the crowd, Hitchen donned a suit of armour before entering the stocks. He paid the under-sheriff and his minions to blockade the pillory with carts to hold the crowd at bay. Yet the sheriff's men were soon overpowered by a howling mob, who vaulted and clambered over the carts to get at Hitchen. They managed to detach part of his armour, then to tear off his clothes to expose his skin. After Hitchen had been in immediate danger of his life for half an hour the under-sheriff called up reinforcements, got control of the situation and took him down before his hour had elapsed.[59]

There were many similar incidents of mob fury. A 60-year-old man in the stocks for attempted buggery was assaulted by the crowd, stripped naked, bespattered in mud, then left to hang almost lifeless until he was taken back to Newgate.[60] On another occasion a man in the pillory for a sexual assault on a child escaped with his life only because of the fearless and resolute actions of magistrates and constables.[61]

By far the most important of all eighteenth-century secondary punishments was transportation, in which minor criminals or those reprieved from the death sentence were banished to foreign lands as indentured labour. Transportation overseas was a feature unique to British penal culture. Apart from Russia, with the vast spaces of Siberia at its disposal, no other civilized nation matched England in the scale and extent of transportation.[62] The punishment originally developed as the English equivalent of French and Spanish galley service and was at first exclusively used against people deemed dangerous to the social order: Irish Catholics in Cromwell's time, Jacobites after 1688.[63] The few transportees that there were up to the 1650s were sent to North America.

The pace quickened during the Restoration. Transportation was stepped up to prevent the automatic discharge of those eligible to plead benefit of clergy. Until 1706 the literacy test was still employed. This meant that the English penal code was unacceptably brittle. There was an impossibly wide chasm between capital punishment and clergyable discharge after branding on the thumb. Transportation, on the other hand, allowed for the removal of men dangerous to society without debasing the overall coinage of capital punishment. In the minds of its more thoughtful exponents, transportation also seemed to offer a slender hope of rehabilitating the criminal.[64]

But by the end of Charles II's reign, the transportation policy was running into serious difficulties because of the opposition of the American colonists themselves. The colonists regarded the convicts as a menace and passed laws to prevent their settlement on American soil. In addition, there was a conflict between the penal requirements of the English government and the profit motive of the merchants to whom they contracted the transportees. These merchants made their profits by selling the convicts as indentured labour in Virginia, Maryland and the West Indies. But this meant that (naturally) they wanted to take only the fit and the able-bodied, leaving the human jetsam in the hands of the authorities.[65]

For these reasons the use of transportation as a punishment largely went into abeyance during the first thirty years of the 'Glorious Revolution'. In 1718 the government revived it in spectacular fashion. The legislation that year is widely regarded as a turning point in the history of transportation.[66] The addition of so many capital offences to the Code had led to an unbearably inflexible either/or in punishment: either the hangman's rope or the picayune penalty of clergyable discharge after branding. By the second decade of the eighteenth century, the government had finally grasped the point that social stability cost money. Transportation was expensive if it was to be run properly; on the other hand the huge expansion in credit since 1688 made an expensive policy of secondary punishment more feasible.[67]

The 1718 Transportation Act enabled courts to order clergyable felons to be transported to America for seven years instead of being whipped or burnt in the hand. Non-clergyable felons could now be transported for fourteen years instead of being sent to the gallows. Those who had received a capital sentence which was later commuted were normally transported for life. If a clergyable felon returned from transportation before the seven years had elapsed, he (or she) would expect to receive a further sentence, this time of fourteen years. Non-clergyable felons who returned before their time could expect to be executed.[68]

Embracing the principle of entrepreneurship which their own ideology so lauded, the authorities put the transportation business into the hands of a London merchant named Jonathan Forward. Forward would be paid £3 for every convict he took across the Atlantic from London and the Home Counties. Similar contracts were to be established between provincial magistrates and other entrepreneurs.[69] The rate of profit was high, since convicts could be sold to plantation owners in Virginia for a minimum of £10 a head. Once their sentences were completed, the felons could either stay on as settlers or return to England, provided they could pay discharge fees to their masters and two local magistrates. The problem was that such fees were normally beyond the reach of convicts who were paid no wages during their indentures.[70]

For the first half of the century transportation was a thriving business. Some 30,000 people were shipped to America. When Virginia tried to stop the import of transported felons by passing laws that would make their settlement in the territory impossible, Forward protested to the London government. The 1723 Virginia Act was disallowed.[71] Forward waxed fat on the profits from the business for twenty years. In 1739 he was succeeded by Andrew Reid, who enjoyed an eighteen-year halcyon period. The less profitable later years were managed by John Stewart (1757-72) and Duncan Campbell, whose incumbency lasted just three years until 1775, when the American war brought the transportation system to an end.[72] After 1727 the government subsidy rose to £5 per head. With inflation at virtually nil at the American end, Campbell in the early 1770s could still expect to receive an average price of £10 for male convicts from American planters, and £8-9 for women. But because there were no regulations governing the transport of felons to America, men like Forward, Reid, and Campbell would already have made a handsome profit from the government fee alone by the time they landed their human cargoes on the other side of the Atlantic.[73]

The effect of transportation on sentencing policies was dramatic. Whereas 60 per cent of those convicted of clergyable offences had been branded and dismissed before 1718, the same proportion of such felons was transported after the 1718 Act.[74] Judges began to use transportation sentences routinely unless good cause could be shown why branding and whipping followed by discharge was more appropriate. The overall effect was to tighten the screws on petty crime. Some examples will help to make clear the offences for which felons were transported. Charles Scoldwell received seven years for stealing two ducks.[75] Joseph Hodges and Richard Probin got a similar sentence for petty confidence trickery.[76] Richard Swift was transported for a receiving offence that would certainly have been punished by death before the 1718 Act.[77] Another man, sentenced to death for forgery, was reprieved and transported instead because he helped save a ship in danger of foundering in a winter storm in the Irish Sea.[78]

The deterrent value of transportation was thought to be high: it gave pause particularly to those who were not abashed by the prospect of branding or whipping. As for capital property offences, the main effect of the coming of transportation was to mitigate the more bloodthirsty aspects of the Code by providing a more nuanced hierarchy of sanctions. In Surrey in 1736-53 179 men and women were sentenced to death for property offences, but 100 of them had the sentence commuted to transportation.[79]

The new punishment, in short, allowed death sentences to be commuted without destroying the overall credibility of the Bloody Code. Despite the extension of capital statutes, the supreme penalty was now largely reserved for murder, highway robbery, burglary, horse-theft, and gang crimes. This effect was not immediately apparent, since hanging levels continued very high in the early 1720s owing to peculiar, non-repeatable factors, such as the coincidence of threats to the Hanoverian succession with an urban crime wave. But as one of the leading authorities on eighteenth-century crime and punishment has remarked: 'Transportation created a penal system that could never again operate without a centrally dominant secondary punishment.'[80]

Transportation was typically used to punish grave crimes which did not quite seem to merit the gallows. The example of disreputable clergymen is an instructive one. The first half of the eighteenth century saw a sustained battle to clear up the exact legal status of marriage. Apart from customary concubinage ('common-law marriage') and secret contracts which could not be declared invalid in law, there was the widespread practice of the 'Fleet marriage'. Certain clergymen made a living as professional matchmakers. For an agreed sum of money these parsons would disgrace their calling by marrying *any* couples anywhere, in clandestine ceremonies in alehouses, coffee-houses, or even in brothels. A favourite haunt for these venal clerics was the Fleet prison, where debtors were lodged. Frequently every single person at such 'weddings' was roaring drunk. But the clandestine marriage was big business. Fleet marriages were both legally valid and very cheap, at a time when official weddings were heavily taxed. These corrupt parsons often employed barkers to solicit on the streets for custom. Advertising hoardings around the Fleet announced 'Marriages performed within'. Touts called out to passers-by 'Sir, will you be pleased to walk in and be married?' Other services provided by the venal clerics included back-dating of the registration of marriage (to legitimize children already born out of wedlock) and the provision of men for women wishing to marry in a hurry.[81]

It might be thought that this state of affairs was such an obvious threat to property that it would be taken in hand immediately after 1688. Clearly, if clandestine marriages were recognized, albeit unwillingly, by the law, there was nothing to stop adventurers of either sex from ensnaring heirs and heiresses to great fortunes. There was also a clear danger of bigamy, with its implicit threat to social mores and cohesion.[82] Yet numerous attempts to bring in a coherent law on marriage were defeated in the House of Commons. The reasons for this were fourfold. The gentry feared that the aristocracy would maintain a closed elite, impervious to intermarriage. The aristocracy feared that their own stock might degenerate if the law was drawn so tightly around marriage that no new blood could be infused into their own scions. There was also a general fear that abolishing the right of minors to marry whomsover they pleased would lead to loveless marriages on the European model and, probably, institutionalized adultery and the cult of *cicisbeism* or the *cavaliere servente*. Finally, if marriage could occur only by special licence then the expense and inconvenience would deter people from it and lead to an increase of concubinage, bastardy, and infanticide among the poor.[83]

Yet marriage was finally put on a clear legal foundation with Lord Hardwicke's Marriage Act of 1753. The main provisions of this Act were that only church weddings, properly solemnized, were legally valid; and that no marriage of persons under 21 was valid without parental consent. From this era dates the flight to Gretna Green by runaway couples, for in Scotland the new Marriage Act did not apply.[84] More pertinently, the

1753 Act stipulated that anyone solemnizing matrimony without a special licence or without calling the banns would be deprived of benefit of clergy (in this case, literally).[85]

The first to fall foul of the Act was a tawdry pair of decayed clergyman, the Reverend John Grierson and the Reverend Mr Wilkinson. Technically they could have received the death penalty, but the 'lag in consciousness' argument was accepted. In other words, it was thought unacceptable that people should be hanged in 1754 for what had been perfectly legal the year before. Grierson and Wilkinson each received a sentence of fourteen years' transportation.[86]

The most obvious drawback to transportation as a sanction was that a convicted felon could avoid the punishment by returning to England before his time was up. Returning from transportation was such a headache to the authorities that four years after the 1717 Transportation Act a second statute offered a fixed reward of £40 to anyone whose action led to the arrest and conviction of a returned transportee. Such people were, as we have seen, regularly employed by Jonathan Wild, especially as false witnesses. They were ideal material: if they did not toe the line, he could denounce them to the authorities.

Returning from transportation was a risky business for an unaided individual. To return from a sentence of fourteen years or upwards attracted an automatic death sentence on conviction.[87] As late as 1800, there was no relaxation in the severity of the law on this point.[88] To return to major crime on illegal return simply exacerbated matters. In 1751 William Parsons, who had been educated at Eton and was the son of a baronet, was hanged for highway robbery after return from transportation. This aggravated crime was so serious that not even the influence of his father and family could save him.[89]

For these reasons returning from transportation was usually associated with hardened criminals linked to a network of organized crime. Smugglers were particularly prone to return, not just because the rewards of their trade were so great but because of the legal loophole that returning from transportation after conviction on a smuggling offence did not become non-clergyable until the 1746 Smuggling Act.[90] Five Sussex smugglers shipped to America in August 1738 were back in England by November of the same year.[91] Members of the Poulter gang, who specialized in pickpocketing, horse-stealing, burglary, and petty fraud during the 1750s, boasted that they were able to book their return passage immediately on arrival in the New World.[92] A similar situation obtained with the Coventry gang in the 1760s; its members who were transported to America habitually returned immediately.[93]

But quite apart from the relative ease with which practised criminals could evade the punishment, there were many critics who thought that transportation was not really a sensible penalty at all. The hardliner Paley considered it a trivial punishment: 'Exile is in reality a slight punishment to those who have neither property, nor friends, nor reputation, nor regular means of subsistence at home.'[94] Also, Paley argued, what sort of a punishment was it that left the felon in no worse a position than his original one? There was also the consideration that since the convict was removed from the gaze of others, his fate could have no exemplary effect.[95]

Opposition to transportation was by no means confined to the hardliners, but ran the entire gamut of social opinion. Bernard Mandeville thought that a better solution was to exchange the felons who were being transported under existing law for the unfortunate innocent Christians being held as slaves in Morocco, Tunis, and Algiers.[96] The liberal reformer Eden agreed. The most dangerous criminals should indeed be exchanged for the Christian slaves of Islam; less serious felons should be put to work on schemes of public improvement and in the mines and dockyards. According to Eden, transportation was 'often beneficial to the criminal and always injurious to the community'. In other words, whereas the kingdom was deprived of a subject and his future income, the criminal was transported to a new country where he could be happy and healthy. He went so far as to suggest that some people actually committed trivial clergyable offences in hopes of getting themselves transported.[97] Colquhoun was also sceptical of the value of transportation as deterrent. He mentioned the expense and the resistance of the receiving countries.[98]

Hence arose the paradox that at the very height of transportation's apparent success, in the 1750s and 1760s, it was increasingly being called in question. Some of the objections were philosophical, others practical. Eden's point seemed particularly telling. Those who were transported actually seemed better off than the industrious poor at home, making transportation an inducement to crime rather than a deterrent. Bigger, faster ships reduced the terrors of the Atlantic, while at home the male transportee's family was maintained at the expense of the parish. Moreover, in the case of members of organized gangs, the punishment simply did not work. With the aid of a supportive gang, a convicted felon could pay the captain of the ship a shade over the £10 expected from his sale in America for both his freedom and return.[99] The rate of return from transportation reached a peak in the years 1763-75. This was because these were years of peace coinciding with the greatest volume of transportation to America and the highest tonnage of transatlantic shipping so far recorded.[100] The return of such men was particularly dangerous to society, since they were desperate, with nothing to deter them from the most outrageous crimes, as they would be hanged anyway if caught. In addition, the rewards paid for their apprehension were not big enough to warrant the time and energy necessary for thief-takers to track them down.

There was also a powerful economic argument against transportation. On the one hand, it was clear that the punishment drew off surplus population and therefore, presumably, lowered the general levels of pauperism and crime. But at the same time, by depriving families of fathers who were glad to be free of the burden of maintenance anyway, it led to more poverty in families and greater levels of female and juvenile crime. Besides, by the 1750s social commentators had largely changed their minds about the supposed evils of overpopulation. In the first place, England no longer appeared overpopulated when there was not sufficient manpower to equip the army and navy properly during the Seven Years War.[101] Second, population was now increasingly seen as an index of a nation's greatness. Sending large numbers of able-bodied males to America seemed to make less and less sense.

But the most important factor of all governing the elite's attitude to transportation was the crisis in America, which entered an acute phase after 1765. One of the ways in which London hoped to bring the recalcitrant colonists to heel was by restricting the flow of labour to the New World. Formal emigration was discouraged; transportation began to shudder to a halt. By the late 1760s men condemned to death were being offered pardon on condition of service in the armed forces.[102] In 1772 the government stopped paying Campbell the bounty of £5 per head.

With the outbreak of war in America in 1775 transportation ceased completely. Since Newgate gaol was quickly filled to overflowing, an alternative secondary punishment was urgently sought. At first those earmarked for transportation were kept on board ships in the Thames pending a final decision on their fate. Some were freed on condition they would go into voluntary exile. Others, including many women were given free pardons. Still others were obliged to join the army and navy.[103]

The next year an Act was introduced to replace transportation by confinement at hard labour. Male prisoners were to be lodged in prison hulks on the Thames.[104] The most common form of hard labour was raising sand, oil, and gravel from the river-bed. Like transportation itself, the new punishment was 'privatized', being contracted out to an entrepreneur who hired his own overseers and warders. Having received convicts at so much a head, the contractor had to find and run his own prison ships. In view of his losses sustained on the abortive transportation contract, the government gave the job to Duncan Campbell. He bought two ships, the *Justitia* and *Censor* and anchored them in the Thames near Woolwich. There he received his first batch of convicts in August 1776.[105]

Those who complained of the 'luxury' of transportation were certainly given no chance to bring their accusations of featherbedding against the prison hulks. The convicts were fed on bread and water or low-calorie food and small beer, and compelled to wear prison uniform. Men who would previously have been transported for seven years were condemned to this regime for between three and ten years, depending on judges' discretion. The only ray of hope was the proviso that anyone showing signs of rehabilitation would be released early. Among the first victims of this harsh new punishment were George Barrington and Peter Le Maitre. George Barrington received three years on the hulks for stealing a watch.[106] Le Maitre was sentenced to five years' ballast-heaving. His crime was robbing medals from the Ashmolean Museum in Oxford while he was a don at the university.[107]

Yet the prison hulks were, by common consent, an unsatisfactory solution to the pressing problem of secondary punishment. The hideous conditions endured by the prisoners and the high mortality rates outraged a public whose sensibilities had become more civilized over the century. Duncan Campbell reported that between August 1776 and March 1778 he had received 632 men on to the hulks, of whom 176 had died, 24 escaped, and 60 been pardoned.[108] Security was a permanent headache. The ending of transportation meant that there a whole cadre of hardened criminals on the doorstep of the capital. Many escaped to the safety of London's rookeries. Those who failed to escape were transformed by criminal osmosis from petty felons to professionals. Others fought pitched battles with warders. Moreover, the hulks were unpopular with Campbell himself, who found his profit margins pinched. The government, meanwhile, felt it had got a raw deal. It paid Campbell £38 a year for each prisoner, but their forced labour produced nothing like that in exchange-value.[109]

The experiment of turning female prisoners and the sick and disabled to hard labour in houses of correction was also unsuccessful. Clearly some other solution had to be found. The 1779 Penitentiary Act virtually conceded defeat on the prison hulks and reduced the sentence to a year.[110] The preamble to the Act explicitly looked forward to the return of transportation.

But the end of the war in America in 1783 merely exacerbated the problems. The independent colonists made it clear that they would not accept convicts in their domains. Apparently it took the English elite some time for this message to sink in, for in September 1784 we hear of 96 male convicts being taken on board ship at Woolwich, outward bound for America.[111] In some desperation, and against the advice of those who feared that a renewal of transportation would lead to serious depopulation in England, the authorities cast around for alternatives. Canada, the Falklands, West Africa, the West Indies, and the East Indies were all mentioned as possible transportation sites. A handful of men actually was transported to Africa in 1784.[112] These countries answered one of the requirements of transportation, in that passage to them would replicate the (real or supposed) terrors of the North Atlantic crossing, but they were ineligible on other counts. Meanwhile high anxiety continued at the prospect of thousands of recidivists, toughened by work on the hulks yet unemployable because of the stigma of criminality, prowling the towns and highways of England.[113] What, then, was the answer?

This was the context in which the Cabinet in 1786 agreed to establish a colony at Botany Bay in the new land of Australia charted sixteen years earlier by Captain Cook. Australia had in fact first been mentioned as a possibility in February 1779, but the high costs involved and lack of apparent benefit to the mother country had led to the rejection of the idea.[114] In 1786 these objections were swept aside by the need to find an outlet for a surplus criminal population; the years 1784-5 had seen another of the periodic 'moral panics' as troops returning from the American war turned to crime on discharge in England.[115]

The choice of Botany Bay as destination for transported convicts is properly a subject for the historian of Australia rather than English crime and punishment. But the best efforts of ingenious historians to see the development of Australia as a far-sighted example of early imperialism have not seriously dented the fundamental proposition that the disposal of convicts was always the primary motive in opening up the land of the Southern Cross.[116] The fleet that sailed for Botany Bay in 1788 took with it the prisoners who had been in limbo since 1784, men not dangerous enough to hang but too much of a social menace to pardon.[117] Some were veterans of the Woolwich hulks like George Barrington, who had fulfilled the direst prophecies about future recidivism by graduating from petty pickpocketing to the more skilled variety at racetracks.[118] Another noteworthy alumnus of the first Fleet was Henry Sterne, the 'gentleman thief' – a Raffles-like master pickpocket who fleeced aristocrats on major social occasions.[119] Particularly noteworthy were the numbers of 'social criminals' transported. This was to be a feature of the next century. Australia was always a favourite place of exile in the minds of the elite for dissenters and intractable members of the nascent English working class.[120]

From the elite point of view the Botany Bay experiment was a success. True, it was expensive as the costs of an entirely new colony had to be borne. On the other hand, the problem from returning transportees was far less because of the sheer distance from Australia.[121] The colony also solved the problem of female criminals, for whom the hulks had never been possible as a punishment. The consequence was that transportation came right back into the picture as a major secondary punishment after 1788.[122]

Incredibly enough, the dispatch of a felon to Botany Bay who did not return illicitly did not necessarily mean that the person was never seen again in an English court. In 1799 Jean Prévôt, an 18-year-old Frenchman, stabbed to death James Wilcox, captain of the *Lady Jane*

Shore, off the coast of Africa while on the way to Australia. When brought back to England for his trial, Prévôt requested a jury half composed of foreigners, as was his right. At first proceedings stalled, since all foreigners summoned to jury service declined. The anger of Lord Elden, who threatened refusers with contempt of court finally secured the presence of six foreigners on the jury. Prévôt's tactics were in vain. The mixed jury found him guilty of wilful murder and he was executed.[123]

Yet exile to Australia was never as significant a part of penal policy as transportation to America had been earlier. Quite apart from the cost, the rapidly expanding population in England at the end of the eighteenth century meant that the authorities baulked at the sheer number of offenders to be dealt with. It was clear that some other effective secondary punishment had to be devised.

The 1779 Penitentiary Act, along with its other provisions, recommended the building of a new kind of house of correction, to be called a penitentiary.[124] The combination of hard labour and solitary confinement was supposed to produce rehabilitation. But the Act was not implemented, since the commissioners charged with setting up the penitentiary could not agree on a site.[125] Yet is was clear that the 1779 statute marked a turning point in the history of imprisonment. To understand how radical a departure it involved, we must look at the situation that obtained at the beginning of the eighteenth century.

In 1700 there were three principal institutions for depriving citizens of their liberty: the gaol proper, where prisoners were lodged until their trial; the debtors' prison; and the bridewell or house of correction. Gaols were run on private enterprise lines, through a system of sub-contracting, much as in parts of the USA today. Prison governors and turnkeys made a handsome profit out of extortion: there were fees payable on entry and discharge from a gaol and a sliding scale of fees to obtain superior prisoner accommodation.[126] There was no internal discipline in prison except that imposed by the inmates. It was a private enterprise paradise: a prisoner got exactly what he paid for; with money everything was possible. Even to survive adequately in gaol required money. When a new prisoner was brought in, he had to pay 'garnish', or cash for drinks all round. If he failed to do so, he was stripped of his clothes, which were divided among the inmates. If a prisoner was freed by the courts, he still had to pay gaolers' discharge fees before they would strike off his fetters. Many totally innocent people stayed on in gaol after being found not guilty in court simply because they could not pay the release fee.[127]

When John Howard conducted his famous investigation into the state of English prisons, he found that abuses were legion. The food provided to prisoners was deficient; if they were not to starve, they had to rely heavily on their families. Sewage and heating were inadequate, there was no proper water supply. Gaols were overcrowded and there was a serious lack of bedding. Because the buildings were antiquated and dilapidated, there were few courtyards for taking exercise. To economize on prison guards many warders kept their charges chained to the floor. To make matters worse, there was little ventilation since the prison governors wanted to save money by avoiding the window tax. In such pestiferous circumstances, disease raged. Worst of all was the dreaded 'gaol fever', a virulent form of typhus, that raged through the army during the Seven Years War and killed eight times the number of battle casualties.[128] This fever was so feared that shrewd physicians refused to enter Newgate and warned that a plague could spread from the gaol and infect the whole of London.[129] The ordinary of Newgate and other clergymen who ministered to the spiritual needs of prisoners were particularly at risk and often refused to attend prisoners under sentence of death when an outbreak of gaol fever was suspected.[130] In April 1750, at the so-called 'Black Assize' at the Old Bailey, two prisoners from Newgate with typhus infected the entire courtroom. The disease swept away at least fifty people, including the judge, all the trial lawyers, all twelve jurymen and many of the spectators.[131]

Nor was it easy to escape from prison. The problem was not deterrence, for prison-breaking was usually a clergyable offence, except in certain clearly specified categories: helping to escape those already condemned to death, or those convicted of high treason, murder, smuggling, or the writing of threatening letters. The real threat came from the heavily armed keeper and his turnkeys. Celebrated gaolbreaks like Jack Sheppard's were the exception rather than the rule. In 1735 a highwayman and four accomplices tried to break out of Surrey County Gaol. After a ferocious shoot-out with pistols followed by hand-to-hand combat with cutlasses, the prison authorities overpowered the five would-be escapees.[132]

The one iniquity commented on all by criticis of the prison system was the utter lack of segregation of the sexes. This produced rampant promiscuity, large-scale amateur prostitution, and a spate of illegitimate births, augmented by the women's practice of 'pleading the belly' to secure a pardon. Outside London, there was a further problem. London had its distinctive debtors' prisons: the Fleet, King's Bench, the Marshalsea.[133] In the provinces there were no separate gaols for debtors, so that those imprisoned for debt were thrown in with hardened felons.[134] Prisons had enormous numbers of debtors. They had to be confined at their creditors' expense and could carry on their trade or business from inside the gaol, with their property outside legally safeguarded. One social critic estimated that 40,000 debtors were arrested annually, most of them for trifling amounts.[135] As John Howard pointed out, until the heterogeneous collection of 'prisoners' coexisting in the same gaol was sorted out, and some discrimination exercised in their treatment, prison could never become a rational place of punishment.[136]

Yet in some ways the most interesting of all the institutions of detention was the bridewell or house of correction, for this was the embryo from which the modern prison grew. Houses of correction were originally established in the reign of Elizabeth, to punish and reform the poor who refused to work. Their original purpose was to confine and control the hosts of 'masterless men' thrown on to the highways by the dissolution of the monasteries. The host of detainees was later swollen by the break-up of feudal retinues and, in the eighteenth century, by enclosure and the eviction of cottagers. The steady population growth in the context of an overstocked labour market did not help matters.[137]

From the very earliest days there had been a rehabilitatory element in the houses of correction: to teach the poor 'the habits of industry'. Entrepreneurs contracted with the county for the labour of the imprisoned. The problem was that forced labour produced low productivity and low profits. The consequence was that most of the time the entrepreneurs did not bother to exercise their option, and no work was enforced in the bridewells. The problem for the inmates was usually not forced labour but starvation, since the authorities frequently provided no food, in disgust at the contractors' failure to use the labour.[138]

For this reason, once the underlying economic circumstances altered, the bridewell went into abeyance. During the Restoration whipping, branding, and the pillory replaced confinement in houses of correction as the principal secondary punishment. But the Glorious Revolution saw a revival of the bridewell. The years 1690-1720, like 1590-1640, were a time of high unemployment, expanding population, rising prices, and falling wages.[139] At such times the bridewell was likely to come back into vogue, as it had the effect of withdrawing labour from a saturated market. In 1701 Timothy Nourse advocated forcing minor criminals to work there: pickpockets, pimps, whores, sheep-stealers, coney-catchers, hedge-breakers.[140] In the 1720s, additionally, the coincidence of a crime wave in London and sharply escalating costs of poor relief in the counties brought the house of correction back on to the penal agenda.[141]

Yet, as we have seen, it was transportation that filled the secondary punishment vacuum from 1718 to 1775. Imprisonment as a punishment largely vanished during these years. Only with the closing of America to convicts, and the realization that the sheer number of felons would in any case rule out transportation as a total long-term solution, did the authorities begin to pay close attention to the possibility of a new type of prison: the penitentiary. But even before the 1779 Penitentiary Act there had been signs of the way the penal wind was blowing. In 1764 there were repeated clamours for a new type of bridewell where productive labour would be compulsory. This was in part an overspill from the war years, when shortages of labour had led penal theorists to advocate a programme of public works for criminals: in coalmining, diverting rivers, building canals. Females could spin yarn and the children of felons set to work in woollen manufactures.[142] And the Fieldings themselves had begun to toy with a new type of penal institution dedicated to solitary confinement. It seemed to them that there was no appropriate penalty for petty larceny. Transportation was too harsh, while whipping merely hardened the criminal. They agreed with Timothy Nourse that the devil provided work for idle hands, especially in a place of detention.[143] On the other hand, for once the Fieldings agreed with Mandeville, in finding Newgate merely a 'crime school'. As Mandeville expressed it 'nothing but the utmost corruption can be expected from a company of forty or fifty people in a prison, who, every one of them, singly considered, were all the worst of thousands before they met'.[144]

It can be seen, then, that the late 1770s mark a decisive watershed in penal theory and in particular the theory of the prison. Before 1775 imprisonment was rarely used. There were occasional short sentences for such crimes as manslaughter, commercial fraud, perjury, rioting, or labour combination. But medium-level or serious crime was almost invariably dealt with either by execution or transportation. The main function of imprisonment in the first three-quarters of the century was as a weapon in the magistrates' armoury. The 1744 Vagrancy Act in particular gave JPs a single power, that is, of imprisonment (in place of the multiplicity of previous ones) to deal with beggars, gypsies, peddlars, strolling players.[145] Magistrates sitting in summary session without a jury could hand down sentences of imprisonment for vagrancy, desertion of family, bastardy, minor trade embezzlement by workers, minor game offences, and for a host of crimes where customary practice clashed with property rights: the theft of turnips and other field produce, the taking of firewood from private premises, etc.[146]

After 1780 the notion of imprisonment, designed as a serious punishment *per se* began to take hold. The years 1780-1800 saw a withering away of the old corporal secondary punishments, especially branding and the pillory, partly as a result of the increasing rejection of violence in society at large. The emphasis on exemplary punishments switched to rehabilitation. Imprisonment also served the cause of Enlightenment rationalism like Bentham's. It allowed the punishment to fit the crime and permitted distinctions to be drawn between degrees of culpability. By 1800 a term of imprisonment was the most likely sentence for conviction in a non-capital property case. Paradoxically, this meant that the consequences of conviction were more serious by the end of the century. Criminals were being imprisoned or transported where a hundred years ago they might have been whipped and released. In assault cases, imprisonment increasingly supplanted fines. A verdict of manslaughter in a homicide case usually led to a gaol sentence rather than a discharge. Women, too, felt the sharp end of the new penal theory. Instead of being pardoned or discharged, female felons tended to be imprisoned or, more frequently, sent to a house of correction for hard labour.[147] The brittle system of punishment in 1700, where a crevasse yawned between the supreme penalty on one side and branding on the thumb on the other, gave way by 1800 to a much more flexible and finely nuanced apparatus of social control.

16

Crime and Social Change

Hell is a city much like London
A populous and smoky city.
                    Percy Bysshe Shelley, *Peter Bell the Third*

Poverty, the great crime, never to be pardoned in England.
            Richard Ford, *A Handbook for Travellers in Spain*

Every society gets the criminals it deserves.
                                    Alexandre Lacassagne

Any account of crime in the eighteenth century which regarded it as a self-contained phenomenon, unrelated to general issues of social structure, would be severely one-dimensional. Yet this area is the most difficult of all to explicate. The causal lines are tangled. It is quite clear that there must be some relationship between criminality and changing social and economic circumstances, if only because what society regards as a crime is itself a function of the general socio-economic arrangements it endorses. Yet the links between crime and punishment on one hand, and, say, the development of the state and of capitalism itself on the other do not reveal themselves easily. However, for simplicity's sake, we may identify three areas of especial importance for their impact on crime: population growth, general economic development, and politics itself. The most significant subsection of the political category is warfare, which merits a chapter to itself.

The steadily rising population in the eighteenth century was not a uniform affair.[1] Rather than a population 'explosion', it was more of an implosion, with the surplus population drifting into the cities from the countryside, especially under the impact of increasingly frequent harvest failures.[2] This tendency was especially marked after the mid-century. The volume of crime in London showed a distinct relationship with rising population, while remaining relatively inelastic to other factors.[3] The Old Bailey Proceedings of 1763 recorded 433 trials of people for murder, burglary, robbery and theft, of whom 243 were convicted and 47 sentenced to death. The 1768 Proceedings returned figures of 613,246 and 54 respectively. By 1770 the number of death sentences had risen to 61.[4] It has to be remembered that this increase took place during 'normal' years, when there were no special factors at play that might have inflated the crime rate.

In general the main influence of population increase on crime was via urbanization. In the days before the growth of 'monster cities', property crime was rare. Crimes against the person could be dealt with for the most part by summary justice or informal sanctions. In the cities both motive and opportunity for crime multiplied. On the one hand, people no longer lived in a face-to-face community, but the logic of this had not yet filtered through to law enforcement processes. On the other, the actual circumstances of life in an urban environment, where overcrowding and competition for space, jobs, and amenities went hand in hand with vastly increased aspirations, can almost be said to have propelled the poor into crime.[5] In London, additionally, the threat to the social order seemed to come not from a few individuals but from an organized criminal subclass – Defoe's 'troop of human devils'.[6] Furthermore, the more subtly graduated social hierarchy added to the problem. Social stratification ran the gamut from beggars to nabobs. In London there were tradesmen, shopkeepers, artisans, merchants, financiers, plus a vast number of people employed in 'service' jobs. This human farrago heaped up 'contradictions' and tautened conflict. The mixture of poverty, population implosion, relative deprivation, revolution of aspirations, and nuanced hierarchy produced an explosive human brew in the capital.

In the first half of the century, this was overwhelmingly a London problem. But in the second half, urbanization reproduced the same problems elsewhere. Organized crime and the failure of traditional methods of law enforcement produced in provincial cities by the late 1700s the same sort of lamentations about the 'immorality of the mob' that had been heard in the metropolis in the late 1600s.[7] In the 1770s and 1780s, renewed population growth and the greater concentration of the workforce began to create in the North and the Midlands social tensions that had hitherto been considered peculiar to London.[8]

The combination of urbanization with resistance to a professional police force produced for a while an extreme form of atomized individualism. The weakness of central government in the eighteenth century was partly technological (it lacked the infrastructure to make its writ run from Land's End to John O'Groats), partly administrative (there was no professional bureaucratic class), and partly cultural (in the resistance to standing armies, professional police, and 'arbitrary power'). The Jacobite risings had shown clearly the feebleness of central government; the nexus of local magnates and provincial hegemony was bound together in a nation-state by the thinnest of administrative tapes.[9]

It was this that accounted for the power of the local 'mafias': the coiners in Yorkshire, the wreckers in Cornwall, the smugglers in Sussex.

In the age before the rise of the great cities, there had been a collective approach to law enforcement. The 'hue and cry' and the *posse comitatus* were the most obvious signs of this corporate responsibility for crime. But it was precisely these institutions that were most obviously made anachronistic by the onset of urbanization. The social control exercised by the old 'organic' community was disappearing even as crime rates rose. The state relied purely on self-interest, private prosecutions, and the reward system. As one student of social control has said, 'Partly as a remedy for defective policing and partly as its cause, social control was formally delegated to the entire population. The inhabitants of England were turned policemen on themselves.'[10]

Yet arguably more important even than urbanization *per se* in its impact on crime was industrialization. Although some historians have recently sought to query the usual chronology, wherein the years around 1760 see the 'take-off' of the Industrial Revolution, there can be no serious doubt that the last years of the eighteenth century saw the final process of transformation of the old feudal residues of England into a full-blooded capitalist society. Commercial capitalism was well established in the seventeenth century. Financial capitalism came in with a bang at the 'Glorious Revolution' of 1688. Finally, the last forty years of the eighteenth century saw the entrenchment of industrial capitalism.[11]

The ramifications of the final conquest by capitalism were manifold. The triumph of market forces and the enthronement of the profit motive meant the destruction of old folkways and customary rights in favour of new work discipline and the iron laws of wages and prices.[12] 'Time is money' became the watchword. The new working classes felt the acute stress of regimented assembly-line work in the new factories. Division of labour appeared in stark form. Alienation became severe as the old part-time 'total man' vanished, to be replaced by 'units of labour' shorn of their 'species-essence'.[13]

The destruction of customary rights and the struggle to substitute a wage economy for the old system of irregular and *ad hoc* payments underlay many of the new conflicts between masters and men. These were largely resolved only by making the older practices criminal.[14] A famous example concerns the law of embezzlement. Many eighteenth-century enterprises involved outworkers – those who worked at home in their own cottages and fashioned the raw materials supplied by their employers. Typical outwork trades were textiles, tool making, iron and steel smelting, and tailoring. In traditional practice, the outworkers were entitled to keep all scraps left over from the work as legitimate 'perks'. In the new climate, however, employers insisted that this residue was their private property which had to be returned.[15] The ulterior aim of capital was not to allow labour a window to an alternative economy, to tie workers down rigidly to a wage economy. To enforce this aim, the authorities passed more and more embezzlement laws, prescribing stiffer and stiffer sentences for non-compliance. Employers banded together in anti-embezzlement associations and hired inspectors who had powers to enter workers' houses. In the woollen trade alone, eleven new embezzlement statutes were passed from 1725 to 1800, more than in the whole previous history of the industry.[16] And the severity of these statutes increased. In 1749 the penalty for embezzlement was fourteen days in a house of correction. By 1777 the penalty had increased to three months' imprisonment.[17]

A similar conflict between traditional irregular payments and the new wage economy lay behind the conflict between masters and servants over the practice of tipping. The rising opposition to 'vails' or tips coincided with the early years of the Industrial Revolution.[18] Vails were demanded by servants not just from house guests when they departed, but from ordinary dinner guests. The cost of dining at the best houses was anything from ten shillings to a guinea, depending on the rank of the master of the house. Servants of the professional and middle classes were normally given a vail of one shilling.[19] To venture from one's house for a social visit was a consideration for any but the very well off. Some servants made £100 a year in tips.[20]

The resistance to vails by the prosperous classes gradually grew, not just in private houses but also in taverns and coffee houses. In 1764 the nobility, gentry, and clergy of Wiltshire all agreed to cease giving vails to their servants and to visit the appropriate sanctions on them if they refused to accept the innovation quietly.[21] Not all of them did take kindly to the winds of change: one gentleman in north Wiltshire was obliged to dismiss his butler and two footmen after they behaved insolently to the first visitor who stopped tipping.[22] Even worse was the disturbance in Ranelagh pleasure gardens in London in May 1764 when a number of servants pelted their masters with stones and brickbats because they had been forbidden to take vails. In the fracas several men were wounded and four were arrested and lodged in Newgate.[23] But by 1766 the battle against tipping was as good as won.[24] The withering away of vails was another factor leading to the drift to the cities. Discontented rural servants joined the throng in the 'great wen'.[25]

Clearly it was difficult for the labouring classes to understand that they were now in the remorseless grip of market forces. But if they did not comprehend abstractions, they needed no clerisy of advisers to tell them that the new machinery of the Industrial Revolution was a threat to their livelihood. Industrial riots in the second half of the century, apart from the great 'general crisis' of 1768, invariably turned on the threat posed by machinery. Weavers, cloth-workers, and framework knitters were in the forefront. Experimental spinning machines were broken at Frome and Warminster in 1776-81. In 1768 at Blackburn spinners attacked the house of James Hargreaves and destroyed his spinning jennies.[26] In 1779 came a more sustained campaign against Richard Arkwright's machines for carding and roving. In October 1779 a mob destroyed the machinery at his Birkacre factory, caused £4,400 worth of damage and put the entire factory out of action. Troops were despatched to Lancashire. In the ensuing confrontation of military and rioter two men were killed and eight wounded.[27] This incident also demonstrates the pace of technological change. The spinning jennies of under twenty spindles, which a decade before had been considered fair game, were left untouched, since these were now considered 'just' machines.[28]

Arkwright was always a major target for industrial rioters. Large numbers of framework weavers attacked his Nottingham mill in 1779. In 1788 the framework knitters of Leicester destroyed one of his cotton spinning machines that had been adapted to the spinning of woollen yarn.[29] Meanwhile the introduction of the flying shuttle in the West Country provoked riots at Trowbridge in 1792 and at Frome and Chippenham in 1801-3. And in March 1792 a crowd of hand-loom weavers burned down Grimshaw's factory in Manchester for using Cartwright's power loom.[30]

There were thus two strands, not always distinct, in the resistance by workers to the Industrial Revolution. One was hatred of technological innovation and the new labour-saving machinery. The other was a foot-dragging resistance to work-discipline and punctuality. The authorities chiefly responded by taking industrial relations under the umbrella of criminal law.[31] The law had long protected the most unscrupulous masters against their exasperated men. Master weavers cynically kept wages down by employing large numbers of apprentices straight from the workhouses and routinely dismissing those surplus to requirements so as to browbeat the others. Yet if any of the apprentices so much as raised a hand to their master, it meant seven years' transportation.[32] In 1764 the screws were tightened further. It was made a capital offence to break into a house, shop, or cellar with intent to steal or destroy any linen or cloth, any manufacturing tools or implements, or to cut any goods with malice aforethought when they had been put out to bleach or dry.[33] The same penalties were ordained two years later in the case of woollen and silk manufacture.[34] All three industrial statutes were later consolidated in a single enabling Act in 1782.[35] Finally in 1788 stocking frames were protected by the criminal law.[36] All these statutes represented an attempt to deal by law with the discontents of wage-earners threatened by new labour-saving machinery. The only hopeful sign about these attempts to dragoon the working class through the majesty of the law is that the death penalty was abandoned as a sanction.[37]

Yet it was not just the *type* of economic change, to an industrial market economy, that affected crime. Arguably even more important was the rate of change, which intensified social stresses. This was seen most clearly in the relationship between town and country. While the expansion of markets provided new jobs in the cities, in spinning, weaving and stocking-knitting, in the countryside the enclosure of commons led to the flight from the land so vividly conjured up in Goldsmith's *Deserted Village*.[38]

> Ill fares the land, to hast'ning ills a prey,
> Where wealth accumulates, and men decay
> Princes and lords may flourish, or may fade;
> A breath can make them, as a breath has made;
> But a bold peasantry, their country's pride,
> When once destroy'd can never be supplied.[39]

Enclosure was a two-phased process. Between 1745 and 1780 the open-field Midland counties were enclosed for pasturage. Then from the late 1780s the open fields, wastes, and commons of the South and East were enclosed for cereals. Three groups of people particularly suffered from the change. First, there were those who worked strips of land on commons which were now fenced off. Then there were the wage labourers who by custom kept animals or poultry on the common to supplement their meagre income. Finally, there was a sub-class of squatters who occupied shacks on common land, and who scratched a living by catching rabbits and burning charcoal.[40]

The effect of enclosure has long been a subject of fierce academic controversy. Some have argued that enclosure may actually have created extra jobs in the countryside, and that other factors, such as the Poor Laws and increasing population itself, were more important triggers leading to the drift to the cities. The crucial question seems to be the extent of tillage and common land lost to enclosure. Although the sheer acreage taken over in this way may be disputed, there can surely be no disputing the vehemence of the widespread opposition to enclosure.[41] In some instances it spilled over into violence. Troops were summoned to Northamptonshire in 1765 after enclosure fences were cut down.[42] And whether the perceptions of countrymen were statistically correct or not, there is no question but that enclosure had a powerful *psychological* effect, leading men and women to conclude that there was no longer any future in rural areas for landless people. For our purposes, enclosure is especially significant, since it increased the pressure on urban resources and brought into the cities precisely the social groups most likely to turn to crime.[43]

Enclosure was not the only rural manifestation of the new economic order. Profitability demanded a substantial improvement in infrastructure. The new turnpikes or toll roads, like enclosure, confronted customary rights with the profit motive.[44] The frequent response of the common man, finding that for the first time he was being charged for taking his livestock to market, was to destroy the toll-booths on the turnpikes.[45] Sometimes, as in the case of the Kingswood colliers, the opposition to turnpikes was more subtle. The riots of 1742-8 seem to have derived from fears for the future, especially that 'stomach taxes' would impede the growth of a promising manufacturing area. Apprehension that Bristol and Gloucestershire would be economically 'marginalized' by the new turnpikes explains the peculiar bitterness of the confrontations there between colliers and authorities.[46]

The violence of the rate of change can also be seen in the general functioning of the eighteenth-century English economy. It is a common-place that crime showed a constant correlation with periods of dearth and high prices. Yet an examination of rioting shows that the most important trigger for 'criminal' behaviour was not the absolute level of prices but the rate and direction of price movements.[47] Riots typically broke out not in the months of highest prices but when the rate of increase in prices was most rapid. This usually occurred during pre-harvest and post-harvest months, when anxiety about food prices was at its height.[48]

The correlation of food riots with harvest failure, slump and depression has already been touched on. But by concentrating on the great outbursts of the 1760s, we have perhaps underplayed the extent to which this was a persistent feature of the eighteenth century. When food prices rose in 1727, the tin-miners of Cornwall plundered the granaries of Falmouth. In 1737 Cornish tinners again assembled at Falmouth to prevent the export of corn. In 1738 there was serious rioting at Tiverton. In 1748 and 1753 attacks on corn dealers were reported in Wales and elsewhere.[49] The Tyneside keelmen rioted in 1709 after a harvest failure. In the more serious near-famine of 1739-40 Northumberland and Durham were in a virtual state of insurrection. Women took a leading part in the rioting. Ships were boarded, warehouses broken into, and the Guildhall at Newcastle reduced to ashes.[50]

But although the years 1739-41 were especially bad, generally until 1750 there had been a good run of harvests and low prices. What this situation masked was an underlying tendency towards severe economic fluctuations.[51] In the eighteenth century this was not just a function of the cycle of booms and slumps intrinsic to capitalism. It also resulted from backward technology. Before the age of steam, for example, large numbers of ships could be detained in port for long periods by contrary winds. Then, when the winds were favourable, all the ships would clear from port together. This meant that at one moment there could be work in plenty, the next moment almost nothing. Primitive technology also meant that most employment was seasonal. Even the lower reaches of schoolmastering were a seasonal affair, as pupils came and went according to the employment or unemployment of their parents. And it is a commonplace of sociology that unemployment and underemployment breed crime.

Once again we can appreciate the intellectual vacuity of the Fieldings' animadversions on crime. For them, the root cause of crime was the love of 'luxury' by the working class; it followed that the payment of low wages would strike at the capacity of the 'lower orders' to indulge in the said luxury. But, quite apart from the fact that 'luxury' was so deeply embedded in eighteenth-century culture that the demotic taste for it had nothing to do with wages, the Fieldings missed the crucial point that the economic wealth of England depended on a high level of effective demand. Here Defoe, with whom the Fieldings are usually at one, was much shrewder. He correctly saw that effective demand required high wages.[52] Defoe always had a much better grasp of economic affairs than the Fieldings.

The underlying profile of backward technology, low effective demand and violent economic oscillations was thrown much more clearly into relief in the years after 1750. There were very serious periods of dearth in 1756-7, 1766-8, 1772-4, 1782-4, 1795-6, and 1800-1.[53] All of these periods of high prices saw a clear increase in property crime, especially theft, and violent rioting. In 1756-7 corn mills were destroyed, bakers and grain dealers roughly handled, and Quaker meeting houses (the Quakers were heavily involved in the wheat trade) pulled down. In 1766-8 it was the Irish who bore the brunt of public ire, as in the fights between sailors and coal-heavers. So alarmed were the authorities by the cycle of dearth and rioting that they called in to the Tower the work of every journeyman gunsmith, done or undone, lest the weapons fall into the wrong hands.[54] Again in 1774 the Irish were singled out as a target, for allegedly being willing to work for low rates of pay. There were pitched battles between English and Irish haymakers at Kingsbury, Hendon, and Edgware.[55]

The fundamental nature of the English economy plus the impact of the Industrial Revolution clearly had a direct effect on English criminality. Yet it would be severely reductionist to explain *all* changes in levels and kinds of crime in the eighteenth century by reference to the socio-economic system alone. There were also powerful cultural factors at play. If the Industrial Revolution was the key factor in the economic and social sphere, the Enlightenment played that role in the arena of beliefs, myths, images, and ideologies.

The level of routine physical violence in the eighteenth century was very high. Children were beaten in schools and within the family. There was a great tolerance of cruelty, especially in spectator sports like prize-fighting, or in 'recreations' involving animals, like bear-baiting, goose-riding, or cock-fighting.[56] The ghastly ritual of Tyburn alone points to a very high acceptance of violent behaviour. For this reason it would be an elementary error to try to retrieve a profile of minor criminality from court records alone. Literary evidence, carefully used, can be a surer guide. The famous Homeric pastiche in *Tom Jones*, where Fielding dresses up rural fisticuffs in mock-heroic language, lifts a corner on a world where casual violence was largely taken for granted.[57]

Yet there is much evidence that attitudes to violence began to change in the later eighteenth century. The work of Rudé and E. P. Thompson, upgrading the 'mob' to the 'crowd', shows that even though rioting intensified in the second half of the century, the political consciousness of rioters increased. They were seldom mindlessly violent, but were discriminating in their targets. The *locus classicus* is, of course, the Gordon riots (see above pp. 233–8). This much more focused violence undoubtedly owed something to the revolution in attitudes in England in the later eighteenth century, a revolution Laurence Stone has characterized as the triumph of 'affective individualism'.[58] There was an increase in tenderness in domestic relations, and less tolerance for the vicious beating of wives and children. There was also increasing distaste for slavery, blood sports, and capital punishment and a gathering concern with prison reform.[59]

This had a direct effect on crime. There seems to have been a decline in murder from 1780 on, together with a decrease in offences reported as homicide. Francis Place testified to the dramatic changes in the general level of violence during 1780-1820. He acknowledged the part played by manufacturing and commerce, but was inclined (surely wrongly) to attribute the decline in violent crime to the rise of full-time professional police forces.[60] Part of the answer to this universally noticed change in society lies in improved scientific knowledge, especially in medicine. In the late seventeenth century many homicide cases were brought to court that were not well grounded in legal evidence. One hundred years later court indictments were much more carefully formulated. Improved medical knowledge had tightened up the causal links between homicide and reasons for death. It was therefore a waste of time to bring vaguely formulated cases into court.[61]

But another part of the answer for the decline in murder cases was that violence itself declined and people became more disposed to settle disputes peacefully. Colquhoun's famous figure of 115,000 criminals (see above p. 248) actually masked a decrease in *violent* crime (murder, armed robbery, hold-ups at the point of a weapon), and an increase in 'economic' crimes against property. At least three causal tributaries can be identified as feeding into this broad river of lessening violence. To begin with, Enlightenment thought emphasized culture over biology. In place of 'nature red in tooth and claw' and Hobbes's 'war of all against all', Montesquieu, Rousseau, Helvétius, and a host of others pointed up the crucial role of environment in social formation. Education was the key to a process of transcending the legacy of biology, of replacing instinct with intellect, unreason with reason. If men behaved like beasts, perhaps this was because they were treated like beasts. The influence of Enlightenment criminologists like Beccaria was particularly strong here.[62] By the 1790s the overwhelming intellectual response to the Bloody Code was that it was untenable: not only did it manifestly not work; it was also arbitrary, unfair, cruel, and inhumane.[63]

Second, the triumph of capitalism after the Industrial Revolution meant that the State had to play an increasing role. The Walpolian period of graft and venality can be seen as a 'half-state', characteristic of the situation where organized corruption replaces violence (as in the Gramscian model) on the road to full legitimacy.[64] After 1760 it was more important than ever that the State act as monopolist of violence. Manufacturers, merchants, and bankers all required an increased sense of discipline and conformity in their workers. Chaos was the enemy of the market, of commerce, and of industry. It was in the interest of the State to clamp down on all manifestations of individual violence and to reinforce pacific attitudes.[65] After all, in a straight Hobbesian fight of labour against capital, capital could not hope to win. Capital had the crucial weapons of money, military fore, and information. It had to make sure that labour was deprived of its one trump card: organized numbers. The most obvious way to achieve this was to insinuate the idea that all violence other than that employed by the State was illegitimate. It has long been a lament of professional criminals that the law is made by those who are physically weak but mentally strong.[66] Echoing Nietzsche's condemnation of Christianity as a conspiracy of cowards to geld the strong, they allege that the law entrenches the privileged with its weapons intact, but declares the weapons of the unprivileged to be illegitimate.[67] Undoubtedly the first phase of this consolidation of state power was under way by the 1790s, and undoubtedly it contributed to the lessening of individual violence. The logic of the situation would, however, only be accepted with the introduction of a professional police force. To that extent the late eighteenth-century elite can be seen to be caught up in a contradiction between its culture (superstructure) and the necessities of its economic system (the base).

Third, the rise of Methodism undoubtedly played a part in constraining the popular taste for violence. This does not mean that we should pre-date Halévy and use Methodism to explain the absence of revolution in eighteenth-century England. But it does mean that we should take religion seriously as a mass motivator.[68] It is tempting to see the suppression of prize-fighting and the London bear-gardens in 1756 as owing something to John Wesley's influence.[69] Certainly Horace Walpole thought so. Writing in 1760 he condemned mindless cruelty to animals in this way:

> We cannot live without destroying animals – but shall we torture them for our sport, sport in their destruction? I met a rough officer at his house t'other day, who said he knew such a person was turning Methodist, for in the middle of a conversation he rose, and opened the window to let out a moth – I told him I did not know that the Methodists had any principle so good, and that I, who am certainly not on the point of becoming one, always did so too.[70]

Yet, arguably the greatest consequences of eighteenth-century social change were felt in the sphere of punishment. The 1780s saw a number of dramatic changes, undertaken at the urging of the reformers. Hangings were 'rescued from the mob' and transferred from Tyburn and other public sites to the prison yard at Newgate and elsewhere. In this way the State asserted its hegemony by ending its tacit collusion with the mob.[71] The authorities wrested control of prisons from an inmate subculture that had made them thieves' seminaries. As one student of the subject has put it, the old division of power between inmates and keepers was broken up by the substitution of the rule of rules for the rule of customs.[72] Moreover, the glimmerings of a professional police force, intended to destroy the autonomous criminal underworld of London, began to be seen.

The decline in violence in society at large was matched by an increasing rejection of violent non-capital punishment. Branding was abolished in 1779. Whipping declined from 17 per cent to 11 per cent of Old Bailey sentences from 1775 to 1790. The pillory was used much less. Public scourgings or ritual degradations were thought on one hand to give offence to the citizen imbued with the thought of the Enlightenment and on the other to lessen the credibility of the law in the eyes of the poor and dispossessed.[73] Until the French Revolution stopped sympathy for reform dead in its tracks, the increasing distaste for violence threatened to make inroads on capital punishment itself. After 1787 the number of pardons began to increase again. By 1800 only a little over 10 per cent of those sentenced to death in London were actually executed.[74]

Most of all, there was a switch in emphasis in penal theory from exemplary punishments to reform or rehabilitation of the criminal: Michael Ignatieff has dubbed this 'the substitution of the pains of intention for the pains of neglect'.[75] This was part of the process of bureaucratic rationalization, adumbrated by the Fieldings' proposal for a professional police force, John Howard's prison reform schemes, and the theories of Beccaria. There is no question but that the eighteenth-century squirearchy would have preferred to continue the old system of law enforcement and administration, where landed Justices of the Peace controlled small, semi-autonomous local areas. But the rapid growth in urbanization and industrialization removed direct contact with squires and parsons. The logic of social change required a whole new professional bureaucratic structure: in place of parish constables there would be a professional police force; instead of JPs there would be stipendiary magistrates; in place of houses of correction there would arise a network of penitentiaries. In sum, the old face-to-face method of paternalist social control was no longer adequate; a new form of discipline was as necessary in the new cities as in the factories.[76]

A necessary part of a bureaucratic system of arrest, prosecution and punishment is a rational approach to offenders. Exemplary punishments meant treating the masses literally *en masse*: there was no question of making each punishment fit each crime; the theory was that you hanged one man in ten to deter the other nine. Under a rationalistic system of punishment, however, rehabilitation was bound to move nearer to the centre stage, as attention was now focused on the correct penalty for *each* crime, not just the genus of crimes to which a particular specimen belonged. The overall aim of punishment came to be that of dealing with the individual prisoner: breaking his spirit, weaning him away from 'luxury', 'getting his mind right'.[77]

But in emphasizing the disjuncture in penal theory in the 1780s, it is important not to overstate the case and to play down the element of continuity with the early 1700s. The revolution in punishment could never have been a total triumph of Weberian rationality for two main reasons. In the first place, the old JP-centred system was not quite as negligible as has sometimes been maintained. In the second place, neither the central government nor the counties, using devolved powers, possessed the necessary infrastructure or technology to make a decisive break with the past. Lacking either the economic muscle or the necessary centralized power to push through a wholesale revolution, the State was forced to postpone the universal imposition of the penitentiary to a later date.[78]

Yet if the penal 'revolution' of the 1780s was more gradual than has been presented in certain over-schematized accounts, the changes it wrought were real. Most of all they seemed symbolised in the new institution of the penitentiary. Imprisonment emerged as the pre-eminent penalty for most serious offences. Its novelty was that it imposed a greater social distance between the confined and the outside world than had even been attempted in the carefree days of Newgate.[79] It appeared as the penologists' main hope of a punishment that would square deterrence with reform, terror with humanity. It allowed the authorities to fit the punishment to the crime and to allow distinctions to be drawn between degrees of culpability.

By 1800 a prison term was the most common sentence in non-capital property cases. The advent of the penitentiary made an immediate impact on sentencing. A verdict of accidental homicide or manslaughter in a murder case most often led, by the end of the century, to imprisonment rather than discharge. Prison also replaced fines in many assault cases. The new institution made its mark on women too, for female offenders now tended to be put behind bars where in a previous era they would have been discharged or pardoned.[80] All in all, the net effects of the penitentiary were to make the consequences of conviction in a law court more serious by the end of the eighteenth century. People were being imprisoned or transported where a hundred years earlier they would have been whipped and released. This was because the State now possessed a large range of penal options. In 1700 the authorities had little room to manoeuvre between ordering execution and short-lived and lightly-considered punishments such as whipping. In 1800 their arsenal of social control was far more sophisticated.[81]

Having to navigate between the tug of Enlightenment hostility to capital punishment on one hand, and the limited capability of transportation to deal with a rapidly rising population on the other, the authorities were bound to turn with interest to the new institution of the penitentiary. Some historians of crime would like to leave it at that, and locate changes in types of punishment entirely within the structure of justice administration itself.[82] But we may still ask, what were the social forces pushing society in the direction of bureaucratic rationalization in the first place? And why the peculiar penal solution of imprisonment?

The discipline required by the Industrial Revolution claimed its first casualties among those Colquhoun preferred to call the indigent rather than the poor, in other words among those who could not stand the pace of regimented work. It is no accident that pauperism in England reached new depths at the same time as the 'penal revolution'.[83] But the authorities were determined that the able-bodied would not be allowed to opt out of work. They tried to compel putative paupers to work rather than go on parish relief by imposing workhouse tests. The distinction between workhouses, meant to house the poor, and bridewells (houses of correction) was progressively blurred.[84] The next link in the chain was the prison proper: as has been well remarked, 'the early form of the modern prison was bound up with the manufacturing houses of correction.'[85] Increasingly, the young came under scrutiny. Apprentices who were convicted of being idle or disorderly had little choice but to turn to crime (boys as footpads, girls as prostitutes). There is a clear link between 'juvenile delinquency' (a term first used in 1776) and the triumph of capitalism.[86]

The combination of population growth, enclosure, the flight from the land and the population implosion into the cities provided, as we have seen, an unprecedented labour supply, allowing manufacturers to make substantial wage cuts. The old sixteenth-century fears about a shortage in the labour supply were a thing of the past. There was thus no economic disincentive about incarcerating those who would not submit to the new industrial disciplines. But the novelty of the idea of imprisonment as a social sanction can be seen to link with the triumph of capitalism which, as Marx pointed out, used as one of its crucial indices the concept of 'labour-time'. Under feudalism there was no conception of human labour measured in time. Therefore there could be no notion of deprivation of time as retribution for crime. Sanctions were visited on the obvious targets: life, physical wholeness, money, status. Execution, maiming, attainder, and exile were the mainstream punishments. In the Middle Ages imprisonment was recognized as an appropriate punishment only by Canon Law.[87] Capitalism made possible a conception of man in the abstract and of abstract human labour measurable in time. Deprivation of time as a punishment is a function of 'labour-time'. As the Russian Marxist Pashukanis put it, 'For it to be possible for the idea to emerge that one could make recompense for an offence with a piece of abstract freedom determined in advance, it was necessary for all concrete forms of social wealth to be reduced to the most abstract and simple form, to human labour measured in time.'[88]

It is important to be clear that these were implications of social change of which the contemporary actors were not conscious. This is not an objection to the interpretation advanced above. Before Marx, no one understood clearly how capitalism operated. But the lack of a theory of surplus value did not mean that eighteenth-century entrepreneurs failed to generate profits successfully or to exploit their workers. Like adaptive organisms, social institutions spawn the subsidiary institutions required for their growth. In this sense capitalism can be said to have produced the penitentiary. Thus far and no farther can one go with structuralism. Theories of the penitentiary that give no scope for the human actor end in a dessicated reification of an abstract category like 'power', as if the said 'power' had an open arena in which to make a clean sweep.[89] Yet as E. P. Thompson and others have cogently pointed out, power in the eighteenth century could not operate in this way. Precisely because the Law was the ideological centrepiece in English society, the elite had as it were, made a rod to beat their own backs. They were the prisoners of 'equality before the law' as well as its beneficiaries.[90]

Two further aspects of the advent of imprisonment as *the* punishment in England by the end of the century need to be examined. The first concerns the 'negative capability' of incarceration, filling a vacuum too large to be spanned by transportation. The other deals with the relationship between the penitentiary and Enlightenment thought.

How far incarceration can be considered 'structural' in the first sense depends on the deeper meaning we assign to transportation. There are grounds for making the guarded observation that England's imperial expansion and her successes in the Treaty of Utrecht may have had some influence on the passage of the 1718 Transportation Act.[91] As so often the interpretative issue is one of structure and conjuncture. Was transportation embraced so eagerly in the 1720s purely because of the post-war crime wave and fears about the Hanoverian succession, or were deeper forces at play? Certainly the correlation between the rise of transportation and the beginnings of England's empire is striking. In this light transportation can be seen as serving the interests of the mother country at a time when the colonies were highly valued as markets for English manufactures and as sources of new raw materials and sub-tropical agriculture.

That transportation was not simply a functional adaptation to the technicalities of crime-solving can be seen from the selective way it was meted out as a punishment. Contemporaries were often puzzled at the lack of uniformity in sentencing. Sometimes theft was rewarded by a whipping, sometimes by transportation. Why the difference? Some have speculated that there was method in the apparent chaos. In other words, to put it bluntly, the most potentially valuable units of labour were not transported. Apprentices and servants were less likely to be transported than paupers and vagabonds who turned to crime.[92] Interestingly, this involved a collision between economic interest and the political culture. Crime by servants or apprentices was held to be, *ceteris paribus*, more serious than that by other working people, as it breached the sacred trust between ruler and ruled, superior and inferior. Nevertheless, servants were a valuable commodity, and there are many instances of masters requesting judges to order physical chastisement rather than transportation.[93]

We have also noted above that transportation can also be seen as an aspect of mercantilism. The golden age of transportation was in the fifty years after 1718. By the late 1760s, transportation to America (whether for seven years, fourteen years, or life) accounted for 70 per cent of all Old Bailey sentences (if commuted death sentences are included). The loss of the American colonies shook thinking on transportation to its foundations. As we have seen, transportation was returned to in the 1780s only with great reluctance. This is why the imperial argument concerning transportation to Australia has to be regarded as a completely different matter from the early imperial argument for transportation to the New World (see above pp. 291–3).

But it was not just that mercantilist thought began to lose ground at the end of the century, and with it the taste for transportation. The new penology of the Reformers was also inimical to transportation. The emphasis was now on rehabilitation rather than deterrence. Yet by definition sending a convict to the far ends of the earth could not be rehabilitatory in terms of the usefulness of the reformed criminal to the society he had originally offended. For all these more profound reasons, transportation gradually lost its role in the schema of punishment. In the 1790s it was ordered in less than 50 per cent of guilty cases, as compared with over 70 per cent just before its suspension in 1775. By the last decade of the century transportation was the penalty for major offences only. Imprisonment almost wholly replaced it as the penalty for minor property offences.[94]

The triumph of the idea of the penitentiary was a triumph for the work of the reformers, especially John Howard. Two things prevented the concept from sweeping the board. One was the perennial niggardliness of governments. Bentham's proposal for a whole spectrum of panopticons (or panoptica) for the confinement of every dependent social category (criminals, paupers, lunatics, children) had been decisively turned down by the mid-1790s.[95] From the viewpoint of the more enlightened reformers this was just as well. The authoritarian element in Bentham's thought deeply worried the far more radical William Godwin. He particularly opposed solitary confinement and was at pains to deny Bentham's key idea that punishment directed at the mind was more legitimate and more acceptable than punishment of the body.[96] As Godwin pointed out, surely unanswerably, no man could be reformed by solitude, since rehabilitation was a social process, a matter of persuasion and example rather than force.

The other impediment to the spread of the penitentiary as an institution of rehabilitation, as envisaged by the reformers, was the French Revolution. The elite became convinced, especially after the 'terror' of 1793, that all moves towards social reform were a mistake. Events in France seemed to demonstrate that reform begat revolution and revolution begat dictatorship. In England the social brakes were slammed on. The reform movement shuddered to a halt. The Bloody Code was granted a new and unexpected lease of life.

The relationship between crime and punishment and social structure and change is so complex that a summary of the main indicators seems necessary. What is revealed is a widening of the moral gap between the State and the individual. As monopolist of violence the State could tax, press men into the armed services, enclose land, discipline the workforce in factory and workhouse, and loot and pillage in India. At the same time it was prepared to crack down hard on a poor woman who stole a handkerchief. The impact of the Enlightenment was arguably greater on individuals than on the State. Where in individual behaviour it induced an increasing distaste for violence, Enlightenment thought largely fell on stony ground with the elite. The rulers of England were less interested in creating the rational society imagined by Bentham and Beccaria, where people could calculate in a utilitarian way the likely consequences of their actions, than in reinforcing attitudes of deference and dependence, on which the authority of the propertied classes was held to depend. Once again we can observe a 'contradiction' between base and superstructure, between economic imperatives and political culture. The new industrial system after 1760 worked on regularity and predictability. Yet the criminal law worked on unpredictability and an exemplary model of decimation. To the commercial and manufacturing sectors who suffered most from property crime, this capricious irregularity of the law seemed incoherent and self-defeating.[97]

The economic picture of eighteenth-century England is peculiarly opaque in its details, but some general outlines seem clear enough. By the beginning of the century England had escaped what one historian has called the 'biological *Ancien Régime*, famine and the pressure of population on an inelastic supply of food and land'.[98] This avoidance was largely due to convertible husbandry, fodder crops, rotation, and fen drainage. When the expansion in manufacturing took place, the increasing population did not bear down on a static food supply.

The Industrial Revolution produced urban conglomerates and new manufacturing regions. Population growth, an organized factory system, the flight from the countryside after enclosure, all contributed to new levels of urbanism, pauperism, and criminality. A large and mobile class of wage earners sprang up, some parts of the old society disintegrated, there was a rapid accumulation of wealth, and the rise of a 'new poor'. From 1760 to 1815 the rate of change was very swift, but wage levels remained depressed.

Throughout this time, at the topmost levels of society the elite easily held its own. As Roy Porter has remarked, 'The century did not witness any dramatic transformation of the social structure, rather a gradual change . . . the league table of wealth and esteem (headed by the great landowners) was much the same in 1800 as a century earlier.'[99] But, since poverty is a traditional parent of crime, there was a significant development at the bottom of the social pyramid.

The increased pauperism of the late eighteenth century was the product of a number of factors. Colquhoun saw that if people were forced through the prism of work discipline, the result would inevitably be a large rump of indigent unemployables. Yet society insisted on this solution. The Protestant work-ethic triumphed. All forms of outdoor relief were increasingly replaced by confinement at forced labour in the workhouse. The idea was to force the recalcitrant to accept work discipline by making the workhouse regime so unpleasant that people would do any work rather than enter it.[100] The predominant theory of mercantilism provided an ideological justification for these harsh elite attitudes. It popularized the idea of the utility of poverty: that a nation's wealth ultimately depended on having large numbers of badly-paid labourers who could be socialized into drudgery.[101] Again we see the failure of Enlightenment notions to penetrate the carapace of the elite. Rousseau's fulminations against the misguided idea that social inequality resulted from natural inequality quite failed to shake the aplomb of England's rulers. They rested on the inappropriate biblical quotation 'The poor you have always with you.'[102] To them social hierarchy was a simple reflection of individual innate talents. They conveniently ignored the fact that almost all the wealthy were the recipients of inherited wealth, so that the question of individual abilities did not even enter into the matter.

The harsh end-of-century economic climate exacerbated the plight of the poor. The wartime disruption of export trades in the 1790s led to increased taxation, soaring inflation, and unemployment. As price inflation easily outstripped wages, more and more workers were thrown on the scrapheap. It began to look as though the Industrial Revolution, so far from eliminating poverty, was producing a permanent sub-class of paupers.[103] The fact that the period 1763-99 was far more turbulent than the first two-thirds of the century testifies to the growth in the numbers of the poor and their subsequent criminalization.[104] When the French Revolution frightened the rulers of England so badly, they dug in for a protracted battle against lawlessness. Even though the judiciary itself had now virtually proclaimed open scepticism about the efficacy of capital punishment, all thought of reform went into abeyance. Paradoxically, the elite spurned the ideas of a man whose main motive was to tighten up the social control made necessary by the Industrial Revolution. Bentham's *Panopticon* brought together a number of authoritarian threads: control by the illusion of constant surveillance of guards, inculcation of work discipline, and the utilitarian end of showing a profit.[105]

The eighteenth century saw the final triumph of property rights over customary or use-rights. The previous rights of the poor and marginal were transmogrified into crimes. Collecting firewood, using a short cut or taking a rabbit for the pot became the crimes of wood-theft, trespass, and poaching. This process was not unique to England, however, but was part of the general absorption of western Europe into a market economy.[106] Much of the Bloody Code, including the notorious Waltham Black Act, can be seen as an unconscious adaptation to the march of capitalism. As agriculture became commercialized, so did the desire of landlords to make a profit from their woodlands, ponds, and commons property they had previously ignored or allowed the poor to use.[107] In one sense, then, the statutes added to the Code during the century were merely an organic process of adaptation to new circumstances, a functional recognition of the supremacy of property rights to customary rights.

Yet, because of the heterogeneous nature of capitalism, with its three main branches, industrial, commercial and financial, the law reflecting this state of affairs contained contradictions.[108] We have seen how draconian were the laws against forgery. Two-thirds of convicted forgers were executed; except for murder, no offence was more relentlessly punished. The proliferation of forgery and counterfeiting statutes was necessary to protect the new financial institutions and their offshoots, the novel system of exchange and paper credit.[109] It might have been, expected, then, that the complex and fragile network of credit would require the law to intervene heavily on the side of creditors and debtors. Attempts were indeed sometimes made to recover debts from the estates of those who died without making provision for the oustanding sums they owed. But, quite apart from the increasing distaste for visiting the sins of the father on the sons (which we have observed in the case of suicide), a law permitting such transfers of assets would be an attack on private property itself, since it would make property rather than persons liable for debts. It was thought better to allow creditors to be defrauded than to allow private property itself to be assailed.[110] Besides, many social critics like the Fieldings had scant sympathy for large-scale creditors, whom they held to be guilty of seducing the 'herd' into luxury, into the consumption of things they could not afford. Once again the Fieldings showed their slender grasp of economics. Even early capitalism found the generation of credit essential to sustain effective demand and hence profits.

Fully to trace the impact of the Industrial Revolution and other social changes on English crime in the eighteenth century would be a Hegelian task. Obviously there is a sense in which every aspect of society links ultimately with every other one. But one of the most interesting recent debates has been that over the impact of modernization on sexual crime. There are two conflicting paradigms. On one model pre-industrial societies required late marriages and deferred sexual gratification. The resultant frustration led to high levels of rape. Once western societies were industrialized, the argument runs, they were in a better position to manage population growth, more liberal sexual attitudes were permitted, premarital sex tolerated and early marriage encouraged. Hence there was less frustration and less rape.[111]

The other, more convincing (to this author at least) model is to argue that sexuality played less of a role in pre-industrial societies, since it is in part a cultural construct. Sex has become an obsession only in the modern world. Freud can be shown to link with Marx precisely because reified sexuality (as observed, say, in contemporary California) depends on the generation of surplus value. This would explain, among other things, why the records do not show the eighteenth century as being particularly rape-obsessed, and why women do not seem to have gone in constant fear of rape.[112]

The final issue in the relationship between crime and social structure concerns the unique experience of eighteenth-century England. We have noted above that many societies experienced similar problems during the transition from feudal residue to full-blooded capitalism. Yet each society had a unique national history; its political culture was both cause and effect of that uniqueness. What was different about England that accounted for the peculiarities of its criminal law?[113]

Much of the difficulty arises from the enunciation of general laws, of which England is then found to be an 'exception'. The rule of thumb holds that the kind of social control involved in holding crime in an iron grip is a prerequisite for industrial 'take-off'.[114] We have seen some of the reasons why this must be so in a general sense. It is impossible to subject labourers and factory-hands to time constraints and work discipline if there is an easy escape route into crime. Yet we have also seen that London was virtually an open city for criminals. How can this conundrum be resolved?

There can be many answers to this. Some allege that the general level of social control in eighteenth-century England was very high, but that the picture is distorted by a megalopolis like London. Others point out, surely convincingly, that there is no obvious correlation between crime and economic performance.[115] In the USA, not only do high levels of crime and violence coexist with high economic performance, but the former may be said to be both parasitic and patterned on the latter. It is a favourite sport to demonstrate that Marxism must logically lead to Stalinist dictatorship.[116] It is less often underlined that the Mafia has a much closer organic relationship to American capitalism.[117]

In any case, attempts to link crime directly with economic development usually fall into the reductionist trap. It is important to distinguish closely between necessary and sufficient conditions. Economic factors create the necessary substratum for crime, but its nature depends overwhelmingly on cultural factors. Any attempt to link crime with social change must be multicausal. So, for example, the criminal experience of eighteenth-century England becomes clearer once a number of different elements: industrial take-off, Enlightenment thought, English empiricism, the undue preponderance of London, are compounded. On the one hand crimes of violence diminished because of a greater distaste for violence in society at large. On the other, crimes against property increased as different types of property proliferated in a concentrated form in the new cities. There was a transition from mindless, casual, occasional, or seasonal delinquency to skilled felony. The threat from gangs of violent criminals roving the countryside was past, if we except the 'gentlemen of the road', whose very characteristic was that they largely eschewed violence. Instead there arose smaller and more professional full-time criminals: pickpockets, forgers, coiners, receivers.

As capitalism disgorged new forms of wealth, new types of criminals arose to take advantage of it. For cultural reasons the elite chose to cling to the old rough-and-ready empiricism of the Bloody Code instead of following Bentham and others down the road of rationalistic social control and the professional police force. This helps to explain why so many sanguinary statutes were added to the Code in a fit of absence of mind. In terms of adaptation and reponse, this can be seen as society's covering the gap left by the absence of a police force. But it would be overly structural-functionalist to push the argument farther than that. The fact that the elite *did* not conspire to add fresh property-protecting statutes to the Code should not be taken as evidence for a comatose or moribund ruling class. As we have seen, the elite did have conscious intentions, and these were altogether more subtle than the mere substitution of a draconian legal system for a French lieutenant of police.

17

The Impact of War

An empire founded by war has to maintain itself by war.
Montesquieu, *Considérations sur les causes de la grandeur des Romains et de leur décadence*

Laws are silent in time of war.

Cicero, *Pro Milone*

There never was a good war or a bad peace.
Benjamin Franklin, letter to Quincy, 11 September 1783

For forty-two of the hundred years from 1700 to 1800 England was at war with France. From 1701 to 1713 there was fought the War of Spanish Succession. The War of Austrian Succession occupied 1740-8. The titanic global struggle with France was then renewed in the Seven Years War (1756-63). The revolt of the American colonists in 1775 ushered in a further eight years' warfare. Finally, from 1793 to the close of the century England was locked in bitter conflict with Revolutionary France. The economic and social dislocation caused by war is a well-known phenomenon.[1] Criminality too felt the shock. One of the few certain propositions that can be advanced about eighteenth-century crime is that, at least until the 1790s, its level rose in peacetime and declined in wartime. Crime peaked especially in the immediate post-war years when troops were demobilized: this can be observed clearly in the years 1674-6, 1698-1700, 1747-51, 1763-5, and 1782-4.[2]

The most obvious effect of war was on manpower, specifically on the young males who in normal circumstances featured so prominently in criminal indictments. Those most likely to turn to crime were swept into the armed forces. There they saw active service from India to the Caribbean. The removal of such a large chunk of the potentially criminal classes could not fail to affect crime levels. The high wartime mortality, especially from disease, further reduced the criminal classes.

War did not simply siphon off *potential* criminals. The authorities used the greater powers available to them in wartime to expel many known criminals. Those who might have been prosecuted in peacetime were allowed to enlist instead.[3] In the countryside, the pretext of national emergency allowed the gentry to get rid of known poachers who could not be convicted for lack of evidence. Local justices of the peace would simply direct press-gangs to the right addresses.[4]

When peace came, the manpower drain that had produced low crime rates during the war was reversed. There were also other indirect factors at work, making the correlation between post-war demobilization and 'crime waves' a causal one. At the simplest level, there was the problem of vast numbers of veterans to be reabsorbed into peacetime society. Following the Treaty of Ryswick in 1697, 106,000 men were demobilized from military service. In 1713-14, after the War of Spanish Succession, 157,000 were discharged. In 1749-50, some 79,000 came home from the wars. After the Seven Years War, in 1764-5, society had to absorb 155,000 veterans. Finally, after the American colonists won their independence, 160,000 men returned to English shores from the Americas.[5]

On paper, this rate of discharge did not seem too alarming. The 79,000 demobilized after the War of Austrian Succession represented only 1 per cent of the population. Even the higher rates after the Seven Years War and the war in America represented just over 2 per cent. This, plus the fact that the total enlisted in a major conflict like the Seven Years War constituted no more than 5 per cent of the male population, has led some scholars to be sceptical about the impact of demobbed men on the crime rate.[6] But a more telling consideration is that the discharged soldiers and sailors made up a much larger proportion of the male labouring poor. The truly relevant statistic is that the veterans returning home after the Seven Years War represented 30 per cent of *that* social segment.[7]

The increase in post-war crime was most marked in serious offences. In peacetime highway robbery was up 52 per cent, burglary 54 per cent, and horse-theft 62 per cent.[8] The longest period of peace in the century – between 1713 and 1739 – was also the time of the greatest public concern over a mounting crime wave.[9] These were the years when Defoe used most of his energies as a social critic, pouring out works that warned of an imminent social and moral collapse.[10]

The other main consequence of the resumption of peace was that North Atlantic traffic returned to normal. The sea lanes were once again open to merchant shipping. Naturally, this allowed more criminals to return illegally from transportation than was possible in wartime. In war, men were in any case conscripted rather than transported. Those who had been transported before the war remained effectively sealed off in America. There was little shipping available for the journey to England, and the passage was fraught with dangers from enemy privateers. Most transportess chose to stay put until the hostilities were over.[11]

But the return to peacetime society of army and navy veterans was not a quantitative matter alone. There was also a *qualitative* element. It was not just the sheer numbers of men who returned, but the attitudes they brought back with them. At worst they had been brutalized by their experiences in war. At best they had acquired new self-confidence through their martial skills. What is more, they had had novel experiences and their eyes had been opened to a world beyond their parish or hundred. 'How you gonna keep 'em down on the farm, now that they've seen Paree?' asks the old-music hall song, and it expresses a fundamental truth. The core notion for the maintenance of stable hierarchy in eighteenth-century England was deference. Yet it is deference that wartime experience, with its cross-class mingling, most of all breaks down. The most eloquent historical testimony to this was the Labour-voting servicemen of World War II, but it is always an ineluctable consequence of the trans-class solidarity bred by struggle with an external enemy. Men who had seen the officer class at close quarters, under fire, and were not necessarily impressed, could not return to the old deference/hierarchy nexus. They preferred to make a living by crime rather than touch their forelocks to the village squire. This was recognized in the eighteenth century and was considered by the elite a worrying development.[12]

These were the direct effects on crime of the transition from peace to war. There were also indirect effects, deriving from economic dislocation and adjustment. War stimulated the demand for certain goods at the very time it artificially depressed the labour supply through conscription, the industries that benefited being textiles (needed for uniforms, hats, sails, etc), the provisioning trade and, in general, any enterprise that stood to gain from the English stranglehold on France.[13] At the same time, the closing of markets for sources of imported goods stimulated the domestic economy. The silk trade, for instance, experienced dramatic upsurges during hostilities, as Britain wrested the trade from her European competitors. London's silk industry expanded rapidly to satisfy temporary wartime needs. This happened in 1706-11, 1741-3, and 1756-62.[14] But with peace came the multiplier effect of renewed competition in overseas trade and reduced demand for labour. Such violent fluctuations were more damaging in their social effects than a steady decline, as they aroused aspirations among the labouring poor only to dash them abruptly in peacetime. The expectations thus aroused were likely to be fulfilled by crime.

The other main criminal economic consequence of war was to give smugglers a free hand. High wartime duties encouraged contraband. For example, the standard rate of tax on imports (10 per cent) was raised to 20 per cent in 1747, 25 per cent in 1759, 30 per cent in 1779, and 35 per cent in 1782 (during the American war).[15] These high duties created a vast differential between prices in England and in France. The inevitable consequence was a thriving contraband trade. The Irish, who were supposed to send their wool only to England, shipped a lot of it to the Continent. The English themselves delivered openly to Scotland and the Orkneys, then trans-shipped wool to Holland, Flanders, and France. Smuggling in wartime was a relatively simple matter. Not only could it be masked by privateers operating under letters of marque; the Navy was fully stretched in the theatre of war and was in no position to help the revenue services in enforcement work.[16]

All these aspects of the relationship between war and criminality can be brought into sharper focus by a study of the particular consequences of each of the great eighteenth-century wars. It was William III's war with Louis XIV from 1689 to 1697 that effectively halted transportation, until the punishment was revived and institutionalized in 1718. Since ships were forced to sail to and from America in convoys, the number of sailings was drastically cut down.[17] Demobilization after the Treaty of Ryswick (1697) brought benefits to the criminal classes. Because of the insupportable pressure on gaols, and the uncertainties over the future of transportation, some prisoners got an absolute pardon for offences for which they might well have been hanged in normal circumstances.[18]

Yet the most often noticed consequence of William's war was that men used their military skills for criminal purposes once back in England. Jack Wilmer honed his burgling skills to a fine point by robbing churches in the Low Countries while campaigning in Flanders.[19] His experiences in Flanders also had an effect on John Simpson (executed 1700). Contemptuous thereafter of civilian life and all its modalities, he organized a military-style gang of burglars in London after 1697, which enjoyed considerable success for a while.[20] The anonymous author of *Hanging Not Punishment Enough* noticed that army veterans were not usually prepared to return to their old way of life. Instead of an analysis in terms of defiance and lack of deference, he produced that hardy annual of conservative demonology 'too lazy to work'.[21]

The aftermath of the War of Spanish Succession produced a similar pattern of criminality. In 1713-14 veterans were being discharged just at the moment when a harsh winter, a poor harvest, and a rise in the price of bread combined with a fever epidemic.[22] Many, like Henry Powell (executed 1715) immediately turned to highway robbery.[23] William Burk, a naval veteran of the Caribbean and Baltic, lasted a little longer on the road (until 1723) but eventually met the same fate.[24] Another veteran, Thomas Phillips, joined the Spigott gang and met his fate with the gang's founder.[25]

The low level of crime experienced during 1740-8, after the high wave of the 1720s, made the impact of the home-coming veterans after the War of Austrian Succession even more traumatic. During the war there was a steady decline in the numbers indicted in the courts, as young men were heavily recruited into the armed services or vital war work, such as shipbuilding, and in the dockyards, in sail-making, in making uniforms, and in provisioning.[26] Levels of crime were extraordinarily low. No one at all was hanged in the county of Surrey between spring 1744 and spring 1747.[27] After the war capital punishment resumed its former level. The demand for labour winnowed out people normally detained under poor law and vagrancy statutes. Houses of correction which were full in peacetime were almost empty during the war.

On the other hand, war tended to produce strikes in the shipbuilding industry. The demand for ships grew; the bargaining power of shipyard workers consequently increased. The outbreak of war in 1739 triggered a spate of strikes. At Portsmouth in 1742 the Riot Act was read to striking shipwrights who tried to deter 'working shipwrights'. Both this disturbance and one at Woolwich were ultimately supressed by the military. Troops acted as strike-breakers.[28]

The shipyard situation was exceptional. Generally, in the war of 1739-48, any increase in crime tended to be related directly to military exigencies. There were riots over army recruiting and pressing.[29] But civilian crime fell away noticeably. Yet immediately peace was declared a crime wave commenced.[30] Not only did the wartime jobs come to a sudden end; the already contracting labour market had to take the impact of tens of thousands of demobilized soldiers and sailors, all champing at the bit for civilian employment and unwilling to take no for an answer.[31] Baulked of the rewards of their service and the compensation for their wounds, they increasingly turned to crime. Shrewd obervers conceded that it was impossible for such a legion of disgorged veterans to find jobs.[32]

The criminality of veterans led to fresh outbreaks of moral panic.[33] Walpole wrote to Mann in great alarm that the disbanded soldiers and sailors had all taken to the highways and streets of London to rob.[34] For the veterans, who were now the despised flotsam of polite society where yesterday they had been its alleged saviours, it was the last straw when petty pickpockets and sneak-thieves, who had sat out the war in the stews of London, dared to prey on them. This was the genesis of the infamous Boscawen Penlez riot in 1749, when sailors who had been cheated pulled down bawdy-houses (see above pp. 223–4)

By the early 1750s it had become a commonplace that the crime rate rose when soldiers and sailors returned from the wars.[35] But, so far from attempting to deal with the real problems of reabsorbing a hundred thousand men into civilian life, the authorities simply responded by offering higher and higher rewards for the apprehension of criminals of whatever stripe, be their offence never so trivial. In 1750 the bounty paid for the arrest and conviction of journeyman footpads was as high as

£100.[36] Inevitably, such largesse led merely to a fresh rash of bogus 'thief-taking' scandals.[37]

Among the bumper crop of military men turned criminal after the Treaty of Aix-la-Chapelle in 1748 was John Poulter, alias Baxter. The Poulter gang was organized along military lines to produce spectacular yields from diversified crime. Poulter and his associates first tried smuggling in Dublin, then switched to highway robbery in England. They cut a spectacular swathe through the country. First they were in Yorkshire, Cheshire, and Shropshire. The burghers of Trowbridge, Halifax, Stockport, Chester, Whitchurch, Grantham, and York all felt their lash. Then they switched venues entirely to Devon. After a cooling-off period as footpads in Exeter, they returned to the north of England, highway robbing in York, Durham, and Newcastle. When pursuit became too hot here, the gang set up operations in Bath. For a time they concentrated on the systematic fleecing of racegoers, practising palming, pickpocketing, and confidence trickery. But a successful period of conmanship in Berkshire led to their being overexposed in that part of England. They switched crimes again, this time to horse-stealing.[38]

By 1753 they were based in Bristol, having run the entire gamut of crime from forgery to highway robbery. But Poulter's luck was running out. Arrested in an Exeter tavern, he was imprisoned. Brutal ill-treatment by the gaoler led him to break out of gaol with some of his manacles still on. He had to travel as far as Glastonbury before he could find a blacksmith to strike off his leg-iron. By now he was suffering from the effects of malnutrition while in gaol. No longer the criminal genius of yore, he made a bad mistake at Wookey near Wells in Somerset, was arrested, tried, and hanged, in 1755.[39]

The Seven Years War was really the second half of a contest, whose first part had been terminated in 1748 to give the combatants a breathing space. Not surprisingly, then, the years 1756-63 mirrored those of 1740-8. Again the level of crime fell away.[40] Again capital punishment dwindled almost to nothing.[41] Once more young males were pressed into the armed services.[42] And again the interruption to shipping meant that judges were far less likely to order transportation.[43] Economic circumstances making for a reduction in crime also reproduced themselves. The French silk trade was virtually ruined, to the great advantage of the weavers of Spitalfields. Contraband burgeoned, especially the smuggling of tea, thought to have been dealt a mortal blow by Henry Pelham in 1745. An increase in duty on tea to help pay for the war led to the revival of a trade long thought moribund.[44] Indeed, smuggling may well have been vital to the French war effort. The export of silver bullion from England through the Channel Islands during the war is thought to have enabled Louis XV to prolong the struggle, even after the disasters of England's *annus mirabilis* in 1759.[45]

There was one species of wartime 'crime' that had not occurred in the 1740s. The passing of a Militia Act in 1757 was followed by severe rioting, especially in the East and North Ridings of Yorkshire.[46] These disturbances were largely caused by the understandable fear that men drafted to the militia would be sent to serve abroad, although the ideological camouflage used by the rioters was concerned with 'arbitrary power'. The fear was widespread. Apart from Yorkshire, there were outbreaks in Lincolnshire and Nottinghamshire, and lesser incidents in Bedfordshire, Hertfordshire, Cambridgeshire, Norfolk, Middlesex, Huntingdonshire, Gloucestershire, and Kent.[47] The worst violence came at Hexham in 1761 when established militiamen opened fire on rioters. Twenty were killed and nearly one hundred wounded when the final tally came in. One of the rioters was executed.[48]

The treaty of Paris in 1763 that brought the Seven Years War to an end also unleashed once more a horde of battle-hardened veterans on the job market. This time the authorities knew better what to expect, even though economic die-hards like Adam Smith flatly denied that the arrival home of 100,000 veterans could have any relevance to the crime figures.[49] More down-to-earth commentators were more perceptive. As the *Gentleman's Magazine* remarked ironically, the veteran returning from the wars who found another man in his job 'must sue for hard labour, or he may starve. If human nature cannot submit to that, cannot he lie down in a ditch and die? If this disbanded brave man should vainly think that he has some right to share in the wealth of his country which he has defended, secured or increased, he may seize a small portion of it by force – and be hanged.'[50]

The attitude of returning veterans was even more uncompromising than in 1748-9. The long years of war had inculcated the notion that violent settlement of disputes was permissible. Men who returned from the wars to find their wives living with other men were liable to solve the problem with the pistol or cutlass. A merciful nature seemed to bring few rewards. One sailor who came home to find his wife living with a cobbler, gave the man eight days to make other arrangements. Finding the cobbler still in place when the time had expired, the sailor threw him out neck and crop. The cobbler returned surreptitiously and cut the sailor's throat from ear to ear. Miraculously, the sailor's life was saved by swift work at the Edinburgh Royal Infirmary.[51]

Occasionally, though, such disputes were settled peacefully. In a similar case where a man returned from the wars to find his wife living with another man, a bizarre Solomonic accord was entered into. The soldier waived his marital rights for eight guineas, leaving the wife free to marry, provided her lover ceased to sleep with her forthwith.[52]

A common response to unemployment was once again to take to the road. War service had equipped many would-be highwaymen with the necessary martial skills. One of them related when captured that he had learned his horsemanship with Burgoyne's Light Horse.[53] Another held up a coach on Finchley Common armed only with a knife. Inside the coach were two men and two women. He took eight and a half guineas from the men but instead of robbing the ladies, treated them to the story of his life. He had served in the Navy during the war but was now destitute. This was his first and last robbery, and his only purpose in life was to get safely home to Ireland. When the two women cowered at his ruffianly appearance, he reassured them:

> Nay, ladies, don't be frightened, I never did the least injury to a woman in my life, nor ever will, damme. As for your money, keep it to yourselves; all that I shall ask from you will be a kiss apiece, and if you grudge me that, I am sure you are neither sensible nor good-humoured.[54]

One of the most significant features of the aftermath of the Seven Years War is the frequent appearance of *sailors* in criminal indictments and reportage. One of the first military victims of Tyburn (in 1762) was an ex-sailor.[55] Another sailor, who had learned his military skills at the siege of Havana and had been mentioned in despatches, became a highwayman.[56] There was perhaps particular bitterness among the heroes of Lagos and Quiberon that they, who had saved England from invasion and destroyed the naval might of France, should be thrown on the scrapheap once hostilities were over.

For once the authorities revealed some sensitivity to the feelings of its fighting men. In July 1764 a seaman was condemned to death at Plymouth for taking part in a mutiny, along with twenty-four comrades, on the *Crown* warship. Following the custom beloved of the authorities, he was reprieved on the morning he was due to hang.[57] Meanwhile urgent consideration had already been given to the plight of discharged seamen. Proposals were made that 20,000 of them should be given preferential employment in the whale fisheries.[58] But this alone was not enough. It was decided that naval veterans should be allowed to work at trades without having gone through an apprenticeship.

This ill-considered piece of positive discrimination merely heightened industrial tensions without resolving any of the underlying problems. The obvious place for returning sailors to find work was in the merchant marine, but significant reductions were made in the labour force there even as the Royal Navy veterans were being discharged.[59] This led to a situation where unemployed merchant seamen and unemployed naval tars mingled in anger and disappointment in London's dockland. The labour surplus was simply used by the merchant navy owners to force down the wages of those still in work. This festering sore led straight to the sailors' strike of 1768.[60]

The plight of the sailors was just one corner in a polygon of economic disasters that hit the nation in the years 1763-6. The growing troubles with the American colonists curtailed the export of goods embargoed by the London government, especially from the iron industry. The disruption of the American market combined with general high prices and a string of bad harvests to produce very high levels of theft.[61] The French silk trade, virtually ruined during the war, revived. The chill winds were felt in Spitalfields.[62] In fact France gained twice over from the coming of peace, for the mania for French fashions and millinery in the early 1760s led to increased smuggling of these items.

Meanwhile there was crisis in the agricultural sector. The boom caused by government victualling contracts during the Seven Years War, followed by changing terms of trade for agricultural products and wildly fluctuating market demand for farm commodities produced, by 1766, both high prices *and* uncertainty about future prospects.[63] The result was the hunger riots of 1766-7. What particularly worried the authorities was that the rioters were well disciplined and organized and led by men with wartime military experience.[64] By 1766 there were three distinct groups of veterans, all among the most alienated members of the English lower class, involved in hunger riots. All of them were familiar with the official military mind, were skilled in the use of weapons, knowledgeable in military tactics, and bold enough to face regular troops. These were ex-soldiers, ex-sailors, and ex-militiamen. Sailors already had a reputation for militancy and would not act against their former comrades.[65] Heavily outnumbered troops would be likely to throw in their lot with disgruntled veterans who spoke the same language. Most unreliable of all, from the authorities' point of view, was the militia, which was composed of the very same elements as the hunger rioters.[66] The 'general crisis' of the late 1760s (see above p. 228) had its powerful echoes in the countryside.

The consequences of the Seven Years War which predisposed returning veterans to crime are so manifold and variegated that a brief recapitulation may be in order. In the first place, ex-servicemen were severely alienated and disillusioned by the situation they found when they returned home. Most of them had joined the ranks in the first place after impressment, to avoid starvation or to escape hanging after the 1756-7 food riots. In addition, militiamen were angry that the government had broken its promise that the militia would be used for home duty alone. When these men came home, not only did they find no improvement, but in many cases conditions were actually worse. Frequently they found their old jobs occupied by others. Even worse, employers had taken advantage of labour shortages during the war to force higher productivity: they actually increased production with a reduced labour force.[67]

At the same time the 'positive discrimination' applied in favour of veterans by the government proved short-lived. Acts of Parliament had been passed to allow veterans to work on the Thames or in various city trades. But not only were the ex-servicemen dumped on industries that already suffered a glut of labour; more serious, the trade guilds struck back. By 1766 successive legal judgements, qualifying the statutes, had effectively removed the veterans' right to enter a trade without an apprenticeship.[68] The phenomenon whereby discharged sailors demanded special rights in a contracting labour market, and at a time of rising prices, was peculiarly explosive. Its consequences were not seen only in the capital. There were seamen's strikes on the Tyne and on the Wear, and a particularly serious one on Merseyside, during the 1760s.[69]

All this was at a time when the price of basic foodstuffs, like meat and grain, was soaring. Men who had joined the armed forces to escape high prices and scarcity now confronted the same problems as before the war, but without the corresponding equanimity. The rise in aspirations, the widening of horizons, and particularly the higher dietary standards enjoyed in the forces made them much less willing to accept their lot.[70]

Most important of all, the years after 1763 saw England in the grip of a sustained economic crisis. The war had created an inflated demand for textiles, shipbuilding , hardware, and coal. All these industries suffered cut-backs after the war. The rapid expansion in labour opportunities in 1756 gave way to large-scale unemployment in 1763. There were two additional consequences of the war. It exacerbated the realignment of trade that was already taking place by the mid-century, for example in the cloth trade. And by removing the French as a military factor in North America, it precipitated conflict with the American colonists. The Stamp Act and later the Townshend duties led to a non-importation agreement in America.[71] English exports plummeted alarmingly. But the American crisis was only part of the general economic depression, at its height in 1765-70. Other factors included instability in India and the economic malaise of Germany. Small wonder, then, that the mid-1760s experienced a crime wave in tandem with a general industrial crisis. Old Bailey committals were 35 per cent higher in 1763-8 than in the war years.[72] The only surprise is that the figure was not higher.

We have already seen that the outbreak of war in America in 1775 ended transportation and meant that prisoners earmarked for secondary punishment had to be employed on the Woolwich hulks instead. The records are full of felons sentenced to ballast heaving and other forms of hard labour on the Thames who in normal circumstances would have been destined for the New World.[73] But the superannuated prison ships could accommodate only 60 per cent of those due to be transported in 1775. Moreover, typhus ravaged the hulks and carried off about one prisoner in four. Expecting an early victory over the Americans, and consequently the return of transportation, the authorities did not bestir themselves on the convict problem until 1779, and not seriously until the war was over.

Merseyside was again an arena of industrial conflict. The outbreak of the American war and the resulting trade embargoes happened to coincide in 1775 with the end of the whaling season. Widespread unemployment in Liverpool led to looting and rioting.[74] Troops were called in. In a violent confrontation, seven sailors were killed and between forty and fifty taken prisoner.[75]

The other obvious impact of the American war in the criminal area was on smuggling. The number of smugglers working the south coast of England increased threefold during 1775-83, as naval and military manpower was diverted to the war effort. By common consent, smuggling was a greater problem during the American war than in any other period of hostilities. It was useless to try to use the militia to staunch the trade, since most of them were smugglers anyway. The authorities tried to cut down the numbers of smugglers by offering them their freedom on condition that they served in the fleet. But most smugglers made a laughing-stock of the law by proving 'unsuitable' within weeks. So instead of being imprisoned they were able to get discharged and to return to their old ways. In 1778 the government stopped up this obvious loophole. From then on, smugglers were released from the armed services only when each candidate for discharge had found two substitutes, one each for the Army and Navy.[76]

The worst effects on the crime rate always came when the end of a long war coincided with a time of dearth. So it was in 1782-3. Even in industries still prosperous, like iron, the level of theft shot up.[77] Demobilization combined with trade depression following the loss of the most important colonial market led to the most serious crime wave since the 1720s. The number of offenders committed for trial at the Old Bailey in 1783-6 was almost 40 per cent higher than in the previous three years.[78] The year 1784 brought a judicial reign of terror. Twenty-four men were sentenced to death at the Old Bailey sessions in April (of whom nine were committed and fifteen executed).[79] In the spring assizes of 1784, there were eighty-eight capital convictions in ten towns, including twenty-one in Winchester alone.[80] We have already seen that the number of convicts held in Newgate and other prisons brought the penal system close to collapse, since to execute them all meant forfeiting England's reputation as a civilised nation. (see above pp. 292-3).[81]

Even small streams of criminality fed into this mighty river. The men who had served their time on the hulks were released into society instead of being banished to America. Since the prison ships were a veritable university of crime, the role of ex-Woolwich prisoners in the crime wave of the mid-1780s was considerable.[82] Walpole was lamenting the situation even before the bulk of soldiers returned from America. In September 1782 he wrote

> We are in a state of war at home that is shocking. I mean from the enormous profusion of housebreakers, highwaymen and footpads – and what is worse, from the savage barbarities of the latter, who commit the most wanton cruelties. This evil is another fruit of the American war . . . In short the grievance is so crying that one dare not stir out after dinner but well armed. If one goes abroad to dinner, you would think one was going to the relief of Gibraltar.[83]

As in the mid-1760s there were two main factors at work in the upsurge of crime in the mid-1780s. One was economic crisis, especially the consequences of the loss of America, in the form of a decline in trade and a glut of labour.[84] The second was that most of the criminals were veterans with military experience.[85] Even when ex-servicemen did not take to the road, their general demeanour was violent and combative. In September 1784 the watch was compelled to stand by powerless when a large body of angry demobbed soldiers went on the rampage in Smithfield. They knocked down every man they met and tore the clothes from the back of every woman.[86] The one attribute conspicuously absent in the behaviour of veterans was deference. In April 1783 some 700 sailors met at the Admiralty to demand payment of their prize money. They then proceeded to unrig any outward-bound ships manned by foreigners or landsmen. It was intolerable to the sailors that pinch-penny masters should be able to avoid coming to them to fill their ships' crews.[87]

Members of the elite wrung their hands in despair at this fresh war-linked crime wave. Arthur Young thought they were weeping crocodile tears: surely it was obvious to anyone with half a brain what would happen if there was no staggered demobilization of 160,000 men?[88] Jonas Hanway spotted that it was the heightened consciousness produced in the lower classes by war service that was largely responsible. But he spoiled his perception by returning to that old staple of the Fieldings: the mania for 'luxury'. According to Hanway, the poor soldiers had to thieve and rob to pay for the debased tastes they had picked up from too close an association with their 'betters' on active service.[89] The one thing none of the commentators was willing to do was elaborate a social critique of crime, showing its inevitable links with economic conditions, including the artificial ones in wartime. All too often, even the most perceptive simply echoed Walpole's homiletic lamentations about the evils of the age.[90]

The wars with revolutionary France in the closing decade of the century are of peculiar interest for the student of crime. For the first time in the century the general proposition that crime declines in wartime broke down. There were two main reasons for this. In the first place, the economic crisis of the 1790s was so acute that not even the normal palliation of wartime demand was able to defuse an explosive conflict between capital and labour. In the second place, crime became 'politicized'. The moribund laws on treason were revived. New measures were passed to deal with political rioting, sedition, and mutiny. This was because a fresh challenge to the elite had arisen. To the endemic economic collision between England and France in America, Africa, and Asia a further dimension was added. The French Revolution produced a new breed of selfconscious revolutionaries. England and France were thereafter locked in an ideological struggle: monarchy against democracy, hierarchy versus equality, property against the 'rights of Man'. The new revolutionary ideas were particularly dangerous since they bade fair to subvert the 'lower orders' in England. The elite's response was to add a new genus of political 'crime' to those proscribed by the Code.[91]

The 1790s began with inflation and a serious trade depression. Several disastrous harvests coincided with the beginning of the protracted and expensive war with revolutionary France in 1793. This time war did not ward off the worst effects of economic crisis, but exacerbated them. There were especially severe recessions in 1793 and 1794. Inflation reached record levels by the end of the decade. The price of wheat went up from sixty shillings and six pence a quarter in 1794 to ninety-one shillings and eight pence in 1795, and to 142 shillings and ten pence in 1800. In other words, the family that was paying six and a half pence for a four pound loaf at the beginning of the war was paying a shilling and four pence seven years later. The spread of political radicalism, together with grain riots and rocketing food prices produced an upsurge in crime unlike anything seen in previous wars. This time the working class did not wait until peace came before jettisoning the values of deference and subordination. For this reason the 1790s were a key decade in the formation of a new English proletariat.[92]

The war with France provided discontented workers with an opportunity to make up wage levels eroded by employers during peacetime. Motive and opportunity went together. The authorities were partially hamstrung by the war and could not so readily use troops to break strikes. At the same time, the radical ideas spreading across the Channel provided an ideological support for class struggle. No less than a third of all eighteenth-century strikes in England occurred in this decade. For the first time the elite went in fear of genuine social revolution.

In theory there was no reason why strikes should come into the criminal arena. They did so when violence took place. As always in industrial relations, this violence was perceived in a one-sided way. 'Violence' was a category used selectively by the elite. It applied to the desperate violence of workers trying to hold their own in an unequal struggle. It did not apply to the brutal methods routinely used by the troops to strike-break. Heavy-handed military intervention always threatened to produce loss of life disproportionate to the public order the soldiers were supposedly maintaining, as in the Bristol toll-bridge riots of 1793 which left eleven protesters dead.[93] Nor did it it apply to the 'violence' of the law, which so protected employers, and so hedged labour combinations about with restrictions, as to make physical violence by workers the *only* feasible way of achieving change. The point can be illustrated by a brief examination of the strikers of the 1790s. In the vanguard were colliers, miners, and keelmen.[94] These men attacked pits and destroyed tools to ensure solidarity and prevent strike-breaking by their fellows. Yet it is quite clear that violence was not their first reaction. They turned to it as a last resort when the employers and authorities (inevitably) proved obdurate and unyielding.[95]

But it was not just industrial disputes that led to rioting and consequently the co-option by the elite of social protest into 'crime'. Economic depression and the polarization of attitudes for and against the French Revolution led to the Birmingham 'Priestley Riots' of 1791, when 'church and king' mobs set on dissenters.[96] The ideological element seemed absent in London, which was spared from rioting until 1794. It was only when the impact of war in the form of disruption of trade and higher taxation combined with its immediate human impact in the form of forced recruitment that the capital exploded.

By 1794 there was an acute shortage of manpower in the armed services. Personnel in the Royal Navy alone had shot up from 16,613 in 1792 to 87,331 in 1794. To attract recruits the military offered bounties as high as £30 a head. These bounties lay at the root of the anti-crimp-house riots of 1794. Crimps were agents who traded in recruits, taking their fees from the bounties of recruits whom they had ensnared into enlistment through debt.[97] Large-scale crimping and kidnapping of men for recruitment led to savage riots in London. These were the worst disturbances seen in the capital since the Gordon riots; it took the authorities three days to suppress them. Although there were no fatalities, the riots resulted in four executions.

It was already clear by 1794 that the war with revolutionary France was unlike any previous war in the century. In this war, the crime rate did not slacken, rather it seemed to increase. Naturally, some of the old features were reproduced. A reduction of crime in London's dockland was reported.[98] On the other hand, smuggling throve. Contraband helped to skew the financial aspect of the war. Smugglers brought silver coin into England from Spain and South America, fuelling domestic inflation. But they also supplied France with the gold, without which she would have been hard put to pay her troops. Napoleon on St Helena praised the smugglers for their vital work.[99] Where fifty years before, the smugglers had been heroes to the Jacobites, now they occupied the same place in the pantheon of the Jacobins. The only contraband trade to come to an end during the French wars of 1793-1815 was the 'owling' of wool.[100]

To confront the *levée en masse*, English society had to gear itself for 'total war' – or as close to it as a relatively weakly centralized state could come in the 1790s. This total war itself produced mixed consequences for crime. For the first time, naval impressment penetrated inland beyond the coastal areas. For the first time, consequently, many poachers were drained off from the countryside.[101] But the sustained threat of invasion from 1795-1805 had 'spin-off' effects on rioting. Large numbers of soldiers, bivouacked all along the south and east coast to meet the expected French landings, strongly affected the price of corn and other basic provisions. Serious food riots were the response to rocketing prices.[102]

That the war had increased rather than decreased crime levels can be seen from two significant pointers. The normal pattern was that crime burgeoned in peacetime and fell away during a war. Yet in 1794, a war year, the Old Bailey records show that 1,060 were brought to trial there, twice as many as in 1764, a war year.[103] It is true that policing and detection methods had improved, and that more prosecutions were being brought. Even so, the statistic is remarkable. Even more telling is the age profile of the offenders. Traditionally most offenders were in the 18-25-year-old age group. But in the 1790s, 60 per cent of those charged with property offences at the Surrey assizes were over 25.[104] This is a powerful circumstantial argument for the thesis that the wars with France produced unprecedented levels of dearth and deprivation. Part of the explanation for the failure of crime to wither away, as in former conflicts, is, of course, obvious. Previous wars had been fought far from home, especially in North America or, in the case of Europe, with continental allies. In the 1790s England stood alone and on the defensive. Fear of invasion meant that most of the troops were cooped up within English shores.

One unfortunate consequence was that elite attitudes hardened. Much of the ground made by Enlightenment thought since 1750 was lost. The tendency not to execute forgers, for example, petered out. The Bloody Code returned in all its vigour. Nowhere can this be seen more clearly than in the resurrection of an area of crime long though defunct: high treason.

The 1790s brought a great rash of trials for sedition and treason. At first those put on trial were men who overtly sympathized with republicanism or Jacobinism.[105] The elite hoped in this way to detach the anti-war spirit of the radical societies from general unrest about the *consequences* of the war. The authorities were shrewd enough to see that the common man had no particular liking for the French; what he objected to was the impact of the war in the form of trade depression and increasing inflation, plus the dubious methods of recruitment. The radical societies, for their part, hit back with the argument that these economic consequences were not genuine results of the conflict with France; the government was engineering a *pacte de famine* to starve unwilling recruits into the army.

At first the authorities were remarkably successful. Juries accepted the argument that to plot for republicanism as a form of government was an implicit act of treason, since *ipso facto* the establishment of a republic meant dethroning the king. Two men, whose sole crime was that they had associated as 'Friends of the People' to advocate a French-style citizen's republic, were executed in 1793 under the old gory sentence of hanging, drawing, and quartering.[106] Two factors helped the government. The execution of Louis XVI was fresh in people's minds. Also, invasion fever gripped the country: the cry 'the French are coming' was not yet the old hat it was to be by the end of the decade.

The years 1793-4 also saw several successful prosecutions for sedition. William Hodgson, Daniel Holt, and the Reverend Mr Winterbottom received two years' imprisonment, respectively for publishing seditious pamphlets and preaching a sermon in favour of revolutionary France.[107] In a number of other cases, sedition was punished by fourteen years' transportation. This very soon became the normal sentence for routine sedition cases.[108] The case of Thomas Muir and the Reverend T. F. Palmer excited peculiar interest, because of the ingenuity of the defence offered. Muir conducted his own defence and began by challenging all the jurors. When he was overruled by the judge, he challenged the evidence of the prosecution witnesses as an obvious 'put-up' job. The prosecution demonstrated that Muir had compared the British economy unfavourably with the French one and had argued for peace. Muir defended himself by alleging that the charges against him and Palmer for sedition were a pretext to mask the real irritation felt by the authorities that both men were radical reformers and supported the cause of the United Irishmen. But, Muir contended, if the cause of radicalism was itself a crime, why had not the Duke of Richmond and Pitt the Younger been put in the dock in earlier years? The judge responded to Muir's 'impertinence' by accepting the song but not the singer. The Reverend Palmer received seven years on the strength of the mitigation argued for in the defence plea. The contumacious Muir received fourteen years.[109]

But in 1794 the authorities' run of success came to an end. After an epic nine-day trial, Thomas Hardy, founder of London's Corresponding Society, was found not guilty of high treason.[110] The attorney-general had confidently advanced the old catch-all 'proof' of his guilt in the form of 'constructive treason' – that the mere advocacy of popular sovereignty logically entails laying hands on a king, as he is bound to resist republicanism.[111] The argument had been accepted by juries before, but a change of temper was evident in this case. The jury decided that the government was coming dangerously close to discretionary powers and rejected the prosecution argument. To the horror and stupefaction of the elite, Hardy's acquittal was followed by that of Horne Tooke and John Thelwall on similar charges.[112]

It was clearly time for sterner measures. In May 1794 the Habeas Corpus Act was suspended. Habeas Corpus did not in itself guarantee freedom from arrest without due charge and without subsequent trial, but it *did* enable a dubious arrest to be tested in the courts. Its suspension cut the ground from under the argument that English liberty was far superior to anything enjoyed in revolutionary France. It was accepted that Habeas Corpus could be suspended only in times of dire national emergency. There were just two precedents: the Jacobite crises of 1714-5, 1722, and 1745-6; and the American war, when between 1777 and 1783 the Act was put in limbo to enable the authorities to deal with treason and piracy. The 1794 action was presented as a justified response to fears over domestic Jacobinism and foreign invasion. In reality it represented the elite's admission that normal legal processes would not necessarily permit it to victimize, marginalize, or warn off Jacobins and partisans of Tom Paine's *Rights of Man*.[113]

In 1795 the authorities went further. Pitt unleashed his 'white terror' in the notorious 'Two Acts'. The pretext was a demonstration of *lèse-majesté* directed at George III. There were groans and hisses from the crowd as the royal carriage passed by on the way to the opening of Parliament. A stone was thrown from the crowd which shattered one of the carriage windows. One Kidd Wake was tried for this offence, and on conviction was sentenced to fines, the pillory, and five years' hard labour.[114] Yet it was widely suspected that the stone-throwing incident had been engineered by a government *agent-provocateur* to provide an excuse for Pitt to bring in the Two Acts.[115]

In the first of the two Acts (the Treasonable Practices Act), it was made a treasonable offence to incite hatred or contempt towards the king, constitution, or government, whether by speech or writing.[116] The second Act (the Seditious Meetings Act) forbade meetings of more than fifty people unless they had notified the magistrates. The magistrates in turn were empowered to veto speeches, arrest speakers, or disperse meetings.[117] In both cases the penalty for transgression was death.

The Treasonable Practices Act was meant to prevent further defences like that in the Hardy case. It extended the law of treason to include anyone who by speech or writing 'compassed or devised' the death, bodily harm, deposition, or imprisonment of the king, who sought to pressurize him into changing his ministers or to overawe parliament. In a word, the death penalty was ordained for anyone inciting hatred of the king, his heirs, his government, or the constitution. In theory 'abstract advocacy' of republicanism, say, in the manner of a Rousseau or a Hume, as distinct from 'speech mixed with action', was still permissible, though recognized as an offence meriting seven years' transportation. The problem was that the Seditious Meetings Act defined 'seditious libel' so loosely that the said libel could be anything from wishing that George III met the same fate as Louis XVI had to inveighing against press gangs.[118]

It was clear that many categories of rioting could now be designated as high treason. At the time of the Gordon riots, Chief Justice Mansfield had given his opinion that any attempt to force the repeal of a law by intimidation or violence was in effect levying war against the king and therefore high treason. Mansfield's judgment was formally enshrined in the Treasonable Practices Act.[119] This was pure legal sleight of hand. Technically, in law treason depended on the intention behind the act, not the act itself. The express intention of the treasonable party had to be attested to by two witnesses. In theory, then, rioting could only be proved to be treasonable if it could be shown that the crowd was politically conscious in the modern sense: that it wanted, not the rectification of some immediate grievance, but the root and branch dismantling of the regime. The obvious snag for the authorities in the eighteenth-century here was that most riots at that time were spontaneous rather than planned.[120]

The 'Two Acts' have habitually been considered a decisive destruction of traditional English liberties and a radical disjuncture with the past, signifying loss of nerve by the elite. But, looked at in another way, they can be seen as continuous with the rest of the Code in that they *threatened* offenders with punishment but did not guarantee it. As E. P. Thompson has remarked, it was the bark Pitt wanted, not the bite.[121] However, it would be a mistake to consider the 'Two Acts' as having negligible importance; after all, there were nearly 200 prosecutions for treason and sedition in ten years. Many radicals were victimized or warned off. Whether the period after 1795 constitutes a reign of terror is more debatable.

It was the unforgettable year 1798 that complicated matters. Invasion threats, the rise of Napoleon, the great insurrection in Ireland combined with food riots and the threat of famine in England, produced an atmosphere of general crisis. Francis Place coined the phrase 'Pitt's reign of terror' to cover the wave of arrests that year. Once again Habeas Corpus was suspended, there was a succession of Acts curbing the press, political societies and workers combinations, and five men were tried for high treason.[122] It was of peculiar interest that the Act banning the United Societies and other corresponding societies received the royal assent on the same day as the Combination Act.[123]

Of the five men tried for high treason, only Father James Coigley was found guilty and executed. The other four: John Binns, Arthur

O'Connor, John Allen, and Jeremiah Leary were acquitted, mainly because the government did not want to blow the cover of the 'mole' it had in place among the United Irishmen.[124] A more serious high treason case in 1800 also foundered. James Hadfield was tried for shooting at the king in Drury Lane Theatre. Hadfield had been an orderly in the Duke of York's service. This, plus his obvious insanity, saved him from the gallows. He was found not guilty by reason of insanity, but ordered detained at the king's pleasure.[125] This is not an impressive record for a reign of terror based on treason trials. To a large extent Place's description is a misnomer. Unlike the modern state, Pitt's England lacked the technology, bureaucracy, and enforcement procedure to make truly repressive legislation bite. To that extent, the Two Acts can be seen to be of a piece with the rest of the Code. The point was not to punish every offence, but to make the occasional awful example to warn off and deter others.[126]

Moreover, the statistical evidence does not show the elite as having lost its grip and in a state of panic. The 200-odd prosecutions for sedition during the 1790s pale beside the vast numbers in the Jacobite period. Jacobite printers risked capital punishment for the mildest pamphlets arguing the Pretender's case. Jacobin printers, on the other hand, usually got no more than two years in gaol.[127] This is another way of saying that the elite never regarded Jacobin revolution as being as serious a threat as Jacobite reaction.

The 1790s produced yet another significant change in the criminal law resulting from war with France. Mutinies in the armed forces reached their height in this decade. This had not hitherto been a significant problem. The most famous mutiny in the high eighteenth century, on the *Bounty*, took place in mid-Pacific; the phenomenon of rebellion by servicemen was not associated with these islands. But the worst army mutinies to date took place in the 1790s; two men were executed for the offence in 1795.[128] England could absorb discontent in the Army, so long as it was safe behind its wooden walls. But the Navy's behaviour was now about to change too.

There had been rumblings of discontent in the Navy for some time, but it took the war with France to bring them to a head. The Two Acts introduced a quota system for seamen in 1795. By this time wartime inflation had greatly eroded sailors' wages. The shape of things to come was evinced by a minor mutiny on board HMS *Defiance* in 1796, after which four men were executed.[129] There were some in the Navy who thought they should take a leaf out of the civilian book. There had been serious riots against the balloting system (for raising men for the militia) and against the militia itself, principally because it was feared militiamen would be sent abroad.[130] These had given the authorities pause. In addition, wartime expansion of the Navy had brought into the service men who could focus the discontent and channel it into a practicable strategy. By 1797 there were veterans of strikes and industrial combinations below deck, plus a number of Irishmen with experience in the United Irishmen.

This combustible cocktail exploded in April-June 1797 with the mutinies at Nore and Spithead.[131] The authorities responded with the Mutiny Act, prescribing the death penalty for resistance to the properly constituted military hierarchy, for the seduction of servicemen from their duty and allegiance, and for anyone who gave aid, comfort, or even communicated with mutineers. The bill was rushed through Parliament in four days.[132] When the mutinies were suppressed, the leader of the 'floating republic' at the Nore, 'Admiral' Richard Parker, was executed, together with twenty-two other mutineers.[133]

For the first time it can truly be said that the elite panicked badly. They swept Pitt, at first inclined to be moderate, along in the direction of draconian repression.[134] This time, it was the bite as well as the bark. The slight tremor of army mutiny, detectable in 1797 in London, Reading, and Maidstone, conjured visions of general revolt in the armed services and concentrated reactionary minds.[135] The death sentences passed on many of the twenty-two mutineers were especially controversial from the standpoint of justice. Robert Fuller, one of those executed, was simple-minded and illiterate. Although the jury found him guilty, they recommended mercy because his offence had occurred so soon after the passage of the Mutiny Act. The judge pronounced the death penalty, but it was then respited pending an appeal. But the appeal judges insisted that the execution be carried out.[136]

Once again the utter uselessness of the death penalty as deterrent was demonstrated. Since the Admiralty did little about the underlying causes of the mutiny, it was not surprising that even the 1797 spectacle of the Bloody Code in full swing did not put an end to shipboard disturbances. Another serious mutiny took place in the Bantry Bay squadron in December 1801. In two separate trials eleven mutineers were sentenced to death and hanged, while punishments of two hundred lashes were meted out to their accomplices. In a sinister echo of the Gordon riots, it transpired that none of the mutineers was older than twenty.[137]

The impact of warfare on crime in the eighteenth century shows clearly the brittleness of English society and the relatively primitive nature of its industrial economy. The absorption of returning veterans into peacetime society is never easy, but modern societies ease the transition by demobilization gratuities, resettlement allowances, the 'GI bill', and so on. In the eighteenth century men were expected to adjust from living at a surplus in the Caribbean, North America, or the Pacific, enjoying higher dietary levels and unprecedented living standards, to destitution in the slums of London. Both mechanically (because of the influx of returning veterans) and psychologically (because of raised consciousness and aspirations), this was an unreal expectation. Moreover, in a modern consumer society, the pent-up economic demand during the war produces an artificial boom in post-war years, even in conditions of shortage, removing one of the motives for property crime. Lack of effective demand on one hand, and of the necessary economic infrastructure on the other, meant that in the eighteenth century the post-war years were times of severe contraction and unemployment.

The 1790s provide an exception to the general eighteenth-century trend, largely because of the depth of the economic recession and because of the military 'implosion'. Whereas in previous wars, soldiers and sailors were dispersed throughout the globe, in the 1790s large numbers of them were cooped up in the British Isles, awaiting an invasion from France. The other important factor is the 'politicization' of crime. Ideological conflicts between elite values and those of Jacobin France, the inchoate English industrial working class and the United Irishmen, led to the introduction of a number of statutes augmenting the scope of treason and mutiny offences. The increase in crime during the war with revolutionary France, against the normal trend, was thus partly a function of the direct military consequences of the war, and partly of the extension of the criminal law to cover new political offences. The century that began with Jacobitism as *the* great treasonable offence ended by putting Jacobinism in its place. As Edward Coxe remarked in 1805:

> To make the wrong appear the right,
> And keep our rulers in;
> In Walpole's time, 'twas Jacobite,
> In Pitt's, 'tis Jacobin!

Whether the idea was to put the clock back or move it forward, the elite would always fight murderously to maintain the status quo of hierarchy, deference, and obedience.

Afterword

It will be clear from the foregoing that my preference in eighteenth-century historical analysis is for the 'empirical Marxism' of E. P. Thompson, Douglas Hay, Peter Linebaugh, and others of that school. The Thompson approach seems to me to avoid the dessicated inanition of the new historical scholasticism, of which G. P. Elton is the leading theoretician, if not always the practitioner. This too often consists of a dry nominalism that eschews all universals and comparative models. It is true that every historical event is by definition unique, but an overemphasis on its uniqueness – 'everything is what it is and not another thing' to quote Wittgenstein – produces a Jane Austen version of history.

While Thompson's approach denies the absolute sovereignty to the perceptions and self-assignations of individual actors that liberalism and its offshoots (such as utilitarianism) require, he also avoids the egregious mistake of dissolving the human subject entirely into structures. Thompson is a famous critic of hypostasized system building *à la* Althusser (see the outstanding polemic in *The Poverty of Theory*). Those sympathetic to the Thompson critique are unlikely to find much of value to the historian in formal Marxist sociology. Certain of the new Marxist criminologists seem to have fallen into the fallacy of taking up a mirror-image position on original sin. Just as for the diehard conservative 'the law is the law is the law' and all crime is an undifferentiated homogeneous mass of 'evil', so for the radical Marxists all crime is simply deviance. The 'new criminologists' seem to make a number of errors which eventually have the effect of diverting attention from the very real socio-economic causation of most crime, the traditional Marxist line.[1] In the first place structures are reified so that the human subject disappears.[2] The disembodied human subject then responds at all points with hyper-rationality, there is only 'economic' crime, no *crime passionnel, acte gratuit,* or motiveless crime. Crimes against the person are dissolved into other social categories: rape becomes a symbolic act of male dominance, murder in war time becomes a patriotic act.[3] Psychiatry and psycho-analysis are drained of all individual meaning and becoming merely instruments of social control: schizophrenia is merely an extreme form of deviance, etc.[4] Finally, in flat defiance of the warnings of Freud in

Civilisation and its Discontents, the myth of a golden age of crime-free society is advanced.[5] To the obvious objection that Marx himself saw the criminal classes as hopeless revolutionary material and preferred to consign them to the *lumpenproletariat*, the new Marxists make a distinction between formal and orthodox Marxism. In other words, Marxism as method leads to conclusions different from those espoused by the historical Marx. The clear implication is that Marx would have seen the error of his ways if schooled in a seminar run by the new criminologists. This is 'natural selection' Marxism with a vengeance!

In sum, the assault from the Left on 'empirical Marxism' is so resolutely ahistorical as to be negligible from the viewpoint of eighteenth-century crime. We have already seen some of the absurdities to which a hardline Marxism of law as 'nothing but' the interests of the ruling class can lead. More formidable is the challenge from the Right. Far from regarding the Law in the eighteenth century as 'nothing but' the interests of a ruling class, certain historians of crime regard it as scarcely at all connected with the interests of the ruling class. Some go even farther and deny that there was such a class.

We may sum up the critique of the Right towards the Hay/Thompson approach under four headings. The first argument alleges that the Hay/Thompson account of the genesis of the statutes in the Bloody Code is misleading. The second argument is that the eighteenth-century law was not class law but demonstrated a 'multi-use' right. The third argument casts doubt on the existence of a single elite capable of concerting the Code as in the Hay/Thompson model. The fourth rebuts the notion that rioters were moral agents and hence genuine 'social criminals'.

The first thesis is that there was no systematic attempt to plug every loophole in the panoply of elite authority. An examination of the provenance of the capital statutes shows them to be sloppily drafted, rarely debated, and to be very often afterthoughts to other legislation. This argument has a certain *ad hoc* force, but depends too heavily on a very crude model of what is involved in eighteenth-century social control and government direction. Only in a totalitarian society can an elite oversee every single detail of a legislative programme. The well-attested need of Walpole, the Pelhams, and other ruling cliques to control Parliament without a modern party machine shows the legislature as relatively more important than the executive, as compared with a modern situation. This in turn reflects the lesser central control available to an eighteenth-century English government. It is unreal to expect such a government to intervene at all points in law-making. The real test is whether any of the 'unconscious', 'absent-minded', 'organic' legislation collided with overall elite interests. The answer to this must be a resounding no.

   The idea that eighteenth-century laws on property crime evinced a 'multi-use right', not restricted to the elite, is a staple of the anti-Thompson faction.[6] The argument is that a detailed examination of court records shows the 'lower orders' keen to participate in the legal process and in no way subscribing to the view that the criminal law was class law.[7] One notable study provides an analysis by occupation of quarter sessions prosecutors in Essex.[8] The author finds a high level of involvement by labourers (one fifth of all Essex quarter sessions prosecutors), which is *prima facie* remarkable, since such men had no servants and few goods and chattels. Moreover, a third of all prosecutors in the Essex quarter sessions in the years 1748-1800 could not sign their names. Nor was it the case, as might be supposed, that these prosecutions by the poor were all paid for by employers, landlords, or local associations for the prosecution of felons. In many cases the courts themselves encouraged wide popular participation in the court by helping poorer prosecutors in property crime cases.[9]

   Yet it is abundantly clear that the use of the legal system by a broad spectrum of social groups does not invalidate the idea that the system itself was ultimately controlled by a tiny elite. The key to this issue is whether the perceptions of actors are to be considered the last word, as in liberal theory. Does the fact that Essex labourers did not regard the law as class law close the book on the entire argument? One does not have to believe in 'false consciousness' to see that there is a problem here. Political scientists have devoted much attention to phenomena like Poujadisme in France and working-class conservatism in England, on the assumption that members of the proletariat and the lower-middle class often vote for parties opposed to their own objective interest. If there is no 'objective interest', as opposed to the perceived or supposed ones of individual actors, the problem does not even arise. Yet those sociologists who have studied working-class conservatism, on the assumption that it is a genuine social problem, have not usually been Marxists.[10] Indeed their studies tend to reinforce the Hay thesis, for one of the key components in working-class conservatism is deference, precisely the state of mind aimed at by the eighteenth-century elite. The enthusiastic embrace of the law by the Essex labourers can more plausibly be attributed to 'false consciousness' and the success of elite hegemonic ideology than to a genuine 'multi-use right'. As for Poujadisme, most studies concentrating on this phenomenon show that the most rabid defenders of a reactionary status quo are those who have clawed their way to the first rung on the social ladder, and are therefore pathologically fearful of the genuine 'have-nots' just below them.[11] The relationship of Essex labouring prosecutors to Essex criminals may in this respect be likened to the relationship of the Irish to the blacks in nineteenth-century USA.

   The third argument is that there was no single elite to concert such a hegemonic ideology. Various groups in society conflicted with, co-operated with, and gained concessions from each other.[12] There was competition for power between aristocratic magnates, the gentry and farmers, industrialists, merchants, financiers, professionals, and many others. In so far as an elite existed, it was plural, not singular. In any case, most of the discretion in criminal cases was exercised by people who were not members of the elite, for example, prosecutors and juries.[13]

The debate is strongly redolent of the one that took place in the USA at the end of the 1950s between Robert Dahl and C. Wright Mills, over whether the US political elite was a single entity or a plurality of independent, intersecting cliques. To some extent the argument will always turn on methodology. An approach via 'decision making' will produce a plurality of elites. An approach via 'power' will find a unitary ruling class.[14] But beyond this, the arguments directed against the existence of a single elite in eighteenth-century England are peculiarly simplistic. There is a sleight-of-hand tendency by critics of the Right to turn the theory of a single ruling elite into paranoid conspiracy theory. But it is quite clear that the notion of conspiracy is unnecessary in locating a single elite. Michael Ignatieff has written:

> One can speak of a ruling class in the sense that access to strategic levers of power was systematically restricted according to wealth and inheritance, but one cannot speak of its acting or thinking as a collective historical subject . . . choral unanimity was rare even in moments of universally recognised crisis.[15]

To which the answer is, the strong sense of 'ruling class' Ignatieff refers to is unnecessary in order to sustain the Hay thesis.

To establish the reality of a single co-ordinating, but not necessarily initiating elite, all we need to do is correlate the verifiably highest position in society with reputational status. An examination of the eighteenth-century elite shows that those at the top of the social hierarchy also possessed the desirable resources: the elite, as the name suggests, were those who had the best of what there was to have. They also shared a common consciousness of belonging to the top social stratum, common values, common culture, and shared assumptions about the natural order of things. The point is made by a cursory glance at the correspondence between, say, Archbishop Herring and Lord Chancellor Hardwicke during the '45, between Lord Chesterfield and the Duke of Newcastle, or Benjamin Franklin and the Duke of Cumberland.[16] Those at the apex of the various pyramids of power in eighteenth-century England did intersect with each other. Their interaction was salient and produced a feeling of solidarity. A self-conscious elite developed pronounced feelings of superiority, fortified by intermarriage.[17] It is abundantly clear from, say, the writings of Hume that the debates over Court and Country ideology or Whig and Tory theory were debates about means rather than ends, except when the spectre of Jacobitism appeared.

There is another point to consider in the argument about the elite. We have already had occasion to query the thesis that eighteenth-century authorities in England resorted to a draconian Bloody Code solely through reluctance to use a regular police force. The proposition that other elites maintained themselves without extending the death penalty *only* because they employed professional police neglects the crucial point that most of them did not in fact maintain themselves, as the convulsion of the French Revolution demonstrated. This alone should highlight the one-dimensionality of regarding the absence of police in England as *the* salient cultural factor. An examination of the other cultural features points strongly towards a single elite. For why did England uniquely escape revolution or serious civil disturbance in the eighteenth century? Is not part of the answer, at least, the skill of England's rulers? Such adroitness would not be possible if there was merely an unconnected plurality of competing elites. Why not credit the English elite with singular subtlety in its mixture of bark and bite, stick and carrot?

The fourth argument is that not even Thompson's advocacy is enough to support the proposition that rioters were genuine 'social criminals'. In his celebrated article Thompson saw food riots in particular as the long-drawn-out resistance of an older moral economy, based on the needs of the consumer, to the profit-oriented world of *laissez-faire* and to the dislocating and extortionate mechanisms of an unregulated market economy.[18] Thompson's location of the rioter in the pantheon of genuine 'social criminals' has attracted especial criticism. First, it is alleged that the food rioter was not a representative example of the common people as a whole: food rioters were a minority section among urban dwellers.[19] Second, it is objected that rioters did not base their claims to legitimacy on ancient paternalistic practices, nor did they seek to restore the 'just price' of some earlier golden age. All they wanted was to restore the price of the previous year or to achieve a compromise price between 'normal' and 'crisis' levels.[20] Third, rioters cannot be considered as a vanguard for 'plebeian culture' against the patrician values of the elite, as Thompson argues.[21] John Brewer has argued that the Wilkesites in particular were neither patrician nor plebeian, that they were in but not of the magic circle of the elite, that Thompson's dichotomy therefore will not work.[22]

It is clear that a lot of this is nitpicking. As David Phillipps has well said, 'Rather than offer alternative theoretical approaches to those of the revisionists, most of them (namely, the critics of the Right) simply take refuge in a detailed but sterile empiricism, as if this somehow refuted the larger theoretical overview.'[23] Brewer's point is not particularly telling. One might just as well say that the existence of the Social Democratic or Liberal Party made it impossible to interpret British politics as a struggle between Right and Left. As for rioters in general and their putative status as social criminals, one has to distinguish between the immanent and transcendent aspect of social movements. Of course it is true that, pinned down at a particular moment of time, the rioter can appear an ephemeral actor concerned with the issues of the day. But every social movement has an element that projects into the future, an aspect that portends something else, what one might call the historical *nisus*. Few of the members of the 1871 Paris Commune were genuine social revolutionaries. Does that mean that Marx was suffering from romantic delusion when he hailed the Commune as the harbinger of genuine revolution? In the eighteenth century full self-conscious revolutionary aims came in only with the French Revolution. Lacking the ideas of the Jacobins still to come, the English rioters naturally turned for inspiration to an older moral tradition. It was the lack of a proper ideological support or inspiration that turned these inchoate revolutionaries back to the myth of the 'Golden Age'.

Notes

ABBREVIATIONS

Some abbreviations have been used for frequently cited publications and documents:

Acts of Parliament: '5 Anne c.6' refers to the sixth statute passed in the fifth year of the reign of Queen Anne.

NNC: *New Newgate Calendar* (1818 edition)

CNC: *Complete Newgate Calendar* (Crook and Rayner, eds, 1926)

Add. MSS: Additional manuscripts, British Library

RA Stuart: Royal Archives, Stuart papers

Walpole Correspondence: Horace Walpole's correspondence is referred to in the collection edited by W. S. Lewis, in 39 vols (Yale, Newhaven, 1934-7).

Hanging Not Punishment Enough: The full title is *Hanging Not Punishment Enough for Murtherers, Highwaymen and Housebreakers: Offered to the due consideration of the two Houses of Parliament* (1701).

The place of publication for all books listed is London, unless otherwise stated.

INTRODUCTION

1 Leon Radzinowicz, *A History of Criminal Law and its Administration from 1750*, 5 vols (1948-86) i, p.4.
2 Ibid., p.5.
3 5 Anne c.6.
4 Jerome Hall, *Theft, Law and Society* (1935) pp.34-5.
5 3 & 4 Wm & M.c.9.
6 10 & 11 Wm III c.23.
7 12 Anne c.7.
8 Philip Yorke, *The Life and Correspondence of Philip Yorke, Earl of Hardwicke*, 3 vols (1913) i, p.135.
9 Tobias Smollett, *Complete History of England* (1848 ed.) ii, pp.279-80.
10 William Lecky, *A History of England in the Eighteenth Century* (1920) vii, p.316.
11 Radzinowicz, op.cit., i., pp.22-3.
12 A whole host of such cases is cited in Samuel Romilly, *Observations on the Criminal Law of England* (1810).
13 *Gentleman's Magazine* 1790 p.1185.
14 Patrick Colquhoun, *Treatise on the Police of the Metropolis* (1800) pp.284-6.
15 Martin Madan, *Thoughts on Executive Justice* (1785) p.137.
16 J. S. Cockburn (ed.) *Crime in England 1550-1800* (1977) p.185.
17 Erskine May, *The Constitutional History of England*, 11th edn (1896) iii, p.393.
18 Cobbett's *Parliamentary History of England* 9 (1777-78) cols 234-42.
19 Romilly, op.cit.; pp.65-7.
20 Colquhoun, op.cit., pp.90-1, 225-31.
21 ibid., pp.292-4.
22 A useful contrast is afforded by comparison of the cases in N. N. C.vi., pp.162-4, 170-1, 187-8, 198-200, 368-73.

23 J. H. Langbein, 'Albion's Fatal Flaws', *Past and Present* 98 (1983) pp.96-120, (at p.106).

24 Sir William Blackstone, *Commentaries on the Laws of England*, 4 vols, 9th edn (1783) iv, p.248.

25 Douglas Hay, 'Property, authority and the criminal law,' in D. Hay, E. P. Thompson, and P. Linebaugh (eds) *Albion's Fatal Tree* (1975) pp.17-63.

26 Authority may be construed as a secondary or indirect interest, in contrast to the primary or direct interest of property. An historical analogy may make the point clearer. It has often been queried why the USA fought such a sustained and bitter war in Vietnam when no obvious economic or national interests were directly at stake. The most plausible answer is that the war was fought for reasons of credibility, to impress on any future enemy that the USA was prepared to defend its real interests elsewhere, in Asia and the Middle East. A similar indirect motive was at work with the English elite. Those, like Madan, who called for punishments to be certain, missed the point that the elite was normally more concerned with the law's bark than its bite.

27 Hay, op.cit., pp.46-8.

28 As Anatole France famously pointed out, the Law in its majestic equality prohibits rich and poor alike from stealing bread and sleeping under bridges. Cynicism about the link between 'equality before the law' and genuine equality is usually considered peculiarly Marxist, but is in fact a staple of all critiques of liberalism. See, for example, my 'The Ideology of Peronism', *Government and Opposition* 19 (1984) pp.193-206.

29 E. P. Thompson, *Whigs and Hunters* (1975) p.267.

30 Blackstone, op.cit., iv, p.377.

1 LONDON

1 E. A. Wrigley, 'A simple model of London's importance in changing English society and economy 1650-1750', *Past and Present* 37 (1967) pp.44-70; cf. also E. A. Wrigley, 'The growth of population in eighteenth-century England: a conundrum resolved'. *Past and Present* 98 (1983) pp.121-50.

2 M. D. George, *London Life in the Eighteenth Century* (1925) pp.22-6.

3 Wrigley, 'Simple Model' op.cit., cf. also E. A. Wrigley and R. S. Schofield, *The Population History of England 1541-1871* (1981), also D. C. Coleman, *The Economy of England 1450-1750* (Oxford, 1977).

4 Daniel Defoe, *Tour through the Whole Island of Great Britain* (1724-6) i, pp.314-16.

5 Walpole to Mary Berry, 8 June 1791, *Walpole Correspondence* 11, pp.283-9.

6 Henry Fielding, *An Inquiry into the Causes of the late increases of Robbers* (1751) p.76.

7 George, op.cit., pp.81-5.

8 ibid., p.97.

9 Fielding, op.cit., p.94.

10 This is a specialized field. But see Pat Rogers, *Grub Street: Studies in Subculture* (1972); J. J. Ricketts, *Popular Fiction before Richardson* (Oxford, 1969); Peter E. Neuberg, *Popular Literature* (1977); Peter Burke, *Popular Culture in Early Modern Europe* (Temple Smith, 1978).

11 NNC iii, pp.236-7.

12 *Gentleman's Magazine* 1763 pp.304-5.

13 *London Chronicle*, 5-7 June 1764.

14 *London Chronicle*, 22-25 December 1764.

15 A. P. J. Grossley, *A Tour to London or new Observations on England*, trans. Nugent (1772) 2 vols, i, p.62.

16 D'Archenholz, *A Picture of England* (Dublin, 1790) p.210.

17 But the notion *was* starting to take a grip on the upper classes; see Laurence Stone, *The Family, Sex and Marriage in England 1500-1800* (1977).

18 George Rudé, *Hanoverian London 1714-1808* (1961); cf. also A. J. Weitzman, 'Eighteenth-century London: urban paradise or fallen city?', *Journal of the History of Ideas* 36 (1975) pp.369-80; Robert B. Shoemaker, 'The London "mob" in the early eighteenth century,' *Journal of British Studies* 26 (1987) pp.273-304.

19 CNC iii, pp.265-6.

20 For these and other details see Jack Lindsay, *The Monster City; Defoe's London 1688-1730* (1978).

21 Daniel Defoe, *Lives of Six Notorious Street Robbers* in Robbens (ed.) Defoe, *Works* (Boston, 1903) 16, pp.347-81.

22 See *Walpole Correspondence* 32, p.308.
23 *London Chronicle*, 21-23 June 1792.
24 *London Chronicle*, 19-21 June 1792.
25 For representative executions of footpads see NNC v, pp.135-8.
26 See the cases in the 1790s, when punishment was in general becoming less severe: NNC vi, pp.198-200.
27 NNC vi, p.120.
28 *Whitehall Evening Post*, 23-26 January, 22-24 March 1768; *London Chronicle* 24-26 March 1768.
29 See the cases at NNC vi, p.593.
30 *Public Advertiser*, 13 July 1784.
31 *Walpole Correspondence* 33, pp.29-30.
32 *London Chronicle*, 27-30 September 1794.
33 William Shenstone, *Works* (1769) iii, p.83.
34 F. Lacombe, *Observations sur Londres et ses environs* (1777) p.15.
35 For a good 'daily life' survey see E. J. Burford, *Wits, Wenches and Wantons: London's Low Life, Covent Garden in the Eighteenth Century* (1986).
36 *Gentleman's Magazine* 1795 p.657.
37 CNC ii, pp.218-20.
38 CNC ii, pp.184-91.
39 A. B. F. Baert, *Tableau de la Grande Bretagne*, 4 vols (Paris, 1800) iv, pp.219-20.
40 *Gentleman's Magazine* 1765 p.145.
41 *Public Advertiser*, 30 January 1765.
42 *Public Advertiser*, 10 January 1764.
43 *Gentleman's Magazine* 1784 p.635.
44 *London Evening Post*, 27 June 1738.
45 *Morning Chronicle & London Advertiser*, 31 August 1784.
46 *London Chronicle*, 11-13 September 1764.
47 *London Chronicle*, 19-21 January 1764.
48 Lytton Strachey and Fulford, (eds) *Greville Memoirs* 1814-60, v, p.147.
49 *London Chronicle*, 6-8 September 1764.
50 *General Advertiser*, 25 August 1750.
51 See Hugh Philipps, *The Thames about 1750* (1951).
52 For Hogarth and London daily life see Jack Lindsay, *Hogarth* (1977); Peter Quennell, *Hogarth's Progress* (1955); Henry B. Wheatley, *Hogarth's London* (1909).
53 Sir J. G. Broadbank, *History of the Port of London*, 2 vols (1921) i, p.83.
54 NNC vi, pp.733-5.
55 Patrick Colquhoun, *A Treatise on the Commerce and Police of the River Thames* (1800) p.198.
56 A. G. Goede, *A Foreigner's Opinion of England* (trans. Horne, 1821) 3 vols, i. pp.214-16.
57 *The Discoveries of John Poulter alias Baxter* (1753).
58 See John L. McMullan, *The Canting Crew: London's Criminal Underworld 1550-1700* (New Brunswick, 1984); cf. also George Parker, *A view of society and manners in High and Low Life* (1781), vol.2. For the 'canting' language itself see Francis Grose, *A Classical Dictionary of the Vulgar Tongue* (1785).
59 *Hanging not Punishment Enough* (1701) p.15.
60 William Blizzard, *Desultory Reflections on Police* (1785) pp.30-1.
61 For a general discussion see A. K. Colon, 'The concept of criminal organisations', *British Journal of Criminology* 17 (1977) pp.97-111.
62 Patrick Colquhoun, *Treatise on the Police of the Metropolis*, (1800) pp.189-92.
63 See, for example, *Gentleman's Magazine* 1784 p.710.
64 Saunders Welch, *A Report on the Subject of Robberies* (1758) p.61.
65 *Gentleman's Magazine* 1750 p.377.
66 *Gentleman's Magazine* 1759 p.91.
67 Ralph Wilson, *A Full and Impartial Account of all the Robberies committed by John Hawkins* (1722) pp.14-15.
68 *Gentleman's Magazine* 1741 pp.356, 441, 498.
69 For these see Colquhoun, *Commerce and Police of the River Thames*, op.cit. p.50.
70 For a comprehensive examination of the subject see Radzinowicz, op.cit., ii. pp.353-78.
71 C. H. George, 'The Making of the English Bourgeoisie 1500-1750', *Science and Society* 35 (1971) p.396.
72 M. D. George, op.cit., p.20; cf. also pp.27-42. See also Dorothy Marshall, *The English Poor in the Eighteenth Century* (1926).
73 Tobias Smollett, *Complete History of England* (1848 ed.) iii, p.81.
74 Sidney and Beatrice Webb, *The History of Liquor Licensing in England* (1903) p.39.
75 *Gentleman's Magazine* 1760 p.21.
76 W. L. Clay, *The Prison Chaplain* (1861) p.37.
77 For evidence of concern see Bernard

Mandeville, *An Enquiry into the Causes of the Frequent Executions at Tyburn* (1725) p.21; Stephen Hales, *A Friendly Admonition to the Drinkers of Gin, Brandy and other distilled spirituous liquors* (1734).

78 George Rudé, '"Mother Gin" and the London riots of 1736', in G. Rudé, *Paris and London in the Eighteenth Century* (1970) pp.201-21.

79 Lord John Hervey, *Memoirs of the Reign of George II* (1848) ii, p.314; Philip Yorke, *Life and Correspondence of Philip Yorke, Earl of Hardwicke*, 3 vols (1913) i, p.138.

80 Paul Langford, *The Excise Crisis* (Oxford, 1975).

81 *Memoirs of the Life and Times of Sir Thomas Deveril Knight* (1748) pp.38-40.

82 RA Stuart 190/189, 192/2. The Jacobites were particularly sanguine about developments in Britain at this time, since the agitation over the Gin Act coincided with the Porteous riots in Scotland (RA Stuart 189/50, 190/160-1, 191/12).

83 See Anon., *Serious Thoughts in Regard to the Publick Disorders* (1751) p.38

84 24 Geo 2 c.40.

85 25 Geo 2 c.36. A magistrate's license was required for all places of amusement (Smollett, op.cit., iii, pp.330-1.

86 26 Geo 2 c.31.

87 William Lecky, *A History of England in the Eighteenth Century* (1920) ii, p.104.

88 S. and B. Webb, op.cit., p.38.

89 M. D. George, op.cit., p.325.

90 Edward Cadogan, *The Roots of Evil* (1937) pp.20-32.

91 The *locus classicus* for this adaptation of the Whig theory of history is the monumental work by Radzinowicz.

92 M. D. George, op.cit., p.17.

93 Rudé, *Hanoverian London* op.cit., pp.134-7.

94 See *London Evening Post*, 26 August, 12 October 1738.

95 See Malcolm Falkus, 'Lighting in the Dark Ages of English economic history: town streets before the Industrial Revolution', in D. C. Coleman and A. H. John (eds) *Trade, Government and Economy in Pre-Industrial England: Essays presented to F. J. Fisher* (1976) pp.187-211.

96 Ferri de Constant, *Londres et les Anglais* (Paris, 1804) 4 vols, iv, pp.170, 174.

97 Baert, op.cit., iv, pp.217-21.

98 Ferri de Constant, op.cit., i, p.27; d'Archenholz, op.cit., pp.82-3.

99 For recognition of this fact by foreign observers see Charles Nodier, *Promenade from Dieppe to the Mountains of Scotland* (1822) p.33; C. P. Moritz, *Travels in England* (1782, ed. P. E. Matheson, 1924) p.21.

100 James Thomson, *The Seasons* (1726).

101 Colquhoun, *Commerce and Police of the River Thames*, op.cit., p.46.

102 Alexander Pope, *The Second Satire of Dr John Donne* (1713).

103 Samuel Johnson, *London* (1738).

104 See Raymond Williams, *The Country and the City* (1973).

2 LAW ENFORCEMENT

1 De la Corte, *Voyage philosophique d'Angleterre fait en 1783 et 1784*, 2 vols (Paris 1784) i, p.112; J. Fieve, *Lettres sur l'Angleterre* (Paris, 1802) p.50.

2 For the continental bugbear see Alan Williams, *The Police of Paris* (1979).

3 For the evolution of the idea of police in the eighteenth century see P. Pringle, *Hue and Cry: the Birth of the British Police* (1955); D. Runbelow, *I Spy Blue: The Police and Crime in the City of London from Elizabeth I to Victoria* (1971).

4 J. B.le Blanc, *Letters on the English and French Nations* (trans. 1747) 2 vols, ii, p.297.

5 J. and B. Hammond, 'Poverty, crime and philosophy', in A. Turberville (ed.) *Johnson's England* (Oxford, 1933) p.301.

6 For this theme see R. C. Jarvis, *Collected Papers on the Jacobite Risings*, 2 vols (Manchester, 1972) *passim*.

7 Sir John Fortescue, 'The Army', in Turberville (ed.) op.cit., pp.68-70; cf. Pringle, op.cit., p.52.

8 E. P. Thompson, 'The moral economy of the English crowd', *Past and Present* 50 (1971) p.121.

9 J. R. Western, *The English Militia in the Eighteenth Century* (1965).

10 V. Wheeler-Holohan, *The History of the King's Messengers* (1935).

11 J. L. Tobias, *Crime and Police in England 1700-1900* (1979) p.27.

12 Lionel K. J. Glassey, *Politics and the Appointment of Justices of the Peace 1675-1720* (Oxford, 1979).

13 Sir William Blackstone, *Commentaries on the Laws of England*, 4 vols, 9th ed. (1783) iv, p.282.

14 Norma Landau, *The Justices of the Peace 1679-1760* (Berkeley, 1984).

15 Leon Radzinowicz, *A History of Criminal Law and its Administration from 1750*, 5 vols (1948-86) ii, pp.155-61.

16 ibid., ii, p.195.

17 Daniel Defoe, *Street Robberies Considered* (1728) p.39.

18 *London Evening Post*, 7 November 1738.

19 Tobias, op.cit., pp.36-8.

20 ibid., pp.39-43.

21 J. M. Beattie, *Crime and the Courts in England 1660-1800* (Oxford, 1986) pp.67-72.

22 Max Beloff, *Public Order and Popular Disturbances*, (1938) pp.24-6.

23 Blackstone, op.cit., i, p.343.

24 ibid., iv, p.122.

25 8 Geo 2 c.16.

26 Radzinowicz, op.cit., ii, pp.164-5.

27 A. B. F. Baert, *Tableau de la Grande Bretagne* (Paris, 1800) 4 vols, iv, p.368.

28 Beattie, op.cit., pp.41-50.

29 Anon., *Proposal for regulating the night watch within the city and liberty of Westminster and . . . to prevent the frequent robberies and riots committed in the streets* (n.d. but c.1750).

30 Radzinowicz, op.cit., ii, p.35.

31 *London Gazette*, 16-20 July 1754.

32 Radzinowicz, op.cit., ii, pp.36,91.

33 ibid., ii, pp.98-101.

34 For rewards offered in Surrey in this period see Beattie, op.cit., pp.50-5.

35 For a full range of the pardons offered see Radzinowicz, op.cit., ii, pp.40-56.

36 ibid., ii, pp.155-61.

37 See the outstanding study by Gerald Howson, *Thieftaker General: the rise and fall of Jonathan Wild* (1970). My account draws heavily on this work.

38 See the well-known 'lives' of Wild by Fielding and Defoe.

39 Hitchen later turned on Wild and denounced him. See Charles Hitchen, *A True Discovery of the Conduct of Receivers and Thieftakers in and about the City of London* (1718).

40 *Select Trials at the Old Bailey* (1742) i, pp.230-1.

41 Howson, op.cit., pp.68-9.

42 Bernard Mandeville, *An Inquiry into the causes of the frequent executions at Tyburn* (1725) p.4.

43 NNC ii, pp.13-84.

44 Howson, op.cit., pp.84-6.

45 Mandeville, op.cit., pp.1-9.

46 4 Geo I c.11.

47 Blackstone famously overrated the effects of the 'Jonathan Wild Act': iv, p.132.

48 For those executed by Wild's contrivance during this period see NNC i, pp.268-72, 311-16, 353-7.

49 Howson, op.cit., p.171.

50 NNC i, pp.171-85.

51 For Carrick and his gang see Daniel Defoe, *Lives of Six Notorious Street Robbers* (1726).

52 NNC i, pp.283-95.

53 See Eveline Cruickshanks (ed.) *The Jacobite Challenge* (Edinburgh, 1988) pp.92-106.

54 Howson, op.cit., p.197.

55 For Sheppard see Christopher Hibbert, *The Road to Tyburn: the story of Jack Sheppard and the eighteenth-century underworld* (1957).

56 NNC i, pp.392-410.

57 Along with Hibbert, see also Daniel Defoe, *The History of the Remarkable Life of Jack Sheppard* (1724); Horace Bleackley, *The Trial of Jack Sheppard* (1933).

58 Hibbert, op.cit., pp.107-15.

59 ibid., p.136-49.

60 See his *Jack Sheppard* (1839).

61 Howson, op.cit., pp.233, 252-3.

62 Anne c.3.

63 Abel Boyer, *The Political State of Great Britain*, 60 vols (1711-40) 29, pp.505-6.

64 Howson's argument is that at 42 Wild was a burnt-out case: 'By 1725 he had top fractures in his skull and his bald head was covered with silver plates. He had seventeen wounds in various parts of his body from swords, daggers and gun shots, contracted in the innumerable affrays, set-tos and riots he always seemed engaged in. His throat had been cut. He was suffering from some sideeffect of syphilis and an incompetent attempt at curing it; on top of all, he had gout, he was in prison and his world had unaccountably started to collapse about his ears.' (Howson, op.cit., pp.245-6).

65 10 & 11 William 3 c.23.

66 Radzinowicz, op.cit., i, p.683.

67 Howson, op.cit., pp.249-50, 264-7.

68 Boyer, *Political State*, op.cit., pp.507-10; cf. also *Select Trials*, op.cit., (1742) ii, pp.284-6.

69 *Daily Journal*, 5 July 1725; *Daily Post*, 5 February 1726.

70 C.de Saussure, *A Foreign View of England in the Reigns of George I and George II*, ed. Van Muyden (1902) p.132.

71 For thief-taking in Surrey see Beattie, op.cit., pp.55-9.

72 *Gentleman's Magazine* 1732 p.1029; 1733 p.493.

73 For an extended discussion see Radzinowicz, op.cit., ii, pp.326-32; cf. also Patrick Pringle, *The Thieftakers* (1958).

74 Radzinowicz, op.cit., ii, p.339.

75 NNC iv, pp.56-9.

76 CNC iii, p.237.

77 Joseph Cox, *A Faithful Narrative of . . . that Bloody-Minded Gang of Thieftakers, alias Thiefmakers* (1756) pp.20-1.

78 And in so doing clearly flouted the strict letter of the law. Blackstone argued that perjury in such cases was tantamount to murder (op.cit., iv, p.196).

79 NNC iv, pp.90-9.

80 For a general survey of the Fielding magistracies see R. Leslie-Melville, *The Life and Work of Sir John Fielding* (1934).

81 John Fielding, *An Account of the Origin and Effects of a Police set on foot by his Grace the duke of Newcastle in the Year 1753 with a plan presented to his Grace by the late Henry Fielding* (1758).

82 See Anthony P. Babington, *A House in Bow Street: Crime and the Magistracy 1740-1881* (1969).

83 Henry Fielding, *Journal of a Voyage to Lisbon* in Leslie Stephen (ed.) *Works* (1882) vii, p.13.

84 ibid., p.46; cf. also W. L. Cross, *Fielding* (1918) ii, p.226; iii, p.13.

85 T. A. Critchley, *A History of Police in England and Wales 900-1966* (1967) pp.32-5.

86 John Fielding, *A Plan for Preventing Robberies within Twenty Miles of London* (1755) p.1.

87 See John Fielding, *Thieving Detested: Being a True and particular description of the various methods and artifices used by Thieves and Sharpers . . . with proper caution to guard against such destructive measures, etc.*

88 W. Melville-Lee, *History of the Police in England*, op.cit., p.367.

89 Gilbert Armitage, *The History of the Bow Street Runners* (reprinted 1932).

90 Fielding, *A Plan for preventing Robberies*, op.cit., p.5.

91 Leslie-Melville, *Life and Works of Sir John Fielding*, op.cit., p.86.

92 30 Geo 2 c.24 (1757) and 39 & 40 Geo 3 c.99 (1785).

93 Add. MSS.38,334 ff. 77-9.

94 See Ben Sedgly and Timothy Beck, *Observations on Mr. Fielding's Enquiry into the late increase of robbers etc . . . to which are added considerations on the nature of government in general; and more particularly the British Constitution . . . in opposition to what has been advanced by the Author of the Enquiry, etc.* (1751).

95 P. Pringle, *Hue and Cry: the Birth of the British Police* (1965) pp.183-94.

96 Radzinowicz, op.cit., iii, pp.47-54.

97 N. McKendrick, J. Brewer, J. H. Plumb (eds) *The Birth of a Consumer Society* (1982); cf. also T. H. Breen, '"Baubles of Britain": the American and consumer revolutions of the eighteenth century', *Past and Present* 119 (1988) pp.73-104. For an American perspective on crime during this period see Douglas Greenberg, *Crime and Law Enforcement in the Colony of New York 1691-1776* (Cornell, 1974).

98 On the treatment of crime by the eighteenth-century press see Jeremy Black, *The English Press in the Eighteenth Century* (1987) pp.81-2.

99 John Styles, 'Sir John Fielding and the problem of criminal investigation in eighteenth-century England', *Transactions of the Royal Historical Society* (1983, 5th series, 33) pp.127-49 (at pp.129-31).

100 Black, op.cit., pp.99-108.

101 Styles, op.cit., pp.136-9.

102 ibid., pp.142-3.

103 ibid., pp.145-9.

104 David Philips, 'A just measure of crime, authority, hunters and blue locusts: the revisionist social history of the crime and the law in Britain 1780-1850', in Stanley Cohen and Andrew Scull (eds) *Social Control and the State* (1983) pp.50-74.

105 Colquhoun, *Treatise on Police*, op.cit., p.298.

106 See Eugène François Vidocq, *Mémoires* (1828).

3 HOMICIDE

1 'All homicide is presumed to be malicious, until the contrary appeareth upon evidence.' (Sir William Blackstone, *Commentaries on the Laws of England*, 4 vols, 9th ed. (1783) iv, p.201.

2 Blackstone, op.cit., iv, pp.178-82.

3 P. E. H. Hair, 'Deaths from violence in Britain: a tentative secular survey', *Population Studies* 25 (1971) pp.5-24.

4 Blackstone, op.cit., iv, pp.182-3.

5 ibid., p.184.

6 J. M. Beattie, *Crime and the Courts in England 1660-1800* (Oxford, 1986) p.95.

7 ibid., pp.92-3.

8 H. B. Baker, *History of the London Stage* (1904) p.72.

9 C. N. C. ii, pp.262-4.

10 Blackstone, op.cit., iv, p.193.

11 See the cases in Leon Radzinowicz *A History of Criminal Law and its Administration from 1750*, 5 vols (1948-86) i, pp.695-8.

12 See the cases in NNC i, pp.171-6; vi, pp.476-80.

13 Blackstone, op.cit., iv, pp.205-7.

14 NNC i, pp.275-80; iv, pp.275-80.

15 Blackstone, op.cit., iv, pp.207-8.

16 See Thomas A. Green, *Verdict according to Conscience: Perspectives on English trial by Jury 1200-1800* (Chicago, 1985) esp. ch.6.

17 NNC iv, pp.186-8.

18 *London Chronicle*, 7-10 July 1764.

19 *General Evening Post*, 12-14 October 1784.

20 *Public Advertiser*, 30 October 1784; *Whitehall Evening Post*, 30 October 1784.

21 NNC iv, pp.368-77.

22 A. Hayward (ed.) *Autobiography of Mrs Piozzi* (1869) i, p.97.

23 Boswell's *Life of Johnson*, ii, p.97.

24 NNC v, pp.318-23.

25 NNC i, pp.337-40.

26 NNC vi, pp.564-8.

27 CNC iii, p.197.

28 See Kathleen Jones, *Lunacy, Law and Conscience 1744-1845* (1955).

29 Nigel Walker, *Crime and Insanity in England: The Historical Perspective* (Edinburgh 1968) pp.56-7.

30 ibid., pp.66-72.

31 J. M. Kaye, 'The early history of murder and manslaughter', *Law Quarterly Review* 83 (1967) pp.365-95; 569-601.

32 Beattie, op.cit., p.105.

33 ibid., pp.105-6.

34 Montesquieu, *L'Esprit des Lois*, Book 6, ch. 16.

35 NNC iv, pp.175-82.

36 CNC ii, pp.296-300.

37 See the cases in NNC i, pp.227-9, 308-11; iii, pp.249-57; iv, pp.50-5.

38 NNC v, pp.17-24.

39 How far the prejudice had grounds in Jewish criminality is discussed in Todd M. Endelman, *The Jews of Georgian London 1714-1830. Tradition and Change in a Liberal Society* (Philadelphia, 1979) pp.192-226, 297-300.

40 NNC i, pp.6-10.

41 *Gentleman's Magazine* 1735 p.558.

42 *Public Advertiser*, 5 April 1764; see also *The Genuine Account of the Trial, Confession and Dying Words of William Corbett* (1764).

43 See the cases in NNC i, pp.72-6, 78-80; vi, pp.209-11, 374-6.

44 NNC vi, p.411.

45 NNC i, pp.166-8.

46 John Brewer, 'The Wilkites and the law 1763-74', in J. Brewer and J. Styles, (eds) *An Ungovernable People* (1980) p.148.

47 ibid., p.149.

48 An appeal was a private suit that, unlike the original indictment, could not be thwarted by a royal pardon. 'The king can no more pardon it than he can remit the damages recovered on an action of battery.' (Blackstone, op.cit., iv, p.316.)

49 *Gentleman's Magazine* 1734 pp.273, 702.

50 See the cases of James Hall (executed 1741), Matthew Henderson (executed 1745), and William Bennington (executed 1795). NNC iii, pp.41-5, 90-4; vi, pp.373-4.

51 NNC iv, pp.239-42.

52 NNC i, pp.229-32.

53 NNC i, pp.242-7.

54 CNC iii, pp.243-4.

55 NNC i, pp.261-3.

56 NNC vi, pp.526-7.

57 CNC iii, pp.244-8.

58 NNC i, pp.341-5.

59 NNC iii, pp.67-9.

60 NNC iv, pp.131-47.

61 NNC ii, pp.219-24.

62 NNC iv, pp.70-4.

63 *London Chronicle*, 7-10 January 1764.

64 NNC vi, pp.736-7.

65 See NNC i, pp.67-72, 301-5; ii, pp.274-8, 323-30, 377-82; iv, pp.365-8; vi, 110-12, 373-4, 751-5.
66 NNC vi, pp.735-6.
67 CNC iii, pp.244-8.
68 See NNC iii, pp.1-9; vi, pp.191-9.
69 NNC vi, pp.154-7.
70 London Chronicle, 5-8 May 1764.
71 NNC i, pp.413-16.
72 NNC iv, pp.23-6.
73 NNC vi, pp.115-16.
74 NNC v, pp.147-50.
75 NNC vi, pp.419-21.
76 NNC vi, pp.483-5.
77 Walpole, Memoirs of the Reign of George III, ii, p.248.
78 London Chronicle, 8-13 April, 13-15 April 1779.
79 Annual Register 1779 p.206.
80 CNC iii, pp.149-50.
81 London Chronicle, 14-16 August 1764.
82 NNC vi, pp.548-50.
83 See, for example, P. J. Grossley, A Tour to London, or new observations on England (trans. Nugent 1772) 2 vols, i, p.60.
84 G. L.le Sage, Remarques sur l'etat présent de l'Angleterre (Amsterdam, 1715) p.132 (le Sage visited England in 1713-14).
85 J. H. Meister, Letters written during a residence in England (trans. 1799) p.120; A. B. F. Baert, Tableau de la Grande Bretagne, 4 vols (Paris, 1800) iv, pp.218-19.
86 P. E. H. Hair, op.cit.
87 Beattie, op.cit., p.89.
88 See Alan MacFarlane, The Justice and the Mare's Ale: Law and Disorder in seventeenth-century England (Oxford, 1981).
89 J. A. Sharpe in 'Domestic homicide in early modern England,' Historical Journal 24 (1981) pp.29-48 raises the possibility of an increased murder rate in the twentieth century as opposed to the sixteenth and seventeenth centuries. But his methodology has been criticized by Beattie, op.cit., pp.105-6, who argues for a constant rate.
90 Beattie, op.cit., pp.110-12, 136-9.
91 Blackstone, op.cit., iv, p.189.
92 Michael Zell, 'Suicide in pre-industrial England', Social History 11 (1986) pp.303-17.
93 See John Adams, An Essay concerning Self-Murder (1700); John Cockburn, A Discourse of Self-Murder (1716).
94 Blackstone, op.cit., iv. p.189.
95 ibid., p.190.
96 R. W. Malcolmson, Life and Labour in England 1700-1780 (1981) pp.83-93.
97 Michael MacDonald, 'The secularisation of suicide in England 1660-1800', Past and Present 111 (1986) p.88.
98 Lester G. Crocker, 'The discussion of suicide in the eighteenth century', Journal of the History of Ideas 13 (1952) pp.47-72.
99 MacDonald, op.cit., p.83.
100 Caleb Fleming, A Dissertation upon the Unnatural Crime of Self Murder (1773) p.17.
101 Gentleman's Magazine 1749 p.341.
102 Gentleman's Magazine 1754 p.507.
103 Walpole Correspondence 20 p.461.
104 London Chronicle, 5-8 November 1774.
105 London Chronicle, 15-17 August 1776.
106 London Chronicle, 23-25 June, 30 June-2 July 1772.
107 London Chronicle, 4-7 August 1764.
108 Gentleman's Magazine 1737 p.315.
109 CNC iv, pp.159-64.
110 Reginald Blunt (ed.) Mrs Montagu, 'Queen of the Blues', 2 vols (1923) i, p.126; cf. also London Chronicle, 21-24 August 1765.
111 Walpole Correspondence 24 p.293.
112 Scots Magazine 1783 p.335.
113 CNC iv, pp.165-8.
114 Walpole Correspondence 25 p.386.
115 London Chronicle, 22-25 January 1780.
116 London Chronicle, 3-8 October 1778.
117 Lloyd's Evening Post, 1-3 January, 6-8 January 1772.
118 Walpole Correspondence 25 pp.386, 408.
119 George Cheyne, The English Malady (1734).
120 Walpole Correspondence 10 pp.166-7.
121 Roland Bartel, 'Suicide in eighteenth-century England: the myth of a reputation', Huntingdon Library Quarterly 23 (1960) pp.145-58, argues that England's notoriety for suicide was based on a myth. For a different view see Peter Laslett, The World We Have Lost Further Explored (1983) p.177.
122 Michael MacDonald, Mystical Bedlam: Madness, Anxiety and Healing in Seventeenth Century England (1981) p.278.
123 Isaac Watts, A Defence against the Temptation to Self-Murther (1726) pp.iii-iv.
124 See, for example, Whitehall Evening

Post, 12-15 June 1784; *Gentleman's Magazine* 1762 pp.151-3.

125 MacDonald, 'Secularisation of suicide', op.cit., p.67.

126 MacDonald, 'Secularisation of suicide', op.cit., pp.50-97, esp. pp.70, 76, 80, 82; cf. also Michael MacDonald and Donna Andrews, 'The secularisation of suicide in England 1660-1800', *Past and Present* 119 (1988) pp.158-70.

127 See, for example, John Tortin, *A Sermon on Different Subjects*, 7 vols (1787) v, pp.147-8; William Rowley, *A Treatise on Female, Nervous, Hysterical, Hypochondriacal, Bilious, Convulsive Diseases . . . with thoughts on Madness, Suicide, etc.* (1788) pp.342-3. Most famous of all the apologists was David Hume in 'Of Suicide'. For a survey of the 'great figures' in English thought and literature who wrote in justification of suicide see S. E. Sprott, *The English Debate on Suicide: from Donne to Hume* (La Salle, 1961).

128 Rousseau,*Du Contrat Social*, Book 2, ch. 5.

129 James Heath, *Eighteenth-Century Penal Theory* (1963) p.237.

130 ibid., p.252.

131 John McManners, *Death and the Enlightenment* (Oxford, 1981) ch.12.

132 See for example Francis Ayscough, *A Discourse against Self-Murder* (1755); George Gregory, *A Sermon on Suicide* (1797); John Herries, *An Address to the Public on the Frequent and Enormous Crime of Suicide* (1774); Charles Moore, *A Full Inquiry into the Subject of Suicide*, 2 vols (1790).

133 Boswell's *Life of Johnson*, iv, p.225.

134 William Lecky, *A History of England in the Eighteenth Century* (1920) iii, pp.139-40.

135 Quoted in Radzinowicz, op.cit., i, p.217.

4 HIGHWAYMEN

1 *Walpole Correspondence* 33 p.296; cf. also ibid., 29 p.160.

2 RA Stuart 158/69.

3 RA Stuart 123/59.

4 NNC i, pp.252-4.

5 NNC iii, p.236.

6 Andrew Michael Ramsay, *Essay on Civil Government* (1732) p.69.

7 Leon Radzinowicz, *A History of Criminal Law and its Administration from 1750*, 5 vols (1948-86) i, p.637.

8 Walpole to Mann, 3 January 1746, *Walpole Correspondence* 19 p.193.

9 4 & 5 Wm & Mary c.8.

10 For general surveys showing the factors that made the eighteenth century the highwayman's 'golden age' see Patrick Pringle, *Stand and Deliver: the Story of the Highwaymen* (1951); Christopher Hibbert, *Highwaymen* (1967).

11 Robert Phillips, *Dissertation concerning the Present State of the High Roads of England, especially those near London* (1736).

12 *Morning Chronicle*, 11 November 1784.

13 Max Beloff, *Public Order and Popular Disturbances*, (1938) p.23.

14 NNC ii, pp.296-314.

15 Pierre Marc de Gaston, duc de Lévis, *L'Angleterre au commencement du dix-neuvième siècle* (Paris, 1814) pp.33-4.

16 NNC ii, pp.369-76.

17 CNC ii, pp.273-9.

18 J. C. Ferri de St. Constant, *Londres et les Anglais*, 4 vols (Paris, 1804) iv, p.167.

19 Ralph Wilson, *A Full and Impartial Account of all the Robberies committed by John Hawkins, George Sympson . . . and their companions* (1722).

20 *Public Advertiser*, 29 February 1764.

21 *Memoirs of Charles Lewis, Baron de Polnitz*, 2 vols (trans. 1738) ii, p.456.

22 Gerald Howson, *Thieftaker General: the rise and fall of Jonathan Wild* (1970) pp.175-6.

23 CNC ii, pp.208-11.

24 *Public Advertiser*, 1 March 1764.

25 *London Chronicle*, 18-21 August 1764.

26 *London Chronicle*, 4-7 August 1764.

27 *London Chronicle*, 18-21 August 1764.

28 *Gentleman's Magazine* 1763 p.200.

29 J. M. Beattie, *Crime and the Courts in England 1660-1800* (Oxford, 1986) p.153.

30 *London Evening Post*, 23 February 1738.

31 *London Chronicle*, 15-18 December 1764.

32 *Walpole Correspondence* 33 p.413.

33 CNC ii, pp.202-5.

34 Hibbert, op.cit., p.35.

35 *London Chronicle*, 10-13 November 1764.

36 CNC ii, pp.114-16.

37 CNC ii, pp.157-61.

38 CNC iii, pp.194-7.

39 *London Chronicle*, 28-31 January 1764.
40 There is very full detail for Turpin's career in these years in D. Barlow, *Dick Turpin and the Gregory Gang* (Chichester, 1973). See also *London Evening Post*, 21 December 1734-11 March 1735, *passim*.
41 NNC ii, p.338.
42 NNC ii, p.340.
43 *London Magazine*, 24 May 1737.
44 NNC ii, p.342.
45 CNC iii, pp.88-97.
46 For Ainsworth and others see Keith Hollingsworth, *The Newgate Novel 1830-1847* (Detroit, 1963).
47 William Plunkett, *A Complete History of James MacLaine* (1750).
48 *A Genuine Account of . . . James MacLaine* (1750).
49 *Gentleman's Magazine* 1750 p.391.
50 *Daily Advertiser*, 10 November 1749; *St James's Evening Post*, 9-11 November 1749.
51 *Genuine Account*, op.cit., p.15.
52 Plunkett, op.cit., p.44; *Genuine Account* op.cit., pp.17-19.
53 *Daily Advertiser*, 28 September 1750; *Gentleman's Magazine* 1750 p.473.
54 Walpole to Mann, 18 October 1750, *Walpole Correspondence* 20 p.199.
55 Same to same, 4 December 1750, *Walpole Correspondence* 20 p.206.
56 *A Genuine Narrative of . . . William Page* (1758).
57 ibid., pp.19-20, 35-7.
58 NNC iv, pp.107-21.
59 *Gentleman's Magazine* 1758 p.143.
60 ibid., p.192.
61 Anon., *The Life of John Rann, alias Sixteen Strings Jack* (1864).
62 Boswell's *Life of Johnson*, iii, p.477.
63 ibid., iv, p.552.
64 NNC v, pp.138-45.
65 Boswell's *Life of Johnson*, iii, p.38.
66 Add. MSS. 27, 826 f.107.
67 NNC vi, pp.570-7.
68 P. Nougaret, *Londres, la cour et les provinces de l'Angleterre, d'Ecosse et d'Irlande* (Paris, 1816) 2 vols, ii, p.239.
69 Baretti, *Journey from London to Genoa*, 2 vols (1770) ii, p.266.
70 F. Lacombe, *Observations sur Londres et ses environs* (1777) p.1.
71 John Wesley, *Journal*, vi, p.177.
72 See for example, *London Chronicle*, 9-11 October 1794.
73 For representative robberies in these locations see *Gentleman's Magazine*

1735 pp.106, 162; N.N.C. i, pp.80-3; iii, pp.46-55, 95-103.
74 See, for example, N.N.C. ii, pp.161-2, 228-9; *St James's Chronicle* 4-7 June 1791; John Cary, *Cary's New Itinerary* (1798); Daniel Lysons, *The Environs of London* (1792-96); G. S. Maxwell, *Highwayman's Heath* (1936). Cf. also *Walpole Correspondence* 12 p.104; 24 p.47.
75 *Walpole Correspondence* 42 p.109.
76 Pepys, *Diary*, 11 April 1661.
77 Daniel Defoe, *Tour through the Whole Island of Great Britain* (1724-6) i, p.143.
78 ibid.
79 William Cobbett, *Rural Rides*, 8 January 1822.
80 William Albert, *The Turnpike Road system in England 1663-1840* (1972).
81 Philip S. Bagwell, *The Transport Revolution from 1770* (1974).
82 Wroth, *The London Pleasure Gardens of the Eighteenth Century* (1896).
83 Add. MSS. 27, 826 f.189; cf. also J. A. Chartres, 'The capital's provincial eyes: London inns in the early eighteenth century', *London Journal* 3 (1977) pp.24-39.
84 Pierre Marc Gaston, duc de Lévis, op.cit., p.30.
85 *Public Advertiser*, 4 January 1764.
86 César de Saussure, *A Foreign View of England in the Reigns of George I and George II*, ed. Van Muyden (1902).
87 Duc de Brunswick, *Promenade autour de la Grande Bretagne* (1795) p.126.
88 Ralph Wilson, *A Full and Impartial Account of all the Robberies committed by John Hawkins, etc* (1722) pp.19-20.
89 ibid., p.17.
90 B. Faujas de St Fond, *A Journey through England and Scotland to the Hebrides*, ed. Sir Archibald Geikie, 2 vols (1907) i, pp.60-3.
91 *London Chronicle*, 14-16 October 1784.
92 *Walpole Correspondence* 11 p.283.
93 ibid., 24 p.47; 32 p.207.
94 *London Chronicle*, 12-14 July 1764.
95 Faujas de St Fond, op. cit.
96 CNC ii, pp.113-14.
97 NNC iv, pp.191-8.
98 NNC v, pp.7-13.
99 See the many examples cited in Captain Alexander Smith, *A Compleat History of the Lives and Robberies of the most Notorious Highwaymen* (1719; reprinted 1933).
100 Abbé le Blanc, *Letters on the English and*

French nations, 2 vols (1747) ii, p.296.

101 Duc de Brunswick, op.cit., p.111.

102 Jacques Casanova, *Mémoires*, trans. Machen (1928) ix, p.170.

103 Johann Wilhelm von Archenholz, *A Picture of England* (1789) ii, p.80.

104 Walpole to Mann, 26 November 1782, *Walpole Correspondence* 25 pp.343-4.

105 J. Fievée, *Lettres sur l'Angleterre* op.cit., p.109; de la Corte, *Voyage philosophique d'Angleterre fait en 1783 et 1784*, 2 vols (1786) i, p.13.

106 See F. J. McLynn, *The Jacobite Army in England 1745: the Final Campaign* (Edinburgh, 1983).

107 Boswell's *Life of Johnson*, iii, pp.239-40.

108 *London Chronicle*, 13-16 October 1764.

109 NNC ii, p.113.

110 *Gentleman's Magazine* 1754 p.242.

111 CNC ii, pp.152-4.

112 CNC ii, pp.257-60.

113 CNC ii, pp.240-1.

114 *London Chronicle*, 17-19, 26-28 July 1764.

115 *London Chronicle*, 5-7 July 1764.

116 *London Chronicle*, 11-13 January 1781; *Daily Advertiser*, 15 January 1781.

117 *Daily Advertiser*, 15 November 1774; *Gentleman's Magazine* 1774 p.538.

118 CNC iii, pp.71-2.

119 P. Burke, *The Romance of the Forum* (n.d.) pp.153-6.

120 *London Chronicle*, 4-6 October 1774.

121 *London Chronicle*, 6-8 October 1774; *Daily Advertiser*, 6 October 1774.

122 *London Chronicle*, 7-9 February 1764.

123 *London Chronicle*, 25-28 February 1764.

124 CNC ii, pp.155-7.

125 *London Chronicle*, 5-8 May 1764.

126 Beattie, op.cit., p.37.

127 See the cases of Joseph Guyant and Joseph Allpren in 1772 (NNC v, pp.91-7).

128 Radzinowicz, op.cit., i., p.214.

129 NNC iii, pp.15-30.

130 NNC i, pp.382-7.

131 NNC v, pp.123-5, 132-5.

132 CNC iii, pp. 210-11.

133 NNC iii, pp.95-103.

134 *London Chronicle*, 19-21 July 1764.

135 *London Chronicle*, 24-26 July 1764.

136 A. Andrews, *The Eighteenth Century* (1856) p.274.

137 CNC ii, pp.230-3.

138 CNC iii, pp.97-9.

139 CNC ii, pp.226-30.

140 *Walpole Correspondence* 22 p.147.

141 CNC ii, pp.129-30.

142 *Hanging not Punishment Enough* (1701) p.18.

143 For a general survey of the years up to 1722 see E. P. Thompson, *Whigs and Hunters* (1975) pp.190-218.

144 *Weekly Journal*, 13, 20 June 1719.

145 Howson, op.cit., p.5.

146 George Rudé, 'Mother Gin and the London riots of 1736', in G. Rudé (ed.) *Paris and London in the Eighteenth Century*, (1970).

147 See *London Evening Post*, 21-23 February 1748; 14-17 January 1749.

148 *Walpole Correspondence* 20 p.188.

149 *Walpole Correspondence* 42 p.109.

150 *Daily Advertiser*, 18 September 1750.

151 *Walpole Correspondence* 11 p.74.

152 Walpole to Dalrymple, 2 May 1763, *Walpole Correspondence* 15 p.90.

153 *London Chronicle*, 23-26 June 1764.

154 ibid.

155 *London Chronicle*, 7-9 August 1764.

156 *London Chronicle*, 15-17 November 1764.

157 *Gentleman's Magazine* 1769 p.508.

158 George Rudé, *Hanoverian London 1714-1808* (1961) p.97.

159 *Walpole Correspondence* 35 p.355.

160 Walpole to Stafford, 3 October 1782, *Walpole Correspondence* 35 p.367; same to same, 23 October 1782, 35 p.525; Walpole to Lady Ossory, 31 August 1782, 33 p.353. Cf. also Walpole to Conway, 20 August 1782, 39 p.391; Walpole to Ossory, 1 October 1782, 33 p.355; Walpole to Mason, 20 September 1782, 29 p.273.

161 *Walpole Correspondence* 33 pp.369-70, 382.

162 Sophie von la Roche, *Sophie in London* (1786, trans. Clare Williams 1933) p.235.

163 *London Chronicle*, 14-16 October 1784.

164 *Walpole Correspondence* 33 pp.371, 476.

165 *St James's Chronicle*, 5-7 July, 12-14 July, 23-26 July 1785.

166 NNC vi, pp.213-15.

167 NNC vi, p.199.

168 NNC vi, pp.460-2, 470-1, 496-7.

169 NNC vi, pp.539-40, 558.

170 NNC vi, pp.728-33.

171 NNC vi, pp.570-7.

172 NNC vi, pp.737-42.

173 V. A. Gatrell, Bruce Lenman, and Geoffrey Parker, *Crime and the Law:*

the social history of crime in Western Europe since 1500 (1980) p.317.

174 Borrow, *Romany Rye*, ch. 24.

175 See the differential amounts being offered in 1740 (*Gentleman's Magazine* 1740 p.198; 1746 (*Gentleman's Magazine* 1746 p.437; 1755 *Gentleman's Magazine* 1755 p.153).

176 Beattie, op.cit., pp.54-5.

5 PROPERTY CRIME

1 *Walpole Correspondence* 22 p.143.

2 An exception was a fire in a wig-maker's in Downing Street in 1742, when the firemen's efficiency attracted general praise (*Daily Advertiser*, 14 July 1742)

3 *Gentleman's Magazine* 1745 p.218.

4 *Daily Advertiser*, 29 June 1752.

5 Add. MSS. 32, 728 f.190.

6 *Daily Advertiser*, 19 June 1789.

7 *London Chronicle*, 12-17 January 1792.

8 *London Chronicle*, 8-10 December, 10-12 December 1789.

9 *London Chronicle*, 3-5 July, 5-8 July 1760.

10 *Daily Advertiser*, 9 May 1785.

11 *London Courant*, 24 January 1782.

12 Leon Radzinowicz, *A History of Criminal Law and its Administration from 1750*, 5 vols (1948-85) i, p.9.

13 31 Geo 2 c.42.

14 10 Geo 2 c.32.

15 12 Geo 3 c.24.

16 Sir William Eden, *Principles of Penal Law*, (1771) p.271.

17 *London Evening Post*, 10-12 January 1738.

18 See, for example, N. N. C. iii, pp.202-10; vi, pp.104-5, 114-15.

19 *London Chronicle*, 15-18 December 1764.

20 NNC vi, p.96.

21 *London Chronicle*, 1-3, 8-10, 17-19 March, 14-16 April, 10-12 May 1768.

22 See NNC i, pp.95-9.

23 *London Chronicle* 5-7 May 1763; *Daily Advertiser*, 9 May 1763.

24 *Public Advertiser*, 15 December 1781.

25 Sir John Clapham, *An Economic History of Modern Britain* (1939) 2 vols, i. p.286.

26 43 Geo 3 c.58.

27 NNC vi, pp.23-64.

28 See the cases cited by Radzinowicz, op.cit., i, pp.688-94.

29 *London Chronicle*, 8-11 September 1764.

30 *Annual Register* 1777 pp.28-31, 166.

31 *London Chronicle*, 6-8 February 1777.

32 John Latimer, *The Annals of Bristol in the Eighteenth Century* (1893) p.427.

33 *London Chronicle*, 11-13 February 1777.

34 NNC v, pp.228-35; Mahon, *History* vi, p.216.

35 CNC iii, pp.69-71.

36 CNC iii, p.248.

37 See Sir William Blackstone, *Commentaries of the Laws of England*, 4 vols, 9th ed. (1783) iv, pp.223-38.

38 ibid., iv, p.240.

39 Radzinowicz, op.cit., i, pp.41-7.

40 5 Anne c.31; 12 Anne c.7.

41 4 Geo 3 c.37.

42 For the many executions for burglary and housebreaking see NNC i, pp.63-6, 83-6; ii, pp.139-53, 232-51, 314-18; iii, pp.55-63, 166-70, 242-6; iv, pp.242-6; v, pp.270-8, 292-6, 305-11, 324-9, 348-52.

43 NNC v, pp.87-91.

44 NNC i, pp.99-104.

45 NNC vi, p.123.

46 CNC ii, pp.246-9.

47 Gerald Howson, *Thieftaker General: the rise and fall of Jonathan Wild* (1970) pp.190-1.

48 Derek Barlow, *Dick Turpin and the Gregory Gang*, op.cit., pp.43-99.

49 J. M. Beattie, *Crime and the Courts in England 1660-1800* (Oxford, 1986) p.165.

50 ibid., p.164.

51 For executions for this offence during this period see NNC iv, pp.268-73, 362; v, pp.13-17, 97-102, 110-14, 145-7.

52 George Rudé, *Hanoverian London 1714-1808* (1961) p.97.

53 *Annual Register* 1770 p.78.

54 William Lecky, *History of England in the Eighteenth Century* (1920) iii, p.325.

55 *Daily Advertiser* 9 January 1772.

56 *Walpole Correspondence* 32 p.77.

57 ibid., 32 p.213.

58 ibid., 31 p.185.

59 ibid., 31 p.298.

60 CNC iv, pp.183-4.

61 Beattie, op.cit., p.163.

62 See the case of Richard Thomas, executed in 1794 (NNC vi, p.200).

63 CNC iii, pp.221-2.

64 *Walpole Correspondence* 23 p.285.

65 ibid., 14 pp.189-90.

66 Walpole to Gray, 25 March 1771, *Walpole Correspondence* 14 p.189.
67 Radzinowicz, op.cit., i, p.633.
68 12 Anne c.7.
69 NNC iv, pp.268-73.
70 Beattie, op.cit., p.174.
71 ibid., p.175.
72 NNC vi, pp.162-4, 170-1, 187-8.
73 NNC vi, pp.368-73.
74 NNC vi, pp.198-200.
75 NNC i, pp.17-23.
76 10 & 11 William 3 c.23.
77 *Public Advertiser*, 18 January 1764.
78 *Public Advertiser*, 3 March 1764; *Gentleman's Magazine* 1764 p.144.
79 *London Chronicle*, 14-17 July 1764.
80 *London Evening Post* 7-9 March, 1-3 June 1738.
81 See, for example, NNC i, pp.24-7, 272-5; iii, pp.170-4; vi, pp.439-40, 449, 722.
82 *Gentleman's Magazine* 1769 p.165.
83 R. A. E. Wells, 'Sheep rustling in Yorkshire in the age of the industrial and agrarian revolutions', *Northern History* 20 (1984) pp.127-45.
84 14 Geo 2 c.6.
85 NNC iv, pp.188-91.
86 *London Chronicle*, 10-12 July 1764.
87 22 Geo 2 c.33.
88 *London Chronicle*, 10-12 July 1764.
89 *London Chronicle*, 24-27 March 1764.
90 NNC vi, pp.203-6.
91 NNC vi, p.554.
92 NNC vi, p.722.
93 CNC ii, pp.235-9.
94 NNC vi, pp.551-4.

6 WOMEN AS VICTIMS OF CRIME

1 See, for example, John Brown, *An Estimate of the Manners and Principles of the Times* (1757); Jonas Hanway, *The Defects of Police: the cause of immorality* (1775).
2 Sir William Blackstone, *Commentaries on the Laws of England*, 4 vols, 9th ed. (1783) iv, p.64.
3 Henry Fielding, *Works*, ed. Leslie Stephen, (1882) vii, pp.179, 233, 269.
4 *Covent Garden Journal*, 4 January, 4 February 1752.
5 *Covent Garden Journal*, 10 March, 21 October, 28 October 1752.
6 Blackstone, op.cit., iii, p.139; iv, p.65.
7 *Gentleman's Magazine* 1750 pp.457-9.
8 Patrick Colquhoun, *Treatise on the Police of the Metropolis* (1800) p.48.
9 ibid., p.626.
10 Cobbett's *Parliamentary History of England*, 20 (1778-80): House of Commons, cols 597-601; House of Lords, cols 592-7.
11 ibid., 35 (1800-01) cols 225-300.
12 John Wesley, *Works* (1771) iv, pp.87-8.
13 See the discussion in P. G. Bouce (ed.) *Sexuality in Eighteenth Century Britain* (Manchester, 1982).
14 W. Bonger, *Criminality and Economic Conditions* (1916) pp.668-9.
15 Boswell's *Life of Johnson*, iii, p.470.
16 ibid., iii, pp.17-18.
17 Bernard Mandeville, *A Modest Defence of Public Stews or an Essay upon Whoring as it is now practised in these kingdoms* (1724), esp. pp.12-15.
18 Boswell's *Life of Johnson*, iv, p.75.
19 ibid., i, p.457; iv, pp.321-2.
20 Peter Linebaugh, 'The Tyburn riot against the surgeons', in D. Hay, E. P. Thompson, and P. Linebaugh (eds) *Albion's Fatal Tree* (1975) p.96.
21 Colquhoun, op.cit., pp.337-45.
22 ibid., p.629.
23 J. A. Sharpe, *Crime in Early Modern England*, (1984) pp.114-15.
24 Anon., *Thoughts on Means of Alleviating the miseries attendant upon common prostitution*(1799).
25 Colquhoun, op.cit., p.340.
26 *London Chronicle*, 8-11 September 1764.
27 *Walpole Correspondence* 18 p.70.
28 *Gentleman's Magazine* 1742 p.386. For an entertaining recent survey see E. J. Burford, *Wits, Wenches and Wantons: London's Low Life, Covent Garden in the Eighteen Century* (1986).
29 Gerald Howson, *Thieftaker General: the rise and fall of Jonathan Wild* (1970) pp.44-5.
30 *Walpole Correspondence* 9 p.19.
31 See Anon., *Satan's Harvest Home* (1749).
32 Saunders Welch, *A Proposal to render effectual a plan to remove the nuisance of Common Prostitutes* (1758), esp. pp.58-9.
33 Leon Radzinowicz, *A History of Criminal Law and its Administration from 1750*, 5 vols (1948-86) ii, p.198.
34 *London Chronicle*, 17-19 May 1764.
35 NNC i, pp.29-31.
36 *London Chronicle* 31 January-2 February 1764.

37 *London Chronicle*, 3-5 May 1764.
38 *London Chronicle*, 10-13 November 1764.
39 Walpole to Mann, 17 September 1778, *Walpole Correspondence* 24 p.413.
40 Howson, op.cit., p.46.
41 *London Chronicle*, 9-12 June 1764.
42 25 Geo 2 c.36.
43 *London Chronicle*, 2-4 February 1764.
44 Saunders Welch, op.cit., pp.23-6.
45 See NNC ii, p.27.
46 For a general survey of the changing economic role of prostitution see·T. E. Jones, *Prostitution and the Law* (1951).
47 NNC i, pp.58-63.
48 Blackstone, op.cit., iv, p.29.
49 NNC v, pp.153-5.
50 NNC iv, pp.304-7.
51 NNC i, pp.367-75.
52 NNC i, pp14-17.
53 NNC vi, pp.441-3.
54 NNC vi, pp.196-8.
55 NNC vi, pp.105-8.
56 NNC iv, pp.128-30.
57 NNC iv, p.3-9.
58 NNC i, pp.116-18.
59 NNC iv, pp.10-23.
60 Blackstone, iv, pp.165-6.
61 NNC iv, pp.64-70.
62 William Lecky, *A History of England in the Eighteenth Century* (1920) vii, p.322.
63 For the historical background see N. Bashar, 'Rape in England between 1550 and 1700', in *The Sexual Dynamics of History* (1980) pp.28-46.
64 J. M. Beattie, *Crime and the Courts in England 1660-1800* (Oxford, 1986) p.124.
65 Blackstone, op.cit., iv, p.215.
66 NNC v, pp.311-18.
67 NNC v, pp.241-6.
68 *London Chronicle*, 1-4 September 1764.
69 Beattie, op.cit. p.127.
70 NNC ii, pp.209-18.
71 See A. Simpson, 'Masculinity and control: the prosecution of sex offences in eighteenth-century London', Ph. D. thesis, NY Univ., 1984; cf. also Anna Clark, *Women's Silence, Man's Violence: Sexual Assault in England 1770-1845* (1987).
72 Beattie, op.cit., p.130.
73 ibid., p.128.
74 NNC vi, pp.527-8.
75 NNC vi, pp.464-6.
76 NNC vi, pp.361-3.
77 NNC vi, pp.508-15.

78 NNC vi, pp.524-6.
79 NNC vi, pp.757-8.
80 As when a woman returning from Bath on horseback in 1764 was pulled from her horse and raped by a footpad (*London Chronicle*, 14-17 January 1764).
81 See a brilliant discussion of the topic by Roy Porter, 'Rape – does it have a historical meaning?' in R. Porter and Sylvana Tomaselli (eds) *Rape* (1986) pp.217-23.
82 Beattie, op.cit., p.104.
83 Blackstone, op.cit., iv, p.212.
84 NNC v, pp.115-16.
85 NNC v, pp.251-4.
86 Cf. Blackstone: 'There is also one species of battery more atrocious and penal than the rest, which is the beating of a clerk in orders or clergyman on account of the respect and reverence due to his social character as the minister and ambassador of peace.' (op.cit., iv, p.217).
87 CNC ii, pp.265-70.
88 Beattie, op.cit., p.433.
89 Porter and Tomaselli, *Rape*, op.cit., p.7.
90 Sir William Eden, *Principles of Penal Law*, (1771) pp.261, 269.
91 Beattie, op.cit.. pp.130-2.
92 Radzinowicz, op.cit., i, pp.436-42.
93 See the Discussion in Bonger, op.cit., pp.644-7.
94 Peter C. Hoffer and N. E. Hull, *Murdering Mothers: Infanticide in England and New England 1558-1803* (NY, 1981) include children up to the age of nine years. Beattie, in a convincing critique of this approach, argues that this unacceptably extends and attenuates the notion of infanticide (Beattie, op.cit., p.113).
95 21 Jac.1 c.27.
96 Pierre Marc Gaston, duc de Lévis, *L'Angleterre au commencement du dix-neuvième siècle* (Paris, 1814) p.122.
97 R. W. Malcolmson, 'Infanticide in the eighteenth century', in J. S. Cockburn (ed.) *Crime in England 1550-1800*, (1977) pp.187-209.
98 ibid., p.202.
99 NNC vi, pp.69-72.
100 Radzinowicz, op.cit., i, pp.431-3.
101 Blackstone, op.cit., iv, p.65.
102 Daniel Defoe, *Augusta Triumphans: or the way to make London the most flourishing city in the universe* (1728) p.9.

103 Malcolmson, op.cit., p.205.
104 NNC i, pp.138-40.
105 *London Chronicle*, 12-14 June 1764.
106 NNC iv, pp.151-9.
107 Beattie, op.cit., p.117.
108 Malcolmson, op.cit., pp.187-209.
109 ibid., p.198.
110 Defoe, op.cit., pp.9-10.
111 Beattie, op.cit., pp.119-20.
112 D. Seaborne Davies, 'Child-killing in English law', in L. Radzinowicz and J. W. C. Turner (eds) *The Modern Approach to Criminal Law* pp.301-43.
113 Beattie, op.cit., p.121.
114 ibid., pp.84-5.
115 *London Chronicle*, 28-31 July 1764.
116 Blackstone, op.cit., iv, p.198.
117 Cobbett's *Parliamentary History of England* 17 (1771-74) cols 699-700.
118 NNC vi, pp.218-20, 415, 487-8.
119 For the later story see Lionel Rose, *Infanticide in Britain 1800-1939* (1986).

7 WOMEN AS CRIMINALS

1 NNC vi, pp.468-70.
2 M. D. George, *London Life in the Eighteenth Century* (1925) p.231.
3 *Gentleman's Magazine* 1767 p.433.
4 NNC iv, pp.308-18.
5 NNC iv, pp.219-27.
6 J. M. Beattie, *Crime and the Courts in England 1660-1800* (Oxford, 1986) p.106.
7 W. Bonger, *Criminality and Economic Conditions* (Bloomington, Indiana, 1969) p.58.
8 ibid., p.160.
9 Beattie, op.cit., p.101.
10 NNC iv, pp.358-61.
11 NNC i, pp.333-7.
12 NNC vi, pp.402-10.
13 NNC vi, pp.187, 212-13, 215-17.
14 See Otto Pollock, *The Criminality of Women* (NY, 1950).
15 NNC i, pp.135-8.
16 NNC iv, pp.27-9.
17 NNC iv, pp.280-6.
18 CNC ii, pp.148-52.
19 NNC i, pp.151-65.
20 Sir William Blackstone, *Commentaries on the Laws of England*, 4 vols, 9th ed. (1783) iv, p.75.
21 See *London Magazine* 1735 pp.390, 451; cf. N.N.C. iii, pp.277-80.
22 NNC iv, pp.246-52.
23 Leon Radzinowicz, *A History of Criminal Law and its Administration from 1750*, 5 vols (1948-86) i, pp.476-77.
24 Blackstone, op.cit., iv, p.93.
25 W. Andrews, *Bygone Punishments* (1931) p.92.
26 A. Marks, *Tyburn Tree* (1908) pp.235-6.
27 NNC iii, p.301.
28 NNC ii, pp.99-129.
29 Beattie, op.cit., p.97.
30 NNC vi, pp.451-5.
31 NNC vi, pp.515-21.
32 Andrews, op.cit., pp.94-5.
33 Cobbett's *Parliamentary History of England*, (1777-78) cols 234-42.
34 *Gentleman's Magazine* 1786 p.524; *Gentleman's Magazine* 1789 p.272; W. Andrews, op.cit., p.92; W. C. Sydney, *England and the English in the Eighteenth Century* (1892), ii, pp.300-1; H. Bleackley, *The Hangmen of England* (1929) pp.138-9.
35 NNC i, pp.258-60; Marks, op.cit., p.231.
36 NNC vi, p.528.
37 NNC vi, pp.550-1.
38 NNC i, pp.145-7.
39 Boswell's *Life of Johnson*, ii, p.217.
40 NNC vi, pp.471-2.
41 NNC i, pp.123-5.
42 NNC vi, pp.713-21.
43 *London Chronicle*, 24-27 March 1764.
44 NNC v, pp.150-2.
45 NNC iii, pp.395-7.
46 Cobbett's *Parliamentary History of England*, op.cit. (1777-78) cols 234-42.
47 Peter King, 'Decision-makers and decision-making in the English criminal law, 1750-1800', *Historical Journal* 27 (1984) pp.25-58 (at pp.41-2).
48 CNC ii, pp.205-6.
49 Howson, *Thieftaker General: the rise and fall of Jonathan Wild* (1970) p.277.
50 ibid., p.42.
51 CNC ii, pp.169-71.
52 NNC vi, pp.193-4.
53 CNC iv, pp.25-6.
54 *London Chronicle*, 18-20 September 1764.
55 NNC v, p.289.
56 *London Chronicle*, 8-10 March 1764.
57 NNC iii, pp.86-90.
58 NNC i, pp.306-8; iii, pp.246-9.
59 NNC ii, pp.382-9.
60 *London Evening Post*, 2 November 1738.
61 Howson, op.cit., p.157, 161.
62 CNC ii, pp.171-2.
63 CNC iv, pp.97-8.

64 King, 'Decision-making', op.cit., p.35.
65 John Howard, *The State of Prisons* (1784) p.484.
66 Beattie, op.cit., pp.436-9.
67 ibid., p.535.
68 J. M. Beattie, 'Crime and the Courts in Surrey, 1736-1753', in J. S. Cockburn (ed) *Crime in England 1550-1800*, (1970) pp.182-3.
69 G. R. Elton, Introduction to Cockburn, op.cit., p.13.
70 Beattie, *Crime and the Courts in England*, op.cit., pp.436-9.
71 J. M. Beattie, 'The criminality of women', *Journal of Social History* 8 (1975) pp.80-116.
72 Bonger, op.cit., p.60.
73 Beattie, *Crime and the Courts in England*, op.cit., p.535.
74 *Public Advertiser*, 21 December 1784.
75 'A woman must not wear man's clothes, or a man go clad as a woman; all such things are hateful to God.' (Knox translation).
76 *London Chronicle*, 25-28 August 1764.
77 *London Chronicle*, 11-13 December 1764.
78 *London Chronicle*, 4-7 August 1764.
79 *London Chronicle*, 6-8 December 1764.
80 *London Chronicle*, 24-27 November 1764.
81 Beattie, 'The criminality of women', op.cit., p.90.
82 NNC vi, pp.348-89.
83 *Gentleman's Magazine* 1785 pp.151, 662.
84 CNC iii, pp.136-7.
85 *Gentleman's Magazine* 1777 pp.348, 402.
86 CNC iv, pp.16-17.
87 *London Chronicle*, 10-12 October 1799.
88 NNC vi, pp.580-93.
89 *London Chronicle*, 31 October-2 November 1799,
90 *London Chronicle*, 3-5 December 1799.
91 *Gentleman's Magazine* 1750 pp.532-3.
92 NNC i, pp.247-8.
93 Beattie, *Crime and the Courts in England*, op.cit., pp.237-43.
94 K. D. M. Snell, 'Agricultural seasonal unemployment, the standard of living, and women's work in the South and East 1690-1860', *Economic History Review*, 2nd series 34 (1981) pp.407-37.
95 John Stevenson, *Popular Disturbances in England 1700-1870* pp.101-2.
96 Douglas Hay, 'War, dearth and theft', *Past and Present* 95 (1982) p.135.
97 Ivy Pinchbeck, *Women Workers and the Industrial Revolution 1750-1850* (1930) pp.168-9.
98 Hay, op.cit., p.144

8 CRIMES OF THE POWERFUL

1 Quoted by Philip Jenkins in 'Into the Underworld? Law, crime and punishment in English Society', *Social History* 12 (1987) pp.93-102.
2 Peter Laslett, *The World We Have Lost Further Explored* (1983) pp.19, 66.
3 Gerald Howson, *The Macaroni Parson* (1973) p.124.
4 Some of the most important statutes directed against forgery were 2 Geo 2 c.25 (1729); 7 Geo 2 c.22 (1734); 31 Geo 2 c.25 (1757) and 18 Geo III c.18 (1778).
5 Leon Radzinowicz, *A History of Criminal Law and its Administration from 1750*, 5 vols (1948-86) i, p.642-50.
6 NNC iii, pp.151-5, 158-61, 174-80, 258-64, 284-90, 294-7, 302-6, 378-82; iv, pp.325-9, 363-5; v, pp.24-39, 62-77; vi, pp.65-7, 92-3, 97-8, 417-18, 437-9, 480-1, 491-2, 528, 536-9.
7 NNC iv, pp.232-9, 300-3.
8 NNC iv, pp.198-206.
9 *London Chronicle*, 20-23 February, 24-26 March 1768.
10 NNC vi, pp.555-7.
11 NNC vi, pp.521-4.
12 NNC vi, pp.124-7.
13 8 Geo I c.22.
14 See the cases at N.N.C. iv, pp.103-6; vi, pp.540-2, 568.
15 Especially 31 Geo 2 c.22 (1757); 4 geo 3 c.25 (1763); 33 Geo 3 c.30 (1797).
16 NNC vi, pp.437-9.
17 NNC iv, pp.30-7.
18 NNC vi, pp.178-82.
19 NNC vi, pp.201-3.
20 NNC vi, pp.596-710.
21 CNC ii, pp.255-7.
22 NNC iv, pp.147-51.
23 NNC iv, pp.252-7.
24 *Public Advertiser*, 30 March 1775; *Lloyd's Evening Post*, 27-29 March 1775.
25 *Lloyd's Evening Post* 5-7 April 1775.
26 *London Chronicle*, 4-6 April 1775.
27 *Gentleman's Magazine* 1775 pp.278-84.
28 *Annual Register*, 1775 pp.222-3.
29 NNC v, pp.155-80.
30 H. Bleackley, *Some Distinguished Victims of the Scaffold* (1905) pp.66-7.

31 NNC v, pp.181-5.

32 *Annual Register*, 1776 p.231.

33 Walpole to Mason, 13 March 1777, *Walpole Correspondence* 28 p.289.

34 Boswell's *Letters* (ed. 1857) pp.223-30.

35 See Gerald Howson, op.cit., for a definitive account.

36 NNC v, pp.105-110.

37 NNC v, pp.207-27.

38 Boswell's *Life of Johnson*, iii. pp.144-8.

39 *Scots Magazine* 1777 pp.105-6; *Annual Register* 1777 pp.232-40.

40 Walpole, *Memoirs of the Reign of George III*, ii. pp.124-5; Wraxall *Historical Memoirs*, (1836) iv, p.249.

41 J. H. Jesse, *George Selwyn and his Contemporaries* (1844) iii, p.195; cf. also J. Campbell, *The Lives of the Chief Justices*, iii, p.320.

42 John Wesley, *Journal*, 25 May 1777.

43 H. Bleackley, *The Hangmen of England*, (1929) p.120.

44 CNC iv, pp.156-8.

45 NNC v, pp.246-50.

46 There is a huge bibliography on the Dodd case, conveniently assembled in Howson's exemplary *Macaroni Parson*, (1973).

47 5 Geo 2 c.30.

48 Especially 28 Geo 2 c.13 (1755) and 37 Geo 3 c.124 (1797).

49 NNC im pp.147-50.

50 NNC v, pp.254-61; cf. also the case of John Perrott in 1761 (NNC iv, p.206-13).

51 See *Annual Register* 1778 p.36. Cf.also the cases chronicled in *London Magazine* 1766 pp.51, 132-3; 1768 pp.53, 164.

52 See NNC iv, pp.59-63.

53 4 Geo I c.12; 11 Geo. I c.29.

54 NNC vi, pp.884-94.

55 NNC ii, pp.206-9.

56 27 Geo 2 c.15.

57 See the exhaustive study by E. P. Thompson, 'The Crime of Anonymity', in *Albion's Fatal Tree* (1975) pp.255-344.

58 Jenkins, op.cit., p.99.

59 Laurence Stone, *The Crisis of the Aristocracy* (1965) pp.242-50. Cf. also J. C. D. Clark, *English Society 1688-1832* (Cambridge, 1985) pp.106-18.

60 Sir William Blackstone, *Commentaries on the Laws of England*, 4 vols, 9th ed. (1783) iv, pp.145, 185.

61 ibid., p.199.

62 Donna Andrews, 'The code of honour and its critics: the opposition to duelling in England 1700-1850', *Social History* 5 (1980). See also Victor Kiernan, *The Duel in European history* (1988).

63 J. M. Beattie, *Crime and the Courts in England 1660-1800* (Oxford, 1986) p.98.

64 CNC iii, pp.178-80.

65 *London Chronicle*, 4-7 February 1764.

66 *London Chronicle*, 7-9 February 1764.

67 *London Chronicle*, 18-21 February 1764.

68 *London Chronicle*, 1-3 March 1764.

69 *Annual Register* 1779 pp.235-6.

70 *London Chronicle*, 27-30 November 1779; cf. also *London Evening Post*, 25-27 November 1779; *Public Advertiser*, 2 December 1779.

71 *London Chronicle*, 23-25 March 1780.

72 *Public Advertiser*, 23 March 1780.

73 Percy Fitzgerald, *Life and Times of John Wilkes* (1888) i, pp.95-107.

74 Walpole, *Memoirs of the Reign of George III*, i, p.152.

75 *London Chronicle*, 15-17 November 1763.

76 *London Chronicle*, 23-25 August 1763.

77 *Whitehall Evening Post*, 21-23 March 1780.

78 Francis Ayscough, *Duelling and Murder Repugnant to Revelation, Reason and Common Sense* (1774).

79 Isaac Watts, *Self-Murther and Duelling the Effects of Cowardice and Atheism* (1728).

80 Walpole, *Memoirs of the Reign of George III*, op.cit., i, p.202.

81 Henry Fielding, *Tom Jones*, Book VII, ch. 3.

82 Boswell's *Life of Johnson*, ii, pp.179-80.

83 ibid., ii, p.226.

84 ibid., iv, p.211; v. p.24.

85 ibid., v, pp.578-9.

86 *Walpole Correspondence* 23 pp.255-6.

87 *Public Advertiser*, 16, 20 January, 3 February 1773.

88 Walpole, *Memoirs . . . George III*, op.cit., i, pp.17-18.

89 *London Chronicle*, 13-15 January 1774.

90 *Walpole Correspondence* 17 pp.172-3.

91 *London Chronicle*, 19-21 November, 21-26 November, 19-22 December 1778.

92 *London Chronicle*, 13-18 November 1777.

93 *Walpole Correspondence* 18 pp.191-2.

94 T. B. Howell, *A Complete Collection of State Trials*, 34 vols (1816-28), 19 pp.1185-91.

95 *Walpole Correspondence* 25 p.96.

96 ibid., 17 p.248.
97 Alfred Spencer, (ed.) *The Memoirs of William Hickey* (1913-25), i, pp.287-97; cf. also Mary MacCarthy, *Fighting Fitzgerald* (1930).
98 *Public Advertiser*, 20 March 1775.
99 *Gentleman's Magazine* 1786 pp.346-7, 518-20.
100 *Walpole Correspondence* 9 p.108.
101 William Wilberforce, *Life* (by his sons) (1838) i, pp.280-4.
102 *Walpole Correspondence* 20 p.289.
103 Wilberforce, op.cit., i, p.356; ii, p.93.
104 *Whitehall Evening Post* 21-23 December 1784.
105 *London Chronicle*, 19-21 November 1778.
106 *Gentleman's Magazine* 1783 p.892.
107 *Gentleman's Magazine* 1783 p.362.
108 *Gentleman's Magazine* 1752 p.90.
109 C. G. Butler, *Colonel St Paul of Ewart, Soldier and Diplomat* (1911).
110 A posthumous pamphlet, *Vindication of an Innocent Lady* (1751) rebutted the charge.
111 *Walpole Correspondence* 20 p.563.
112 ibid., 20 p.496.
113 *London Chronicle*, 11-13 June 1782.
114 Beattie, op.cit., p.89.
115 J. A. Sharpe, *Crime in Early Modern England*, (1984), pp.97-9.
116 *London Chronicle*, 18-21 August 1764,
117 Peter King, 'Decision-makers and decision-making in the English criminal law, 1750-1800', *Historical Journal* 27 (1984) p.47.
118 *Walpole Correspondence* 19 p.387.
119 See, for example, *London Chronicle*, 15-18 December 1764.
120 NNC vi, pp.108-9.
121 *Gentleman's Magazine* (March, 1731).
122 NNC iv, p.329-54.
123 NNC v, pp.186-200.
124 Walpole to Mann, 24 April 1776, *Walpole Correspondence* 24 p.196.
125 CNC iii, p.76.
126 *The Trial of Laurence, Earl Ferrers* (1760) pp.39-40.
127 *Gentleman's Magazine* 1760 p.232.
128 *Daily Advertiser*, 24 April 1760.
129 *Gentleman's Magazine* 1760 p.234.
130 NNC iv, pp.159-70.
131 *Gentleman's Magazine* 1760 p.235.
132 *Walpole Correspondence* 21 pp.400-2.
133 *Gentleman's Magazine* 1760 p.236.
134 Howell, op.cit., 16 pp.767 *et seq.* Cf. also J. Campbell, *Lives of the Lord Chancellors and Keepers of the Great Seal of England*, 8 vols (1845-69).
135 J. H. Plumb, *Sir Robert Walpole* (1961), ii, p.110.
136 For Wharton see Leslie Melville, *Philip, Duke of Wharton* (1913). Cf. also Mark Ord-Blackett, *Hell-Fire Duke* (1982).
137 Gerald Howson, *Thieftaker General: the rise and fall of Jonathan Wild* (1970) pp.281-2.
138 E. P. Thompson, *Whigs and Hunters* (1975) p.218.
139 John Carswell, *The South Sea Bubble* (1960) p.210.
140 ibid., p.264.
141 Thompson, op.cit., p.217.
142 Quoted in ibid.
143 Bernard Mandeville, *The Fable of the Bees*, ed. Philip Harth (1970) p.183.
144 Neville Williams, *Contraband Cargoes* (1960) pp.176-7.
145 J. H. Plumb, *The Growth of Political Stability in England* (1970) p.21.
146 Quoted by John Brewer, 'The Wilkites and the Law', in J. Brewer and J. Styles, *An Ungovernable People*, (1980) p.128.
147 *The Craftsman*, no.320, 19 August 1732.
148 See P. J. Marshall, *The Impeachment of Warren Hastings* (Oxford, 1965).
149 *Journal of the House of Commons* 38 pp.987, 1004-5, 1039, 1042, 1054-5, 1065, 1138.
150 *London Chronicle*, 1-3 May 1783.
151 *Journal of the House of Commons* 39 pp.81, 398, 520.
152 Walpole to Mann, 30 April 1783, *Walpole Correspondence* 25 p.400.
153 Namier and Brooke (eds) *History of Parliament: The Commons 1754-1790* (1964), iii, p.283.
154 Walpole, *Memoirs of the Reign of George III*, iii, p.159; cf. Boswell's *Life of Johnson*, ii, p.339.
155 Boswell's *Life of Johnson*, v, p.106.
156 ibid., iv, pp.213-14.
157 Walpole to Mann, 26 August 1785, *Walpole Correspondence* 25 pp.603-4.
158 Walpole to Mann, 30 April 1783, *Walpole Correspondence* 25 p.400.
159 Walpole to Mann, 6 October 1774, *Walpole Correspondence* 24 p.47.

9 HIGH TREASON

1 Sir William Blackstone, *Commentaries on the Laws of England*, 4 vols, 9th ed. (1783) iv, pp.75-91.

2 13 & 14 William 3 c.3.

3 1 Anne c.17.

4 2 & 3 Anne c.20.

5 6 Anne c.7.

6 17 Geo II c.30.

7 9 Geo II c.30.

8 29 Geo II c.17.

9 20 Geo II c.46.

10 NNC i, pp.10-15.

11 NNC i, pp.125-31.

12 NNC i, pp.206-21.

13 NNC i, pp.187-206.

14 NNC i, pp.232-9.

15 NNC i, pp.249-52.

16 NNC i, pp.316-21.

17 W. A. Speck, *The Butcher: The Duke of Cumberland and the Suppression of the '45* (1981) p.177; cf. also Annette M. Smith, *Jacobite Estates of the Forty-Five* (Edinburgh, 1982).

18 Blackstone, op.cit., iv, p.380.

19 See John Prebble, *Culloden* (1961) ch.5.

20 See S. Schafer, *The Political Criminal: the problem of Morality and Crime* (1974).

21 Cobbett's *Parliamentary History of England* 1777-78, cols 234-42.

22 There is a huge literature on the trial of the Jacobite rebel lords. Fundamental is *The Whole Proceedings in the House of Peers upon the indictment against William, Earl of Kilmarnock . . . and Arthur Lord Balmerino* (1746). Cf. also Add. MSS. 32, 707 f. 505; *Daily Advertiser*, 30, 31 July 1746; T. B. Howell, *A Complete Collection of State Trials*, 34 vols (1816-28) 18 pp.338-850; *Walpole Correspondence* 9 pp.40-2; 19 pp.280-9; Boswell's *Life of Johnson*, i, p.180.

23 *The Whole Proceedings in the House of Peers upon the Impeachment . . . against Simon Lord Lovat* (1747); *Journal of the House of Commons* 25 pp.211-56.

24 Adam Wilkinson, *Official Diary* (Camden Society, 3rd series, 22, 1912).

25 *Daily Advertiser*, 26 July, 25 August, 30 August 1746; 8 April, 10 April 1747.

26 J. S. Cockburn (ed.) *Crime in England 1550-1800*, (1977) p.336.

27 *Gentleman's Magazine* 1753 p.292; Walpole, *Memoirs of the Reign of George II*, i, p.133.

28 Boswell's *Life of Johnson*, i, p.146.

29 See F. J. McLynn, 'Jacobitism and David Hume', *Hume Studies* 9 (1983) pp.171-99.

30 Blackstone, op.cit., iv, pp.382-5.

31 Quoted with approval by Sir William Eden in his denunciation of forfeiture: *Principles of Penal Law* (1771) pp.46-9. For a defence of the practice by one of the Whig hardliners of the '45 see Philip Yorke, *Some Considerations on the Law of Forfeiture for High Treason* (1748).

32 McLynn, op.cit.

33 Rohan Butler, *Choiseul* (1981) p.624.

34 Blackstone, op.cit., iv, pp.115-16.

35 Historical Manuscripts Commission, v, pp.188-9.

36 RA Stuart 253/51.

37 R. C. Jarvis, *Collected Papers on the Jacobite Risings* (Manchester, 1972), ii, pp.169-88.

38 Walpole to Mann, 27 September 1745, *Walpole Correspondence* 19 p.116.

39 Carl L. Klose, *Memoirs of Prince Charles Stuart, Count of Albany* (1845) p.238.

40 RA Stuart 78/181.

41 Apart from the *Calm Address* see RA Stuart 169/19.

42 *A Full Collection of the Proclamations and Orders Published by Order of Charles, Prince of Wales* (Glasgow, 1746) p.29.

43 RA Stuart 228/129.

44 RA Stuart 130/133.

45 RA Stuart 205/16.

46 Howell, op.cit., 18 p.499.

47 For a full discussion see F. J. McLynn, *France and the Jacobite Rising of 1745* (Edinburgh, 1981).

48 See the cases at NNC ii, pp.10-13; iii, pp.180-8; iv, p.318-22; v, pp.77-82.

49 *Morning Post*, 7 March 1777.

50 8 & 9 William 3 c.26, made permanent in 7 Anne c.25. See also Blackstone, iv, p.90.

51 15 Geo 2 c.28. See also Blackstone, iv, p.91.

52 D. MacPherson, *Annals of Commerce* (1805), iii, p.193.

53 R. Ruding, *Annals of Coinage* (1840) ii, p.80.

54 MacPherson, op.cit., iii, p.512.

55 T. S. Ashton, *An Economic History of England: The Eighteenth Century* (1955) p.175.

56 See the cases of Maurice Standford and Henry Palmer (NNC vi, pp.492-3).

57 See the case of David Roberts in 1739 (NNC ii, pp.359-69).

58 John Styles, 'Our traitorous money-makers: the Yorkshire coiners and the law 1760-1783', in J. Brewer and J.

Styles (eds) *An Ungovernable People*, (1980) pp.172-249.

59 Leon Radzinowicz, *A History of Criminal Law and its Administration from 1750*, 5 vols (1948-86) i, pp.652-4.

60 In 1779 Rowland Ridgley was executed for high treason for having in his possession a puncheon, on which was impressed the head side of a shilling (NNC v, pp.344-6).

61 John Hewitt, *The Proceedings of J. Hewitt, Alderman . . . in the year 1756 . . . Being a particular account of the gang of coiners apprehended in the counties of Oxford, Warwick and Stafford, pursued by the author . . . the extraordinary adventures of Thomas Lightowller* (Birmingham, 1783).

62 Styles, 'Our traitorous moneymakers', op.cit., pp.192-3.

63 Ashton, op.cit.m pp.169-71.

64 Styles, 'Our traitorous moneymakers', op.cit., pp.181-2.

65 *Morning Advertiser*, 11 March 1746.

66 H. L. Roth, *The Yorkshire Coiners 1767-1783* (Halifax. 1906).

67 J. A. Sharpe, *Crime in Early Modern England*, (1984) pp.140-1.

68 Styles, 'Our traitorous moneymakers', op.cit., pp.186-90.

69 ibid., pp.186-249 *passim*.

70 ibid., pp.201-4.

71 T. W. Hanson, 'Cragg Coiners', *Transactions of the Halifax Antiquarian Society* (1909) pp.85-106.

72 Styles, 'Our traitorous moneymakers', op.cit., pp.215-18.

73 Roth, op.cit., pp.11-69.

74 This reinforces the general argument of Douglas Hay, 'Property, authority and the criminal law', in D. Hay, E.P. Thompson, and P. Linebaugh (eds) *Albion's Fatal Tree* (1975) pp.17-63.

75 For Rockingham see R. J. S. Hoffman, *The Marquis, a study of Lord Rockingham 1730-82* (NY, 1973); P. Langford, 'The Marquis of Rockingham', in H. Van Thal, (ed.) *The Prime Ministers*, 2 vols (1974) i, p.130; C. Collyer, 'The Rockinghams and Yorkshire Politics 1742-1761', *Thoresby Society Miscellany* 12 (1953) pp.373-4.

76 Styles, 'Our traitorous moneymakers', op.cit., pp.226-7.

77 *Journal of the House of Commons* 34 pp.378, 383, 389.

78 13 Geo 3 c.71.

79 *Daily Advertiser*, 14 July 1773; 6 June 1775.

80 Styles, 'Our traitorous moneymakers', op.cit., p.233.

81 As Sir William Meredith pointed out in his famous speech in May 1777 (see Cobbett's *Parliamentary History of England* 1777-78, cols 234-42. For confirmation of his predictions see the cases of John Benfield and William Turley (NNC vi, pp.68-9).

82 Styles, 'Our traitorous moneymakers' op.cit., pp.197-200.

83 Robert W. Malcolmson, 'A set of ungovernable people: the Kingswood colliers in the eighteenth century', in Brewer & Styles, op.cit., p.121.

84 Blackstone, op.cit., iv, p.75.

85 Eden, op.cit., pp.141-4.

86 Montesquieu, *L'Esprit des Lois*, Book 12, ch. 8.

87 J. Cox, *Three Centuries of Derbyshire Annals* (1890) 2 vols, ii, pp.41-2.

10 SMUGGLING

1. W. A. Cole, 'Trends in eighteenth century smuggling', *Economic History Review* 1958 pp.395-409.

2 W. Bonger, *Criminality and Economic Conditions* (1916) p.576.

3 Adam Smith, *An Inquiry into the Nature and Causes of the Wealth of Nations*, 2 vols, ed. R. H. Campbell and A. S. Skinner, (Oxford, 1976) ii, pp. 553, 881-2.

4 *Walpole Correspondence* 30 p.331.

5 Adam Smith, op.cit., ii, p.898.

6 Neville Williams, *Contraband Cargoes* (1959) p.103.

7 *The Report, with the Appendix, from the Committee of the House of Commons appointed to enquire into the Frauds and Abuses in the Customs to the Prejudice of Trade and the Diminution of Revenue* (1733) (hereinafter 1733 Report).

8 *Gentleman's Magazine* 1751 pp.232-3.

9 F. E. Halliday, *A History of Cornwall* (1963) pp.263-4.

10 T. Shaw, *A History of Cornish Methodism* (Barton, 1967) pp.28-31; R. F. Wearmouth, *Methodism and the Common People of the Eighteenth Century* (Epworth, 1945) pp.258-9.

11 1733 Report p.65.

12 R. C. Jarvis, 'Illicit trade with the Isle of Man 1671-1765', *Transactions of the Lancashire and Cheshire Antiquarian*

Society 58 (1948) pp.245-65.

13 *London Chronicle*, 26-28 July 1764.

14 *London Chronicle*, 15-18 December 1764.

15 1733 Report pp.13, 61-4.

16 Williams, op.cit., pp.168-9.

17 *London Chronicle*, 8-11 December 1764.

18 For the Porteous riots see Add. MSS. 33, 49 ff. 17-117; T. B. Howell, *A Complete Collection of State Trials*, 34 vols, (1816-28) 17 pp.923-94; NNC ii, pp.264-75. Cf. also D. G. Isaac, 'A study of popular disturbances in Britain 1714-54', Ph.D. thesis, Univ. of Edinburgh (1953) pp.130-41; H. T. Dickinson and K. Logue, 'The Porteous riot 1736', *History Today*, April 1972 pp.272-81.

19 Eveline Cruickshanks and Erskine Hill, 'The Waltham Blacks and Jacobitism', *Journal of British Studies* 24 (1985) pp.358-65.

20 See RA Stuart 88/98; 91/79.

21 RA Stuart 111/2.

22 Williams, op.cit., pp.87-8.

23 Lord Teignmouth and C. G. Harper, *The Smugglers. Picturesque Chapters in the History of the Smugglers* 2 vols, (1923) i, pp.2, 7, 11.

24 W. D. Cooper, 'Smuggling in Sussex', *Sussex Archaeological Collections*, 10 pp.69-94.

25 George Bridges, *Plain Dealing or the Whole Method of Wool Smuggling Clearly Discovered* (1744).

26 William Lecky, *A History of England in the Eighteenth Century* (1920) iv, pp.47, 59; v, pp.295-6, 305, 309-10.

27 *London Chronicle*, 14-16 August 1764.

28 Adam Smith, op.cit., i, p.223.

29 Gray to Walpole, 28 March 1738, *Walpole Correspondence* 13 p.156.

30 Sir Matthew Decker, *Serious Considerations on the Several High Duties* (1743).

31 *Journal of the House of Commons* 25 (1745-50) pp.104-5.

32 'First report from the committee appointed to enquire into the illicit practices used in defrauding the Revenue', *Parliamentary Papers 36 Reports VI. House of Commons 58* (1783) (hereinafter First Report 1783).

33 *Walpole Correspondence* 25 p.578.

34 *Gentleman's Magazine* 1785 p.399.

35 *Journal of the House of Commons 1745-50* pp.101-10.

36 First Report 1783 H.C.58.

37 H. and L. Mui, 'Smuggling and the British tea trade', *American Historical Review* 74 (1968) pp.44-73 (at p.50).

38 First Report 1783 H.C.58 p.5.

39 D. MacPherson, *The Annals of Commerce* (1805) iv, p.49.

40 A. L. Cross, *Eighteenth Century Documents Relating to the Royal Forests, the Sheriffs, and Smuggling, Selected from the Shelburne MSS in the William L. Clements Library* (Univ. of Michigan Publications, History and Political Science VII, NY, 1928) pp.299-304.

41 MacPherson, op.cit., iv, p.336.

42 H. D. Traill, *Social England* 6 vols (1893-1897) iv, p.472.

43 Cooper, op.cit., p.90.

44 See *London Chronicle*, 11-13 September 1764.

45 *London Journal*, 8 April 1721.

46 See Hervey Benham, *The Smugglers' Century* (Chelmsford, 1986).

47 *London Journal*, 22 April 1721.

48 Williams, op.cit., p.100.

49 *London Journal*, 30 June 1722.

50 First Report 1733 pp.18-19.

51 For the importance of this see *Walpole Correspondence* 35 p.191.

52 Cross, op.cit., pp.237-40.

53 24 Geo 3 c.47.

54 Alfred Rive, 'A short history of tobacco smuggling', *Economic History* No.4 (1929) pp.554-69.

55 ibid., pp.558-60.

56 First Report 1733 pp.6-9.

57 Rive, op.cit., p.560.

58 24 Geo 2 c.41.

59 Cross, op.cit., pp.246-50, 253-5.

60 Rive, op.cit., pp.567-9.

61 A. P. Wadsworth and Julia de L. Mann, *The Cotton Trade and the Industry of Lancashire 1660-1780* (1958) p.139.

62 Kenneth Ellis, *The Post Office in the Eighteenth Century* (1958).

63 Traill, op.cit., iv, pp.716-17.

64 *Walpole Correspondence* 4 pp.439, 453.

65 *London Chronicle*, 25-27 December 1764.

66 *London Chronicle*, 16-18 December 1764.

67 *Walpole Correspondence* 33 p.64.

68 *Walpole Correspondence* 10 pp.288-9.

69 Cole to Walpole, 5 January 1766, *Walpole Correspondence*, i, p.101.

70 Williams, op.cit., p.137.

71 5 Geo I c.11.

72 Cross, op.cit., pp.319-21.

73 9 Geo 2 c.35.

74 12 Geo 2 c.21.

75 19 Geo 2 c.34.

76 Sir William Eden, *Principles of Penal Law*, (1771) pp.204-5.

77 Williams, op.cit., p.104.

78 *London Chronicle*, 2-4 February 176.

79 24 Geo 3 c.47.

80 Cal Winslow, 'Sussex smugglers', in D. Hay, E. P. Thompson, and P. Linebaugh (eds) *Albion's Fatal Tree*, (1975) pp.119-66.

81 *Journal of the House of Commons* 25 (1745-50) pp.101-4.

82 Walpole to Montagu, 26 August 1749, *Walpole Correspondence* 9 pp.96-9.

83 Cooper, op.cit., pp.83-9.

84 Adam Smith, op.cit., i, p.128.

85 Teignmouth and Harper, op.cit., i, pp.50-102.

86 *Gentleman's Magazine* 1747 p.198.

87 For full details see G. P. R. James, *The Battle of Goudhurst* (1845).

88 *Gentleman's Magazine* 1747 p.397.

89 C.N.C. iii, pp.155-8.

90 *Gentleman's Magazine* 1749 p.359.

91 *Gentleman's Magazine* 1748 p.475.

92 NNC iii, pp.188-98.

93 Anon., *A Full and Genuine History of the Unparalleled Murders of Mr William Galley and Mr David Chater by Fourteen Notorious Smugglers* (1749).

94 The Duke of Richmond's involvement in this case requires a study to itself. Some preliminary pointers can be obtained from a reading of his papers for this period, especially the correspondence with the Duke of Newcastle (Add. MSS. 32, 711-18).

95 Winslow, op.cit., pp.160-3.

96 NNC iii, pp.216-22.

97 NNC iii, pp.223-7.

98 Winslow, op.cit., p.166.

99 NNC iii, pp.375-8.

100 Walpole, *Memoirs of the Reign of King George II*, i, p.3.

101 See F. J. McLynn, *France and the Jacobite Rising of 1745* op.cit.

102 Add. MSS. 32, 709 ff. 273-4; 32, 711 f. 211.

103 *Walpole Correspondence* 35 p.141.

104 *Gentleman's Magazine* 1749 p.138.

105 *Walpole Correspondence* 35 p.137.

106 Cross, op.cit., pp.253-5.

107 Rive, op.cit., p.560.

108 Cross, op.cit., pp.255-6.

109 G. D. Ramsay, 'The smugglers' trade: a neglected aspect of English commercial development', *Royal Historical Society Transactions*, 5th series 2 (1952) pp.131-57.

110 Leon Radzinowicz, *A History of Criminal Law and its Administration from 1750*, 5 vols (1948-86) ii, pp.64-7.

111 E. E. Hoon, *The Organisation of the English customs system 1696-1786* (1968 ed.) p.182.

112 'First report from the committee appointed to enquire into the illicit practices used in defrauding the Revenue', *Parliamentary papers 36 reports VI House of Commons 58* (1783) (hereinafter First Report 1783) p.5.

113 Quoted in Cross, op.cit., p.255.

114 'Third Report from the committee appointed to Enquire into the Illicit Practices used in defrauding the Revenue', *House of Commons 60* (1784) (hereinafter Third Report 1784) p.6.

115 Cross, op.cit., pp.255-6.

116 R. C. Jarvis, 'Customs cutters of the North-West', *Transactions of the Lancashire and Cheshire Historical Society* 99.

117 Hoon, op.cit., pp.180-2.

118 N. A. M. Rodger, *The Wooden World; the Anatomy of the Georgian Navy* (1986) p.171

119 Adam Smith, op.cit., ii, pp.884-5.

120 Hoon, op.cit., pp.177-8.

121 H. and L. Mui, op.cit., p.56.

122 First report 1783 p.5.

123 Hoon, op.cit., p.232.

124 *Walpole Correspondence* 35 p.458.

125 Cross, op.cit., pp.308-21.

126 Hoon, op.cit., pp.36-7, 49, 64, 65.

127 Cross, op.cit., pp.289-94.

128 Winslow, op.cit., pp.144-6.

129 Anon., *A Free apology in behalf of the smugglers, so far as their case affects the Constitution, by an enemy to all oppression, whether by tyranny or Law* (1749) pp.12-14.

130 Hoon, op.cit., p.233.

131 Paul Muskett, 'Military operations against smuggling in Kent and Sussex 1698-1750', *Journal of the Society for Army Historical Research* 52 (1974) pp.89-110.

132 Cross, op.cit., pp.289-94, 308-21.

133 Winslow, op.cit., pp.142-4.

134 ibid., pp.128-9.

135 Williams, op.cit., p.133.

136 See E. K. Chatterton, *King's Cutters and Smugglers* (1912).

137 Rodger, op.cit., p.171.

138 *London Chronicle*, 8-11 September 1764.

139 J. R. Western, *The English Militia in the Eighteenth Century* (1965) p.433.

140 Cross, op.cit., pp.306-7.

141 Pepys, *Diary*, 30 April 1660; William Cobbett, *Rural Rides*, 3 September 1823.

142 Hoon, op.cit., p.89.

143 ibid., p.233.

144 *General Evening Post*, 31 August-2 September 1784.

145 NNC vi, pp.528-9.

146 NNC vi, pp.723-8.

147 D. Arnold Foster, *At War with the Smugglers: the career of Dr. Arnold's father* (1936).

148 Hoon, op.cit., p.271.

149 Cole, op.cit., p.402.

150 Ramsay, op.cit., p.135.

151 H. and L. Mui, op.cit., p.73.

152 *Gentleman's Magazine* 1749 p.138.

153 Winslow, op.cit., pp.150-4.

154 *Daily Advertiser*, 5 June 1780.

155 *Walpole Correspondence* 20 p.289.

156 ibid., 20 p.261.

157 NNC iv, pp.74-90.

158 NNC iv, pp.99-103.

159 Eveline Cruickshanks and Howard Erskine Hill, loc.cit.

160 *Gentleman's Magazine* 1747 p.496.

161 *Gentleman's Magazine* 1751 pp.232-3.

162 *General Evening Post*, 7-9 September 1784.

163 *Gentleman's Magazine* 1757 p.528.

164 *Gentleman's Magazine* 1765 p.94.

165 6 Geo 3 c.5.

166 Tobias Smollett, *Complete History of England*, iii, p.303; Lecky, op.cit., v, pp.295-6.

167 W. D. Cooper, op.cit., pp.89,91.

168 Montagu to Walpole, 13 June 1965, *Walpole Correspondence* 10 p.158.

169 J. A. Picton, *Memorials of Liverpool* (1873) pp.242-3.

170 *Annual Register* 1758 p.113.

171 J. G. Rule, 'Wrecking and coastal plunder', in D. Hay, E. P. Thompson, and P. Linebaugh (eds) *Albion's Fatal Tree* (1975) pp.167-88.

172 Sir William Blackstone, *Commentaries on the Laws of England*, 4 vols, 9th ed. (1783) i, pp.291-3; cf. also ii, p.14, iii, p.106, iv, p.235.

173 *Annual Register* 1774 pp.113-14.

174 Quoted in Rule, op.cit., p.176.

175 26 Geo II c.19.

176 See Edward Carson, *The Ancient and Rightful Customs* (1972).

177 Daniel Defoe, *A Tour through the Whole Island of Great Britain* (Everyman edition, 1974) 2 vols, i, p.244.

178 See J. Pearce, *The Wesleys in Cornwall* (Truro, 1964) pp.158-9. Cf. also Wesley Journal, 17 August 1776.

179 MacPherson, op.cit., (1805) iii, p.40.

180 See the many cases cited in A Hamilton Jenkins, *Cornish Seafarers* (1932); J. Vivian, *Tales of the Cornish Wreckers* (Truro, 1969); G. G. Smith, *The Wreckers: or a Tour of Benevolence from St Michael's Mount to the Lizard Point* (1818).

181 *Journal of the House of Commons* 12 (1735) p.603.

182 See the copious details contained in the 1753 petition to Parliament (*Journal of the House of Commons* 26 (1753) p.289.

183 *Gentleman's Magazine* 1782 p.44

184 See *Gentleman's Magazine* 1775 p.202; *Annual Register* 1782 p.219.

185 *Journal of the House of Commons* 25 pp.204, 705, 738, 745.

186 'Debate on Mr Burke's Bill to prevent the plundering of shipwreckers', Cobbett's *Parliamentary History of England* 18 (1774-7) cols 1298-1302 (27 March, 30 April 1776).

187 Sir William Eden, *Principles of Penal Law* (1771) pp.112-13.

188 Rule, op.cit., p.186.

189 See the cases of wealthy wreckers at Anglesey and Hereford in 1774-5 (*Annual Register* 1774, p.148; 1775, pp.113, 154). For the participation of wealthy Cornish farmers see *Gentleman's Magazine* 1751 p.41.

190 Rule, op.cit., p.184.

191 Quoted in ibid., p.185.

11 POACHING

1 See Gertrude Himmelfarb commenting on the appeal of John Buchan's *John MacNab*: 'It is a parable about authority and property and the perpetual challenge to which they are both subject.' (G. Himmelfarb, *Victorian Minds* (1968) p.265.

2 Sir William Blackstone, *Commentaries on the Laws of England*, 4 vols, 9th ed. (1783) iv, p.415.

3 ibid., iv, p.174.

4 See Joseph Chitty, *A Treatise on the*

Game Laws and on Fisheries, 2 vols (1812).

5 22 & 23 Car.2. c.25.

6 To judge from the arrogant and high-handed attitude of contemporary fox-hunters, it seems that in practice hunting rights still do count for more than those of private property.

7 P. B. Munsche, *Gentlemen and Poachers* (1981) pp.15-19.

8 Blackstone, op.cit., iv, p.416.

9 Douglas Hay, 'Poaching and the game laws on Cannock Chase', in D. Hay, E. P. Thompson, and P. Linebaugh (eds) *Albion's Fatal Tree* (1975) p.248.

10 Chester and Ethyn Kirby, 'The Stuart game perogative', *English Historical Review* 66 (1931) pp.239-54.

11 *Walpole Correspondence* 10 pp.209, 235, 241, 267.

12 Blackstone, op.cit., iv, p.174; B. A. Holderness, *Pre-Industrial England, Economy and Society 1550-1750* (1976) pp.43-4.

13 Chester Kirby, 'The English game law system', *American Historical Review* 38 (1933) pp.240-62.

14 J. C. Cox, *The Royal Forests of England* (1905); C. E. Hart, *Royal Forest* (Oxford, 1966); P. A. J. Pettit, *The Royal Forests of Northamptonshire* (Northants Record Society 23 (1968).

15 *Gentleman's Magazine* 1752 pp.90, 190.

16 Montagu to Walpole, 24 December 1765, 19 February 1766, *Walpole Correspondence* 10 p.188.

17 A. L. Cross, *Eighteenth-Century Documents Relating to the Royal Forests, the Sheriffs, and Smugglers, Selected from the Shelburne MSS in the William L. Clements Library* (Univ. of Michigan Publications, History and Political Science VII, NY, 1928) pp.37-46, 111-17.

18 Leon Radzinowicz, *A History of Criminal Law and its Administration from 1750*, 5 vols, (1948-86) ii, pp.95-6.

19 See Charles Chevenix Trench, *The Poacher and the Squire* (1967).

20 E. P. Thompson, *Whigs and Hunters*, (1975) pp.63-6, 68-75.

21 ibid., p.63-70.

22 NNC i, pp.362-7.

23 Thompson, op.cit., pp.142-6.

24 ibid., p.173.

25 *London Gazette*, 20-24 July 1725; 7-10 August 1725.

26 Thomson, op.cit., p.233.

27 Daniel Defoe, *The Great Law of Subordination Considered; or the Insolence and Unsufferable behaviour of servants in England duly Enquired into* (1724) pp.271-3.

28 Blackstone, op.cit., iv, p.180.

29 *London Chronicle*, 11-14 February 1764.

30 *London Gazette*, 17-20 August 1724; 3-6 June, 30 August-2 September 1726; 23-27 July 1733.

31 Hay, op.cit., pp.194-5.

32 ibid., p.196.

33 William Taplin, *Observations on the Present State of the Game Laws in England* (1772) p.30.

34 *Whitehall Evening Post*, 6-9 November 1784.

35 Munsche, op.cit., p.83.

36 ibid., p.210.

37 ibid.

38 Blackstone, op.cit., ii, p.419; iii, p.362.

39 Peter King, 'Decision-makers and decision-making in English criminal law 1750-1800', *Historical Journal* 27 (1984) pp.53-4.

40 See the anonymous pamphlet, *Thoughts on the Present Laws for preserving game* (1750).

41 Hay, op.cit., pp.213-17.

42 See W. Menzies, *A History of Windsor Great Park and Windsor Forest* (1864); C. H. Hart, *The Commoners of Dean Forest* (Gloucester, 1951); C. Mackie, *Norfolk Annals* (Norwich, 1901).

43 *London Gazette*, 4-7 August 1733.

44 Chester Kirby, 'The attack on the English game laws in the forties', *Journal of Modern History* 6 (1932) pp.18-37.

45 Blackstone, op.cit., iv, pp.281-2.

46 ibid, p.415.

47 ibid.

48 For the social composition of the Blacks see Thompson, op.cit., pp.84-115.

49 'Most poachers were poor, if only because most Englishmen were poor.' (Hay, op.cit., p.200). For poverty as the spur to poaching see ibid., pp.200-2.

50 Thompson, op.cit., p.163.

51 *Walpole Correspondence* 34 pp.64, 69.

52 Quoted in Hay, op.cit., p.216.

53 5 Anne c.14.

54 Munsche, op.cit., pp.22, 56.

55 ibid., pp.56-64.

56 ibid., p.65.

57 Cross, op.cit., p.40.

58 Hay, op.cit., pp.220-1.

59 *Gentleman's Magazine* 1773 p.98.

60 Hay, op.cit., pp.228-30.

61 ibid., pp.230-4.

62 Munsche, op.cit., p.25.

63 H. Zouch, *An Account of the Present Daring Practices of Night Hunters and Poachers* (1783) p.10.

64 16 Geo 3 c.30.

65 Munsche, op.cit., p.24.

66 ibid., p.69.

67 ibid., p.73.

68 Chester Kirby, 'English game law reform', in *Essays in Modern English History in honour of Wilbur Cortez Abbott* (Cambridge, Mass. 1941) pp.345-80.

69 S. and B. Webb, *English Local Government (vol. 1) The Parish and the County* (1963) p.598; J., L., and B. Hammond, *The Village Labourer* (1948) p.184.

70 Quoted in L. and B. Hammond, op.cit., p.188.

71 G. E. Mingay, *English Landed Society in the Eighteenth Century* (1963) pp.120, 249.

72 Thompson, op.cit., pp.258-69.

73 *Some Considerations on the Game Laws and the Present Practice in Executing them, with a hint to the non-subscribers* (1753) p.26.

74 Munsche. op.cit., pp.231 *et seq.*

75 Thompson, op.cit., *passim.*

76 Hay, op.cit., p.212.

77 ibid., p.250.

78 Zouch, op.cit.

79 Pat Rogers, 'The Waltham Blacks and the Black Act', *Historical Journal* 17 (1974) pp.465-86.

80 Thompson, op.cit., *passim.*

81 Munsche, op.cit., p.66.

82 There is a very good discussion on this point in J. A. Sharpe, *Crime in Early Modern England* pp.125-31. They may, however, sometimes have been 'political criminals'. The notion that Jacobitism played a role with the Waltham Blacks (first canvassed in Cruikshanks and Erskine-Hill, loc.cit.) has received support from a study of deer-stealing in Buckinghamshire. See John Broad, 'Whigs and deer-stealers in other guises: a return to the origins of the Black Act', *Past and Present* 119 (1988) pp.56-72.

12 RIOTING

1 See in general Max Beloff, *Public Order and Popular Disturbances* (1938), esp. pp.34-55. For the Jacobite riots see G. Holmes, 'The Sacheverell riots', *Past and Present* 72 (1976).

2 1 Geo 1 st.2 c.5.

3 Henry Fielding, *Works*, ed. Leslie Stephen (1882) vii, pp.225-33.

4 ibid., vi, p.133.

5 For a general survey of the use of the army against eighteenth-century crowds see T. Hayter, *The Army and the Crowd in Mid-Georgian England* (1978).

6 But see, for the not negligible levels of crowd violence Robert B. Shoemaker, 'The London "Mob" in the Early Eighteenth Century', *Journal of British Studies* 26 (1987) pp.273-304.

7 T. S. Ashton, *Economic Fluctuations in England 1700-1800* (Oxford, 1959) pp.17, 144, 147.

8 D. G. G. Isaac, 'A study of popular disturbances in Britain 1714-1754', Ph.D. thesis, Univ. of Edinburgh (1953) pp.92-103.

9 The plight of the weavers is explained in a number of pamphlets that appeared in 1719-20: *The Just Complaints of the Poor Weavers* (1719); *The Case of the Linen Drapers and other dealers in Printed Calicoes and Linen* (1720); *The Case of the Printers of Calicoes and Linens* (1720).

10 Isaac, op.cit.

11 7 Geo I c.13.

12 *Gentleman's Magazine* 1736 pp.242, 285.

13 *London Chronicle*, 12-14 July, 16-19 July 1774.

14 M. D. George, *London Life in the Eighteenth Century* (1925) pp.113-25.

15 8 Geo 2 c.30.

16 *London Gazette*, 10-14 February 1735.

17 15 Geo 2 c.33 (1742); 20 Geo 2 c.47 (1747); 27 Geo 2 c.16 (1754); 7 Geo 3 c.40 (1767).

18 E. P. Thompson, *Whigs and Hunters*, (1975) pp.256-8.

19 For Hardwicke's ludicrous judgement see J. Campbell, *Lives of the Lord Chancellors, and Keepers of the Great Seal of England*, 8 vols (1845-69) p.49.

20 Robert W. Malcolmson, 'A set of ungovernable people: the Kingswood colliers in the eighteenth century', in J. Brewer and J. Styles (eds) *An Un-*

governable People, (1980) pp.85-127.

21 John Wesley, *Journal* iv, p.75.

22 *London Evening Post*, 1-4 July 1749.

23 Peter Linebaugh, 'The Tyburn riot against the surgeons', in D. Hay, E. P. Thompson, and P. Linebaugh (eds) *Albion's Fatal Tree* (1975) p.89-102.

24 NNC iii, pp.236-42.

25 Fielding's own account of the riots is in *Works*, op.cit., vi, pp.405 *et seq*.

26 Quoted in Linebaugh, op.cit., p.93.

27 R. B. Rose, 'Eighteenth-century price riots and public policy in England', *International Review of Social History* 6 (1961) pp.277-92.

28 *Gentleman's Magazine* 1756 pp.457 *et seq*.; 1757 *passim*.

29 R. A. E. Wells, 'Counting riots in eighteenth-century England', *Bulletin of the Society for the Study of Labour History* 37 (1978) pp.68-71.

30 W. J. Shelton, *English Hunger and Industrial Disorders: A Study of Social Conflicts during the first decade of George III's reign* (1973) pp.21-49.

31 A. Charlesworth, *An Atlas of Rural Protest in Britain* (1983).

32 John Stevenson, *Popular Disturbances in England* 1700-1870 (1979) pp.91-112.

33 *London Chronicle*, 12-14 March 1761; *Gentleman's Magazine* 1761 pp.137-8; 187-8.

34 *Gentleman's Magazine* 1763 pp.31-2, 97.

35 Ashton, op.cit., p.147.

36 *Correspondence of George III*, ed. Sir John Fortescue (1927-8) i, p.95.

37 *Gentleman's Magazine*, 1765 p.244.

38 *Annual Register* 1765 p.41.

39 Walpole, *Memoirs of the Reign of George III*, ii, pp.110-13.

40 J. H. Jesse, *Memoirs of George III* 3 vols (1867) i, pp.291-4.

41 *Gentleman's Magazine* 1765 p.296.

42 Jesse, op.cit., p.294.

43 *London Chronicle*, 22-25 September 1764.

44 4 Geo 3 c.37.

45 For this reason I have not dealt with the Wilkesite agitation. For an admirable account see George Rudé, *Wilkes and Liberty* (Oxford, 1962).

46 George Rudé, *Hanoverian London 1714-1808* (1961) p.205.

47 Shelton, op.cit., p.5.

48 M. D. George, 'The London Coalheavers', *Economic History, Supplement to Economic Journal* 1. no.4 (1926-9) pp.229-48.

49 *Annual Register* 1768 pp.101-2, 108-9.

50 ibid., p.136.

51 Walpole, *Memoirs of the Reign of King George III*, iii, pp.148-9.

52 *London Chronicle*, 30 July-2 August 1768.

53 *Daily Advertiser*, 14 June 1768.

54 *Annual Register* 1768 p.92.

55 ibid., pp.105-17.

56 *St James's Chronicle*, 12-14 May 1768.

57 *London Chronicle* 7-10 May, 10-12 May 1768.

58 *St James's Evening Chronicle*, 14-17, 17-19, 24-26 May 1768.

59 *St James's Chronicle*, 2-4 June, 17-19 June 1768.

60 Shelton, op.cit., pp.165-185.

61 *Gentleman's Magazine* 1768 pp.347, 422.

62 *Annual Register* 1769 p.57.

63 ibid., pp.136-86.

64 ibid., p.136.

65 ibid., p.138.

66 ibid., p.161.

67 *Gentleman's Magazine* 1769 pp.606-7.

68 *Annual Register* 1771 pp.193-5.

69 Shelton, op.cit., p.200.

70 Rudé, *Wilkes and Liberty*, op.cit., pp.65-103.

71 For this point see Add. MSS. 30, 866 *passim*.

72 A. V. Dicey, *Laws of the Constitution* (1885) p.308.

73 *Annual Register* 1768 pp.108-9, 112, 136-8, 227-33.

74 Walpole, *Memoirs of the Reign of George III*, iii, pp.232-3.

75 For all these very good reasons a discussion of the Wilkes riots is largely out of place in a book about eighteenth-century *crime*.

76 *Annual Register* 1780 pp.254-6.

77 Cobbett's *Parliamentary History of England* 21 pp.654-9.

78 ibid., p.657.

79 *Daily Advertiser*, 5, 6 June 1780.

80 *Gentleman's Magazine*, 1780 p.266.

81 Cobbett's *Parliamentary History of England* 21 pp.665, 668-9.

82 *Gentleman's Magazine* 1780 p.26.

83 N. W. Wraxall, *Historical Memoirs* (1836) i, pp.363-4.

84 *London Chronicle*, 1-3 June 1780.

85 For some other pointers on attitudes during the Gordon riots see Add. MSS. 38, 214 f. 51; H M C, Lothian p.367.

86 The sequence of events can be followed in J. P.de Castro, *The Gordon Riots* (1926); cf. also Christopher Hibbert, *King Mob* (1958).

87 De Castro, op.cit.. pp.82-6, 122.

88 *Memoirs of the Life of Sir Samuel Romilly* (1840) i, p.123.

89 *Lloyd's Evening Post*, 5-7 June 1780.

90 ibid.

91 *Public Advertiser*, 9 June 1780.

92 *London Courant*, 9 June 1780.

93 De Castro, op.cit., pp.136-7.

94 *Lloyd's Evening Post* 7-9 June 1780.

95 De Castro, op.cit., p.138.

96 William Vincent alias Thomas Holcroft, *A Plain and Succinct Narrative of the late Riots and Disturbances* (1780) p.36.

97 Wraxall, op.cit., i, pp.336-7.

98 *London Courant*, 9 June 1780.

99 De Castro, op.cit., pp.141-4, 154, 158.

100 Walpole to Lady Ossory, 8 June 1780, *Walpole Correspondence* 33 p.190.

101 *London Courant*, 9 June 1780.

102 Wraxall, op.cit., i, p.356.

103 Cobbett's *Parliamentary History of England* 21, pp.690-98.

104 De Castro, p.180.

105 ibid., p.263.

106 *Public Advertiser*, 13 June 1780.

107 *Annual Register* 1780 pp.262-3.

108 NNC v, pp.72-8.

109 *New Annual Register* 1780 pp.62-7.

110 *Gentleman's Magazine* 1780 p.343.

111 *London Chronicle*, 8-10 August 1780; *Annual Register* 1780 pp.285-7.

112 Walpole to Mann, 24 July 1780, *Walpole Correspondence* 25 pp.75-6.

113 *Daily Advertiser*, 7, 14, 17 July 1780.

114 *Daily Advertiser*, 7 February 1781.

115 *London Chronicle*, 10-15 June 1780.

116 W. Belsham, *Memoirs of the Reign of George III* (1795), iii, p.22.

117 *Letters of the first Earl of Malmesbury*, 2 vols (1870) i, pp.466-7.

118 De Castro, op cit., pp.51-6, 69-70.

119 Leon Radzinowicz, *A History of Criminal Law and its Administration from 1750*, 5 vols (1948-86) iii, pp.89-137.

120 *London Chronicle* 10-12, 12-15 August 1780; Cobbett's *Parliamentary History of England* 21, pp.694-8.

121 I. R. Christie, *The End of North's Ministry* (1958) p.24.

122 S. Maccoby, *English Radicalism 1762-1785* (1955) p.321.

123 Christopher Hibbert, *The Road to Tyburn: the story of Jack Sheppard and the eighteenth-century underworld* (1957) p.20. This is a succinct version of the interpretation of the riots advanced in his *King Mob* op.cit.

124 De Castro, pp.213-36.

125 *London Chronicle*, 6-8 June 1780.

126 Walpole to Mason, 29 June 1780, *Walpole Correspondence* 29 pp.61-3; cf. also same to same, 24 September 1780, 29 p.82.

127 For an able argument along these lines see John Nicholson, *The Great Liberty Riot of 1780* (1985).

128 George Rudé, 'The Gordon riots: a study of the rioters and their victims', *Transactions of the Royal Historical Society*, 5th series, 6 (1956).

129 George Rudé, 'Some financial and military aspects of the Gordon riots', *The Guildhall Miscellany* 6 (1956) pp.31-42; George Rudé, 'The London "Mob" of the Eighteenth Century', *Historical Journal* (1959) pp.1-18.

130 Walpole to Mann, 14 June 1780, *Walpole Correspondence* 25 p.63.

131 *London Chronicle*, 14-16 July 1791; *St James's Chronicle*, 16-19 July 1791.

132 John Latimer, *The Annals of Bristol in the Eighteenth Century* (1893). pp.501-4.

133 NNC vi, pp.544-8.

134 George Rudé, *The Crowd in History: a Study of Popular Disturbances in France and England 1730-1848* (NY, 1964) esp. pp.47-65.

135 E. P. Thompson, *The Making of the English Working Class* (1986 edn) pp.67-83.

136 E. P. Thompson, 'Eighteenth-century English society: class struggle without class?' *Social History* (1978) pp.133-65.

137 Peter Linebaugh, 'Eighteenth-century disorders', *Bulletin of the Society for the Study of Labour History* 28 (1974) pp.57-61.

138 E. P. Thompson, 'The moral economy of the English crowd in the eighteenth century', *Past and Present* 50 (1971) pp.76-136.

139 Thompson sees the food riots of 1795-6 and 1800-1 as 'the last desperate attempt by the people to reimpose the older moral economy as against the economy of the free market.' *(The Making of the English Working Class*, op.cit., p.63).

13 THEORIES ON CRIME AND PUNISHMENT

1 Edward Carpenter, a great late Victorian criminologist, held that nine-tenths of all crime was due to 'the desire for property or the disappointment of being deprived of it', and to drink. The remaining one-tenth was due to the great human passions, of hatred, malice, revenge, etc. which are themselves 'often connected or entangled with property'. (Edward Carpenter, *Prisons, Police and Punishment: an Inquiry into the Causes and Treatment of Crime and Criminals* (1905) pp.47-63.

2 William Godwin, *Enquiry concerning Political Justice and its Influence on Morals and Happiness* (1797), ed. F. E. L. Priestley (Toronto, 1946), i, pp.14-24, ii, pp.453-67.

3 Michael Ignatieff, *A Just Measure of Pain: the Penitentiary in the Industrial Revolution 1750-1850* (1978) p.66.

4 ibid., p.67.

5 For this debate see especially J. G. A. Pocock, *The Machiavellian Moment* (1975); H. T. Dickinson, *Liberty and Property* (1977).

6 Alexander Pope, *Imitations of Horace*, Epistle II (1737).

7 The argument from moral depravity has never died. As late as 1926 G. T. Crooke, editor of the *Complete Newgate Calendar* could be found arguing that sport was *the* great barrier to crime as it gave the working classes something to do (what he would have made of football hooliganism is another matter). Crooke provided an anecdote to show that men could even be converted from Marxism (obviously in itself a crime) by acquiring an interest in cricket. See Crooke's introduction to vol. 1 of CNC

8 Henry Fielding, *An Inquiry into the causes of the late increase in Robbers*, Fielding, *Works*, ed. Leslie Stephen, (1882) vii, pp.171, 179.

9 ibid., pp.163-4.

10 See Vincent J. Liesenfeld, *The Licensing Act of 1737* (Madison, Wisconsin, 1984).

11 Daniel Defoe, *The Poor Man's Plea* in relation to all the Proclamations for a Reformation of Manners, etc. (1698) pp.8-10.

12 *London Journal*, 20 April 1728.

13 NNC ii, p.249.

14 Ronald Leslie-Melville, *The Life and Works of Sir John Fielding* (1934) pp.279-82, 285-6.

15 *Gentleman's Magazine* 1773 p.464; cf. also W. E. Schultz, *Gay's Beggar's Opera* (1923) pp.244-9.

16 Boswell's *Life of Johnson*, ii, pp.367-8.

17 ibid.

18 NNC iv, p.197.

19 Boswell's *Life of Johnson*, ii, p.176; iii, p.293.

20 Bernard Mandeville, *Fable of the Bees*, i, pp.90, 166.

21 ibid., i, pp.103-4.

22 ibid., i, p.87.

23 Boswell's *Life of Johnson*, ii, pp.169-70; cf. also iii, pp.226, 282.

24 ibid., iii, p.291.

25 ibid., ii, pp.217-18.

26 See Hector Monro, *The Ambivalence of Bernard Mandeville* (Oxford, 1975) esp. pp.84-93. Cf. also M. M. Goldsmith, *Private Vices, Public Benefits: Bernard Mandeville's Social and Political Theory* (Cambridge, 1985).

27 Benjamin Rush, *An Enquiry into the Effects of Public Punishments upon Criminals and upon Society* (Philadelphia, 1787).

28 John Wesley, *Journal*, 21 January 1767.

29 Patrick Colquhoun, *A Treatise on Indigence* (1806) pp.7-8.

30 Patrick Colquhoun, *Treatise on the Wealth of the British Empire* (1814) pp.111-12; *A Treatise on Police of the Metropolis* (1800) pp.515-18.

31 Colquhoun, *Treatise on Police*, op.cit., pp.562, 613.

32 See the absurd lists of human deficiencies among the indigent in Colquhoun's *A Treatise on Indigence*, op.cit., pp.11, 23, 239.

33 See the criticisms by Francis Place (Add. MSS. 27, 826 f. 169; 27, 827 ff. 47-8).

34 For a general review see James Heath, *Eighteenth Century Penal Theory* (Oxford, 1963).

35 Fielding, 'An Inquiry', etc. *Works*, op.cit., vii, pp.187-218.

36 ibid., p.263.

37 ibid., p.260.

38 Quoted in Leon Radzinowicz, *A History of Criminal Law and its Administration from 1750*, 5 vols (1948-86) ii, p.19.

39 Fielding, *Works*, op.cit., vii, pp.268-9.

40 Fielding, *Journal of a Voyage to Lisbon*

in *Works*, op.cit., vii, p.18.

41 Cesare Beccaria, *Dei Delitti e Delle Pene* (1764), trans. J. A. Farrer as *Crimes and Punishments* (1880) pp.165-8.

42 William Paley, *Principles of Moral and Political Philosophy* (1817) Book VI, ch. 9.

43 ibid., p.408.

44 ibid., pp.420-1.

45 Martin Madan, *Thoughts on Executive Justice*, (1785) pp.42-3.

46 Paley, op.cit., pp.131-2, 412-13.

47 Sir William Blackstone, *Commentaries on the Laws of England*, 4 vols, 9th ed. (1783) iv, pp.17-18.

48 For a general survey see Franco Venturi, *Utopia and Reform in the Enlightenment* (Cambridge, 1971), esp. pp.100-16. For Montesquieu's thought see especially *L'Esprit des Lois*, vol.1, Book VI. ch. 13.

49 ibid., ch. 16.

50 ibid., Book XII, ch. 4.

51 ibid., Book XII, ch. 18.

52 For a defence of this practice see Philip Yorke, *Some Considerations on the law of Forfeiture for High Treason* (1748), written in the aftermath of the post-'45 treason trials.

53 Beccaria, *Crimes and Punishments*, op.cit., p.168.

54 ibid., p.186.

55 ibid., pp.213-14.

56 ibid., pp.169-73.

57 See Jean-Jacques Rousseau, *Du Contrat Social*, (1762) Book II, ch. 5.

58 Sir William Eden, *Principles of Penal Law*, (1771) pp.7-8.

59 ibid., p.8.

60 ibid., pp.46-9.

61 Blackstone, op.cit., iv, pp.4-5, 18-19, 251.

62 ibid., iv, p.371-2.

63 ibid., iv, pp.383-4.

64 *Memoirs of the Life of Sir Samuel Romilly* (1818) i, p.88.

65 Samuel Romilly, *Observations on the late publication entitled Thoughts on Executive Justice* (1786) p.59.

66 John Howard, *Account of the Principal Lazarettos in Europe* (1789) p.222.

67 Jeremy Bentham, *Rationale of Punishment* (1830).

68 See the assessment of Bentham's relationship to the other late eighteenth-century legal reformers in Radzinowicz, op.cit., i, pp.355-96.

69 Bentham, op.cit., p.82.

70 Bentham, *Panopticon or the Inspection House* (1791) p.39.

71 See Hay, 'Property, authority and the criminal law', in Hay, Thompson, and Linebaugh (eds) op.cit., p.25.

72 For a discussion of this distinction see Leon Radzinowicz, *Ideology and Crime* (1966).

73 Antonio Gramsci, *Quaderni del Carcere*, ed. Valentino Gerratana (Turin, 1975) p.1638.

14 EXECUTION

1. Leon Radzinowicz, *A History of Criminal Law and its Administration from 1750*, 5 vols (1948-86) pp.1-3.

2 Douglas Hay, 'Property, authority and the criminal law', in D. Hay, E. P. Thompson, and P. Linebaugh (eds) *Albion's Fatal Tree* (1975) p.22.

3 Sharpe, *Crime in Early Modern England*, (1984) p.65.

4 Radzinowicz, op.cit., i, pp.151-9.

5 David Philips, 'A new engine of power and authority: the institutionalisation of law enforcement in England 1780-1830', in V. A. C. Gattrell, Bruce Lenman, and Geoffrey Parker (eds) *Social History of Crime in Western Europe since 1500* (1980) p.158.

6 Hay, op.cit., p.42.

7 J. M. Beattie, *Crime and the Courts in England 1660-1800* (Oxford, 1986) p.516.

8 A. Andrews, *The Eighteenth Century* (1856), p.271.

9 J., L., and B. Hammond, 'Poverty, crime and philanthropy', in A. S. Turberville (ed.) *Johnson's England*, (Oxford, 1933) pp.314-22.

10 John Howard, *State of the Prisons in England and Wales* (1771) pp.479-85.

11 Sir William Blackstone, *Commentaries on the Laws of England*, 4 vols, 9th ed. (1783) iv, p.17.

12 Beattie, op.cit., pp.424-5.

13 Walpole to Mann, 24 February 1781, *Walpole Correspondence* 25 p.131.

14 For the crime wave in these years see *Gentleman's Magazine* 1783 pp.891, 973-4; 1784 p.955; 1786 p.990.

15 *Annual Register* 1785 p.247.

16 Michael Ignatieff, *A Just Measure of Pain: the Penitentiary in the Industrial Revolution 1750-1850* (1978) p.87.

17 *Gentleman's Magazine* 1785 p.379.

18 Howard, op.cit., pp.45, 56.
19 Hay, op.cit., pp.23-6. For the symbolic significance of hanging and the connection between the body and the body politic see Randall McGowen, 'The body and punishment in eighteenth-century England', *Journal of Modern History* 59 (1987) pp.651-79.
20 Beattie, op.cit., p.146.
21 O'Brien, *The Foundation of Australia* (1937) pp.99-100.
22 Andrews, op.cit., pp.269-70 provides a long list of execution venues.
23 This middle ground is covered in exhaustive detail in Beattie, op.cit., pp.199-400.
24 See NNC iii, pp.210-16.
25 CNC iii, p.120.
26 Martin Madan, *Thoughts on Executive Justice*, (1785) pp.144-5.
27 CNC iii, pp.177-80.
28 Madan, op.cit.. p.26
29 *Gentleman's Magazine* 1784 pp.311, 633.
30 Madan, op.cit., pp.26-30.
31 Quoted by Hay, op.cit., pp.17-18.
32 Quoted in E. P. Thompson, *Whigs and Hunters* p.211.
33 CNC iv, p.111.
34 Boswell's *Life of Johnson*, iv, p.359.
35 NNC vi, pp.134-9.
36 Radzinowicz, i. pp.195-7.
37 W. Eden Hooper, *Newgate and the Old Bailey* (1935) examines the topography of Newgate.
38 W. J. Sheehan, 'Finding Solace in eighteenth-century Newgate', in J. S. Cockburn (ed.) *Crime in England 1550-1800* (1977) p.243.
39 B. L. Muralt, *Lettres sur les Anglais et les Francais*, ed. Von Greyerz (1897) pp.76, 714-15.
40 Peter Linebaugh, 'The ordinary of Newgate and his account', in Cockburn (ed.) op.cit., pp.246-69. However, Randall McGowen, '"He beareth not the sword in vain": religion and the criminal law in eighteenth-century England', *Eighteenth Century Studies* 21 (1987-8) pp.192-211 takes seriously such religious sentiments, as also the assize sermons.
41 NNC iv, p.260.
42 Boswell's *Life of Johnson* iv, p.329.
43 John Wesley, *Journal* vii, p.41.
44 Peter Linebaugh, 'The Tyburn riot against the surgeons', in Hay, Thompson, and Linebaugh (eds)

op.cit., p.66.
45 Cesar de Saussure, *A Foreign View of England in the Reigns of George I and George II*, trans. Van Muyden (1902) p.127.
46 Radzinowicz, op.cit., i, pp.168-70.
47 Jonathan Swift, 'Clever Tom Clinch going to be hanged'.
48 Quoted in Samuel Richardson, *Familiar Letters on Important Occasions* (1928 ed.) p.218.
49 *Celebrated Trials* (1825) iii, p.471.
50 H. Bleackley, *The Hangmen of England* (1929) p.27.
51 M. D. George, *London Life in the Eighteenth Century* (1925), p.16.
52 Richardson, op.cit., p.218.
53 W. Andrews, *Bygone Punishments* (1931) p.11.
54 ibid.
55 Swift, op.cit.
56 'To Hyde Parke, where great plenty of gallants. And pleasant it was only for the dust.' Pepys, *Diary*, 22 April 1664. Cf. also Thomas Shadwell, 'The Answer': 'And then in Hyde Park do repair/To make a dust and take no air'. *Poems on Affairs of State* (1698).
57 Thomas Brown, *Amusements, Serious and Comical*, VI, 'The Walks' (1700).
58 Sir Charles Petrie, *The Four Georges* (1946) p.195.
59 D'Archenholz, *A Picture of England*, (Dublin, 1790) pp.187-9.
60 Radzinowicz, op.cit., i, p.175.
61 Ferri de Constant, *Londres et les Anglais*, (Paris, 1804) i, pp.303-4; iv, pp.181-6.
62 C. L. Pollnitz, *Mémoires* (1738) pp.458-9.
63 F. Lacombe, *Observations sur Londres et ses environs*, pp.185-7.
64 J. H. Meister, *Letters written during a residence*, pp.61-2.
65 J. P. Grossley, *A Tour to London*, i, pp.172-3.
66 *London Chronicle*, 5-7 June, 9-12 June 1764.
67 *Daily Advertiser*, 10-11 April 1747.
68 Richardson, op.cit., p.219.
69 William Lecky, *History of England in the Eighteenth Century* (1920) vii, p.322.
70 *Walpole Correspondence* 22 p.165.
71 J. H. Jesse, *George Selwyn and his Contemporaries* (1843) i, pp.5-12.
72 S. Parnell Kerr, *George Selwyn and the Wits* (1909) pp.122-30.

73 Boswell's *Life of Johnson*, ii, p.93.
74 Radzinowicz, op.cit., i, pp.178-81. See also J. A. Sharpe, 'Last dying speeches: religion, ideology and public execution in seventeenth-century England', *Past and Present* 107 (1985) pp.147-67. For Jacobite dying speeches see Daniel Szechi, 'The Jacobite theatre of death', in Eveline Cruickshanks and Jeremy Black (eds) *The Jacobite Challenge* (Edinburgh, 1988) pp.57-73; cf. also Pieter Spierenburg, *The Spectacle of Suffering* (Cambridge, 1984); David Cooper, *The Lesson of the Scaffold* (Athens, Ohio, 1974).
75 W. Andrews, op.cit., p.27.
76 CNC ii, pp.265-70.
77 *Public Advertiser*, 20 April 1768.
78 *Weekly Journal or Saturday's Post*, 9 September 1721.
79 de Saussure, op.cit., pp.124-5.
80 Meister, op.cit., p.61.
81 John Wesley, *Journal*, 9 October 1748.
82 *Celebrated Trials* (1825) iv, p.359.
83 *Gentleman's Magazine* 1736 p.422.
84 *Annual Register* 1763 p.96.
85 See *Gentleman's Magazine* 1740 p.570; 1767 p.90; *London Magazine* 1740 p.560.
86 NNC ii, pp.153-6.
87 CNC iii, p.110.
88 NNC i, pp.89-92.
89 A. Marks, *Tyburn Tree: its History and Annals* (1908) pp.221-2.
90 Linebaugh, 'The Tyburn riot and the surgeons', op.cit., pp.102 *et seq.*
91 *Gentleman's Magazine* 1733 p.213.
92 Linebaugh, 'The Tyburn riot and the surgeons', op.cit., p.102.
93 *Gentleman's Magazine* 1767 p.276.
94 H. Bleackley, *The Hangmen of England* (1929) pp.74-5.
95 NNC vi, p.515.
96 For a wide-ranging discussion see Ruth Richardson, *Death, Dissection and the Destitute* (1988).
97 Linebaugh, 'The Tyburn riot against the surgeons', op.cit., pp.70-8.
98 NNC ii, p.81.
99 Richardson, op.cit., p.219.
100 *General Evening Post*, 18 September 1750.
101 de Saussure, op.cit., pp.126-7.
102 *Hanging Not Punishment Enough* (1701) pp.9-24.
103 Timothy Nourse, *Campania Foelix or, a discourse of the benefits and improvements in husbandry* (1700) pp.229-31.
104 George Olyffe, *An Essay humbly offered for an Act of Parliament to prevent capital crimes and the loss of many lives and to promote a desirable improvement and blessing in the nation* (1731).
105 Charles Jones, *Some Methods Proposed towards putting a stop to the flagrant crimes of Murder, Robbery and Perjury* (1752).
106 Beattie, op.cit., p.526.
107 NNC vi, p.515.
108 A. Hartshorne, *Hanging in Chains* (1891).
109 Blackstone, op.cit., iv, p.202.
110 25 Geo 2 c.37.
111 Hartshorne, op.cit., p.14.
112 NNC vi, p.121.
113 W. Andrews, *Bygone Hertfordshire* (1898), pp.225-9.
114 Hartshorne, op.cit., p.96.
115 *Celebrated Trials* (1825), v, p.368.
116 Radzinowicz, op.cit., i, pp.476-7.
117 For a discussion on the variants in the sentence for treason see Radzinowicz, op.cit., i, pp.220-1. For the prisoners of the '45 see Sir Bruce Seton and J. G. Arnot, *The Prisoners of the '45*, 3 vols (Edinburgh, 1929).
118 Blackstone, op.cit., iv, p.92.
119 For the treatment of the Manchester regiment see John Prebble, *Culloden* (1961) ch. 5. For the later 'civilized' development see Radzinowicz, op.cit., i, pp.225.
120 *Whitehall Evening Post*, 4 October 1759; cf. also Marks, op.cit., pp.63-5.
121 Bernard Mandeville, *An Inquiry into the causes of the Frequent Executions at Tyburn* (1725) pp.36-7.
122 Fielding, *Works*, op.cit., vii, p.265.
123 Richardson, op.cit., pp.219-20.
124 Boswell's *Life of Johnson*, iv, pp.188-9.
125 William Paley, *Principles of Moral and Political Philosophy*, (1817) p.434,
126 Michael Ignatieff, *A Just Measure of Pain: the Penitentiary in the Industrial Revolution 1750-1850* (1978) p.89.
127 *Gentleman's Magazine* 1783 p.974.
128 *Gentleman's Magazine* 1783 p.1060.
129 Radzinowicz, op.cit., i, pp.201-5.

15 SECONDARY PUNISHMENT

1 Sir William Blackstone, *Commentaries on the Laws of England*, 4 vols, 9th ed. (1783) iv, pp.394-6.

2 J. M. Beattie, *Crime and the Courts in England 1660-1800* (Oxford, 1986) p.431.

3 Martin Madan, *Thoughts on Executive Justice*, (1785) p.137.

4 Henry Fielding, *Works*, ed. Leslie Stephen (1882) vii, pp.261-4; Patrick Colquhoun, *Treatise on the Police of the Metropolis* (1800) pp.294-6.

5 *Gentleman's Magazine* 1788 p.316.

6 Walpole, *Memoirs of the Reign of George II*, i, pp.175-6.

7 Boswell's *Life of Johnson* i, p.347.

8 Cesare Beccaria, *Crimes and Punishments*, trans. J. A. Farrer 1880, pp.189-91.

9 Blackstone, op.cit., iv, p.397.

10 Sir John Fortescue (ed.) *Correspondence of King George the Third, 1760-1783* (1927) i, pp.395, 507; ii, pp.375, 379, 380-1.

11 Douglas Hay, 'Property, authority and the criminal law', pp.40-9.

12 ibid., p.52.

13 Colquhoun, *A Treatise on the Police of the Metropolis* (1800) pp.294, 296.

14 Similarly, it was clergyable if the shop-keeper saw the shoplifter taking goods. Thefts from a warehouse were clergy-able if the goods were simply stored there, but non-clergyable if they were put on display. Thefts from a stable were capital only if the goods were habitually kept there and integral to the work of a stable. Similarly, the Act that removed clergy for stealing from a ship in a navigable river was held to apply only when *goods* were uplifted, not rigging or tackle.

15 *London Chronicle*, 18-20 September 1788.

16 Beattie, op.cit., p.433.

17 Peter King, 'Decision-making and decision-makers in English criminal law 1750-1800', *Historical Journal* 27 (1984) p.39.

18 See N. Walker, *Crime and Insanity in England. vol.1. The Historical Perspective* (1968).

19 King, op.cit., p.41.

20 *Gentleman's Magazine* 1742 p.660.

21 J. J. Langbein, *Torture and the Laws of Proof: Europe and England in the Ancien Regime* (Chicago, 1977).

22 *Annual Register* 1770 pp.163-5.

23 Blackstone, op.cit., iv, pp.325-9.

24 *Hanging Not Punishment Enough* (1701).

25 G. Olyffe, *An Essay humbly presented for an Act . . . to prevent capital crimes and . . . promote a desirable improvement and Blessing to the Nation* (1731).

26 10 & 11 Wm 3 c.23.

27 H. Bleackley, *The Hangmen of England*, (1929) pp.61-2.

28 Blackstone, op.cit., iv, pp.378-80.

29 CNC iv, pp.175-6.

30 CNC iv, pp.125-6.

31 Arthur N. Gilbert, 'Military and civilian justice in eighteenth-century England: an assessment', *Journal of British Studies* 1978 pp.50-5.

32 *Annual Register* 1772 p.116.

33 Beattie, op.cit., pp.544-6.

34 E. P. Thompson, 'The moral economy of the eighteenth-century crowd', *Past and Present* 50 (1971) pp.76-136.

35 *London Evening Post*, 19 September 1738.

36 *Gentleman's Magazine* 1762 pp.43, 81; 1763 p.144.

37 Boswell's *Life of Johnson*, iii, p.315.

38 CNC iii, pp.122-4.

39 *Gentleman's Magazine* 1732 pp.774, 823.

40 *Gentleman's Magazine* 1756 pp.90, 116, 166, 297-300.

41 *Annual Register* 1771 p.96.

42 Cobbett's *Parliamentary History of England* 21 (1780) pp.388-91; J. A. Woods (ed.) *The Correspondence of Edmund Burke*, iv, pp.230-1.

43 Add. MSS. 27, 826 ff. 173-5.

44 CNC iii, pp.225-6.

45 CNC iv, p.3.

46 NNC iii, pp.359-65.

47 Laurence Stone, *The Family, Sex and Marriage in England 1500-1800* (1977) pp.541-2.

48 See, for example, *London Chronicle*, 18-20 October 1764.

49 *London Chronicle*, 22-24 March, 19-21 July, 28-31 July, 4-6 September 1764.

50 Blackstone, op.cit., iv, p.215.

51 Randolph Trumbach, 'London's Sodomites: homosexual behaviour and urban culture in the eighteenth century', *Journal of Social History* 11 (1977) pp.1 et seq.

52 Gerald Howson, *Thieftaker General, the rise and fall on Jonathan Wild* (1970) pp.62-3.

53 *London Chronicle*, 7-9 June 1764.

54 Arthur N. Gilbert, 'Buggery in the British Navy 1700-1861', *Journal of Social History* 10 (1976) p.72.

55 Beattie, op.cit., pp.433-4, 515; see also A. D. Harvey, 'Prosecutions for Sodomy in England at the beginning of the nineteenth century', *Historical Journal* 21 (1978) pp.939-48.
56 NNC v, p.102.
57 Peter Laslett, *The World We Have Lost Further Explored* (1983) pp.156-8.
58 *London Chronicle*, 25-28 February 1764.
59 NNC ii, p.49; cf.also Howson, op.cit., p.288.
60 *Gentleman's Magazine* 1762 p.549.
61 *Public Advertiser*, 27 January, 7 February 1764.
62 For international historical comparisons, showing the tendency for transportation to increase as a punishment in the nineteenth century, see Radzinowicz, v, (1986, with Roger Hood) pp.485-9.
63 H. B. Simpson, 'Penal servitude: its past and its future', *The Law Quarterly Review* 15 (1899) pp.33-50.
64 A. E. Smith, *Colonists in Bondage: White Servitude and Convict Labour in America 1607-1766* (Chapel Hill, 1947, reprinted 1971) pp.93-5.
65 ibid., pp.97-106.
66 Sir William Holdsworth, *A History of English Law* (1938) 11, p.573.
67 See P. G. M. Dickson, *The Financial Revolution in England: A Study in the Development of Public Credit, 1688-1756* (1967).
68 4 Geo I c.11,19.
69 J. D. Butler, 'British colonists shipped to American colonies', *American Historical Review* 2 (1896) pp.12-37.
70 Smith, op.cit., pp.113-15.
71 ibid., pp.119-22.
72 Roger Ekirch, *Bound for America: The Transportation of British Convicts to the Colonies 1718-1775* (Oxford, 1987).
73 A. E. Smith, 'The transportation of convicts to America', *American Historical Review* 39 (1933-4).
74 Beattie, op.cit., p.507.
75 CNC iv, pp.214-17.
76 CNC iv, pp.218-21.
77 NNC iv, pp.296-9.
78 *London Chronicle*, 5-8 May 1764.
79 J. M. Beattie, 'Crime and the Courts in Surrey, 1736-53', in J. S. Cockburn (ed.) *Crime in England 1550-1800*, (1977) p.179.
80 Beattie, *Crime and the Courts in England*, op.cit., p.513.
81 See J. S. Burn, *The Fleet Registers* (1833) *passim*.
82 See G. E. Allemann, *Matrimonial Law and the Materials of Restoration Comedy* (Pennsylvania, 1942).
83 Cobbett's *Parliamentary History of England*, (1780) 15 cols 2-81.
84 Stone, op.cit., p.35.
85 26 Geo 2 c.33.
86 CNC iii, pp.250-60.
87 NNC i, pp.263-6.
88 NNC vi, pp.578-9.
89 NNC iii, pp.306-51.
90 19 Geo 2 c.34.
91 Neville Williams, *Contraband Cargoes* (1959) p.109.
92 *The Discoveries of John Poulter, alias Baxter* (Sherbourne, 1753) p.28.
93 J. Hewitt, *A Journal of the Proceedings of J. Hewitt, Senior Alderman of the City of Coventry and one of his Majesty's Justices of the Peace for the said City and County in his Duty as a Magistrate*, 2 vols (Birmingham, 1790) i, pp.117-220.
94 William Paley, *Principles of Moral and Political Philosophy* (1817) pp.420-2.
95 ibid., p.543.
96 Bernard Mandeville, *An Inquiry into the Causes of the Frequent Executions at Tyburn* (1725) pp.50-1.
97 Sir William Eden, *Principles of Penal Law*, (1771) p.33.
98 Colquhoun, op.cit., pp.478-81.
99 *The Discoveries of John Poulter*, op.cit. p.28.
100 Douglas Hay, 'War, dearth and theft', *Past and Present* 95 (1982) p.143.
101 Stephen Gradish, 'Wages and manning: the Navy Act of 1758', *English Historical Review* 9 (1978) pp.46-67.
102 Roger Ekirch, 'The transportation of Scottish criminals to America during the eighteenth century', *Journal of British Studies* 24 (1985) pp.366-74.
103 S. R. Conway, 'The recruitment of criminals into the British Army, 1775-1781', *Bulletin of the Institute of Historical Research* 58 (1985) pp.46-58.
104 16 Geo 3 c.43.
105 For full details on the working of the prison hulks see W. Brand Johnson, *The English Prison Hulks* (1957).
106 NNC v, pp.264-70.
107 CNC iv, pp.107-8.
108 O'Brien, *The Foundation of Australia*, op.cit., pp.132-4.
109 Brand Johnson, op.cit., p.9.
110 19 Geo 3 c.74.
111 *General Evening Post*, 4-7 September

1784.

112 *Public Advertiser*, 8 March 1784.

113 Margaret Weidenhofer, *The Convict Years: Transportation and the Penal System 1788-1868* (Melbourne, 1973) p.21.

114 O'Brien, op.cit. pp.161-2

115 A. G. L. Shaw, *A Study of Penal Transportation from Great Britain and Ireland to Australia and other parts of the British Empire* (1966) pp.45-57.

116 The imperial proposition is argued in Alan Frost, *Convicts and Empire: A Naval Question 1776-1811* (Melbourne, 1980). For a rebuttal see Mollie Gillen, 'The Botany Bay decision 1786: convicts not empire', *English Historical Review* 97 (1982) pp.740-86. Some of the evidence is set out in Manning Clark (ed.) *Select Documents in Australian History 1788-1850* (1950).

117 John Cobley, *The Crimes of the First Fleet Convicts* (Sydney, 1970); cf. also Charles Bateson, *The Convict Ships 1781-1866* (Glasgow, 1959).

118 NNC vi, pp.98-103, 171-3.

119 CNC iv, pp.168-70.

120 George Rudé, *Protest and Punishment: the story of the Social and Political Protesters transported to Australia 1788-1868* (Oxford, 1978).

121 ibid., p.64.

122 See J. Cobley, *The Convicts 1788-92* (Surry Hills, 1965). This chapter was written before Robert Hughes's *The Fatal Shore* came to hand. There is nothing in Hughes to challenge the established picture, but the book in general is so good that it is now the place where anyone interested in Botany Bay, 1788, should start.

123 NNC vi, pp.559-63.

124 For a discussion see Sean McConville, *A History of English Prison Administration 1750-1877* (1981), esp. ch. 5.

125 Robin Evans, *The Fabrication of Virtue: English Prison Architecture 1750-1840* (Cambridge, 1982) pp.118-31.

126 Michael Ignatieff, *A Just Measure of Pain: the Penitentiary in the Industrial Revolution 1750-1850* (1978) pp.33-8.

127 John Howard, *State of the Prisons in England and Wales* (1771) op.cit. p.4.

128 *Gentleman's Magazine* 1763 pp.602, 633.

129 W. J. Sheehan, 'Finding solace in eighteenth-century Newgate', in J. S. Cockburn (ed.) *Crime in England 1550-1800*, (1977) pp.229-45.

130 *London Chronicle*, 10-12 April, 28 April-1 May 1764.

131 Peter Linebaugh, 'The ordinary of Newgate and his account', in Cockburn (ed.) op.cit., p.253.

132 *Gentleman's Magazine* 1735 p.498.

133 Joanna Innes, 'The King's Bench prison in the later eighteenth century: law, authority and order in a London debtor's prison', in J. Brewer and J. Styles, *An Ungovernable People* (1980) pp.250-98.

134 John Howard, *State of the Prisons* (1784) pp.235-41.

135 Colquhoun, op.cit., pp.390-3.

136 Howard, op.cit., p.35.

137 Michael Ignatieff, *A Just Measure of Pain: the Penitentiary in the Industrial Revolution 1750-1850* (1978) pp.11-14.

138 ibid., pp.31-3.

139 T. S. Ashton, *An Economic History of England: The Eighteenth Century*, (1955) p.39.

140 Timothy Nourse, *Campania Foelix or a discourse of the benefits and improvements in husbandry* (1700) p.229.

141 G. Rusche and O. Kirchheimer, *Punishment and Social Structure* (1939) p.24.

142 *London Chronicle*, 11-14 February, 11-13 October 1764.

143 Nourse, op.cit., p.229.

144 Mandeville, op.cit., p.16.

145 17 Geo 2 c.5.

146 Ignatieff, op.cit., p.25.

147 Beattie, *Crime and the Courts in England*, op.cit., pp.611-13.

16 CRIME AND SOCIAL CHANGE

1 E. A. Wrigley, 'The growth of population in eighteenth-century England: a conundrum resolved', *Past and Present* 98 (1983) pp.121-150.

2 M. Weisser, *Crime and Punishment in Early Modern Europe* (revised edn 1982) pp.107-110.

3 Sir William Besant, *London in the Eighteenth Century* (1902) pp.494-533.

4 George Rudé, *Hanoverian London 1714-1808*, (1961) p.96.

5 A. J. Weitzman, 'Eighteenth-century London: urban paradise or fallen city?', *Journal of the History of Ideas* 36 (1975) pp.369-80.

6 See Jack Lindsay, *The Monster City;*

Defoe's London 1688-1730 (1978).

7 P. J. Corfield, *The Impact of English Towns 1700-1800* (Oxford, 1982).

8 J. M. Beattie, *Crime and the Courts in England 1660-1800* (Oxford, 1986) pp.14-15.

9 See R. C. Jarvis, *Collected Papers on the Jacobite Risings* (1972) *passim*.

10 Paul Rock, 'Law, order and power in late seventeenth and early eighteenth century England', in S. Cohen and A. Scull, *Social Control and the State* (Oxford, 1983) pp.191-221 (at pp.200-1).

11 See David S. Landes, *The Unbound Prometheus: Technological Change and Industrial Development in Western Europe from 1750 to the Present* (Cambridge, 1969); Robert W. Malcolmson, *Life and Labour in England 1700-1780* (1981). Cf. also Maxine Berg, Pat Hudson, Michael Sonenscher (eds) *Manufacture in Town and Country before the Factory* (Cambridge, 1983).

12 Weisser, op.cit., pp.110-13.

13 E. P. Thompson, 'Time, work, discipline and industrial capitalism', *Past and Present* 38 (1967) pp.56-97.

14 W. G. Carson, 'Early British Factory Acts', in G. Geis and E. Stotland (eds) *White Collar Crime* (Beverley Hills, 1979) pp.142-73; cf. also John Rule, *The Experience of Labour in Eighteenth-Century Industry* (1981), esp. ch. 5.

15 John Styles, 'Controlling the outworker: the embezzlement laws and industrial outwork in eighteenth-century England', in Berg, Hudson and Sonenscher (eds) *Manufacture in Town and Country*, op.cit.

16 T. S. Ashton, *An Economic History of England: The Eighteenth Century* (1955) p.102.

17 ibid., p.210.

18 *Gentleman's Magazine* 1760 p.76.

19 Dorothy Marshall, 'Manners, meals and domestic pastimes', in A. Turberville (ed.) *Johnson's England* (Oxford, 1933) i, p.342.

20 *London Chronicle*, 15-17 May 1764.

21 *Gentleman's Magazine* 1764 p.449.

22 *London Chronicle*, 13-16 October 1764.

23 *London Chronicle*, 10-12 May 1764.

24 *Gentleman's Magazine* 1766 p.43.

25 J. J. Hecht, *The Domestic Servant Class in Eighteenth-Century England* (1956) pp.158-68.

26 L. and B. Hammond, *The Skilled Labourer 1760-1832* (1919) pp.145-6.

27 *Annual Register* 1779 pp.228-9, 233.

28 R. S. Fitton and A. P. Wadsworth, *The Strutts and the Arkwrights 1758-1830* (Manchester, 1973).

29 L. and B. Hammond, op.cit., pp.222-5.

30 ibid., pp.159-61.

31 P. Mantoux, *The Industrial Revolution in the Eighteenth Century* (1937) p.82.

32 By 12 Geo 1 c.34 (1725).

33 4 Geo 3 c.37.

34 6 Geo 3 c.28.

35 22 Geo 3.c.28.

36 28 Geo 3 c.55.

37 Leon Radzinowicz, *A History of Criminal Law and its Administration from 1750*, 5 vols (1948-86) i, pp.479-84.

38 L. and B. Hammond, *The Village Labourer* (1948) p.73.

39 Oliver Goldsmith, *The Deserted Village* (1770).

40 See J. M. Yelling, *Common Fields and Enclosures in England 1450-1850* (1977); M. Turner, *English Parliamentary Enclosure* (1980).

41 W. E. Tate, 'Opposition to parliamentary enclosure in the eighteenth century', *Agricultural History* 19 (1945) pp.137 *et seq*. Cf. also G. Slater, *The English Peasantry and the Enclosure of Common Fields* (1907).

42 *Gentleman's Magazine* 1765 pp.391, 441.

43 J. D. Chambers, 'Enclosure and the labour supply in the industrial revolution', *Economic History Review*, 2nd series 5 (1952-3) pp.319-43.

44 For the turnpikes in general see W. Albert, *The Turnpike Road System of England 1663-1844* (Cambridge, 1972).

45 *Gentleman's Magazine* 1749 pp.376-7; 1753 p.343.

46 Robert W. Malcolmson, '"A set of ungovernable people": the Kingswood colliers in the eighteenth century', in J. Brewer and J. Styles (eds) *An Ungovernable People*, (1980) Cf. also D. G. G. Isaac, 'A study of popular disturbances in Britain 1714-1754', Ph.D. thesis, Univ of Edinburgh (1953) ch. 5 and 6.

47 T. S. Ashton, *Economic Fluctuations in England 1700-1800*, (Oxford, 1959).

48 J. S. Cockburn (ed.) *Crime in England 1550-1800* (1977) p.160.

49 J. Walter and K. Wrightson, 'Dearth and the social order in early modern

England', *Past and Present* 71 (1976) pp.22-42.

50 J. M. Fewster, 'The keelmen of Tyneside in the eighteenth century', *Durham University Journal* 19 (1957-58).

51 G. E. Mingay, 'The agricultural depression 1730-1750', *Economic History Review*, 2nd series 8 (1956) pp.323-38.

52 Daniel Defoe, *The Complete English Tradesmen* (1726) p.317.

53 D. E. C. Eversley, 'The Home Market and Economic Growth in England 1750-1780', in E. L. Jones and G. E. Mingay (eds) *Land, Labour and Population in the Industrial Revolution* (1767); J. D. Chambers and G. E. Mingay, *The Agricultural Revolution 1750-1880* (1966).

54 *Annual Register* May-June 1768, *passim*.

55 M. D. George, *London Life in the Eighteenth Century* (1925) p.357.

56 See J. A. Sharpe, 'The History of violence in England: some observations', *Past and Present* 108 (1985) pp.206-15; Laurence Stone, 'Interpersonal violence in English society 1300-1980', *Past and Present* 101 (1983) pp.22-33; Ted Robert Gurr, 'Historical trends in violent crime: a critical review of the evidence', *Crime and Justice: An Annual Review of Research* 3 (1981) pp.295-353.

57 Henry Fielding, *Tom Jones*, Book 4, ch. 8.

58 Laurence Stone, *The Family, Sex and Marriage in England 1500-1800*, (1977) esp. ch. 6-9.

59 J. H. Plumb, 'The new world of children in eighteenth-century England', *Past and Present* (1975) pp.64-75; Robert Malcolmson, *Popular Recreations in English Society 1700-1850* (Cambridge, 1973) pp.89-157; Randolph Trumbach, *The Rise of the Egalitarian Family: Aristocratic Kinship and Domestic Relations in Eighteenth Century England* (NY, 1978).

60 Mary Thrale (ed.) *The Autobiography of Francis Place* (Cambridge, 1972) pp.14-16,74-82.

61 Beattie, op.cit., pp.107-112.

62 Philip Jenkins, 'Varieties of Enlightenment criminology', *British Journal of Criminology* 24 (1984) pp.112-30.

63 Keith Thomas, *Man and the Natural World: Changing Attitudes in England 1500-1800* (1983) pp.143-91.

64 E. P. Thompson, *The Poverty of Theory* (1978) p.165.

65 Adam Smith, *An Inquiry into the Nature and Causes of the Wealth of Nations*, 2 vols, ed. R. H. Campbell and A. S. Skinner (Oxford, 1976) p.437.

66 Piers Paul Read, *The Train Robbers* (1979 edn.) p.318.

67 A number of recent works deal with this issue: J. Q. Wilson and E. Hernstein, *Crime and Human Nature* (NY, 1985); John Hagan, *Modern Criminology* (NY, 1985); George Vold and Thomas Bernard, *Theoretical Criminology* (Oxford, 1985).

68 J. Walsh, 'Methodism and the mob in the eighteenth century', in G. J. Cuming and D. Parker, *Popular Belief and Practice* Studies in Church History VIII, (Cambridge, 1972); cf. also R. F. Wearnmouth, *Methodism and the Common People of England* (Epworth, 1945).

69 William S. Boulton, *The Amusements of Old London*.

70 Walpole to Dalrymple, 28 June 1760, *Walpole Correspondence* 15 p.70.

71 Peter Linebaugh, 'The ordinary of Newgate and his account', in Cockburn (ed.) op.cit.

72 Michael Ignatieff, 'State, civil society and total institutions: a critique of recent social histories of punishment', in S. Cohen and A. Scull (eds) *Social Control and the State: Historical and Comparative Essays* (1983) pp.75-105.

73 Michael Ignatieff, *A Just Measure of Pain: the Penitentiary in the Industrial Revolution 1750-1850* (1978) p.90.

74 ibid.

75 ibid., pp.100, 113.

76 Dario Melossi and Massimo Pavarini, *The Prison and the Factory: Origins of the Penitentiary System* (1981) p.3.

77 Beattie, op.cit., p.617.

78 Margaret de Lacy, *Prison Reform in Lancashire 1700-1850* (1986).

79 Ignatieff, 'State, Civil Society and Total Institutions', op.cit., pp.79-83.

80 Beattie, op.cit., pp.611-13.

81 ibid., pp.619 *et seq*.

82 ibid.

83 G. Rusche and O. Kirchheimer, *Punishment and Social Structure*, (1939) p.95.

84 Melossi and Pavarini, op.cit., p.35.

85 Rusche and Kirchheimer, op.cit., p.65.

86 Wiley B. Saunders (ed.) *Juvenile Offenders for a Thousand Years* (Chapel

Hill, Univ. of N. Carolina, 1970) pp.40-91.

87 Melossi and Pavarini, op.cit., pp.4-5.

88 Quoted in ibid., p.55.

89 This is surely a serious objection to the interpretation put forward in Michel Foucault, *Discipline and Punish: the Birth of the Prison* (1977).

90 See the brilliant essay with which E. P. Thompson ends *Whigs and Hunters* (1975) pp.258-69.

91 Although Beattie, *Crime and the Courts* p.625 argues strenuously that the empire *always* answered the purely domestic requirements of England, not vice versa.

92 Rusche and Kirchheimer, op.cit., p.32.

93 See J. J. Hecht, op.cit.

94 Ignatieff, *Just Measure*, p.92.

95 For the vast scope of the panopticon proposals see Bentham, *Works* (NY, 1962) iv, pp.1-71.

96 For this authoritarian and repressive element in the panopticon see Gertrude Himmelfarb, 'The Haunted House of Jeremy Bentham', in *Victorian Minds* (NY, 1968) pp.32-81.

97 Cockburn, op.cit. p.186.

98 Roy Porter, *English Society in the Eighteenth Century* (1982) p.27.

99 ibid., p.112.

100 Melossi and Pavarini, op.cit., pp.37-8.

101 A. W. Coats, 'Changing attitudes to labour in the mid-eighteenth century', *Economic History Review* 11 (1958) pp.35-51.

102 D. A. Baugh, 'Poverty, Protestantism and political economy: English ettitudes towards the poor 1660-1800', in S. B. Baxter (ed.) *England's Rise to Greatness* (California, 1983).

103 See the extended discussion in Gertrude Himmelfarb, *The Idea of Poverty* (1983).

104 Rusche and Kirchheimer, op.cit., pp.95 *et seq*.

105 Melossi and Pavarini, op.cit., pp.40-3.

106 See Karl Marx, 'Proceedings of the Sixth Rhine Province Assembly Debates on the law on theft of wood', *Rheinische Zeitung* (1842) in Marx, *Collected Works* (1975) i, pp.224-63.

107 For traditional rights see B. Bushaway, *By Rite: Custom, Ceremony and Community in England 1700-1880* (1982).

108 See in general D. F. Greenberg, *Crime and Capitalism* (1981); T. Platt and P. Takagi (eds) *Crime and Social Justice* (1981); K. Tribe, *Genealogies of Capitalism* (1981).

109 Sir William Blackstone, *Commentaries on the Laws of England*, 4 vols, 9th edn (1783) iv, pp.248-50.

110 Paul H. Haagen, 'Eighteenth-century English society and the debt law', in Cohen and Scull (eds) op.cit. pp.222-47.

111 E. Shorter, 'On writing the history of rape', *Signs* 3 (1977) pp.471-82.

112 Roy Porter, 'Rape – does it have a historical meaning?' in R. Porter and Sylvana Tomaselli (eds) *Rape* (1986) pp.216-36.

113 For a general assessment of this problem, unrelated to crime and punishment, see E. P. Thompson, *The Poverty of Theory*, op.cit., pp.35-91.

114 For this see W. W. Rostow, *The Stages of Economic Growth* (1960).

115 V. A. C. Gattrell, Bruce Lenman, and Geoffrey Parker, *Crime and the Law. The Social History of Crime in Western Europe since 1800* (1980) p.7.

116 A notable recent exponent of this line of reasoning is Lezek Kolakowski, *Main Currents of Marxism*, 3 vols (1978).

117 Some try to deny the link between American capitalism and organized crime by asserting that the latter could never become 'hegemonic' in the Gramscian sense. This ignores the fact that most regimes create their own legitimacy through the educational system, the media, etc. So although capitalism and, say, the Mafia are distinct *sociologically*, they do not differ significantly morally or philosophically (for the rule of law is a 'fetter' on untrammelled profit-making). To adapt Clausewitz, organized crime is the pursuit of profit by other means.

17 THE IMPACT OF WAR

1 J. M. Winter (ed.) *War and Economic Development* (1975).

2 J. M. Beattie, 'The pattern of crime in England, 1600-1800', *Past and Present* 62 (1974) pp.47-95.

3 Arthur N. Gilbert, 'Army impressment during the War of Spanish Succession',

The Historian 38 (1976) pp.696-700.

4 P. B. Munsche, *Gentlemen and Poachers*, (1981) p.88.

5 T. S. Ashton, *Economic Fluctuations in England 1700-1800* (Oxford, 1959) op.cit. p.189.

6 A. H. John, 'War and the English Economy 1700-1763', *Economic History Review*, 2nd series, 7 (1955) pp.329-44.

7 Douglas Hay, 'War, dearth and theft', *Past and Present* 95 (1982) pp.117-60 (at p.139).

8 ibid., p.144.

9 J. M. Beattie, *Crime and the Courts in England 1660-1800* (Oxford, 1986) p.215.

10 Daniel Defoe, *Conjugal Lewdness or Matrimonial Whoredom* (1727); *Street Robberies Considered: the Reason of their being so Frequent* (1728); *An Effectual Scheme for the Immediate Prevention of Street Robberies and Suppressing of all other Disorders of the Night* (1730).

11 Hay, op.cit.

12 John, op.cit.

13 Ashton, op.cit. p.52.

14 ibid., pp.74-5.

15 T.S. Ashton, *An Economic History of England: The Eighteenth Century*, (1955) pp.162-3.

16 E. E. Hoon, *The Organisation of the English Customs System 1696-1786* (1968 edn) p.232.

17 John Ehrmann, *The Navy in the War of William III 1689-97* (Cambridge, 1953) pp.113-14.

18 Beattie, *Crime and the Courts*, op.cit., p.483.

19 CNC ii, pp.163-5.

20 NNC i, pp.10-14.

21 *Hanging Not Punishment Enough*, op.cit. p.24.

22 See R. E. Scoullar, *The Armies of Queen Anne* (1966).

23 NNC i, pp.179-81.

24 NNC i, pp.322-6.

25 NNC i, pp.255-8.

26 J. M. Beattie, 'Crime and the Courts in Surrey 1736-1753', in J. S. Cockburn (ed.) *Crime in England 1550-1800* (1972) pp.159-60.

27 Beattie, *Crime and the Courts in England*, op.cit., p.232.

28 John Stevenson, *Popular Disturbances in England 1700-1870* (1979) pp.126-7.

29 See D. A. Baugh, *British Naval Administration in the Age of Walpole* (Princeton, 1975); cf. also John Prebble, *Mutiny* (1975); Christopher Lloyd, *The British Seaman* (1970).

30 *Journal of the House of Commons* 26 (1750-4) p.27.

31 John Howard, *An Account of the Principal Lazarettos of Europe* (1780), Appendix.

32 ibid.

33 *Gentleman's Magazine* 1748 p.293.

34 Walpole to Mann, 31 January 1750, *Walpole Correspondence* 20 p.111.

35 *Gentleman's Magazine* 1751 p.423.

36 *Gentleman's Magazine* 1750 pp.41-2.

37 NNC iv, p.90.

38 *The Discoveries of John Poulter, alias Baxter*, (1753).

39 NNC iv, pp.74-90.

40 *Gentleman's Magazine* 1757 p.43.

41 *Gentleman's Magazine* 1758 p.240.

42 Stephen Gradish, *The Manning of the British Navy during the Seven Years War* (1980); H. C. B. Rogers, *The British Standing Army of the Eighteenth Century* (1977).

43 J. S. Cockburn (ed.) *Crime in England 1700-1800* (1977) pp.185, 336.

44 John Howard, op.cit.

45 For a detailed examination of this aspect of the French war effort see James C. Riley, *The Seven Years War and the Old Regime in France* (Princeton, 1986).

46 J. R. Western, *The English Militia in the Eighteenth Century*, op.cit.

47 *Gentleman's Magazine* 1757 p.431.

48 CNC iii, p.316.

49 Adam Smith, *An Inquiry into the Nature and Causes of the Wealth of Nations*, 2 vols, ed. R. H. Campbell and A. S. Skinner (Oxford, 1976) i, p.470.

50 *Gentleman's Magazaine* 1763 pp.119-20.

51 *London Chronicle*, 28 April-1 May 1764.

52 *London Chronicle*, 6-9 October 1764.

53 *Gentleman's Magazine* 1762 p.44.

54 *London Chronicle*, 31 January- 2 February 1764.

55 NNC iv, pp.227-32.

56 *Gentleman's Magazine* 1765 p.391.

57 *London Chronicle*, 17-19 July 1764.

58 *Annual Register* 1763 p.59.

59 Ralph Davis, 'Seamen's sixpence: an index of commercial activity 1607-1828', *Economica*, new series 23 (1956) p.328.

60 W. J. Shelton, *English Hunger and Industrial Disorders*, op.cit. pp.184-92.

61 Hay, op.cit. p.136.

62 *London Chronicle*, 18-21 May 1765.

63 Ashton, op.cit., pp.22, 60, 181-2.

64 Shelton, op.cit., p.124.

65 ibid., pp.126-7.

66 ibid., p.135.

67 Arthur Young, *The Farmer's Tour through the East of England*, 4 vols (1771) ii, pp.77-8.

68 Ashton, op.cit., p.152, 187.

69 R. B. Rose, 'A Liverpool sailors' strike in the eighteenth century', *Transactions of the Lancashire and Cheshire Antiquarian Society* 68 (1958) pp.87-92.

70 Some far-sighted critics had warned that this would be the inevitable consequence of enlisting tens of thousands of the labouring poor into the Army and Navy (*Gentleman's Magazine* 1756 p.625). For the superior diet of sailors in the Seven Years War see Rodgers, *The Wooden World* (1986) op.cit.

71 See Piers Mackesy, *The War for America* (1964) for a general survey.

72 Michael Ignatieff, *A Just Measure of Pain: the Penitentiary in the Industrial Revolution 1750-1850* (1978) op.cit. p.46.

73 NNC v, pp.235-40, 296-302, 329-39.

74 J. A. Picton, *Memorials of Liverpool* (1873) i, pp.696-7.

75 Rose, op.cit.

76 Neville Williams, *Contraband Cargoes*, (1959) pp.150-1.

77 Hay, op.cit. p.138.

78 Leon Radzinowicz, *A History of Criminal Law and its Administration from 1750* 5 vols (1948-86) iii, pp.1-11.

79 *Gentleman's Magazine* 1784 p.379. Of the executed, twelve were burglars, two were footpads, and one posed as someone else to get his wages.

80 *Gentleman's Magazine* 1784 p.224.

81 'Convicts under sentence of death in Newgate and the gaols throughout the kingdom increase so fast that, were they all to be executed, England would soon be marked among the nations as the bloody country.' (*Gentleman's Magazine* 1784 p.224.)

82 *London Courant*, 31 August 1782.

83 Walpole to Mann, 8 September 1782, *Walpole Correspondence* 25 pp.316-17.

84 *Gentleman's Magazine* 1782 p.450; 1783 p.973; 1784 p.712.

85 See *Whitehall Evening Post*, 2 January, 1 March, 17 May 1783.

86 *General Evening Post*, 4-7 September 1784.

87 *Whitehall Evening Post*, 19 April 1783.

88 Arthur Young, *Autobiography* (ed.) M. B. Edwards (1898) pp.470-1.

89 Jonas Hanway, *Solitude in Imprisonment* (1776) p.63; *The Defects of Police* (1775) p.11.

90 See, for example, Patrick Colquhoun, *Treatise on the Police of the Metropolis* (1800) p.32.

91 See in general Clive Emsley, *British Society in the French Wars 1793-1815* (1979).

92 This is of course the starting point for E. P. Thompson's monumental *The Making of the English Working Class* (1963).

93 John Stevenson, op.cit. p.166.

94 ibid,. pp.127-9.

95 ibid., pp.129-35.

96 R. B. Rose, 'The Priestley riots of 1791', *Past and Present* 18 (1960) pp.68-88.

97 John Stevenson, 'The London 'crimp' riots of 1794', *International Review of Social History* 16 (1971) pp.40-58.

98 Colquhoun, op.cit., p.100.

99 Williams, op.cit. p.165.

100 Cooper, 'Smugglers in Sussex', *Sussex Archaelogical Collections*, p.91.

101 Munsche, op.cit. p.138.

102 Stevenson, op.cit., pp.97-8.

103 George Rudé, *Hanoverian London 1714-1808* (1961) p.97.

104 Beattie, *Crime and the Courts*, op.cit., p.248.

105 See the list of those tried for sedition, libel, and treason in Clive Emsley, 'An aspect of Pitt's 'Terror': prosecutions for sedition during the 1790s', *Social History* 6 (1981) pp.155-84 (at pp.176-84).

106 NNC vi, pp.220-42.

107 NNC vi, pp.157-62, 164-9.

108 NNC vi, pp.173-8, 188-91.

109 NNC vi, pp.140-8.

110 *Memoir of Thomas Hardy* (1832) pp.36-43.

111 Howell, *State Trials*, op.cit., 24 p.252.

112 NNC vi, pp.246-361.

113 Clive Emsley, 'Repression, terror and the rule of law in England during the decade of the French Revolution', *English Historical Review* 100 (1985) pp.801-26.

114 NNC vi, pp.424-6.

115 See Place's opinion (Add. MSS. 27, 808 ff. 41-9).

116 36 Geo 3 c.7.

117 36 Geo 3 c.8.

118 Emsley, 'An aspect of Pitt's terror', cit.

119 W. S. Holdsworth, *A History of English Law* (1938) viii, pp.302-22.

120 George Rudé, *The Crowd in History: a Study of Popular Disturbances in France and England 1730-1848* (NY, 1964) p.244.

121 E. P. Thompson, op.cit., p.147

122 Add. MSS. 27, 808 f.110.

123 Thompson, op.cit., pp.216-17.

124 Marianne Elliott, *Partners in Revolution: the United Irishmen and France* (New Haven 1982) pp.182-9.

125 NNC vi, pp.711-13.

126 Emsley, 'Repression, terror and the rule of law', op.cit., pp.820-1.

127 See T. B. Howell, *A Complete Collection of State Trials*, 34 vols (1816-28) 15, pp.1323-1403.

128 NNC vi, pp.399-402; cf. also Prebble, op.cit.

129 NNC vi, pp.446-7.

130 Western, op.cit. pp.294-302.

131 See B. Dobree and G. E. Mainwaring, *The Floating Republic* (1935); J. Dugan, *The Great Mutiny* (1966).

132 37 Geo 3 c.70.

133 NNC vi, pp.497-508.

134 Radzinowicz, i, pp.487-93.

135 *London Chronicle*, 13-16, 25-27 May 1797.

135 Emsley, 'Repression, terror and the rule of law', op.cit. pp.814-15.

136 NNC vi, pp.758-817.

AFTERWORD

1 Bonger's *Criminality and Economic Conditions*, op.cit., is singularly stimulating and insightful. Doubtless there is nothing particularly 'Marxist' about it, as it puts forward a commonsensical view of crime as being largely socioeconomic in causation, but containing also a residue of crimes against the person deriving from psychopathological foundations. But the condemnation of Bonger in Ian Taylor, Paul Walton, and Jock Young, *The New Criminology* (1973) pp.222-36 seems excessive. Reading the two different Marxist approaches to crime together, one is immediately struck by Bonger's much greater grip of the sort of reality familiar to historians, to say nothing of his superior lucidity.

2 Daria Melossi and Massimo Pavarini, *The Prison and the Factory: Origins of the Penitentiary System* (1981) *passim*.

3 Taylor, Walton, and Young, op.cit., pp.145-6.

4 ibid., p.36.

5 ibid. pp.235-6.

6 See, for example, J. Styles and J. Brewer (eds) *An Ungovernable People* (198) p.20.

7 J. M. Beattie, 'Judicial records and the measurement of crime in eighteenth-century England', in L. A. Knapla (ed.) *Crime and Justice in Europe and Canada* (1980) p.136.

8 Peter King, 'Decision-makers and decision-making in English criminal law, 1750-1800', *Historical Journal* (1984) pp.25-38.

9 ibid., pp.32-4.

10 See Mackenzie and Silver, *Angels in Marble* (1968); Nordlinger, *Working Class Conservatism* (1967).

11 See the classic study by S. M. Lipset in *Political Man*

12 King, op.cit., pp.26, 58.

13 J. H. Langbein, 'Albion's Fatal Flaws', *Past and Present* 98 (1983) pp.96-120.

14 In this connection the title of Peter King's article cited above is itself significant.

15 Michael Ignatieff, 'State, civil society and total institutions: A critique of recent social histories of punishment' in S. Cohen and A. Scull (eds) *Social Control and the State: Historical and Comparative Essays* (1983) p.94.

16 *Correspondence between Archbishop Herring and Lord Chancellor Hardwicke during the '45, English Historical Review* 19, (1904); *Private Correspondence of the Earl of Chesterfield and the Duke of Newcastle* (Royal Historical Society, Camden series, xliv, 1930); Leonard W. Labaree and Whitfield J. Bell, Jr (eds) *Papers of Benjamin Franklin* (New Haven, 1961).

17 A very vivid, if impressionistic, picture of this self-confidence is given in Smollett's *Humphrey Clinker* during the hero's visit to Bath (Penguin edn, 1967, p.65).

18 E. P. Thompson, 'The moral economy of the English crowd', *Past and Present* 50 (1971) pp.132-4.

19 J. Stevenson, 'The moral economy of the English crowd: myth and reality', in Anthony Fletcher and John Stevenson (eds) *Order and Disorder in Early Modern England* (Cambridge, 1985) pp.218-38.

20 J. Bohstedt, *Riots and Community*

Politics in England and Wales 1790-1810 (Harvard, 1983) p.211.

21 E. P. Thompson, 'Patrician society, plebeian culture', *Journal of Social History* (1974) pp.382-405.

22 John Brewer, 'The Wilkesites and the law 1763-74, a study of radical notions of government', in J. Styles and J. Brewer (eds) *An Ungovernable People* (1980) p.169.

23 S. Cohen and A. Scull (eds) *Social Control and the State: Historical and Comparative Essays* (1983) p.68.

Index

OXFORD

MORE OXFORD PAPERBACKS

Details of a selection of other Oxford Paperbacks follow. A complete list of Oxford Paperbacks, including The World's Classics, Twentieth-Century Classics, OPUS, Past Masters, Oxford Authors, Oxford Shakespeare, and Oxford Paperback Reference, is available in the UK from the General Publicity Department, Oxford University Press (RS), Walton Street, Oxford, OX2 6DP.

In the USA, complete lists are available from the Paperbacks Marketing Manager, Oxford University Press, 200 Madison Avenue, New York, NY 10016.

Oxford Paperbacks are available from all good bookshops. In case of difficulty, customers in the UK can order direct from Oxford University Press Bookshop, 116 High Street, Oxford, Freepost, OX1 4BR, enclosing full payment. Please add 10 per cent of the published price for postage and packing.

PAST MASTERS

General Editor: Keith Thomas

The *Past Masters* series offers students and general readers alike concise introductions to the lives and works
of the world's greatest literary figures, composers,
philosophers, religious leaders, scientists, and social and
political thinkers.

'Put end to end, this series will constitute a noble ency-
clopaedia of the history of ideas.' Mary Warnock

HOBBES

Richard Tuck

Thomas Hobbes (1588–1679) was the first great English political philosopher, and his book *Leviathan* was one of the first
truly modern works of philosophy. He has long had the reputation of being a pessimistic atheist, who saw human nature
as inevitably evil, and who proposed a totalitarian state to
subdue human failings. In this new study, Richard Tuck shows
that while Hobbes may indeed have been an atheist, he was
far from pessimistic about human nature, nor did he advocate
totalitarianism. By locating him against the context of his age,
Dr Tuck reveals Hobbs to have been passionately concerned
with the refutation of scepticism in both science and ethics,
and to have developed a theory of knowledge which rivalled
that of Descartes in its importance for the formation of modern
philosophy.

Also available in Past Masters:

Spinoza   Roger Scruton
Bach   Denis Arnold
Machiavelli   Quentin Skinner
Darwin   Jonathan Howard

OXFORD LIVES

Biography at its best—this popular series offers authoritative accounts of the lives of famous men and women from the arts and sciences, politics and exploration.

'SUBTLE IS THE LORD'
The Science and the Life of Albert Einstein

Abraham Pais

Abraham Pais, an award-winning physicist who knew Einstein personally during the last nine years of his life, presents a guide to the life and the thought of the most famous scientist of our century. Using previously unpublished papers and personal recollections from their years of acquaintance, the narrative illuminates the man through his work with both liveliness and precision, making this *the* authoritative scientific biography of Einstein.

'The definitive life of Einstein.'
Brian Pippard, *Times Literary Supplement*

'By far the most important study of both the man and the scientist.' Paul Davies, *New Scientist*

'An outstanding biography of Albert Einstein that one finds oneself reading with sheer pleasure.' *Physics Today*

Also in the Oxford Lives series:

Peter Fleming: A Biography Duff Hart-Davies
Gustav Holst: A Biography Imogen Holst
T. H. White Sylvia Townsend Warner
Joyce Cary: Gentleman Rider Alan Bishop

POLITICS IN OXFORD PAPERBACKS

Oxford Paperbacks offers incisive and provocative studies of the political ideologies and institutions that have shaped the modern world since 1945.

GOD SAVE ULSTER!
The Religion and Politics of Paisleyism

Steve Bruce

Ian Paisley in the only modern Western leader to have founded his own Church and political party, and his enduring popularity and success mirror the complicated issues which continue to plague Northern Ireland. This book is the first serious analysis of his religious and political careers and a unique insight into Unionist politics and religion in Northern Ireland today.

Since it was founded in 1951, the Free Presbyterian Church of Ulster has grown steadily; it now comprises some 14,000 members in fifty congregations in Ulster and ten branches overseas. The Democratic Unionist Party, formed in 1971, now speaks for about half of the Unionist voters in Northern Ireland, and the personal standing of the man who leads both these movements was confirmed in 1979 when Ian R. K. Paisley received more votes than any other member of the European Parliament. While not neglecting Paisley's 'charismatic' qualities, Steve Bruce argues that the key to his success has been his ability to embody and represent traditional evangelical Protestantism and traditional Ulster Unionism.

'original and profound . . . I cannot praise this book too highly.'
Bernard Crick, *New Society*

Also in Oxford Paperbacks:

Freedom Under Thatcher Keith Ewing and Conor Gearty
Strong Leadership Graham Little
The Thatcher Effect Dennis Kavanagh and Anthony Seldon

HISTORY IN OXFORD PAPERBACKS

Oxford Paperbacks' superb history list offers books on a wide range of topics from ancient to modern times, whether general period studies or assessments of particular events, movements, or personalities.

THE STRUGGLE FOR THE MASTERY OF EUROPE 1848–1918

A. J. P. Taylor

The fall of Metternich in the revolutions of 1848 heralded an era of unprecedented nationalism in Europe, culminating in the collapse of the Hapsburg, Romanov, and Hohenzollern dynasties at the end of the First World War. In the intervening seventy years the boundaries of Europe changed dramatically from those established at Vienna in 1815. Cavour championed the cause of *Risorgimento* in Italy; Bismarck's three wars brought about the unification of Germany; Serbia and Bulgaria gained their independence courtesy of the decline of Turkey— 'the sick man of Europe'; while the great powers scrambled for places in the sun in Africa. However, with America's entry into the war and President Wilson's adherence to idealistic internationalist principles, Europe ceased to be the centre of the world, although its problems, still primarily revolving around nationalist aspirations, were to smash the Treaty of Versailles and plunge the world into war once more.

A. J. P. Taylor has drawn the material for his account of this turbulent period from the many volumes of diplomatic documents which have been published in the five major European languages. By using vivid language and forceful characterization, he has produced a book that is as much a work of literature as a contribution to scientific history.

'One of the glories of twentieth-century writing.' *Observer*

Also in Oxford Paperbacks:

Portrait of an Age: Victorian England   G. M. Young
Germany 1866–1945   Gorden A. Craig
The Russian Revolution 1917–1932   Sheila Fitzpatrick
France 1848–1945   Theodore Zeldin

HISTORY IN OXFORD PAPERBACKS

As the Oxford Paperbacks' history list grows, so does the range of periods it covers, from the Pharaohs to Anglo-Saxon England, and from Early Modern France to the Second World War.

EGYPT AFTER THE PHARAOHS

Alan K. Bowman

The thousand years between Alexander the Great's invasion in 332 BC and the Arab conquest in AD 642 was a period of enormous change and vitality in the history of Egypt. The Hellenistic era under the powerful Ptolemies ended with the defeat of Antony and Cleopatra in 30 BC, and Egypt became a province of Rome.

Throughout the millenium, however, many of the customs and belief of old Egypt survived, adapting themselves to the new rulers, who were in turn influenced by Egyptian culture. The heritage of the Egypt of the Pharaohs remained a vital force in the history of the land until the coming of Islam.

A vast collection of papyrus texts has survived from this period recording not only the great events but the everyday letters, lawsuits, accounts, and appeals of ordinary Egyptians. From these texts and from the evidence of archaeology, Dr Bowman draws together the Egyptian, Greek, and Roman strands of the story, presenting a masterly survey of the history, economy, and social life of Egypt in this thousand year span.

'eminently readable . . . should be studied by anyone who is seeking details of everyday life in the Roman period' *British Archaeological News*

Also in Oxford Paperbacks:

A History of the Vikings Gwyn Jones
A Turbulent, Seditious, and Factious People Christopher Hill
The Duel in European History V. G. Kiernan

LAW FROM OXFORD PAPERBACKS

Oxford Paperbacks's law list ranges from introductions to the English legal system to reference books and in-depth studies of contemporary legal issues.

INTRODUCTION TO ENGLISH LAW
Tenth Edition

William Geldart
Edited by D. C. M. Yardley

'Geldart' has over the years established itself as a standard account of English law, expounding the body of modern law as set in its historical context. Regularly updated since its first publication, it remains indispensable to student and layman alike as a concise, reliable guide.

Since publication of the ninth edition in 1984 there have been important court decisions and a great deal of relevant new legislation. D. C. M. Yardley, Chairman of the Commission for Local Administration in England, has taken account of all these developments and the result has been a considerable rewriting of several parts of the book. These include the sections dealing with the contractual liability of minors, the abolition of the concept of illegitimacy, the liability of a trade union in tort for inducing a person to break his/her contract of employment, the new public order offences, and the intent necessary for a conviction of murder.

Other law titles:

Freedom Under Thatcher: Civil Liberties in Modern Britain
Keith Ewing and Conor Gearty
Doing the Business Dick Hobbs
Judges David Pannick
Law and Modern Society P. S. Atiyah

PAST MASTERS

General Editor: Keith Thomas

Past Masters is a series of authoritative studies that introduce students and general readers alike to the thought of leading intellectual figures of the past whose ideas still influence many aspects of modern life.

'This Oxford University Press series continues on its encyclopaedic way . . . One begins to wonder whether any intelligent person can afford not to possess the whole series.' *Expository Times*

KIERKEGAARD

Patrick Gardiner

Søren Kierkegaard (1813–55), one of the most original thinkers of the nineteenth century, wrote widely on religious, philosophical, and literary themes. But his idiosyncratic manner of presenting some of his leading ideas initially obscured their fundamental import.

This book shows how Kierkegaard developed his views in emphatic opposition to prevailing opinions, including certain metaphysical claims about the relation of thought to existence. It describes his reaction to the ethical and religious theories of Kant and Hegel, and it also contrasts his position with doctrines currently being advanced by men like Feuerbach and Marx. Kierkegaard's seminal diagnosis of the human condition, which emphasizes the significance of individual choice, has arguably been his most striking philosophical legacy, particularly for the growth of existentialism. Both that and his arresting but paradoxical conception of religious belief are critically discussed, Patrick Gardiner concluding this lucid introduction by indicating salient ways in which they have impinged on contemporary thought.

Also available in Past Masters:

Disraeli   John Vincent
Freud   Anthony Storr
Hume   A. J. Ayer